T0307928

SALT LAKE SCHOOL OF THE PROPHETS 1867–1883

The Council House in Salt Lake City, circa 1867, where early meetings of the Salt Lake School of the Prophets were held.

SALT LAKE SCHOOL OF THE PROPHETS

1867–1883

DEVERY S. ANDERSON, EDITOR

SIGNATURE BOOKS | 2018 | SALT LAKE CITY

To my older brothers, James Anthony Anderson
and Stephen William Anderson

Jacket design by Ron Stucki

Signature Books is a registered trademark of Signature Books Publishing, LLC. Printed in the USA on paper certified by the Sustainable Forestry Initiative.
www.signaturebooks.com

FIRST EDITION | 2018

LIBRARY OF CONGRESS CATALOGING-IN-PUBLICATION DATA

Control number: 2018022685

contents

EDITOR'S INTRODUCTION

Although age and mounting anti-polygamy raids had tamed Brigham Young to a degree, he could still be fierce, even in his seventies. The source of his animus in 1872 was declining attendance at the all-male School of the Prophets, which he had founded five years earlier. Nor was he happy that information about the school's otherwise secret proceedings was leaking to the outside world. He had had enough and decided to dissolve the school and reorganize it, each member having to reapply for membership and demonstrate his worthiness to attend. It was typical of the way Young had run the school for five years, adapting to circumstances rather than being confined by precedent.

All three iterations of the School of the Prophets, under the direction of three different church presidents—Joseph Smith, Young, and John Taylor—were reflections of the personalities and beliefs of the leaders who stood at their head. The original school organized by Smith in Kirtland, Ohio, was formed because of a revelation. The overall purpose of the school was the education of new missionaries preparing to enter the mission field. Some of the ceremonies introduced to the school were later seen as foreshadowing the Nauvoo temple endowment, and there was an emphasis on spiritual as well as secular instruction. By contrast, Young's Salt Lake school was more pragmatic in how it attempted to oversee local politics and economics, and in how members discussed, debated, and resolved theological questions. It was not unusual for the school to consider crop rotations or the differences between gold ore and quartz gold. In 1883, Taylor's effort to revive the school began much like Smith's school, with a revelation, leading to a review of the records to ensure the new school adhere to divine precedent, even if the revelation had not always been carefully followed in the past. Under Smith, a separate branch of the school was established in Missouri; under Young and Taylor, branches were established throughout Utah Territory.

JOSEPH SMITH'S SCHOOLS, 1833–37

The idea for the Schools of the Prophets predated Joseph Smith.

Harvard and Yale were initially seminaries where clergymen were trained, and they were sometimes referred to as "schools of the prophets," drawing on the Bible (1 Sam. 19:18–24). By the time the First Great Awakening occurred in the 1740s, suspicions regarding secularism in elite educational institutions prompted the founding of rival schools, which retained the term *prophet* in referring to teachers of religion. All of these schools functioned as seminaries at first and built up the secular structures around the divinity-school core as time went on.[1]

So too was Smith's School of the Prophets meant to prepare men for the ministry. The school's directive appeared in two revelations, the first received during a conference of priesthood holders in Kirtland, Ohio, on December 27–28, 1832, the second on January 3, 1833; together the two revelations now form Section 88 of LDS editions of the Doctrine and Covenants. The December revelation commanded the men to "teach one another the doctrine of the kingdom." If they did so correctly, with God's grace attending them, they would be "instructed more perfectly in theory, in principle, in doctrine, in the law of the gospel, in all things that pertain unto the Kingdom of God, that are expedient for you to understand." This knowledge would extend beyond theology to teach "things both in heaven and in the earth," although temporal knowledge would be conveyed through a religious lens. They were also told to build a house and see to it that it became "a house of prayer, a house of fasting, a house of faith, a house of learning, a house of glory, a house of order, a house of God" (vv. 77–79, 119). The earliest interpretation of this "house of God" was a schoolhouse to train lay missionaries and ministers; references to the building as a "temple" would come later.

The second part of section 88, the portion dictated six days later in January 1833, elaborated on the "school of the prophets, established for their instruction in all things that are expedient for them, even for all the officers of the church, or in other words, those who are called to the ministry in the church." Those received into the school needed to be "clean from" sin and were to be initiated through "the ordinance of washing of feet … to be administered by the president or presiding elder of the church" (vv. 127, 138–40).

1. Darowski, "Schools of the Prophets," 1–3.

Smith shortly thereafter sent a letter to William W. Phelps in Independence, Missouri, where the church was attempting to erect a model society. Smith enclosed the December revelation, which he called "the Olieve leaf which we have plucked from the tree of Paradise, the Lords message of peace to us." He may have included the January revelation, which he also referenced by pointing out to Phelps that "the Lord commanded us in Kirtland to build an house of God, & establish a school for the prophets, this is the word of the Lord to us, & we must—yea the Lord helping us we will obey, as on conditions of our obedience, he has promised <us> great things."[2]

Smith hoped the school would unite the priesthood, because the church organization was beginning to show fractures. During another conference of high priests, this one on January 13, he assigned his brother Hyrum and Orson Pratt to chastise the Missouri leaders for criticizing the church and to inform them that "the School of the Prophets will commence if the Lord will in 2 or 3 days."[3] It would be eight days, but a school did materialize; the first meeting was held in the upstairs level of a store owned by early convert Newel K. Whitney. In fact, the Smith family lived upstairs adjacent to the school room. Those in attendance on Tuesday, January 22, 1833, were twelve high priests and two elders from among the elite of the church's leadership.[4] They were so overjoyed that they spoke in tongues and offered unrestrained praise to God.[5]

The next day Smith introduced the washing of feet, as performed by Jesus for his disciples (John 13). The gesture had been picked up by prelates in the earliest Christian centuries and was still being practiced here and there in the 1830s, although generally as a sign of humility rather than purification and cleansing. It was criticized in the sixteenth century by Martin Luther, who saw in it a contrived servility, whereas

2. Smith to Phelps, Jan. 3, 1833, in Godfrey et al., *Joseph Smith Papers: Documents 2*, 366–67, which notes that the revelation may have been called the "olive leaf" because it countered "the stark apocalyptic imagery of the 25 December revelation" predicting slave rebellion and war (334).

3. Godfrey et al., 372–78.

4. They were Zebedee Coltrin, Levi Hancock, Orson Hyde, Lyman Johnson, John Murdock, Sidney Rigdon, Hyrum Smith, Joseph Smith Sr., Samuel H. Smith, William Smith, Ezra Thayer, Frederick G. Williams, and Newel K. Whitney, along with Joseph Smith Jr.

5. *History of the Church*, 1:322–23; Backman, *Heavens Resound*, 264.

Mennonites thought it was an important sacrament from primitive Christianity. The Pittsburgh Baptist Church under Walter Scott, with which Sidney Rigdon had associated as a minister, performed feet washing as a gesture of brotherly love and hospitality.[6] After Smith had ritually washed everyone's feet, he told them to do the same, and he "pronounced them all clean from the blood of this generation."

After the inauguration of the school, twenty-five members met regularly through the winter and spring until April 1, 1833, with plans to reconvene in the fall. Orson Hyde had served as instructor, Smith as principal or presiding officer, and school members had followed a specific academic curriculum, although occasionally the classes were interrupted by revelations and visions. For instance, fifty years later, Zebedee Coltrin asserted that he and other men had seen Jesus walk through the room in plain clothing, as well as God in a vision that was so intense he thought the fire might consume them. Although no specific message was delivered at the time, Smith told the men that having seen the Father and the Son meant they were now qualified to be called apostles.[7]

During one of the school's sessions on February 27, 1833, Joseph received by revelation what is known today as the Word of Wisdom, an admonition to abstain from tobacco, strong drink, and hot drinks (D&C 89). Coltrin remembered that twenty-one men were present, of whom twenty used tobacco. In a dramatic move, they collectively threw their pipes into the fire. Parley Pratt opened a similar school that summer in Missouri with some sixty members meeting "in the open air, under some tall trees, in a retired place in the wilderness." Pratt's group also had spiritual manifestations, reporting that they "prayed, preached and prophesied, and exercised ourselves in the gifts of the Holy Spirit."[8]

The Ohio school closed its doors less than three months after it opened. Problems were developing in Missouri and time and resources had to be diverted to calm the increasingly restive situation. Eventually school members in Ohio had to help resettle refugees who were expelled from Jackson County in November.[9] In the school itself, they had encountered disruptive disagreements. A revelation dated June 1, 1833,

6. Grow, "Clean from the Blood of This Generation," 131–39.
7. See Oct. 3, 1883, entry, herein.
8. Patrick, "School of the Prophets," 9–10; Pratt, *Autobiography*, 100.
9. *History of the Church*, 1:340.

two months after the school's closure, reported that "my servants sinned a very grievous sin; and contentions arose in the school of the prophets; which was very grievous unto me, saith your Lord; therefore I sent them forth to be chastened" (D&C 95:10).

Despite these impediments, members still followed the instructions given in the revelation of January 1833, slightly modified in the June revelation, and built a school house in December 1834 that occupied the first floor of a two-story building. The second story housed the church's print shop. There were now two departments called the School of the Elders (the seminary preparing men for missions) and the Kirtland School (which emphasized temporal education). Subjects included arithmetic, geography, grammar, and spelling, and students used well-known textbooks such as *Kirkham's Grammar* and Noah Webster's Dictionary.[10] Enrollment grew beyond expectations to March 1835, when the school graduated a class of missionaries and sent them off on the missions they had been preparing for.[11]

Smith announced a new term on November 3, 1835. This time the two branches were called the School of the Elders, for training prospective missionaries, and the School of the Prophets, for more advanced instruction. Sidney Rigdon, an educated counselor in Smith's First Presidency, was brought in to help administrate. The divinity school, or School of the Prophets, came to offer two main classes in English grammar and biblical Hebrew.[12] To provide texts to study, Oliver Cowdery ordered Bibles and Hebrew books from New York. A Hebrew instructor was engaged, but did not teach, and then another was found: Joshua Seixas of Hudson, Ohio. Seixas agreed to teach a seven-week course for $320. In January 1836 the schools moved into the recently completed Kirtland House of the Lord, and by February a second Hebrew class was added for another thirty students. Shortly before the House of the Lord opened, new ceremonies consisting of washing and perfuming the body, followed by anointing the individual's head with oil and pronouncing blessings and sealings upon him, became part of the purification process preparatory to the building's dedication in March.

10. *History of the Church,* 2:200.
11. Patrick, "School of the Prophets," 11.
12. William E. McLellin to his wife, Dec. 18, 1835, qtd. in Patrick, 12.

The washing of feet would be reintroduced on March 29 following the building's dedication.[13]

A final school in Smith's lifetime commenced in November 1837 with classes in arithmetic, English, geography, grammar, biblical Greek, and writing. Student membership numbered over 130.[14] But over the next seven years, Smith would not attempt another school. This was partly because of the 1838 Mormon War in Missouri and Smith's incarceration in that state for four months in 1838–39 and partly because of his divided attention as the church grew and his responsibilities increased.[15] For instance, relocating the church to Commerce (renamed Nauvoo), Illinois, in 1839 meant building a city from the ground up. The School of the Prophets would not be reorganized in Nauvoo, but one discerns a possible evolution in rituals from the washing of feet in Kirtland to the washing and anointing prior to the dedication of the Kirtland House of the Lord to the temple-related washing, anointing, endowment, and sealings in Nauvoo. Different in scope and purpose from the School of the Prophets, the Nauvoo temple may be understood as an outgrowth of the initial project to purify and sanctify the Saints.[16]

It is also worth noting what the original school accomplished with men who possessed little to no formal education, such as learning Hebrew from a respected scholar. It must have been an exhilarating experience. Smith biographer Richard L. Bushman summed up the institution this way: "The School of the Prophets tells more about the desired texture of Joseph's holy society than anything he had done thus far—and more of what he was up against. The directions to quell excessive laughter and all light-mindedness implicitly reflect the rough-hewn characters who had joined him in the great cause. Few were polished—and he would never teach them gentility—but he wanted order, peace, and virtue."[17]

---

13. Anderson and Bergera, *Joseph Smith's Quorum of the Anointed*, xvi–xvii; Buerger, *Mysteries of Godliness*, 11–34

14. Patrick, "School of the Prophets," 14–15.

15. See Gentry and Compton, *Fire and Sword*; LeSueur, *Mormon War in Missouri*; Baugh, *Call to Arms*.

16. For more, see Anderson and Bergera, *Joseph Smith's Quorum of the Anointed*; Ehat, "Joseph Smith's Introduction of Temple Ordinances."

17. Bushman, *Joseph Smith*, 211–12.

BRIGHAM YOUNG'S SCHOOLS, 1867–74

Twenty years after the church began its settlements in the Great Basin, Brigham Young revitalized the school in conjunction with the reorganization of the University of Deseret (later called the University of Utah). The proto-university was founded in 1850 in the home of John Pack at the corner of West Temple and 100 North streets, but closed two years after its founding.[18] From the start, the purpose of the Utah iteration of the School of the Prophets was less sacral than it had been in Kirtland. "It is purposed to open a school in the Council House, in Great Salt Lake City, on the 2d day of December next," announced the *Deseret News* on November 21, 1867, "to be called the School of the Prophets." The curriculum was to include a range of secular topics, including "Mathematics, Architecture, Chemistry, Mineralogy, Geology, Geography, Grammar, Penmanship, Book-keeping in all its practical details in commercial and other business transactions ... together with Lectures on International and Commercial Law and other such subjects."[19] It seems the moniker School of the Prophets was originally intended to be applied to the school generally and that the theology class spun off from the rest of the curriculum.

Young explained that the school "will be dictated and controlled by the Chancellor and Regents of the University of Deseret, the whole being under the guidance of the Holy Priesthood; and hence, it may properly be called the 'School of the Prophets.'"[20] But again, it was not long before the religious side of the school differentiated itself from the secular side and became its own entity, increasingly more like the Kirtland seminary, although it was also clear that the church president intended to use the school for political and economic as well as religious purposes.[21]

The nature of the school's founding was probably what resulted in the initial membership of 900 men, and soon an enrollment exceeding 5,000 when those of the other branches of the school throughout

18. Grethe Ballif Peterson, "University of Deseret," in Ludlow, ed., *Encyclopedia of Mormonism*; Jenson, *Encyclopedic History*, 190. For more on the founding and history of the university, see Chamberlin, *University of Utah*.

19. "School of the Prophets," *Deseret Evening News*, Nov. 21, 1867, 2.

20. "Remarks," *Deseret Evening News*, Dec. 3, 1867, 1.

21. Patrick, "School of the Prophets," 21. See also Leonard J. Arrington's discussion in *Great Basin Kingdom*, 245–51.

the territory were added to the sum.[22] Branches existed in American Fork, Beaver, Brigham City, Fort Ephraim, Grantsville, Logan, Nephi, Ogden, Parowan, Paris, Payson, Provo, St. George, and Tooele, and each had its own local officers and community-specific programs.[23] These schools often took on the form of town hall meetings led by priesthood officers, with discussions of community problems, issues of church government, and theological questions. The content of the discussions was intended to be kept confidential, primarily out of concerns that non-Mormons not be alerted to the schools' political/economic agenda, and no one was admitted without a membership ticket.

The early minutes and summaries of Utah meetings show a concern over the arrival of the transcontinental railroad, the predicted outcomes and proper procedures for partisan elections, and relations with Native Americans. There is also a persistent emphasis on individual spiritual improvement and adherence to the rules of the school, which were regularly read and agreed upon as new members were admitted. Some of these rules are contained in appendix 1 of this volume. They include temperance in the use of alcohol and tobacco, obedience to priesthood leaders, and not permitting livestock to intrude on neighbors' properties.

One of the matters for the church presidency was the growing tendency for young people not to wait to marry inside the temple. They "spoke of cleanliness of person, before going to get endowments; a woman should not go for a week after her menses were upon her, a man should not have intercourse with his wife for several days but should be clean in body and exercised in spirit previous thereto; his clothing should be changed once or twice before going there."[24]

Another topic was how to treat "outsiders," meaning both non-Mormons expected soon to flock to Utah because of the arrival of the railroad and former Mormon merchants who protested Young's attempt to organize a communal economy. Support for home-grown products and Zion's Cooperative Mercantile Institution (ZCMI) was encouraged within the school, where the "preamble and constitution of Zions Cooperative Institution were read by sections and discussed and unanimously approved" on October 24, 1868. Three weeks later, "Elder

22. Campbell, *Establishing Zion*, 319–20.
23. See appendix 1 in Patrick, "School of the Prophets," 142–43.
24. Jan. 31, 1868, entry.

Franklin D. Richards presented the by-laws of Zions Mercantile Institution. The constitution was read and the by-laws read and approved."[25]

Where church members shopped became a test of loyalty. Young was easily provoked by people who bought goods from non-Mormons. "Bro. Wilkinson was charged with having bought goods from a Jew," it was reported in one meeting. "He confessed, asked forgiveness and promised not to do so any more." At the same time, Utah profited from selling goods to miners and immigrants as they passed through the territory, so church leaders were anxious to see that this source of revenue was not interrupted. Young "asked the Mormon merchants on Main Street to sell their goods so low that they will catch all the transient trade."[26]

Despite attempts to maintain cohesion in the territory by remaining aloof from the nation, school meetings reveal the reality of a church in distress, unavoidably entangled with the rest of the country. In 1862, when the US Congress passed the Morrill Act classifying polygamy as a felony, the act remained ineffectual because of LDS control over local courts. But soon more legislation would follow and set the church and national government on a collision course. As this drama unfolded, the School of the Prophets was where a strategy of resistance was forged.

In 1857, when US President James Buchanan sent troops to Utah Territory to seize control of the government from then-Governor Brigham Young, it began a sixteen-year period of turmoil during which eight non-Mormons, one after another, served as territorial governor. Resisting the pressure to conform to national expectations, the school took on the character of the previous Council of Fifty, the theo-politcal organization that had secretly run territorial affairs during the early exploration and settlement of the Great Basin.[27] For instance, the school decided who would run for elective office—decisions were made without consulting proposed nominees, on the assumption that they would do their duty.[28]

The minutes reveal the disproportionate concern Young and others felt when in 1869 two of Joseph Smith's sons, Alexander and David,

25. See entries for Oct. 3, Oct. 24, Nov. 14, 1868; Bradley, *ZCMI*.

26. May 29, 1869, entry.

27. See Hansen, *Quest for Empire*, and Rogers, *Council of Fifty*. For more on the Council of Fifty during Joseph Smith's day, see Grow et al., *Joseph Smith Papers: Administrative Records* and Grow and Smith, *Council of Fifty*.

28. Quinn, *Mormon Hierarchy: Extensions*, 280.

came to Utah as missionaries for the Reorganized Church of Jesus Christ of Latter Day Saints (later Community of Christ). The young men engaged in tense private discussion with Young regarding polygamy and other practices, after which he lambasted their mother, Emma Hale Smith Bidamon, in the School of the Prophets and elsewhere, for misleading them and others about her late husband's theological innovations. David Smith responded in editorials he submitted to local newspapers.[29]

Of even more concern was an underground movement within the LDS Church challenging Young's plenary control of ecclesiastical and economic policies. William S. Godbe, one of the members of the school, initially made some "good remarks on the benefits of the [economic] co-operation" on December 12, 1868, but a year later on October 25, 1869, Godbe and colleague Elias Harrison would be cut off from the church and school for allegedly working against the church's cooperative economic endeavor. Two days earlier the men had been among six who were required to stand before the initiates and answer the charge of "not [regularly] attending the school" and of writing articles questioning Young's policies. All six were expelled from the school, and then Godbe and Harrison were abruptly excommunicated.[30]

The dissidents had founded a tabloid newspaper called the *Utah Magazine,* which was dedicated to the news, to publishing opinion pieces, and to providing an outlet for creative expression such as fiction and poetry. In January 1870 the men would change the name of the paper to the *Mormon Tribune*, and in time it would become the *Salt Lake Tribune.* Godbe's and Harrison's excommunications spawned what was called the New Movement and the independent Church of Zion, attracting a few hundred like-minded former Mormons. In time the movement died out, but not before becoming a thorn in Young's side. In the January 29, 1870, meeting of the School of the Prophets, English convert Thomas Armstrong, announced that "he was about to take a very important step [and] leave his connexion with this organization and join the New Movement—he therefore handed over his Ticket, as

29. Newell and Avery, *Mormon Enigma*, 285. For more, see Avery, *From Mission to Madness.*

30. Campbell, *Establishing Zion*, 324. For a study of the Godbeite movement, see Walker, *Wayward Saints*. Minutes of their trial appear in appendix 2 in this volume.

a member of the School of the Prophets." Young responded that "it was a very painful thing to see men fall away and become deceived—but this apostacy was the thin[n]est whitewash of anything he had ever been acquainted with." Young and others spoke often against those who left the church, the Godbeites being uppermost in their minds.

By 1872 Young had decided that the schools were too large and too lax in their admission policies. Members in Provo had misplaced their admission cards. Others had spoken outside of the school with people unaffiliated with it, the details of conversations sometimes becoming mangled in the retelling. Albert K. Thurber found that "every thing that is said here is reported to our enemies contrary to our conversations."[31] Young was worried that word of their economic and political strategies would continue to leak. This was another indication, he thought, of self-satisfied members with nothing better to do than to gossip; he lamented "the growing worldly mindedness and careless indifference that is manifest among the wealthy Elders of Israel—instead of building up the Kingdom of God." Young said that "the Devil showed himself in their midst," leading him to dissolve all the schools throughout the territory.[32]

Three months after ending the schools, Young reestablished the Salt Lake City school with safeguards intended to prevent the problems they had encountered. Meeting with advisors on November 4, 1872, he said he wanted to start over and fill the school with "men who loved the Lord and did not have Babylon in their hearts, but were determined to keep the commandments of the Lord." Those wishing to become members should be "willing to enter into the Order of Enoch [economic communalism] and to build up a city upon that principle, to hold all that they have subject to the dictation of the Holy Priesthood." Those not so willing would be invited to leave.

Elsewhere in the territory, the schools that had dissolved remained dormant, but the Salt Lake school was reorganized with a membership that, at its peak, reached nearly 250.[33] The minutes of this more exclusive group indicate a greater interest in theology and spiritual matters than previously, but it continued to address political and economic concerns

31. Patrick, "School of the Prophets," 30, 32.
32. Aug. 23, 1872, entry.
33. Patrick, "School of the Prophets," 35.

as well. Blending religion and economics was the whole idea behind the communal system Young was inventing on the foundation of Joseph Smith's experiments with cooperative projects. Apostle George A. Smith proposed to the School of the Prophets in November 1873 that those "willing to be one in Temporal things" should form an "Order of Enock," a joint-stock company "conducted by a Committee of Trustees." They would grow their own food, raise their own livestock, make their own clothing, and rid themselves "of all unnecessary imported articles." These efforts, with "all things controuled by the Trustees," meant that "the Lord will pour untold wealth into our hands."[34]

The Order of Enoch was the name for the cooperative approach Young was pushing with ZCMI, for instance, also known as the United Order, which he imagined could be tailored to each community's needs. As more than 200 United Orders sprang up that year, some were organized like trade unions and others were completely communal. Despite the leaders' enthusiasm for this endeavor, they were never able to gain control of all means of production and distribution of goods. Still, over twenty cooperative organizations formed in Salt Lake City alone during May–June 1874.[35]

Supervision of these orders became so important that the School of the Prophets was transformed into a committee overseeing the cooperative movement. The rules that had governed the School of the Prophets were altered slightly and sent out to all branches of the United Order.[36] The various trade and mercantile groups were incorporated under territorial law, with guidance from the body that had been the School of the Prophets, making sure local branches of the United Order adhered to all relevant civil laws.[37] The last meeting of the group named the Salt Lake School of the Prophets was held on June 1, 1874, and the next day the same group met as officers of the city's cooperative ventures. The

34. Nov. 17, 1873, entry; see also the entry for November 11, 1872, for the differentiation of "three laws given" at various times: "The first, the more perfect law, given in 1831," was the law of consecration, meaning that one forfeited all property to the church. "The second, the Order of Enoch," granted a percentage of ownership based on what one contributed to the common fund. The third was the lesser law of tithing. See also 448n40 in chapter 6.

35. See Arrington, Fox, and May, *Building the City of God*, 407–19, for lists of all known United Order organizations.

36. Arrington, Fox, and May, 142.

37. Patrick, "School of the Prophets," 109.

minutes of the Salt Lake United Order from June to September 1874 comprise appendix 3 in this volume. It was a short-lived experiment, however, since by fall virtually all urban branches of the United Order had dissolved. The Saints were evidently unprepared for such a radical shift from practicality to idealism.

JOHN TAYLOR'S SCHOOL, 1883

Nine years later, and six years after Brigham Young's death in 1877, church president John Taylor received a revelation on April 28, 1883, commanding him to reconvene the School of the Prophets. Taylor reported that there were matters to resolve that "belong to my Priesthood; but more properly to the School of the Prophets," once the members had become "acquainted with my laws." Membership was to be limited to those who were trying to live by all the commandments. Those who were not "shall not have a place in my school, for I will be honored by my Priesthood; and let my laws be made known unto them as may be deemed expedient."[38]

With that counsel, Taylor ordered a search of the historical records and revelations to ensure that the new school would meet all revelatory requirements and previous expectations of protocol. The minutes of the organizational sessions and two meetings to initiate members tell us as much about the previous schools in Kirtland and Utah as they do about the 1883 organization.

The meetings to plan organizing a school were held in the summer of 1883. At the first meeting reports were made by First Presidency counselor George Q. Cannon and secretary George Reynolds on what they had found in the historical records regarding the schools. Cannon read the revelation of 1833, as well as some New Testament passages describing how Jesus washed his disciples' feet. Knowing the challenges the previous schools had faced in Ohio and Utah, Cannon suggested, "before sitting down, that if we do organize such a School, I am decidedly in favor of being very choice in our selection of who shall be members." Discussions followed regarding whether it was necessary to repeat exactly what had gone before, and whether some rituals, such as washing and anointing, had pertained to the school or to the temple. At a subsequent meeting, Zebedee Coltrin, one of the original members of

38. Aug. 2, 1883, entry.

the school in Kirtland, recounted what he recalled of the experiences the Kirtland members had collectively enjoyed.

The First Presidency asked the presidents of stakes to join them and the Twelve Apostles on October 11, 1883, to be introduced to the concept of a school and invited to participate. It is considered the first meeting of the 1883 school, and the next day, in what would be the second and final meeting, these men gathered in the Endowment House on Temple Square in Salt Lake City to be initiated through the washing of feet, performed by Taylor. The minutes record that Taylor "girded himself with a towel and proceeded to wash the feet of Bro. Zebedee Coltrin, explaining that he did so because Bro. Coltrin was a very aged member of the Church and had belonged to the School instituted by Joseph, and had had his feet washed by the Prophet." While holding Coltrin's hand, Taylor told him, "Thy sins be forgiven thee." Afterward Coltrin placed a towel around his waist and washed Taylor's feet, thus creating "a link connecting the old school with the present."[39] After the others' feet had been washed, the sacrament was administered, and members hailed each other with the greeting prescribed in section 88 of the Doctrine and Covenants:

> Art thou a brother or brethren? I salute you in the name of the Lord Jesus Christ, in token or remembrance of the everlasting covenant, in which covenant I receive you to fellowship, in a determination that is fixed, immovable, and unchangeable, to be your friend and brother through the grace of God in the bonds of love, to walk in all the commandments of God blameless, in thanksgiving, forever and ever. Amen. (verse 133.)

Those present did not anticipate that this would be their last meeting. Why, after receiving a commandment of God to organize the school, would they suddenly abandon the project? The records are silent, but a likely answer is that church leaders were coming under increased surveillance by federal marshals over the practice of polygamy, making it more dangerous to meet together. Over the following years, many of them would go into hiding.[40]

In fact, another school organized two months later was meant to

39. Oct. 12, 1883, entry.
40. Patrick, "School of the Prophets," 137.

exist simultaneously with the Salt Lake City institution, even though the latter was now inactive and would not meet again. The second school met in the remote town of St. George, before train or even adequate road led to the area, which offered a degree of safety to those who took part. The minutes of the December 23–24, 1883, meetings are in appendix 4, showing how a branch located 300 miles from church headquarters operated. Unfortunately, the St. George school met the same fate and ended after two inaugural meetings.

Despite the inability to maintain a consistent organization, the School of the Prophets left an impact on both the church and territory, especially during the time when the rank-and-file were included, as ideas and programs filtered down from top to bottom. The minutes reveal that the most important issues facing church leaders at the time were the disruption they anticipated resulting from the influx of non-Mormon outsiders who would arrive with the railroad, mounting pressures from the federal government, and a determination to maintain a theocracy in an increasingly democratic American West. It is hoped that this volume will serve to illuminate some of the developments during this period between the early and later pioneer periods.

THE DOCUMENTS

At the top of a document listing the members of the School of the Prophets in Utah, we are informed that the school "opened Dec[embe]r 9th 1867 at the City Hall at 6 oclock p.m.,"[41] According to the daily scrapbook called the Journal History, subsequently kept by the Church Historian's Office, there were several organizational meetings a week earlier, as the school's purpose and format were decided upon. References to these meetings are also found in personal diaries and a few incidental documents outlining the rules of conduct and qualifications for admission. These materials comprise chapter 1 in this compilation. By 1883 the minutes for 1867–69 were missing, according to George Q. Cannon's 1883 report that they could not "find any minutes of these meetings. It is a very singular thing that they cannot be found, and we cannot account for it."[42] All extant minutes for the school, from January

41. "Names of Members of the School of the Prophets," SotP, bx 1, fd 2.
42. See Aug. 2, 1883, entry.

1870 on, are reproduced in this volume and are housed at the Church History Library. They begin in chapter 2.

As this book went to press, LaJean Purcell Carruth, a specialist of the publications division of the LDS Church History Department and an expert at reading nineteenth-century shorthand, informed me that she had recently transcribed extensive shorthand notes, 150,000 words in number, made by George D. Watt at thirty meetings of the School of the Prophets held from December 2, 1867, through May 15, 1868. Watt was a church secretary who would embrace Godbeism and the New Movement in 1869. His notes consist of fifty-eight sermons made primarily by Brigham Young, but also by George Q. Cannon, Heber C. Kimball, Orson Pratt, George A. Smith, Erastus Snow, John Taylor, Daniel H. Wells, Lorenzo Young, and a few others. He also occasionally reported pieces of discussions between members.

Except for the December 2, 1867, meeting, which was published in the *Deseret News*, it appears that Watt never transcribed his shorthand notes for these meetings.[43] To give a flavor of Watt's record, Matthew J. Grow, director of publications for the LDS Church History Department, kindly provided Carruth's translation/transcription of Brigham Young's sermon delivered on December 20, 1867, which appears here as appendix 5.

The minutes in the records of the Salt Lake School of the Prophets cover four and a half years from January 1870 through June 1874, after which the school went dormant for nine years. When it reconvened in 1883, they again kept minutes, and those are available online and included as chapter 7 herein. When I began working on this volume, none of the minutes were available for research at the Church History Library, and I began with a photocopy of Edyth Romney's typescript located in the Leonard J. Arrington Papers at Utah State University. Romney was a retired employee of the Church Historical Department whom Arrington, official Church Historian, engaged to prepare typescripts of important documents. Although Romney did well deciphering faded ink and dated handwriting, there were mistakes. It was a pleasure to proof the typescript against the scans of the originals minutes when those became available online. Because the scans of the 1883

43. LaJean Purcell Carruth to Devery Anderson, June 18, 2018.

minutes were partly redacted, I sometimes used typescripts made available by Merle H. Graffam and also D. Michael Quinn, and filled in the redacted text using {braces} to alert the reader to the source of those.

EDITORIAL PROCEDURES

Except where listed below, I retained the original spelling and punctuation and only added new words or punctuation within square brackets. I took a mostly unobtrusive approach to reproducing the original the documents except where additional clarity was needed:

> Where sentences were missing periods, I silently inserted them. If a period was followed by a lowercase initial letter, I silently corrected that.
>
> Clerks sometimes closed sentences with a dash. I converted these to periods.
>
> When a word was repeated, I removed the repetition, rendering "the the" simply as "the." However, when a phrase or sentences was repeated, I explained this in the annotation.
>
> I standardized the entry dates (*December 9, 1867; Monday*), regardless of how they were written in the original record.
>
> For editorial changes on the original manuscript, such as crossed-out words and words added above the line, I indicated them with ~~strike-throughs~~ and ^carets.^ I ignored marks made by later editors, archivists, or historians who, for instance, underlined portions of the Journal History.
>
> I ignored superscriptions (14th instead of 14th).
>
> Occasionally a space was left to write in a word later, which was never done, which I indicated as [space]. Large gaps, either vertical or horizontal, are noted in the annotation.

ACKNOWLEDGEMENTS

I am indebted to the Special Collections and Archives staff of the Merrill–Cazier Library (Utah State University) for providing the transcript of the 1870–74 minutes of the School of the Prophets, the basis from which I began this project many years ago. I am also grateful to the LDS Church History Library for subsequently scanning the minutes and making them available online, including the 1883 minutes. I have received invaluable support from the Smith–Pettit Foundation and Signature Books, whose editors John Hatch and Ron

Priddis helped to make this a better work. Historian Ardis E. Parshall assisted in identifying hard-lo-locate individuals mentioned in the minutes, after I gave up looking for them. Bryan Buchanan helped to proof the galleys and caught errors (both small and large) I and other proofers had missed. I benefited from helpful suggestions by Gary James Bergera and others. Finally, as helpful as the staff of the LDS Church History Library has been—especially LaJean Purcell Carruth and Matthew Grow— as well as staff and others at other institutions, I alone am responsible for this work.

SELECTED MEMBERS OF THE SALT LAKE SCHOOL OF THE PROPHETS

According to an undated attendance roll, Salt Lake City's School of the Prophets hosted, at its peak, nearly 1,000 members. This number fluctuated, but the size of the school makes a complete biographical register impossible. The following list includes members mentioned in the minutes, including those who were later expelled, such as William S. Godbe and his followers.

Albion, James (1806–92), was born in Lancashire, England, and became an independent minister in London. He was baptized in 1841, immigrated to Utah in 1857 as a handcart pioneer, and lived in the Salt Lake 16th ward. He was killed when he was run over by a horse and carriage.

Albiston, John (1814–91), was born in Cheshire, England, and converted to Mormonism in 1840. In 1854 he immigrated to Utah, where he labored on public-works projects in Grantsville and Ogden.

Albrand, Wilhelm Frederick John (1828–1903), was born in Mecklenburg, Germany. Baptized in 1852, he immigrated the next year to Salt Lake City, where he worked as a gardener.

Alexander Jr., Alva (1799–1890), was born in Acworth, New Hampshire. He converted to Mormonism in 1841 and in 1852 arrived in Utah, where he and his sons built a lumber mill in Salt Lake City's Mill Creek area.

Allen, William Lund Nuttle (1825–93), was bishop of Salt Lake's 21st ward. He had been in the Nauvoo Legion during the War with Mexico and helped pioneer the settlement of southern Utah and northern Arizona.

Alsop, Thomas Hill (1835–95), was born in England and joined the LDS Church in 1856, emigrating the next year. He lived in the southern part of the Salt Lake Valley near present-day Draper. He was a farmer, surveyor, and school teacher.

Anderson, David Patterson (1838–1914), was born in Scotland and migrated to Utah in 1856 as a member of the Willie Handcart Company. In the 18th ward in Salt Lake City, he was the choir director. He was a carpenter by trade.

Anderson, George Alexander (1837–1906), was born in Scotland, migrated to Utah in 1855, and was a member of Salt Lake's 20th ward.

Andreason, Ole Christian (1840–1904), was from Denmark. He settled in Sevier County, a remote area of Utah, but relocated to Salt Lake City by 1870. He was a shoemaker.

Andrus, Milo (1814–93), was born in Elizabethtown, New York, and joined with the Mormons in 1832. While on one of several missions, he served as acting stake president in St. Louis.

Angell, Truman Osborne (1810–87), was born in North Providence, Rhode Island, and baptized in 1833. In Nauvoo he was a carpenter who helped build the temple, and in Utah he became an architect, eventually the church's chief architect responsible for the St. George, Salt Lake, Manti, and Logan temples, among other edifices.

Argyle, Joseph (1818–1905), born in Leicestershire, England, came in 1856 to Utah, where he worked as a tinsmith.

Armstrong, Thomas Columbus (1817–1900), was born in England and appeared in Utah in 1856. A store clerk, he was also a member of the seventies quorum.

Arnold, Henry (1822–88), was born in Herefordshire, England. He was baptized in 1842 and traveled to Utah ten years later. A member of a bishopric, he was also an owner of the Globe Bakery and Saloon.

Ashby, Benjamin (1828–1907), was born in Salem, Massachusetts. He was baptized into the LDS Church in 1841, came to Utah in 1848, and served a mission to England in 1853.

Asper, William (1836–1910), born in Newville, Cumberland, Pennsylvania, was baptized in 1861. In Utah he worked as a carpenter on the Salt Lake Theatre; he was on the committee that oversaw construction of the Assembly Hall on Temple Square.

Atkinson, William (1812–79), bishop of the South Bountiful ward, was known for having been the captain of a wagon company in 1853.

Attwicks, James (1804–81), was born in England. After migrating to Utah in 1853, he settled in Salt Lake's 16th ward and was employed as a tailor.

Atwood, Millen (1817–90), was from Mansfield, Connecticut. He had been a member of the LDS Church only six years when he arrived in Utah in 1847 as one of the pioneer company. In 1856 he was captain of the first successful handcart company to reach the Great Basin. He was bishop of the Salt Lake City 13th ward.

Atwood, Miner Grant (1823–87), was born in Mansfield, Connecticut. A year after his 1849 baptism, he immigrated to Utah and became a member of the Salt Lake high council and served several missions.

Atwood, Samuel Frink (1825–1906), born in Wellington, Connecticut, was baptized into the LDS Church in 1849 and came to Utah the next year. From 1870 to 1902, he was the bishop of Kamas, fifteen miles east of Parley's Park (Park City).

Baldwin, James (1791–1875), was born in England, baptized in 1840, and ten years later migrated to Utah, where he was a high priest in the 17th ward.

Ball, John Price (1828–90), from Leicestershire, England, migrated to Utah in 1862 and settled in Cache Valley as a shoemaker and grocery store owner.

Barber, George (1826–90), was living in London when he was baptized in 1849. After serving a mission to India, he settled in central Utah in the agricultural town of Nephi. He was later made manager of a church-run cooperative store on the northern edge of the territory in Cache Valley.

Barfoot, Joseph Lindsey (1816–82), was born in Warwick, England. An advocate of science and mentor to professor/apostle James E. Talmage, he ran the Deseret Museum beginning in 1870.

Barlow, Israel (1806–83), born in Granville, Massachusetts, was baptized in 1832, two years after the church's founding. He came to Utah in 1848. As a missionary in England from 1853 to 1855, he served as president of the Birmingham conference (district).

Barlow, James Madison (1812–93), of Kentucky, was traveling west to seek gold in California when he was converted to Mormonism in Salt Lake City, where he became a jeweler and metal worker.

Barnes, Mark (1809–90), was born in Herts, England. He presided over the French mission in the late 1850s, not arriving in Utah until 1860, then working as a gardener and carpenter.

Barney Jr., Royal (1808–90), was born in Ellisburgh, New York. He joined the LDS Church a year after its founding and followed the progression of the church from Ohio to Illinois. He was endowed in the Nauvoo temple in 1846. Six years later he moved to the Great Basin.

Barrell, Charles Henry (1819–1901), was born in Cannington, England. In 1868 he appeared in Utah and found work laboring on the Salt Lake Temple. He eventually became an aide to apostle George Q. Cannon.

Barton, Peter (1845–1912), of Lancashire, England, became a leading businessman in Davis County, north of Salt Lake City, and was bishop of Kaysville for thirty years.

Bean, Joseph William (1814–83), was converted to Mormonism in 1843 in England. He emigrated in 1859 and soon found himself called to help fight Indians in the Black Hawk War. He was a member of the bishopric of the Salt Lake City 11th ward.

Beesley, Ebenezer (1840–1906), was born in Oxfordshire, England. His family converted to Mormonism in 1849. A decade later they were in Utah, and he became a music teacher and compiler of song books used in Sunday School and the Mutual Improvement Association. In 1880 he became director of the Tabernacle Choir.

Benson, Ezra Taft (1811–69), was born in Mendon, Massachusetts. He converted to Mormonism in 1840 and became a member of the Quorum of Twelve Apostles six years later; the next year he entered the Salt Lake Valley as one of the original pioneers. He was eventually sent to Cache Valley to preside over the church there. His great-grandson of the same name would become church president in 1985.

Bernhisel, John Milton (1799–1881), was born in Pennsylvania. A physician who graduated from the University of Pennsylvania School of Medicine, he was appointed to be Utah's first territorial delegate to Congress, serving in that position for ten years (1851–59, 1861–63).

Bird, Edmund F. (1847–1934), born in Boston, Massachusetts, was baptized at eight years of age in 1855. He became a carpenter and builder in Utah.

Bleazard, John Hopwood (1803–71), born in Yorkshire, England, and trained as a wheelwright and ship carpenter, spent two years at Winter Quarters, Nebraska, 1848–50, helping immigrants by mending wagons before continuing on himself to Utah. He lived in the Salt Lake 17th ward, where he operated a brewery. He married nine wives.

Boyle, Henry G. (1823–1902), was born in Tazewell, Virginia. After his baptism into the LDS Church in 1843, he served fourteen missions, including one as president of the Southern States Mission from 1875 to 1878.

Brimhall, Norman Guiteau (1820–1907), was born in Watertown, New York. He was baptized in 1847, arrived in Utah in 1855, and settled in the Ogden area as a millwright.

Brimley, Richard (1822–1905), was born in Lancashire, England, and was baptized into the LDS Church in 1838. It was thirty years later that he migrated to Utah, where he was bishop of the Salt Lake 5th ward from 1877 to 1884.

Brinton, David (1814–78), was born in Dillworth, Pennsylvania, and baptized into the LDS Church in 1840. In 1856 he was ordained bishop of the Big Cottonwood ward in Salt Lake County.

Britton, Richard (1814–89), immigrated to Utah from England in 1852. He was a jeweler.

Broadhurst, Samuel (1820–85), arrived in Utah from Lancashire, England, in 1853. A wheelwright, he was an early settler of the Cottonwood/Millcreek area of the Salt Lake Valley.

Brockbank, Isaac (1837–1927), was born in Liverpool. His conversion to Mormonism occurred the same year the pioneer company arrived in the Rocky Mountains (1847), and he immigrated to America five years after that. He was vice president of one of the United Orders in 1874.

Brown, Abiah William (1840–1924), was born in Ohio. In Utah he was employed as a school teacher.

Budge, William (1828–1919), of Lanark, Scotland, converted to Mormonism in 1857. He helped settle Bear Lake Valley, Idaho, and served as a bishop and stake president there. He also served as president of the European Mission, 1878–80, and was president of the Logan, Utah, temple, 1906–18.

Bunting, James Lovell (1832–1923), born in Norfolk, England, was baptized in 1853. In 1870 he was sent to colonize southern Utah. His occupation was that of a shoemaker, and he volunteered time as an officiator in the St. George temple.

Burnham, Charles Carroll (1838–1926), was born in Illinois and immigrated in 1850 to Draper, Utah.

Burt, Andrew Hill (1828–83), of Fifeshire, Scotland, converted at nineteen and journeyed to Utah when he was twenty-three, becoming a ward bishop and Salt Lake City chief of police. He was killed at fifty-four years of age by a man he was arresting over public drunkenness.

Burton, Robert Taylor (1821–1907), was born in Ontario, Canada, and converted to the LDS Church when he was sixteen. In 1862 he was appointed by Abraham Lincoln to be the US internal revenue collector for Utah, serving until 1869. He was also a regent for the University of Deseret and a member of the territorial legislature.

Butler, Alva Kelly (1845–1909), was born in Winchester, Indiana. His family immigrated to Utah when he was eleven. He became a lumber mill owner and bishop of the Granite ward in Salt Lake City.

Bywater, George Gwillyn (1828–98), was born in Glamorganshire, Wales. After arriving in Utah in 1854, he became a train conductor for the Utah Central Railway.

Cahoon, Andrew (1824–1900), a son of Reynolds Cahoon, became bishop of Salt Lake's South Cottonwood ward. The father was on the committee in Kirtland, Ohio, that oversaw construction of a building (ultimately the Kirtland Temple) for the School of the Prophets. The son was born forty miles east of Kirtland.

Caine, John Thomas (1829–1929), born on the Isle of Man, joined the LDS church in 1847, arrived in Utah in 1852, clerked for the territorial legislature, helped to found the *Salt Lake Herald* in 1870, served on the territorial council, was city recorder, was a delegate to the US House of Representatives, and briefly was a member of the Utah Senate.

Calder, David Orson (1823–84), a Scottish convert, became the business manager for the *Deseret News* in 1873, twenty years after his arrival in Utah. In 1875 he became director of ZCMI.

Call, Anson (1810–90), originally from Vermont, converted in 1836 and settled in Bountiful, Utah, where he was a farmer, merchant, probate judge, and bishop.

Campbell, Robert Lang (1825–74), was born in Scotland, converted to Mormonism in 1843, and served as a secretary to Brigham Young, as a clerk in the Church Historian's office, and as chief clerk of the Utah House of Representatives.

Cannon, Angus Munn (1834–1915), was born in Liverpool. A news agent for the *Deseret News*, he was best known as president of the Salt Lake Stake, a position he held for twenty-eight years.

Cannon, George Quayle (1827–1901), was born in Liverpool, where his family converted in 1840. He became publisher of the *Deseret News*. Ecclesiastically he was a member of the Quorum of Twelve Apostles and a counselor to Brigham Young, John Taylor, Wilford Woodruff, and Lorenzo Snow in succession.

Carlisle, Joseph (1826–1912), was born in Sherwood, England. He was baptized a Mormon in 1849 and left England in 1851, arriving in Utah in 1853. He had a farm south of Salt Lake City.

Carrington, Albert (1813–89), converted to Mormonism in 1841. He was an apostle, a secretary to Brigham Young, Church Historian, editor of the *Deseret News,* and president of the Perpetual Emigrating Fund. In the minutes of the School of the Prophets, he comes under questioning for his relationships with women other than his wives; he was excommunicated in 1885.

Chapman, Welcome (1805–93), was a Vermont native, baptized into the LDS Church quite early, about 1831. He appeared in Utah in 1848, a year behind the pioneer company. Eventually he helped settle the administrative seat of Sanpete County, the town of Manti.

Clark, John (1832–1923), was born in Clinton, Ohio. He converted in 1842. When he moved to Utah and settled in Provo, he became, among other pursuits, an Indian interpreter, serving in all of Utah Territory's Indian wars.

Clawson, Hiram Bradley (1826–1912), converted to Mormonism with his mother. He became a clerk to Brigham Young managing the church president's private business interests. He was also involved in building the Salt Lake Theatre.

Clayton, William (1814–79), became closely associated with Joseph Smith as his personal scribe, after Clayton's conversion in England. Clayton was among the earliest polygamists in the church. For several years in Utah, he was treasurer of ZCMI. He was originally from Lancashire.

Clinton, Jeter (1813–92), was born in Whitewater, Indiana, converted to Mormonism, and moved to Utah in 1850, where he was a physician and coroner, as well as an alderman, justice of the peace, and member of the Council of Fifty.

Cluff, William Wallace (1832–1915), was born in Ohio and baptized in Nauvoo, Illinois, in 1842. He became a bishop and stake president in the mountains east of Salt Lake City (Summit County) and was president of the Coalville Co-operative Mercantile Institution for thirty-three years.

Collins, Robert H. (1822–89), was from England. After conversion and emigration, he became a private in the Mormon Battalion during the Mexican–American War.

Coltrin, Zebedee (1804–87), was an original member of the Kirtland School of the Prophets who was from New York but lived forty miles from Kirtland at his conversion. Following the Mormon migration to the Great Basin in 1847, he settled in Spanish Fork.

Corbett, Daniel (1809–92), was born in Farmington, Maine. He arrived in Utah in 1849, serving as a counselor in the bishopric of the Salt Lake 2nd ward.

Crismon, Charles (1807–90), was an early convert who built the first grist mill in Salt Lake City in 1848 along City Creek. The following year he followed the Gold Rush to California, then helped settle the Mormon colony at San Bernardino. He returned to Utah before moving to Arizona in 1877.

Crockwell, John Daniel Madeira (1820–85), of Ohio, lived in Salt Lake's 14th ward. He is sometimes identified as "Dr."

Cummings, James Willard (1819–83), was born in Wilton, Maine, baptized in 1841, and the following year served a mission to St. Charles, Illinois. He managed the Deseret Woolen Mill in Utah.

Curtis, Theodore (1815–1903), was born in Connecticut and migrated to Utah in 1848. He was a carpenter and a wheelwright.

Despain, Solomon Joseph (1823–95), was born in Alabama. He converted in Illinois and was sent on an eight-year mission to Arkansas and Tennessee. When he arrived in Utah, he settled in Little Cottonwood Canyon, becoming bishop of the Granite ward. He later helped settle Arizona. He had four wives and twenty-seven children.

Dinwoodey, Henry (1825–1905), was born in Latchford, England, and came to Utah in 1855 as a carpenter. He owned a successful furniture store in downtown Salt Lake City.

Dunbar, William C. (1822–1905), was born in Inverness, Scotland, and remained until his conversion to Mormonism in 1840. In Utah he worked by day as a clerk and news correspondent (later as a founder of the *Salt Lake Herald*) and at night he played the bagpipe, sang, and told comedic stories to theater audiences.

Dunford, George (1822–91), was born in Wiltshire, England, joined the LDS Church in 1847, and served as a branch president there after his conversion. He operated a number of stores in St. Louis before becoming a successful retailer in Utah.

Edlefson, Niels Christian (1827–98), was born in Denmark. He helped settle the Bear Lake region of northern Utah and southern Idaho.

Eldredge, Horace Sunderlin (1816–88), converted to Mormonism in 1836 in New York. He came to Utah in 1848 and was appointed territorial marshal, assessor and collector of taxes, and a brigadier general in the militia prior to becoming superintendent of ZCMI.

Ellerbeck, Thomas Witton (1829–95), was born in Lancashire, England. He moved to Utah in 1851 and became a clerk in Brigham Young's office in charge of keeping the files pertaining to the Union Pacific Railroad in Utah. He was involved in constructing the first waterworks system in the city.

Evans, David (1804–83), of Maryland, converted to Mormonism in 1833, and for a while attended the School of the Prophets in Kirtland, Ohio. In 1851 he was called to settle the town of Lehi, Utah. He said he laid out the city with a pocket compass and square. For over thirty years, he was the town's bishop.

Evans, Samuel (1789–77), was born in Wales, where he converted in 1844 and left for America ten years later, settling on a farm in Lehi, Utah.

Eyring, Henry (1835–1902), a German immigrant, served several proselytizing missions back to Europe after his immigration to the United

States. He helped settle St. George, Utah. After being pursued by federal marshals for having two wives, and living in exile in Mexico, he died in the Mormon polygamist settlement of Colonia Juárez.

Fackrell, Joseph Crumb (1822–1900), was born in Vermont and migrated to Utah in 1852. He worked a farm in Bountiful, Utah, until his death there.

Farr, Lorin Freeman (1820–1909), was born in Waterford, Vermont, and converted to Mormonism in 1837. After he arrived in Utah, he was sent by Brigham Young to preside over the church in Ogden as president of the Weber Stake. He also became the mayor of Ogden.

Felt, Nathaniel Henry (1816–87), was from Salem, Massachusetts. In 1847, four years after his conversion, he was sent to preside over the St. Louis branch and to assist LDS immigrants arriving there. Three years later he continued his own journey to Utah and helped found the town of Parowan. He was then called to be a traveling bishop, similar to being in the Presiding Bishopric today.

Fenton, Thomas (1822–90), was born in Nottinghamshire, England. He migrated to America three years after his 1848 conversion. An avid gardener, he established orchards and nurseries in Utah Territory.

Fielding, Amos (1792–1875), was an English convert who acted as a church emigration agent until 1845. In Nauvoo, Illinois, he became a charter member of the Council of Fifty. In 1869 he began manufacturing ink in Utah. Then he once again became a church agent in England.

Findlay, Alexander (1820–1911), born in Scotland, immigrated to Utah in 1848, becoming a farmer in southern Utah.

Folsom, William Harrison (1815–1901), was born in Portsmouth, New Hampshire, and worked for his father's contracting business until 1842 when, at age twenty-six, he converted to Mormonism and moved to Nauvoo, Illinois. After proving useful in helping construct the temple, he went on to design some of the early buildings in Salt Lake City. He was in the presidency of the Salt Lake Stake.

Fox, Jesse Williams (1819–94), was born in New York and was baptized a Mormon in 1840. He arrived in Utah ten years later to teach school in Manti and eventually at the University of Deseret. He became the Salt Lake City surveyor and a counselor in the Salt Lake Stake.

Frost, Burr (1816–78), a blacksmith, was born in New Haven, Connecticut, and converted to Mormonism in 1842. He helped settle the southern Utah town of Parowan. He was one of the early missionaries to Australia.

Gardner, Archibald (1814–1902), was born in Scotland. He arrived in Utah in 1847 to build the first sawmills in the region. He became bishop of the West Jordan ward.

Gates, Jacob (1811–92), was born in St. Johnsbury, Vermont, where he was trained as a carpenter and joiner. Three years after the church's founding, he converted, and sixteen years later in 1849 made the trek to Utah, but he was soon called on a mission to England. He later moved to St. George, Utah.

Gerber, John Theophilus (1837–1920), was born in the Midwest to Protestant missionaries from Switzerland ministering to Swiss emigrants. The entire family converted to Mormonism and made the journey to Utah in 1854. John was sent back to Switzerland on a mission before he married in 1864 (adding a plural wife the next year) and settled down as a Utah farmer, growing crops and fathering sixteen children.

Godbe, William Samuel (1833–1902), was born in Middlesex, England. He worked as an engineer and sailor prior to his conversion to Mormonism in 1850. He immigrated to Salt Lake City a year later and became a successful merchant. In 1868 he and other merchants criticized Young's plan to collectivize the economy and was eventually excommunicated for his outspoken opposition.

Goddard, George (1815–99), was born in Leicester, England, where at age thirteen he began an apprenticeship as a grocer. He operated a successful store in Salt Lake City, and in time he became assistant superintendent of the church's Sunday School Union and secretary to the School of the Prophets.

Gowans, Hugh S. (1832–1912), was a Scottish convert who became the stake president in Tooele, Utah. He also served a mission in his native Scotland.

Grant, Heber Jeddy (1856–1945), was born in Salt Lake City, the son of Brigham Young's counselor Jedediah M. Grant. Heber became an apostle in 1882. In 1918 he became president of the LDS Church and served in that position for twenty-seven years.

Groo, George Washington (1848–1922), was born in New York and was trained as a bookkeeper. He was a clerk in the mining industry in Utah.

Groo, Isaac (1827–95), was born in New York, converted to Mormonism in 1852, and traveled to Utah two years later. From 1856 to 1858, he served as a member of the city council, and from 1859 to 1864 he was street supervisor and water master. He was also the city recorder and a regent of the University of Deseret.

Grow, Henry (1817–91), was born in Morristown, Pennsylvania. He was baptized LDS in 1842 and came to Utah in 1851. A prominent architect in Utah, he designed and built the Social Hall, New Tabernacle, and a suspension bridge over the Weber River, among many other well-known structures.

Hancock, Levi Ward (1803–82), was one of the first seven presidents of the Seventy from 1835 to 1882, and a member of the Kirtland School of the Prophets. He was among the pioneer settlers of Manti, Utah.

Hardy, Leonard Wilford (1805–84), was born in Massachusetts, migrated to Utah in 1850, and worked as a store clerk. He was bishop of the Salt Lake 12th ward beginning in 1851. From 1856 to 1884 he was a counselor to Presiding Bishop Edward Hunter.

Harrington, Leonard Ellsworth (1816–83), born in New York, was baptized a Mormon in 1840 and came to Salt Lake City in 1847. Three years later he moved to American Fork, becoming that town's mayor for twenty-nine years.

Harrison, Elias Lacy Thomas (1838–1900), converted to Mormonism as a teenager in Essex, England. He became a celebrated architect and co-editor of the *Peep O'Day* newspaper that criticized some LDS Church policies, resulting in his excommunication, along with William S. Godbe.

Hatch, Abram Chase (1830–1911), was born in Lincoln, Vermont, and was baptized in 1841. Occupationally he was a freighter who moved goods across the Great Plains by wagon train. From 1877 to 1901 he was president of the Wasatch Stake.

Henrie, William (1799–1883), was a member of Brigham Young's 1847 pioneer company and a resident of Bountiful, Utah.

Hickenlooper, William Haney (1804–88), was born in Pennsylvania. A Mormon since 1839 and a member of the Mormon Battalion during the Mexican War, he became bishop of the Salt Lake 6th ward and a city councilman, his occupation engineering, in addition to the cooperative business he ran.

Hills, Lewis Samuel (1836–1915), was born in South Amherst, Massachusetts, and came to Utah in 1862. He was engaged as the bookkeeper for a bank called Hooper, Eldredge and Company that began in a small adobe building in Salt Lake City. Hills later helped establish the Deseret National Bank.

Hilton, David (1831–1904), was born in England, migrated to Utah in 1855, and was a store clerk.

Hoagland, Abraham Elias Lucas (1797–1872), was trained in Hillsboro, New Jersey, as a blacksmith. He was baptized in 1841 and became a bishop in Winter Quarters, Nebraska, in the mid-1840s, then bishop of the Salt Lake 14th ward from 1851 to his death.

Holman, John Greenleaf (1828–88), was a member of Brigham Young's 1847 pioneer company and an early rancher in Pleasant Grove, Utah.

Hooper, William Henry (1813–82), was born in Maryland and became a bank clerk and merchant there. He converted to Mormonism in Illinois, moved to Utah in 1850, and soon became the territorial secretary (1857), then the territory's delegate to the US Congress (1859–61, 1865–73), and on his return from Washington the superintendent of ZCMI.

Howell, Thomas Charles Davis (1814–1902), was born in Waynesboro, North Carolina. He was converted in 1844 and enlisted in the US Army two years later as part of the Mormon Battalion. He lived in Utah for a while and then moved to Franklin, Idaho, where he became a justice of the peace.

Hulse, Benjamin Robinson (1815–97), born in Brookhaven, New York, converted to Mormonism in 1840. He ended up in the Mill Creek area of Salt Lake City.

Hunter, Edward (1793–1883), was a well-to-do Quaker in Pennsylvania who was engaged in the mercantile business until his conversion to Mormonism in 1840. He became the presiding bishop of the LDS Church in 1851 and served in that position until his death.

Huntington, Dimick Baker (1808–79), of Watertown, New York, was a blacksmith and farmer who converted to Mormonism in 1835 and for over forty years served as a missionary to Native Americans; he was prominent at the peace conference that led to the end of Utah's Black Hawk War.

Hyde, Orson (1805–78), was one of the original members of the Quorum of Twelve Apostles in 1835. He served a mission to Palestine in 1841. In Utah he presided over settlements in Sanpete and Sevier Counties.

Jenkins, Thomas (1829–1905), was born in Herefordshire, England, and converted to Mormonism in 1838. He came to Utah ten years later, and from 1866 to 1875 he was one of the city's ward bishops. He had five wives and twenty-seven children.

Jennings, William (1823–86), was born in Yardley, England. He became a prominent merchant in Utah, who invested in the cooperative movement Brigham Young pushed for in 1868. He later became mayor of Salt Lake City for one term.

Jeremy, Thomas Evans (1815–91), was a Welsh farmer who immigrated to Utah in 1849.

Jones, Daniel Webster (1830–1915), born in Fayette, Missouri, was baptized in 1851. He helped translate portions of the Book of Mormon into Spanish. He was one of the pioneer settlers of Mesa, Arizona.

Kelsey, Eli Brazee (1819–85), was born in Portsmouth, Ohio, and was baptized in 1843. Once in Utah, he found his faith wavering; his association with William Godbe and the Godbeites led to his excommunication.

Kesler, Frederick (1816–99), was born in Pennsylvania. He joined the LDS Church in 1840, came to Utah in 1851, and became bishop of the Salt Lake 16th ward for forty-three years. He owned and ran a flour mill in Bountiful.

Kimball, David Patten (1839–83), was born in Nauvoo, Illinois, a son of Heber and Vilate Kimball. A teamster by trade, he pioneered the settlement of northern Arizona as the presiding elder in St. David and then a member of the St. Joseph Stake presidency to his death at age forty-four. He had also previously been a stake president in northern Utah.

Kimball, Heber Chase (1802–68), converted to Mormonism in 1832 and became one of the original members of the Quorum of Twelve Apostles three years later. In 1847 he became first counselor to Brigham Young. He died shortly after the organization of the Salt Lake School of the Prophets.

Kimball, Heber Parley (1835–85), was born in Kirtland, Ohio, a son of Heber and Vilate Kimball. In 1874 he became superintendent and manager of the Utah Western Railroad. During the Black Hawk War, he served as a militia colonel.

King, Thomas Jefferson (1806–76), was born in Massachusetts. He migrated to Utah in 1854, was a farmer, and lived in Layton.

Lambert, Charles (1816–92), from Yorkshire, England, was a stonecutter before his conversion to Mormonism in 1843. He continued his occupation in St. Joseph, Missouri, and Salt Lake City, although the house he built for himself in Utah was made of adobe. He also farmed and was involved in the early effort to refine sugar beets.

Laney, Isaac (1815–73), was born in Franklin, Kentucky, joined the LDS Church in 1838, and survived the massacre at Hawn's Mill in Missouri later that year. He migrated to Utah in 1847.

Larson, Christian Grice (1828–1911), a Danish convert to Mormonism, settled in Spring City, Utah, where he milked cows, raised sheep, grew plums, and was ward bishop. He filled several missions back to Scandinavia. About 1880 he moved his families to Castle Valley and became president of the Emery Stake.

Lawrence, Henry William (1835–1924), was born in Canada. In the 1850s in Utah, he became a successful merchant. He later became a city counselor, a member of the ZCMI board of directors, and founder of the *Utah Magazine*. When the magazine became critical of Brigham Young, it resulted in his Lawrence's excommunication.

Layton, Christopher (1821–98), of Befordshire, England, converted to Mormonism in 1842. He was a member of the Mormon Battalion during the Mexican War and afterward founded the town of Kaysville, Utah. He became general superintendent of the Utah Central Railroad and director of ZCMI. In the 1880s he pioneered the settlement of Thatcher, Arizona, where he served as president of the St. Joseph Stake from 1883 to 1898.

Leach, James (1815–1911), was born Lancashire, England. He came to Utah in September 1847, two months after the first pioneers arrived, and worked in an adobe yard. For a time he was acting bishop of the Salt Lake 2nd ward.

Little, Feramorz (1820–87), was born in New York. After his conversion and immigration to Utah, he contracted with the federal government to carry the mail between the territory and the Midwestern states. He became superintendent of the Utah Central and Utah Southern railroad lines. He also owned a saloon and gristmill and was part-owner of a hotel and several lumber mills. In 1876 he was elected Salt Lake City mayor.

Little, Jesse Carter (1815–93), was one of the few well-educated early Mormon converts. He studied at Ipswich Academy in New Hampshire and taught school in the East before traveling to Utah in 1847. A year before that, he was the one who persuaded US President James K. Polk to enlist Mormons in the conflict with Mexico. In Utah he practiced law and was a member of the Presiding Bishopric, 1856–74.

Luce, Ephraim Grant (1799–1880), was baptized by future church president Wilford Woodruff in Maine in 1838. Ephraim and wife, Lydia, saw a son die at Winter Quarters. When she and the other children left for Utah in 1849, it was without her husband, whom she soon divorced. He arrived in 1851 and married two other women, living with them in Salt Lake City and Spanish Fork.

Lyman, Francis Marion (1840–1916), was born in Illinois to apostle Amasa M. Lyman and his wife Louisa. He was a manager of several businesses, including the Deseret National Bank, ZCMI, and Zions Savings Bank and Trust, and was ordained an apostle in 1880.

Maiben, John Bray (1826–1910), was a medical student in Brighton, England, at the time of his conversion to Mormonism in 1848. He became the bishop of Manti, Utah. In 1877 he was added to the Sevier Stake presidency. Later he would be called to the Manti temple presidency.

McAllister, John Daniel Thompson (1827–1910), was born in Delaware and trained as a blacksmith. In 1851 he arrived in Utah (he was baptized in 1847), where he became superintendent of Brigham Young's woolen mills and the Utah territorial marshal. He was also a prominent member of the Deseret Dramatic Association. In 1877 he was sent to St. George as stake president.

McKean, Theodore (1829–97), born in New Jersey, was baptized into the LDS Church in 1851. He became the Salt Lake County surveyor, territorial road commissioner, deputy territorial marshal, and US collector of internal revenue.

McKenzie, David (1834–1912), was born in Edinburgh, Scotland, and converted to Mormonism in 1853. He came to Utah the next year and became one of the pioneer thespians associated with the Deseret Dramatic Association. For many years he was a clerk and bookkeeper in the church president's office. From 1879 to 1887, he managed the Salt Lake Theatre.

McLelland, Thomas (1819–90), was born in Londonderry, Ireland. He traveled to Utah seven years after his 1841 conversion and became bishop of the Salt Lake 7th ward in 1862; seven years after that he was elected to the city council.

McRae, Alexander (1807–91), was born in North Carolina and converted to Mormonism fairly early, in 1835. He was a body guard of Joseph Smith in Illinois, a county sheriff in Iowa, and the territorial prison warden in Utah, as well as bishop of the Salt Lake 11th ward.

Merkley, Christopher (1808–93), was born in Ontario, Canada. He was baptized in 1837 and moved to Utah in 1849. He owned a store and photography business.

Merrill, Albert (1815–73), was born in New York, lived in Nauvoo, and immigrated to Utah in 1852, where he was a farmer and local seventies leader.

Miller, Reuben (1811–82), was born in Redding, Pennsylvania. In 1843 he converted to Mormonism and was given leadership of a branch near Chicago. At Joseph Smith's death, he associated briefly with James J. Strang, then switched his allegiance to Brigham Young. He immigrated to the Mill Creek area of the Salt Lake Valley in 1849 and became the bishop and a county commissioner.

Miner, Aurelius (1832–1913) was born in Connecticut and studied law in New York. In 1854 he decided to see the West. Stopping in Salt Lake City, he ended up being converted and marrying a daughter of apostle Orson Hyde. He stayed in the city and became the county's prosecuting attorney and then deputy attorney general for the territory, but was disbarred in 1885 for having married a plural wife.

Mitchell, Frederick Augustus Herman Frank (1835–1923), was born in Sheffield, England, and baptized in 1845. He was the US Deputy Mineral Surveyor from 1887 to 1900.

Morris, Elias (1825–98), was a stone mason from Wales who worked for several years on the Salt Lake Temple and built houses, including the officers' homes at Fort Douglas. He was bishop of the Salt Lake 15th ward.

Morris, George (1816–97), was from Cheshire, England. He converted in 1841, crossed the plains to Utah in 1848, and worked in Salt Lake City as a shoemaker and house builder.

Morris, Richard Vaughan (1830–82), a Welshman who had worked as a bookkeeper for six years in Liverpool, became in Utah—after converting in 1849 and immigrated in 1855—the accountant for the Deseret Telegraph Company, auditor of the Utah Central Railroad, and president of the Utah Soap Factory. He was bishop of the 19th ward.

Muir, William (1822–96), was born in Scotland. After he converted to Mormonism in 1842, he went to California to work in the mines, then retrieved his family from Winter Quarters at the border of Nebraska and Iowa and brought them to Bountiful, Utah, in 1849.

Murphy, Emanuel Master (1809–71), was born in South Carolina and baptized in 1836. In 1857 he was appointed to help gather the scattered Saints in Tennessee and bring them to Utah. In doing so, he released his slaves, although he brought two of them with him to Utah, arriving in the territory in 1860.

Musser, Amos Milton (1830–1909), of Pennsylvania, was baptized into the LDS Church in 1851, a few years after his mother's conversion to the church. Arriving in Utah that same year (1851), Amos found work in the tithing office, but he was called on a mission to India the year after that. On his return he was called to be a a traveling bishop (similar to the Presiding Bishopric today), and in 1902 he became Assistant Church Historian.

Naisbitt, Henry W. (1826–1908), was born in England, converted to Mormonism in 1850, and relocated four years later in Utah, where he became a business associate of William Jennings. He was also involved with Jennings in ZCMI, and he was a well-known lecturer on Mormonism at the Salt Lake Tabernacle.

Neal, George Augustus (1794–1874), of New Hampshire, immigrated to Utah in 1852 and was bishop of Salt Lake's 14th ward.

Nebeker, Peter (1822–85), was from Delaware. Baptized into the LDS Church in 1848, he settled on the west side of Salt Lake City and raised cattle and chickens, and planted the first apple orchard in the valley. In the 1860s he worked as a teamster on the church wagon trains.

Neslen, Robert Francis (1832–1912), converted to Mormonism in 1852 in Suffolk, England. He became a successful merchant, a member of the Salt Lake Tabernacle Choir, and a costumer and actor at the Salt Lake City Theatre.

Noble, George Omner (1844–1911), was born in Nauvoo, Illinois, to Joseph and Sarah Noble. The family migrated to Utah in 1847. His father had been one of Joseph Smith's bodyguards and had secretly married the church president to Louisa Beaman in April 1841 in the church's first official plural marriage.

Noble, Joseph Bates (1810–1900), was born in Massachusetts. A convert since 1832, he was one of the first seventies in the church in Kirtland, Ohio. At Winter Quarters, Nebraska, he became a bishop. A proponent of plural marriage, he had eleven wives and fathered thirty-one children.

North, Levi (1817–91), was baptized in Ohio in 1839. He immigrated to Utah in 1852 and pioneered the Mill Creek area of Salt Lake City. He served a mission to White Mountain, Nevada.

Nuttall, Leonard John (1834–1905), was born in Liverpool and was baptized in 1848. In Salt Lake City he became a county recorder, probate judge, and bishop. He was then sent to the southern edge of the territory to what is known as the Arizona Strip to serve as stake president in Kanab. Later he became territorial superintendent of public schools and secretary to church presidents John Taylor and Wilford Woodruff.

Pack, John (1809–85), of New Brunswick, Canada, converted to Mormonism in 1836. He helped build the first dancing hall and one of the earliest flour mills in Salt Lake City. In 1856 he pioneered the settlement of Carson Valley, Nevada. The first classes of the University of Deseret (University of Utah) were held in his home in downtown Salt Lake City.

Park, John R. (1833–1900), was born in Ohio, where he graduated from Ohio Wesleyan University. He went on to receive an MD from the New York University medical school. He arrived in Utah in 1861 and was baptized the next year. In 1869 he became president of the University of Deseret (University of Utah).

Parker, Robert (1820–1901), was born in England and migrated to Utah in 1856. He became postmaster in Utah's Washington County.

Parry, Caleb (1824–71), from Wales, joined the Mormon Church in 1846. When he arrived in Utah in 1849, he joined the territorial militia and participated in the Indian wars from 1850 to 1855. He also worked as a stone mason on the Salt Lake temple, after which he served a mission to England.

Paxman, William (1855–97), was born in Salt Lake City and became a stake president. In the meantime, on a mission to New Zealand, he supervised the translations of religious texts into the native Maori language.

Peck, Lucius Wheaton (1821–91), was born in Vermont and migrated to Utah in 1848. He was a schoolmaster.

Peck, Martin H. (1806–84), was from Massachusetts. In Utah, arriving in 1848, he became the sealer of weights and measures in Salt Lake City.

Picknell, John Harris (1813–78), was an English butcher who arrived in Utah in 1855.

Pixton, Robert (1819–81), of Manchester, England, became acquainted with Mormons on a ship while sailing to America in 1841. He followed the Mormons to Illinois, becoming converted and submitting to baptism the next year. A year after that, his wife and child arrived from England. In 1846 he joined the Mormon Battalion. He and his family were soon engaged in helping to settle southern Utah.

Pratt, Abinadi (1845–1914), was a son of apostle Parley P. Pratt. In the minutes of the School of the Prophets for September 2, 1871, Abinadi offers to write out wills for members of the school, apparently for a price. On October 28, 1871, he speaks out against "billiard saloons and [against] acquiring loose and wicked habits." He died in the state mental hospital in Provo.

Pratt, Milando Merrill (1848–1930), was born in Iowa, a son of Orson and Mary Ann Pratt, and served on the high councils of the Salt Lake Stake from 1873 to 1904 and the Liberty Stake from 1904 to 1911. Toward the end of his life, he became a stake patriarch.

Pratt, Nephi (1846–1910), was born in Nauvoo, Illinois, to Parley and Belinda Pratt. He was sent to Fillmore to help bolster the church in that part of the territory, and served missions to England and (as mission president) the Pacific Northwest, where he was living when he died. When not on a mission, he worked for a sewing machine company.

Pratt, Orson (1811–81), was one of the church's original Twelve Apostles in 1835. After Brigham Young became church president, the two clashed periodically over theology. Pratt, whose views leaned toward mainstream Christian fare, supported himself and his families in part through the sale of his theological books and pamphlets.

Preston, William Bowker (1830–1908), was born in Virginia. Baptized in 1857, he was in Utah the next year and served in the Utah War. He became a bishop in Logan, then president of the stake, and eventually Presiding Bishop for twenty-three years.

Pyper, Alexander Cruickshanks (1828–82), was a Mormon convert from Scotland. He built a silk factory in Salt Lake City, managed some of Brigham Young's business interests, and was a bishop and local judge.

Raleigh, Alonzo Hazeltine (1818–1901), of New Hampshire, became a brick mason in Boston and then in New York, where he converted to the LDS Church in 1842. In Utah he was bishop of the Salt Lake 19th ward and president of the Deseret Dramatic Association, as well as a justice of the peace.

Rawlins, James (1794–1874), of North Carolina, immigrated to Utah in 1848 and lived and farmed in the Big Cottonwood area.

Redi, Thomas Hand (1826–1920), was born in Scotland. From 1852 on, he farmed and resided variously in Beaver, Duchesne, and Salt Lake City.

Reynolds, George (1842–1909), from England, worked in the office of Brigham Young and agreed in the late 1870s to challenge the constitutionality of the 1862 Morrill anti-bigamy act. He was found guilty, and the ruling was upheld by the US Supreme Court. In 1890, he was sustained as one of the seven presidents of the seventy.

Rich, Charles Coulson (1809–83), was an early convert from Kentucky who was baptized LDS in 1832. Two years after his October 1847 arrival in Utah in a wagon company he captained, he became one of the Quorum of Twelve Apostles. In the early 1860s, after exploring the Bear Lake Valley, he moved his families there.

Richards, Franklin Dewey (1821–99), born in Massachusetts, was baptized into the LDS Church in 1838, and eleven years later he became a member of the Quorum of Twelve Apostles. He was sent to Ogden to preside over the church there, and he simultaneously founded the *Ogden Junction* and served as a local judge. He served as LDS Church Historian from 1889 to his death.

Richards, Howe Phineas (1788–1874), was a brother of apostle Willard Richards and father of apostle Franklin D. Richards. In Massachusetts he was a county coroner. He was baptized in 1837 and moved to Utah in 1848.

Richards, Levi (1799–1876), of Massachusetts, was baptized in Kirtland, Ohio, in 1836. Like his brother Willard, he was a botanical doctor and Joseph Smith's personal physician. In Utah he was active on the Council of Health.

Richards, Samuel Whitney (1824–1909), was a brother of Franklin D. Richards, also baptized a Mormon in 1838. He was a Salt Lake City alderman and judge. In Liverpool he presided over the British and European missions and edited the *Millennial Star*.

Riggs, Obadiah H. (1843–1907), was born in Pennsylvania. Both he and wife Emma Louise became professors of education at the University of Deseret. He later became territorial superintendent of public schools. He is mostly remembered as the father of Emma Ray Riggs, who married future LDS president David O. McKay. However, Obadiah left the LDS Church, became RLDS, studied medicine in Brooklyn, and became a physician in Cincinnati.

Riser, George (1818–92), born in Germany, immigrated with his family to the United States in 1831, and was baptized in 1842. After settling in Utah in 1850, he became a shoemaker. Four years later he was called back to Europe to preside over the German mission.

Rockwood, Albert Perry (1805–79), was born in Holliston, Massachusetts, and was baptized in 1837. He immigrated to Utah in 1847 and was one of the first Seven Presidents of the Seventy from 1845 to 1879. He was a director of the Deseret Agricultural and Manufacturing Society, and also served as a warden of the Utah Territorial Penitentiary.

Rowberry, John (1823–84), was born in Bishop's Grove, Herefordshire, England. He was baptized into the LDS Church in 1840, arrived in Utah in 1849, and settled in the Tooele Valley, where be was called as bishop. He was later named as a stake patriarch and was a member of the Utah legislature for several years.

Rushton, Edwin (1824–1904), was born in Leek, Staffordshire, England, and converted to Mormonism in England in 1840. He arrived in Salt Lake City with his family in 1851. He farmed and raised livestock. In about 1890, he wrote an account of a sermon allegedly delivered by Joseph Smith in 1843, termed the "white horse prophecy," which foresaw cataclysmic end times. Rushton's narrative is generally regarded as spurious.

Schettler, Paul Augustus (1827–84), was born in Coblentz, Prussia, immigrated to the United States, and joined the LDS Church in 1860. He served as treasurer for Salt Lake City for twenty years.

Sharp, John (1820–91), was born in Clackmannanshire, Scotland, and converted to Mormonism in 1847. In Utah he was ordained bishop of the Salt Lake City 20th ward. In 1867, he became a subcontractor of the Union Pacific Railroad. He became president of the Utah Central Railway in 1873, and later was a director for the Union Pacific. In 1885, he pleaded guilty to unlawful cohabitation (polygamy), despite church officials' request that he plead not guilty, and was asked to resign as bishop, which he did.

Shaw, Osmond Broad (1822–88), born in England, immigrated to Utah in 1852. He was a member of the 26th Quorum of the Seventy and a painter.

Shearer, Daniel (1791–1874), was born in Stillwater, New York. He was an early convert to Mormonism, lived in Nauvoo, Illinois, and immigrated to Utah. He was a whip maker by profession.

Sheets, Elijah F. (1821-1904), joined the LDS Church in 1840 and served missions to Indiana, Illinois, Pennsylvania, and Britain. He immigrated to Utah in 1847, helped to settle Iron County, but returned to Salt Lake City, where he was a member of the city council. He was bishop of 8th ward for almost fifty years.

Shipp, Milford Bard (1836–1918), joined the LDS Church in 1857 and later served several LDS missions. He was a physician and an attorney. He married Ellis Reynolds (1847-1939) in 1866, who became one of Utah's first female medical doctors.

Shurtliff, Lewis Warren (1835–1922), was born in Sullivan, Ohio, where his family converted and then immigrated to Utah in 1850. He served in the Utah State Legislature from 1896 to 1898 and was elected judge in Weber County. He was a bishop in Plain City, later president of the Weber Stake.

Silver, William John (1832–1918), was born in London and immigrated to Utah in 1859. He was president of the 13th quorum of the seventy, and worked as a mechanical engineer, manufacturing machinery and helping to construct mills and power houses. He built iron fences and built the first steam engine in Utah.

Smith, Elias (1804–88), was born in Royalton, Vermont, and was a cousin of Joseph Smith. He baptized into the LDS Church in 1835.

He served as Salt Lake County probate judge from 1852 to 1882, and postmaster of Salt Lake City from 1854 to 1858. He was also president of all high priests in the church from 1870 to 1877.

Smith, George A. (1817–75), a cousin to Joseph Smith Jr., was called as an apostle at age twenty-two. In Utah, he was Church Historian (1854-71) and replaced Heber C. Kimball in 1868 as Brigham Young's counselor in the First Presidency.

Smith, Joseph F. (1838–1918), son of Hyrum and Mary Fielding Smith, was ordained an apostle in 1866, and served in the First Presidency under John Taylor, Wilford Woodruff, and Lorenzo Snow, before assuming the office of church president himself in 1901.

Smith, Lot (1830–92), was born in Willamstown, New York, and was baptized in 1851. He was a member of the Mormon Battalion and president of the Little Colorado Stake from 1878 to 1887. He was also a member of the 74th quorum of seventy.

Smith, Silas Sanford (1830–1910), was born in Stockholm, New York, and was a cousin of Joseph Smith and George A. Smith. He came to Utah in 1847 and was a member of the Utah legislature for over twenty years as well as a member of the Council of Fifty. From 1883 to 1892, he was president of the San Luis Stake.

Smith, Willard Gilbert (1827–1903), was born in Amherst, Ohio, and baptized in 1835. He came to Utah in 1849, after serving in the Mormon Battalion. He was later ordained a bishop in Morgan, Utah, and then was stake president from 1877 to 1893.

Smoot, Abraham Owen (1815–95), was born in Kentucky and converted to Mormonism in 1835. He was a bishop in Salt Lake City and later a stake president in Provo. He had been mayor of Salt Lake City and became mayor of Provo, as well as a member of the territorial legislature and a justice of the peace.

Snow, Erastus (1818–88), was an early missionary for the church in New England and Pennsylvania. He became a member of the Council of Fifty and was ordained an apostle in 1849, in which capacity he oversaw the settlement of southern Utah.

Snow, Lorenzo (1814–1901), converted to Mormonism in 1836, was a member of the Utah legislature from 1853 to 1882, and a founder of Brigham City. In 1898 he was ordained fifth president of the LDS Church.

Snow, Zerubabbel (1809–88), was born in St. Johnsbury, Vermont, and converted to Mormonism in 1832. In 1869 he was elected attorney general of Utah Territory.

Spencer, Howard Orson (1838–1918), was born in Middlefield, Massachusetts, and was baptized into the LDS Church in 1846. He served as a counselor in the Kanab (Utah) Stake presidency from 1877 to 1884.

Staines, William Carter (1818–81), was born in Higham Ferrers, Northhampton, England, and converted to Mormonism in 1841. He arrived in Utah in 1847, where he gardened and farmed. He was Territorial Librarian and helped to guard the overland mail route. He served on the city council, filled as LDS mission to England, and later was Church Emigration Agent.

Stenhouse, Thomas Brown Holmes (1824–82), was born in Scotland and converted to Mormonism in 1845. He served several missions for the church and published articles and newspapers defending Mormonism. He was a regular writer for the *Deseret News* and a regent of the University of Deseret. He later joined the Godbeite Movement and, with his wife, Fanny, was subsequently excommunicated from the church.

Stevenson, Edward (1821–97), was born in Spain and immigrated to America with his family in 1827. He joined the Mormons in 1833, came to Utah in 1847, and served several missions for the church in the United States and abroad. He also served as one of the Seven Presidents of the Seventy.

Stewart, Isaac Mitton (1815–90), was born in New Jersey, immigrated to Utah in 1852, and was a bishop in Willow Creek/Draper, Salt Lake Valley.

Stewart, Levi (1812–78), was born in Edwardsville, Illinois, and was baptized into the LDS Church in 1837. He was in Utah by 1850 and labored as a farmer and merchant.

Stoker, John (1817–81), born in Madison Lake, Ohio, and baptized in 1836. He immigrated to Utah in 1849 and was called as bishop of the East Bountiful (Utah), ward. He also served a mission to Virginia.

Stout, Hosea (1810–89), was born in Kentucky and converted to Mormonism in 1838. He was chief of police in Nauvoo, Illinois, Winter Quarters, and later in Salt Lake City. In Utah, he served as Speaker of the House in the Utah Territorial Legislature.

Taylor, George Edward Grove (1810–74), immigrated from England to Salt Lake City with members of his family in 1866. In Salt Lake, he was a member of the 13th ward and worked as a tailor in a shop next to the old Salt Lake Theatre.

Taylor, George John (1834–1914), born in Canada, was a son of John Taylor, a publisher and editor, and manager of his father's business affairs. He taught at the University of Deseret, was a member of its Board of Regents, was chief clerk of Utah's territorial legislature, and was Salt Lake County coroner.

Taylor, John (1808–87), was born in England and immigrated to Canada, where he was converted to Mormonism in 1836. He was ordained an LDS apostle in 1838 and, later in Utah, served in the legislature and in other civic offices. He succeeded Brigham Young as head of the LDS Church and briefly reconstituted the School of the Prophets in 1883.

Taylor, Thomas (1826–1900), was born in Oldham, Lancashire, England, and converted to Mormonism in 1840. After immigrating to Utah, he returned to England and served a mission from 1862 to 1865, and then was appointed church immigration agent in New York. He was a leading merchant in Salt Lake City and served as bishop of the 14th ward from 1871 to 1886.

Teasdale, George (1831–1907), was born in London, England, and joined the LDS Church in 1852. He taught school at the Salt Lake Dramatical Association and was a member of the Tabernacle Choir. In 1882, he was called as a member of the Quorum of the Twelve Apostles. In business, he was the manager of many different stores, including ZCMI.

Thompson, Ralph (1811–72), was born in Aycliffe, England, and was one of the early British converts of 1837. He came to American and to Utah, where he was a woolen manufacturer and weaver.

Thorne, William (1814–1907), immigrated to Utah in 1851 and was a farmer. He also served as bishop in Salt Lake City.

Tripp, Enoch Bartlett (1823–1909), born in Maine, converted to Mormonism in 1845. He immigrated to Utah and lived in Salt Lake City and the South Cottonwood area where he was a farmer.

Turnbow, Samuel (1804–90), born in Lexington, Kentucky, converted to Mormonism in 1840. He served a mission to Mississippi in 1844 and went west with the church, arriving in Utah in 1847. He was a member and served in the bishopric of Salt Lake's 14th ward and was a farmer.

Tuttle, Newton (1825–1905), was born in Connecticut and migrated to Utah in 1854. He was farmer living in Bountiful, Utah.

Twede, Christian Frederick Nielsen (1828–1907), was born in Copenhagen, Denmark, and immigrated to Utah in 1854. He lived in Salt Lake, central Utah, and Utah Valley, and worked a variety of jobs.

Van Cott, John (1814–83), a native of New York, joined the LDS Church in 1845 and arrived in the Salt Lake Valley in 1847. He was a Seventy and served as president of the Scandinavian Mission from 1852 to 1856, and again from 1859 to 1862. When he returned, he was named as a president of the Seventy. Following his appointment, he filled a brief mission to Scandinavian church members living in Sanpete county in central Utah.

Wallace, George Benjamin (1817–1900), born in New Hampshire, converted to Mormonism in 1842. He was ordained president of the Salt Lake Stake in 1874. From 1877 until his death, he served as president of the high priests quorum in that stake.

Watt, George Darling (1815–81), was born in England and learned Pitman shorthand. He served as one of Brigham Young's secretaries and recorded many of Young's and others' sermons. He aligned with the Godbeites, fell out of Young's favor, and was excommunicated in 1874.

Weiler, Joseph (1836–85), was born in East Nantmeal, Pennsylvania, and was baptized in 1846. He came to Utah in 1848 and was Sunday school superintendent of the Salt Lake City 4th ward.

Wells, Daniel Hanmer (1814–91), was born in New York and lived among the Mormons in Nauvoo, Illinois, before his conversion in 1846. He immigrated to Utah in 1848 and later served as second counselor to Brigham Young in the First Presidency from 1857 to 1877. Wells was the mayor of Salt Lake City during the time the School of the Prophets met under Young.

Wheeler, Edward (1820–88), was born in England and immigrated to Utah in 1856. He was a horse doctor.

Whitney, Horace Kimball (1823–84), was born in Kirtland, Ohio, to Newel K. Whitney and Elizabeth Ann Smith Kimball. He arrived in the Salt Lake Valley in 1847. He was a member of the Nauvoo Legion, a member of the Deseret Dramatic Association, and was a talented musician. He worked as a printer for and manager of the *Deseret News*.

Whittaker, Thomas William, Sr. (1816–86), was born in England. As a young man, he was a sailor. After joining the LDS Church in San Francisco, he was called on a mission to Tahiti, and in 1856 he immigrated to Utah, settling in Centerville. He was a builder and carpenter.

Wickens, James Brown (1824–91), was born in England and immigrated to Utah in 1862. He was a carpenter.

Willis, William (1810–77), born in Kineton, Warwickshire, England. He was baptized in 1848 and was a laborer and gardener.

Winberg, Anders Wilhelm (1830–1909), immigrated to Utah from Denmark in 1854. He was a blacksmith and lived in Salt Lake's 19th ward.

Winder, John Rex (1820–1910), was born in Biddenham, England, and converted to Mormonism in 1848. In 1853, he came to America with his family and settled in Utah. He worked as a boot and saddle maker and went into the tanning business with several partners, including Brigham Young. He was later a member of the First Presidency under Joseph F. Smith.

Winter, Thomas (1812–82), was born in Portmouth, Hampshire, England, joined the Mormons in 1844, and immigrated to the United States in 1849. He and his family journeyed to Utah the next year. He served as bishop of the Salt Lake City 5th ward.

Wood, Daniel (1800–92), born in Dutchess County, New York, converted to Mormonism while living in Ontario, Canada, in 1833. He moved to LDS headquarters in Ohio, Missouri, and Illinois, before immigrating to Utah in 1848. He helped to settle Woods Cross, north of Salt Lake City, and became is most wealthy citizen.

Wood, Robert Stewart (1815–?), was born in New York. He was a member of the 14th ward when he was called to help settle northern Utah with Lorenzo Snow and Charles C. Rich, and therefore stopped attending the Salt Lake City School of the Prophets after 1870.

Woodruff, Wilford (1807–98), converted to Mormonism in 1833 and was ordained an apostle in 1839. He was an assistant church historian during this time. He was ordained president of the LDS Church in 1889 and issued the Manifesto ostensibly ending plural marriage in 1890. He maintained a voluminous diary.

Woolley, Edwin Dilworth (1807–81), converted to the LDS Church in 1837. In Utah he was a business manager to Brigham Young, a member of the Utah territorial legislature, and Salt Lake County recorder. He helped to organize the Deseret Telegraph Company and in 1853 was called as a bishop, a position he held until his death.

Woolley, Samuel Amos (1825–1900), was born in Newlin, Pennsylvania, and was baptized in 1840. He came to Utah in 1848 and helped to settle Parowan. He was called as a bishop in 1864. He also ran the church tithing office in Salt Lake City.

Young, Brigham (1801–77), joined Mormonism in 1832 and was ordained one of the original members of the Quorum of Twelve Apostles in 1835. He took over leadership of the main body of the followers of Joseph Smith after Smith's 1844 assassination. He resurrected the School of the Prophets primarily in response to calls for greater economic and mercantile diversity.

Young Jr., Brigham (1836–1903), was a son of Brigham Young. In 1851, he was called to be a high councilor in the Salt Lake Stake. He was ordained an apostle in 1864 but not added to the Quorum of the Twelve Apostles until 1868, setting up a future controversy over seniority and presidential successions with Joseph F. Smith (who, though ordained after Young Jr., joined the quorum before him).

Young, Franklin Wheeler (1839–1911), was born in Winchester, Illinois, and was a son of Lorenzo Dow Young. He immigrated to Salt Lake City with his family in 1847. He was called as bishop of the Payson, Utah, ward in 1859, at age nineteen. He was a bookkeeper at Morgan's Commercial College and ZCMI.

Young, John Willard (1844–1924), was born in Nauvoo, Illinois, and was ordained an apostle at age nineteen, although he never joined the Quorum of the Twelve. He became an additional counselor to his father, Brigham Young, in 1873, and then First Counselor in 1876. He helped to develop four railroads in Utah, and established Salt Lake City's first streetcar line.

Young, Joseph (1797–1881), Brigham Young's older brother, was senior president of the First Council of Seventy and a member of the Nauvoo Council of Fifty. He arrived in Salt Lake City, where he spent most of his life, in September 1850 and in 1870 served an LDS mission to Britain.

Young, LeGrand (1840–1910), born in Nauvoo, Illinois, was a son of Joseph Young. He came to Utah in 1850 and was a member of the 3rd Quorum of Seventy. He was a Salt Lake City councilor for two terms. He was a lawyer and also a judge for the 3rd District Court in Utah.

Young, Lorenzo Dow (1807–95), a brother of Brigham Young, was a gardener and blacksmith. He arrived in the Great Salt Lake Valley in 1847 with the first company of Mormon pioneers. He was a bishop in Salt Lake City for twenty-seven years and later a stake patriarch.

Young, Phineas Howe (1799–1879), another of Brigham Young's older brothers, arrived in Utah in 1847 and was bishop of Salt Lake City's 2nd ward until 1871.

Young, Seymour Bicknell (1837–1924), born in Kirtland, Ohio, was a son of Joseph Young and nephew to Brigham Young. He came to Utah in 1850 and in 1854 helped to settle Cache Valley, Utah. He practiced medicine and was Brigham Young's and others' physician and medical advisor.

Young, Willard (1852–1939), was born in Salt Lake City to Brigham Young and his eighth wife, Clarissa Ross. He graduated from West Point in 1875 and was an instructor there from 1879 to 1883. Later, in Utah, he was a university president, city and state engineer, and supervised LDS Church building activities.

Young, William Goodall (1827–83), born in Canandaigua, New York, was a son of Lorenzo Dow Young. He was baptized in 1835, immigrated to Utah in 1847, and was the first person to start a farm in the Pleasant Green area. In 1874, he was ordained bishop of the Big Cottonwood ward in Utah.

CHAPTER ONE

"WISDOM THAT COMES FROM GOD"

1867–1869

Sec[tion] 88 Doc[trine] & Cov[enants][1]

Memo[randum] regarding School of the Prophets

The President is to be in the House first, and it would seem, is to bow alone in prayer. When the prayer is finished, the members of the School are admitted, and when they have taken their places he arises, and standing in his place in the house, with uplifted hands, salutes the brethren in the following words: "Art thou a brother (or brethren)? I salute you in the name of the Lord Jesus Christ in token or remembrance of the everlasting Covenant, in which Covenant I receive you to fellowship, in a determination that is fixed, immovable and unchangeable, to be your friend and brother through the grace of God, in the bonds of love, to walk in all the commandments of God blameless, in thanksgiving, for ever and ever. Amen."

The members of the School (who are found worthy) with uplifted hands to heaven, return the salutation, by repeating the same prayer and covenant, or by saying "Amen" in token of the same.

December 2, 1867; Monday[2]

A meeting of the school of the Prophets was held in G[reat] S[alt] L[ake] City, addressed by Brigham Young, Heber C. Kimball and Daniel H. Wells.

1. This undated loose sheet explaining how the school is to open is in SotP 6, bx 1, fd 6. It directly quotes LDS Doctrine and Covenants 88 (hereafter D&C), which sets out "the order of the house prepared for the presidency of the school of the prophets, established for their instruction in all things that are expedient for them."

2. With the exception of January 20, 1868, the minutes for the first two years of the School of the Prophets are not extant (see introduction). Unless otherwise noted, all dated entries in this chapter are extracted from the Journal History (hereafter JH), a multi-volume scrapbook of primary and other documents in the Church History Library (hereafter CHL). Digital scans of the JH are available online at the CHL website.

The following was published in the Deseret News:[3]

This morning at 9 o'clock a meeting convened in the Council House[4] in this city to inaugurate the opening of the classes advertised by the Board of Regency, in connection with the University of Deseret.[5] There were present Presidents Brigham Young, H. C. Kimball and D. H. Wells, Elders Orson Pratt, Wilford Woodruff, George Q. Cannon and Joseph F. Smith of the Twelve Apostles, Chancellor [Albert] Carrington, several members of the Board of Regents, with a large number of the Bishops and leading men of the city.

President Young made some remarks at the commencement, which we will publish at length to-morrow; after which he offered the following

OPENING PRAYER

O God, our Father who lives in the heavens, in the name of Jesus Christ we approach Thee this morning as Thy children, and we come to Thee as our Father and God, even the God and Father of our Lord Jesus Christ and the Father of our Spirits. We thank Thee for the blessings which Thou hast given unto us, and we pray Thee in the name of Jesus to look in mercy upon us. Bless, O Lord, these Thy servants, and wilt Thou be compassionate unto us, and bless us with the out pouring of Thy Spirit as the time has now arrived when we can commence again a [s]chool here on this esrth [earth] for the improvement of the minds of Thy servants, the Elders of Israel [male priesthood holders] in all truth that pertains to heaven and earth, through the Priesthood of the Son of God, and by the

3. The *Deseret News* was founded in Utah in 1850, with apostle Willard Richards as editor. It was established by Brigham Young to provide communication throughout the Mormon colonies where there was otherwise intellectual and physical isolation. It began as a weekly paper, then semi-weekly in 1865, and in 1867 a daily under the name *Deseret Evening News*. It remains in print, still owned by the LDS Church. Crawley, *Descriptive Bibliography of the Mormon Church*, 2:146–50.

4. The Council House (not to be confused with Utah's territorial government building, the Council Hall) was built on the corner of Main Street and South Temple, a short walk from Brigham Young's homes and across the street from Temple Square. It was finished in 1850 and had several functions, including hosting temple rites until the Endowment House was built five years later. The Council House burned down in 1883. "A Destructive Fire," *Deseret News*, June 27, 1883.

5. The University of Deseret, later named the University of Utah in 1894, was established in February 1850, and is the oldest state university west of the Missouri River. It closed due to a lack of funds from 1852 until 1867, but in 1869 it established itself permanently and continued to expand as it acquired additional acreage from the federal government. Chamberlin, *University of Utah*.

learning which we have in books that hath been revealed in days of old, and in this our day. Inasmuch as we enjoy these privileges, we ask Thee to inspire the hearts of Thine Apostles, Elders, High Priests, and Seventies, and pour out Thy Spirit upon the Bishops and every servant of Thine that their eyes may be opened to see and understand things as they are. Bless all who take an interest in the improvement of the minds of Thy people, and wilt Thou instruct them by the revelations of Thy Spirit; for we realize that we are ignorant, and our opportunities to be taught in the learning of men on earth have been few.

We have had the privilege of the gospel revealed unto us through Thy servant Joseph [Smith],[6] and of gathering from the nations privilege, to assemble ourselves together where we can improve our lives, and instruct each other in the knowledge of all truth. We ask Thee to give unto us the revelations of Thy Holy Spirit to enable us to commence this school, which is the School of the Prophets, the school of the Saints of the Most High, and we ask that the revelations of the Lord Jesus Christ may rest on those who take the charge of this school in its different branches.

Bless the Chancellor and Regency of the University of Deseret with wisdom that comes from Thee, and all who shall assist in any way in guiding and upholding this institution, that Thy servants and handmaidens may receive instruction which is contained in books, and which flows from the revelations of Thy Spirit. Bless all who shall join this school at this time, and all who shall hereafter join it.

Bless and preserve Thy people throughout the Territory of Utah, and throughout the whole earth; O Lord preserve thy people in the Gospel of the Lord Jesus; especially Thy people in these mountains and prepare them to go back and redeem the centre stake of Zion.[7] We ask thee to hasten this time, and aid thy people to improve, that they may the sooner be able to build up and redeem the waste places of

6. Joseph Smith Jr. (1805–44) founded the original School of the Prophets in Kirtland, Ohio, in 1833 and the school met intermittently (also under the name School of Elders) until 1837. Smith and his brother Hyrum were assassinated in Carthage Jail, Illinois, in 1844. Patrick, "School of the Prophets"; Bushman, *Joseph Smith*.

7. Mormons were driven out of Missouri after clashing with locals in the Mormon War of 1838. For years after, church leaders spoke often of returning to redeem Zion and reclaim the land as their own to prepare for the second coming of Christ. See Gentry and Compton, *Fire and Sword*.

Zion, according to Thy word. Prosper us in these things, O Lord, and bless us in building a Temple[8] to Thy name in this land, and in giving endowments to Thy people. Pour out Thy Spirit upon Thine Apostles, that they may be of one heart and one mind in all things, that we may be more thoroughly instructed from on High in the revelations of the Lord Jesus Christ, looking unto and trusting in Thee for the result in all things, both in the affairs of life and learning, and in the procuring of the necessaries of life for our families, and bless all the substance which Thou hast given to Thy people, and which Thou dost desire they shall enjoy upon the earth.

Bless all who manifest an interest in the building up of Thy kingdom in every land: bless the land we occupy, even the valleys of the mountains, with every facility therein contained for Thy people, and bless the whole land of Zion, even the land of Joseph, and bless and multiply Thy Saints until this land shall be filled with those who love and serve Thee. Extend these blessings to all the subjects of our prayers. Preserve us on the earth to do Thy will on earth, and with the sanctified in glory bring us into Thy presence through Jesus our Redeemer. Amen.

The President then stated the nature of the school now being organized, and the objects in view in organizing it.

President H. C. Kimball[9] made a few remarks, in the course of which he spoke of the necessity of good order and strict decorum being enforced amount [among] the pupils, whether old or young. He felt well about the opening of the School of the Prophets here and said if we are not all prophets, we ought to be, for it is the duty of all Latter day Saints to live so that they may act under the guidance and dictation of the Holy Ghost, that constitutes a man a prophet.

President D. H. Wells said he felt the importance of the school now being organized, and was glad to assist in promoting it. It is the privilege and duty of the Latter-day Sain[t]s to become acquainted with every true principle pertaining to all science and learning; and it is more incumbent upon the elders of Israel than upon any other men

8. The Salt Lake Temple, first begun in 1853, was not finished until 1893. In the meantime, the St. George Temple was finished in 1877, followed by Logan in 1884, and Manti in 1888.

9. When the Church Historian's Office compiled the index to the Journal History, they underlined names and subjects for inclusion; I have omitted these underline marks since they were not part of the original documents.

in existence because they are engaged in a greater work than any others, —the building up and establishing the kingdom of God upon the earth. There are men of great attainments in many of the sciences in the outside world, but it is rare that such men, through pride and the circumstances by which they are surrounded, join the church; hence their knowledge and abilities are not available in the kingdom of God. This augments the necessity for the Elders of Israel to become proficient in the sciences. Yet, the wisdom of the world is not so very desirable, being so mixed up with vain philosophy. It is for the servants of God to acquire knowledge that is really useful, divested of all folly, and bring it into active service in the kingdom of God. By listening to the oracles of God, and following in the channel that He has appointed, the Elders of Israel have the privilege of acquiring true wisdom, even that which emanates from God. He exhorted all to support the school, with the utmost of their ability and energy; and prayed that the blessing of God might attend their exertions.

Chancellor Carrington spoke briefly upon the objects designed in the commencement of this school. He rejoiced that the Presidency had seen fit to make a move in this direction, and had met with the brethren at its opening.

Professor [David O.] Calder then gave an outline of the course of instruction that would be imparted and the time during each day that would be devoted to it. Every day in the week but Saturday, school will be held from 9 a.m. until 11 a.m. from 2 to 4 p.m. and from 7 till 9 in the evening. Book-Keeping will be one of the first branches taught; not book-keeping in the restricted sense, which merely teaches how to make correct entries in a day book, journal and ledger; but all the branches in actual use, and as practiced in the great business marts of the world. No text books will be used; but in the school the students will have a little commercial world of their own, in which, after going through the primary department, they will be initiated into the various transactions of actual business.

The meeting was dismissed with prayer by Pres. D. H. Wells. [In another meeting] Pres. Brigham Young at the Council House opened the school to be commenced under the auspices of the [University of Deseret board] regency, the rooms were not quite completed. ~~bu~~ David O. Calder, who was to be the principal, announced that they would

^probably^ be ready in a week. Pres. Young dedicated the school to the Lord, and the names of the pupils were taken.

REMARKS[10]

By President Brigham Young, on Monday Dec. 2, 1867, at the opening of the High School [School of the Prophets], established by the Chancellor and Regents of the University of Deseret.

Reported by G[eorge] D. Watt.

The morning is damp, and our room not very comfortable, and it is likely our exercises will be short. The Bishops and leading men of the city should all have been present.

In the early part of the year 1832 [1833], I think in January, Brother Joseph Smith, the prophet, commenced a school, denominated the "School of the Prophets." It was so called, because it was expressly designed for the education of the Elders of Israel in the science of Theology, and the design was to connect with this branch every other branch of useful learning. The circumstances which led to the bringing forth of the Word of Wisdom[11] took place in that School of the Prophets. Brother Joseph Smith had a small room over his kitchen, which, if I recollect aright was about ten feet by fifteen, where he held the school. The members of the school were in the habit of using tobacco extensively, which became very offensive. The prophet began to reflect on this disagreeable habit of the Elders, and sometime after, how long I know not, he inquired of the Lord, and the "Word of Wisdom" was given. I was not present at that school, but I was conversant with many who were. That school broke up, as nigh as my memory serves me, in the latter part of February, or the beginning of March following.

We now propose starting a school which will embrace every department of a useful and practical education. It will be dictated and controlled by the Chancellor and Regents of the University of Deseret, the whole being under the guidance of the Holy Priesthood; and hence, it may properly be called the "School of the Prophets." Our school will

---

10. This portion of the entry was clipped from the *Deseret News* and glued into the JH. I have retained the capitalization and italics used by the *News*.

11. The well-known Mormon prohibition against the use of tobacco, liquor, and "hot drinks," had its origins in the Kirtland School of the Prophets. For more, see Dirkmaat, et al., *Joseph Smith Papers: Documents, Volume 3*, 11–24; Peterson, "Historical Analysis of the Word of Wisdom."

commence in this house, and it will grow and multiply its departments as our facilities, or room for classes shall increase, for the education of the old, of the middle-aged and of the youth. I expect through the faithful exertions of the brethren, and the blessings of heaven, this institution will be greatly prospered. We should improve our minds in the knowledge of all truth that is now known to the children of men, and constantly seek in addition to this, wisdom that comes from God.

This is not a common and unimportant meeting. I expect to see nothing in this school that will be contrary to the most refined attainments. We have met to establish a school for the Elders of Israel, that they may be instructed in the things of the Kingdom of God. We expect this school to continue and extend until our faith and union are one. I am not a learned man, after the learning of this world, although I am not ignorant of the nature of the learning that should be disseminated among the human family. An education in mathematics, philosophy, and the sciences is incomplete without the knowledge of man, the design of his creation, and the object of his Creator in fitting the earth for his habitation, as it was, as it is, and as it will be. The first lessons for the Elders of Israel should be the study of themselves, and to learn God; for to know God, and Jesus Christ whom He has sent, is eternal life; and then to learn how to apply our lives constantly and faithfully to His service and requirements, which will result in leading us back into His presence; for this is in reality the great object and purpose of man's existence here. From this great leading branch of a true education grow all truths in science and in art, which pertain to the world we inhabit and to the animate and inanimate substances which compose its fullness.

From the different classes in this school, persons will be selected to form a class to be instructed in theology, that we may learn to be of one heart and of one mind, both the teachers and the scholars. The First Presidency of the Church of Jesus Christ of Latter-day Saints, and the Twelve Apostles will be scholars as well as professors in this high school, learning first to know the mind and will of God, and then to distribute this knowledge freely to those who are capable of receiving it, that the students may be educated in theology or the science of life—of life that was, that is, and that is to come. As soon as practicable, every branch of learning essential to the attainment of a complete and finished education, will be introduced into this school. Elder David O.

Calder has been assigned the preceptorship of the mercantile branch of education in this college. He will commence at once to give lessons in the different branches of this department of learning, viz. Book-keeping, Commercial Calculations, Penmanship, Business Correspondence, Commercial and International Law, Banking, Insurance, Exchange, Brokerage, Commission, Jobbing, Forwarding, Railroading, Expressing,[12] Telegraphing, Phonography and Post Office. Other branches will be introduced as the school enlarges and the facilities for teaching increase, among which we may name Geology, Chemistry, Languages, the science of Physic, or the healing art, which will lead into the study of Natural Philosophy, Botany, Anatomy, Surgery, etc., to a knowledge of the nature and functions of every part of the human system, the causes and character of disease and the remedies to be applied. There are very few indeed, if any, who know how to administer proper remedies to the sick, for the effectual destruction of disease, and the restoration of sound health, unless they are instructed by revelation from God. Some will, doubtless, have time and patience to enter into and continue the study of the advanced branches of Mathematics; but the more common, and generally useful branches of education, will be taught in this school, and we more particularly call the attention of the elders to these. While we are thus engaged in the pursuit of this class of knowledge we will still continue our practical lessons in agriculture, and horticulture, and in the development of the beauties of the floral kingdom; increasing the qualities of our meat-bearing animals, taking advantage of the experience of others, and improving upon all the blessings which our Heavenly Father has bestowed upon us. All these different branches o[f] education, which will be introduced into this School of the Prophets, will be at all times under the supervision of the Priesthood, which, under the Almighty, stands at the head of all things.

In the school particularly devoted to the Elders of Israel I shall invite the Bishops, and select others from the Elders to fill the class. There are but few of the Elders in attendance this morning. They very likely think that it is a matter of no great importance, and education is but a dry subject anyhow, and the morning is wet and the roads muddy. Allow me to say that there are very few of the Elders in this room who have

12. That is, carrying mail and goods by horse.

eyes to see the importance of this little meeting and the mighty results to which it will lead. We are not awake to this matter as we ought to be, and as I trust ere long we shall be. If we were I do not hesitate to say that we would soon be prepared to go back to Jackson County to build up the centre stake of Zion, and to receive the fullness of the blessings of the Lord which He will bestow on all those who are worthy. Those who manifest a lively interest in the things of God will be selected for an education to fit them for the great work which will be entrusted to them. We have now got a fair commencement for the attainment of those blessings God has in store for the faithful. The First Presidency and the Twelve are agreed, are one in heart and mind, and are better prepared than ever to perform those great and important duties, that are resting upon us. The salvation of the inhabitants of the earth rests upon the Elders of Israel, to build up the Zion of God in the last days, and the sanctifying of the people. This is the work which is before us, and for us to prepare to perform, that we may be ready to meet the Son of Man at His coming. We have established ourselves in these mountains, and supplied ourselves with the substantial comforts of this life, and it is now time for us to look a little more fervently for the salvation of the human family, and our own perfection. I will close these few remarks and call upon others to address you.[13]

December 9, 1867; Monday

A meeting of the school of the prophets was held in the City Hall. Pres. Brigham Young and Daniel H. Wells and Elder Geo. A. Smith spoke.

December 13, 1867; Friday

The school of the Prophets held ~~at~~ a meeting in the City Hall.

Class in Theology. This class met last night, and instructive addresses were delivered by Presidents B[righam] Young and H[eber] C. Kimball. Remarks were also made by Elders W[ilford] Woodruff, G[eorge] A. Smith and G[eorge] Q. Cannon. The class was organized with a President, two Vice-Presidents, and two Secretaries. Presidents B. Young,

13. Brigham Young valued vocational education as a practical means to build up the Mormon kingdom. He tended to oppose public schools, and, until 1890 when Utah adopted a public school system, education in the territory was almost exclusively controlled by Latter-day Saints through Mormon wards and leaders. Buchanan, "Education among the Mormons."

H. C. Kimball, and D[aniel] H. Wells, being elected the Presidents. Tickets of admission were also issued.[14]

December 16, 1867; Monday

A meeting of the school of the Prophets was held in the City Hall. Elders Orson Pratt, Pres. Brigham Young and Jos. F. Smith spoke.

December 20, 1867; Friday

A meeting of the school of the Prophets was held at 1 p.m. Pres. Brigham Young, Elder Jos. W. Young and several others were present.

December 23, 1867; Monday

Pres. Brigham Young preached at the School of the Prophets on sustaining the brethren and letting the outsiders alone.[15] [Blank] "He spoke in a heavenly manner, he then called upon Elder John Van Cott and the first 13 bishops in G[reat] S[alt] L[ake] City who all expressed themselves on the subjects sustaining the position taken by Pres. Young.["]

December 27, 1867; Friday

I attended the School of the Prophets in the Afternoon. We had speeches from Presidet You[n]g & the Bishops upon trading with our Enemies.[16]

December 30, 1867; Monday

In the Afternoon I Attended the School of the Prophets. The Subje[c]t treated upon was trading with our Enemies. Presidet You[n]g spoke & several of the Bishop[s] George Godard[,] J[ohn] Taylor[,] C[harles] C Rich & H[eber] C Kimball.[17]

January 3, 1868; Friday

I Attended the School of the Prophets in the Afternoon & we had some Excellent teaching from Presidet Young upon the principle of union of our being one & building up the kingdom of God.[18]

---

14. This second paragraph is taken from the *Deseret News*, Dec. 18, 1867.

15. That is, non-Mormons and dissidents challenging Mormon business hegemony. Themes of mercantile cooperation and patronizing the shops of non-Mormons would dominate the school for much of 1868–69. By the end of 1869 the opposition was fierce enough that Young moved to have independent merchants like William S. Godbe excommunicated. See Walker, *Wayward Saints*, and appendix 2, herein.

16. From WWJ, Dec. 27, 1867.

17. WWJ, Dec. 30, 1867.

18. WWJ, Jan. 3, 1868.

January 6, 1868; Monday

I attended the School of the Prophets. The following Persons spoke[:] Preside[n]ts Young & Wells also O[rson] Pratt[,] G[eorge] A. Smith, Elias Smith, Wm S Godby, & President Daniel Spencer. We had a good time.[19]

January 20, 1868; Monday[20]

The school of the prophets met in the afternoon, when Pres. Brigham Young and Daniel H. Wells and Elders Orson Hyde and Pres. Heber C. Kimball, Phineas H. Young, Geo. A. Smith, Jos. Young, Erastus Snow, and Geo. Q. Cannon spoke. Pres. Young also made a few concluding remarks.

The School of the Prophets[21]
Met at the 14th Ward Meeting House[22] at
1 oclock pm as for public notice

After singing prayer by Elder Jno Taylor. Singing after the roll was called.

Prest. B[righam] Young. See Geo. D. Watt.[23]

D[aniel] H. Wells, heartily coincides with the principles advocated by Prest. B Young, he always understood it was his duty to abide the counsel of the Prophet of God, to offer aid & comfort to our enemies, in the eyes of Nation[s] would be regarded as treason and we should be dealt with as Traitors, contrasted the mild, gentle leadership of Prest. Young, to the harsh and severe tone of Joseph [Smith] and many have taken the advantage of it.

On Adoption he supposed it had reference to the linking together

19. WWJ, Jan. 6, 1868.

20. The meeting of the territorial legislature disrupted the schedule of the school and there were no gatherings for two weeks.

21. These undated minutes follow the roll book in SotP 6, bx 1, fd 2. Several clues indicate that the minutes were from this meeting, including the list of speakers matching the list from the JH. These are the only surviving minutes from the 1867–69 meetings of the school.

22. The Fourteenth Ward was home to several apostles and prominent members. The large meeting house, called "one of the finest in the city at the time," was built in 1861 on First South. The ward school house, where the School of the Prophets also met at times, was constructed from adobe in 1852 and located one block southwest from the Council House. Jenson, *Encyclopedic History of the Church*, 749.

23. School member George D. Watt kept shorthand notes of Young's sermons, often (but not in this case) for later publication in the *Deseret News* or *Journal of Discourses*, and between December 1867 and May 1868 took minutes for the School of the Prophets. Like many of his notes, his minutes were never transcribed and are in his own papers rather than in the school's collection at the Church History Library. For a sample sermon, see appendix five.

of the Priesthood ~~now living~~ that it might reach back to the link that had long since been broken, that it might present one unbroken chain.[24] He considered that any children begotten by him before he rec[eive]d the priesthood, they would require to be sealed to him, in Order to graft them in as lawful heirs, but all begotten after he had ~~been sealed~~ gone through the [temple] Sealing Ordinances, he did not think his offspring begotten after this, there would be no necessity for them to be sealed as they were lawful heirs.

Prest. O[rson] Hyde[:] Much approved of the principle of Oneness now advocated, and intended to carry it out. Alluded to the recommendatory item in the local papers,[25] which seemed to encourage the saints to patronize our enemies, but desired to leave this point for other hands to handle it. The Doctrine of Adoption he knew but little about and should decline touching it until the line is chalked out.

Heber C Kimball[:] Was one with Prest. Young and propose Carrying it out himself as far as linking was concerned. Unless we take a course to become one, will see corrosion. The time will shortly come, when the Lord will choose a people from the midst of this people that will serve him. Spoke of our selfishness which had to give way and we become one.

Phineas H Young[:] Has had no other desire for the last 30 years but to ~~be~~ build up the Kingdom of God & to bless his family, his friends, and even his enemies (if he had any) was the object of his life. After alluding to some parts of his experience, he prayed for the blessings of God to rest upon him.

Elder Geo A Smith[:] Said the Elders of Israel should learn well what is right and then do it to day, tomorrow, and for ever.

Prest. Jos[eph] Young[:] The oneness [of the Law of Adoption].

Elder Erastus Snow[:] Said pertaining to our Temporal affair he was anxious to see carried out that we had been enriching our open enemies was a stubborn fact. The outside enemies of this people can accomplish nothing against us until we nourish, feed and sustain those in our midst.

---

24. The Law of Adoption, as taught by Brigham Young and others, allowed Mormons to be sealed to one another as families outside of traditional bloodlines and therefore be linked together in one cohesive family chain. See Irving, "Law of Adoption," and Stapley, "Adoptive Sealing Ritual in Mormonism."

25. Hyde is suggesting that the *Deseret News* should not carry advertisements for non-Mormon goods or shops, something George Q. Cannon refutes later in the meeting.

It is our business to do as we are told, but it is not our business to attempt to do every thing we see Bro Brigham do. Many things may be lawful for him to do, which, were he to attempt to do, would endanger his ~~life~~ Salvation. Strongly urged the practice of sustaining ourselves.

Elder Geo Q Cannon[:] As an Editor, he thought it would be very unwise to refuse the advertisements of our Enemies (would be likely to enkindle a fire in our midst ^&^ which would be carried to the states)[26] that would do more harm than good. Editing a paper was some thing lik[e] an Hotel, he has to admit all parties without asking any questions and should they refuse to admit such into their columns, it would be construed into a species of oppression that [blank].[27]

Prest. B Young[:] ~~See Geo D Watt~~ spoke of the wealth ^that^ had been accumulated by several of our merchants and by him self also, and therefore they ought to use it for the building up ~~for~~ ^of^ the Kingdom of God. He wanted the merchants to give liberally for the gathering the poor saints [to Utah].

The Editors here were as good men as any other and to refuse advertisements would be very poor policy, for that would only be the means of sustaining the Union Vedette.[28] We must sustain ourselves and build each other up, and by and by we'll have as much wealth as to buy not only the states but the World.

The meeting was then adjourned ~~for~~ till Friday at one Oclock p m.

After singing Benediction by [blank].

January 24, 1868; Friday

The School of the Prophets met in the 14th Ward School House. Pres. Brigham Young, John Taylor, Heber C. Kimball, Elders Wilford Woodruff and Robt. Pixton spoke. The latter related dreams and visions which he had received which Pres. Young endorsed.

W[ilford] Woodruff[:][29] I feel thankful for the privilege of speaking a few words to this school. I wish to refer to the first doctrin preach[e]d

26. That is, would potentially create calls for investigations by Congress or other federal officials.

27. Cannon's comments end abruptly, followed by three blank lines, then Young's closing remarks follow on the next page.

28. The *Union Vedette* was published by soldiers stationed at Camp Douglas. It was the first daily paper in the territory and openly opposed polygamy and LDS leaders.

29. The remainder of the entry is from WWJ, Jan. 24, 1868.

that Adam was our Father & God.[30] In the Revelation Called the ollive leaf[31] it says that the Devil gathered together the Hosts of Hell And Michael the Ark angel gathered to gether the Hosts of Heaven and he overcame the devil & his Angels & this is the Battle of the Great God." Who is this Michael the Ark Angel[?] It is Adam who was Michael in the Creation of the World.

Again in regard to the redemption of the dead I believe it will take all the ordinances of the gospel of Christ to save [one] soul as much as another. Jesus himself obeyed all the ordinances of the Gospel that he might fulfill all righteousness. Therefore those who have died without the gospel will have to receive the gospel in the spirit world from those who preach to the Spirit[s] in Prision, & those who dwell in the flesh will have to attend to all the ordinances of the gospel for & in their behalf by Proxy & it will take 1000 years with Jesus Christ at the head of all the Prophets & Apostles before the work will be finishing attending to all the ordinances for all the dead who have died without the gospel.

Again Co[nce]rning Revelation. I Believe it to be the privilege of Evry Apostle & Elder who bears any portion of the Holy Priesthood to have the Holy Ghost & Revelation to guide them in all things. But I do not Believe that the Lord will Reveal to any man a New Principle, doctri[ne] or Law, to govern the Church & kingdom of God on the Earth Except through the Mouth of the Prophet Seer, Revelator, Preside[n]t & Law giver unto the Church. This is his place & position to receive the word of the Lord & give it unto the people. There are some keys which the Prophet Joseph held which No other man held while he lived & there are some which Preside[n]t Brigham Yo[u]ng holds which No other Man holds The keys of the sealing power for instance. But he permits other Apostles to administer in this ordinance.

Again their is another subje[c]t I wish to speak off [of]. There is one subject up[o]n my mind & has been for years that is contrary to my Practice & the Practice of this People & that is Concerning the Sabbath.

I have never thought that the Jews or ten Tribes of Israel would Ever

30. Brigham Young had first taught in 1852 that Adam and God the Father were one and the same, calling Adam "our Father and our God, and the only God with whom we have to do." JD, 1:50–51. For more, see Buerger, "Adam–God Doctrine."

31. D&C 88 was termed by Joseph Smith as an olive leaf because it was "the Lords message of peace to us." Godfrey et al., *Joseph Smith Papers: Documents, Volume 2*, 334.

keep the gentile Sabbath [Sunday]. That is the first day of the week. When I was Baptized into this Chu[r]ch I was keeping Saturday for the Sabbath. But I knew that the Latter day Saints were the tru[e] Church of Christ & if I had imbibed 100 tradition[s] I would have given them up for this. I dont know as the Latter Day Saints will Ever keep this day & it does not make any difference whether they do or not for the Lord will dictate them Just as he please in all those things.

But when Moses received this Commandment to keep the seventh day of the week The Lord [said] this Law shall remain as a Statute Betwe[e]n me & the House of Israel forever throughout all your Generation. I have Never found this Commandme[n]t Changed By any revelation from God. Jesus & the Apostles kept the 7 day of the week Called the Jewish Sabbath. Yet the Apost[l]es did meet in some Instances on the first day of the week to Break bread &c. Constantine Changed the day of worship from the seventh to the first day of the week about 600 years after Christ.

We received a Revelation in the doctrins & Coven[an]ts in the Early age of this Chirch to Meet upon the Lords day to Break Bread &c. But the Lord did not reveal which day of our time was the Exact d[ay] that the Lord Commanded Israel to keep.

At the Close of the rema[r]ks Preside[n]t Young read the revelation and said that there had been so much Change in time that we do not know the Exact time that was the seventh day. Presid[en]t Yo[u]ng made many rema[r]ks upon vario[u]s subje[c]ts.

January 27, 1868; Monday

The School of the Prophets met in the 14th Ward School House. Pres. Young gave liberty for the Twelve [Apostles] and others to ask questions. Pres. Erastus Snow asked pertaining the rights of the Bishops, the High Council and the members of the Quorum of Twelve. Pres. Young spoke and recapitulated some of the sayings of Joseph [Smith] the Prophet pertaining to the Priesthood.

I attended the school of the Prophets. Many remarks wer[e] made upon the order of the Priesthood. Preside[n]t You[n]g[:] a man being ordained to the High Priesthood does not deprive him of any office which he held before. I have a right to officiate as a priest teacher or Deacon. Preside[n]ts of the seventies might act as Bish[o]p[s,]

Councellors to the [stake president] or act as High Councellor without Being ordained a High Priest.[32]

January 31, 1868; Friday

The school of the prophets met in the 14th Ward School House. Pres. Brigham Young, Heber C. Kimball and Daniel H. Wells and the Twelve Apostles and others were present. Pres. Brigham Young and counselors spoke; also Hiram B. Clawson, B[isho]p Edwin D. Woolley, Daniel Evans[33] and Erastus Snow. Prests. Young, Kimball and Wells spoke on the impropriety of the youth of Zion marrying [for time only] instead of getting sealed [for eternity]. He also spoke of cleanliness of person, before going to get [temple] endowments; a woman should not go for a week after her menses were upon her, a man should not have intercourse with his wife for several days, but should be clean in body and exercised in spirit previous thereto; his clothing should be changed once or twice before ^going^ there.

Pres. Brigham Young nominated Abraham O. Smoot to go to Provo[34] to act as president, mayor and Bishop of that place, and John Taylor to go there as judge and a number of others as city councilors.

February 3, 1868; Monday

The school of the Prophets met in Salt Lake City; the subject of astrology,[35] witches, and witchcraft was discussed. Pres. [Brigham] Young declared that there were witches in the midst of the people by whose influence suffering and distress were wrought upon many.[36]

February 7, 1868; Friday

The school of the prophets met in the 14th Ward school house, Pres. Daniel ~~F.~~ ^H.^ Wells presiding. Elders Orson Pratt, Orson Hyde, Geo.

---

32. This second paragraph comes from WWJ, Jan. 27, 1868.

33. Other documents clarify that this is David, not Daniel Evans. David Evans was bishop of Lehi, Utah; for more, see the biographical register.

34. Provo was first settled as Fort Utah in 1849 with Ellis Eames as the town's first mayor in 1851, largely as a fruit farming community.

35. Wilford Woodruff noted in his diary that "it was decided that Asstrology was in oposition to the work of God." WWJ, Feb. 3, 1868.

36. According to D. Michael Quinn, "By affirming the reality of witches, Young inadvertently encouraged [some] Mormons ... to use house-amulets against witches ... Pioneer Mormon belief in witches also led to other counter-charms, including ritual magic against witchcraft." Quinn, *Early Mormonism and the Magic World View*, 222.

Q. Cannon, Jos. ~~Wells~~ ^Young^ and Pres. Wells spoke on the Word of Wisdom, especially on the eating of meat.[37]

February 10, 1868; Monday

The school of the prophets met in the 14th Ward School House. Among those present were Daniel H. Wells, Orson Hyde, Orson Pratt, Lorenzo Snow, Erastus Snow and Geo. Q. Cannon.

These brethren except Bro. Snow all spoke on the principles of union, reference being made to the alteration in the [Salt Lake] city ticket, substituting Edwin D. Wooley's name for LeGrande Young. Pres. Jos. Young also spoke on unity and the alteration of todays city election ticket.[38]

February 14, 1868; Friday

A meeting of the school of the Prophets was held in the 14th Ward, commencing at 1 o'clock p.m. the First Presidency and several of the Apostles and others were present. Pres. [Brigham] Young investigated the cause of division in the late [Salt Lake] City election when the name of La Grande Young was stricken out and the name of Edwin D. Woolley substituted and he cried strongly against the spirit of division at the [election] polls.[39]

February 17, 1868; Monday

A fine meeting of the school of the prophets was held in the 14th Ward commencing at 1 o'clock p.m. Elder Geo. A. Smith and Brigham Young spoke. Pres. Daniel H. Wells and Elder Geo. Q. Cannon made statements and full confession relative to their not being energetic and alive sufficiently to the importance of putting down the division at the [election] polls. Several of the colleagues and others who had voted the scratch ticket[40] made humble confessions.[41] Pres. Young and [Heber

---

37. The Word of Wisdom counseled that meat should only be eaten sparingly outside of winter. See D&C 89:12–13.

38. Brigham Young was traveling in Provo during the election and did not approve of swapping Young's name with Woolley's, who was elected as an alderman (see Feb. 14, 1868, entry). Daniel H. Wells was re-elected as mayor.

39. Wilford Woodruff recorded the next day that Young "rebuked (in the Strongest terms) D. H. Wells and all the men who were prese[n]t for not stoping the opposition. I never herd him speak in such power & spirit." WWJ, Feb. 15, 1868.

40. That is, a ballot with a candidate's name struck through or erased.

41. Young had not authorized the substitution of Edwin D. Woolley to replace his

C.] Kimball spoke nicely and a very interesting, profitable and heavenly meeting was the result.

February 22, 1868; Saturday

I attend[e]d the School of the prophets in the Afternoon but was near sick.[42]

February 24, 1868; Monday

I attended the scho[o]l of the Prophets In the afternoon. Preside[n]t [Brigham] Young request[e]d the Twelve to Bring in rules & regulations to govern the School of the Prophets.[43] The following Persons prese[n]t[e]d rules[:] O[rson] Hyde, L[orenzo] Snow, & W[ilford] Woodruff prese[n]ted 10 Commandments. They were all read Before the School.[44]

February 28, 1868; Friday

A meeting of the school of the Prophets was held in the afternoon. Elder Daniel H. Wells, John Pack, Pres. Heber C. Kimball and Geo. Q. Cannon spoke on agriculture, horticulture, etc.

March 2, 1868; Monday

A meeting of the school of the prophets was held in the 14th Ward school house. Pres. Daniel H. Wells, Geo. D. Watt and Jos. A. Young spoke.

March 9, 1868; Monday

A meeting of the school of the Prophets was held. Pres. Brigham Young, Heber C. Kimball and Daniel H. Wells, Elders Geo. A. Smith, Geo. Q. Cannon and a full school was present. Prests. Wells and Young preached, and a number of rules were read to which the school unanimously subscribed.

March 13, 1868; Friday

The school of the Prophets met, the First Presidency being present.

---

nephew LeGrand Young. For more, see Quinn, *Mormon Hierarchy: Extensions of Power*, 263–64. Those who confessed admitted to being not "energetic & alive" enough to "putting down the division at the polls." HOJ, Feb. 17, 1868.

42. From WWJ, Feb. 22, 1868. The territorial legislature was still in session and no School of the Prophets meetings were mentioned in the JH or the HOJ.

43. The rules are included as appendix 1 and were transcribed from the original. They were re-read several times as new members joined the school, including at the September 19, 1868, meeting and printed in the Journal History under that date.

44. WWJ, Feb. 24, 1868.

Prests. [Brigham] Young and [Heber C.] Kimball and Elders Geo. A. Smith and Geo. Q. Cannon preached under a heavenly influence which prevailed throughout the meeting. Bishop [Edwin D.] Woolley also made a few remarks. Bro. Cha[rle]s Crismon's son was called to go onto the Sevier and locate on the abandoned settlement,[45] taking some of the right kind of men with him.

March 16, 1868; Monday

The First Presidency attended the school of the Prophets at which the speakers were Pres. Brigham Young, Geo. D. Watt, Phineas and Lorenzo D. Young and Cha[rle]s Crismon ~~spoke~~. The subjects dwelt upon by the speakers were silk culture, pisiculture [sericulture: raising silkworms], wool growing and machinery. The rules of the school were again read by Geo. Q. Cannon and all voted to sustain ~~him~~ ^them^.

March 20, 1868; Friday

At the school of the prophets held from 1 to 4 o'clock Pres. Daniel H. Wells, Elders John Taylor, Orson Pratt and Wilford Woodruff preached the subjects being in the interests of the kingdom, etc. Orson Pratt encouraged the brethren to seek after the spirit of prophecy.

March 23, 1868; Monday

At the school of the prophets in the afternoon Pres. Daniel H. Wells, Elders John Taylor, Geo. Q. Cannon, Edward Hunter, Orson ~~Hunter~~ ^Pratt^, Wilford Woodruff and Edwin D. Woolley spoke on the subjects treating on home manufactures, being dwe~~a~~lt upon in a very interesting manner.[46]

March 27, 1868; Friday

The school of the Prophets met in the afternoon, Pres. Brigham Young presiding. Pres. Brigham Young, Elder John Taylor and Pres. Daniel H. Wells spoke; the spiritual and temporal duties of the saints were the subjects, the rules of the school were read to which the new members subscribed.

45. The settlement, located at present-day Richfield, in Sevier County, had been established in 1864, but it and surrounding towns were abandoned following confrontations with Ute Indians during the Black Hawk War of 1865–68.

46. Woodruff wrote that he "spoke vary plain upon following the fashions of the day." WWJ, Mar. 23, 1868.

March 30, 1868; Monday

At the school of the Prophets Elder Orson Pratt, Tho[ma]s W. Ellerbeck, Robt. L. Campbell and Geo. B. Wallace, ~~Marius~~ ^Morris^ John Pack, Jos. Young and Pres. Brigham Young spoke, their subjects being agriculture, manufactures, etc. The presidency reported that by this weeks end he would have transpla^n^ted about 100,000 mulberry trees.[47]

April 3, 1868; Friday

At the school of the Prophets held in the 14th Ward School House the First Presidency and a full school were present. Elder Albert Carrington delivered a fine lecture on the laws of health, etc. Pres. [Brigham] Young spoke a few words. Elder [John] Al^b^is^t^on delivered a short lecture on the first principles of the Gospel. He is the son of Patriarch [John] Al^b^is^t^on. The class was adjourned for a week.

April 10, 1868; Friday

The school of the Prophets met at ~~10~~ 1 o'clock p.m. in the 14th W[ar]d Meeting house. Pres. Brigham Young, Amos Fielding ^and^ Dr. John M. Bernhisel occupied the time speaking on diatetics [nutrition], hygiene, etc. Elder [George Q.] Cannon read the rules of the school, as some new members were being admitted all the time.

April 13, 1868; Monday

The school of the Prophets met as usual. ^Daniel H. Wells, Orson Pratt,^ Geo. A. Smith, Heber C. Kimball, and Erastus Snow spoke.[48] 200 new members had recently joined the class.

April 17, 1868; Friday

The School of the Prophets met in the old Tabernacle.[49] About 60 new members joined the school. Elder Geo. Q. Cannon read a chapter in the new Testament and one of the revelations in the Doctrine and

47. Mulberry trees provided habitation for silkworms. Salt Lake City's desert climate allowed the trees to flourish, and in the post-Civil War era both Mormons and non-Mormons alike hoped silk manufacture would boost the local economy. "Grape, Mulberry, and Cotton, *Union Vedette*, Nov. 9, 1867; "Culture of Silk," *Deseret News*, Mar. 25, 1868.

48. Brigham Young had traveled to Provo and did not attend this meeting.

49. The Old Tabernacle sat on the southwest corner of Temple Square and was finished in 1852. It resembled a rectangular barn on the outside and a theatre on the inside, with ascending seats. The new tabernacle, still in use on Temple Square, was finished in 1867. Peterson, "Accommodating the Saints at General Conference," 7–8.

Covenants. Elders John Taylor, Orson Pratt and Pres. Daniel H. Wells preached and Elder Geo. Q. Cannon made a few remarks.

April 20, 1868; Monday

R[obert L. C[ampbell] ... afternoon at School [of the Prophets].[50]

May 1, 1868; Friday

Afternoon I attended the school of the prophets.[51]

May 4, 1868; Monday

I attended the school of the Prophets in the Afternoon.[52]

May 8, 1868; Friday

The school of the Prophets was held in the old Tabernacle; Pres. [Brigham] Young occupied the most of the time contrasting the favorable situation of the saints here with the world, and counselling the saints to live their religion. Pres. [Heber C.] Kimball made a few remarks. A committee was organized to ^form^ ~~organize~~ parties for killing grasshoppers.

May 11, 1868; Monday

At the school of the prophets Pres. Daniel H. Wells, Heber C. Kimball and Pres. Brigham Young preached. A number of new members were admitted at every meeting of the class.

May 18, 1868; Monday

Attended the school of the Prophets in the Afternoon. A rainy day. The subject of Labor was talked abo[u]t.[53]

May 22, 1868; Friday

Pres. Brigham Young gave to the school of the prophets the term of the railway[54] contract and adknowledged the hand of the Lored in giving this people the privilege of performing the work, thus keeping

50. From the HOJ, Apr. 20, 1868.
51. WWJ, May 1, 1868.
52. WWJ, May 4, 1868.
53. WWJ, May 18, 1868.
54. The Union Pacific Railroad, part of the Transcontinental Railroad authorized by Congress in 1862, began serious work in 1865 and laid about a mile of track each day. The transcontinental project was finished in 1869, the Union Pacific heading west from Omaha, Nebraska, and the Central Pacific coming east from Sacramento, California. The two lines met at Promontory Summit west of Brigham City, Utah. The Union Pacific became the major railroad company in Utah.

away from our midst the swarms of scalawags[55] that the construction of the railway would bring here.

A good influence pervaded the meeting and all present seemed to feel the same. When the president expressed the hope that the job might be completed creditably with the saints, that in the halls of Congress it might be announced that no part of the national railway was completed more satisfactorily. The brethren in mass clapped their hands approving of the president's remarks.

Elder Wilford Woodruff records the following in his journal: "Pres. Young has taken a job in making the railroad from the mouth of Echo [Canyon] to this city or to the lake; it was spoken of today in the school."

May 25, 1868; Monday

I attend[e]d the Meeting of the Prophets in the Afternoon.[56]

May 28, 1868; Thursday

At the school of the Prophets held this day the building of the Union Pacific Railroad and the union of the people, the establishing of wagon and carriage shops and furniture ware was discussed. Pres. Brigham Young, Geo. Q. Cannon, Daniel H. Wells spoke upon the subject.

May 29, 1868; Friday

At a meeting of the school of the Prophets President [Brigham] Young and President [Daniel H.] Wells, and Elder Geo. Q. Cannon preached. The President wished the brethren to establish carriage manufactories, shops, furniture manufactories; to send for their timber to the [United] States and have the best carriages and furniture for sale here. Questions were answered by the President about the railroads, also with reference to the hourly expected telegrams, and letting out of contracts.

Brother George Q. Cannon spoke on the necessity of the Bishops directing in the temporal affairs in the Wards, and exhorted the letting outside [non-Mormon] stores alone.

---

55. Young appropriated the post-war term for Southerners profiteering by colluding with Northerners during Reconstruction. He feared the influx of outsiders the railroads would bring.

56. WWJ, May 25, 1868.

June 6, 1868; Saturday[57]

At the meeting of the school of the Prophets, at 1 p.m., in the old Tabernacle, President Brigham Young, Heber C. Kimball and Daniel H. Wells were present. Pres. Young preached, also Elder Geo. A. Smith, Subject, the Josephites[58] and the New Translation of the Bible.[59] Pres. Young said the family of Joseph [Smith] would be placed in circumstances where they would have to seek the Lord and be sufficiently humble to get revelation from him so they would yet see their true condition.

June 13, 1868; Saturday

At a meeting of the school of the Prophets held in Salt Lake City, Pres. Brigham Young presiding, the subject of the new translation ^of the Bible^ was introduced and spoken of; also the railroad, etc.[60]

June 20, 1868; Saturday

The School of the Prophets met at 1 p.m. President [Brigham] Young spoke of the new translation of the Bible and said it was not complete. Dr. [John M.] Bernhisel testified that the Prophet [Joseph Smith] told him that he wished to revise it. Emma Smith[61] let Dr. Bernhisel have the new translation to peruse it, for three months; during this time the Doctor copied much of it. Orson Pratt compared many of the sayings in the new and old translations. George A. Smith testified that he had heard the prophet Joseph say, before his death, that the new translation was not

57. After usually meeting twice a week on Monday and Friday, the school now began meeting weekly on Saturdays, with some exceptions.

58. "Josephites" referred to members of the Reorganized Church of Jesus Christ of Latter Day Saints (now Community of Christ), formed in 1860, with Joseph Smith III as prophet and president. Although several Mormon groups were formed after the death of Joseph Smith and ascension of Brigham Young, the Reorganized Church became the largest and, at the time, most worrisome to Utah Church leaders because of the affiliation of immediate family members of Joseph Smith. The two churches clashed over polygamy, which the Reorganized Church claimed Smith had neither practiced nor sanctioned.

59. The New Translation of the Bible, also called Joseph Smith's Inspired Version, was begun in June 1830 and mostly finished by July 1833. It was never published during his lifetime, although extracts appeared in LDS periodicals. The manuscript was published by the Reorganized Church of Jesus Christ of Latter Day Saints in 1867.

60. Wilford Woodruff recorded that he left the meeting early to attend to Heber C. Kimball, who was gravely ill, "intirely speechless" and "would not live long." Kimball died on June 22. WWJ, June 13, 1868.

61. After her husband's death, Emma Hale Smith (1804–79) remarried, ceased her affiliation with the church, and later joined the Reorganized Church. Newell and Avery, *Mormon Enigma*.

complete; that he had not been able to prepare it, and that it was probably providentially so. The roll was called, which took half an hour.[62]

June 27, 1868; Saturday

At the School of the Prophets Pres. Brigham Young, Geo. Q. Cannon, Geo. A. Smith and John Taylor spoke. Bro. [Orson] Pratt made a confession of his error in printing Mother Lucy Smith's[63] book[64] without first consulting Pres. Young. Extracts from Bro. Pratt's writings were read.

July 4, 1868; Saturday

The school of the prophets met ^in Salt Lake City^ at 2 p.m.[65] Elder Orson Pratt made a full confession before the School of his error in opposing doctrines revealed; said whenever he had done so and excused himself because of what was written [in scripture], his mind became darkened and he felt bad. He asked forgiveness of Pres. [Brigham] Young, of the Twelve [Apostles] and the whole school. Pres. Young expressed his satisfaction with Elder Pratt's confession and preached in relation to Adam, etc. Elder [Wilford] Woodruff spoke and felt happy at Bro. Pratt's position and present feelings.[66]

July 11, 1868; Saturday

At the School of the Prophets Pres. Brigham Young gave a good exortation on the necessity of laying up bread stuff, unity, etc., and gave a good account of the progress of the railroad. The only difficulty was

---

62. By now the school had hundreds of members.

63. Lucy Mack Smith (1776–1856), born in New Hampshire, was the mother of Joseph Smith Jr. After the murders of Joseph and Hyrum Smith in June 1844, and the departure of the main body of the church to the west two years later, she remained in Nauvoo and dictated her memoirs, which became *Biographical Sketches of the Prophet Joseph Smith,* published in Liverpool, England, in 1853.

64. Orson Pratt published Lucy Smith's *Biographical Sketches of Joseph Smith* in Liverpool in 1853. Young believed it was, as described by Elias Smith, "a tissue of lies from beginning to end," and he was incensed by Lucy's favorable treatment of her youngest son, William, who had been excommunicated, and what Young saw as Pratt's insubordination. Young now began a campaign to recall and destroy the book, and he championed a revised version, which did not appear until 1902. See Anderson, *Lucy's Book.* For more on the younger son, see Walker, *William B. Smith.*

65. Wilford Woodruff noted that, in addition to the School of the Prophets meeting, "We had a great Celebration of our Nations Birth day." WWJ, July 4, 1868.

66. Young and Pratt had long differed on certain doctrinal issues, such as Young's controversial "Adam–God" teachings. For more, see Bergera, *Conflict in the Quorum,* and Buerger, "Adam–God Doctrine."

that the engineers were not staking off the road fast enough. Many of the brethren had to go east on Nounan's contract.[67] Brigham Young Jr. also spoke, followed by A. Milton Musser and Emanuel Murphy.

July 18, 1868; Saturday

At a School of the Prophets held in Salt Lake City, Geo. Q. Cannon, Levi W. Hancock, Wilford Woodruff and Pres. Daniel H. Wells spoke. The nomination of [Salt Lake] county officers, delegate to [US] Congress, etc. was made unanimously. Unity and the sustaining of ~~one of the~~ ^leading and^ living oracles of the Church were the pr~~e~~incipal topics treated upon.

July 25, 1868; Saturday

At a School of the Prophets various brethren spoke on medicine, and hygiene. Elder Geo. Q. Cannon who presided[68] preached on the laws of health, etc.

August 1, 1868; Saturday

At the School of the Prophets Pres. Brigham Young preached as did also Elder Geo. A. Smith and Pres. Daniel H. Wells, on the Saints sustaining themselves, etc.

August 8, 1868; Saturday

At the School of the Prophets, which met in S[alt] L[ake] City, Pres. Brigham Young, Geo. Q. Cannon, Geo. A. Smith and John Pack spoke. Elder Jesse C. Little announced that the beef contract at Camp Douglas[69] had been let to Orustein and Popper[70] at $14.68 per hundred [pounds].

---

67. Joseph F. Nounan (1837–1909), a Salt Lake City non-Mormon banker and business man, was one of several principal subcontractors on the Union Pacific Railroad. Young charged the subcontractors tithing and the church netted an $88,000 profit from the railroad construction. Bain, *Empire Express*, 495.

68. Brigham Young was traveling in Provo and did not attend.

69. Camp Douglas (renamed Fort Douglas in 1878) was established on Salt Lake City's east bench in 1862 by Colonel Patrick Edward Connor and the California Volunteers, sent to Utah to oversee the Mormons during the Civil War. The Saints were thought largely by the soldiers to be religious fanatics of questionable loyalty. The first Indian battle involving the troops stationed there, against a band of Shoshones, took place the next year. Other campaigns followed, continuing up to the 1890s. Maxwell, *Civil War Years in Utah*, 166–70.

70. Jacob Ornstein (1831–1885) and Charles Popper (1845–1909) were Jewish butchers who had emigrated from what is now the Czech Republic, arriving in Utah Territory in 1864–65.

August 15, 1868; Saturday

The School of the Prophets held an interesting session.[71]

August 22, 1868; Saturday

The School of the Prophets met in S[alt] L[ake] City, Elders Dimick, B. Huntington, Orson Pratt, and Prest. D[aniel] H. Wells preached. Bro. Huntington informed the school that with Sup[erintenden]t [Franklin H.] Head[72] he had visited the few Indians who still remained at war, and concluded peace with them. Black Hawk[73] was there and was still in for peace. They recited their wrongs from the time John Murdock[74] abused them in Manti [Utah], and told deliberately about their killing this one and that one. Bro. Pratt spoke very spiritedly on the blessings that awaited them. Bro. Wells recapitulated many scenes in their Indian campai[g]ns—told of the time they killed 27 in Utah Co[unty], and exhorted the Saints to divest themselves of any revengeful feelings towards the Lamanites [Native Americans]; and related many interesting incidents in the late San Pete Campai[g]ns, and spoke of the bad feelings many of the Saints had towards the Indians who were ignorant and full of heathen traditions.

August 29, 1868; Saturday

The School of the Prophets met as usual in Salt Lake City. Pres. Brigham Young and Daniel H. Wells and Elders Geo. A. Smith and ~~Brigham~~ ^Joseph^ Young preached on the duties of the saints, the ~~sultes~~ ^rules^ of the school were read and sustained by vote.[75]

71. Wilford Woodruff recorded that "G[eorge] A Smith spoke 22 M. Capt [William H.] Hooper spoke 60 minuts[,] G[eorge] Q Canon 15 Minuts[,] Presidt [Brigham] Y[o]ung spok[e] 25 Minuts." WWJ, Aug. 15, 1868.

72. Franklin H. Head (1832–1914) was appointed by US President Andrew Johnson as superintendent of Indian Affairs in Utah in 1865. He was an advocate for the Mormons but not for the Indians; in later years he called them "savages … treacherous, revengeful … imbued with the idea that every kind of labor is absolutely degrading." Head, "What Shall We Do with Our Indians?" 222. He later lived in Chicago where he was an industrialist and president of civic groups and literary societies.

73. Black Hawk (d. 1870), a Ute chief, became an enemy to the Mormons after he witnessed the suffering of his tribe at the hand of the LDS settlers. The resulting Black Hawk War began in April 1865 when Indians killed five Mormons and drove off a large herd of cattle. The Native American force, made up of several tribes, grew, and the conflict lasted for seven years. Black Hawk was seriously wounded in a battle near Salinas, Utah, in 1866, and died four years later. Peterson, *Utah's Black Hawk War*.

74. This is either John M. Murdock, who fought in the Black Hawk War, or John R. Murdock, residing at the time in Beaver, Utah.

75. Levi Hancock and Abraham O. Smoot also spoke. WWJ, Aug. 29, 1868.

September 5, 1868; Saturday

R[obert] L. C[ampbell] ... at [School of the] Prophets meeting.[76]

September 12, 1868; Saturday

The School of the prophets met in the old Tabernacle, Salt Lake City, at 1 p.m. Elder Geo. A. Smith, Brigham Young and Daniel H. Wells, preached. Dimick B. Huntington, Andrew Cahoon, Loren Farr and Dan Wood also made a few remarks.

September 19, 1868; Saturday

The School of the Prophets met as ^usual^ ~~usual~~ in ~~S.L.~~ ^Salt Lake^ City.[77] Orson Pratt, Geo. B. Wallace, Geo. D. Watt, Edwin D. Wooley and Amos Fielding spoke. By direction of Geo. A. Smith the rules of this class were read and a copy of them filed. They are as follows:[78]

September 26, 1868; Saturday

R[obert] L. C[ampbell] ... aft[ernoon] at School of the Prophets.[79]

October 3, 1868; Saturday

At the School of the Prophets Pres. Brigham Young, Elders Geo. A. Smith and Geo. Q. Cannon preached on sustaining the brethren, and letting outsiders alone.

The president and school voted that those who dealt with outsiders [non-Mormons] should be cut off [excommunicated] from the Church. The president declared that he had tried to control the merchants, but could not do it; he said they would go to hell, if they did not turn a short corner.[80]

---

76. HOJ, Sep. 5, 1868. Brigham Young, Wilford Woodruff, George Q. Cannon, and other leaders were traveling west of Salt Lake City in Grantsville.

77. Brigham Young and others were traveling through the territory to establish local chapters of the School of the Prophets. The local bishop was usually made president of the school. In Sanpete County, Young continued to counsel against "traiding with the Gentiles or I will Cut you off from the Church." He also admonished everyone to "Stop dri[n]k[in]g Coffee, tea, whiskey, Tobaco for this is the word of God unto you & you will be Cut off." WWJ, Sep. 18, 1868.

78. The rules were reprinted in the Journal History at this point. They are found here in appendix 1.

79. HOJ, Sep. 26, 1868. Brigham Young, Wilford Woodruff, and other leaders were traveling south.

80. Brigham Young had warned the Saints not to trade with anyone "who does not pay his tithing and help gather the poor and pray in his family," concerned that the arrival of the transcontinental railroad would bring competition and disruption. These

October 10, 1868; Saturday

G[eorge] A. S[mith] ... preached at School of the Prophets. R[obert] L. C[ampbell] copying letter, attending School [of the Prophets].[81]

October 17, 1868; Saturday

At the School of the Prophets held in Salt Lake City, Pres. Brigham Young and Geo. A. Smith preached on cooperation.[82]

October 24, 1868; Saturday

At the School of the Prophets held in S[alt] L[ake] City a preamble and constitution of Zions Cooperative Institution[83] were read by sections and discussed and unanimously approved. Pres. [Brigham] Young spoke of the foolishness of the brethren refraining from selling wheat to their brethren [in favor of outside markets].

October 31, 1868; Saturday

In the School of the Prophets Pres. Brigham Young spoke of ^the^ Silk Worm Culture, Home Manufacturers, etc, followed by Geo. D. Watt and Pres. Geo A. Smith. Bishop Reuben Miller spoke on farming ^and^ agricultural interests, and was followed by Pres. Brigham Young.

November 7, 1868; Saturday

The School of the Prophets met at 1 p.m. in the old Tabernacle. Elder [Edwin] Rushton spoke on the manufacture of silk. He and all his father's family had been raised in the manufacture of sewing silk and he desired to go into the movement with his whole heart. Pres. Geo. A. Smith preached on hiring school teachers who were not Latter-day Saints, and placing the children of the saints under their influence which was wrong. On motion of Pres. Geo. A. Smith, Bartlett Tripp was voted to go on a preaching mission.

---

remarks set the stage for a cooperative merchandising endeavor sponsored by the church. See Campbell, *Establishing Zion*, 317–18; Walker, *Wayward Saints*.

81. HOJ, Oct. 10, 1868. The meeting was overshadowed by a reunion of Zion's Camp that evening. Thirty-nine men and three women who participated in the 1834 march gathered at the Social Hall.

82. The HOJ clarified that the subjects were "unity, Zion's co-operative store."

83. Zion's Cooperative Mercantile Institution (ZCMI) was Young's answer to non-Mormon merchants. His plan was "to bring goods here and sell them for as low as they can possibly be sold and let the profit be divided among the people at large." Because of the wide array of products available at ZCMI, it was called America's first department store. Campbell, *Establishing Zion*, 318. For more on the history of ZCMI, sold to Macy's in 1999, see Bradley, *ZCMI*.

November 14, 1868; Saturday

At the School of the Prophets Elder Franklin D. Richards presented the by-laws of Zions Mercantile Institution. The constitution was read and the by-laws read and approved. Pres. Geo. A. Smith preached and exhorted the bishops and Elders to live their religion. Pres. Brigham Young and Daniel H. Wells were also present.

November 21, 1868; Saturday

At the School of the Prophets Pres. Daniel H. Wells and Geo. A. Smith, Elder [blank] Leonard[84] and Pres. Brigham Young spoke on the subject of consecration; the true principle of consecration was to hold emphatically everything we possessed upon the altar for the use and benefit of the Kingdom of God, and men shall be as stewards over that which they possess, not that everything shall be common or that all men shall be made equal in all things, for to one is given one talent, to anothor two, and to another five, according to their capacity.

November 28, 1868; Saturday

At the School of the Prophets held in the afternoon the subjects of trading with outsiders was discussed. Bro. [blank] Wilkinson[85] was charged with having bought goods from a Jew. He confessed, asked forgiveness and promised not to do so any more.

December 12, 1868; Saturday[86]

At 1 o'clock p.m. the School of the Prophets met as usual. The report of the Committee on establishing a uniformity of prices was read. Hiram B. Clawson, W[illia]m S. Godbe and Henry W. Naisbitt made some good remarks on the benefits of the co-operation.

Pres. [Daniel H.] Wells spoke of the small pox in San Francisco & the danger of its introduction. W[illiam] Bernhisel spoke of the benefits of vaccination: the greatest blessing ever revealed to man.[87]

December 19, 1868; Saturday

84. Although Lyman Leonard and Bradford Leonard were listed as members of the school, this is probably Truman Leonard, an early missionary to India who settled in Farmington. See Leonard, "Truman Leonard."

85. William B., Robert M., and Moses Wilkinson were all listed in the rolls of the school.

86. Although the school likely met December 5, nothing is mentioned in the JH, the HOJ, or WWJ.

87. This second paragraph was taken from the HOJ from this date.

At the School of the Prophets Pres. Brigham Young, Elder Geo. Goddard and Bishop Edwin G. Woolley spoke on the manufacture of pails, wooden buckets, etc, to which Pres. Brigham Young replied encouraging home industry.[88]

December 26, 1868; Saturday

The School of the Prophets met at 1 o'clock p.m. in the Old Tabernacle. Prest. Brigham Young introduced the business and desired that there might be no occasion to speak harshly to his brethren. His language might sometimes be unbecoming, but the principles he advanced were correct. He alluded to ink and match manufactures, and hoped the brethren would make them so good that the public, for their own good, would be compelled to buy them.

Bro. [George D.] Watt spoke on silk culture; Bishop [Edward] Hunter made a few remarks on domestic manufactures, repeating the words of the Lord: "Let your garments be plain, and the beauty thereof be the workmanship of your own hands, etc". Prest. Geo. A. Smith gave a lengthy speech, replete with good exhortations to his brethren and talked considerably on domestic manufacture.

January 2, 1869; Saturday

R[obert] L. C[ampbell] … P.M. at School of the Prophets.[89]

January 9, 1869; Saturday

At the School of the Prophets Elder Franklin D. Richards preached on Domestic Economy, followed by John Pack on stock raising. Pres. Brigham Young followed and advanced many good items on home manufacture.

January 16, 1869; Saturday

The school of the Prophets met in Salt Lake City, of the First President [Presidency] there were present Brigham Young, Geo. A. Smith, Daniel H. Wells, of the Twelve [Apostles]: Orson Hyde, Orson Pratt, John Taylor, Wilford Woodruff, Cha[rle]s C. Rich, Ezra T. Benson, Lorenzo Snow, Erastus Snow, Franklin D. Richards, Geo. Q. Cannon,

88. The HOJ of this date added that Goddard "said he had manufactured good ink for years, but few of his brethren patronize him."

89. HOJ, Jan. 2, 1869. Most leaders were north in Ogden meeting with civic leaders and railroad officials and establishing a branch of the School of the Prophets.

Brigham Young Jr. and Jos. F. Smith. The meeting was held in the old Tabernacle, Salt Lake City. Elder Chas. C. Rich made a few general remarks, followed by David Evans, bishop of Lehi [Utah], who gave a statement of the prosperity and financial success of the Lehi co-operative store. Elder Erastus Snow gave a relation of his labors in all the counties of Utah Territory south of Utah County.

January 23, 1869; Saturday

The School of the Prophets met in S[alt] L[ake] City. Pres. Geo. A. Smith spoke on the necessity of the brethren getting out their naturalization papers.[90] Elder Franklin D. Richards read the bill introduced into [US] Congress by Mr. Ashley[91] for the cutting and parceling of Utah [Territory].[92] The meeting adjourned at an early hour.

February 6, 1869; Saturday

Attended the school of the Prophets & addressed the school. Was follow[e]d By C[harles] C. Rich & Erastus Snow.[93]

February 13, 1869; Saturday

I spent the Afternoon in the school of the prophets.[94]

February 20, 1869; Saturday

Attended School of Prophets at 1.P.M.[95]

February 27, 1869; Saturday

A session of the School of the Prophets was held in G[reat] S[alt] L[ake] City. Pres. Geo. A. Smith preached on the necessity of having

90. If the thousands of male LDS immigrants became naturalized (legal US citizens), they could vote and give the church increased political power, especially when leaders continued to fret over the expected influx of outsiders from the Transcontinental Railroad.

91. James Ashley (1824–96) had served Ohio in the US House of Representatives from 1859 to 1869 and chaired the Committee on Territories and had been appointed governor of Montana Territory.

92. Utah Territory, although initially smaller than the proposed state of Deseret, included most of present-day Nevada and portions of Wyoming and Colorado. Throughout the 1860s the territory was divided and parceled out to other territories. Ashley, an avowed opponent of the LDS Church, wished to carve up the territory further, but this time Utah would retain its present boundaries.

93. WWJ, Feb. 6, 1869. The meetings of the territorial legislature may have cut into the school's normal activities this month.

94. WWJ, Feb. 13, 1869.

95. FDRJ, Feb. 20, 1869.

good arms and training as a militia; also on the necessity of obtaining naturalization papers by the foreign[-born] brethren.

March 6, 1869; Saturday

At the School of the Prophets held in the old Tabernacle, S[alt] L[ake] City, Pres. Daniel H. Wells spoke on unity in temporal things and the importance of having our youth educated by those full of faith in the holy gospel. Pres. [Brigham] Young spoke at length on many important subjects.

March 13, 1869; Saturday

At a session of the School of the Prophets held in S[alt] L[ake] City new tickets were issued to the members. Elder Jesse C. Little gave an account of the success attendant upon his [freighting] mission east for carriage and wagon material. He had 50 tons of material on the road.

March 20, 1869; Saturday

The School of the Prophets met in the old Tabernacle, S[alt] L[ake] City. New tickets were distributed among the members. Lewis S. Hill gave an account of the way pre-emption claims and homesteads are claimed; the difference between the one and the other.[96] Elder Jesse C. Little spoke on the land business. Several spoke on the same subject and questions were asked [of] Bro. L[ewis] S. Hills who is receiver. A committee ^consisting^ of Jesse C. Little, Hosea Stout and Aurelius Miner was appointed to post to themselves upon the land question and report to the people what steps were necessary to take to preserve their homesteads being claimed by the railway companies.[97]

March 27, 1869; Saturday

At the School of the Prophets which met in Salt Lake City Elders Daniel H. Wells, John Taylor and Wilford Woodruff spoke on the introduction of home manufacturers, on the necessity of labor becoming

---

96. The Preemption Act of 1841 provided a way for male settlers already living on government land to buy that land (up to 160 acres) at an affordable price. It was largely supplanted by the Homestead Act of 1862, which allowed the purchase of 160 acres after a settler had improved the land for five years. The Homestead Act excluded women and former Confederate soldiers. McPherson, *Battle Cry of Freedom*, 193–95.

97. Settlers in the West often improved land before it could be surveyed, creating confusion about ownership. Railroad land grants ceded millions of acres to rail companies, including limited-fee rights of way. White, *Republic for Which It Stands*, 144–45.

cheaper in order that our manufacturers might fairly compete with outside manufacturers, Elder Orson Pratt preached a short sermon on the necessity of some of the Elders learning the living languages and the Hebrew to qualify them for future usefulness in sending the Gospel to all nations. A fine spirit prevaded the meeting. Pres. Brigham Young was not well enough to come to the meeting, but sent text to be preached upon by those who occupied the time. The president had been somewhat indisposed.

April 3, 1869; Saturday

The School of the Prophets met at 1 p.m. in the old Tabernacle. Elder Geo. D. Watt gave a lengthy account of his late southern and northern tours, preaching seri-culture [silkworm raising]; and replied to charges against him [that he was] deprecating Zion's Co-operative; and admitted his indiscretion and injudicious use of words.[98] President Brigham Young spoke mildly in relation to Geo. D. Watt's course; said so long as a man's intentions were good, we could afford to overlook his indiscretion.[99] Brother Joseph Young made a few remarks pertaining to the unwise sayings of brother Watt.

April 10, 1869; Saturday

The School of the Prophets met at 1 p.m. Elder Erastus Snow preached on the interests of the Southern Mission and Pres. [Daniel H.] Wells on the futility and wickedness of opposing co-operation [church cooperatives], or any measure instituted by the servants of God. Elder Geo. Q. Cannon read John Pack's letter to his son-in-law in Cache Valley [Utah] burlesquing [mocking] co-operation. Bro. Cannon made some pungeant remarks on the same and read the rules. Pres. Brigham Young followed on the same subject as Pres. Wells and Elder Cannon and showed how much easier it is to distroy than build up.

April 17, 1869; Saturday[100]

98. Wilford Woodruff noted that "Watt spoke about 2 Hours in his own defense." WWJ, Apr. 3, 1869.

99. Watt had left Young's employ as a clerk and was opening his own store. Unable to compete with ZCMI, he publicly criticized the cooperative movement. He would later join with the Godbeites and leave the mainstream church. Watt, *Mormon Passage of George D. Watt*, 234–39.

100. Brigham Young, Daniel H. Wells, George Q. Cannon, Wilford Woodruff, and

At the School of the Prophets held in S[alt] L[ake] City Elder A. Milton Musser spoke on paying endebtedness to the Perpetual Emigrating Fund.[101] Bro. Wm. S. Muir also spoke on the same subject, Elder Robt. Campbell spoke on school and the Deseret alphabet,[102] Geo. D. Watt on the Deseret alphabet and Geo. B. Wallace ~~and~~ ^on^ agriculture and horticulture.

April 24, 1869; Saturday[103]

At the School of the prophets held in S[alt] L[ake] City, Elder John Taylor presiding, remarks were made concerning the homestead laws of the United States by Hosea Stout and others, Elder Jos. F. Smith delivered a very good address. Elder Taylor's health was improving.[104]

May 8, 1869; Saturday[105]

At the School of the Prophets in S[alt] L[ake] City the land questions were ~~thought~~ ^talked^ over and explanations given relative to the mode of procedure in relation thereto.[106]

May 15, 1869; Saturday

At the School of the Prophets in S[alt] L[ake] City Pres. Brigham Young and Geo. A. Smith ^and^ Delegate Wm. H. Hooper occupied the time in speaking.[107]

May 22, 1869; Saturday

The School of the Prophets held their usual meeting in S[alt] L[ake]

---

other leaders were in Springfield, Utah, to dedicate a new meetinghouse and did not attend this meeting.

101. The Perpetual Emigrating Fund loaned money to immigrants, for which the church expected to be repaid. The fund was dissolved with the passage of the Edmunds–Tucker Act of 1887, though, by then, much of the debt had been forgiven.

102. The Deseret alphabet was phonetically based, intended to help immigrants learn English. It never found widespread use.

103. Brigham Young and other leaders were still away and did not attend this meeting or the May 1 and 8 meetings.

104. The HOJ for this date adds that George A. Smith, himself ill, "considered it wisdom to remain at home."

105. The school also met May 1, but no details remain about the gathering.

106. See Mar. 20, 1869.

107. Wilford Woodruff wrote that "a Letter was read from John Pack ridiculeing Cooperation & the work of God for which He was Cut off from the Church." It is unclear if this was the same letter mentioned at the April 10, 1869, meeting or another. WWJ, May 15, 1869.

City. Elder Geo. Q. Cannon, Presidents Geo. A. Smith, Daniel H. Wells and Brigham Young spoke; and also Elder Wilford Woodruff. The President asked of the Bishops in the City individually if they had traded outside the general co-operative. Bishop Phineas H. Young had bought one sack of sugar at the Elephant Store.[108] Those who had done so were requested to leave their tickets [of admission to the school]. Geo. D. Watt and Bishop Young spoke. Benediction by Geo. A. Smith.[109]

May 29, 1869; Saturday

Pres. Geo. A. Smith and Brigham Young preached in the school of the Prophets, S[alt] L[ake] City. B[isho]p Edwin D. Woolley made a few remarks also. The first speaker dwelt mostly on Military matters. President Young endorsed his remarks on military, and made some very good remarks on co-operation, asking the Saints to do all their trading at their ward stores, and asked the Mormon merchants on Main Street to sell their goods so low that they will catch all the transient trade.[110]

June 5, 1869; Saturday

At the School of the Prophets held at the Old Tabernacle, S[alt] L[ake] City, ~~held~~ ^commencing^ at 1 p.m., Pres. [Brigham] Young spoke of the impossibility of competing with foreign productions while labor was so high. He also spoke of the necessity of having confidence and referred to his seeking at all times to build up the kingdom, never going across the street [to non-Mormon shops] to make a bargain for himself. Elder [George Q.] Cannon sustained the presidents remarks on the necessity of reducing wages. Pres. ^Geo. A.^ Smith endorsed Pres. Young's remarks. Dimick B. Huntington also spoke.

June 12, 1869; Saturday

The School of the Prophets held a session this afternoon in Salt Lake City. The subject of cheap labor and home manufacture was discussed.

---

108. The Elephant Store was on the east side of Main Street, operated by non-Mormon Isaac Trumbo. Brigham Young's brother Phineas was required to give up his ticket to the school. WWJ, May 22, 1869.

109. The HOJ also noted that "Elder John Pack's confession [was] read" at the meeting. See his restitution, July 3, 1869, entry.

110. By transient trade, Young meant those passing through briefly on their way to the coast.

Elders Albert P. Rockwood, Jos. Young, Geo. B. Wallace and many others spoke; Jos. F. Smith presided.

June 26, 1869; Saturday[111]

At the School of the Prophets Pres. Daniel H. Wells, Elder Geo. Q. Cannon and Wilford Woodruff and Bro. Geo. A. Smith spoke, giving reports of the journey north, etc.

July 3, 1869; Saturday

The School of the Prophets met in the Old Tabernacle, S. L. City at 1 p.m. The First Presidency and several of the Twelve [Apostles] and others were present making a full school. Pres. [Brigham] Young spoke in relation to John Pack's case;[112] he being present made a confession which was finally accepted. The speakers were Geo. A. Smith, Jos. F. Smith, John Taylor and Brigham Young. A committeeman from each trade was elected to submit to the trades the proposition of reducing the wages of the mechanics in order that Utah might be able to compete with the manufactures of the [United] States.

July 10, 1869; Saturday

At the School of the Prophets held in the old Tabernacle reports of the meetings of the [manufacturing] Trades, etc., were read. President ^Brigham^ Young talked much on the policy of lowering wages, etc. President Geo. A. Smith entered his protest against the 13th Ward Meeting house, or any other meeting house being let out for shows, performances, etc., which was endorsed by Pres. Young, who gave a short history of the building of the Social Hall, Theatre, etc.: and how he had headed off Artemus Ward,[113] Parepa Rosa,[114] etc, who wanted to perform

111. If an intervening meeting was held June 19, 1869, no record was made. Brigham Young, Wilford Woodruff, and other leaders were traveling in northern Utah and southern Idaho on a preaching mission.

112. Pack had criticized the cooperative movement and had been "cut off" (see May 15, 1869 entry), but quick restorations to full fellowship in the church were common if the accused made a public confession.

113. Artemus Ward (1834–67), pen name for Charles Farrar Browne, was a prominent satirist and comic. He gained popularity in England for letters he wrote to *London Punch* humor magazine.

114. Epuphrosyne Parepa Rosa (1836–74) was a Scottish opera singer. In 1866 she came to America on tour and became popular with the American public.

at the Tabernacle.[115] He also gave a recapitulation of the plans he gave the Ward School Houses, which are now called Meeting Houses.[116]

July 17, 1869; Saturday

At the School of the Prophets held in the Old Tabernacle, the brethren who spoke alluded to the visit of the sons of the Prophet Joseph [Smith],[117] and the conduct of Emma Smith, widow of the martyred prophet [Joseph Smith], was c[a]nvassed.[118]

July 24, 1869; Saturday

The School of the Prophets met as usual at 1 p.m. Pres. Brigham Young and Geo. A. Smith occupied most of the time, unity, home-manufactures etc., being the topics. President Young alluded to Emma Smith's prevailing on Joseph [Smith] to take off his garments before he went to Carthage [Jail, Illinois], Hyrum Smith and John Taylor did the same;[119] but Willard Richards[120] being charged by Joseph never to put

---

115. Both Ward and Rosa eventually performed in the Salt Lake Theatre, not in the Salt Lake Tabernacle. Young enjoyed the theater but objected to using church buildings for performances.

116. Each Mormon community in the territory had a tabernacle, then later adapted one-room school houses for various meetings. Some even had municipal offices and a jail and were called "ward meeting houses." Richard T. Ely, "Economic Aspects of Mormonism," *Harpers*, Apr. 1903; Arrington and Bitton, *Mormon Experience*, 216.

117. During the summer of 1869, Smith's sons Alexander and David Hyrum arrived in Utah on a mission for the Reorganized Church of Jesus Christ of Latter Day Saints. They were greeted by their cousin, Presiding Patriarch John Smith, and met with Brigham Young and other church officials. In their preaching, they held well-attended public meetings in the non-Mormon-owned Independence Hall, while opposition meetings were organized and held by their cousin Joseph F. Smith, son of Hyrum Smith.

118. Conversations about Emma Smith and her "conduct" were mostly a rehashing of what Brigham Young reportedly said to Alexander and David Smith during their tense meeting when Young called her a "liar, yes, the damnedest liar that lives" and repeated the old charge that their mother had tried to poison their father. Newell and Avery, *Mormon Enigma*, 285. Young had made similar charges in LDS conference sermons in 1866 and 1867.

119. Church members who have participated in temple ordinances covenant to wear the garment day and night and it is said to offer protection to those who wear it. Brigham Young believed that Joseph Smith was left vulnerable to the bullets fired in Carthage Jail and blamed Emma Smith for that. Hyrum Smith was also killed and John Taylor wounded at Carthage. Current LDS teachings emphasize that the protection is a spiritual one, meant to serve as a reminder of covenants and help safeguard against temptation.

120. Willard Richards (1804–54) was a first cousin to Brigham Young. He became a close associate of Joseph Smith and served as his personal secretary and as Church Historian and Recorder. He was called as an apostle and later served in the First Presidency with Brigham Young from 1847 until his death.

them off, would not, for said Joseph: ["]Willard, the day will come when bullets will whistle by you on each side, and men will fall on each side of you, but you shall be preserved.["]

[Letter read into the record:] W[illiam] S. Warren,[121] of Parowan, said, in our hearing at his house, in the 17th ward, about the 12th of July, 1869: 1st: That a man who wouldn't buy goods where he could get them the cheaptest was a fool. 2nd. That the reduction of the prices of labor and produce was introduced to build up such men as Presidents Brigham Young, Daniel H. Wells and W[illiam] H. Hooper. 3rd. That the prices were kept up when the President had lumber to dispose of, now he has none, and it has to be brought down. 4th. It has come to that pass now that the poor brethren must either starve or apostatize.

Sabith F. Hyde, Angeline Hyde,
Provo 17th Ward[122]

July 31, 1869; Saturday

At the School of the Prophets, Pres. Geo. A. Smith and Brigham Young, Bishop [William R. S.] Warren and Elder A. Milton Musser spoke. Geo. A. Smith was voted to be lieutenant-governor of the state of Deseret.[123] Bishop Warren's suspension of the previous week was continued.[124]

August 7, 1869; Saturday

The First Presidency attended the School of the Prophets and several hundreds of the school were present. Pres. [Brigham] Young occupied much of the time. ~~as did also~~ Prests. Daniel H. Wells, Geo. A. Smith and Elder George Q. Cannon ^also spoke^.

---

121. William R. S. Warren (1818–82) was bishop of Parowan, Utah, but was temporarily living north to work on the railroad spur from Ogden to Salt Lake City. He was friends with former apostle Amasa Lyman; both had helped colonize San Bernardino, California. Warren was suspended from the school because of his comments in Provo opposing Young's cooperative plan. He was later excommunicated, joined the Godbeite movement, and eventually left Utah. See Orton, *William Reed Stockbridge Warren.*

122. This letter to the school was reprinted in the *Mormon Tribune* (later *Salt Lake Tribune*), Apr. 16, 1870, and was quoted by William R. S. Warren as part of a lengthy rebuttal to the charges against him.

123. The church began a renewed effort to obtain statehood under the name Deseret. George A. Smith's nomination as lieutenant governor was part of a proposal endorsed at a mass meeting in Salt Lake City on October 7, 1869. A memorial was sent to Congress petitioning for statehood, but it was ignored. "Grand Mass Meeting of the Citizens of Utah," *Deseret News*, Oct. 13, 1869.

124. See July 24, 1869.

August 14, 1869; Saturday

This P.M Attended School of Prophets & spoke about [blank]. Tho[ma]s G. Thayner and Father [Nels] Nelson also spoke very plainly about several matters pertaining to our cooperative matters.[125]

I met with the school of the prophets.[126]

August 21, 1869; Saturday

The School of the Prophets met as usual in S[alt] L[ake] City. Elder Joseph F. Smith, Presidents Geo. A. Smith, Brigham Young, and Daniel H. Wells ~~also~~ preached. Elder Geo. Q. Cannon spoke first, introducing the subject of Josephitism, and read David H. Smith's[127] letter to the reporter, published at Corinne [Utah].[128] Many interesting items were rehearsed by Presidents Smith and Wells.

President Young spoke but little. Said he would not allow a word to be spoken on this subject, were it not for the sake of many who are young in the Church, and are unacquainted with the things which transpired in the days of Joseph [Smith].

August 28, 1869; Saturday

At the School of the Prophets Pres. Brigham Young, Geo. A. Smith and Daniel H. Wells preached. Committees were appointed to draft a series of resolutions.[129]

September 4, 1869; Saturday[130]

1 PM Attend school of Prophets. Pres Joseph Young[,] Edward Stevenson and Loren Farr [occupied the time].[131]

---

125. FDRJ, Aug. 14, 1869.

126. WWJ, Aug. 14, 1869.

127. David Hyrum Smith (1844–1904) was born in Nauvoo, Illinois, five months after the death of his father, Joseph Smith Jr. He was a singer, poet, and painter, and became prominent in the Reorganized Church. He later developed a mental illness and lived in an asylum the remainder of his life.

128. David Smith's letter to the *Utah Daily Reporter* was published August 15, 1869. It responded to a public meeting held by Joseph F. Smith on August 8 denouncing Emma Hale Smith and defending polygamy. See Avery, *From Mission to Madness,* 104–08.

129. Franklin D. Richards wrote that he "spoke about 45 minutes on saving grain." FDRJ, Aug. 28, 1869.

130. Gaps exist in the JH between August 28 and October 16; I have supplemented those with entries from the HOJ, WWJ, and FDRJ. No meeting was held October 9 due to General Conference. Apostle Ezra T. Benson died on September 3, 1869, in Ogden, Utah, and it is likely his death was also a topic at this meeting of the school.

131. FDRJ, Sep. 4, 1869.

I attended the school of the Prophets in the After noon. Presidet [Brigham] Yo[u]ng was prese[n]t & spoke to the School.[132]

G[eorge] A. S[mith] in [historian's] office and at School [of the Prophets].[133]

September 11, 1869; Saturday[134]

R[obert] L. C[ampbell] ... at School [of the Prophets]. J[oseph] F. S[mith] Recording sealings and at School [of the Prophets].[135]

September 18, 1869; Saturday[136]

At School of the Prophets—Elders John Taylor, John Sharp, Jun & James Sharp spoke.[137]

September 25, 1869; Saturday

I went to the City & attended the School of the Prophets many speeches were made upon Cooperation & other things.[138]

October 2, 1869; Saturday

AM at School of Prophets & spoke half an hour on several subjects.[139]

October 16, 1869; Saturday

The School of the Prophets met as usual in S[alt] L[ake] City, and was addressed by Pres. Brigham Young who related a dream which he had had concerning the bishops and gave an earnest and solemn appeal to the brethren to wake up from their lethargy. A number of the brethren were disfellowshipped until they should attend and give reasons for their absence [from the school] and their grumbling.

132. WWJ, Sep. 4, 1869.

133. HOJ, Sep. 4, 1869.

134. Brigham Young, Wilford Woodruff, Franklin D. Richards, and most other leaders were in Brigham City for meetings on this day.

135. HOJ, Sep. 11, 1869.

136. Brigham Young and other leaders were still in the northern part of the territory.

137. HOJ, Sep. 18, 1869.

138. WWJ, Sep. 25, 1869. The HOJ noted that some men, including Elias Smith, John Sharp, and John Taylor, were assigned as emissaries to work with the Union Pacific Railroad on land claims and other contracts in Omaha, Nebraska. Franklin D. Richards noted in his diary that Thomas C. Stayner of the Godbeite movement was excommunicated. Because neither explicitly says these events occurred in the School of the Prophets, they are not included here.

139. FDRJ, Oct. 2, 1869.

October 23, 1869; Saturday

The School of the Prophets met as usual in the old Tabernacle S[alt] L[ake] City. The following named brethren were called upon to answer to charges brought against them for not attending the school and other things: Robt. F. Neslen, W[illia]m C. Dunbar, Geo. D. Watt, Tho[ma]s B. H. Stenhouse, Wm. S. Godbe and Elias L. T. Harrison. The two last named were not excommunicated from the Church but were summoned to appear before the city [high] council on Monday at 10 a.m.[140] The others were restored to fellowship.

October 30, 1869; Saturday

The School of the Prophets met as usual at 1 p.m. Henry W. Lawrence made a statement of his position [regarding William Godbe] and Pres. Daniel H. Wells, Elders John Taylor and Geo. Q. Cannon spoke at length.[141]

November 6, 1869; Saturday

The School of the Prophets met at 1 p.m. and was addressed by Elders John Taylor and Geo. Q. Cannon and Pres. Daniel H. Wells.

November 13, 1869; Saturday[142]

The School of the Prophets met as usual.[143]

November 20, 1869; Saturday

G[eorge] A. S[mith] in [historian's] office and at School [of the Prophets].[144]

I attended the school of the prophets. D[aniel] H Wells spoke 20 Minuts, Brother [William W.] Player a few mome[n]ts[,] J[ohn] Taylor 38, W[ilford] Woodruff 18 Min[u]t[e]s[,] Joseph Yo[u]ng 16[,] G[eorge] A Smith 18.[145]

---

140. For the minutes of Godbe's and Harrison's trial, see appendix 2. The case was heard by the high council in the city's Council Hall.

141. Brigham Young and other leaders were traveling south and did not attend.

142. William H. Shearman, part of the Godbeite movement, relinquished his ticket to the school on this day, writing, "As under existing circumstances, it will not be pleasant or profitable for me to longer attend the 'School,' I feel it my duty to return my ticket." Shearman to George Goddard, Nov. 13, 1869, SotP, 6, bx 1, fd 6.

143. Wilford Woodruff recorded that Daniel H. Wells and Brigham Young both spoke for over an hour each. WWJ, Nov. 13, 1869. Franklin D. Richards wrote that he spoke for fifty minutes. FDRJ, Nov. 13, 1869.

144. HOJ, Nov. 20, 1869.

145. WWJ, Nov. 20, 1869. Joseph F. Smith wrote that topics included the Godbeites and the railroad. JFSJ, Nov. 20, 1869.

November 27, 1869; Saturday

R[obert] L. C[ampbell] ... at School [of the Prophets]. J[oseph] F. S[mith] recording sealings & at School [of the Prophets].[146]

December 4, 1869; Saturday

The School of the Prophets met and were addressed by Geo. Q. Cannon, Wilford Woodruff, John Taylor and Brigham Young.

P.M. at School [of the Prophets]. The question of adoption was raised. Elders P[hineas] H. Young & Geo Q. Cannon and Prest. D[aniel] H. Wells spoke on the subject also the question of sealing. If a woman be sealed to two men, whose will she be? Answer—his who has the best claim upon her thro[ugh] faithfullness and Priesthood. Elder Woodruff, Prest. B. Young & Elder Orson Pratt spoke on the Subject of the power or authority of the Holy Preisthood.[147]

December 11, 1869; Saturday

The School of the Prophets met in S[alt] L[ake] City. Wilford Woodruff opened the school by prayer. Questions were asked by several of the members. The following is a synopsis of President [Brigham] Young's remarks; He said a bill of divorce given to many is no better than a piece of blank paper. A woman who is sealed [married for eternity] to a good man that bears the Priesthood, if that man honors that Priesthood, if she leaves him of her own accord, and she is sealed to a dozen other men, the first man will hold her in the resurrection, if he wants her ~~unless she should be sealed to a man of a higher Priesthood than the first man~~. But even a man holding the office of a Deacon may magnify that calling so that he would be more worthy and have a higher exaltation than many High Priests. It is not so much the office a man holds, as it is the magnifying of that portion of the office he does hold. Some ordinations cannot be given without a Temple. All children born before parents are sealed at the altar, will have to be sealed to their parents in order to make them legal heirs. Those who are born after their parents are sealed are legal heirs. Man also will have to be sealed to man until the chain is united from Father Adam down to the last Saint. This will be the work of the Millenium and Joseph Smith will be the man to

146. HOJ, Nov. 27, 1869.

147. This second paragraph is taken from JFSJ, Dec. 4, 1869.

attend to it or to dictate it. He will not minister in person, but he will receive his resurrected body and will dictate to those who dwell in the flesh and tell what is to be done, for he is the last Prophet who is called to lay the foundation of the great last dispensation of the fullness of times. Some may think what I have said concerning Adam strange, but the period will come when this people will be willing to adopt Joseph Smith as their Prophet, Seer, Revelator and God, but not the Father of their Spirits, ~~for that was our Father Adam~~. Many questions are asked about divorces. I will say that many men and women want to be sealed that should not be, for they will not stay together. But if I was to stop it, there would be a fuss; now what is to be done? They will be sealed and then they will separate. Some give them bills of divorce. I charge nothing for sealing, but I charge $10.00 for bills of divorce. If they will break the commandments and make me break them, they shall pay ten dollars. For President Joseph Young asked President Brigham Young, if he was justified in giving Bills of Divorce. President Young answered: – Yes, I am, I do not force them to separate, I give them good counsel and tell them what to do. No man has a right to put away [divorce] a wife except for adultery. But when a woman will have a man against his will, he does not put her away, but she puts herself away, and he that marries her commits adultery.[148] I am justified in giving them bills of divorce, for they will separate against my counsel. And the woman is responsible herself and not I.

He said in relation to Joseph Smith receiving the plates of the Book of Mormon, that he did not return them to the Box from which he had procured them, but he went in a cave in the Hill Comorah with Oliver Cowdrey and deposited the plates upon a table or shelf; and in that room were deposited a large amount of gold plates, containing sacred records. When they first visited that room the sword of Laban was hanging upon the wall, and at the last visit the sword was drawn from its scabb[a]rd and lay upon the table and a messenger, who was the keeper of the room, informed them that that sword would never be restored to its scabb[a]rd until the Kingdom of God was established

148. That is, a woman who has a sexual relationship with someone who is not her husband is the cause of the inevitable divorce and anyone who might marry her after that is committing adultery.

upon the earth, and reigned triumphant over all. Joseph Smith said that cave contained tons of choice treasures and records.[149]

December 18, 1869; Saturday

The School of the Prophets met as usual and was addressed by Pres. Brigham Young who spoke principally on honesty, making good remarks. The sale of estray cattle having been discussed lately, a vote was passed to the effect that there should be no more drives of stock, unless the people signified their wish to have it so and the school also.

December 25, 1869; Saturday

The School of the Prophets met. Many questions were asked by the members and answered by President Brigham Young. Elder Lorenzo Young asked if the spirits of negroes were neutral in Heaven, as some one had said that the Prophet Joseph [Smith] said they were? President Young said; No, they were not, there were no neutral spirits in Heaven at the time of the rebellion, all took sides. If any one says they heard the Prophet Joseph say that the spirits of the blacks were neutral in Heaven, he would not believe them, for he heard Joseph say to the contrary. All spirits are pure that came from the presence of God. The posterity of Cain are black because he committed murder. He killed Abel and God set a mark upon his posterity.[150] But the spirits are pure that enter their tabernacles and there will be a chance for the redemption of all the children of Adam, except the sons of perdition.[151] Wilford Woodruff made a speech upon apostasy.

149. According to Cameron J. Packer, "At least 10 different accounts, all second-hand, refer to this cave and what was found there." Packer, "Cumorah's Cave."

150. For Mormon racial teachings, see Bush Jr., "Mormonism's Negro Doctrine"; Mauss, *All Abraham's Children*; Reeve, *Religion of a Different Color*.

151. In LDS theology, "Lucifer is perdition," and those who supported him in opposition to God the Father and Jesus Christ during a pre-earth Council in Heaven "were thus followers (in other words sons) of perdition." McConkie, *Mormon Doctrine*, 746.

CHAPTER TWO

"THE RISING GLORY OF ZION"

1870

January 1, 1870; Saturday[1]

Theological Class met in the Tabernacle at One o clock pm. Present Prest. B[righam] Young presiding. After singing Prayer by Elder Jos[ep]h F. Smith. Singing.[2]

Elder B Young [Jr.] who had been absent over two months, exprest thankfulness to return, he had been East, and spoke of some half hearted friends in New York, who on the arrival of the News about the Godbe & Harrison Movement,[3] thought it would prove a death blow to Cooperation. He said there never was a more bitter spirit in the United States [against the Mormons] than exists at the present time. He also spoke of the beneficial effects that will result, by the Elders recently being sent forth to disseminate correct principles among the people. He Met with Col ^T[homas]^ Kane,[4] who expressed his full faith in

1. Unless otherwise noted, entries in this and subsequent chapters are from the original minutes in SotP.

2. Secretary George Goddard opened the minutes of each meeting using the same format: where the meeting was held (usually in the still-standing tabernacle, built in 1867, or in the old tabernacle, not torn down for another seven years), the time, which leader was presiding, singing by the school members, a prayer, and then more singing by the congregation.

3. The Godbeites, named after leader William S. Godbe, were a resistance movement against LDS isolationist economic policies and an attempt to integrate Utah into the national economy. Godbe and his supporters began *Utah Magazine*, then *Mormon Tribune* (later *Salt Lake Tribune)*, and in 1870 formed the Church of Zion with former LDS apostle Amasa M. Lyman at its head. Many of those involved in the movement were excommunicated from the LDS Church. Walker, *Wayward Saints*.

4. Thomas L. Kane (1822–83), born in Philadelphia, was an ally to the Mormons. He intervened to help create the Mormon Battalion, to help petition for statehood, to stop the Utah War, and later to help Brigham Young write his will. He served as a Union officer during the Civil War. For more on the relationship between Kane and Young, see Grow and Walker, *Prophet and Reformer*.

the final triumph of Mormonism, and adverted to the corrupt Men who constitute the present Senate of the United States &c.

Elder Geo Q. Cannon said, if we thought that God was not with us, he had no doubt we should ^feel^ very bad. And after alluding to the recent~~l~~ triumph of the American Arms, in subduing over 11 Millions of people, during the late rebellion [American Civil War], he believed the President [Ulysses S. Grant] & his Cabinet ~~h~~ entertain the belief that it would be but an easy task for them to wipe out of existence the 150 or 200 thousand that live in these vallies[5]—he was satisfied there would be another crusade made against us, before the cup of this Nation would be filled, and thus prepare them for the judgments of God that hang over it. There is no honour or integrity left, almost every man in power and trust are as corrupt and dishonest as hell—but they are afraid of the growth and influence of the Kingdom of God. He then spoke of the fearfulness that exist to some extent among us, and the unwise letters they write to their friends in the East.

The Man recently appointed to be our Governor[6] [John W. Shaffer] and who will shortly arrive, while in Orleans threatened the Orchestre in the Theatre that unless they would play tunes which they might have a strong National hatred to,[7] he would have every one of them arrested and cast into prison. This was the kind of tune, we might shortly be expected to play to, they had erected a God, and will try to make us bow to, or else threaten and endeavour to destroy us.

Prest. D[aniel] H. Wells spoke of the warfare [Utah War] that has, and will continue to exist, but we will maintain our ground against all aggressors.

He said that the basis upon which this Apostatized [Godbeite] Movement rested ^was^ viz that Prest. Young will either loose his power, or die soon but he (Prest. Wells) felt to prophecy that neither

---

5. Plural marriage was a frequent topic in the US Congress and the government took several measures to oppose it, including passing legislation, sending federal officials to Utah territory who were hostile to the church, carving up the territory, and rejecting pleas for statehood. Gordon, *Mormon Question*.

6. John W. Shaffer (1827–70), appointed by Ulysses S. Grant as seventh territorial governor of Utah, was an active Republican and determined to stop what he saw as rebellion by the church. However, he died during his first year in office.

7. In the aftermath of the Civil War, Southerners continued to oppose nationalism and Reconstruction. Shaffer, then stationed in New Orleans, ordered the orchestra to play patriotic songs.

one nor the other will take place. There were many in our midst who lacked integrity, and although, neither the Josephites, nor the present Movement, can catch them, something in the future will occur that will take away all those who cannot stand the trying times that yet await us. God will have a tryed people, and all who ^are^ not honest cannot possibly stand, but let us be firm and faithfull, and observe our Covenants, and the word of wisdom, and greater blessings would be poured out upon us. Let us bear up in our faith, prayers and actions. The Man God has appointed as Our leader, he is a choice ruler and we should esteem him—and pray for his life to be lengthened out. We do not expect justice from the hands of the wicked—but let our course be onward and upward, and the strength of the wicked will be broken. Let us prove to God & Angels that we are worthy of ^the^ trust reposed in us. All that can endure the ordeals will be saved and all who cannot will not.

~~Elder, said about~~

Several remarks were made by different members on the truth of the Doctrine of Celestial Marriage [polygamy].[8] And on the principle of Infidelity and Spiritu[a]lism which [William] Godbe, [Elias] Harrison & [Eli] Kelsey were preaching.[9]

Meeting was adjourned for one week at one oclock pm. After singing Benediction by Elder John Taylor. Geo Goddard Sec[re]t[ar]y.[10]

January 8, 1870; Saturday

Theological Class met in the Tabernacle at One oclock pm. Present Prest. D[aniel] H. Wells presiding, ^Prest. B[righam] Young absent through ^sickness^. After singing Prayer by B[isho]p E[dwin] D Woolley. Singing.

Prest. D H Wells enquired if any member of the school wished to present anything.

Bro [William] Henry said he would like to hear something about Sacrifices.

---

8. Joseph F. Smith recorded that Robert Howlett of the 11th ward told the school that he had a vision that "polygamy or Patriarchal Marriage is of God." JFSJ, Jan. 1, 1870.

9. The leadership of the Church of Zion embraced spiritualism, participated in séances, and hosted prominent national spiritualists. See Lyman, *Thirteenth Apostle*, 625–68.

10. Goddard, after taking notes, would sign his name and add either "Secty" or "Clerk"; I have not included his signature in future entries. Readers should assume, unless otherwise noted, that Goddard recorded the minutes.

Elder Orson Pratt said that [animal] Sacrifices were instituted by the Almighty many generations before the Crucifixion of the Savior, and since that time the Sacrament of Bread and Wine was substituted. There are many ways of sacrificing besides the shedding of blood. We may sacrifice property, and other things for the sake of building up of the Kingdom of God. Though from many passages in the old Testament, he was inclined to believe that the Children of Israel would in the last days be required to offer sacrifices as in days of old.

Prest. D. H. Wells said that Prest. Young was very ill, and hoped the faith and prayers of the brethren would be exercised for his recovery. As for Sacrificing, he said, that he expected, for him to obtain eternal salvation, it would cost him not only all that he had, but all that he will ever have, though he did not deem it a sacrifice, for it was simply an exchange for the better—to keep the law of God would ^bring^ superior pleasure and satisfaction to all those who are enlightened by the spirit of the Lord, than can acrue to any person by indulging in the gratification of Carnal desires. He expected it would be a rough passage when he entered the road to eternal life, and any saint having an idol between him and his God, it will certainly have to be torn from him, before he can enter into the Celestial Kingdom of our God.

Before Jesus Comes again, he expected the Jews would be gathered again in unbelief to rebuild ~~R~~ Jerusalem, and offer sacrifices, as of old.

Elder Orson Hyde from Sanpete [County] felt to rejoice that we lived in this day, and such opportunities as these were afforded us. He complained that many he met yesterday between here and Cottonwood were under the influence of strong Drink, which grieved him very much. Which forced the reflection on his mind, is it necessary for us to receive the chastening hand of the Almighty. As far as his influence extended, in connexion with his brethren, he would seek in the right place and way to dry up this snare of the adversary. He felt that it was right for us to come out from the Wicked world and its practices.

Elder W[ilford] Woodruff said we all stood in need of Faith, especially at the present time, we have ^had^ good peace for a great many years, and he had no doubt but every one would sooner or later be tried to the very core. We should be prepared for every thing that may come along. We are the friends of God, and the World is it [at] war with us, and he was glad of it. God has put into our hands the Gospel of Christ, the Kingdom of God and that makes the world mad, as for Polygamy, they did not care so much for it, as for the dust under their feet. If it requires the United States to shed more blood of the Saints, before their cup is full, they will shed it, there never was a more corrupt Nation dwell on the face of the earth, than that which now exists on this covenant.[11] And the Saints should never in their prayers forget to pray for Colfax,[12] and the Government in the right way. We have everything to encourage us in doing right—to keep the word of Wisdom, And whatever is required of us.

No man ever apostatizes from this Church without transgressing the laws of God, either secretly or openly. The Spirit of God will never leave any one without sufficient cause.

Prest. Young is not without Revelation, he is not without the power and Spirit of God. He has councilled the Saints for a great many years by the mind and will of God, and if everything had to be done by Revelation, many of us would now be living under great condemnation.

Brigham Young Junr bore testimony to the evil effects of drinking Beer and Whiskey on the states road especially.[13] And he hoped that an influence would be exerted ~~to f~~ over the County authorities to prevent a license being granted again to either Whiskey or Beer Saloons on that road.

The Meeting was adjourned for one week at One o clock pm. After singing Benediction by Elder Geo Q. Cannon.

January 15, 1870; Saturday

Theological Class met at the Tabernacle at One oclock pm. Prest. B[righam] Young, Presiding. After singing Prayer by Elder B Young Junr. Singing.

Prest. D[aniel] H. Wells, gave an opportunity for any member of the School to bring anything forward for the benefit of the ~~school~~ same.

11. The minutes say *covenant* but Woodruff may have meant *continent.*

12. Schuyler Colfax (1823–85) was elected vice-president of the United States in 1868 with President Ulysses S. Grant. During an October 1869 visit to Salt Lake City, he spoke against polygamy, saying that "our country is governed by law, and no assumed revelation justifies any one in trampling on the law" (qtd. in Walker, *Wayward Saints,* 213). He later failed to secure the nomination for a second term in 1872 because of charges of corruption in connection with the Crédit Mobilier scandal. For more, see White, *Republic for Which It Stands*, 255–65.

13. That is, on the emigrant road through Utah from the eastern states to southern California, and not local roads where local government, and therefore the church, could exercise more control.

B[isho]p David Evans of Lehi, said it was necessary for us to be able at all times, to give a reason for the hope that is within us. Celestial Marriage some Elders are preaching, that a Man who has not got 3 wives, cannot possibly have an ~~opportunity~~ exaltation. Others are preaching that a Man with only one wife can only obtain a very small exaltation. His views however from studying the Revelation, are that if a Man who is faithful to his religion and though he may have but one wife, he will be able to pass the Angels & God, and become exalted. At the same time, those who assume the greatest responsibilities in this probation will be entitled to higher degrees of exaltation hereafter.

Elder Erastus Snow, said, in the south [southern Utah] they had schools organized throughout the Country, they are well attended, and have been very useful. There is an increase of Union, peace, & contentment, they are striving to build up the Kingdom—and be saints—both old and young appear to appreciate the blessings bestowed upon them. They are comparatively free from the Spirit of apostacy & outside influences.

In the more populous cities and settlements where contact with unbelievers is more common than in many other places—more vigilence and watch care is necessary by the Elders to shield and protect our Wives and families. We have had Many years of peace and quiet, while the outside world has been rent asunder with broils and contentions. ~~And~~ but now there is considerable talk outside, and apostacy commenced within, the Spirit of the Holy One teaches ~~to~~ us to pray, and every Spirit that is of God, confesses that Jesus is the Christ and that Joseph Smith was a Prophet. And the more we pray, the more will we be enlightened.

The world seems much agitated over our Social System [plural marriage], ^&^ ~~seemed~~ ^are^ determined that it shall not be an article of [our] religion. And that which pertains to the union of the sexes shall be classed among temporalities &c.

~~The re~~ In all the civilized Nations, Marriages are recognized as a religious rite.[14] But we as Latter day Saints are to be an exception to that, and not allowed to be Married except as ^a^ civil contract, thus divesting it altogether of a religious Character. These puny efforts have generally originated by those [dissidents] who have been fostered & fed in our midst. We should neither fatten nor sustain Lawyers—Merchants,

14. For a history of marriage practices, see Coontz, *Marriage, a History.*

Doctors, Bankers, &c in our midst—who are not with us in the building up of the Kingdom of God.

B[isho]p Jo[h]n Sharp spoke of a spirit of grumbling that he had met with since the finishing up of the Railroad.[15] Some are talking of us as being divided into [social] Classes—he had always considered we were brought here to be one.

He then spoke on Home Manufacture. Much had been said and done by Prest. Young to have us become self sustaining. Those now engaged in Manufacturing, complain of Wages ^being^ too high and the employees complain of Wages too low. Simple reason suggests that we reason together and try to do each other good. But unless something is done soon—our Mechanics will be all idle for the want of having work to do, because Manufacturers under existing circumstances cannot possibly compete with foreign markets, and will have to close those establishments. Labour can be just as easily imported from the East and West as Merchandise and unless we can bring our minds to this fact, and become willing to submit to the pressure of circumstances, we shall see sorrow and poverty to our hearts content. God, through his servants must dictate us, in all things and he will most assuredly lead ^us^ ~~to~~ back to God and the Lamb.

Elder Geo Q. Cannon then read a Letter from a Member of the [US] Senate,[16] which had been addressed to ^the^ Prest[17] [Ulysses S. Grant] & Members of that body—who urges very strong commercial and humane reasons, why that Obnoxious Bill now before ~~th~~ Congress, Called Culloms Bill[18] should be immediately slaughtered.

---

15. The Transcontinental Railroad was finished when the Union Pacific Railroad and the Central Pacific Railroad met and laid the golden spike at Promontory Summit, Utah, in a ceremony in May 1869. In January 1870 the Utah Central Railroad—the spur bringing the railroad from Ogden to Salt Lake City—was also completed. WWJ, Jan. 10, 1870. For more on the transcontinental railroad, see Bain, *Empire Express*.

16. Joseph F. Smith wrote that the letter was from a merchant and not a senator, though many senators did oppose Cullom's bill. JFSJ, Jan. 15, 1870.

17. Ulysses S. Grant (1822–85) held the office of US president from 1869 to 1877. He was a quartermaster in the Mexican War and entered the Civil War as colonel, later to be appointed general in chief of all US armies. Although his two-term presidency was rife with corruption, Grant was personally honest, unaware of the scandals, and loyal to a fault. Chernow, *Grant*.

18. The Cullom Bill sought to end plural marriage and Mormon theocracy in Utah. It required that anyone practicing polygamy be fined and imprisoned, denied the benefits of the homestead and preemption acts, required a loyalty oath from non-polygamists, and sought to replace the police force with federal marshals. The bill passed the US

Prest. D H Wells recommended those brethren to whom the Utah Central Railroad Co May be indebted, to purchase Bonds which ^will^ be ready in a few days, rather than let them be sent to a foreign Market and sold among strangers. He would rather the Road was owned by the Saints, and the Bonds would draw a Gold interest payable semi annually. All in favour of sustaining Prest. Young in having the Bonds of that road held by our own people, hold up your right hands. And all hands were uplifted.

If we will only do right, and sustain the Servants of God, No matter what the Government do or any body else, they cannot hurt us. And inasmuch as we prove faithfull in handling the things of this world, we shall be found worthy of being entrusted with the eternal riches. But as soon as a difficulty or trial comes, and we fly the track, No Matter how much wealth we may have, and Wives and children, we shall never obtain an exaltation in the Kingdom of our God.

Meeting was then adjourned for One week at One oclock pm. Benediction by Bishop David Evans.

January 22, 1870; Saturday

Theological Class met at the Tabernacle at One o clock pm. Present Prest. D[aniel] H Wells presiding. After singing Prayer by Elder [Amos] Fielding. Singing.

Prest. Wells gave permission for any member of the School to present anything on their minds but no one rising He said, that as some had complained that for every member of the school [to be told] ^to vote one way or the other^ had regarded it as a species of Tyrrany ~~to be expected to Vote one way or the other~~, when any measures were presented He would simply say that it had been a Legislative Maxim for ages, and therefore we were not alone in this practice. He then combated ^the^ Notion of a One Man power, so much objected to of late, by reference to a supreme power exercised in heaven.

Man being a religious being ~~a religious being~~, the Devil ministers to him, to suit his Notion, and thus create as many religions as the Morbid cravings of corrupt minds may seek after. If the universal ideas of those

House of Representatives but failed in the Senate. While most Senators who spoke out against the bill said they sympathized with its intents, they believed the railroad would bring outsiders to Utah and dilute the Mormon influence. Walker, *Wayward Saints,* 214–15; Gordon, *Mormon Question*, 274n6.

recently gone out from us prove right in the end, we all certainly stand as good a chance, as any of them. But if they are rejected ~~exe~~ We shall assuredly be in a better condition than they. Salvation does not come from the multitude, but from God our Heavenly Father.

They do not compr^e^hend God, nor his purposes not even so much as the barbarous tribes around us. No Man ever attains to the highest state of Glory, but those who "abide the Law of that Glory.["] There was no other principle of salvation, that he [Wells] was acquainted with, but a full compliance with the law of God, under every circumstance, no matter what obstacles or difficulties may come across our path way. The first lesson we have to learn, is to govern ourselves, then we will be able to govern others. When the Kingdom of God is fully established, all men will not be latter day saints, but every man will be protected in his rights. Some say that a cloud was gathering, and will shortly burst, no matter how soon, there will no faithful saint be injured one particle. We will live as a people, and prosper, and go on to build up the Kingdom of God. When he embraced the Gospel, the wife of his youth could not see it, and would not come out with him. He therefore left her behind, though his heart had bled for her thousands of times, for she was a good woman.[19] May God bless us and enable us to see the light, that we may walk therein and be saved is my prayer.

<u>Prest. Jos[ep]h Young Senr</u> said the fellowship of saints was private property, and if any one deviates from a correct course, so as to lose the spirit of God, he should be perfectly justified to withdraw his fellowship from such a one. The same thing was done throughout all Christendom, then why should any body complain—and make such a hue and cry, that we will ^not^ fellowship them.

<u>Elder W[ilford] Woodruff</u> in his acquaintance with Joseph Smith & Brigham Young, said he never knew either to give any council but what always came out true, instancing ~~the~~ Sidney Rigdon[20] whom Joseph

19. Wells married Eliza Robinson in 1837 in Illinois and had one child together. He was later baptized a Mormon, but she was not.

20. Sidney Rigdon (1793–1876) was a close associate of Alexander Campbell and helped to found the Disciples of Christ, or "Campbellite," movement. He encountered Mormon missionaries in 1830 and quickly became a close associate of Joseph Smith. He offered himself as a guardian to the church after Smith's death but was rejected and soon excommunicated. He went on to found his own Mormon-oriented group in Pennsylvania.

wished to through [throw] off &c. We have got to follow the Lord—the Celestial law must be abided or we never can be exalted.

Prest. Young is our Lawgiver and stands between us and God, and if God has Any revelation to give to man, he will not give it to ~~him~~ ^me^, nor Billy Godbe, but it will come through Prest. Young. He will speak through his Mouthpiece. God has placed him as our leader in temporal as well as in other things—we shall be dictated by revelation and council And those who abide it ~~and~~ will be saved.

Bro [William] Henry gave a short exhortation to faithfulness.

B[isho]p David Evans said after he had read the Manifesto of Godbe & Co[mpany][21] which refers to the spiritual labours of Jos[ep]h Smith the Prophet, reminded him of a great many ~~of~~ Temporal labours which Joseph had preformed, such as kicking men behind for their insults, ^&c.^ And as for Tithing, & Consecration which he knew that Joseph had revealed to him—he was fully satisfied that they [the Godbeites] knew nothing at all about it—and their entire system amounted to about the same.

Elder Geo Q. Cannon regretted that Men who had ^been^ loved and esteemed for years, should turn round and fight against the work of God. Though he had recently rejoiced in the fact, that an issue had been raised, and much good will result, by having the question of Authority settled in regard to ~~the~~ the priesthood, and our allegience to it. Those remaining in our midst will certainly have a better understanding of the powers of the living priesthood, and be better prepared to render what is term[ed] unconditional obedience. I do hope the Elders of Israel will be willing in the day of Gods power. We have long since been praying that God will permit us to take part in building up the waste places of Zion. And he is now seeking to prepare us as a people for that event, Only let us learn cheerfully the principle of obedience. God has the greatest blessings in store for us.

I have never seen so much power And wisdom Manifested through Prest. Young & his Councillors[22] than at the present time—and there

21. The "Manifesto of W. S. Godbe and E. L. T. Harrison" was published in the *Utah Magazine* on November 27, 1869. See Walker, *Wayward Saints,* 179–81.

22. Young had three counselors, George A. Smith, Daniel H. Wells, and Joseph F. Smith.

never was more union in the twelve [apostles] that [than] now. Let us rejoice and be exceeding glad, for great things are in store for us.

B[isho]p John Sharp, deals much in temporalities—and then explained how the hand of the Lord had been plainly made manifest. In the location of the terminus of the U[nion] P[acific] R[ail] R[oad] and also the construction of our Utah Central, though at the same time, it involved an indebtedness on Prest. Young and others, who were exceedingly anxious to liquidate, but for want of available means, it was impossible [to] pay at present. Though he ^Bro Sharp^ was perfectly willing to turn over his dwelling House and lot in the 20th ward, at a fair valuation and take Utah Central Bonds.

Prest. D. H. Wells expressed similar statements, and offered Lumber, his House & lot or Anything else he had, with a view of paying up those debts. The Latter day Saints should be reasonable &c.

Elder J[esse] C. Little strongly urged the necessity of Brethren turning over their loose property to pay some of those debts, that Prest. Young & others are owing on that Railroad—that their hands may be liberated—let us all lift, and work together—until we are free, and prepared for some thing else.

Elder John Taylor explained some of the difficulties that himself and Bro Sharp met with in Boston, while trying to obtain a settlement with the Railway Comp[an]y—and was confident that the best had been done, that could be, though it was hard on some of the working men.

Elder F[eramorz] Little said that every Workman they had employed on the railroad, had been Supplied with Grain & Flour, as they needed, and they did not suffer for the necessary's of life but the President and some of his brethren had such a burden on their shoulders, that if we did not join issue, and relieve them, we shall be damned.

Elder F Little made a few remarks on Labour—advocating the principle that men should be willing to receive for ^their^ labour, a remuneration that others can afford to give, and rather work for very little, than be idle.

School adjourned for One week at 1 o clock PM. After singing Benediction by Elder Orson Hyde.

January 29, 1870; Saturday

Theological Class met at the Tabernacle at One oclock PM. Present

Prest. B[righam] Young presiding. After singing Prayer by Elder J[ohn] W Young. Singing.

Prest. Orson Hyde said the laws of our Country ~~require all~~ requires us to swear or take a certain Oath under certain circumstances, but it also permits an affirmation in lieu of either, should ^there^ be any religious scruples in the mind of a person towards taking an oath. He would like to hear a few remarks on the subject, as the Savior said ["]Swear not at all.["]

Elder W[ilford] W. Woodruff. Moved and was Seconded That this Meeting be turned into a Caucus Meeting, for the purpose of ~~making~~ Nominating our City Officers, preparatory to the forthcoming Election.

Elder Geo Q Cannon fully approved of this, as it was much better to unite upon a whole ticket of Officers, rather ^than^ to divide and split up on the day of Election. We have the power to be united, and may as well use our Priesthood for this purpose.

Moved by Geo Q. Cannon[,] Seconded by W. W. Woodruff ^& carried unanimously^ That Bishop E[dward] Hunter be Chairman for the occasion, and that Paul A Schettler be the Secretary. Carried.

Elder Orson Pratt suggested that we might at least increase our votes one Hundred per cent, to anything we have ever had, he then mentioned a law in which Females, born Citizens, have a right to vote. Those who are married to Citizens, have a right. The United States ^make[s]^ it a Law for Ladies to vote, and contrould by the Territorial Legislature.[23]

Moved & Seconded That a Committee be appointed to Nominate the Mayor and Officers of the City—Carried Unanimously. Moved, seconded and Carried[:] That Geo Q. Cannon, W. W. Woodruff and J[esse] C. Little be said Committee. ~~Carr[ie]d unanimously~~ Moved, seconded & Carried That the Chairman Make a speech.

E[dward] Hunter, Chairman, spoke on the subject of Union, shewing the importance of it, especially when directed in a good ~~direction~~ cause.

The Committee then presented the names of City Officers as Follows[:][24]

23. Wyoming became the first territory to enact women's suffrage the previous year. Utah gave women the right to vote weeks after this meeting on February 12, 1870.

24. The nominees were all members of the School of the Prophets.

D[aniel] H Wells Mayor of Salt Lake City			
Isaac Groo Councillor of the	1st Municipal Ward		
S[amuel] W. Richards	2	"	
A[lonzo] H Ra~~u~~leigh Alderman	3	"	1 Contrary vote
Jeter Clinton	4	"	
A[lexander] C. Pyper	5	"	
Theo[dore] McKean	C[ouncilo]r		
Tho[ma]s Jenkins	C[ouncilo]r		
R[obert] T. Burton	C[ouncilor]		
John Clark	C[ouncilo]r		
Henry Grow	C[ouncilo]r		
Heber P. Kimball	"		
Louis S Hills	"		
Thomas McLelland	C[ouncilo]r		
John R Winder	C[ouncilo]r		
City Recorder	Robert Campbell		
Treasurer	Paul A Schettler		
Marshall	J[ohn] D. T. McAllister		

It was moved ^by a Stone cutter^ and Seconded That the above Officers serve as a source of Honour, and their fees appropriated to the benefit of Common Schools.

Mayor Wells, said with the exception of the Recorder and Treasurer whose time was entirely absorbed, and therefore had a fixed salary. The City Officers were not remunerated except for lengthy sessions, neither was any ~~approp~~ salaries provided for, in the City Charter.

It was then Moved and carried by general applause That the Stone Cutters devote as much of their time gratis [for free], as the City Council do, and the proceeds of their labour appropriated to the poor fund or Common Schools.

Prest. Jos[ep]h Young was determined to sustain his brethren in anything that is introduced by the Servants of God whose superior wisdom dictated their policies. When the School of the Prophets was first commenced the order of Enoch[25] was talked about, and he

25. The "United Order of Enoch" was the cooperative movement initiated by Brigham Young. Although attempted in some form earlier in church history, and talked about in these early meetings of the School of the Prophets, it was not until February 1874 that Young was able to successfully establish it in Utah. It began in St. George and was practiced in some 200 other communities before it faded out.

thought the sooner it was established the better, as procrastination was the thief of time.

Elder Jos[ep]h A Young related a dream, and then applyd it, to shew the necessity of the Elders keeping out of the devils pressure. Elder J. A. Young then adverted to the present financial difficulties that the lack of U[nion] P[acific] R[ail] R[oad] Co[mpany] paying their debts, had thrown Prest. Young, himself and others into, but there was no Man who laboured on the Railroad but ~~what will~~ who will sooner or later obtain it. He hoped therefore that those to whom they were indebted, would be patient, and they would surely get their pay. He then shewn up the great advantages of owning a railroad to do our own freighting, as a people; ~~and the fearful al~~ He then called upon the brethren to be faithfull to the interests of the Kingdom of God. Be united.

[Thomas C.] Armstong said, as he was about to take a ^very^ important step viz. to leave his connexion with this organization and join the New Movement [Godbeites]. He therefore handed over his Ticket, as a member of the School of the Prophets.

Prest. B Young said the way to obtain Life eternal was clearly pointed out by Joseph [Smith] the Prophet, it was a very painful thing to see men fall away and become deceived—but this apostacy was the thinest ~~of~~ whitewash of anything he had ever been acquainted with.

God can never save men in their sins—but to hell they are bound to go. The apostates have got nothing worthy of anybody seeking after. He wished they had honesty enough to repent. If they had not light enough ^to prevent it^, they might possibly repent.

He then spoke of their Railroad indebtedness, and intended to have a meeting next Saturday of all the Creditors for the purpose of giving such explanations as is necessary, to bring about a pacific [peaceful] feeling.

The School was then adjourned for two weeks at One oclock pm.[26] After singing Benediction by Elder Geo Q. Cannon.

26. There was no meeting the following week so railroad creditors could meet "in lieu of the School of the Prophets." JH, Feb. 5, 1870. Young had signed contracts with the Union Pacific and Central Pacific Railroads, and more recently with the Utah Central Railroad, to have the Saints grade the tracks and construct bridges and tunnels but he had not yet been paid. He asked the workers to accept tithing credit and bonds instead of cash. Arrington, *Great Basin Kingdom*, 265–75.

February 12, 1870; Saturday

Theological Class met ^at^ the Tabernacle at One oclock pm. Present Prest. B[righam] Young presiding. Singing. Prayer by B[isho]p Lorenzo Young. Singing.

Last Saturday Prest. Young met his Railroad Creditors for the purpose of making satisfactory arrangements with them, hence the postponement of the School By request of Prest. Young.

Elder G H [John Greenleaf] Holman of Pleasant Grove [Utah] was called for, and responded. He had previously written a letter, to solicit the privilege of expressing his views on Celestial Marriage. He referd to a paragraph on page 46 ^in G[eorge] A. Smiths pamphlet^[27] then 118 page Book Mormon, which seems to condemn David, Solomon &c for plurality, but he believed it had reference to the excess they carried it to[,][28] then Page 37 Pamphlet. Then page 118 B[ook] [of] Mormon then 21 paragraph 5 page ^74th pages^ 112 page Revelation on Celestial Marriage, read the whole of it—and which plainly shows that it reveals the law of plurality, and that no man in Monogamy can ~~never~~ enter into an exaltation, according to his understanding of the Revelation.

B[isho]p L[eonard] Harrington said, there was one difficulty in viewing the revelation That any woman married to a man, under the New Covenant is not entitled to a full exaltation, unless the first wife, properly sealed by Him who has authority, ~~is~~ has obeyed the Celestial Law, can the Marrying of a second wife make the first marriage valid?

The subject was discussed by Elder Orson Pratt Bishop David Evans of Lehi & Jos[ep]h F. Smith.

Prest. B Young said that men and women will be saved in the Celestial Kingdom without even being Married at all—others with only one wife, and some again with many wives. ~~If s~~ Whoever continues faithful~~l~~ to the end, will have all ^the^ exaltation they can possibly enjoy. Let every person so live as to enjoy the Holy Ghost, and please God our Father. That the Revelation, though the greatest ever given to man, more ~~that~~ than that will yet be given when we are ready to receive it.

27. Smith's pamphlet, published by the Church Historian's Office, gave a brief overview of LDS history, reprinted Joseph Smith's 1843 revelation on polygamy (D&C 132), and answered a series of questions. Page forty-six of the pamphlet answers the question, "Is a plurality of wives in any case lawful under the Gospel?" Smith, *Rise, Progress and Travels*.

28. The Book of Mormon's condemnation of polygamy (Jacob 2:27–30) allows for future unforeseen circumstances.

We are so imperfect, that should our own views be crossed, we become angry, and fly like glass. He hoped He should see the time when this will not be the case.

B[isho]p L[orenzo] Young strongly recommended faithfullness to all latter day Saints—seeing that such a pressure exists against us, both outside and inside of us.

The School was adjourned for One week at One o clock pm. Benediction by Elder J[esse] C. Little.

February 19, 1870; Saturday

Theological Class met at the Old Tabernacle at One o clock pm. Present Prest. B[righam] Young presiding. After singing Prayer by Elder W[ilford] Woodruff. Singing.

Prest. Geo A Smith expressed his gratitude for another privelege of meeting again in the School, since this School was organized, he realized that we had made some progress. God had placed the Keys of priesthood in the Church, and had gathered his people from all parts of the earth, with a great variety of traditions, which he illustrated by the practice of some of our Judges, whose judgments were rendered in accordance with the rulings of Courts in the particular state they happened to hail from.

So with traditions made upon the minds of others who received their impressions from some religious Teachers, as to what is right and what is wrong. When the Elders of Israel are permitted to fall into darkness, it is a true sign of their having indulged in iniquity. Perhaps there is no more aptitude to sin among the Elders, than in the habit of buying and selling—and there was no safer principle for each to be guided by, that To do unto others, as we would that others should do unto us. We as Latter day saints have got to lay aside all our cheating propensities, if not, the Spirit of the Lord will leave us. Some have committed the sin of Adultery, and however much they may have repented, they cannot obliterate the fact of its existence, and in that much, they cheat themselves of a blessing. He then rehearsed the many blessings that had attended us since we came into these vallies, and yet how little we seemed to appreciate them. He also traced the gradual development of apostacy which inevitably resulted in the Spirit of Murder towards the leaders of the people.

He then spoke of the efforts being made in Congress to raise thousands of Volunteers to come and wipe us out, this was all right, for the President had far better have thousands of hypocrites and dishonest persons to leave the Church, leaving but a few honest faithful saints to build up the Kingdom of God. Zions Ship is not going to sink, for such is not the case—dont be excited, the Power that has sheltered the Saints ever since Jos[ep]h Smith rec[eive]d the plates, will be exerted in our behalf, if we'll only live our religion and do what is right. The only principle that can possibly hold together a community, is the Holy Priesthood—there are many false Spirits gone abroad and all who desire it may go after them, and be duped by them. &c

Elder Geo Q. Cannon spoke of the mean class of Men, selected recently, to fill the official offices in this Territory. One honorable exception, however he was pleased to make mention of viz. Mr. Man[n],[29] the Secretary ~~and~~ who has recently been acting as Governor, the Lord has ^so^ overruled circumstances as to make of him a friend rather than an enemy.

He spoke of the gigantic measures now being sought to be thrust upon us, to annihilate the great work of God, he was much rejoiced to see the remarkable calmness and serenity that sits upon the Countenance of Prest. Young under the Most trying circumstances, it is also observable among the Saints, ~~also~~. It is not always Known in what way the Lord will deliver his people when threatening circumstances surround us, but depend upon it, He will put hooks in the jaws of our enemies, and bring out the Saints of God triumphantly.

~~The following questions were then read and answered by Elder Geo Q. Cannon~~[30]

Elder W Woodruff said we were approaching a very interesting time, and as the Lord will have a tried people. We shall ^have^ a severe test to prove and try the saints—something that make us look around us, and ascertain where we ~~shal~~ stand. The Nation on this Continent is nearly ripe in iniquity, and will certainly be destroyed, according to the Revelations given to Joseph [Smith]. Men that are not ground[ed] in their faith by revelation, must past [pass] away in the trying hour—every weapon that is formed against us, will not prosper. Let the Elders

29. Stephen A. Mann (1837–81), born in Vermont, served as acting governor of Utah Territory between Charles Durkee (1865–69) and John Wilson Shaffer (1870).

30. The remainder of the page is blank.

read the revelations and become acquainted with them—that we may see what is coming. The Lord does not require us to make war upon our enemies until he reveals it from heaven.

He could afford to lay down his temporal life, rather then forfeit his eternal salvation. If it was necessary let Prest. Young and others be hid up in these Mountains. But he did not think the Lord was going to destroy the faithful Saints of God. But let every faithful Man of God be willing to assume his share of responsibility, instead of throwing everything on the shoulders of Prest. Young. There was a very wicked spirit in this City, which was connected with the same lying spirit at Washington [DC].

When [Schuyler] Colfax was here,[31] he had the pleasure of preaching the Gospel to him and warn him against shedding innocent blood. Let us stand valiently and bear our testimony, and leave the event in the hands of God. Let us go before the Lord, and pray that Hypocrites and liars may be gathered out.

Prest. B Young said that He & Bro Geo A Smith was about to leave for the South next week, and expected to be away during the Months of March and April. He then besought the brethren during their absence, to be faithful and humble before God—and be united with Bro [Daniel H.] Wells who will be left here ~~to~~ in charge of matters and things. Himself and some others intended to have wintered in the South ~~last win~~ about a year ago—but circumstances in connexion with the Railroad rendered it impossible.[32] They were going to investigate the southern Country, to ascertain where the streams of water are, where timber, and lime rock is. He was all the time looking after the Welfare of Zion and all her interests—there was no danger whatever from without, according to his feelings—but there was from within.

He could not tell what was coming, but from the Moment he first beheld this Valley, he had the calmest and most serene feelings that this was the home of the Saints and would be. He expected to find a place in the south to establish a beautiful City &c &c.

School was adjourned for one week at one o clock pm after singing Benediction by Prest. Geo A Smith.

31. See Jan. 8, 1870, entry.

32. Young would have a permanent home built in St. George, Utah, in 1871 and would often spend winters there in his later years.

February 26, 1870; Saturday

Theological Class met at the old Tabernacle at one o clock pm. Present Prest. D[aniel] H. Wells presiding (Prests B[righam] Young and Geo A. Smith having started on the 24th on a southern trip to Dixie [southern Utah]). After singing Prayer by Elder Isaac Groo. Singing.

Prest. D H. Wells then read a Petition to Congress for the removal of John P. Taggart[33] as U.S. Assessor of Internal Revenue, on account of his Officious and despotic manner towards the inhabitants of this Territory.

The ~~paper~~ signatures of the Members of the School was then obtained by Bro R[ichard] V. Morris.

Elder Orson Pratt alluded to some of the peculiarities, that characterize us as a people, in contrast with other religionists. He also refer'd to the obnoxious character of the individual [John P. Taggart] whose removal was asked for in the Petition, said he was entirely unfit to occupy the high trust reposed in him.

He analized the Cullum Bill[34] and showed the effect it would have upon the Male portion of this community, depriving them of every religious and civil right. Whatever course that Congress may take in regard to us, one thing is ~~course~~ certain. If we should be called to pass through affliction the Lord will sooner or later remove them from us—but the future is dark to us. The Prophet Joseph [Smith] did not know of many things pertaining to the future of this people—such was wisdom in God.

He reviewed the blessings of the Lord since we came into these Vallies. Touched on the subject of Union in Temporal things, and the difficulties of bringing it about. Many apostatized in consequence of it. But the Lord had been dealing with us according to our traditions, the time will come, and that is not far off, when the Order of Enoch will not only ^be^ believed in, but practised to the very letter. He looked forward with much pleasure, when deep rooted selfishness will be uprooted.

By carrying out the old Gentile fashons we see a distinction of Classes in our midst, which is the root of all evil &c.

33. John P. Taggart (1830–89) was part of the first wave of government-appointed gentiles who arrived in Utah and a prominent member of the group known as the "Federal Ring." Ulysses S. Grant made him the assessor of internal revenue, responsible for determining how much federal income tax Utahns should pay. Brigham Young argued the church should be exempt from having tithing receipts taxed, but the government disagreed. To counteract Taggart, Young suggested eliminating tithing altogether. Brunson, "Brigham Young vs. the Bureau of Internal Revenue."

34. See Jan. 15, 1870, entry.

Prest. D H Wells said the Kingdom of God upon the earth, has to struggle for its existance, it [h]as to be established by his people. And they have first to be informed in their judgments pertaining to the first principles of the Gospel, act upon them, cast out in many instances by their friends, and gather together with many traditions. We have to live by the light of the Spirit, through the living oracles. Shown the necessity of the brethren taking out their Citizenship Paper, by referring to the results of the last Election. A Mans whole interest should be devoted to the building up of the Kingdom of God. He would rather that truth & righteousness should prevail, instead of being trampled under foot. He spoke of the unfriendly legislation that Congress was engaged in towards us. He would rather the bill passed ~~in~~ ^with^ all its obnoxious clauses, in preference to a modification.

He then urged upon the brethren to be in readiness for any emergency by having Guns and Ammunition on hand to use at a Moments notice. If we will only be up and doing, and act as a saint of God, be in readiness to defend the Kingdom of God, there is no danger of the enemy taking advantage of us. Those who have neglected to supply themselves with a Gun &c—had better go to, and get one, with at least a thousand rounds of ammunition—and attend to every duty that devolves upon us. And he would venture to affirm, that we shall never be called on to use them. Let us pray for and sustain Prest. Young, he is ^a^ wise and Merciful ruler, and there is not one among all the hosts of Israel, so suitable to fill his place, according to his Knowledge of him for the last 20 years.

He condemned the habit that many still indulge in of patronizing our enemies—when shall we have wisdom enough to use the blessings of the earth in a way that God our Heavenly Father approves. Let us get wiser in our day and generation. The Kingdom will be established in these Mountains and God will fight our battles—he then closed by an energetic exhortation to faithfulness.

After singing Benediction by B[isho]p E[dwin] D. Woolley.

March 5, 1870; Saturday

Theological Class met at the Tabernacle at One o clock pm. Present Prest. D[aniel] H. Wells presiding. After singing Prayer by Bishop D[avid] Brinton. Singing.

Elder Horace S Eldredge having just returned from a visit to the East where he had been 5 days—said he was pleased to return and again come to the School of the Prophets, he found that a great deal of prejudice had been allayed among the more influencial, and men of business. He called upon W[illiam] H. Hooper, our [Congressional] delegate, who through the blessing of God had been restored to health again, his labours were very great, especially in preparing to meet the Cullum Bill when the right time comes. H. S. E[ldredge] felt to use his time, & means for the building up of the Kingdom of God.

Elder Jacob Gates, was thankful to return from his Mission, ~~where~~ he started from here on the 1st of Nov[embe]r, he had visited his relatives & friends, and had endeavoured to gather in and comprehend the spirit of the people, which he had learned to some extent, mostly by fireside conversation, and some little by public preaching.

He also spoke of the irrational views entertained by the religious people in the [United] states. He appreciated the society of those who are Members of the Church of Jesus Christ of Latter day saints, far more than those of his blood Kin. He rejoiced that God had given us such a leader as Brigham Young, he had no disposition to turn aside from the truth, having spent the greater portion of his life in this Kingdom, he did not ~~with~~ wish to turn a fool in the evening of his days. Finding fault with our leaders, had a tendency to weaken our own faith, and that was very undesirable, we should rather strive to build up and strengthen each other.

Elder John Taylor was pleased to hear the remarks of his brethren. From the testimony of the scriptures, the world would wax worse and worse. This is backed up by the testimony of the Elders who have been labouring among the people. He then compared the inestimable blessings of the Gospel which we here enjoy to the empty and shallow pretensions of the religious professors of the age. We are here, as the friends and representatives of God and righteousness, and virtue &c and we feel that God is our friend, he has organized his Holy Priesthood, who are men who hold communion with God. He has shewn us how we can secure the salvation of ourselves and family. When we cast our eyes upon the tomb and the grim monster death, we realize that they will simply convey us from this to a higher and happier sphere of existence.

Cullum & others had undertaken to fight against God and his truth and they will find it a rough job. Though we are a weak and feeble people, he does not wish to Kill us, but to use us for his purpose. The Power of God will be felt among all Nations, and when Thrones and Empires will have crumbled to ruin, Truth and righteousness will prevail, while life and thought and being last, or immortality endures.

Elder Geo Q Cannon said the Church had been organized near 40 Years [April 6, 1830], about the same time, the Lord kept the children of Israel travelling in the wilderness, he hoped the time was not far distant when at these schools [of the Prophets], there may be a continual stream of inspiration made manifest of things that has been hid for many generations.

Nothing prevents it but a lack of union on our part in the observance of what we call Temporal things, for instance,—how many in this School strictly carry out the simple requirements of the Word of Wisdom. There is much depending on us as members of this school, as to how soon Zion will be redeemed. We are burthened with great responsibilities, and some day not far distant we shall be called to account for the same.

He was oftentimes astonished to see the steadfastness, courage, and faithfulness of our leader [Brigham Young] under all circumstances—and how patient and long-suffering he was towards the slothfullness and apathy of his brethren.

The Meeting was then adjourned for one week at 1 o clock p.m. After singing Benediction by Elder Jos[ep]h F. Smith.

March 12, 1870; Saturday

Theological Class met at the Tabernacle at One o clock pm. Present Prest. D[aniel] H. Wells presiding. After singing Prayer by Elder Jacob Gates. Singing.

Elder Geo Q. Cannon then read the rules of the School, and made some excellent remarks on the nature and obligation that each Member of the School enters upon, whenever, with uplifted hands, covenants to observe. He repudiated the idea of a self sufficient spirit, as being a barrier to progress, but while we can view our own weaknesses or defects by the light of the spirit, there is room for us to advance. If we loved our Lord our God with all our hearts, there would be no duty unperformed; How long will it be before we are prepared to go back to build up the Zion of our God, this land was given us, on purpose to give us a preparation or experience, that we may become fitted to return, and build up the Centre stake[35] of Zion. The rules of the School just read, when we can thoroughly be guided by them—will be followed by others far more stringent than these are. What is it to keep the Word of Wisdom according to the Spirit and meaning thereof, was asked by a Member of the school.

Prest. D. H. Wells said when a person was melted down under a conviction of sin—is ready to ask What shall we do Lord. He then enumerated several duties that is strictly binding on all Latter day Saints. We may do many things, that in their very nature will ~~be a~~ have a tendency to benefit, bless, and exalt us in ~~the~~ his presence. Amongst them is the privilege of Cooperating together to build up Zion—the payment of Tithing, the allaying of an unhallowed appetite, by abstaining from Tobacco, Tea, Coffee, Whiskey &c—serve God with a willing heart—twas a great privilege to know how to serve God. He mentioned his own experience in leaving off the use of Coffee—and also quoted the promise the Lord made to those who observed the Word of Wisdom, viz That ~~when~~ the destroying angel should pass by, and not hurt us.

We must comply with his will or law, and find our way back into the presence of God or we can reject it, and go along the broad road that leads to death. The rules are not very stringent, and he wished to know who would observe them. The vote was then put to the school, and every Member apparantly, with uplifted hands voted to sustain them.

Elder John Taylor said there was more importance in those things we have been hearing, than we are apt to attach to them. In his visits away from home he is often asked to take Tea and Coffee, and in some houses he notices they drink it all around him, and it gives him very peculiar feelings for some of them are members of the School of the prophets. He strongly advocated cleanliness in our habits, in our houses, our persons, our food, &c so that we can become fit subjects for those who are arrayed in white [God and Christ]. Why were we required to come out from the world, but for the purpose of laying aside every evil practise (that so prevails in the Gentile World) among them is the Word of Wisdom. If we are preparing for the Kingdom of God, how strange, if we cant observe some of these little things.

35. That is, Independence, Missouri. Mormons believed that prior to the Second Coming, the church would relocate back to Missouri.

He then contrasted the pure and safe principles of ~~the~~ Eternal life, with the shallow and uncertain notions of the World and apostates. He wanted to associate with those who fight the good fight of faith, who dare to keep the commandments of God, with those he wished to live, and with them he wished to die.

Adjourned for one week at one oclock. After singing Benediction by Elder Orson Pratt.

March 19, 1870; Saturday

Theological Class met at the Tabernacle at one o clock pm. Present Prest. D[aniel] H. Wells presiding. After singing Prayer by Elder Geo Goddard. Singing.

Elder W[ilford] Woodruff said, this being a school of ^the^ prophets, should be profitable to those who come here, the spirit of God that each Elder possesses is the Spirit of prophesy. We have had the living oracles in our midst for 40 years on the 6th of April next. And as a people we have got to prepare a place for the coming of the son of man. The United States had been warned ^lately^ by several hundred Missionaries, perhaps for the last time[,] and their testimonies will stand good before God, Angels and Men. The situation of the people required the Servants of God to interfere with temporal things, and council and instruct them in the principle of Cooperation &c, this gives offence to some but all things are necessary from time to time. He then urged the necessity of each one who comes to this school, observing the rules which we have covenanted to observe. We want an increase of faith, so as to meet all the opposition and persecution we may have to encounter.

He then commended the Calmness and composure of our leader Prest. [Brigham] Young, [who] under the most trying circumstances, encouraged the school to put their trust in God, and be united, and do our duty, And our Leaders will be inspired to lead this people in a straight path and Zion will be built up—and the ~~Go~~ blessings of God will rest upon his people, and may He enable each one to do their [duty] is my prayer in the name of Jesus.

Elder Geo Q. Cannon spoke of neglect in some coming late to school—and others excuse them selves in being absent On some trifling pretext. The Spirit of Prophecy, by some, is not well understood, and are more or less exposed to the influence of the adversary. There are rules by which we may become thoroughly acquainted with it. That Spirit is a still small voice, that whispers to our understanding, but to be benefitted by it, and taught by it, we must seek after it, commune with it, observe its whisperings, and carry them out, then everything necessary for a Man as a Husband or Father &c will receive wisdom for every emergency in all our private affairs of life—and if fully developed, that soul will be filled with the spirit of Prophecy, and he will be warned and forewarned of everything that affects his interests.

We are not sufficiently alive to the great privileges that we are entitled to as the Saints and Servants of God, then let us give heed to the voice of the Spirit, that our understandings may not be warped. But that our faith in God may be of the most unwavering kind—and our lives exemplify the great truth that we have received. God has given unto us the Holy Oracles of God, he has given us the Holy Ghost &c and preserved us, hedging us in as with a wall of ~~wi~~ fire, and kept us safe in these Vallies, from the hands of all our enemies. Many have sworn to destroy us, for practising the order of ~~P[lural]~~ Celestial Marriage, and yet God has saved ^us^ from their threats—every man who proves a traitor under all these circumstances will be damned and go [to] the lowest hell.

<u>Elder [William] Henry</u> acknowledged the kind hand of God that had been over him & his family since he had embraced the Gospel, Multiplying his posterity to between 50 & 60, while those of his relatives who backed out from the church many years ago, had been smitten by death, until they were nearly all gone, and the few living, complain of their loneliness.

<u>Elder Orson Pratt</u> referred to the Spirit of prophecy which existed to a great extent in the days of Moses. God is willing that all should enjoy it according to their faithfulness, but it must be obtained by diligence and humility. There are several ways of seeking after the blessings of God. One is by prayer alone—another by prayer and good works combined. We have ^been^ taught a great deal in our temporal matters, since this school was organized. Our standard temporal things was fashioned more after the world, and ~~a~~ much instruction was necessary to lay aside the spirit of selfishness that had grown up in our midst.

He then shown the ^great^ blessings enjoyed by the Ancient Prophets by having the spirit of prophecy and revelation, in connexion with the school of the prophets. He then warned the brethren against false and delusive spirits, which a few ~~of the~~ who had been ~~e~~ members of this school—had been led astray by. They have discarded the ~~temp~~ doctrine of the resurrection of the body, the personality of God &c—in seeking therefore for the blessings of the Holy Spirit, beware of the counterfeit.

Elder S[amuel] A. Woolley, (returned Missionary from the [United] States) Said he had met with uniform respect and kindness from those he had visited. He had done but little good, in regard to convincing people of the truth of the Gospel. But in his conversations he had been influencing many. In correcting false impressions pertaining to our social and political condition, he had sought interviews with Men of wealth and influence, and obtained many opportunities of the Kind—and he made frequent allusions to the corruptions in the present [federal] administrations, and Celestial Marriage. He had tried to live faithfull before God, And when he rec[eive]d a telegram of the death of his son,[36] he was led to enquire, what he had done, to be bereft of his firstborn. But he nevertheless felt to acknowledge ^the hand^ of God, and his kind hand dealings, not only over him, but we as a people.

Prest. D. H. Wells said, now that Wheat and flour are low in price and ~~has suf~~ difficult to sell for Money, they had plenty of it in the Tithing Office, he wished the brethren to send in their tithing Butter, Eggs, Meat &c that the tithing hands may have a little variety of food on their table as well as others—instead of having to peddle off Wheat, or Flour, for which they have to pay $2.00 per bush[el] and $6.00 per 100., and can ~~ob~~ only obtain 90¢ per bush[el] and $2.50 per 100 in exchange ~~for~~ for a little Butter, Eggs or Meat.

Meeting adjourned for one week at 1 o clock. Benediction by Elder Jos[ep]h F. Smith.

March 26, 1870; Saturday

Theological Class met ^at^ the old Tabernacle at 1 o clock. Present Prest. D[aniel] H. Wells presiding. After singing Prayer by Elder Amos Fielding. Singing.

36. Woolley's son, Samuel Henry, died suddenly on March 9 of an unspecified heart condition. Woolley Sr., in Michigan on a mission, wrote of receiving the telegram that "it is almost more than I can bear … no one can fully realise my grief in this far off city." He telegramed back begging them to wait, and he arrived on March 14 by train in Salt Lake, where his son's body "was laid in an air tight coffin and looked very natural." Woolley journal, Mar. 10, 1870, in Woolley Papers; "Local and Other Matters," *Deseret News*, Mar. 16, 1870.

B[isho]p Jno. [John] Sharp, was much pleased to see his brethren again, having been to California to effect a settlement with the ~~Utah~~ Central Pacific Railroad Co[mpany], he had succeeded in obtaining One Hundred Thousand Dollars, which he considered tolerably liberal. In reference to the Cullum Bill, ~~he~~ the people in California cared but little about it, but they would certainly prefer us for their friends rather than enemies.

Elder John Taylor, said he thought that Congress had not sunk so low as to pass such a Bill ~~as~~ against us, as they had done, having passed through the house, they may possibly carry it through the [US] Senate, if so, and it becomes a Law, and they seek to enforce it, how we shall stand it, he did not know—but it was Gods Kingdom, and He had to sustain it, or we should be in a poor fix.

He then rehearsed some of the experience of himself and the other apostles in being called, and sent forth as Missionaries to the Nations of the earth, and spoke of the operations of the Holy Spirit upon the minds of the people among whom they laboured.

In reference to the bill just passed, said it was the Most barbarous of anything that ever emanated from a Legislative body, will a war with us be the result? He knew not and cared less—Zion will prosper, some may have to pass behind the vail, and what of it, we have plenty of friends there, and if do right, we have nothing to fear.

Elder Jos[ep]h A. Young said it seemed that we ^had^ improved this country too much, for the dogs outside were envious of our improvements. He was tired of this eternal doggery, but God was on our side, and he will defend us, as in times past. He believed that we as a people were never more inclined to build ~~it~~ up the Kingdom of God than at the present time. He suggested the idea of having all the Elders of Israel got together by timely notice to give vent to our feelings of indignation against such an ungodly oppressive measure now inaugerating. They are bound to make us independant. They are bound to fight the Kingdom of God until they are used up.

Elder W[ilford] Woodruff, loved to see men valient in a good cause, especially in the testimony of Jesus. He had known Elder [John] Taylor as far back as Kirtland, stand up nobly in defending the Prophet Joseph [Smith]. The spirit made manifest here to day, he had no doubt existed among all the Elders of Israel.

This was the great Kingdom of our God, and our Government will rot and come to Nought, ~~hav~~ being about to fill up the Measure of their iniquity. We do not know what the Lord wants to [do] with us, but we must take it patiently, and whatever the Lord says through his servant Brigham [Young], we will do.

He had been baptized for all his friends, and was ready to go behind the vail, any time, the Lord wanted him. But Zion will prosper and be built up, every latter day Saint should live to build it as far as they have strength and ability. He then prophesied the speedy destruction of this Nation, and the establishment of the Kingdom of God.

Elder [John] Crockwell related the experience he had while on a Mission to the East, when conversing with some on the Cullum Bill, and its probable consequences upon us as a people, and also on the United States.

Elder Geo D Watt said he was now prest [pressed] under the Devils Harrow,[37] but by the help of God he hoped to get from under it. He wanted nevertheless to hang on to his brethren, and the cause of truth that he had espoused.[38] He hoped he should become humbled sufficient by and bye, that Prest. Young will be able to use him. ~~He~~ By possessing a mixture of the blood of English & Scotch, he never could bear to be drove, but kindness and sympathy influences him, and will do, all through his mortality. He hoped to hang on to the old Ship Zion, and endure to the end.

Elder James Cummings said in 1863 or 1864 while secretary to the Act[in]g Governor Amos Read,[39] ~~he s~~ the said Read stated that in 5 Years, Polygamy would not exist on this Continent, & Bro C[ummings] retorted, that in 10 Years, it would govern the whole Nation. He ~~was~~ would rather die, than submit to such infernal oppression that will be entailed upon us by the passing of that cursed bill. As a Nation they have got to join issue[40] with this Kingdom ~~We~~ and fill up the measure

37. A plow-type instrument to break down and level land prior to farming.

38. Watt, no longer in Young's employee as a clerk, would soon leave the church and align with the Godbeites.

39. Amos Reed (1824–87) was the son of John Savage Reed, who defended Joseph Smith in court in 1830. He was sent by the federal government to be secretary of Utah Territory in 1863, and became acting governor in 1865, replacing James Doty for three months until the new appointee, Charles Durkee, arrived.

40. That is, join in the controversy.

of their iniquity. We have no other show, but to prepare for the Contest which was sure to come to pass. If this Kingdom is not the Lords, it will go to the wall. May the Lord help us to do our duty—As he wished to see Zion established.

Elder E[manuel] M. Murphey denounced the Traitors in our midst, as being far more to be dreaded than all the outside enemies and Cullums Bill put together—exhorted the brethren to be faithful.

Elder Geo Q. Cannon said the spirit of fighting seems to be easily brought out ^when circumstances call it forth^ it had not died out during the years of peace we have enjoyed. If any people ever did deserve salvation and deliverance from the hands of our enemies, the Latter day Saints certainly did. Let us keep our tongues still and not implicate ourselves by unwise talking. He then predicted in the Name of the Lord Jesus that our enemies will never drive us from these vallies nor burn our property.

Elder David Kimball said the greatest warfare ~~is~~ he knew anything about was that which pertained to himself, to overcome himself, lest he should not do right. The hoops will be drove tight, and ~~many of~~ the wicked and ungodly will flee away.

He had a long time to live, if he did right—and he had a great desire to do right— ~~he had a good~~, and gave a favourable report of the people of Bear Lake,[41] who were out of debt, very industrious, and had comfortable homes

Elder Orson Pratt expressed the same feelings of resistance to that iniquitous bill, should it pass the Senate, and become a Law, as he would rather turn out and submit to all the privations incident to a war, then tamely ~~submit to~~ ^bear^ the humiliation that it would subject us to.

He then read in the Book of Mormon some of the promises that were made to the righteous who should be oppressed by the proud and wicked nation on this Continent. He had no doubt but the Bill will pass the Senate, and then signed by the President, and if so, he should like to know what course we should have to take that we may be getting ready but the Lord through his Servants will dictate these matters &c.

Prest. D H Wells, said it was easy to make unwise speeches—it seemed natural for men to want to fight—though that was the last resort for us

41. Kimball, with apostle Charles C. Rich, was part of the northern Utah leadership that also oversaw the Paris, Idaho, branch of the School of the Prophets.

to think about. He again exhorted the brethren to quietly secure a Gun and plenty of ammunition. As to submitting to such a state of things, he did not expect to—but how many of even this school are this day trading and sustaining our open enemies in this City, instead of sustaining the servants of God in their Councils &c. But inasmuch as we have sinned as a people, let us repent and do better ^Prest^ D H Wells then expressed a desire to learn what proportion of the school were Polygamists, and on rising upon their feet about one third present were in Polygamy. He then favored ~~the~~ a Mass Meeting of the Elders to discuss on legal grounds the unconstitutionality of passing such a bill as Cullums. He also refered to ^the^ relentless persecution that raged against us in Illinois, and also stated the fact that all the leading men now oppressing us and the principal ^US^ Officials in our midst are from Illinous.[42]

If an unconstitutional Law be passed by Congress, we dont recongnize it as Law, and by shewing up Legal points, why we oppose such, may possibly reach some Legal Court that will decide ~~on~~ in our favour.

It was then moved ^by Geo Q Cannon, Seconded by W Woodruff^ & carried unanimously—That we hold a Mass Meeting on Thursday Next at this place—at One o clock pm. Moved & Carried That a Committee ^of 13^ be appointed and the following were unanimously sustained—John Taylor[,] D H Wells[,] Orson Pratt[,] Hosea Stout[,] Elias Smith[,] A[urelius] Miner[,] J[esse] C. Little[,] Geo Q Cannon, Jos[ep]h A Young[,] Wilford Woodruff[,] Zerub[abbe]l Snow[,] ~~[Orson] Pratt, Jos[ep]h A Young[,] Jos[eph] F Smith~~[,] Sam[ue]l W. Richards[,] ~~J[ohn] M. Bernhishal[,]~~ J[ohn] M. Bernhisal.

The School was adjourned for one week ~~pm~~ at one oclock pm. After singing Benediction by Elder W Woodruff.

April 2, 1870; Saturday

Theological Class met in the Tabernacle at One o clock PM. Present Prest. D[aniel] H. Wells presiding. After singing Prayer by Elder G[eorge] B. Wallace. Singing.

Elder Geo Q. Cannon said no subject had been spoken [more] upon in this school, as that of tr^a^ding with our enemies, had this Council

42. Shelby Cullom, principal author of the Cullom Bill, grew suspicious of the Mormons as an Illinois citizen twenty years earlier. He played a role in driving them from Nauvoo and later said, "We had sent them, bag and baggage, after the Star of Empire." Walker, *Wayward Saints,* 214.

been fully carried out, he did not believe the Cullum Bill would have met with such support as it has, the originators of that bill have been, and are continuing to be sustained by some of our leading men, which he was sorry for. Were he to do it, and trouble comes upon us—he should feel that blood would stain his garments, and he would have to render an account of it in the day of the Lord Jesus. He hoped the time however would come, when the Lord will not permit the righteous to suffer with the wicked. Whenever we become united as one man—we shall not be permitted to be harrassed and perplexed &c.

Elder Jos[ep]h F. Smith spoke of the responsibilities that rested upon the Elders of Israel. Whenever the outside world attempt to bring trouble upon us as a people, he was led to look upon the Conduct of the Saints, and ^if^ he was satisfied that they had Kept their covenants and ~~kept~~ the commandments of God, then we have nothing to fear, but if we have been faulty and not observed the Council of the servants of God, then we shall surely receive the chastisement that is neccessary to purge out from our midst those who offend.

We had great reason to repent, for he well knew that some had been guilty of flagrant offenses, and violation of Covenants which we have in this school. The principles of the Gospel were calculated to reform the world. No man can serve two Masters, God and the Devil. He desired to act moderately, and speak in accordance with the spirit of his calling. He had a desire for the saints to be humble and live their religion, and then there would be no fear from the outside element. The Kingdom of God was bound to be built up on this Continent, and any effort made by the Government of the United States to wipe it out—it would only hasten its final accomplishment—the quicker.

The fact that our enemies are flourishing in our Midst, is a proof that they are sustained by many, who call themselves Latter day Saints. He then urged the brethren of the School to use their utmost endeavours to check this evil, for it was a great and crying sin.

All Saints in these Vallies have all the freedom that any Man in the world can ask for, they are free to do evil or good according to their choice. There is nothing in the world but the Kingdom of God for me. No man though a Millionaire can take one bank note with them when they leave the World. He hoped the Lord would never bless him with great wealth, unless with it, a disposition to build up the Kingdom of God, in preaching the Gospel, Feed the Poor, build the Temple &c. It was a strange thing ~~th~~ to him, for any one who loves the gift more than the giver.

Prest. D. H. Wells said when the world was particularly down upon us, it was a pretty good sign, that we are not very far wrong as a people. Since Cooperation started, quite a number of [non-Mormon] Merchants had been stopped in business—and if we will only sustain Cooperation ourselves, many more will close up.

We have ~~not~~ ^now^ to be wise and prudent in our Course, and we shall see the Salvation of God. The Kingdom, and the greatness of the Kingdom will be given to the saints of the most high God, just as soon as they have learned to use it to carry out his purposes.

In times past we have sustained our enemies with the very Means that God had blest us with, but we have now learned better, and the Devil is mad about it. And just as we are willing to carry out the Council of the ~~Saints~~ Servants of God—we shall prosper and increase in everything. Let us not swer[v]e to the right hand or the left ~~and~~ but put out our fruit trees, and cultivate the land, and all will be right. Because men cannot practise their iniquity with impunity, the Devil and servants are mad about it. The Lord will never permit the evil one to stop his work—but what is coming, will only hasten the great work of the Last days. Prophesies are being fulfilled in this our day. We do not want of our Government, but what is guarranteed to us by the Constitution. And should we ever have to take any violent measure it will only be in self defense. Let us have everything ready, to act at a moments notice, be sure to have a gun, and plenty of Ammunition, it may be necessary some time to use it.

He then notified the School that on the 6th April, a Meeting will be held as usual, [despite] being Conference day.[43]

He then reminded the Bishops to bring in their tithing of Butter, Eggs, Meat &c—and he would like to have the brethren ~~have~~ commence to haul rock as quick as possible to the Temple Block. He then suggested that ~~The Meeting~~ a collection be taken up to defray the expense of disseminating of the Deseret News ~~and~~ with the Petition to Congress in, also the Letters of [US vice president] Colfax and Elders Taylors reply. There was [blank] Dollars subscribed.

---

43. The annual general conference was delayed until May when Brigham Young and other leaders returned, but Daniel H. Wells presided over one meeting to commemorate the fortieth anniversary of the founding of the church.

The School was adjourned for one week at One oclock. After singing Benediction by Elder O[rson] Pratt.

April 9, 1870; Saturday

Theological Class met at the Tabernacle at One oclock pm. Present Prest. D[aniel] H. Wells presiding. After singing Prayer by B[isho]p John Sharp. Singing.

Elder Jos[ep]h F. Smith desired the aid of the spirit of the Lord while he endeavoured to address the school. He who runs well, and ~~runs~~ endures to the end, will most assuredly gain the prize. He desired to use his influence and set such an example to his brethren as will induce them to be more faithfull and humble. God by his power brought this people to this Territory. We have had every opportunity of becoming a wise and righteous people since we came here. God through his servants has sought ^to make^ this people one, and if we have not advanced to that perfection as we ought to, it is not the fault of God our Heavenly Father, but it lies with ourselves. If any of us come short of any blessing it is because of our unfaithfulness.

All mens faith in this Kingdom will shortly be tried to the very centre, and many, he felt satisfied, would fall by the way. He knew that this was the Kingdom of God. He also knew that the sealing power and other principles of the Gospel were true and eternal. He was satisfied that all murmereres and complainers, were ~~the~~ apostates. He could point out members of this School whose conduct clearly proved them to be apostates, and he could call out their names if necessary. The Man who undertakes to build himself without prayer will fail, for this is the Kingdom of God, and God requires us to call upon him. So with a Liar, a Swearer, and negligent, all will fall short of their expectations.

For over twenty years in these vallies, we have lived in peace, and had every opportunity of carrying out the council of the school of the Prophets. He then enumerated several sins that have been indulged ^in^ by the Elders of the Church—especially before the establishment of the school. And since then a "Code of Morals" had been introduced for every member to observe, and to overcome these sins, the Elders must be more faithful and humble. We must adapt ourselves to the law of God, and obey Celestial laws, if ever we enjoy a Celestial Glory so with every other grade of Glory. The Man who drink whiskey, lies or steals will never arrive to that height of Glory, as those who shuns these things and lives up to the moral Law of God &c.

Elder W[ilford] Woodruff said a man must live his religion if he expects to be benefited by it. He was satisfied that a faithful man of God will have his reward. One fault among latter day saints was a looseness in paying his obligations. We should improve in this. No one Apostatizes from this church in a day, it generally commences in a neglect of duty. Many both in and out of the church find fault with Prest. [Brigham] Young and say that he tyrannized over the people, but he had known him for many years, both in public and private, and no one, whom he ever knew had so few failings as Brigham Young. ~~but~~ He had been a great benefactor to the poor, whom he had brought from their poverty in the old country—and placed them in comfortable circumstances in these Vallies. We as a people must keep the commandments of God if we expect to be saints. We must try to overcome our taste for Tea, Coffee[,] Tobacco, Whiskey &c. It was a warfare and will be as long as we live, but the path that leads to eternal life is a narrow one.

Our future condition and exaltation, certainly depends on the course we pursue here. We are the best people on the earth, and he had no doubt but we were trying to improve our lives. He did not believe the wicked will ever disturb us from our homes—if we will only do right and prize our priveleges. He knew this was the Gospel and these are the people of God, and we have the Ordinances—but if Zion needs cleansing, God will cleanse her. He prayed that God would prepare us for whatever is coming—to be true and faithful &c.

Prest. Jos[ep]h Young said their was a great many speculations indulged in at the present time. The Latter day saints were enternally at war with their own faith. We have heard much this afternoon nearly all one side of the Page—true there are a few among us who are reckless and wicked—but what is it in our midst that keeps this people so secure from the shafts that are hurled at them. It was the fact that thousands are now ready to endorse the Law of Enock—and from the fact that ^a^ great and momentous crisis nears us—let us be honest with God and ourselves. Any man who is not willing to honour the Law of God he sincerely wished he would leave us and that forthwith. He never felt more calm & confiding ^we are safe^ if we'll only do right.

Elder Jos[ep]h Young further said, there was private abuses in Families, and also public abuses, that needed correction, and the sooner they are rectified the better.

<u>Elder Amos Fielding</u> mentioned a case of dealing, where a person who purchased an article at an outside store who advertizes sugar at 5 lb for 1.00—and paid 75 c[en]ts more, for it than a better article was bought for at the Co operative Store.

The School was adjourned for one week pm. Benediction by Elder H[orace] S Eldredge.

April 16, 1870; Saturday

Theological Class met at the Tabernacle at 1 o clock pm. Present ~~Prest.~~ Elder Orson Pratt presiding. After singing Prayer by B[isho]p E[lijah] F. Sheets. Singing.

<u>Elder Geo Q. Cannon</u> was thankful to meet once more in peace and safety, notwithstanding the fulminations of the Cullom Bill, and the efforts of our enemies to disturb us. He never felt more like being cheerful than at present. He did not know any reason why we should not be so, even if the Bill had already past [passed], and the troops were on the way here, there is every proba^bi^lity of the Bill passing and receiving the signature of the President. He hoped however that something would come along, that would take off the Hypocrites and Apostates, and the ungodly. We should cultivate the spirit of prayer, and confidence in God our Heavenly Father ~~by~~ and be faithful in all our duties, then the wicked ^& faithless^ in our midst will fear and tremble, while we will be calm and serene.

All the circumstances we are now passing through will develop for us an experience that will increase our faith and Confidence in God, if we do right. Cooperation had accomplished much for Israel [the LDS Church], notwithstanding some had apostatized in consequence [three-and-a-half lines redacted]. He then warned the school against a fault finding spirit, which if not checked, will most assuredly overcome us—we should seek to be faithful in all our duties, which is our only safe guard against falling away. If we thus live, we shall always be ready to receive the councils of the Servants of God, and by the spirit of revelation, anticipate [that] which emanates from their lips.

<u>Elder Orson Pratt</u> suggested that the whole school when they leave here, should go towards the Theatre to meet, and greet Prest. [Brigham]

Young with a hearty welcome, he is expected in sometime this afternoon.[44] From the great wickedness of this nation, and the intense bitterness indulged in towards us, he had no doubt but the Cullom Bill would pass, their object is simply to wipe out and utterly destroy this people, and how far they will be permitted to carry out their design, he could not say—but he did ~~not~~ know that many in this school had held sacred the covenants they had made while some had not done so. He ~~that~~ ^then^ shown by reference to ancient Israel that vows were very sacredly Kept—and even rash vows had sometimes to be observed, rather than break them.

Several years ago, a sacred covenant was made in the Tabernacle by the Latter day Saints—and how many had failed to observe it. This covenant had been made since then, many times by the members of this school—I mean in regard to the word of wisdom.[45] As an individual he was willing to abide the word of the Lord in reference to the course we are to take should the Cullom bill pass—and he fully believed the great majority of the ~~people~~ would be willing to surrender all their property as a Consecration, and ~~be willing~~ to enter upon the Order of Enoch &c.

Bro. Morris then sung a song of his own composing. After singing Benediction by Elder Geo B. Wallace.

April 23, 1870; Saturday

Theological Class met in the Tabernacle at One o clock pm. Present Prest. B[righam] Young presiding. After singing Prayer by Elder Geo Q Cannon. Singing.

Prest. Geo A Smith was thankful to appear before the School again, after visiting the southern part of our Territory, comprizing some 30 thousand Saints. Many had been called years ago, to make settlements below the rim of the basin, some had excused themselves, others had asked to be excused, while quite a number went to fill their Missions, and the amount of work they had performed, was quite astonishing,

44. Young arrived at 4:30 p.m., greeted by hundreds holding banners and flags. The next day, according to Joseph F. Smith, "thousands" were turned away from the Sunday service with the tabernacle overflowing with people to listen to Young. JFSJ, Apr. 16–17, 1870.

45. The covenant made was part of the Mormon Reformation of 1856–57, when church leaders traveled through the territory preaching repentance and recommitment to Mormon ideals, including the Word of Wisdom. Thousands of members were rebaptized as part of movement. Peterson, "Mormon Reformation."

various were the Motives that prompted the establishment of this important Mission, though but few could realize, why they should leave a thickly settled country, and go into a very barren place, and a long way off, from where the comforts of life could be obtained.

He then exposed some of the dangers that many had subjected themselves to, in consequence of going off into an isolated part, without having arms or numbers sufficient to protect themselves against the caprice and plunder of the Savages. They had been absent 52 days from the City, had travelled over 1200 Miles, and constantly employed in councilling the saints in public or in private—teaching the principle of Domestic economy [cooperatives] and how to build up Zion.

Prest. B Young said it was better to do ~~or~~ ^than^ to talk, to build up Zion was the business of the saints. He would like to spend his winters in Dixey [southern Utah], it was a beautiful Country, ~~and~~ whether Cullom's Bill passes or not; he should certainly advise some of the Brethren to go and settle there.

Those who demurred going on a Mission when called, on account of their Farm, Merchandise or anything else, who sooner or later apostatize from this Church. Some few had lately gone overboard, but nothing in comparison to what there will be, when the screws are put down. They were about to select some few ^for^ a Mission to England and Scandinavia, and also for the South. He did not wish for any one to volunteer, for no~~n~~ one would go, where he wanted to send them except to carry out the principle of Co operation, especially in reference to Cattle & Horses. He rebuked the spirit of destruction entertained by some, towards the Indians. It was just as reprehensible as the same Spirit we see in the Gentiles, who want to destroy the Mormons.

He then recommended the[y] let alone policy towards apostates in our midst, not to speak, or write about them, or wish them evil.

The following persons were then called on Missions[:] (Europe) H[orace] S. Eldredge, Geo G. Bywater, David Brinton, Levi North, Rob[er]t F. Neslen, Tho[ma]s Howell, Caleb Parry, N[iels] C. Edlesson, Jos[ep]h Argyle Sen[io]r, South Levi Stewart, with a small Comp[an]y. Scandinavia W[illia]m W. Cluff (to preside).

In response to an enquiry, all those present, who were called, exprest their willingness to go ~~The~~ On Motion, The School unanimously sustained the Brethren whose names had been called to take Missions.

Bro [William] Henry expressed his joy at the return of our Captain from the south, and prayed for, and blest the Missionaries.

The Meeting was adjourned for one week at One o clock pm. After singing Benediction by Pres G[eorge] A. Smith.

April 30, 1870; Saturday

Theological Class met at the Tabernacle at one oclock pm. Present Prest. B[righam] Young presiding. After singing Prayer by Elder David McKenzie. Singing.

Elder Horace S. Eldredge was pleased to be a Member of the School, it had been a source of ~~profit~~ ^benefit^ and blessing to him, though he had not lived up to all the duties he had many times lifted up his hands to attend to, such as attending Ward and Fast Meetings &c. ~~the~~ yet it was his daily effort to overcome his weaknesses until he finally succeeded in honoring every calling and duty required at his hands. He felt thankful for the confidence reposed in him, by calling him to fulfill an important Mission to England which he hoped by the blessing of God to honorably fill.

He never had any desire to go after or listen to, any of the Schisms that have broken off from this Church, lest his mind should come in contact with false doctrines. While on his Mission he particularly desired the prayers of his brethren in his behalf.

Elder Demick Huntington felt thankful to be ~~thank~~ here again, having been on a Mission East, and bore the same testimony as the other Elders, pertaining to the selfishness and darkness of the people. He exhorted the brethren to live their religion, all was right, we are in the right place. He felt to rejoice in God, &c.

Elder Geo Q. Cannon then read the rules of the School.

Prest. Geo A Smith spoke of the rules being simple and exactly adapted to our sanctification, and should be observed. Every man that belongs to the school of the prophets, ought to be man enough to do right because it is right, and to abstain from wrong because it is wrong. And not to let his left hand Know what his right hand doeth.

We have a right to meet here and talk about building up Zion or anything else we please—although some bellow and howl, and threaten us, because we hold these meetings. God will defend us, and when the time comes, a Temple will be built in Jackson County [Missouri] and the City of Zion erected there, though Earth or Hell oppose.

Prest. Jos[ep]h Young rather objected to the first rule of the School which require exact promptness in our attendance ~~or g~~ unless excused by the President, he regarded it as too stringent, and did not wish to be bound by it in ~~his~~ its present form. The Word of Wisdom, he looked upon as being interpreted and acted upon by each Saint. He strongly advocated the Spirit of leniency and Kindness towards our Wives and Children, when they are in error, rather than uncouth and harsh treatment.

Elder Rob[er]t F. Neslen felt proud that he had been called to go forth on a Mission to preach the Gospel, he had been more or less engaged in that delightful labour for 17 Years. He expressed thankfulness for the chastising rod that was administered to him some time ago—by Bro Brigham. He had seen much affliction in his family, and in his body, since that time, and needed much of the consoling influences of the spirit of God. He hoped the prayers of the Saints would be offered in his behalf while on his Mission.

Prest. B Young said at the time that Bro Neslen was chastened, it was like a ^fire^ brand being thrown into the nest and breaking a shell before it had time to hatch.

B[isho]p E[dwin] D. Woolley had voted for the rules of the school a great ~~made~~ many times, and had endeavoured to live up to them—there is nothing very binding on the latter day saints, for every rule is good and wholesome and ought to be observed.

Many Members of this school never darken the doors of a Fast Meeting or Ward Meeting, or pay their fast offering. He never enjoyed his religion better than now—and now was the time, when dangers threatened us, to rally round the standard and sustain, not only the principles but the promulgaters of them.

Elder Geo Q Cannon did not agree with the idea that the Word of Wisdom should be regarded and treated in that loose and lax way, as to be left to our own interpretation of it. He believed that both Tea, Coffee, Tobacco & Spirits was possitively injurious, and though the Word was given 38 years ago, as a Word of Wisdom. After so long an experience we have had, it is now become a possitive Law to refrain from them. He strongly urged a strict observance of the rule that refers to sustain^ing^ ourselves and letting alone the enemies of the saints—for it was perfectly suicidal for us to sustain our open and a vowed enemies.

It was then Motioned & Carried. That Bro Geo Barber of Smithfield

[Utah] go on a Mission to England. Also Peter Evans 9th Ward D[itt]o Edmund F. Bird[,] D[itt]o Ralph Thompson D[itt]o. It was also Motioned & Carried That Bro Levi North be released from a Mission to England that he was appointed to last Saturday. A request was also made for the Sunday School Children to attend the New Tabernacle—tomorrow afternoon, also for as many adults as possible so as to fill up the House. The High Council was requested to Meet at the Seventys Council Hall on Tuesday next at 10 oclock AM.

Prest. B Young then notified the Missionaries that Friday 13th May had been decided upon for them to start to Omaha. He then spoke on the necessity of every Member of the School, observing the rules of it—it was just as easy to observe them as not, but we must have our hearts upon them. We can just as well attend our Ward and fast Meetings and pay our fast offerings as not, if we only want to. The Lord requires us to keep the Sabbath day Holy—and no man is justified in sending his team on a Saturday for wood when they know that it cannot possibly return before Sunday evening. ~~and no one~~ He then call[e]d for a show of hands from those who desired to observe the rules of the School, All hands were uplifted. He then gave some valuable instruction on the Word of Wisdom.

The Meeting was adjourned for two weeks at one oclock pm.[46] After singing Benediction by Elder H[orace] S. Eldredge.

May 14, 1870; Saturday

Theological Class met at the Tabernacle at One o clock pm. Present Prest. Geo A. Smith presiding. After singing Prayer by Elder S[amuel] W. Richards. Singing.

Elder A[lbert] P. Rockwood recommended a systematic organized effort being made to destroy the Grasshoppers, unless it is done, he was satisfied there will be but little raised this season.[47]

Elder W[ilford] W. Woodruff said the best plan he had found to destroy them was to get a large sheet, and a Man at each corner to drag it through the grain, and when caught, bury them—it certainly

46. No meeting was held on May 7 due to general conference.

47. The settlers contended with crickets destroying crops in the valley so often that over time they developed a miraculous story about the crops of 1848 being saved by gulls eating the crickets. Contemporary accounts said little or nothing about the seagull story, but later reminiscences were reshaped to accommodate it. Hartley, "Mormons, Crickets, and Gulls."

was their duty to make an organized effort, and if after that is done, and the Crops are destroyed, we shall have the satisfaction of having done our duty.

Elder John Pack had never seen such destruction by Grasshoppers ~~as~~ in his life, as this season. They had destroyed his wheat, and was going to sow again on Monday—if they take that, he intended to plant Corn. He intended to plough the wheat under and not Harrow it, then, ~~should~~ the first joint [node] is under the surface, and if the Grasshoppers still come, the first joint being under ground it will shoot again.

Elder Ja[me]s Brown suggested a simple method similar to Bro Woodruffs plan.

Prest. D[aniel] H. Wells said one of two things had to be done, one to sit down supinely and bear the loss or by an organized effort, destroy them, and save a partial Crop. He earnestly recommended a persevering effort by a thorough organization.

Elder W. W. Woodruff suggested That the Bishops of the ~~City~~ County get together and devise some practical method for destroying them.

Elder [Daniel] Carns suggested that by putting Axle Grease on the trunk, two feet high on all our fruit trees—the Grasshoppers will not go near them.

Elder Milo Andrus said that Whiskey & water sprinkled on our Trees and Plants will preserve them from injury by the Grasshoppers.

Elder Demick Huntingdon recommended organization[,] we are not yet starved to death, neither shall we be, but the Lord was to try us.

Prest. D[aniel] H. Wells desired the Bishops to meet and organize in sufficient force to destroy them in their respective Wards.

It was Motioned and Carried That we all turn out and assist at the Bishops call. Motioned and Carried That Bro [Samuel] Turnbow be appointed overseer ~~to call out~~ to superintend~~ent~~ and see that a sufficient number of men be called out to accomplish the object.

Prest. Geo A. Smith made a few encouraging remarks, and called upon the brethren to be faithful.

Meeting adjourned for one week at one oclock pm—Benediction by Prest. Geo A Smith.

May 21, 1870; Saturday

Theological Class met at the Tabernacle at One o clock pm. Present

Prest. B[righam] Young presiding. After singing Prayer by Elder B[righam] Young Junr. Singing.

Elder W[ilford] Woodruff reported that a considerable effort had been made during the week by Bro [Samuel] Turnbow and those who had turned out to assist him, in the destruction of the Grasshoppers, and hoped that a union of ~~Gre~~ exertion will ~~be~~ continue to be made that our Wheat may be spared.

B[isho]p A[rchibald] Gardner said they had turned 1600 Sheep into a field, and Kept them as much as possible in a compact body, driving them slowly along, and every grasshopper was literally trappled under foot. This they found the most successful effort they had tried.

Prest. Geo A Smith said the First Presidency had for many years past, tried to inspire the brethren to lay up [store] Grain & Flour against a day ^of^ Famine—which had not been carried out so generally as might have been. He suggested a deep thought on this subject, as something to eat, ~~and~~ ^to^ sustain us should be our first consideration. Another class of enemies were plotting our destruction in their private councils, they may determine to send Armies here to destroy us, and scatter us, and lay waste our habitations, but it would not prove our religion to be false. There are many who expect to fatten on our overthrow, and pick the bones of the Mormons, he believed that some of the Government officials in this City were trying to raise up a friction by brutal ignorance amongst our community so to base a "hue and cry" of insubordination.

It should be our policy to so act, as to give no occasion for offense. If we pursue a straightforward, wise and patient course, we shall be protected and sustained, and all will come off right. He refer'd to varieties of ruling by our Judges in relation to the ~~ju~~ extent of Jurisdiction by Probate Courts, what one decides upon, another will denounce, and each Judge seems to have been impregnated with the law that was common in the state they hailed from. He then contrasted the adjacent Territories with Utah in the way of Taxes and clearly Shown we were highly favoured by husbanding our resources. Keep out of debt &c.

But we will do our duty, and let the worst come, God will reveal in the very day thereof what we should do, if we should have to lose our lives, what better are we than Joseph & Hyrum [Smith], & others.

In view of the coming events, God had instituted the principle of co operation, and those Merchants now trading who are not sustaining it, will surely fall into darkness. Let us unite with all our hearts to take council and build up the Kingdom of God—but not to seek after devils to govern this people. He spoke of the Apostacy in the days of Strang[48] & others.

Elder [James M.] Barlow returned Missionary—was highly gratified to return to Salt Lake City, he was well satisfied with this Country, and this people. Here the will of the Lord can be learned, and his concern was, to make his calling and election sure. He had visit^ed^ his friends in the flesh, but could not take that pleasure with them, as with the people of God, who dwelt in these vallies. He had been well treated in every place where he visited. The Newspapers generally sought to bring this people—into disrespect by false statements. He had endeavoured to give a fair and truthful report of the Latter day Saints—and thus correct their impressions in regard to them.

B[isho]p [Edward] Hunter hoped the brethren would continue their exertions in connection with Bro Turnbow by destroying the Grasshoppers, and we would raise some good crops. Let us continue to plant Corn & Potatoes, even should our wheat be eaten up.

Prest. B Young said when we raise grain, hereafter, let us Keep it, had we done so and we had a seven years supply, let the Grasshoppers come, instead of raising ~~feed~~ wheat for them, leave nothing but oak brush &c for them, and let us go to and build the Temple and ~~the~~ instead of going to the Gold Mines[49]—~~let~~ because they are short of work, let all such come on and haul rock for the temple.

Meeting was adjourned for one week. Benediction by Elder Jno [John] Taylor.

May 28, 1870; Saturday

Theological Class met at the Tabernacle at One oclock p. m. Present

48. James Jesse Strang (1813–56) claimed to be Joseph Smith's successor, though he had just recently converted to Mormonism. He established the splinter Church of Jesus Christ of Latter Day Saints, commonly called Strangites, in Wisconsin and Beaver Island, Michigan, where Strang was ordained king. He was elected to the Michigan state legislature in 1853 but was assassinated three years later. Speek, *"God Has Made Us a Kingdom."*

49. Gold had been recently discovered in a canyon west of Utah Lake. The town of Mercur sprang up as miners flocked to the area. Other mining endeavors were finding success throughout the territory in the Oquirrh Mountains and Park City.

Prest. B[righam] Young presiding. After singing Prayer by B[isho]p E[dwin] D. Woolley. Singing.

Prest. Geo A Smith said at the present moment, the whole civilized world are more or less agitated on the subject of Celestial Marriage which we as a people not only preach and believe in, but more or less practised. We did not receive that doctrine because Ancient Men of God practised it, but on a/c [account] of a revelation given by the Almighty to Joseph Smith. He wished the Elders to speak on the Social Effects of Plurality—on the testimony furnished by the Bible in its favour—&c.

Elder N[athaniel] H. Felt said in the world, the Bible was pretty much ignored—and Jesus Christ regarded as a Mere Man, denying his divinity—but they dont like the Mormons having more wives than one. We have physyological laws to sustain the Doctrine—the Bible also, and more than all, a command given by God Almighty. The brute creation refuses connexion with the opposite sex, but man frequently breaks this pure law of nature—a frequent connexion with a pregnent wife will produce a serious effect on the unborn infant, and no wonder their offspring as they grow up, have such a tendency to a lustful and indsicriminate familiarity between the sexes.[50] This generation is fast running out in consequence of such indulgences

The large proportion of the female sex is generally admitted, and which fact is simply the result of Monogomy. Woman, who according to her organism is prepared to produce offspring—and fulfil the great command of God to Multiply and replenish the earth. She therefore has her claims on God & the Heads of Governments that no law shall ever be made to counteract or prevent her destiny.

Prest. Geo A Smith made a particular request of ~~his~~ the Elders to speak plainly on this subject, to avoid vulgarity, but call things by their right names. He then gave a privilege for any one to come ^to the stand.^

Elder Tho[ma]s H Read ^1st ward^ believed the earth was the Lords and the fulness thereof. Do we respect and carry out the Councils of the Servants of God. Do we sustain ourselves, and are willing to become one. Would ~~the~~ a ^good^ King send a mighty army against

50. Felt was echoing a common belief, called "maternal impression," that whatever happened to a child in the womb of its mother would physically imprint itself on the child. Therefore if parents engaged in intercourse while a fetus was still in the womb, the newborn might have a tendency towards an increased sexual appetite. Pickover, *Girl Who Gave Birth*, 211.

loyal subjects. He did not think he would, but we call this farm and this orchard &c Ours, instead of acknowledging it to be the Lords, He says except ye are one ye are not mine &c.

Prest. B Young said we had been councilled to lay up our grain, and with but very few exceptions—had neglected to carry ^it^ out—and on that a/c [account], the Grasshoppers were suffered to destroy our crops, and he had no objection for them to remain, until the Saints became willing to be one.

Elder A[lbert] Merrill said this was ^a^ fast age, and a great many East were giving way to a suicidal course—by cutting throats, Infanticide &c. A Woman of Child bearing age having a good Husband, was capable of giving birth to from 6 to 12 Children, this would fill up her capability~~—but a man~~ by about the time she was 40 or 45 years old—but a Man during the same length of time had the power to beget hundreds of children, without impairing his physical powers.

Prest. Geo A Smith hoped the Brethren would post themselves on the subject of Polygamy—and other doctrines, so that at future schools they may deliver a 10 minutes meeting, for mutual instruction.

Meeting was adjourned for one week at One oclock pm. After singing Benediction by Prest. Geo A Smith.

June 4, 1870; Saturday

Theological Class met at the Tabernacle at one o clock pm. Present Elder Orson Pratt presiding[,] Prest. B[righam] Young & Council being absent, holding a two days meeting at Box Elder [Brigham City, Utah].[51] After singing Prayer by Elder Sam[ue]l Richards. Singing.

Elder Orson Pratt after making a few preliminary remarks, called on the brethren to deliver their views on the Subject of Plural Marriage as suggested by the 1st Presidency.

The Clerk then read a paper on that subject written by Elder Edw[ar]d Stevenson, it was composed ~~E~~ entirely of Scripture testimony.

Elder Geo B Wallace referd to the 1st pair that God created to be in the Garden of Eden viz Adam and Eve, at which time they were perfect, and immortal beings. Through transgression they forfeited the

51. The completion of the railroad made what would have been an all-day journey north a trip of a few hours; Young's party left Salt Lake in the early morning and was speaking at the bowery in Brigham City at 10:00 a.m. WWJ, June 4, 1870. Box Elder became Brigham City on January 12, 1867.

favour of God, and brought sin and death into the world. The Gospel of the Son of God is intended to reinstate, and restore them to all, that by sin they had lost and will be brought forth in the Morning of the resurrection with the same relationship as existed when they fell, viz Husband & wife and as it is natural for ^more^ women to obey the Gospel than Men, so in the resurrection will every woman come forth united to some Man as her husband. He believed that no one with one Wife will ever become a God. He also believed that no one with only one wife will come forth in the first resurrection.[52] That no ~~woman~~ man could cohabit with his wife while pregnant without ~~a~~ diminishing the strength of body and mind in the infant—½ an hour.

Elder Osmond Shaw exprest full confidence in the scripture testimony's. It [polygamy] has been ^the^ rule and Monogomy the exception since the creation of Man. No Law that ever emanated from God will produce evil. At the present time there is One fifth of all children born, illegitimate. There are one third of all the Marriageble females in England in excess of Males. The Children of Polygamic nations are stronger in Body and Mind then those of Mon^o^gamy— ~~where is the~~

Elder Burr Frost said Abraham when he received the Gospel entered into a Plurality of Wives—and Whenever and Wherever, the Gospel was received, Polygamy ~~was~~ always existed. Spoke of Jesus coming when the time of restitution of all things spoken by the Prophets since the world again [began].

Elder [Anders W.] Winberg spoke of those who have had wives before receiving the Gospel ^and died^, then received it, had More, and the living one to act as proxy for those behind the vail, and ^all^ thus come forth together in the resurrection.[53]

Elder Theo[dore] Curtis shown that Jacob of old was in the Kingdom of God as he proved by the Scriptures.[54] Rachael & Leah his wives, Leah was barren, asked the Lord for Children and it was granted.

52. The first resurrection, inaugurated when Jesus was restored to life, will begin in earnest after Christ's second coming. The second resurrection will include the less faithful, according to LDS theology. Douglas L. Callister, "Resurrection," in Ludlow, ed., *Encyclopedia of Mormonism*.

53. Living members of a family can perform essential ordinances, such as baptism and marriage sealings, for deceased relatives ("those behind the vail"), in other words.

54. Gen. 29–30.

Rachael complained of Jacob for closing up her womb Jacob said God alone could do this. Jacob who had 4 wives, God promised to be with him and would never leave him—and when returning with his wives and children Esaw met him and enquired who all these were, he said, ~~Go~~ these are my wives and children whom God hath given me.

Elder E[manual] M. Murphy spoke much on the subject of personal experience.

Elder Amos Fielding said, the signs of the times require the introduction of Polygamy and God requires it &c. ~~there is~~

Elder Orson Pratt had been instructed by some of the Scriptures testimonies that ~~were~~ had been brought forward. Enock had such a knowledge of Life and Immortality, as to become translated, body and spirit—and [this occurs] as Life and immortality is brought to light through the Gospel. Enock and the ancient worthies must have obeyed the Gospel.

If there is no marrying nor giving in marriage in the next world, he did not know any scripture where it said there shall be no giving, God may possibly give many wives to a good man. We can prove to the world that God sanctions plural Marriage, and that to, for eternity. He was thankful for an additional testimony advanced by Bro Curtis, that God had given wives, children &c to Jacob. God has so ordained it that Females should bring forth their offspring during the most healthy and vigorous portion of their lives, viz from the age of about 17 to 45.

The School was adjourned one week at 1 pm. After singing Benediction by B[isho]p E[dwin] D Woolley.

June 11, 1870; Saturday

Theological Class met at the Tabernacle at one o clock pm. Present Prest. Geo A Smith presiding. After singing Prayer by Elder Geo B. Wallace. Singing.

By request of Prest. Geo A Smith Elder [George] Reynolds read a letter received from a Gentleman residing in California by the name of Allan Tillinghart Wilson, in which, he heartily endorces the doctrine of Plurality of wives, and speaks very highly of those principles which govern the latter day saints, though himself, a man of no religion.

Prest. Geo A Smith in speaking of David & Uriah refer'd to in the above letter, said that David was guilty of adultery as well as Murder, for both of which he had to pay the penalty.[55]

Whenever we leave this valley, he expected we would go to Jackson County [Missouri], although we may have to return in a roundabout direction. The Lord will try us in various ways—the road we should walk in, is that which is already marked out for us. Until our hearts are a little more mellowed around here, we need not expect to go to Jackson County. We must all unite, and stand by the [First] Presidency. The effect of Co operation in our midst, has saved many of our Merchant Brethren from Bankruptcy by inducing a cautious mode of purchase &c. It is our bounden duty to sustain and back up the hands of President [Brigham] Young, and not stand in the way of progress. We are going to learn to do right here, and stay just as long as the Lord wants us. He also spoke of the happy reception the President & party met with at Brigham City [Utah].

Elder Geo Q Cannon read a question from a Member of the School [of the Prophets], enquiring if the Revelation on Celestial Marriage, is not binding on all the Members of the Church. Answer, If any man marries a Wife in the Endowment House he is sealed under this Law, and in taking a second, under the same law also—the revelation is printed and consequently can be read and understood by all—he did not think the question was worth quibling about.

Elder Orson Pratt considered ^it^ a very important thing for the Elders to become well informed on all the principles connected with our faith, and es[pecially] that of Plural Marriage, recommended them to commit to Memory every passage in the old as well as the New ^Testament^ every passage that has any bearing on the subject, so as to become thoroughly familiarized with them, and bring them forward whenever called for. If only one passage was committed to Memory daily, we would soon have our minds well stored with Scripture testimony.

Elder Geo Q Cannon—said the object of marriage, is it for the purpose of propagating our Species or for the purpose of sensual indulgence. Man is differently organized to Women. Man is capable of begetting children until Eighty years old, Woman only capable of bearing children until from 40 to 50 years old. This fact is a very important

55. 2 Sam. 11.

one, it gives a righteous Man a chance of raising a pure seed and many of them, if the Law permits him. Woman, during the period of pregnancy, and Lactation, gives a Man a long period of time to beget children should circumstances permit. It would be an easy thing for a strong man like Moses or ~~others like of like~~ to beget a very numerous offspring, if he had a sufficient number of wives to do so.

The introduction of Polygamy at the present time, he believed would be the means of raising a noble seed—and any man who steps out under the present circumstances, and takes to himself many wives, in the face of so much opposition, shows himself to be of no ordinary character—and such men are more likely to raise up a number of great men, than those who are confined to the Monogamous system. Many of our own Church would have left no son to perpetuate their name, were it not for Polygamy &c.

Elder John Pack believed it to be the duty of every one to keep the commandments of God. Adam & Eve were married by God & commanded to multiply and replenish the earth. Man possesses a greater power of procreation than woman—and therefore indispensable in having more wives than one. He felt under condemnation in cohabiting with his wives at improper times [during menstruation or pregnancy]—and all mankind were under that sin. To carry out the first great command, Man must have the means to do it, viz women in whom to plant seed. Jesus sprang from the loins of David, and God has always honored the great and noble polygamists of past ages. Elder [blank] Believed in ^the^ work of the latter days, he believed in the written ~~tes~~ word, in the Bible, Book of Mormon & Doctrine & Covenants, also on the living oracles.

School was adjourned for one week at 1 pm. Benediction by Elder Geo Q Cannon.

June 18, 1870; Saturday

Theological Class met at the Tabernacle at one oclock pm. Present Prest. Geo A Smith presiding. After singing prayer by B[isho]p A[braham] Hoagland. Singing.

By request of Prest. Geo A. Smith Elder George Reynolds said that where Monogamy was the Law, it compelled a more frequent cohabitation than is right and proper, and as a consequence the Animal passions are very early developed in their offspring—and also a habit of giving way to self abuse [masturbation]. This evil exists to a greater or less extent among the Children of the Latter day Saints—and Parents should certainly warn their children of the evils of such a practise. The practise of Plural Marriage had existed from time immemorial among the Jews—therefore St Paul says ~~H~~ Marriage is honorable in all and the bed undefiled, but Adulterers and whoremongers, God will judge.

Elder L[orenzo] Snow spoke of the first command that God gave to Adam & Eve viz. To Multiply and replenish the earth and could be carried out by man with one wife or more. God commanding plural Marriage in this our day, was the strongest reason for him to carry it out. Plural Marriage was in accordance with nature, and Natural Law will not conflict with divine Law. He thought that in the Majority of cases, the Female during pregnancy would rather repulse than invite cohabitation. The act of generation [impregnation] draws the very best blood that a man possesses.

He believed that Plural Marriage would tend to diminish the evil [of] self-pollution [masturbation]. He was inclined to think that indulgence on the part of man, was less in Plural Marriage than in Monogamy. He also thought that as there were more Marriageable females than Males—so he thought that Plural Marriage made provision for that and should be tolerated.

Elder Orson Pratt said that when plurality was first taught in Nauvoo the following arguments were used, that supposing Male & female be about equal in number—are there not some, more righteous than others. Spirits are begotten in the spirit world, by the righteous—the ~~world~~ wicked have not the privilege of procreating their species [in the pre-mortal existence], and why not the same restrictions in this world. The wicked, here, have the privilege of begetting tabernacles in this life, but not to beget the inteligent spirit in the eternal world.

In the ancient Law, at a time of war, they were commanded not to spare, either Man Woman or Suckling—so that the Jewish nation should not be polluted by a people who were living without law. If the number of Males & females be equal—it is no reason why Plural Marriage should not exist. ^as the lord had determined to raise up a^ righteous seed.

Elder A[lbert] Merrill said in the New Testament that it says that the Heavens must receive Jesus, until ~~th~~ the restitution of all things, spoken of by the Holy Prophets since the ~~days~~ world began. The Revelation on plural Marriage was given through Joseph [Smith] the Prophet, to the Latter day saints only, the outside world has no part or lot in the matter. Elders in Israel should respect and honour the principle, seeing that there is such a great pressure against us outside.

Elder Amos Fielding said if there ever ~~was~~ would be a time when a righteous seed would be raised up, every principle of purity must be sought after and practiced.

Elder [George E.] Taylor for 17 years had studied and partially practised the law that Governs Sexual intercourse. If man should be chaste, should we not study the Laws of chastity. Some kinds of food, such as Meat, Oysters, &c, have a tendency to develope the animal passions. Recommended the members of the school to study the laws of life, and health—or in ~~ot~~ scripture phrase—Man know thyself.

Prest. Geo A Smith spoke of the evil of Masturbation which should be abated and entirely overcome by our people. Many of the Laws given by Moses to the children of Israel—were given because they were not capable of observing a higher law. Many things were commanded in his day, had passed away—but certain high moral principles, continue, and always. Certain ordinances ^& sacrifices^ were done away when Christ came.

A Question had been asked on paper, that if a man married a wife & Mother in the days of Moses ^should be burnt to death^ why was it admissable now?[56]

The Man or woman who inculcates a distaste to polygamy among their children, will be wasted away. No person can speak or use their influence against it, without imbibing the spirit [of] adultery—and the chances are that all those who faithfully and manfully stand up for the law of Celestial Marriage will finally come off conqueror.

Children born under the sealing power, are especially the objects of Satans endeavour to destroy them. He strongly recommended the brethren to keep away from the [gold] Mines. He also urged the study of plural Marriage, on its Physical, Moral & Religious bearing, also all the objections they can find, that are made by the world, and answer them.

---

56. "And if a man take a wife and her mother, it is wickedness: they shall be burnt with fire, both he and they" (Lev. 20:14).

The Rules of the school were then read by Elder Geo Q. Cannon, and sustained by a unanimous show of hands.

Meeting was then adjourned for one week at 1 o clock. After singing Benediction by Prest. Geo A Smith.

June 25, 1870; Saturday

Theological Class met at the Tabernacle at One o clock pm. Present Prest. B[righam] Young presiding. After singing Prayer by ^Elder^ Brigham Young Junr. Singing.

Prest. B Young read the following note. [“]Is it the will of the Lord for us to entirely abstain from Pork, and send our money back to the [United] States to import it?[”]

Prest. Young said it was the will of the Lord for us to preserve our body’s in health as long as we can. It was the will of the Lord ~~to~~ to those who cant do without Pork, to raise it themselves and it was against the spirit of the Lord for us to send back to the States after it. It is the will of the Lord for us to eat Fish, Fowl, Eggs, Butter &c. Many who had ceased raising Pork had not yet succeeded in raising substitutes in its stead.

Prest. D[aniel] H. Wells gave an interesting account of their Northern trip.[57] There was every indication of the blessing of God resting upon the Saints and the settlements they live in. Every prospect of rich crops, and a remarkable increase of posterity among the saints. There was nearly 200 lodges of Indians close by the Saints, and yet nothing had been missed by the brethren, and no one had been molested by them. They begin to realize that we are their friends, and they soon will know that we are their only friends.

Pork was rejected entirely, among the Israelites anciently, but we ~~have~~ had been traditionated to use it, and many felt it difficult to leave it off. The servants of God had been wrought upon to council the saints not only to lay aside the use of Pork, but Tea, Coffee, Tobacco &c—in order that the Saints may become a purer people, and better in our physical condition, &c. The Lord was preparing by railroad speed, a people for the second coming of the Messiah.

Elder W[ilford] Woodruff had a pleasant journey up North. The leading Council given, was ^for^ the Saints to lay up their grain—had

57. See June 4, 1870, entry.

they heeded it before, the Grasshoppers would not have visited us. Woollen and other Factorys were also recommended for the saints to build.

Zion is increasing. We shall soon have a mighty host in these vallies. Parents should teach their children the Gospel of Christ. He hoped the Saints would magnify their callings and build up the Kingdom of God. He would like to have them build one Temple in these vallies—hundreds had got to be built.

If we did our duty, we shall never be driven away from these Vallies. When the time comes, for the Saints to go back to build up Zion in Jackson County [Missouri]—that these vallies will not be vacated entirely, neither will all return to that Country.

<u>Elder Jno [John] Taylor</u> said, as in Nature, in regard to the growth of grain—in the gradual development of infants, so is the growth and progress of the Kingdom of God. We have had to contend with very many obstacles, and ~~the~~ yet we have grown, as may be seen, by contrasting the Past with the present condition of the people. The great majority of the saints of God, are engaged heartily in the work of God. The hundreds now before him, had come, some of them many miles, to be taught and instructed in the things of the kingdom of God.

We enjoy great priveleges in these vallies—and surely must be standing in holy places. We are here, not to build ourselves up—but use every means in our power, unitedly to bring about the purposes of God. We ought to seek to know, what the will of God is concerning us is, and then to do it, whether it makes us rich or poor, no matter, and should it even cost us our lives, we should do it. These were the only principles that actuated the first Elders of the church—When sickness and poverty surrounded them, still they persevered, because the welfare of Mankind was their motive. The Lord reigns and let Israel rejoice—for Zion shall henceforth be the Head and not the tail.

<u>Prest. Geo A Smith</u> said the Enemy of all righteousness was never more busy, than at present among us. There were many Teachers in the different ward[s], and some of the Teachers met at the Bishops meetings—&c. A secret effort was being made to poison the minds of our youth. Especially against the authorities of the Church. It is the duty of every Teacher to give such instructions as to counteract that spirit—teach our children to love the Lord. Let every man, called to act as

Teachers, feel that we have a great and noble calling. Let every Bishop and Teacher be wide awake.

Prest. Geo A Smith, continued—he enquired in which Wards their were Josephite [Reorganized Church] Meetings held, and nine Wards were spoken of. He~~n~~ then asked if all present were willing to do their duty as Teachers if appointed and the majority of hands was uplifted.

It was then Motioned and Carried That every Member of this School, who had been recommended as being good faithful Members—should henceforth act as Teachers—to reprove Sin, and correct error.

Prest. B Young recommended a kind spirit, in the Teachers while trying to correct the errors of ~~his~~ ^their^ Brethren & Sisters—yet while doing their duty, many will regard them as ^their^ enemies. There is a good reason, for every requirement that the Lord makes upon us. If every member in this School will only act as faithful Men of God, a great and good influence may be exerted, among the people.

The Meeting was adjourned for one week at One o clock pm. Benediction by Elder G[eorge] Q Cannon.[58]

July 2, 1870; Saturday

Theological Class met at the Tabernacle at One o clock pm. Present Prest. B[righam] Young presiding. After singing Prayer by Elder Orson Pratt. Singing.

Prest. Geo A. Smith gave out the text for the afternoon viz. Co operation, which subject, he desired the brethren to speak upon for ten minutes.[59]

Elder Miner G Atwood, believed in the principle of Co operation, and had done ever since he obeyed the Gospel. We had all co operated under the same ordinances, viz ^one^ Faith, one Baptism, one Leader &c. He expected to be led and taught in a way that he was ignorant of before. He tried to treasure up what he heard, and then practise it. He never had any unpleasant feeling towards the leaders of Israel.

Elder Millen Atwood said the first teaching he ever received in the Gospel, was that it would take all he possessed, if ever he obtained

58. Joseph F. Smith added that some school members complained of a local Methodist strawberry feast that doubled as a church fundraiser. Zerubabbel Snow "told one of the most appalling stories about a prize being offered to the young lady who should get the greatest number of votes from the boys. The votes being 25¢ each!!" JFSJ, June 25, 1870.

59. Members were sometimes invited to speak in alphabetical order.

salvation. He always thought, that whether he had much ~~and~~ or little, it would sooner or later be required and he wanted to be ready to enter the order of Enoch when the time arrived.

Elder Sam[ue]l Atwood came here on the purpose to learn the ways of the Lord, he did not know them before, but he expected to learn them through the servants of God. He did not know the difference between Temporal & Spiritual things, then why not cheerfully comply with temporal councils. When the things of Heaven are told us, we have understanding to realize it, but we Know nothing of them until some heavenly messenger reveals them, neither do we know how to build up a Temporal Kingdom only as we are taught by those in authority.

Elder W[illiam] L. N. Allen endorsed the above sentiments. He knew the time would come when Co operation would unite and bind us together as one family. And no one denies the right of a good Father to direct and controul his wives and children—so the Leader of the people has a right to direct the temporal affairs of the people.

The principle of Co operation will enable us to build up the Kingdom of God much quicker than by a single handed effort—and if we only had the same spirit as when we first embraced the Gospel in the old Country, we would be willing to carry out whatever was councilled by the Servants of God.

Elder W[illia]m Asper realized ~~wh~~ that Co operation was something of great importance, and implicit obedience to the servants of God is the only way ^by which^ the Kingdom of God can ever be built up. There is something coming in the future, which nothing short of the spirit of God, will enable us to appreciate and endure.

Elder W[illia]m Atkinson, came into this Church for exaltation, and nothing but carrying out the ^council of the^ servants of God will ever bring that great blessing to himself or others. It was for us to co operate in everything that is councilled by the authorities. He had for nearly 20 years been patiently trying to do right, and it was now too late in the day to back out for such a noble cause.

Elder Benjammin Ashby said, if Co operation was not a subject revealed from Heaven, it would not have occupied ~~out~~ our attention to day. If Co operation was heartily enter'd into by us a people, as a general principle—~~and~~ we should soon become the wealthiest people on the face of the earth. It is an eternal principle by which the Gods in eternity are ~~a~~ governed.

Elder David P. Anderson felt proud to be a member in the church and Kingdom of God—was a firm believer in Co-operation, regarded it as a steping stone to our entering in to the order of Enock. He desired to support the Kingdom of God as long as he lived.

Elder Geo Q Cannon read ~~the following~~ ^several^ questions. ~~are we to understand,~~ on the subject of plural Marriage and ^was^ answered by ~~Elder~~ Prest. Geo A Smith and Prest. B Young who said, to understand it require a ^clear^ perceptive mind, susceptible of the spirit of the Lord—A man thrown in circumstances where he cannot enjoy the blessing of Plurality [of wives] [and] yet [is] a firm believer in the doctrine—such a one will certainly not lose his exaltation.

He then gave some excellent council to Husbands towards their wives. Some men so act, as to ask pardon of his wife, which is stooping to an inferior. He then exhorted the brethren to so live before God, and their families, that their wives and children will look up to them, with all confidence & affection.

Prest. Young then gave several simple illustrations, on the principle of plural marriage all showing, that all Men hereafter will be rewarded according to his works. He also gave some good council to Bishops. Presidents, Fathers, Husbands &c. To be prudent and Kind, so that wives, neighbours & others may respect and honour you. There are but few in this Church who can bear reproof without getting angry. When he reproved his brethren, it was for their good.

He believed the Majority of the Members of this School, if they had an opportunity of expressing their views, would express feelings of joy and Hallelujah at the approach of that happy time, when the order of Enoch shall be carried out.

School was adjourned for one week at One oclock pm. Benediction by ~~Eld~~ Prest. Geo A. Smith.

July 9, 1870; Saturday

Theological Class met at the Tabernacle at One o clock pm. Present ~~President B[righam] Young~~ ^Elder O[rson] Pratt^ presiding. After singing Prayer by Elder A[mos] M[ilton] Musser. Singing. (Prest. Young & Council and most of the twelve [apostles] being absent on a preaching mission to Ogden, where a meetings to day and to morrow are to be held.)

Elder Pratt made a few preliminary remarks, touching the subject of Co operation, Tithing, Consecration, Home Manufacture &c, strongly recommending the adoption and practise of sustaining home produced articles. Cooperation should be more extensively carried out, than it has hitherto been.

He then read several questions, to as to whether ^what^ Lamech meant where he said to his Wives, I have slain a young Man to my wounding, and also to my hurt,[60] and also, will Uriah be exalted, and become a God, or will he be an angel?[61] Bro Pratt briefly reply'd.

Elder Albert Carrington felt peculiarly gratefull for the privelege of again appearing before the school of the Prophets. He had spoken much in Europe [as British Mission President] during the last two years. He always trusted to the dic^ta^tion of the spirit of the Lord—and it had never failed him. The Saints throughout the Mission and the Elders too, are living faithfull, and patient under all their trials. The faith, zeal, and finer good works among the Saints in Europe are in a much better condition than ever did ^was^ before. He felt to acknowledge the hand of God in the general success that has attended the Mission during his stay, he also gave an account of some of the Elders who have been released, to return home, for a lack of ability to speak in public.

He also gave a general account of his Mission, and made a special call upon those who had borrowed means of poor Saints in Europe to return ^it to^ them saints as speedily as possible.

Elder C[harles] C. Rich felt, that as a people we had barely commenced co operation. The subject was suggested by the Prophet Joseph [Smith] in the days of Kirtland, that the brethren should unite their labours, & fence in a large farm, and carry out a principle of Union. There was not a settlement in the Territory but might soon have every kind of labour saving machinery, if they would only unite and put their means together.

We ought to adopt such principles as will place us in the march of progress—and individual effort is needed to make it general—and there

60. Gen. 4:23.

61. Another reference to King David arranging for the death of Uriah so he could marry Uriah's widow, Bathsheba. See 2 Sam. 11–12.

is no blessing that will do us good, but what may be obtained if sought after, in the right way. Apostacy which does, and will take place—first commences by giving way to some little sin, then followed by indulging in larger ones, the Spirit of God leaves such, and they go into darkness.

Elder Phineas ~~Young~~ Richards—recommended early to bed, and early to rise, if done, in this City alone would save thousands of dollars in Tallow and Oil.

Elder William G Young, in visiting Wisconsin—noticed their making of ~~Choice~~ Cheese, every Settlement in Cache and Rich Counties [Utah] might just as well open up their factories and export Cheese by the Ton, and thus bring means in our midst—instead of sending away our mean East for that article [cheese].

Elder Tho[ma]s Ellerbeck appreciated faith and good works in any man wherever he saw it, he honoured good men—he himself was not a man of much faith, but had been gaining a little more and more—He had been to England on a visit, and had to return because his time was limited, he would be glad to go back on a two years Mission to preach the Gospel.

The School was then adjourned for one week at One o clock pm. After singing Benediction by Elder W[ilford] W. Woodruff.

July 16, 1870; Saturday

Theological Class met at the Tabernacle at one o clock pm. Present Prest. B[righam] Young presiding. After singing Prayer by Elder B[righam] Young Junr. Singing.

Prest. B Young suggested that nearly two years ago, Jesse C Little was appointed to go East to purchase Wagon Timber &c. and do business since his return for a small [wagon] Company that was formed about that time. He also desired the school to decide whether our ward meeting houses should be used for Theatrical, and other similar purposes, such as the 13th Ward Assembly rooms had been used for &c then the subject of Co operation, he wished to be thoroughly sifted.

Prest. Geo A. Smith arose, and put a Motion and was Carried, That Elder Jesse C Little furnish on Saturday next, a statement of his a/c [account] in the wa~~l~~gon making department. He then called upon B[isho]p [Edwin D.] Woolley to speak on the subject of renting the Assembly rooms.

B[isho]p E. D. Woolley said the only object he had in renting the [13th ward] Assembly rooms was to raise a little means to repair the house. He was very sorry however to have the feelings of his brethren hurt, and would not have done it, had he known it would have had that effect.[62] If the ward was able to build in addition to a Ward Meeting House, another one for fun & frolic. He would prefer Keeping a ward house entirely for sacred purposes.

Prest. B Young said a Theatre and Social Hall had been built for the express purposes of Theatrical plays, and dances, and whoever desires to use them for such uses ^can hire them^ and no Ward Meeting House need ever be used for such purposes—it was not right.

Prest. Geo A. Smith named several places where Meeting Houses was used for Theatrical purposes, viz Lehi—Battle Creek [Pleasant Grove], Fairview [Utah], &c but he himself did not believe in the policy.

On the subject of Co operation he said, there was some doing business under a "Co operative Sign" ~~was~~ in the habit of sending back East for their goods. He did not want to sustain such, for they were deadly opposed to Co operation. The hand of the Lord was certainly among us at the present time, a valuable school was now going on in our midst, and there was a great amount of wickedness, and ~~if~~ all who felt inclined can join in the crowd, but every one will have an opportunity of shewing up their real character~~s~~, as all must stand on their own merits. The Gold Mines ~~will~~ were drawing off a great many but those who fight grasshoppers and cultivate the earth will be far better off, than those who go to the Mines.

He named Amasy Lyman[63] as one who had been councilled not to ~~be~~ purchase a Ranch when he went to California, but he did, and brought upon him a vast amount of trouble. Had he carried it out, he might possibly have become ^a^ wealthy man, but now, there are thousands and thousands of dollars still unpaid on that purchase.[64]

62. Woolley rented the meeting house to the Godbeites for a dance. Arrington and Bitton, *Saints without Halos*, 60.

63. Amasa Mason Lyman (1813–77) converted to Mormonism in 1832 and was ordained an apostle in 1842. In 1853 he built the Mormon community of San Bernardino, California, and later served as European Mission president from 1860 to 1862. He was removed as an apostle in 1867 and excommunicated in 1870 for his alignment with the Godbeites. Lyman, *Amasa Mason Lyman*.

64. Lyman and fellow apostle Charles C. Rich purchased the Rancho San Bernardino from two brothers for a down payment of $25,000. Although Young wanted

Whoever forsakes this church and joins the ranks of Apostates, is as much a murderer as any one who with knife in hand sought the life of the Prophet Joseph [Smith].

Prest. Young warned the school against going to any such places as the "Strawberry Festivals"[65]—for they are dens of iniquity.

He refered to the lies that Apostates live upon, ~~lef~~ let them alone, dont abuse them, and they will soon die out. Had Amasy Lyman carried out the council given him, he would have ~~given~~ been in the Church to day. He intended to use his influence to strengthen Israel until Jesus reigns whose right it is to reign.[66]

After singing Benediction by Elder Geo Q. Cannon.

July 23, 1870; Saturday

Theological Class met at the Tabernacle at 1 o clock. Present Prest. B[righam] Young presiding. After singing[,] prayer by Elder John W. Young. Singing.

In response to a request of Pres[ident] Young last Saturday, that he wished the Members of the School to express their views on the "Necessity there was for the Atonement of Jesus Christ" and put those views on paper if they chose. A Number of Essays on that subject were handed in, and read by the Clerk to the School.[67]

Prest. B Young was pleased with what had been read. There never was an Earth without an Adam. There never was a time when Earths were not coming into existence and going out. There never was a time when there was no Saviour upon an Earth—but man in his finite being cannot comprehend Eternity. God the Father came and begotten a Son of the Virgin Mary, just the same as we beget our children, and

---

them to settle unclaimed land, Lyman and Rich believed by 1853 no suitable land remained in southern California and they had no choice but to buy. They were unable to make the payments and worked tirelessly to raise money, with but little help from Young or church headquarters. Lyman, *Thirteenth Apostle*, xvi, 191, 197.

65. See note under June 25, 1870, entry.

66. Joseph F. Smith noted that "the meeting was resolved into a caucus for the nomination of officers for the Territory, Delegate, Representatives, &c. &c. ... Geo. A. Smith made a speach, explaining the law of Congress in relation to Territorial Elections, making ... an election necessary each year." JFSJ, July 16, 1870.

67. Essays were handed in by John B. Maiben, Grandison Newell, William E. Gooch, Robert Collins, William Lorne, Jacob Peart, Daniel Shearer, and two unnamed individuals, and were inserted in the School of the Prophets minutes under the above date, but are not reproduced here.

consequently Jesus partook of his Fathers divine nature, and was therefore competant in offering a sacrifice to satisfy divine justice.[68]

He spoke of the danger that we are in as a people of again being driven, in consequence of the Spirit of the World that is creeping upon the people. Many who have been on Missions, when they return are full of faith &c, but how soon they forget, and drink into the spirit of the world.

He then spoke of some who were opposed to Co operation, who ~~were~~ he was sorry for—some had complained of him having so many shares in that Institution [ZCMI]. He wished ~~that some of~~ the brethren would step forward, and buy him out, so that he ~~can~~ ^could^ pay up his railroad debts.

We have got the Gospel, but if ^we^ expect to receive the benefits of it, we have got to live according to its precepts. If we are agreed as touching anything that is Council'd by the servants of God, and go to, to perform it. God will own and bless us.

The time will come whether we live to see it or not when the canal from Big Cottonwood [Canyon] will bring water to irrigate the east part of our City and the Utah Lake will be brought out to Davis Co[unty], also to the base of the Western Mountains, and ~~to~~ as far as Tooele [Utah].[69]

He then called on B[isho]p E[dwin] D Woolley to say ~~who~~ whether he did not mean <u>him</u> [Young], when he said last Saturday that there were some who owned thousands of dollars worth of property ^in the 13th Ward^ and would require a half hours sermon preaching to them before a $5.00 donation could be got from them—and also whether he [Woolley] did not build the assembly rooms with an expressed view of running against the Social Hall.

~~B[isho]p E D Woolley said he did ^not^ mean Prest. Young, neither~~

And whether he [Woolley] did not say last Saturday, that Bro Geo A [Smith] was coming over to <u>his</u> side.

Bro E D Woolley denied ~~being each~~ having Prest. Young in his mind when he spoke of some owning a great am[oun]t of property in his

68. Young and other leaders hinted at times that God, with a physical celestialized body, came to earth and impregnated Mary. See JD 8:115; Pratt, *Seer*, Oct. 1853, 158.

69. While irrigation systems never reached Young's lofty goals, over a thousand miles of canals were dug. Bishops, then county water commissioners, oversaw water rights in the territory until statehood.

Ward. He also denied having such a Motive as was suggested, in the building of the Assembly rooms, ^and spoke of the Social Hall which he thought^ was too high in price, and too ~~price~~ small in size. He also denied making such a statement about Geo A Smith.

Elder Geo Q. Cannon said that while Geo A was speaking he heard B[isho]p Edw[i]n D. Woolley—say that Bro G[eorge] A. was coming over to his side.

Elder Jos[ep]h F. Smith confirmed the above statement.

Prest. B Young said the Social Hall was large enough for a dancing Hall—and the Crockery cost $3,000.00, much of which had been broken, they had an expensive boiler, &c—and the price charged for its use, was in accordance with its original cost, and the cost of Keeping it ~~and~~ in comfortable repair—when parties were about to be held there.

Prest. Geo A Smith arose and said, that inasmuch as "He was going over to B[isho]p Woolleys side["] he ^would^ make a Motion That He [Woolley] take a Mission to Europe.

B[isho]p E D Woolley expressed a deep regret at having hurt the feelings of his brethren—and asked their forgiveness. But dont send me on a Mission to atone for what I have done—punish me at home rather.

Prest. B Young said he did not ever remember having sent a Man on a Mission to punish him, but to do ~~him~~ them good, and give them a chance to get the spirit of God. But on account of B[isho]p Woolleys Confession and solicitation, Prest. Geo A Smith withdrew his motion, and another Motion put and carried That He be allowed a further trial as a Bishop.

Benediction by P[resident] Geo A Smith.

July 30, 1870; Saturday

Theological Class met at the Tabernacle at One o clock pm. Present Prest. B[righam] Young presiding. After singing Prayer by Elder John Taylor. Singing.

Elder B Young Junr then read the first ~~Chapter~~ ^Lecture^ out of the Doctrine & Covenants, on the subject of Faith.[70]

Elder Chester Andrews being called upon to speak on the subject of

70. The seven theological Lectures on Faith, likely written by Sidney Rigdon with input and approval from Joseph Smith, were part of the canonized Doctrine and Covenants until 1921. The lectures were first delivered in the Kirtland, Ohio, School of the Prophets. Van Wagoner et al., "Lectures on Faith."

Faith, said He believed that Faith was the principle action, hence we are here to day &c it was also a principle of power also.

Elder Tho[ma]s Allsop. Faith was the gift of God, and in proportion to the way and manner in which we live.

Elder James Atwick when in England was told by a Physician that he would never come to the Valley, but he had faith that he would, and he did. &c.

Elder George Anderson said Faith was the gift of God and we have to live right in order to receive it.

Elder James Albion gave a similar testimony.

Prest. B Young spoke of the high schools and Universitys that we have established, had been held in the Council House and the old Hoopers store.[71] He therefore Proposed for the consideration of the Regency as to whether the large Ward Meeting Houses would not be more suitable places to hold those schools in. He then wished to know whether any of the Brethren are willing to assist him in bearing the burthen of the Railroad, or shall I be under the necessity of selling our Railroad to outsiders.

He then made enquiry of Bro Tho[ma]s Taylor and Bro [George] Dunford[72] whether they did not continue to send back east for their goods, they both answered yes. He said that no one can do these things unless they ^will^ sooner or later apostatize from the church. He then declared himself a candidate for Eternal Life, and all who are willing to go with him, all right[,] if not, He calculates to go without them.

Prest. Geo A. Smith said it had been a cherished idea of our Christian Neighbours, that when a Railroad was built through~~t~~ Utah, that it would evaporate Mormonism in a very short time. He then dwelt on the benefits of the timely introduction of our Cooperative system, which not only prevented our own Merchants from utter ruin, but Kept off outside speculative Merchants, and we ought to stick right to it. He then explained how the indebtedness of ^the^ Railroad, ~~how~~ accumulated upon his [Young's] hands, through the nonpayment of the U[nion] P[acific] R[ail] R[oad]'s Contracts, part of which had been

71. William H. Hooper, owner of the store and member of the School of the Prophets, would soon become superintendent of ZCMI.

72. Both men were merchants. Taylor later ran a successful grocery store and Dunford a clothing store.

paid in Iron, used on the Utah Central line. The brethren should make a united effort to liberate ~~the~~ ^~~his~~ the^ hands of Prest. Young—let us feel that we have one common interest. The earth is the Lords and the fulness thereof, and the saints will ultimately ~~belong to the Saints~~ posses it.

On the Election of next Monday, he wished every man having a team to ~~have itch~~ Hitch it up and carry their neighbors both Male and Female to the Polls.[73] And let that business be the first one before any other.

Elder Geo Q Cannon said we had a good opportunity at the present time of testing our loyalty to the Cause and Kingdom of God—by stepping forward and relieving the hands and taking off the burthen [burden] now on the shoulders of Prest. Young, who was now in his 70th year of age.[74] We live in a critical time—And are liable at any moment to be overpowered by our enemies. He would like to have every Member of the School, hold all they possess at the disposal, for the liquidation of that Railroad indebtedness. God requires it at our hands. ~~The Tribune~~

Prest. D[aniel] H Wells said if ever the Railroad goes into the hands of outsiders, it will never come out again. No accident had yet happened on our line, as the brethren did not smoke, or drink whiskey, but if outsiders had it, our lives would be jeopadized besides bringing young men to run it, and employment given only to half hearted Mormons or Gentiles—&c.

Elder B Young Junr said the U[nion] P[acific] R[ail] R[oad] was owing him indirectly several thousand dollars, and for it was willing to take U[tah] C[entral] R[ail] R[oad] bonds.

Elder J[ohn] W. Young Moved That a Committee of six business men be appointed to carry out this matter.

Elder John Taylor gave some explanations of the Railroad indebtedness—a principle of Co operation was now needed to liberate the hands of Prest. Young. He believed relief can be immediately forthcoming and may God bless Brigham Young, and the curse of God on all those who are his enemies, and the enemies of the Kingdom of God.

B[isho]p John Sharp spoke favourably of the U[tah] C[entral] R[ail] R[oad]—the difficulties of the Superintendant of the running department

73. In February 1870, women in Utah over twenty-one who had lived in the territory at least six months were granted the right to vote. See Jan. 29, 1870, entry.

74. Young was born June 1, 1801.

who have many Claims to meet from the Construction dep[artment]. If we will not purchase bonds on the U[tah] C[entral] R[ail] R[oad] sufficient to pay off the present indebtedness, Prest. Young will be under the necessity of selling off sufficient of the stock to outsiders.

The Motion was carried unanimously regarding the Committee of six—The following were nominated and unanimously sustained[:] W[illiam] H. Hooper—John Sharp—Jos[ep]h F. Smith[,] R[obert] T. Burton, Tho[ma]s Taylor and ^and on amendment, ~~the t~~ by Prest. Young, the twelve apostles^ [and] Jos[eph] A Young.

Elder W[illiam] H. Hooper had had his mind upon the Political business of the Territory while absent from his brethren but was fully satisfied that the Railroad question was one, not strictly confined to a financial view—but a far higher consideration should prompt us to step forward and afford the required relief to Prest. Young. He then offered to take 10,000.00 worth of bonds in Mules & Money.

~~Elder Jos[ep]h. W. Young made a few suggestion as to~~

Prest. B Young then moved and was carried unanimously That every Merchant who is determined to still send back east for their goods should at once take down their ~~sig~~ Co operative signs. The sin of Ingratitude was the greatest sin that Man can be guilty of. Elder W[illiam] H. Hooper exposed the villany of some of General Maxwell's[75] practises in the Land Office &c.

Prest. Young called for a show of hands from all those who are determined henceforth to stop trading ~~who~~ with those Merchants who are opposing Co operation. All hands appeared to be lifted up.

Benediction by Prest. Geo A. Smith.

August 6, 1870; Saturday

Theological Class met at Tabernacle at 1 oclock pm. Present Prest. B[righam] Young presiding. After singing Prayer by Elder Orson Pratt. Singing.

Prest. Young enquired if the Brethren would like to have a settlement made at Soda Springs, on Bear River.[76] They are very desirable,

75. Brigadier General George R. Maxwell (1842–85), non-Mormon registrar of the land office, broke both legs and lost three fingers during the Civil War. He challenged George Q. Cannon for his seat in the US House of Representatives.

76. Soda Springs, in southeastern Idaho, has natural carbonated spring pools and was a popular stop on the Oregon Trail.

and will ultimately become a favourable resort for Invalids, as the Mineral waters are very valuable, and are situated on the Highway for Idaho, on the Bear River, and about 150 miles distant from here

Bishop [Edward] Hunter reported several Mechanics who are among the Emigrants who arrived here ~~a~~ last evening, and hoped their services will be appreciated. He then refer'd to the Emigration Indebtedness[77] which was very large, and spoke of the energy and perseverance of B[isho]p Nichols[78] of Box Elder who had collected considerable of that indebtedness in that locality.

Elder W[illia]m H. Hooper as the Chairman of a Committee appointed last Saturday, said, they had met and attended to the business appointed for them to attend to, and called upon Geo Q. Cannon who acted as Secretary—~~E~~ to report proceedings, ~~at at~~ of said committee.

Elder Geo Q Cannon then read a synopsis of said meetings. Some of the Committee said there was a ^wide^ spread feeling of discontent and distrust in relation to Moneytary matters in connexion with Prest. B Young and ^the^ Railroad. There ^was^ a saying of Prest. Young to the deputation who waited upon him last evening that deeply impressed him viz. By the providences of God I have been led into the present situation I am now in, and verily believed his course had been sanctioned and approved by high Heaven. The ~~gener~~ world generally applaud those who chance to be prospered—and blame those whose enterprizes should happen to be unsuccessful.

If a feeling of distrust & want of confidence exists among the people towards the financial course of Prest. Young—there was the greatest necessity for the Committee going forth, and trying to correct such a false impression.

Prest. B Young said the U[tah] C[entral] R[ail] R[oad] was a good and substantial property and ought to be owned by the Latter day Saints. He had plenty of property himself, and some $200,000.00 was all that was wanted to enable him to pay his railroad debts—and if the brethren ^in Salt Lake County^ were now reduced to the same circumstances, as when they ~~were~~ first came here, there would be enough means to pay 10 times the amount now required. Some say it was not a

77. He means the deficit in the Perpetual Emigrating Fund. See Apr. 17, 1869, entry.

78. Alvin Nichols (1819–99), bishop of Brigham City since 1857, was born in Canada and migrated to Utah in 1852.

Money Making business, but what of that, we ought to take hold of it for the sake of building up the Kingdom of God, whether it pays or not, so with the building of Factories, get^ing^ out Lumber, and anything else that helps to benefit and building up of the community, we should do what we can as public benefactors.

The first 6 months of our railroad, made a profit of Sixty Eight thousand dollars—and trade will increase rather than decrease. Co operative Measures will soon be entered into for the Manufacture of Hats, Boots & Shoes, ~~Fus~~ &c &c to compete with foreign made not only in quality but in price also. By and bye we will have a bank as quickly as we have the Gold and Silver in the depository, before issuing our currency.

There was not a member of that Committee or any one else, who murmurs against the financial concerns of this Church, possesses more or less the spirit of apostacy.

Elder John Sharp Committee Man said there was a great deal of business discussion in the Committee yesterday—and the spirit of darkness reigned to a greater or less extent—and he himself partook of it. He rehearsed the cause of the financial difficulty in reference to Prest. Young and the Railroad.

Prest. B Young then read a Monthly returns of U[tah] C[entral] R[ail] R[oad] which increased from Jan[uary] to June—from $4554.00 to $12489.00 per Mo[nth].

Elder W[ilford] Woodruff said the only way for the Committee to do, was for them to do just what Prest. Young wanted them to do. Let us unite and co-operate as a people, and turn out our means to relieve Prest. Young, and become part owners of the Railroad. The Lord has blest us, and we are all better off, than ever before and let us find out what our duty is and then do it. He was willing to do all he could himself &c.

Prest. Young said our Railroad was now owned by the Latter day Saints, the ground, Materials, cars &c, all that was wanted, was for those who are out of debt to turn round and hand over their means and become part owners.

Elder Lorenzo Young, said he a had a 30 acre Farm with an Orchard of over 500 bearing Apple trees, which he would gladly dispose of in exchange for U[tah] C[entral] R[ail] R[oad] bonds, below a Cash value.

W[illiam] H. Hooper then asked a few questions of Prest. Young in relation to the Bonds and Stock ^for the benefit^ of the Brethren who are disposed to render assistance in that way.

Prest. Young answered the questions satisfactory and to the further understanding of the subject.

Elder Geo Q. Cannon then read the 2nd Lecture on Faith from the Doctrine & Covenants.

Meeting adjourned for one week at 1 oclock pm. Benediction by Prest. Geo A Smith.

August 13, 1870; Saturday

Theological Class met at the Tabernacle At One o clock pm. Present Prest. B[righam] Young presiding. After singing Prayer by Elder James Cummings. Singing.

Elder B[righam] Young Junr said the Committee appointed to visit the settlements last Sunday, had attended to that duty. He then made enquiry, as to how much the price of a Bond was to be, to those who are disposed to invest in them, to relieve the hands of Prest. Young—as some, had been bought on Main St, for considerable less, then the price put upon them by the Directors at fi[r]st viz—80 cents on the Dollar, making $800.00 for each $1,000.00 bond.

Elder John Sharp admitted that some Bonds had been forced on the Market, by those unable to hold them, and were sold at a depreciated value, but that fact does not invalidate their real value, neither can ~~they~~ they be, unless the security was deficient, and in reality they ought to fetch their face.

Prest. Geo A Smith made a few remarks on Faith—and the necessity for every Elder in Israel seeking for wisdom from the Law of the Lord. He then adverted to the Discussion now going on between Elder Orson Pratt and Mr. Newman,[79] and recommended the brethren to study every principle and argument that tends to build up Zion. Do not ever be found fighting against God and his Priesthood &c.

Prest. B Young said it required a greater amount of study and trickstering to make the truth of God into a Lie—but a Child or a Fool can easily speak truth. He was truly thankful to be associated with a people

79. John Philip Newman (1826–99) was a noted clergyman and chaplain of the US Senate. He and apostle Orson Pratt held a three-day debate on polygamy in the Salt Lake Tabernacle.

who desire truth, in preference to fiction. The Lord sustains his people, and the Devil sustains his. All the efforts that our present Officials have made, to bring trouble and disgrace upon us, had signally failed. The Lord was with us, and will defend us, if we do right.

The School was adjourned for One week at One o clock pm. After singing Benediction by Prest. Geo A Smith.

August 20, 1870; Saturday

S[alt] L[ake] City, Old Tabernacle[,] School of Prophets met pursuant to adjournment. After singing prayer by Eld[er] B[righam] Young, jr. Singing of hymn No. 249.[80]

Elder Orson Pratt. Felt thankful for the blessings we as a people enjoyed in these valleys, and the progress we had made here. He thought there never was a time, when the Saints felt as united, as at the present time, and that there were comparatively but very few apostates. Referred to some of them, who had denied the atonement of Christ, and the resurrection of the dead, Spoke of the late discussion about "polygamy," which had lately taken place in the New Tabernacle, and felt pleased by the good order that had prevailed among a congregation of 10 or 11,000 persons.

Prest. Dan[iel] H. Wells Said the declaration of the town site had been filed in the Land Office,[81] but he did not know, how many obstacles would still be put in the way. We might have an answer from Washington [DC] in 16 days, and the people would be notified through the papers. Made some remarks, that there were a good many complaints made lately about people turning out their cattle in the streets, so that they break into their neighbors field and garden, which should be stopped, and the crops saved. Said it was one of the rules of our school that we had covenanted to observe to keep our bars up etc. etc. Spoke of some of our boys contracting bad habits, on the streets, petty thieving etc. & thought a house of correction should be erected to have such boys put in for some time, instead of putting them in the lock-up. Did not wish to accuse any member of the school of trading with outsiders,

80. "What Fair One Is This, from the Wilderness Trav'ling" was hymn 249 in *Sacred Hymns and Spiritual Songs for the Church of Jesus Christ of Latter-day Saints* (Liverpool: Albert Carrington, 1869).

81. Probably for Soda Springs, Idaho Territory. See Aug. 6, 1870, entry.

but the people were doing it, and mentioned the tinner Allen,[82] who had joined the "Godbeites" and had still the Cooperative sign up, which deceived a good many. We all had covenanted, to help the Lord ~~the to~~ ^and^ assist him, to build up his Kingdom, and therefore we could not do as we please.

Prest. Geo A Smith. Hoped that all the excellent remarks made here this afternoon would be reflected upon by all of us. There were many things in regard to our rules, that we should better observe, as for instance he knew that brethren had been attending school here repeatedly, while they had the hardest feelings against each other.

Prest. B Young sen[ior] Asked, if the brethren were studying the lecture in the book of D & C, and advised them to try to gain much knowledge & said there was no book that gave so much useful knowledge in general as the Bible, and the book of Mormon & D & C contained the root of all of our faith. We ought to continue our lectures, but we have so many other things to bring into this school, because here are the headquarters. We want to send some brethren up to Soda Springs [Idaho], which we consider a very important point. The R[ail] R[oa]d may run by there soon, and the springs I believe cannot be beaten in their medical qualities. We intend to go N[orth] S[outh] E[ast] & West and inhabit all these mountains. Next fall we intend to go south and cross the Colorado, and we must not love our land so much, that we cannot go to make a new settlement, or go on a mission.

Spoke how beautiful it would be to have this City built according to the original plan, with each house standing back in the lot and only one house on each lot, a flower garden in front, and the outhouses being in the back of the lot, double rows of shade trees in the middle of the streets etc., and that we should always desire to improve.

Said that at Soda Springs was the very best soil, and that it was right on the bed of a crater, and that he wanted to show that trees, wheat, potatoes, etc could be raised there. Wished we would soon be able to build the temple, but if we co[u]ld not inherit & use it, he rather have it as it is now. But the day must come, when Joseph [Smith] will be again among this people and he will have the keys of the resurrection. Said

82. Joseph Smith Allen (1840–1921) was born in Jackson County, Missouri, and migrated to Utah in 1852. He owned a large hardware store.

he, and his councilors would not be here for a few weeks, & the twelve [apostles] would take charge of the school.[83]

Adjourned to Saturday next at 1 pm. Singing of hymn No 152. Benediction by G[eorge] A Smith.

August 27, 1870; Saturday

Meeting of the School of the Prophets, Salt Lake City. Opened with singing "Come Come ye Saints" Prayer by—Elder R[obert] L. Campbell ~~Pray~~—Singing Come all ye sons of Zion.

~~Br~~ Elder Orson Pratt (who presided) called upon Bro R[obert] L. Campbell to read the 3rd lecture [on faith] Book of Doc[trine] & Cov[enants]. Elder Campbell read the 3rd ~~Section~~ ^lecture^ with accompanying questions and answers.

Elder Orson Pratt delivered the school into the hands of the Brethren to speak on the subjects referred to in the lecture.

Elder Geo Q Cannon spoke on the subject of faith, especially as connected with the Saints coming to these vallies & the building of the U[nion] P[acific] R[ail] R[oad].

Elder Orson followed on the same subject.

Bro [Joseph] Carlisle spoke on faith.

Bishop John Sharp preached a Railroad Sermon.

Elder John Taylor also spoke on the railroad business & read the circular of the President on the matter.

Bishop Sharp made a few remarks.

Closed by Singing the Doxology & prayer by Elder Joseph F Smith. [Minutes kept by] Geo Reynolds, Clerk pr[o] tem.

September 3, 1870; Saturday

Theological Class met at the Tabernacle at One o clock pm. Present Prest. Geo A Smith presiding. Singing. Prayer by Elder E[dward] Stevenson. Singing.

Elder Geo Q. Cannon then read a portion of the Doctrine & Covenants from page 37,[84] containing an account of the attributes of God, a

83. Young, Daniel H. Wells, and George A. Smith left on August 27 to travel through the southern part of the territory on a preaching tour.

84. Cannon was reading the second Lecture on Faith from a reprint of the 1845 Liverpool, England, edition of the Doctrine and Covenants. The book remained unchanged until Orson Pratt revised it in 1876 with permission from Brigham Young.

knowledge of which by Man, was essential for him to possess, to secure salvation and eternal life—for without that knowledge there would be no foundation upon which, Faith in God could rest. He read a number of Questions and Answers on the afore section—or Lecture. The following names were then called upon to speak 10 minutes on the subject of Faith.

Alva Alexander Junr, believed that Faith existed in all inteligent beings, also in Infidels—he himself had faith to go to the stand, but not enough to stay long. &c.

Elder W[illia]m Allbrand made a few remarks.

O. C. Andrearson said Faith was the Gift of God, bestowed by him, according to the faithfulness of his children.

Elder Jos[ep]h Bean by the power of Faith he was present, here, a knowlege of God was revealed to him by reading the [Millennial] Star,[85] which made him rejoice. In many troubles, and in various administrations, he had been enabled to exercise Faith in God, and secured many blessings. No man can exist and prosper, and continue in this church and Kingdom without Faith. He had Faith that the time would come when the pure and comparatively unknown faithful Saints will be become Known.

Elder Truman O Angel thought the subject of Faith was fully set forth in the written word, but every Mans actions in all departments of life were simply an exhibition of Faith. He thought ~~was~~ the church was complete in its organization, he fully believed it was—he believed that Bro Brigham [Young] was in his right place—etc.

Elder Royal Barney has had faith in the Gospel—produced by hearing the word of God. Faith is the Gift of God—made manifest even in Infants—by humility and prayer, a great increase of Faith and power with God may be obtained. He had faith in and believed fully in the present authorities of the Church.

Elder Sam[ue]l Broadhurt had more faith in fixing up a Wagon wheel, than in standing up before his brethren. When he first heard an Elder pray and preach, faith began to spring up—until it ripened into a knowledge. Those who held the power and gift of healing—had it in their clothing, tools &c that they handled. Compared the trial of ancient Israel with that that is shortly coming upon us, did not know but

85. The *Millennial Star* was the longest-running LDS periodical, published by missionaries in England beginning in 1840 and continuing as an official organ through 1970.

in 1870 it would come—related several instances of healing and other instances of answer to prayer &c.

Elder John Taylor said the principles of Faith were as fully explained in the Doctrine & Covenants as possibly could be. No people on the earth exercise so much faith in God, as the Elders of Israel, as evinced by a relation of past experiences. Elder Geo A Smith & Wilford Woodruff were ordained on the ^corner^ stone [of the temple] which had just been laid in Far West [Missouri], before going with the rest of the Twelve [Apostles] on a Mission to England—though many obstacles were thrown in their way and much sickness, yet through Faith they overcame, and accomplished what they were sent to do. He also related several instances of the power of Faith in various ways. Where necessitys existed, and called it forth By Faith, all things spoken of ~~Faith~~ by the Prophets will be fulfilled.

Prest. Geo A Smith said that Prest. Young started South on Saturday Morning last, preached at Provo. Next day at Springville, then to Nephi. Named [said], that at Springville there ^was^ a difficulty between Capitol and Priesthood which is to be settled by the 1st Presidency on his return—another ~~tres~~ difficulty between some, at Juab & Sanpete Counties, about the right of coal—was tried before Prest. Young, and decided—contrary to a previous decision of the High Council. He [George A. Smith] said that Martin Harris[86] ~~h~~ one of the Witnesses to the book of Mormon was here, and would probably speak in the old Tabernacle tomorrow morning.

Judge E[lias] Smith gave some instructions to those Officers who had been shortly elected at the late Elections.[87]

Meeting was adjourned for one week at one oclock pm. After singing Benediction by Pres[ident] Geo A Smith.

---

86. Martin Harris (1783–1875), who financed the 1830 publication of the Book of Mormon, was also one of its scribes and witnesses. He was excommunicated in 1837, rebaptized in 1842, and arrived in Utah on September 6, 1870, causing "considerable interest" among the territory's citizens. "Martin Harris—One of the Witnesses of the Book of Mormon," *Deseret News*, Sep. 7, 1870.

87. The election, held a month previous, had "no opposition vote outside of the four [Salt Lake] city precincts" and the total opposition votes in the city only came to 167, some of which were cast "by persons ineligible to vote." Those elected to county offices from the School of the Prophets included Orson Pratt, John Taylor, Brigham Young Jr., and Joseph F. Smith. "The Recent Election," *Deseret News*, Aug. 10, 1870.

September 10, 1870; Saturday

Theological Class met at Tabernacle at One o clock pm. Present Prest. Geo A Smith presiding. After singing Prayer by Elder G[eorge] B Wallace. Singing.

Elder O[rson] Pratt read Lecture [on Faith] 5 paragraph 45 on the Godhead.

Elder Andrew Burt, said we all ought to try to have faith in God, and in his servants also.

Elder Isaac Brockbank, tried to do honour to his calling, Faith was the leading spring of all our actions, it brought us here—and by obedience ^only^ can make it manifest—his heart was with this people &c.

Elder Mark Barnes had tried for a number of years to do as he was told, Could not say anything so full on the Subject of Faith—as was ~~written or~~ printed in the book of Doctrine & Covenants &c. Faith drawn out and exercised in Prayer, will not only bring down from Heaven an Answer, but Revelation too—as he illustrated in several instances of his experiences.

Elder A[lbert] Carrington then called over a list of Justices of the peace, and Constables, recently elected, who had not ^yet^ qualified, ^&^ desired them to attend to that duty forthwith.

Prest. Geo A Smith was very anxious for the brethren to make themselves posted with the subject of Faith as it is read from time to time out of the Doctrine and Covenants. He had been a close observer of the Power of Faith, and could relate many instances. He made a few remarks on Baptism for the dead—the Lord had commenced the great work, and the Ordinance was being attended to every Wednesday.[88]

Elder A[lbert] Carrington was then called upon to read two short letters on Baptism for the dead, written by the Prophet Joseph [Smith], in the Doctrine & Covenants.[89]

B[isho]p E[dward] Hunter testified that he was present when the Prophet Joseph [Smith] received the last revelation on ~~the~~ Baptism for the Dead. Bro W[illia]m Clayton was present also, and wrote it down

88. LDS proxy baptisms for deceased ancestors were primarily enacted in the Endowment House, built in 1855 and used until its demolition in 1889. Anderson, *Development of LDS Temple Worship*, 30; Brown, "Temple Pro Tempore."

89. The instructions (D&C 128) were written by Smith on September 6, 1842, and copied into his journal on September 11. Hedges et al., *Joseph Smith Papers, Journals Volume Two*, 143–46.

from his lips, and promised to read it to the saints on the following Sunday morning, which he did.

Elder W[ilford] W. Woodruff refered to the many priveleges that latter day Saints enjoy, was glad many were waking up to the subject of Baptism for the dead. He had been baptized and sealed to all his progenitors that he could find out. He then made Comparisons between the beauty and glory of our religion, and the nonsense of what the world called religion. When we pray, we pray to a being who has a Head, a Heart, and a perfect organization.

People apostatize, because they dont Keep the Commandments of God—they dont study the Scriptures. What is not yet revealed will be, a little at a while until we shall receive all ^that^ is essential for our perfection &c.

Elder Orson Pratt spoke on the subject of Authority. The priesthood has been in our possession at least 29 years—especially that portion pertaining to officiating for our dead—and if we use it, for all [ancestors] within our reach, in due time, God will reveal a still further Knowledge of our ancestry. It was our duty to try and find out all we possibly can ourselves, we can then with Faith come before the Lord and ask him to make Known the rest. Was thankful that so many had been stirred ups to attend to these things. The time was not far off, when there will be More Baptismals Fonts, and Temples, than at present.

Elder James Bunting did not believe that principles ~~that~~ intended for us as a people, were ~~not~~ to be demonstrated to us on the same principle as two and two make four. If everything presented to us must be demonstrated to our minds, there certainly would be no room for the exercise of Faith.

Elder James Baldwin, if we all do the best we can until the end, we shall be saved. Hoped we should all be saved in the Kingdom of God.

Meeting adjourned for one week at one o clock pm. After singing Benediction by Elder O[rson] Pratt.

Prest. Geo A Smith Prophesied the time was near by when the Saints would be the ruling power on the face of the earth, all that was wanted, was for them to be faithful and humble before the Lord, and do right.

September 17, 1870; Saturday

Theological Class met at the Tabernacle at one o clock p.m. Present.

Prest. Geo A Smith presiding. After singing Prayer by B[isho]p E[dwin] D. Woolley. Singing.

Elder A[lbert] Carrington then read the 5th Lecture [on Faith] in book of Doc[trine] & Cov[enan]ts.

Elder James Bussell whose name was called out in rotation—said he was a believer and labourer in the Kingdom of the Great God, hoped the Lord would help him to abide therein, and adhere to the end.

Elder Israel Barlow said it had ever been his desire to Know the Mind and will of God concerning him—the Mind of God comes to us through Prest. [Brigham] Young—and if we are spiritually discerned, there are many things we can do without waiting to be commanded. He desired to enjoy the spirit of God by night and day.

Elder Cha[rle]s C. Burnham tryed to shew his faith by his works. Faith was the first principle that leads us on our journey—without it we should never have started. While he did the best he knew how even while a sectarian, he felt that he was justified—but since his connexion with this people, his mind had expanded and the scriptures had been a new book to him.

Elder John H. Bleazard, was called an Infidel in his early days—and he could not see as the Methodists or any other of the Sectarians saw—and he began to think he should be damned. When he did ever so many bad things in the week day—he always kept Sunday. Jesus told Joseph [Smith], three things were necessary for Man to Know, viz ^1st^ That God was a being of Tabernacle 2th, That a just Knowledge of his Character and his attributes. 3rd That our lives should be such as will please him.

Elder John P. Ball Considered we all had faith, or we should not be here, he prayed that all might continue faithfull.

Elder R[ichar]d Brimley had seen the time when he would have deemed it a privelege to stand up before a congregation like the present, especially if half were clergymen; and it rather astonished him how he should have a feeling of dread to stand up before his brethren. Are we in possession of that living faith, we once possessed, if not, let us be diligent to observe what is required at our hands, that we obtain more faith.

Elder R[ichar]d Brittain without faith we cannot take one step towards our own, ~~or~~ salvation, or that of our dead. Was an Infidel in early days could not believe in any of the religions of the day before joining the church. He had a child die of Fever and had been dead 3 days, One of the Elders Anointed it with Oil & prayed over it, and that Child rose up and the next morning was running around as well as ever—that young man ^now lives at American Fork [Utah].^[90]

He also mentioned several instances of the power of Faith, that accompanied his administrations under his own hands. There is nothing required at our hands but what we can accomplish ~~if we it~~ if we only have Faith in God. If we had more faith and less Doctors ~~le~~ far ~~less~~ fewer of our wives and Children would be carried up to that Grave yard. Condemned the use of Drugs instead of Oil, Prayer & faith—the faithlessness of the latter day saints had built up and made ~~him rich~~ Billey [William] Godbe rich and apostatize.

Elder A[lbert] Carrington then read two Proclamations from the [Salt Lake] "Herald," issued by Governor Chaffer [John W. Shaffer]—Announcing that P[atrick] E. Connor[91] had been appointed by him as "Major General" over the Utah Territory—and also forbidding all Musters, Drills being held in the Territory. How long are that miserable "ring" and "Click" [clique] to be among us, to annoy us just so long as we (as a people) continue to foster and mix up with them, only let our faith and works come up to the requirements and this place will become too hot for the miserable scoundrels in our midst.

Prest. Geo A Smith, said Councils had long been given for the Brethren to furnish themselves with good guns and Ammunition, the effort of the Governor and Clique in our midst to bring on a collision and trouble will certainly fail if our Faith and Works are such, as God ~~b~~ will own and bless. He hoped the brethren will be patient and quiet, and all will be well.

Elder W[ilford] W. Woodruff strongly recommended the brethren to exercise Faith and prayer for Governor Chaffer, the Judges, and the other members of the ring & that the Lord would overrule their acts for the good of Israel.

School adjourned for one week at one o clock pm. Benediction by Elder J[ohn] M. Bernhisel.

90. Probably Joseph M. Britton, born 1849 in England.

91. Patrick Edward Connor (1820–91) was appointed colonel of the Third California Infantry and in 1862 helped to found Fort Douglas. He won a brigadier-general star in 1863 for his expeditions against Native Americans, including the Bear River Massacre. He also worked in the mining industry in Utah and Nevada.

September 24, 1870; Saturday

Theological Class met in the Tabernacle at 1 o clock pm. Present Elder Orson Pratt presiding. After singing Prayer by Elder S[amuel] W. Richards. Singing.

The First Presidency ~~& the rest of the Twelve [Apostles]~~ not yet arrived, but are expected momentarily, ~~the Twelve wen~~ from their Southern trip, and some of the twelve [apostles] are gone to meet him.[92]

Elder Orson Pratt read Lecture [on Faith] 7th Paragraph 1.

Elder E[benezer] Beazley, being called upon, rejoiced exceedingly at the privileges he had in connexion with his brethren, as a member of the church. The power of Faith was necessary in the right perfomance of every duty required at our hands. We must walk by faith, and exercise it towards the servants of God. Every ~~Ft~~ month on Fast days, Faith was necessary ~~to~~ not only to abstain from breakfast ~~a~~ but to attend Meeting.

Elder Abiah W. Brown considered the subject of Faith was made sufficiently plain in the ~~the~~ Lecture. No person can possess Faith without works to correspond. To ascertain whether we have Faith or not in God, let us examine ourselves &c—we see many persons whom we have no faith in. And he scarcely Knows who to have faith in, he meant human beings, but he recommended faith in God—whose attributes are so well Known and understood.

Elder Peter Barton felt to rejoice that he had a standing in the Kingdom of God &c.

Elder Charles Barrel had exercised Faith during the past 16 years that he ~~so~~ would sooner or later be gathered with the saints to this place, which lately had been accomplished—for several years he was the only saint living in his Native town, had a family of 8 children and left a faithful testimony behind him.

Elder Alva Butler, required a great deal of Faith to live his religion—&c.

Elder Norman G Brimhall said his Faith had been increased since hearing the Lectures. Had witnessed many instances of the Power of Faith in the healing of the sick. He believed in God, in Jesus Christ, and in the servants of God.

---

92. Brigham Young's party arrived at 2:00 p.m. and was greeted by a large group of supporters. Some, such as George A. Smith, had traveled back to Salt Lake City earlier. JFSJ, Sep. 24, 1870.

Elder W[ilford] W. Woodruff said we are all here by Faith—Utah would never have been inhabited without faith. Joseph Smith brought forth the book of Mormon through faith. He himself, had been sustained and done what he had done since he embraced the Gospel, by Faith. He was one who went up in Missouri to fight the state, to redeem Zion by Faith.[93] All our works had been performed by faith.

He had faith that our enemies would be stirred up to fight against us—but Salvation, such that is promised unto us should stimulate us to exercise faith and our works should correspond to do what God required of us. Some had not faith enough to retain their standing in the church, they had gradually given way to temptation and given way to overt acts, until the Spirit of the Lord was entirely withdrawn from them.

God was going to build up Zion in spite of Earth or Hell. A Man who has received the Holy Ghost had the Apostleship &c and then fall away, had far better have had a Millstone ~~eas~~ put around his neck and cast into the sea. He did not want to live one hour only while he continued in the faith. Let our wants be Known before the Lord, and pray for our friends and enemies also. We will ^have^ plenty of New principles, as fast as we can appreciate and live up to them.

Prest. Geo A Smith who just came in, said he started on Thursday with Jos[ep]h F. Smith & Jos[ep]h A Young, to meet the President—He then stated particulars of the Soldier raid on the peaceable citizens of Provo, on Thursday night—(which appeared in our local papers)[94] breaking and smashing up doors, windows, furniture &c in the Houses of F. D. Mackdonald, E[lijah] F. Sheets, W[illiam] Miller &c. Many of the Brethren who had been called up to quell the riot had neither Guns, or Pistols in readiness. He then warned and cautioned the school against such a state of indifference, as so many of the Provo brethren were found in, when such a state of Terror reigned. He hoped all would make every preparation to prevent any such raids in Salt Lake City

93. Woodruff was referring to Zion's Camp, also called the Army of Israel, a march from Ohio to Missouri in 1834 ostensibly to reclaim Mormon lands appropriated by other settlers.

94. Forty soldiers from Camp Rawlins, an outpost of Fort Douglas, had come to Provo to dance. They became drunk and fired random shots and destroyed property. JFSJ, Sep. 23, 1870; WWJ, Sep. 24, 1870; "Midnight Assassins on the Rampage," and "The Provo Raid," *Deseret News*, Sep. 28, 1870.

occurring without giving a warm reception. If any one should be without arms &c. be sure to get them forthwith.

Meeting adjourned for one week at 1 o clock pm. After singing Benediction by Elder Jno [John] Taylor.

October 1, 1870; Saturday

Theological Class met at the Tabernacle at one oclock pm. Present Prest. B[righam] Young presiding. After singing prayer by B[isho]p Phineas Young. Singing.

Prest. B Young said he had been absent for several Saturdays from the school, he had visited the Southern Country, and had returned in full faith and fellowship with the Kingdom of God, the object of this school was for the Elders to teach and be taught, it was their duty to devote their time, talents &c. for the building up of Zion—but as a people we are slow and tardy in our movements, and do not like to be interfered with in regard to our time, and the use of our means, we think it is enough for us to attend to our spiritual duties, without having our time infringed upon &c.

We are very far from being what we ought to be and yet, are perhaps the best people the Lord has got on the Earth, and if we were willing to become united, we should make more progress.

He then explained a portion of Territory they had recently visited towards the head waters of the Sevier [River][95] &c—a portion of which had been once inhabited but where driven in by the Indians those who return to that country are especially instructed to make them a good strong fort, and not less than 50 men, well armed be left there at all times, so as to protect themselves against Indian raids &c. They had also established a place which they call Look Out, and all the brethren that go there will enter a Cooperative System in regard to their stock to avoid and prevent Thieves from driving it off—and have it better cared for. By and bye he hoped ~~He then explained~~ we would have a quicker and safer mode of travel from the North to the South, and ~~ourselves~~ establish a trade of exchange. Unless we are hindered, we may be able to build a railroad ourselves.

There is a wonderful increase in our settlements, in numbers, and improvements. If we as a people live our religion, faithful to our Covenants

95. The Sevier River begins in Kane County and flows north to central Utah.

& callings—we shall increase and Multiply, and prosper—but if not—look out, for we shall surely be [given] chastisements.

He then gave some good council about labour~~—be willing to be do the work for the Miners in the way of hauling &c~~ let the brethren in this and Davis County try to get all the hauling, and labour for the Miners, and do it so cheap that no outsider can compete, and they will have to leave—and if somebody finds a good lode, work it sufficiently to keep it, but dont run crazy over it—and dont spend what you get among our enemies, but among ourselves. The Clique or Whiskey Ring[96] are sent here to make trouble, to ride over the Law, and try to create a collision with the government but they will accomplish nothing, only flounder and be disappointed.

Let every man attend to his duty, and have no fears. The Governor dont care anything about Polygamy, he's after the Mormons. He wont divide the people and set them against Brigham Young, which was his intention. We will prepare for the building of the Temple, and have Teams hauling rock immediately after Conference—and we will look after [perform ordinances for] our dead.[97]

Many strangers are constantly coming, and are brought under the sound of the Gospel, who would never go near our Elders abroad. Let us do right, and God will fight our battles, and we will grow, and prosper.

He then called upon the County wards to gather up their Means, and buy up some of the Utah Central [Rail Road] bonds, that his hands might be liberated in paying what he was owing his brethren—it was the duty of those who can, to step forward and bear a portion of this burthen.

Prest. Geo A Smith bore testimony to the truths advanced by Prest. Young—and hoped we would profit by them. Let us take hold and carry this railroad, and be ready to build another South. It had already been

96. The Whiskey Ring name given to non-Mormons came from their production of alcohol in Salt Lake City, much to the consternation of Young, who had intended the church to produce and sell liquor to outsiders for a profit. On August 27, 1870, marshal J.D.T. McAllister and others smashed several vats of brandy, whiskey, and wine, claiming they were acting under the law. They were later sued but because the plaintiffs asked for three times the value of the liquor destroyed, the case was dismissed. "Judicial Ruling," *Deseret News*, Oct. 26, 1870.

97. Young vacillated on allowing temple ordinances without a temple. At times, he permitted all ceremonies, including the second anointing, in his own home. But in 1873 he announced that some rites, such as sealings, could only be done in a temple and not the Endowment House or other buildings. Anderson, *Development of LDS Temple Worship*, 27–31.

a great blessing to us, by bringing many strangers to our City, and to our meetings where they hear the Gospel. Our business is to labour in building the rising glory of Zion, with our time, Means, &c.

The Merchants were counciled to unite their interests in supplying the Saints with goods, but many of them howled and fought against the principle of Co operation, and are to this day engaged in open antagonism to that principle. If we will not do our duty as Elders in Israel God will displace us, and raise up others in our stead.

~~I~~ A mans time means home, property and everything else he has got, should be used to build up the Kingdom of God. Let us ~~go~~ observe council, and ^be^ prepared with arms and ammunition, so as to repel any outrage that might be made upon us, either night or day.

He hoped and expected to live long enough to see 16 Railroads terminate in the Centre stake of Zion Jackson Co[unty] [Missouri], and at a Conference, to bring 200,000 people to meeting.

School adjourned for two weeks[98] at 1 o clock. Benediction by Prest. Geo A Smith.

October 15, 1870; Saturday

Theological Class met at the old Tabernacle at One o clock pm. Present Prest. B[righam] Young presiding. After singing Prayer by Elder W[ilford] Woodruff. Singing.

<u>Elder W Woodruff</u> regarded this school was one of the greatest priveleges the Elders can enjoy—we are taught here how to build up the Kingdom of God. We can see the hand of God in inspiring his servant Brigham in opening this school, the Cooperative movement &c which soon developed a secret ~~of~~ plot of apostacy [Godbeites] and which had been revealed to Prest. Young some time before it was ~~making~~ made manifest.

The cup of this Nations iniquity will soon be filled up, and the judgments of God will break it to pieces. He then read a little from page 79 Doc[trine] & Cov[enants]—and by making comparisons with what is found in the Bible, Book of Mormon & Doc[trine] & Cov[enants] pertaining to Father Adam, as to ^who^ he was &c., we can learn much that will strengthen our Faith & Comfort our hearts.

98. The word "two" was written over "one," and "week" was changed to "weeks" due to the upcoming general conference.

Day by day the Gentiles who are constantly coming up to Zion, are fulfilling the scriptures. He hoped every Elder & boy in Israel will have a good rifle and Ammunition, all in readiness to defend ourselves and families, that God and Angels may see that we are willing to do anything that is required of us—but He for one had great Faith in prayers. Let every Saint bear up before the Lord those who are in our midst seeking to destroy us. He believed God will not only hear, but answer the Prayers of his Saints, which are offered up in earnestness & faith.

Elder Geo Q Cannon fully endorsed the doctrine that Father Adam was our God and Father—or as He in many places is called Michael the great Prince—Arch Angel[,] Ancient of Days &c.[99] It was not only wisdom, but perfectly consistent that Adam & Eve should partake of the forbidden fruit and start the work of increase of their species. The above Doctrine had been revealed to him, so that he Knew it was true.

He then spoke of the Magnitude of the Principle of Cooperation—although so many are opposed to it—this is only a preparatory step, to something further that God is waiting to reveal. He very ^much^ regretted the reluctance among many of the brethren to receive some of these principles, which arises from the hardness of their hearts. We ought to be as ready to receive principles from the servants of God, as good, Confiding children are from their Parents. If our hearts are open to receive Council, God will impart more and more. We must ~~t~~ not pride ourselves in our supposed Knowle^d^ge, but like little children, be willing to be taught and instructed.

Elder George[100] felt to believe and receive everything from our President, and rejoiced at the privilege of coming to this school.

B[isho]p Andrew Cahoon of Little Cottonwood, being called upon said he wanted to say something about a report freely circulated through his ward and this City, that he had Apostatized, and turned Godbeite. It is not true! and any man who says so, He is a liar. He hoped no one ~~who~~ would take offence at this. He had not let go. Prest. Young as his Leader—if anything had caused a change in his views, Prest. Young would be the first to know of that change, his honour would not permit

99. Joseph F. Smith recorded that Woodruff "spok[e] a short time on the Subject of Adam being Michael, the arch-Angel &c." and that Young said "he wanted the brethren to meditate on the subject, pray about it and keep it [Adam–God] to themselves." JFSJ, Oct. 15, 1870.

100. Joseph F. Smith identifies this speaker as William Henrie.

him to slight the Man who placed him in ^the^ position he occupies as a Bishop. He was very sorry that such a report should have been circulated about him, not so much on his own a/c [account] as his near friends~~—His belief~~.

God is with the people—and sustains Prest. Young & the twelve [apostles]. He never embraced Mormonism ~~before~~ because his Father & Mother had done so. He had investigated for himself, hence he embraced the Gospel. His feelings remained the same, as they had been, in regard to the present organization. God was [with] this people and he knew it—but the report had injured him, and especially those who circulated it. He had made unguarded and unwise expressions but having made them to particular friends, did not think they would ever have been circulated to his injury.

Prest. B Young said the items of revelation given us to day, are for our meditation. The Saviour said—This is life eternal, To know the only wise God, and Jesus Christ whom he has sent. He wished the brethren to pray to God, for wisdom, to know ~~and find out~~ when ~~and how~~ to speak on that subject. Some of this school were often complaining of the lack of revelation, it reminded him of many who came to him for council having their minds already made up before they come, and expect a blessing from the hands of the Lord, although their hearts are corrupt.

Apostates cannot promote truth, their business and right is to write or talk about Him or his brethren—as their accusers.

Mining. The Mountains are full of Gold and Silver, and when we are nearer to the standard of truth and right and oneness—the Lord will give us all we could ask for. If we do [not] Know who Adam is, how can we Know anything about his Father &c.

Prest. Geo A Smith exprest a desire that whatever is said at this school should be just right, and spoken at the right time.

School adjourned for One Week at One o clock pm. After singing Benediction by Prest. G[eorge] A. Smith.[101]

October 22, 1870; Saturday

Theological Class met at the Tabernacle at One o clock p.m. Prest. B[righam] Young, Geo A. Smith & ^most of^ the twelve [apostles]

101. This concluding paragraph is written in the middle of the page vertically, covering a portion of the main body of text that came before it.

having gone to Provo. Prest. D[aniel] H. Wells presided. After singing prayer by Elder John W. Young. Singing ~~Elder A[lbert] Carringinton~~.

Elder T. [David] McKenzi read a letter from Prest. B Young addressed to the Members of the School, stating the heavy burthen [burden] that still rested upon him with railroad indebtedness, and the very limited aid that he had received from the efforts of the Committee appointed to lay the subject before the brethren, what had been promised through the Bishops, had not ^yet^ been fulfilled—the reason of which he could not account for. Unless something could be done before long to afford him relief, necessity might force the ~~read~~ sale of the U[tah] C[entral] R[ail] R[oad] to Gentile purchasers; ~~the~~ He then asks a questions "whether the brethren are willing to assume the responsibilities of such a sale?["]

Elder A Carrington made some remarks on the above subject—and on the use and abuse of the wealth & riches of this world. The Saints will sooner or later enjoy the wealth of the world, as soon as they are capable of using it for the building up of the Kingdom of God. The hand of God was over us for good, not only in the Construction of the U[nion] P[acific] R[ail] R[oad] but also the Utah Central. Will we unite as a people to lift the load of indebtedness from the shoulders of Prest. Young, and hold that Road ourselves, rather than sell it to outsiders[?]

Elder Brigham Young Junr referd to a universal decision of this school some time ago, that we would hold ~~th~~ and retain the U[tah] C[entral] R[ail] R[oad] in our own possession, but he was not aware that much if anything had been done by the members, by making purchase of bonds to assist Prest. Young in what he is owing to his brethren.

Prest. D H Wells gave notice that a ^two days^ meeting will be held in this or the New Tabernacle on Saturday ^& Sunday^ next at 10 o clock AM and he hoped the Bishops would give publicity to this. It will be for this school to say whether Prest. Young shall or shall not dispose of our railroad to outsiders or not—acts and not words will decide the matter. He himself will very much regret our line of railroad going into our enemies hands.[102]

The Kingdoms of this world will soon become the Kin^g^dom of our

102. Young and the church maintained control of the Utah Central Railroad until the late 1870s. Jay Gould and the Union Pacific would purchase the Mormon-controlled lines in 1879. Cowan, "Steel Rails and the Utah Saints."

God and his Christ. And in the economy of heaven, this will be brought about, and when accomplished, Railroads[,] Steamboats, Horses, ~~Ch~~ Carriages &c will be enjoyed by the saints in the Kingdom of God. Spoke of the unwise course of Latter day Saints patronizing their enemies. He much regretted also that many of our wealthy Merchants were unwilling to use their means for the building up of the Kingdom of God. Let no one among us Covet Wealth, for it is a slippery path to tread, we have many examples of this kind before us. Our enemies will drive us away from our homes, as they have done it before, if they can. This Railroad of ours, is an Engine of safety and protection to us, if we can hold it~~—or if~~ and is a triumph for God and his Kingdom—if it goes into our enemies hands, they will have a powerful Engine to injure, an^n^oy, and finally expel us from our homes. Let the enemy once gain the ascendency in this place, and you'd see how quickly he would hoist every latter day saint from his homes. Few men in this Kingdom can be blest with~~out~~ means, without him going straight way to destruction.

The meeting was then adjourned for two weeks at one o clock pm. ~~Pray~~ Benediction by Elder J[oseph] F. Smith.

November 5, 1870; Saturday

Theological Class met at the Tabernacle at One o clock pm. Prest. ~~Elias Smith~~ Jno [John] W. Young. Prest. of the Stake [presiding] Prest. B[righam] Young ^&c^ being absent on a Missionary tour to Grantsville. Singing. Prayer by Elder Geo Goddard. Singing.

Elder Jno. [John] W. Young gave a general invitation for any member of the School to come forward and express their thoughts on anything pertaining to the Kingdom of God.

B[isho]p Edw[ar]d Hunter was thankful to meet in this school, had not been absent more than 4 or 5 times. Much instruction had been given on temporal dutys—Agriculture &c—he hoped to magnify his calling. We are accountable for the privileges we enjoy, and should therefore treasure up the instructions we receive and put them in practise. He did not think we as a people would be Kicked and Knock'd about, as in Kirtland, Nauvoo or Missouri—but tried in some other way the enemy he thought would try ^us by^ another tact. We must act our part, and be servants of the Lord.

B[isho]p John Sharp said nothing short of the power of God, could enable a man like B[isho]p Hunter of his years, to stand up and bear a faithful testimony, of the truth of the latter day Work. We as a people are the most blest, of any people on the earth, and should be the most grateful; the Lord had granted us ~~a~~ many blessings both temporal and Spiritual in answer to our fervent prayers. We have been preserved from the hand of our enemies—and his care will constantly be over us, so long as we continue to love and serve God.

The Apostates cannot offer us anything worthy of [our] acceptance—they have denied the necessity of the atonement and resurrection of Jesus Christ. May we ever feel humble and gratefull, let us ever feel our dependence on God.

<u>Elder Geo B. Wallace</u> said a great deal of good instruction had been given here from time to time & what applys to us here, applys ~~ed~~ equally to our wives and children. At times the spirit of the Lord rests so fully on an individual, that they can unfold the principles of life to their brethren to their understanding—he failed in language to express his views to ~~th~~ others. When the Council was first given to sustain ourselves instead of our enemies—he reflected on it, and sustained that Council.

He then spoke on Home Manufacture, the necessity of raising pure seed &c. pure stock & budded fruit. While we do cultivate the ground, we may just as well ~~to~~ raise good fruit as bad. We live in the days of regeneration, the time has commenced. He then spoke of whole families living in this City, who never go near a Ward Meeting or come to the Tabernacle especially in a Morning—this is not right.

<u>Elder Elias Smith</u> always deemed it a privilege to attend this school whenever circumstances would permit him—he never went away without being benefit~~t~~ed. He had many years been a close observer of Mankind and was astonished to find so many needed so much preaching to induce them to Keep the commandments of God.

We are slow to carry out the Council of the Servants of God in regard to our deal[ings]. He then ^made^ some appropriate remarks on the improper use that many make of the County and Territorial ^scrip^ by trading it off to outside Merchants, who would hade to have paid their taxes in <u>Money</u>, if the brethren had not taken their Scrip to them.[103] He touched on the

103. To minimize the purchase of imported goods by non-Mormons, communities began issuing their own scrip to buy only locally produced goods and select imported items at approved stores. May, *Utah: A People's History*, 81.

subject of neglecting meetings, paying fast offerings—&c if we fail in carrying out the Council of the Servants of God—we cannot prosper. Let us not be discouraged, let us be faithful, & we will come off victorious.

~~Elder Levi Richards~~

Meeting adjourned for one week at one o clock pm. After singing Benediction by Prest. Elias Smith.

November 12, 1870; Saturday

Theological Class met in the Tabernacle At One o clock PM. Present Elder Orson Pratt presiding Prest. B[righam] Young & Council being absent on a two days meeting at Ogden. After singing Prayer by Elder A[mos] M[ilton] Musser. Singing.

Elder Orson Pratt gave permission for any member of the School to speak from 10 to 15 minutes on any subject that most rested on their minds.

Elder [William] Henry bore testimony to the truth of the Gospel, was pleased with all the instructions he received from the servants of God. All is right in Zion—the Saints are prospering—let us all go on—be faithful, and do our duty.

Elder Robert Collins felt thankful to meet with his brethren, he came regular to school, and hoped to continue so. Spoke of the time when the "Times of the Gentiles shall be fulfilled.["]—~~all~~ the words, the Lord spoken to Joseph [Smith] the Prophet pertaining to the same subject—when he said that this generation shall not pass away when these things should be fulfilled. We have got to Keep the new commandments that God has given us, in order for the work of God to prosper, and these events bro[ugh]t about. He had observed the word of Wisdom, yet he had been a dear lover of Coffee. The Nations who had hitherto refused admission for our Elders to carry the Gospel, will be shaken, turned and overturned, until the bars are down, and permission granted the servants of God to preach there.

Elder W[illia]m Miller spoke of his early experience—when Elder Banks bestowed upon him the Spirit of Prophecy, and in less than 3 weeks after he did have that spirit, and it was plainly Manifest to him that Elder Banks would sooner or later apostatize.[104] He then spoke of

104. John Banks (1806–62) was a British convert who immigrated to Utah and founded Pleasant Grove. He converted to Joseph Morris's Church of the Firstborn and was killed in a battle with the Utah militia. Anderson, *Joseph Morris*.

Charity, which he regarded as sustaining the order of the Kingdom of God. Many would do much towards feeding the poor, but they would do it their own way, and not through the Bishop. Many of such have already apostatized.

Elder T[homas] J. King had seen many rise and fall in this school—there is no end of progress in this Church.

Elder ^Jos[ep]h^ Carlisle said we are anxious to Know the mind and will of God, and what is going to happen. The Gentiles [non-Mormons] dont appreciate us, neither here, nor out in the world—but God does—And will overrule all things for our good and his glory. Speaking of apostacy said, if we are going to apostatize, let us do it up quick. Prest. Young said the spirit of Apostacy was thick around, and even in this School. The Lord was trying us and would try us—he has does well for us—and to live so as to have the light of truth in them, what a blessing it is, let us then rejoice and do right. May God help us to be wise.

Elder A[mos] M[ilton] Musser said our feelings ^&^ views tally with each other, if we have within us the Spirit of the Lord. He has long seen the importance of us becoming one in Temporal things—and we should all echo the same sentiments and practises of our Leaders. We should never patronize those who are opposed to Co operation, but pass them by.

We should also be willing to forego our own appetites, and not continue to indulge in the use of those things which the Lord has forbidden. We should never give way to a spirit of fault finding against the Lords anointed—until we can improve upon the suggestions of Prest. Young. The Lord never gave us the right to find fault. If we as a School would all be united and carry out the word of wisdom, we should soon see the result, by Tea & Coffee being banished out of our Stores.

Elder James Leach said a neglect of duty was a stepping stone to apostacy. We are children of the light, and should cleave unto it.

Elder Orson Pratt—We have much good instruction this afternoon—the same things that have been impressed upon our minds, since we came into this church. It is astonishing to see how slow some children are to learn the most simple duties, so it is with us—hence the necessity of having those duties pointed out and reiterated in our ears—how good it is to be put in remembrance of our duties—even by the weakest of saints.

We are living in an important era—we are certainly nearer by 40 years, than when the Lord spoken to his servant Joseph [Smith]. There are many things not yet revealed to us—but will be in the due time of the Lord. We are living much nearer the time when the "Times of the Gentiles are fulfilled"—than when Joseph the Prophet first received revelations pertaining to them.[105] The time when the Times of the Gentiles are come in, was when the Gospel was first ushered in—in the midst of the Gentiles—but when those times will be fulfilled, the Lord has not yet revealed—but the Gospel will then be sent to the scattered tribes of Israel.

He then read a paragraph from page 250 in the Doc[trine] & Cov[enants]. When the Lord shall take away the Gospel from the Gentiles—it will be taken to the scattered remnants of Israel—and the arm of the Lord will be made bare in their midst.

We are the school of the Prophets raised up from the midst of the Gentiles—and are here for the purpose of being taught and instructed in the operations of the Spirit upon the Mind of man. He had almost a longing anxiety for the time to come, when the Gospel should be sent to the scattered Jews. The descendants of the Jews who persecuted the Saviour, will remain in unbelief, though many of them will be gathered in Jerusalem yet, others whose fore fathers did not persecute the Saviour & the Apostles, will embrace the Gospel before they gather to Jerusalem.

A Question was asked whether a substitute can be taken (for Tea & Coffee) owing to the impurity of the water that runs through our streets—and Elder O[rson] Pratt said, if the water was impure, in itself, why ~~h~~ add poison to make it more pure. Water was the only beverage that came ^so^ free & plentiful from the hands of our Creator for our use, and there was Nothing so well adapted to assuage thirst.

Elder W[ilford] Woodruff commented severely on the wilful practise of Herd boys destroying fences, and damaging the late crops—And shewed the necessity of enter^ing^ into all our operations, the principle of Co-operation. ^[He spoke on] the importation of Bees and Fish.^

Meeting was adjourned for one week at one o clock. Benediction by Elder J[ohn] W. Young.

---

105. That is, the "gentiles" will soon reject the gospel and usher in the second coming of Christ. Variations of the phrase "the times of the gentiles be fulfilled" appears in the New Testament and the Doctrine and Covenants. Monte S. Nyman, "Fulness of Gentiles," in Ludlow, ed., *Encyclopedia of Mormonism.*

November 19, 1870; Saturday

Theological Class met at the Tabernacle at One o clock pm. Present Prest. B[righam] Young presiding. After singing prayer by Prest. D[aniel] H. Wells. Singing.

Prest. Geo A. Smith said that they had recently visited Grantsville & Ogden, at which they had held two days Meetings, all were well attended, and much instruction imparted to the saints, a school of the Prophets was organized in Grantsville—there was great need of preaching among the latter day saints.

Since Joseph Smith received revelations from God, the world had been flooded with false revelations thousands of false spirits had gone forth on the face of the earth—and unless we Keep a strict watch care over ^our^ selves and do our duty, we cannot resist their influence. He had no doubt the Mining excitement now going on in our midst, will prove a great blessing~~s~~ to us as a people, tho' he was sorry so many of our Elders should allow themselves to be carried away with it. He felt anxious to see the rock hauled for our Temple for there never was a time when the people were so well prepared to push forward the Temple.

He also felt anxious for the people to take hold, and relieve the hands of the President of the Railroad indebtedness. He then advocated the general principle of Co-operation, in reference to Merchandize—Woollen Factories, Cheese Factories &c &c. Dont let small difficulties check you in your efforts to accomplish this.

Any member of this school who wilfully divulges what takes place or spoken here lays the foundation ~~of~~ for his own ruin, though the school is not injured by it.

Let us observe the "word of Wisdom," for Prest. Young & Himself were about to continue their labours of preaching & Councling the saints through the Southern Country, and should recommend the saints to observe the same. He prayed for the blessing of Israels God ~~should~~ ^to^ abide upon his people.

B[isho]p E[dward] Hunter refered to the hauling of Rock—there was considerable heavy rock to haul, which would require heavier teams. He also spoke favorably of the effort now being made to improve our stock, by importing a superior variety, and he urged the necessity of selecting out good & suitable men to make selections & purchase in the East, what will be most suitable for this Country.

We must fill our Covenants, not wait to be commanded, or we'll be slothful servants. The Lord will not always strive with men—who are indifferent to his requirements. Let us hasten to do our duty. There will be some labour tithing wanted shortly in extending the Paper Mill Factory—and the wards adjacent to it will be called upon to furnish it.

A Question was asked by a member of the 11th Ward. "How near one may build a Stable to his neighbors house ^and be justified^[?"] B[isho]p [Alexander] McRae & Prest. Geo A Smith reply'd and recommend every person to study his neighbors health and convenience, and by no means to encroach upon each other.

Elder Geo Q Cannon ~~who ha~~ said it was important for the alteration to be made at the Paper Mill, to be attended to forthwith, so as to secure its completion before the winter sets in—and he would be glad for the call to be made forthwith, for the tithing labour necessary to accomplish it.

He felt that the recent two days meetings held here and elsewhere would be attended with the best of results. Our outside enemies had been straining every point to gain an advantage over us as a people—but had signally failed. If we will only do right and attend to our duties, God our Heavenly Father will always bring us off victorious. There ~~h~~ never had been such a united effort made here by the Federal Officers to bring trouble upon us.

The Hand of God is very apparant in the development of our Mineral resources. There is a wise design in the providence of God—by diverting the attention of our enemies from their secret plot. We want time to grow, to increase, to become mighty. The great point for us as a people, is to have the fear of God before our eyes—and not absorbed by the glittering prospects of Gold or Silver that may appear to be looming up. Our feet will be made fast in these mountains, if we will only do right. God is with us—Satan is making a great onslaught on the work of God, ~~by the~~ and some are shook out of the church by it, and hypocrites & unbelievers will still leave us.

Prest. B Young said Bro Geo A Smith and himself would shortly go South, and if the Bishops and all others in Authority will only do their duty. Keep their wives and daughters at home, and not allowed to go out at midnight, subjecting themselves to insult from Soldiers & others. Do not have many parties through the winter, and what you do have, have them in respectable places, such as the Social Hall—the 13th & 14th Ward Houses &c.

The winter will pass off quietly, the saints will not be molested, there may be a little menacing by the outsiders, but nothing of importance, if the brethren will only be wise and attentive to their duties. Be kind, all is right. The present Commander [Patrick Connor] at Camp Douglas will do his duty, there is nothing to fear.

Let the hauling of Rock be continued without a days hinderance, until the last one is placed upon the [Salt Lake] Temple. We shall succeed in rearing it. We will not play the Card that our enemies wish us to. He spoke with much confidence on the ability and judgement of D[aniel] H Wells, as Mayor, his Knowledge of Law, Justice &c, and if the brethren will only hearken to him, and carry out his instructions, we shall have a peaceable winter.[106]

In the course of a little time, we shall have the controuling power in Ida[h]o—and also in the East. We are the Soul, and the Mainspring of the West. The Latter day Saints will stay here, and labour and make it their home. But the balance will go, as ~~the~~ soon as the bottom drops out of these Mines, and become as white pine[107]—& other once boasted Mines, but are now forsaken—Let us be patient, and the victory is ours. Dont have any parties this winter, but keep your Wives and daughters at home—Let us remember. The Kingdom of God or nothing. Try to unite ourselves more & More. The outside rumours of War & bloodshed, ~~do~~ dont pay any attention to—we understand all about it. ~~Many~~ Men go down to the graves by the thousands who are over anxious ~~to~~ about the acquirement of wealth.

Meeting was adjourned for one week at One oclock pm. Benediction by Prest. Geo A Smith.

November 26, 1870; Saturday

Theological Class met at the Tabernacle at One o clock pm. Prest. D[aniel] H Wells presiding. Prest. B[righam] Y[oung] & Geo A Smith

106. George Q. Cannon added that Young "spoke more eulogistically than I think I ever heard him speak about any man before, at least to the man's face. … I was pleased to hear the President speak in this strain of Bro. Wells, for he is a modest, kind & lovely man." GQCJ, Nov. 19, 1870.

107. In White Pine, Nevada, silver was found and the boomtown of Hamilton sprung up. When the ore was mined out, the town shrank just as quickly as it had flourished.

started yesterday for Dixie, to spend the winter there. After singing Prayer by B[isho]p A[lonzo] H. Raleigh. Singing.

Elder Geo Q Cannon spoke of the variety of teachings that are needed to be taught to the Latter day Saints, as are suggested by the spirit of the Lord, and by each days circumstances. The present effort now being made to break up the Kingdom of God, by our enemies in our midst—was now occupying the minds of the saints, especially in this City. Some were defiant, some timid and fearful, others tranquil & serene realizing that God rules—but notwithstanding our care and anxiety to avert impending trouble, God will overrule all things according to his good pleasure.

Owing to several of our Brethren being taken prisoners to Camp Douglas, by the Authority of the [Federal] Clique or Ring,[108] some wanted to fight and Kick up a fuss, but we should learn to Keep quiet, for all things will work for our good, if we only do right—We need not expect to get along without difficulties, but it is for us to take such a course as will be justified by the Heavens.

He did not fear as to the result of the present movements, we continue to enjoy a great many priviledges, such as our public Meetings, prayer Meetings, Washings & Anointings [in the Endowment House] &c and we should therefore be very thankful, and faithful to our duties. Trials are necessary to test us, and to prove us—and purge ~~al~~ out from us everything that is displeasing in the sight of God.

Let us be all united, not only in the hauling of rock for the Temple, but in other temporal labours. We should seek to become more and more united, and in proportion to our efforts, the efforts of our enemies will endeavour to keep pace, so as to prevent it.

A Petition ~~from~~ signed by 47 citizens of Mill Creek & adjacent settlements, asking for a Cattle & Horse Drive was then read by the Secretary.

Elder Orson Pratt made a few remarks on the subject & invited some one to make further remarks, shewing forth their reasons, why there should be a drive—whose names were attached to the petition.

B[isho]p J[oseph] Weiler thought, if a drive can be economically and satisfactorily carried on, more good than harm, may be expected.

108. Utah governor John Shaffer had disbanded local militias, so when men in the Twentieth Ward held a muster of arms, they were detained by the army. "Bound Over," *Deseret News*, Nov. 30, 1870.

Elder A[lbert] P. Rockwood exprest the same views—until we are more perfect than we are at present. He was opposed to a drive.

Elder Jno. [John] Pack, thought from present appearances, most of the Stock now on Jordan Range, if left there, would certainly perish [in the winter], especially the Horned Stock. He was therefore in favour of a Drive.

Elder Seymour B Young thought a public ~~dr~~ good would ~~be~~ result from a drive, and therefore sanctioned one, believing that the many will be benefitted, ~~wh~~ even should the few be exposed to injury & wrong.

Elder A[lbert] Carrington, hoped he should never own stock on West Jordan Range[109]—that way of raising stock, at best, feeds and encourages, and fattens thieves. In his judgement, he was altogether opposed to a public drive, believing ^it^ to be, not only in direct antagonism to the principle of Co-operation—but positively a public nuisance.

Elder James Rawlins, said it had been represent[ed] to him, that the ~~signed~~ petition had originated in this School, or he should never have put his name to it, for he was opposed to a drive.

Elder [Ephraim] Luce had lived 15 years over Jordan—had heard of many drives, and lost all the Cattle he had with them—he was very much opposed to them.

Elder [blank] was this year in favour of a drive, to be carried out according to Prest. Youngs suggestion, viz for the Bishops to send reliable men after them.

B[isho]p [Abraham O.] Smoot was ^not^ in favour of a drive—especially as in former times.

Elder [blank] was in favour of a drive—he had lost more Cattle in Herds than on the range.

Elder A[lbert] Carrington did not deem it wisdom to trouble this school with the question of Stock driving.

B[isho]p A[lonzo] H. Raleigh had no objection to any legitimate means being used for people to prevent injury to their stock. He thought we ought to treat Kindly a petition sent here by so many citizens. And that wisdom sufficient was in this school to devise the best means to collect what stock there now is on the range.

109. The livestock range was southwest of Salt Lake City. The proposal was to drive cattle to the west side of the valley where there was more open land. Others objected that there would not be enough feed or water, and that keeping the cattle corralled in herds was better.

Dr [John] Crockwell thought it would be policy to get all the stock in if possible, to prevent them from dying, and then turn them in, on the [Perpetual] Emigration Fund—as he had done with some of his.

Elder ^Sam[ue]l^ Hill had the understanding last year that all future drives should be sanctioned by this school—hence the petition being sent here. He was in favour of a drive, and that owners of Cattle only, should be employed, so that no expense be incurred in driving it.

Elder Geo Q Cannon suggested a Cooperative Herd being established and entered into before the stock was driven in, so as to have a place provided, and parties prepared to receive ^them^ as soon as the owners have found their own stock.

Prest. D H Wells said, whether we ^have^ stock or anything else, we should esteem them as blessings from the Lord—and should therefore take proper care of them to avoid waste. Said there was no other way of having the ~~driven~~ Stock driven up, except by hiring men to drive it, and that is attended with expense. Therefore there will be no public drive at the present, by his consent. All men will be held accountable for the way and manner they use the blessings of the Lord.

He then councilled Farmers in particulars not to attempt to keep more stock then they can profitably use and take care of. Jordan Range will never be a suitable place for even a Co operative Herd, while it is used by the public to use as a common herd ground—we ought to drill ourselves in the proper management of business and do things right. Let us take care ~~care~~ of our stock—and any owners who choose, may ~~b~~ go after their own, but not disturb other peoples. Owners had far better get up their Stock and dispose of them where they will be taken care of, or else put them in the Emigration Fund.

It was Motioned & Carried "That their be no Cattle drive."

A Notice was read of several bad places on the road leading from the Quarry, and would prevent any more rock being hauled, unless they were repaired. Some one present promised to attend to it.

A notice was given out, of a Public Meeting being held on Monday evening next of which Bro [Wilford] Woodruff was the president.

A few remarks were then made on the subject of trespassing in the Big Field.[110]

---

110. The big field was south of the city at present-day Liberty Park.

Meeting was adjourned for one week at One oclock pm. After singing Benediction by Elder Orson Pratt.

December 3, 1870; Saturday

Theological Class met at the Tabernacle at One o clock pm—Present Prest. D[aniel] H. Wells presiding. After singing Prayer by Elder S[amuel] W. Richards. Singing.

Elder Geo Q Cannon said that only about six months was remaining, before those who have preempted land [from the federal government] will have to pay for it, and it would be well for every one interested to bear it ^in^ mind, and be prepared to make payment, when the time comes, or we shall be liable to lose our propety.[111] So with naturalization, now that the difficulties have thickened around that subject, those who have neglected this important duty, must more or less, feel under condemnation. Let us carry out every requirement and duty that devolves upon us as Elders in Israel, so that in times of trial, we can confidently look for, and expect the Kind interposition of God, our Heavenly Father. For He will most assuredly deliver us, if we carry out the councils and instructions of the servants of God.

Let us learn to appreciate and enjoy the Spirit of God, though we gamy [may] be crowded with many cares in our every day life yet we should learn to Keep them in their proper place, and not thrown off our guard by them &c.

Elder Jos[ep]h F. Smith spoke of the individual and collective responsibilities that rest upon us, that we got to defend ourselves, and stand upon our own resources. The enemy had already got a foothold among us—and are seeking to deprive us of every right and privilege. It will be recreant [unfaithful] therefore for us to favour any scheme that will tend ^to^ strengthen their plans and influence here.

He did not approve of Latter day Saints sending their children to the Day and Sabbath schools of the Sectarians in our midst. He would prefer having children brought up under proper influences, and taught correct principles. We are altogether too loose and careless in this respect, and not near so exclusive as we ought to be—proving the fact

111. See Mar. 20, 1869, entry, for more on preemption.

by reference to what was common among Democrats & Republicans, Protestants and Roman Catholics.[112]

He exprest his determination to sustain ^by^ his prayers and acts those only who are the servants of God. He had no desire to mingle with the ungodly. Let us look after our rights and defend them. If we do right, God will stand by us—and shield us from our enemies.

He had lived long enough, to know there was only one man outside the church, that he would trust further than he could throw a two ~~yet~~ year old Bull by the tail—the one exception was Col T[homas] Kane. Let us be exclusive Latter Day Saints. If we enjoy the spirit of the Lord, we shall be able to judge men aright.

Elder W[ilford] W. Woodruff said the Lord intends to build up Zion, but the enemy is so far on the alert, that we may expect to be met on all sides. The Land question [preemption] is very important, and should not be neglected, or we will suffer by it. Ours is a constant warfare, and has been from the beginning—we have got to watch and guard ourselves, lest the enemy gets an advantage over us. God was going to build up Zion on this Land and we ought to carry out the Council of his Servants. We had got to Labour, and cease to sustain the enemies of our God. Though the Government, through its Officials are seeking to destroy every constitutional right, and deprive us of them. They will certainly find it a dear bought effort, for if we do our duty, God will frustrate their plans, and bring them to shame.

Prest. D H. Wells said we ^are^ not an exclusive people—for we preach the Gospel in all nations. Zion will be redeemed, and the Glory of God will be extended to the ends of the earth. There are many who make no pretensions to religion, and yet are great sticklers for right—such men will be rewarded according to his efforts to sustain the right. If we stand firm to the principles of truth to the end, we shall most assuredly come forth ~~with~~ crowned ~~th~~ with the blessings of Eternal Life.

There is no danger of the Lords forsaking us if ^we^ will only do right. Let us stand firm and faithfull in the hour of trouble—and act in wisdom, and we will be steadfast and the enemy will disappear, and break asunder. Let us be united, and they will be broken. We are entrenched in the strong principles of truth.

112. In other words, since other religious bodies operated their own schools, Mormons should not hesitate to open and operate their own as well.

B[isho]p [Edward] Hunter was pleased with what had been said to day. He urged on the brethren to continue with their heavy teams, in the hauling of Rock for the Temple. Some of our fast meetings were tolerably well attended, and offerings paid, but some were very neglectful.

He was ashamed at the trifling response from the Southern wards to work on the Paper Mill. He therefore called on ^all^ the ~~1st. 2nd. 3rd~~ City Wards to assist immediately on that labour, as it was the presidents wish to have the work done this fall.

Meeting was adjourned for one week at One o clock pm. Benediction by Elder Orson Pratt.

December 9, 1870; Saturday

Theological Class met at the Tabernacle at one oclock pm. Present Prest. D[aniel] H. Wells presiding. After singing Prayer by Elder Phineas H Young. Singing.

Prest. D H Wells, said, a Brother asks, Is it right for us to sell our Lots to outsiders? In answer He said, it was much better to sell to friends, than to enemies. Though they are crowding in upon us, and are trying to obtain a foothold here, of the two He would rather lease the land, on a good rental, and let them make improvements, whilc we retain the right of freehold ourselves.

He then recommended Parents to look after their children, and not allow them to associate with outsiders, in meeting at Beer & Oyster Saloons, for Oyster Suppers &c. Rather indulge them at home a little, than spend their time in Saloons, under bad influences.

He then recommended that our Youth, learn some useful Trade, rather than depend upon Clerkship behind the Counter. Any kind of Mechanical labour will constantly find a Market, and be a source of income. It was also necessary for our young people to learn God and his purposes and become useful in their day and generation. He recommended a Kind and gentle influence rather than a harsh and coercive means, towards our children. Instil into their minds correct principles and endeavour to preserve them from going astray. Learn them some useful trade or profession.

We will endeavour ^to^ preserve ourselves in this City, and not allow it to go into the hands of the wicked. He expected the saints would retain it for God and his Kingdom, as with also, every new Settlement that is opened up. He did not think that our Temple we are now erecting, will ever be wrenched out of our hands, and be desecrated by the wicked. Let us be faithful to God and his Kingdom.

B[isho]p Edw[ar]d Hunter said it was the Lords good pleasure to give us this Land, and it was of the utmost importance for us each to secure a legal title to the same—by paying for it within the time specified for its payment. Let us be in the way of our duty, attend our fast meeting, pay our offerings, Tithings &c.

Elder W[ilford] W. Woodruff said we have not sufficiently realized our Responsibilitys, as parents or Members of the Church. Though he himself had always been used to work, and his wives and children also had to work and be industrious—it was not right for us to allow our children to be out late at night, and mingle with evil associations. They should be taught to respect and honour their parents. He was truly thankful for the institution of Sabbath Schools, and our children should be sent there to learn the principles and doctrine of Christ.

Some of us will soon pass away, and the responsibilities of the Kingdom of God, will fall upon the heads of our children—therefore they should be instructed in everything that pertains to the government of God. Zion will conquer, and prevail, and our duties ^which^ are ^of^ the most various kinds, [will be complete] if we will only attend to them. We shall gain an experience that will qualify us for increasing usefulness. We should teach our Wives, (in our absence) to pray with their ~~fa~~ Children, and teach them to be honest—also that when they find anything, it is not theirs, but seek to find the owner.

We have been greatly blest and softened the hearts of men in our behalf, in times past—and if we do right, God will give ~~our~~ ^us^ power to retain our possessions and keep the balance of Power in this City.

B[isho]p Phineas ^H^ Young, expressed thankfulness to be present at this School. To hear the wise councils and instructions given by the servants of God. Spoke of his early experience in the church, and rejoiced at the glorious prospect before us as a people.

School adjourned for one week at one oclock pm. Benediction by Elder Jos[ep]h F. Smith.

December 17, 1870; Saturday

Theological Class met at the Tabernacle at One o clock pm. Present

Prest. D[aniel] H. Wells presiding. After singing Prayer by Elder Edw[ar]d Stevenson. Singing.

Elder Geo Q. Cannon spoke of the necessity of the Members of the School being occasionally reminded of the obligations we have voluntarily taken upon ourselves by subscribing to the rules, which have many times been read, and still need to be read, to remind us of the same. Many were very lax in their promises, and obligations, and the rights of others. Unless we pay particular attention to the vows we have made, we shall be very loose in our business transactions.

He then administered a timely reproof towards those who indulge in a careless and indifferent ^spirit^ to their promises. He then confess'd his own faults in those respects, and desired to profit by his own remarks.

Elder W[ilford] W. Woodruff sanctioned the remarks of the previous speaker, said no one living in the Zion of Enock would make promises and not fulfill them, and before we can enter into the Order of Enock, we have got to practise the principle of righteousness. If every man would fulfil ~~their~~ their promises to each other, confidence will be increased—both Joseph Smith & Prest. [Brigham] Young have taught us the principles of Honesty and Integrity and we should try to carry them out. The rules of the School are just and good, and we should observe them.

We cannot be saved in the Celestial Kingdom of God, unless we practise principles of righteousness & Honesty—it does not pay any of us, to do wrong. He teaches his children to be honest, and he believes they will grow up as Honest Men. We must not encourage our children to do wrong, if we do, they are ~~lit~~ almost sure to make it manifest as they grow up. Let us set good examples before our Wives and children.

He then recommended the brethren to get up what Horses or Cattle they have over Jordan. If not, we shall certainly lose them, for there is no feed for them there. Put them in Cooperative Herds where they can be taken ~~where~~ proper care of.

Prest. D. H. Wells refered to the close and difficult times that Joseph [Smith] the Prophet had to pass through ~~but~~ from Governors, Lawyers &c, while the Church was in the midst of the World. But since we have been here, under very little restraint, some have developed a principle of dishonesty, which is wrong. He refer'd to some who began to have fears that ~~lest~~ the influence of Prest. Young was on the wane, partly on a/c [account] of having no Muster [of arms] &c. This was not the way to strengthen the hands of the Anointed of God. No person could express such views, without himself being half an apostate. We are silently laying a broad, deep, foundation in these vallies, for God and his Kingdom—and gradually increasing in Wealth, and Influence, and union. There is no cause therefore to indulge in a spirit of fearfulness. The Power of God has been made Manifest in our behalf—and there is no need for faintheartedness.

Our enemies are approaching us in every possible shape, and very different to what ever they did before. They appeal to our selfishness and liberty & freedom, and endeavour to make it appear that we are curtailed in these things.

Those brethren who went to Camp Douglas, by some, are spoken of ~~by some~~ as having done wrong by mustering in the 20th Ward.[113] He was sorry that any should so regard it—for they were merely as representatives of the community in that thing—and should any expense acrue to them in their defence, we should all rally around them, and pay those expenses. We ought to be united, and should stand by each other in defending the rights of the saints. The Federal officers have committed themselves in many things, and he had no doubt but what they had got their foot in, and are already beginning to fear, the course they have been pursuing, will ~~be~~ not be sustained by the heads of departments. Let us therefore stand by each other, shoulder to shoulder, and live our Holy Religion—and fight our enemies by policy, never submitting to the last ~~alterna~~ extremity viz ~~B~~ fight with blows, until every other source failed us, then God would come to our rescue. He then encouraged us to let our passions be our servants, so that they may subserve the object for which they were ~~placed~~ created.

Meeting was adjourned for one week. Benediction by Elder A[mos] Fielding.

December 24, 1870; Saturday

Theological Class met at the Tabernacle at one o clock pm. Present Prest. D[aniel] H. Wells presiding. After singing Prayer by Elder S[amuel] W. Richards. Singing.

Prest. Elias Smith said in the transfer of property from one to another,

113. See Nov. 26, 1870, entry.

we had not been so particular as we ought to have been, in securing good title deeds, and having it properly ~~conveyed~~ recorded. Our enemies are on the alert and looking after such land as is not duly held by parties, who have been careless about their title deed.

Elder John Pack said he had entered a quarter Section of land in Davis Co[unty] [Utah] some time ago—and about 20 persons owned peices of land upon that section—and until he obtained his Patent from Government, it was impossible for him to Deed to them their separate claims.

Elder Z[erubabel] Snow shown the importance of being sufficiently descriptive of the land conveyed from ^one^ to another.

We have a City & County Recorder which contains first ^a^ Certificate of ownership, then a trade is made for land duly recorded by the first owner, but no conveyance is made ^and recorded^ of that trade. The second owner improves that property and occupies it for many years, yet not having had it duly conveyed & recorded to him, is running a serious risk of losing that property. Let us therefore comply with the Laws of our ~~C~~ Territory and enjoy our rights without fear of molestation.

Elders W[ilford] W. Woodruff & Jno [John] Pack made a few more remarks on the same subject.

Prest. D. H. Wells related a circumstance~~s~~ where one Bro was likely to lose a property which he had paid for, ~~a but~~ from a flaw in the conveyance. He then recommended each one to look after their title, and where it was imperfect, to look immediately after it, to avoid trouble and loss. Let us be firm and united, and endeavour to keep our enemies from using us up, and if we do right, God will defend us and protect us. Let us look after our titles, for every day discloses some new effort on their part to an^n^oy and trouble us. It was a great blessing for us to have the Land law extended to Utah.

He then desired the Bishops to have but few parties, and those well ~~attended~~ superintended—have no whiskey there, open and close by prayer.

~~A~~ [Protestant] Schools had been opened up here for the purpose of Sowing the seeds of disaffection. No faithful~~l~~ latter day saints will send their children there. The enemy is seeking to make inroad upon us, by every variety of temptations—and our children should be watched over. May God help us to live our holy religion.

School was adjourned for one week at One o clock pm. Benediction by [blank].

December 31, 1870; Saturday

Theological Class met at the Tabernacle at one o clock pm. Present Prest. D[aniel] H. Wells presiding. After singing Prayer by Prest. Jos[ep]h Young. Singing.

Elder C[harles] C Rich said there was no employment so beneficial for us to learn, as how to be saved. When we can arrive at a point when all will Know how to do right in all things—and really do it, then evil will cease to exist in the world, and God will be honored. This School is the place for us as the servants of God, to be taught in correct principles, that should govern us to day, and not reach after those that pertain to the eternal worlds in the future. No person ~~t~~ can sin with impunity, it will have its influence over us, and our destiny, in proportion as we indulge in it. He regretted the prevalence of harsh, vulgar words which some are in the habit of indulging in. Bad words seldom proceed from a pure heart, but is indicative of an impure fountain from whence such words proceed.

~~the~~ Elder Geo Q. Cannon complained of the improper conduct, manifested at a party recently held at Ballou[']s Hall—and hoped the Bishop and Council of the 14th Ward would controul that Hall hereafter, if even they had to pay the Rent of the Hall.[114] He said that persons who indulge in habits of intemperance should be cut off from the Church. He was in favour of every Hall in the City being closed ~~as~~ against Parties, not immediately under the controul of the Bishop.

Elder W[ilford] W. Woodruff had visited Fort Herriman[115] preached there, and attended a party. He bitterly complained of conduct which he had been eyewitness to in B[isho]p [Archibald] Gardners Ward ^at a party^ and was sorry that B[isho]p Gardner was not present to day. Bishops ought to be the most honest of any people in the Territory—and especially those who have charge of Cooperative Stores, and not permit their Wives and daughters to draw goods out of the store without keeping ~~out~~ any account of it. B[isho]p Gardner ought to be had before B[isho]p [Edward] Hunter and tried for such conduct—in permitting such deviltry to exist in his ward.

114. Joseph F. Smith attended the party with two of his wives and made no note of trouble, only later reporting that a "lady's hat and a quantity of whiskey bottles" were found in the hall. JFSJ, Dec. 31, 1870.

115. Fort Herriman, in use from 1854 to 1858, was a two-acre adobe enclosure that grew into a small farming community on the southwestern edge of Salt Lake County.

B[isho]p [Abraham] Hoagland expressed his determination to put a stop to Ballou's Hall being used for rowdy parties.

Bro A[mos] Fielding believed that Parties held after dark was an abomination in the sight of God—they should be held in the day and closed when night comes.

Elder A[lbert] Carrington was opposed to stringent measures being used in any way towards old or young—dont try to force anybody, but ~~call~~ calmly & Kindly reason with and try to persuade men to do right, and leave off doing wrong. He recommended that parties ~~sh~~ when held, should be well controuled and conducted—and leave off at reasonable hours—commencing as early as you like, but leave off at 12. oclock pm. He could not endorse the stringent measures advocated by Bro Fielding. He deprecated the habit of drinking now being indulged in—He knew from God himself, that ~~the word~~ of word of wisdom was true.

A day was coming when the time of choosing would take place—and after that, a shaking, happy for us, if we so conduct ourselves now, that we will be prepared for that which is to come. Let us try to make our homes happy and attractive to our Children, so that they will prefer home to any other place.

Prest. D. H. Wells said, those who indulge in swearing or drinking should not be allowed a membership in the Church. The party Bro Woodruff spoken about in B[isho]p Gardners Ward, should have been stopp'd, and not allowed to proceed. He would like the brethren to do the hauling from the Mines, for the Gentiles—also work on the Railroad, we need all the work to be done in this Territory, and should underbid strangers, and not allow them to take the work out of our hands. The Moment a ~~so~~ man in this church makes means, as a general thing, learns to smoke, chew, drink and swear, and does not use their wealth for the building up of the Kingdom of God.

It's a fearful thing for a man to be rich in this church—on acc[oun]t of our proneness to give way to our weakness. Those who make means in this Kingdom, are not on hand to build it up. There is an element in our midst growing up here that needs to be check'd, we have had to contend with it for years. We are negligent in paying our Tithing when we are blest and so sure as we do so, we shall be clipt in our glory—and not inherit the blessing of the righteous.

There are but few who get rich out of mining, those who are hired and receive a daily pay for our labour—will earn more, than the majority of the mining community—a very few may get immensely rich, but the Masses of Miners do not get a living.

Let the Bishops and Teachers use all wisdom and watch care over the saints and endeavour to set a worthy example. Whenever a Party is wanted, see that there is no drinking, Swearing nor smoking. The young wants an occasional recreation, and need it—only govern them, and keep them in proper bounds, and they will do good and not harm. The Bishops should be diligent and wise, not be too stringent, and drive the hoops too tight, lest something will burst[116]—but get up some Kind of amusements, Concerts &c to attract and amuse our your folks.

School adjourned for one week at One o clock pm. After singing Benediction by Elder R[obert] L. Campbell.

116. An analogy to barrel-making, where if the metal hoops are tightened to excess, the wood slats separate and the barrel leaks.

CHAPTER THREE

"ONE COMMON LEVEL"

1871

January 6, 1871; Saturday

The School met at the Tabernacle at 1 o clock pm. Present Prest. D[aniel] H. Wells presiding. After singing Prayer by Elder Jos[ep]h F. Smith. Singing.

B[isho]p Arch[ibal]d Gardner said on the 5th Dec[embe]r [1870] they had a Wedding Dance in their Ward House. There was to be no Liquor in or around the premises, but after he had gone home a little before recess, staying about 1½ hour, on his return he heard ~~heard~~ there had been a fuss, arising from a misunderstanding between two brethren, who had taken too much liquor.

They had another party on Christmas eve, and from circumstances he could not well controul, they were over crowded. 123 tickets were issued, and it was impossible to prevent a great noise, he learned since there had been some swearing & taking the name of God in vain, though he never heard it himself. It was a[n] ugly dance, and he was ashamed of it, and had grieved over it ever since. The evil reports that had gone round the whole neighbourhood, branding the ward with a Stigma of disgrace, that made him feel bad ever since.[1]

Elder W[ilford] Woodruff said, he alone was responsible for what was said about B[isho]p Gardners ward Party, he was not present himself, but from reports that reached him, he had stated last Saturday what he did, was pleased with B[isho]p Gardners statement, realized the difficulties that B[isho]ps labour under, especially in the management of Parties, where Liquor happens to get in, if only by a few. He hoped

1. Gardner was called to explain the rowdy Christmas party, reported first at the school at the December 31, 1870, meeting.

B[isho]p Gardner would be blest in controuling his ward, he entertained a high regard for him.

Prest. D. H. Wells spoke of the necessity of saints living their religion in the Kanyon, or in the mines, as in any other place. Have we as much relish for our Religion, and is our Love for truth as warm and unfailing as when we first embraced the Gospel. No ~~mo~~ Latter day Saint will gain respect by stooping down to the low degrading habits of the Gentiles—but should retain the dignity of our Saintship, be honorable, industrious, sober and full of integrity, then we will be prefered to fill places of trust, to outsiders; God has told us what is best for us to do, and as we shall be judged by our works, we shall Only be known by the course of life we pursue. It would be far better for us to have remained in babylon, than to bring with us the sins of the wicked and the ungodly—self government is the first thing we have to learn.

Great blessings are promised to those who observe the Words of Wisdom. He condemned the use of Liquor in strong terms. The reason the City undertook the sale of Liquor was to controul it more effectually than in any other way.[2] They had also put a high tariff or tax, as a license for the sale of Liquor, which really prohibited the sale to only a few. No City in the world is so free from Drunkenness & debauchery, as this City is. The so called Christianity of the age fails to exercise a Controuling check to these great evils, the principles of the Gospel are alone sufficient to stem the torrent of iniquity they are aiming to bring upon us. The foundation is being laid in the vallies of the Mountains, to secure peace and the practise of righteousness, let us be the friends of God, and Coworkers with him, in establishing his Kingdom upon the earth. Great responsibilities rest upon us, in Keeping the commandments of God—and nothing short of this will secure to us an exaltation in the presence of God. No one goes into apostacy, but there is a good and sufficient reason for it—either by committing adultery or some other thing. Some had denied the Very plank upon which the foundation of our holy Religion stands. We have got to stand upon the

2. A Salt Lake City ordinance outlawed private production of spirituous (distilled) beverages for personal or commercial use. Liquor licenses granted to saloons were expensive and proprietors had to purchase their alcohol from the city. The sale of liquor generated more revenue for the city than tax collection, and church leaders defended the practice as a way to control the use of alcohol. Alexander et al., *Mormons & Gentiles*, 55–56; Peterson, *Historical Analysis of the Word of Wisdom*, 54–61.

firm foundatation of truth and integrity—or we never can stand the pie[r]cing glance of the Almighty. Mans iniquity is exposed sooner or later by the all searching eye of the almighty. One single act of stealing can destroy a life time for honesty—~~one act~~ let us be careful of the sacredness of a good reputation—and live so as not to be overcome. The power of truth is ass[a]iling the powers of evil, but in no other sense, we do not assail an individual or a community, but the world assails us, and ^seeks to^ destroy the germ of the Kingdom of God, together with us, our tabernacles &c. let us so order our lives, as not to forfeit our names being reserved in the lambs book of life.

Elder Geo Q Cannon enquired if there was any business to bring before the school.

School was adjourned for one week at one o clock pm. After singing Benediction by Elder G Q Cannon.

January 14, 1871; Saturday

Theological Class met at the Tabernacle at One o clock pm. Present Prest. D[aniel] H. Wells presiding. After singing Prayer by B[isho]p Phineas H Young. Singing.

Prest. D H Wells announced that it was the intention of Professor Orson Pratt to give two Lectures weekly on the subject of Astronomy in this Tabernacle, and as they will be free of charge, he hoped there would be a general turn out of the Citizens to hear him.[3]

He then read a Telegram from ~~the~~ our Delegate W[illiam] H. Hooper, announcing the Decision of the highest authority on the subject of taxing our Tithing receipts which has been attempting to impose upon us by Dr. J[ohn] P. Taggart, assessor of income tax for Utah. That no Tithing property used for Ecclesiastical purposes or benevolent d[itt]o is taxable, only that portion of it that it used for bringing in an income, which income alone is subject to tax.[4]

Elder Orson Pratt spoke of the value and pleasure of acquiring Knowledge, he had studied various branches himself, not with a view of worldly gain, that motive never inspired him, but from the pleasure its acquirement gave him, he had for many years used his many leisure

3. Pratt acted as the company observer and amateur astronomer during the pioneer trek west to calculate the company's position and distance traveled. Self-taught, he lectured and wrote on astronomy periodically.

4. See Feb. 20, 1870, entry.

hours in that direction. His early efforts after joining the church, was the study of the Book of Mormon, which he had pretty thoroughly done, so much so, that he committed many portion of it to memory. After the school of the Prophets had been organized, ~~he~~ he study'd Kirkmans Grammar,[5] Hebrew &c, which studies were intended by the Prophet Joseph [Smith], to furnish aid and assistance to the Elders when they went forth to promulgate the Gospel of the Son of God. An Elder understanding Hebrew was likely to have more influence over the minds of the scattered tribes of Israel who understood the Hebrew Language, by being able to meet them on their own ground. The Prophet Joseph also inculcated the necessity of the Elders studying the History of Nations, so that the spirit of God might more easily impress them [their] minds with what was going to take place. He mentioned that as Joseph used the Urim & Thummim in the translation of the book of Mormon, he wondered why he did not use it in the translation of the New testament. Joseph explained to him that the experience he had acquired while translating the book of Mormon by the use of the urim & thummim, had rendered him so well acquainted with the Spirit of Revelation & Prophesy, that in the translating of the New Testament he did not need the aid that was necessary in the 1st instance.

He then shown the necessity of our Youth acquiring Knowledge of various branches, to fit and quality them to fill responsible places of the Kingdom of God. We are going to become a Mighty Nation, and shall have special duties, to perform in many other Nations, that will absolutely render it necessary for our Knowledge and wisdom in science, & Policy of Governments, to exceed any other people that dwell on the earth.

Elder Phineas Richards was pleased with the prospect of Lectures on Astronomy being about to be given by Bro Orson Pratt. A knowledge of that science would greatly assist any student in their^re^ searches after any other science.

Elder O[smond] Shaw said what Bro Pratt had said, was true—the little study he had devoted to the heavenly bodies—the composition of our own planet &c had afforded him more pleasure than any thing outside of the Gospel of the Son of God.

Elder W[ilford] Woodruff said we had been in school a good

5. This was Samuel Kirkham's *English Grammar in Familiar Lectures,* first published in 1830 and reprinted numerous times since.

while—and ^he^ believed we were approaching a very great and important crisis as a people. He also believed, we were improving and advancing. The Angel told Joseph what would become of certain Nations, quoted many passages of ancient scriptures, and taught him their application. By this means, he was ŧ instructed and taught from a pure and correct fountain. The spirit of revelation grew up in him until he became thoroughly acquainted with it. The same Spirit dwelt in Bro Brigham [Young]—and ^had^ been growing in him for many years. We want to learn God and the spirit of God as well as the sciences, for there are many great Philosophers well versed in the sciences are not only ignorant of God, but are infidel in their principles. Let any one read the prophecies in Isai[a]h, Book of Mormon, Doctrine & Covenants with a prayerful spirit, and we can almost write the future of many Nations. He spoke of the diversity of gifts and qualifications, some quick to discern one thing, and some another. There was a necessity for each one to learn the voice of the Spirit, mentioning two cases ^of^ self preservation in [h]is own experience by listening to and obeying the whisperings of the spirit.

W[ilford] Woodruff continued—adverted to the hand of God in our present peace and quiet we enjoy in this City, notwithstanding the hue and cry of our bitter enemies. In the set time of the Almighty not only this Nation, but other Nations that lift their hands against this Work—will be broken to pieces and come to nought. Prayed that we might all become more acquainted with the Spirit of God, understand his purposes—and be prepared for the great things that are coming to pass.

<u>Elder Anson Call</u> had been absent a short time, on a tour to the [United] States, after dwelling here some 22 years—he found a great change among his old associates, most of whom had turned infidel. No confidence in the Bible. Many had turned spiritualists—nine tenths were disbelievers in the atonement. [They] look'd on him as a good man, moral in his conduct but nothing more—they regard us a very strange people. They had seen us in very peculiar positions—expected that the publication of the doctrine of Celestial [plural] Marriage[6] would certainly procure the entire destruction of the whole Mormon

6. Although practiced by Joseph Smith and some others beginning in the early 1840s, polygamy was kept largely secret until the church officially announced and published its doctrine of plural marriage in 1852.

community and especially so, when the flower of the American Army was sent up to Utah for that purpose. For the U.S. never undertake anything they do not accomplish, but to their utter astonishment, in this, they failed—and you still live. He told them that God dictated and directed us what to do—as in the case of the great Buchanan Army,[7] the word of the Lord selected 24 young men and sent them back to tell the army to stop, and after burning up several of the baggage wagons but fired no gun but simply told the army ^to stop^ and the Army stopp'd.

Elder Geo. Q. Cannon then read a few extracts from a letter just rec[eive]d from Prest. B[righam] Young.

The School was then adjourned for one week 1 o clock pm—After singing Benediction by Elder Geo. Q. Cannon.

January 21, 1871; Saturday

Theological Class met at the Tabernacle at 1 pm. Present Prest. D[aniel] H. Wells presiding. After singing Prayer by Elder Jos[ep]h F. Smith. Singing.

Elder A[lbert] Carrington refered to the conduct of many of our Children. There are quite a number of parents who do not seem to sufficiently appreciate the importance of correctly training our Children to ~~un~~ be taught in all kinds of knowledge. Spoke of the importance of having good, well ventilated School Houses, with every other convenience—then select the very best Teachers. Education is not a system of stuffing in the heads of children, by teaching them, parrot like to recite piece after piece &c but Education consists in leading the minds to exercise themselves, and ~~teaching them~~ endeavour to draw out their full capabilities in the study of all kinds of knowledge. Parents should exercise a wholesome influence over their children, teach them to keep good hours at night—and never trespass on the rights of others—nor indulge in a wanton destruction of shade trees &c. The spirit of evil seems to prompt many of our youth to be very mischievously inclined. The reward of the righteous is a constant peace that flows like a river. Never let us slack up in our efforts to train up our children to forsake every evil practise.

7. The US Army was sent to Utah by President James Buchanan, which helped to usher in the Utah War of 1857–58. For more, see MacKinnon, *At Sword's Point*.

Elder Lorenzo Young[8] admitted the facilities now amongst us for the education of our children [are subpar]—but particularly recommended the practise of parents giving an evening attention to giving instruction to their children. His Mothers council to ~~g~~ him 59 years ago, influencing him in his conduct all through life. Recommended the establishment of Free Schools, where the children of poor parents can be properly educated. Let us teach our children the principle of kindness to each other.

Bro ^R[obert] S.^ Wood bore testimony to the truth of the Gospel.

Prest. D H Wells speaking of free schools, said this was a New Country, and no revenue sufficiently large to sustain free schools—there are many who never pay taxes, and many others so very indifferent about paying them that ~~they~~ ^it^ takes as much to collect them as they are worth. Government, which ~~at~~ makes appropriations for every other Territory & State in the Union for the purpose of Education, but nothing at all for Utah. As a people, no Nation under the sun does so much for the education of the poor as we do as a people. There is no Teacher but what would rather educate the children of the poor, gratis, than they should go uneducated. But there are so many, through the spirit of selfishness, that fancy they cannot educate their children & pay their taxes—when they have 5 acre lots and other valuable property. Spoke favourably of the University [of Deseret],[9] and its influence for good among the people, some of its patrons do not pay up, for the education of their children as they should do. There is constantly a warfare on hand waged against us. The enemy is on the alert and it takes both time and means to ward off their efforts.

Elder Geo Q. Cannon was opposed to the establishment of Free Schools or anything else that would foster and encourage pauperism. As quickly as many persons know that some of their neighbours ~~were po~~ would pay for their Childrens education, it would tend to destroy the spirit of independence.

He then read a portion of a letter receieved from W[illiam] H. Hooper, also a document sent to Washington [DC], by Gen[era]l [George] R. Maxwell, in which he notifies his intention to appear at

8. The surname "Young" is written over "Snow."
9. See Dec. 2, 1867, entry for more on the reopening of the University of Deseret.

head quarters ~~to cont~~ early in March to contest the seat of W[illiam] H. Hooper, and endeavour to prove the illegality of his election.[10]

He warned the school against divulging what had been read, nearly all of this school had received their endowments, and entered into Covenants, not to reveal the Council of the servants of God. Men should school themselves to be wise and prudent, and keep that which should [not] be talked about. It was a thousand times better to teach men how to earn their own living, rather than feed them on Charity. The principle of emigrating our people from the ranks of wretchedness in the old Country—was one, worthy of God who revealed it from the Heavens.

No man either in or out of the Church, can do anything to benefit & bless the saints of God but what will be blest of the Lord. By Union, exe[r]tion & faith we have to meet the enemy. We should be submissive, and pliable in the hands of the priesthood. Our children should be so educated, as to compete in Court Rooms & Halls of Congress with the wisdom of those who are opposed to the Kingdom of God.

In our efforts to establish our own industries, there are no end ~~of~~ ^to^ the difficulties that spring up ~~b~~ as barriers in our way. If we do not do our own business, others will come in and do it. In many ways, we lose power because we do not walk ~~to~~ up to our duties, although God has put such power into our hands, if we will only use it. Many of our poor might just as well be employed as not, if we would only unite our means together, and establish manufacturies, so as to encourage our own Mechanics.

It was a constant drain upon the resources of the Kingdom of God, to keep sending back for Pork, Tobacco &c. which might just as well be raised and manufactured here—when we know better, we ought to do better.

The School was adjourned for One week at 1 oclock pm. Benediction by Elder O[rson] Pratt.

January 28, 1871; Saturday

The Theological Class met in the Tabernacle at one oclock pm. Present Prest. D[aniel] H. Wells presiding. After singing prayer by Elder A. M[ilton] Musser. Singing.

10. Maxwell lost the congressional race to William H. Hooper, who received over 21,000 votes, or nearly 94 percent of the votes cast. Maxwell wrote a memorial to Congress claiming fraud but was told nothing could be done. He ran against George Q. Cannon in 1872 and lost in a similar landslide, with Mormons voting en bloc for the church apostle. Tullidge, *History of Salt Lake City*, 599–600.

Elder W[ilford] Woodruff said, in behalf of the parent association, for the introduction of improved Stock, Bees, Swine, Sheep &c &c, while they were calling ^upon^ other Counties to cooperat~~ive~~ with them in establishing brand associations. It was very necessary for us in Salt Lake County to start in a cooperative effort to herd our stock, so as to have the ranch cleared of all that is now running loose. Have a regular system on an upright principle that every one may have their rights. There [h]as been a great amount of dishonesty practised by individuals who have undertaken to take stock & Sheep on shares, and we want to do away with this.

Elder A M[ilton] Musser Mentioned a case in Corn Creek [Kanosh, Utah] where an old Gentleman who had a little Cash which he put in a Cooperative Store a few Cows and Sheep which he put into different Cooperative Herds, and the income he derived from those sources, he obtained a comfortable living. He strongly recommended the establishment of Cooperative Herds.

B[isho]p [Thomas] Jenkins said he had had a good deal of experience in Horses, and some little in Horned Stock. He strongly recommended an immediate effort to Import good blooded animals, and have the inferior stock removed from the range—thorough blood Durham, short horned, ~~wou~~ Bulls, would do well to introduce~~d and~~ &c.

Elder Geo Q Cannon advocated the necessity of taking good care of what God has put into our hands—and the best way he could suggest was to enter into a cooperative plan, wisely and honorably conducted. A great amount of Stock had been stolen from the range, and a remedy was loudly called for—and no plan is equal to the one now advocated. One advantage will be to avoid an unnecessary competition, in the sale of stock—besides the preservation and increase~~s~~ of our stock that are taken care of in Cooperative Herds. He hailed the organization of these cooperative efforts with a great deal of pleasure, as a means of great good to the community.

Elder Peter Nebeker said if his means had been put in Cooperative herds, before he went on his Mission, he would have saved thousands of dollars—being one of the Committee on Horses. Said they had suggested the idea of having all the Horses removed from off the Jordan Range—and all put in a Herd where they can live and do better than where they now are, leaving the present pasture for Milch Cows for the City. He made some valuable suggestions on the principle of Union or cooperation.

Elder A[lbert] P. Rockwood recommended the various Committees to set about their duties in a business like way, and he would promise and insure them success, get up their bye laws, open up their subscription books.

It was Moved & Seconded That the Committee on Horned Stock take immediate steps to open the books for subscription. Elder Wheeler Horse Farrier [horseshoer], gave some excellent~~s~~ instructions about the management of Horses.

The School was adjourned for one week at One o clock pm. Benediction by Elder S[amuel] W. Richards.

February 4, 1871; Saturday

Theological Class met in the Tabernacle at One o clock pm. Present Prest. D[aniel] H. Wells presiding. After singing Prayer by Bishop A[lonzo] H. Raleigh. Singing.

Elder John Taylor, after several weeks sickness, was pleased to have the priviledge of again appearing before the saints, to speak on the subject of the Everlasting Gospel, which is unchangeable in its general character. Spoke of some who did not like to be interfered with by the priesthood especially in their temporal matters, they also laid aside some of the fundamental principles of the Gospel, such as the necessity for the atonement of Jesus Christ. If we trust to our own understanding and judgment, and yet neglect God, he believed ~~w~~ we should go astray.

There are no people on the face of the earth who know how to save, either themselves or their progenitors, except as God should reveal it—which he has done to Joseph Smith the Prophet, and Brigham Young—and if God revealed these things, then He is our Head, and we meet here to be instructed how to build up the Kingdom of God.

Elder W[ilford] Woodruff felt it was a time when we ought to watch as well as pray. We are having a great influx of strangers in our midst—and among them, many speculators, who are trying to get our land and Houses—by purchase or otherwise. He strongly recommended the brethren who have property to rent, to call on Prest. Wells for Council and always have the writings drawn up by Judge [Elias] Smith or Hosea Stout, and not sign any document drawn up by strangers—for fear we should have advantage taken of us. No amount of Means could tempt him to sell his inheritance—and he hoped the brethren would hold their homes as being most sacred.

The Mines were now being opened and developed, for the special benefit of the Saints, and by and bye if we do right, our eyes will be opened to see ^that^ the hand of the Lord is over us for good. Zion will soon arise and ~~arise~~ shine, and increase. Our enemies are not going to destroy us, nor take away our rights.

Elder Geo Q Cannon thought if we could only look behind the spirit world, we should find the same spirit of rejoicing, among the damned spirits that is now indulged in by many in our midst. That Mormonism was now about to be so pent up, that it would shortly come to an hand [head], being entirely swallowed up by our enemies.

For Years past our private and Public prayers embodied in them that God would hide up the treasures of the earth, and for some time, we seem to have forgotten that prayer, our faith has slacked up. He was satisfied that God heard and answered our prayers, but now in the providence of God, the Mines are opened and the glittering ore is seen almost on the surface, the present appearance of the things, seem to indicate an unprecedented prosperity among the saints, if ^this^ should be the case, the faithful saint, who holds all he has upon the alter, will not be tempted or drawn aside from the truth, by the glittering gold & Silver. If we continue to obey the laws of the Gospel we shall certainly occupy a pinnacle beyond the reach of temptation.

Only let us pursue the course that God has marked out, and the Government will never pass into wicked hands, but we will always retain our supremacy in these Mountains.

Elder Orson Pratt said, sometimes the Lord takes a course to bring about his purposes, that are not understood by the people, especially for the time being—as in reference to the selling of Joseph of old to the Egyptians—and that while the fact was not justifiable by his brethren, yet God turned it to good account.[11] He then refer'd to the opening up of the Mines in our Territory. He was satisfied that the time had now come but those who had been showing up the richness of these Mines to the Gentiles, with a view to our injury (meaning the Godbeites) will

11. See Genesis 37–41 for the biblical account of Joseph sold into slavery by his brothers and his rise as a servant of the pharaoh.

be under the great condemnation, yet God will overrule it for ~~their~~ ^the^ good of the people of God.

Prest. D H Wells was pleased with the good attendance of the brethren, and hoped they would turn out in the morning and afternoons meetings. He also recommended those who had entered Land over Jordan [River] to see to it, and make such improvements as is necessary to secure it—for some parties were here, and would take it up, if we did not attend to it.

Let us do our duty, live our religion, go on in the even tenure of our way—and the Lord will perhaps take the present means, to get us into the Union, so that we can select our own [government] officers, (who knows). He then read a short paragraph from the Lectures on Faith, in the Doctrine & Covenants—shewing that those only who have a Knowledge of what ^they^ are doing is ~~in~~ strictly in keeping with the mind and will of God, will ever attain to eternal life.

He then shown up the folly and wickedness of those who sell their inheritances, on the merest pretext, especially the supposition that Prest. D H Wells had sold a piece of Land to an enemy. He then explained the case, which was entirely satisfactory to the school.

If we do not understand ~~t~~ all the movements of the 1st presidency, let us steer our own course and not talk about ~~not~~ ^them^— and not to presume that what we are told. Prest. [Brigham] Young has done that we have a right to do also, and go headlong to sell out our inheritance. Prest. B[righam] Young has many times bought Houses and Lots of brethren to prevent them from going into the hands of our enemies.

No Latter day Saints who happened to drop into a valuable claim worth one or two hundred thousand dollars, but what would lay down his means at the feet of the Apostles or Bishops—or should do. No man can obtain a Wife, the remission of his sins, or any spiritual blessing, but must obtain them through the priesthood—and should therefore have such confidence in them as to be guided by them in our temporal things.

School adjourned for One week at One o clock pm. After singing Benediction by Elder Orson Pratt.

February 11, 1871; Saturday

Theological Class met in the Tabernacle at One oclock pm. Present Prest. ~~B[righam] Young~~ D[aniel] H. Wells presiding. (~~Who~~ ^President

B[righam] Young and Geo A. Smith^ returned yesterday afternoon from St George [Utah] after an absence of ten weeks.) After singing Prayer by Elder S[amuel] W. Richards. Singing.

Prest. D. H. Wells again urged upon the brethren the necessity of properly securing our land titles or we will certainly lose them. Those who have filed their intentions to secure land whether over Jordan or anywhere else, let them build on it forthwith and have some one, or go themselves and live on it—and secure it legally.

Our enemies have not made any great point against us at present, although they have made many efforts to do so. We have an organized government that have administered Justice here for many years, and our enemies have tried ^to trample^ it under their feet.

Let us hold fast to the Iron Rod, do work for those who come here, mind our own business, be wise in our sayings, be faithful and true to our holy religion, and God will preserve us in our rights.

Elder Jno. [John] Taylor let us not give way to anything, contrary to the principles of righteousness, but seek first the Kingdom of God. What am I doing to further this object, let us ask ourselves this question. The Kingdom will roll ^on^ and let us assist it in its onward march. No person can stay its progress—whether Government or private individuals attempt to stop it—they cannot do anything against it, but for it, it always has been so. He always expected such kind of opposition, the Devil is not dead yet, and he thought we might naturally look for a continuance of opposition, if even we become a State. Let us be alive to our duties, cleave to God and his Kingdom and all will be well.

Prest. Geo A Smith arose, and expressed thanks to meet the School again once more. He and Prest. Young had been spending a few weeks in a milder climate, down in Dixie [southern Utah]. They met with a very warm reception, and renewed many old acquaintances with long settlers in that country. The brethren there never felt better, and Zion is triumphant, notwithstanding there is a necessity for the people to be tried. He hoped the brethren will carry out the Council of Bro Wells, respecting the land titles. The Lord will help those who help themselves. Let us cleave to the Iron Rod. At St. George [Utah] they are building the finest Meeting house in the Territory with sand stone. We are the least taxed and best governed people in the world, let us not go crazy over the mines, let us cultivate our soil. Keep out of debt.

Preserve our lots. Let every man learn his duty, for all must stand ^or fall^ for themselves.

Elder Geo Q Cannon said from the amount of Council given in this school, ought to make us wise and happy people. He knew of no other people, that are so favoured as we are, the kind, fatherly council so unselfishly communicated to us—comes to us so cheaply and frequently ought to be more appreciated.

He hoped we might profit from what we hear for the powers of Earth & Hell are combined to uproot us from this country. He spoke of the deep laid plots and schemes now being laid by our enemies, they ^are^ just as ~~much~~ certain in their estimation of driving us to the wall, and wrestling from us our lands and homes. From the Head of our Government, a great scheme and plot has been working, by appointing every Official that would operate prejudicial to our interests—if possible to create a collision between us and the Government, and thus bring trouble and distress into our midst. Let us act well our part and God will multiply ~~all his unselfish~~ blessings upon all who act unselfishly towards building up the Kingdom of God. ~~we are~~ He then shown up the folly and wickedness of an Elder in Israel ~~in~~ selling their inheritances.

School was adjourned for One week at One o clock pm. Benediction by Elder Orson Pratt.

~~Received Thomas G Spencer~~

February 18, 1871; Saturday

Theological Class met at the Tabernacle at one o clock pm. Present Prest. B[righam] Young presiding. After singing Prayer by B[isho]p L[eonard] W. Hardy. Singing.

Prest. B Young after an absence of 11 weeks from the School, said The Kingdom was onward and upward—though the outside world was never more opposed to ~~the~~ it, since the Angel gave the plates into the hands of Joseph [Smith], Hold on to the Iron Rod, and we need have no fears about the Kingdom. I pray you in Christs stead, put your trust in God, and never apply to Wizards and familiar spirits,[12] who are not only in our midst to day, but have been since the organization of the

12. Joseph F. Smith wrote that Young said, "As in ancient Israel, those that were called witches and wizzards were with this people and would be until the sheep were divided from the goats." JFSJ, Feb. 18, 1871.

Church. God is jealous of his honour and will be sought after by this people. The Devil and his imps have tried their best to destroy the Kingdom during the past winter and will continue to try, but they might ^crack^ down, while they pluck off and try to injure the branches, the Kingdom is taking root.

The climate in the south suited, both himself and bro Geo A Smith, and he hoped to go there again in the fall and stay there during the Winter. They intended to build a Temple there also, so that the aged and young may get their blessings, instead of being under the necessity of coming all the way from dixie to this city.

He also urged upon the brethren to be faithful and diligent in their prayers, for they were just as necessary as if we [were] out in the world preaching the Gospel, and may God bless you my brethren, and I bless you in the name of the Lord.

Prest. D[aniel] H. Wells heartily endorsed the sentiments of Prest. Young, and rejoiced exceedingly that the time had come when the wants of the growing people were about to be met in the building of Temples in other places besides the City. He also urged the necessity of looking after their land claims, and get legal titles, for many are here seeking to jump every claim they possibly can.

If we have stock that we do not need for present use, let us~~e~~ put ^it^ into a Cooperative herd and have it well cared for. He was thankful to see his brethren back from Dixie, and hoped they would live many ~~blessin~~ years to prove a blessing to Israel. We have no other work on hand but to build up the Kingdom of God. Let us therefore cooperate with him, and devote both time and means for God and his kingdom, then we will secure his Confidence & that of his servants.

Elder W[ilford] Woodruff was glad to hear the voice of Prest. Young's voice again, to listen to his councils. The Spirit of God had been with Prest. Wells ~~&~~ during his absence. He also refered to the wicked world who are much opposed to the Kingdom of God as ever, there [h]as been a strong combination among the wicked to bring us into trouble during the past winter, but we have been preserved, and have met in our School, Tabernacle, & Ward Houses, without interruption. It was also a wise suggestion of Prest. Young to introduc~~tione~~ the use of Oxen for during much of our labour instead of Horses as a source of economy.

He also named a few things about the Mines. The hand of the Lord was in it, and much good would have come out of it. Let farmers cultivate the soil, and every Mechanic cleave to his Mechanism by and bye, we shall see the wisdom that God has in permitting them to be opened here & there.

He had been absent a few days looking out a Herd ground for a Cooperative Herd—and hoped the brethren would rally round the effort and help it along. Zion will arise, and triumph on the face of the earth—and all opposition will have to give way—and the Kingdom will be built up. We must attend to our prayers, and our works must be good, and we shall have a home here, and the wicked and ungodly will have no power to prevent it.

Elder O[rson] Pratt spoke of the reckless character of many who are, and will be in our midst.[13] They will steal and murder, and come here entirely on a speculative principle, he hoped we would be careful and diligent over what God has given into our charge.

Elder Ja[me]s Leach expressed confidence in the authorities of the Church—and rejoiced in having the privilege of following the example of good men.

Elder Amos Fielding condemned the use of still slop[14] fed pork which is now being Imported, also Cattle, fed in the same way, neither, was fit ^for^ human food. He also exposed the poisonous character of Whiskey.

Elder [Robert] Collins advocated the same sentiments.

Elder Geo B. Wallace illustrated the principle of economy in the use of Cattle by reference to a Bro, who with 3 yoke of Oxen could haul 6 ton of Coal in six days, and when he traded them off, for Horses could only haul two ton in 7 days. Hence Oxen are the cheapest for farm and other labour.

The School was adjourned for One week at One o clock pm. Benediction by Elder G[eorge] Q. Cannon.

February 25, 1871; Saturday

Theological Class met in the Tabernacle at one oclock pm. Present Prest. B[righam] Young presiding. After singing Prayer by Elder A M[ilton] Musser. Singing.

---

13. That is, those who come on the railroad hoping to work in the mines.

14. Still slop comes "from distilleries, or brewer's slop or brewer's grain; or milk from diseased cows." Thornton, *Law of Pure Food*, 62.

Elder Geo Q Cannon read an advertisement ^in the [Deseret] News^ of a prize Lottery put in by the Exchange & Reading rooms Comp[an]y,[15] for the purpose of raising means for said company, he then warned the school against sustaining and patronizing such money making schemes. He also made a few remarks against sustaining the numerous life insurance company's that are now appealing to our community for patronage, he hoped the brethren would prefer investing in our home institutions, for he did not consider any of the companys of Babylon safe and reliable.

He then read a letter from one of the Members of the school in which the following questions were asked viz What difference is it between patronizing an outside Lumber Merchant and a dry goods Merchant? Prest. D[aniel] H. Wells reply'd that Lumber can be bought just as cheap of the brethren, as of an outsider, for the same kind of pay, and the same degree of promptness in payment—and if we as a people sustain the brethren in the Lumber trade, outsiders would soon be run out, and the same may be said about general Merchants.

Prest. B Young said if he was a Leather Merchant ~~an~~, a Lumber Merchant or anything else, and he could not or would not sell as cheap as the same kind of articles can be imported ^for^ from abroad—he would not blame the brethren for not buying from him—for that ~~not~~ was ^~~not~~^ the principle he had acted upon and intended to. We must come down in our price of labour and profits, and compete with foreign labour.

He thought this Lottery scheme to make money, was a species of gambling, and ought to be put down by the Law Makers. [On] (Insurance Cos.) [he] said there was no trust to be placed in them, many of them are based upon a fabulous foundation, and he hoped the brethren would not invest in them. If there is to be life insurance companys ~~he~~ sustained, let us have one established among ourselves, then if there is anything to be made by it, we will make it ourselves, and keep our means at home.

Have we thought over the subject I ~~understood~~ introduced last Saturday, viz to use Oxen for our Farming, Hauling, Lumbering &c as a Means of economy, and cheapening labour, instead of Horses or Mules.

---

15. The Salt Lake Exchange and Reading Rooms was a short-lived library, founded by Bentham Fabian (1820–76), a member of the Godbeite movement. Walker, "Liberal Institute."

We must learn to economize our labour, and produce what we can at the very cheapest rates, and live within our income.

We are going to build up the Kingdom, turn all the tithing of this Year towards the building of the temple, and we will build other temples, let us be willing to do whatever the Lord our God wants ^us^ to do. Let us try to learn the mind and will of the Lord concerning us. The volition of will is perfectly free but God holds in his own hands the results thereof. If we ever have means let us hold ourselves both ready and willing to use it for any purpose he may require it—~~The~~

Elder G. Q. Cannon bore testimony to the truth of the policy that has been taught to us this afternoon, as the best suited to our present condition—and if we carry it out the wisdom of God will be plainly seen—in the same. There is every prospect of Capitolists coming here, and making extensive investments, and that class of men are not the ones to provoke war, but ~~are~~ will be identical with us, in trying to preserve peace—having great interests at stake—and if we as a people will only do right, the Lord will overrule all things for our salvation &c.

The School was adjourned for one week at one o clock pm. After singing Benediction by Elder Geo Q. Cannon.

March 4, 1871; Saturday

Theological Class met at the Tabernacle at one oclock pm. Present ~~B Prest. B[righam] Young~~ ^Pres[dent] D[aniel] H. Wells^ presiding. After singing Prayer by Elder O[smond] Shaw. Singing.

Elder B[righam] Young Jun[io]r was pleased to be present again in the School, having been in the southern Country for some time past. He, in his travels, was sorry to notice so much Tea, Coffee, Tobacco, & Whiskey being used among the saints. And from the amount of such articles imported he was satisfied there was quite an increase~~s~~ in their use. Some might think the Word of Wisdom was not binding particularly on them, but he certainly regarded it, binding on him to observe. He had met some of his brethren who were hauling ore, and had learned to drink and swear equal to any outsider which he regretted to observe. He had noticed a great increase of strangers in the City since his return, and many were the temptation that our young people are now, and will be exposed to—but there is no one who attend to their duties as saints, will ever be drawn away.

Some were in the habit of talking too much especially about matters spoken in this school. this should not be. We should learn to be wise—and keep our own counsel. There are no men on the face of the earth who should be so wise as the Members of this school.

Our enemies living here, though they have tried to bring us into bondage, have failed every time. At the very time when they seemed to have accomplished something, a Ram was caught in the thicket, their evil designs ^were^ made manifest, and their plot all exploded and destroyed. Thus has God been our friend and will continue to be if we will only do right.

Elder Geo Q Cannon refered again to the efforts of the Insurance Comp[an]ys now being made in our midst—to induce persons to invest their means in Life Policies. He then suggested the propriety of establishing~~nt~~ a Life and Fire Insurance Company among ourselves, and thus secure our means in our own hands. Elder Geo Q Cannon Motioned, and was carried That we Organize a Life Insurance Comp[an]y.[16]

Our various Co operation efforts now being entered into, afford a much safer and better investment than anything of an outside institution. He then adverted to the Co operation Herd about to be started—now is the time to urge it into existance.

Elder W[ilford] Woodruff said these important subjects require our wisdom, patience and perseverance. He spoke of Father Russell ship builder,[17] who before embracing the Gospel had his Life & Ships Insured, but after that drew his interest out, and paid his Insurance Money into the church, and trusted in God, to take care of his life and property. He also explained some particulars about starting the Co operative Herd.

Spoke of the opposition we have had to contend with, from the Government Officials who have tried to bring us into bondage & trouble—but have signally failed. God has heard the prayers of the faithful and delivered us out of the hands of the wicked. He feels that God will continue to break every weapon that is formed against us. Our enemies

16. This last sentence was written vertically on the right side of the page, obscuring the horizonal text already recorded.

17. Joseph Russell (1786–1855) was born in Scotland and immigrated to New Brunswick in his thirties. He was a shipbuilder and founder of a fire insurance company. He joined the LDS Church in 1840 and, after a brief return to the British Isles, relocated to Utah Territory in 1852.

are very short lived, God has cut them off—and will do so. I build up Zion—let us therefore combine and cooperate together and have integrity and shew that [we] are in every [way] worthy of the confidence of both God and man.

Prest. D. H. Wells spoke of another defeat which our enemies have experienced. So many instances that we have Known that God had answered our prayers and turned things in our favour should certainly induce us to be faithful and diligent in our duties. The very heart of our Government have been arrayed against the interest of this people if the Cragin or Cullum bill had passed. The President would sign it, and if neither passes, he would enforce the way of 1862.[18] but neither of these things had been accomplished—how is it? because faithful brethren pray both in ~~the~~ private and in the circle.

If 5[000] or 10,000 dollars can be raised here to start an Insurance Comp[an]y—he would like to have the means invested in the Wagon and Machine business at a low rate of interest.

He spoke of the importance of starting the cooperative Herd. He said if ^we^ will only do our duties, we have nothing to fear from the influx of strangers—the claim jumping[19] now going on, if persisted in, will certainly end in trouble.

He hoped the Lord will bless and prosper Prest. Young and cause him to live long on the earth. There was ^no^ necessity for those who work in the Kanyon to swear steal & get drunk. Those who obtain means can have the privilege of helping roll forth the Kingdom of God.

If we want a blessing let us pay our tithing and attend to our duties, and the Lord will pour us out a blessing, that we will scarcely have room to contain it. The tithing office is empty [of goods], and there is nothing to sustain the workman now employed there. Let each one pay in their tithing in its kind.

The School was adjourned for one week at One o clock pm. After singing Benediction by Elder G Q Cannon.[20]

---

18. The Morrill Anti-Bigamy Act of 1862 prohibited polygamy in the United States, including the Utah Territory, but it remained unenforced. The Cragin Bill of 1867 would have disenfranchised the Latter-day Saints, but it failed to pass the US Congress.

19. A claim jumper seized the land of someone else and claimed the mining rights thereon. For more on the challenges of securing land claims, see Mar. 20, 1869, entry.

20. These final two paragraphs were inserted vertically over text already written horizontally.

March 11, 1871; Saturday

Theological Class met in the Tabernacle at One oclock pm. Present Prest. B[righam] Young presiding. After singing Prayer by Elder B[righam] Young Jun[io]r. Singing.

Prest. B Young wished to agitate the question of donation for emigrating the poor, there was scarcely anything done last year, ~~b~~ in consequence the railroad indebtedness, but we need the labour of our brethren from the old country and I think this will be a good time. In regard to Insurance Institutions, if the brethren feel like Insuring their lives and property, let us do it among ourselves, it will be just as convenient to assist each other in this respect, as to pay out our means to strangers. But he himself felt more like emigrating the poor, and building the Temple. He then Motioned and was carried That we commence to raise a fund to day.

Prest. B Young subscribed	$1,000.00
B Young Junr—	100.00
Howard ^O^ Spencer	50.00
D H Wells	300.00
E. Luddington	1.00
[Total]	$1,451.00

F. Little	100.00	D. R. Allen	25.00
[G.] J.T[aylor] D[itto]	50.00	Thos. Whitaker	5.00
G Goddard	10.00	Joel Parish	10.00
W. E. Pack	40.00	Coop[21] Spears	2.00
Jas. Albion	1.00	Thos J. Jones	1.00
A H Raleigh	100.00	Geo Anderson	2.50
B Y Hamilton	25.00	J. Ladd	10.00
Milan Atwood	20.00	H Tingey	5.00
Chas Edwards	1.00	Jno Groves	1.00
L. Mantile	50	A M. Musser	25.00
Jas Leach	2.00	C Merkley	1.00
Jos McRae	1.00	Jno Eddings	25.00
F. Merrill	1.00	~~Geo G West~~	~~2.00~~
M. Pratt	1.00	T. Curtis Senr.	1.00
A M. Merrill	10.00	L. H. North	1.00
J. W. Johnson	1.00	L. Leonard	2.00

21. "Z[ion]s Coop[erative]" is written in smaller script outside the column.

Chas Keelgell	2.00	P Gunderson	1.00
J. J. Thayn	25.00	W. S Jones	75.00
Geo Hamlin	2.00	S. D. Overton	5.00
G M Keyson	1.00	W. Brown	2.00
A Fielding	5.00	S. Fowler	50
E W Davis	2.75	J. Peart	5.00
Jos. Hartwell	5.00	Jno Swenson	25.00
[Total]	1857.25[22]		2013.00

Jas Russell	50	Brot Forwd	2251.00
S. Williams	5.00	W McLlaughlin	5.00
W. H. Foster	2.00	Jacob Malstrom	1.00
W. J. Smith	1.00	L. Suhnke	2.
J. J. Murphey	5.00	H. W. Despain	5.
W. H. Walker	10.00	Geo D. Keaten	2.
Geo A Neal	100.00	Thos. Birch	1.
T. W. Winter	5.00	Jas. Wall	1.
Jno. Hoffman	5.00	Thos. F. King	1.
R. Golightly	25—	J. B. Noble	10.
F. A. Mitchell	25—	Jno Wilson	1.
C C. Assmussen	25—	S. A. Woolley	15.
Geo C. Riser	5—	Josh. Horne	10.
N. N.	1—	Alvin Vinegar	1.
Jno. R. Standiford	5.00	[Total]	$2,306.00
Jno. Evans	1—		
Robt. Calder	1.		
Jas. S. Brown	5.		
Wm Clark	2.		
Jacob Hen~~y~~sen	5.		
D Huntingdon	2.	Henry Tingey has some	
H Woodbury	2.50	wheat [to donate]	
[Total]	2251.00		

Bros [Wilford] Woodruff, G[eorge] Q. Cannon, D[aniel] H. Wells & Prest. B[righam] Young, spoke on the subjects of the Cooperative Herd, the necessity of its early start. [Also on] the Word of Wisdom, many failing to observe it, especially our young men, the evils of improper associations among our young people, danger of amalgamations,

22. Amounts listed under each column include totals carried over from previous columns.

though earnestly sought by the adversary—skating rink, and parties in the Music Hall and Morgans College [were] denounced on account of the evil tendencies they are fraught with.[23] We must not allow ourselves to be drawn aside into wickedness or the love of this world, but attend to our duties, not become excited, as most men are, who come here greedy after the God of this world.[24]

Prest. Young moved & was carried that no more parties be allowed in Morgans School house—in consequence of improper conduct being allowed there—and that the Music Hall be hired by the Priesthood, so as to have it under control.

School was adjourned for one week at one oclock pm—Benediction by Elder G Q Cannon.

March 18, 1871; Saturday

On Saturday March 18th 1871 Theological Class met at the Tabernacle at One oclock pm. Present Pres~~ent~~[ident] B[righam] Young presiding. After singing prayer by Elder Jos[ep]h F. Smith. Singing.

The following Donations were rec[eive]d towards the [Perpetual] Emigration fund[:]

Wm. J Silver	10.00
Jacob Peart	5.00
N B Sorenson	2.00
Thos. Morris	1.00
[Total]	18.00

Prest. D[aniel] H Wells made a request of the brethren not to bring food with them to school, but to get their dinner before they came.

Elder R[obert] L. Campbell who had just returned from a visit to Canada ~~among~~ to see his relations, whom he had not seen for 26 years, when he first met them, it was a very affecting circumstance. He borne a faithful testimony ~~an~~ to his friends—and had a very pleasant stay with

23. The Music Hall "featured women dancing in provocative ways." Alford and Freeman, "Salt Lake Theatre." Morgan Commercial College, founded by John H. Morgan, was open from 1867 to 1874 when it closed due to competition from the University of Deseret. Dennis Lythgoe, "Education Pioneer," *Deseret News*, June 26, 1998.

24. Joseph F. Smith explained that it was Woodruff who spoke on cooperative herds and Cannon on the Word of Wisdom. "Pres[iden]t Wells followed, on the schemes of the world to make money that no stone would be left unturned to get our money. Skating rinks, life insurence Co[mpany]s and every other thing." JFSJ, Mar. 11, 1871.

his brothers for several weeks, had visited schools, and attended several places of worship.

Elder Ja[me]s W. Cummings had just returned from the furthest ~~end~~ portion of the united States ~~to~~ whither he had been to see his relations, and obtain[ed] a record of his Ancestors.[25] He found them willing to listen to a history of Utah, and especially about its inducements for making money—had travelled 7000 Miles—met with kind friends wherever he went. The business men & influencial ones, have little or no sympathy with the carpet baggers now in our midst,[26] even if we were to kick them out. He had succeeded in obtaining a genealogy of his forefathers for 8 generations back.

In his researches after the manufacture of Woolen Cloth[27] he met with great respect from the leading men in the various factories & Machine Shops, and was shown around them without the least reserve. There are more ~~f~~ Mills in Philadelphia ^& vicinity^ than ~~al~~ in all the New England States put together. He had gleaned a good deal of information pertaining to the Manufacture of Cloth—and brought specimens with him.

He then dwelt on the necessity of advancing our home Manufacture, raising more wool, Factory's Mutton &c &c. He had been away nearly 4 Months, but had never seen the place where he would exchange for his home in Utah.

Prest. D H Wells said the path of worldly prosperity seems to be a path of danger to many in this church. In a career of poverty there are those whose times & what little means they have are on hand for the building up of the Kingdom of God, but let prosperity attend them, and they become cold & indifferent. Many such have left landmarks behind them, so that we can see the wreck of many who did run well for a season, until the Lord blest them with means then they made ship wreck of their faith.

He refer~~r~~ed to the subject of raising and using Oxen instead of Horses or Mules—being much more economical. The wealth of the Country

25. Cummings was born in Wilton, Maine, and had traveled throughout the northeast to learn about mass clothing production for Utah's cooperative movement.

26. That is, the federal officials appointed to oversee Utah.

27. Sheep were able to survive well in the Utah desert, and since machinery could be transported by rail, the result was the completion in 1872 of the Provo Woolen Mills. Arrington, "Provo Woolen Mills."

lies in the ranches and facilities for raising Animals, food &c. He then made a calculation between the cost of working Horses & Mules, & Oxen and shewn that Oxen were more servicable & less costly to keep. He also adverted to the value of increasing our home Manufactures.

Those who perform the work of the miners, such as hauling ore, building smelting works &c will earn more then the Majority of those who own & ^find means to^ work the Mines.

Elder G[eorge] Q Cannon Notified the brethren to send delegates from all the precincts of the county to attend a Meeting at the City Hall at ½ past 6 oclock on Monday night.

School was adjourned for one week at one o clock pm. Benediction by Elder B[righam] Young Jun[io]r.

March 25, 1871; Saturday

Theological Class met in the Tabernacle at One o clock pm. Present Prest. B[righam] Young presiding. After singing prayer W[ilford] W. Woodruff. Singing.

Towards emigration fund[:]

James Wood	$ 2.00
Wm. Mc Camp	5.00
Jno. [John] Thomson	1.00
Rd. Golightly	25.00
Jane Thomson	50
Neils Nelson	2.00
B[isho]p Hoagland	25.00

Prest. B Young said he would like, through the school, to effect an organization for permanent labour on the Temple. He wished to caise [raise] a Corps of Masons and other labourers, who attended to their prayers, pay their tithing and do right, speak well of the anointed of God &c. No others need apply, for they ~~would~~ ^will^ not be wanted to labour on the temple. He wanted every branch and portion of the priesthood to back up, and sustain the Counsels of the first presidency, and endeavour to have them carried out.

Prest. D[aniel] H. Wells had named the subject to a number of the Masons and wished them to hand in their propositions, as the labour hereafter is to [be] performed on the Temple [and] will be done on piece work instead of by days work.

And that while the workmen are expected to sustain their families by their labour, he did not wish them to make exorbitant calculations, but realize that we are here to build up the kingdom of God. Let us fall in with the ways of the Lord instead of carrying out our own will. Almost everything that emanates from the Lord is sure to meet with opposition from the world, and those saints who are governed by a worldly spirit.

B[isho]p Edward Hunter was pleased with the disposition shewn last season in the hauling of Rock, and hoped the same liberal spirit will continue, and deem it a privilege ^to lend^ ~~let~~ a helping hand, and accomplish what the Lords servants require of us.

Elder W Woodruff said we ought to rejoice in the privelege of living in a day when we can assist in building a Temple to the name of the Most high—no one since the days of Solomon has had such a privelege. Many efforts have been made to destroy us in this generation, but the hand of God has been outstretched towards us and delivered us from the hands of our enemies. We are abundantly able to do what is required of us if we are only willing.

He felt anxious to respond to the call made last Saturday for funds to emigrate the poor—but having no ready means on hand was the only cause he did not. He would give 1,000 lb. Flour to help feed the hands that work on the Temple.

It was quite a privelege to help build up the Kingdom of God. We cannot take behind the vail any of our property with us, but we can take with us, those blessings that have been put on our heads by the servants of God, if we will only live for them.

Anson Call will give 1,000 lb. flour for the ^Temple.^

Prest. Geo A Smith said it was often the case, that when ~~th~~ the Elders of Israel got tolerably well off they forgot the Lord. For the want of a better understanding, many do not pay a correct tithing—it should always be done at the place and time when we receive our income.

There is much excitement on the Gold and Lead Mines, but do not forget the Lord brethren. Dont drink Tea, Coffee, Whiskey, nor smoke tobacco—nor break the rules of this school. The only way to secure the blessings of the Lord upon us, is to pay our tithing and do right.

Many needed instructions on the principle of self government, ~~a~~ it is not right to give way to passion so as to abuse any one sufficient to call for an acknowledgement.

Spoke of an Elder of Israel who has entered into the most sacred obligation towards his wife—and yet in a moment of passion would try to break those solemn ties, and turn a cold shoulder towards her, this was a disgracefull and lamentable circumstance. ~~We~~ The only way ^we^ can ever govern a Kingdom, is to learn to govern ourselves. Recommended a kind and respectfull treatment towards our wives, ^so^ as to gain a suitable influence over them. Polygamy is a great school for men & women to learn how to govern themselves—that we ^may^ secure the confidence and respect of our families.

Prest. B Young wished the Bishops present to make Known the subjects of the Emigration Fund and labour, and means for the Temple in their respective wards, and report success at Conference.

Hyrum Woolley donated $20.00 towards the Temple.

Benidiction by Prest. Geo A Smith. School adjourned for one week.

April 1, 1871; Saturday

Theological Class ^met^ at the Tabernacle at 1 oclock pm. Present Prest. B[righam] Young presiding. After singing Prayer by Prest. D[aniel] H Wells. Singing.

Emigration Donations[:]

Gustava Leach	50	Wm B Vance	5.00
Mary D[itt]o	50		
C Assmussen	25.00		

Elder L[orenzo] Snow excused ^himself^ for partial inattendance at the ~~business~~ ^school^, on account of business. He stated that he expected shortly to go to Washington [DC] to test the recent rulings of Judge [James B.] McKean, in relation to the setting aside of our Territorial Marshall and General Attorney, and the jurisdiction of our Probate Courts.[28] When these things w~~h~~ere tested before the supreme court of the United States, we could not go further, but have to abide its decisions. He then bore testimony to the truth of the great work of God in which he was engaged.

28. Territorial Chief Justice James B. McKean (1821–79) saw opposition to polygamy as a moral and Christian duty, and he used territorial laws against adultery to indict polygamists. But after he dismissed Mormon officials and empaneled only non-Mormon jurors, the US Supreme Court found his actions unconstitutional. Turner, *Brigham Young*, 364–71; Fitch, *Utah Problem*.

Elder Harrison [from] Cache Valley, spoke well of the saints in that County, (many had been cut off) but the members of the Church were more alive to their duties, the school and other Meetings were well attended. The power and spirit of God rested upon Prest. Young which he proved by the fact of Elders being sent forth by the spirit and power of the priesthood that is upon them, and the promises made by them are verily true and are sure to come to pass. He bore a strong and faithful testimony to the truth.

B[isho]p Andrew Cahoon felt thankful for the privelege of a few moments to speak. He felt a good influence whenever he came to this school. He loved his brethren—will be 47 years old in August—had been in the Church 37 years—had been a Bishop 17 years. He had been charged as being an Apostate,[29] if so, He certainly ought himself to find it out. Visited the first presidency yesterday, and they questioned him somewhat, he felt well in their presence. He ~~desired~~ detested an apostate, for he regarded such as a bitter enemy to this people. The spirit of accusation that meets him, he feels had a strong desire for B[isho]p Cahoon to apostate [apostatize]—and had been circulating, that such was the case. No man can do so, without being an enemy to the Kingdom of God. Since his appointment as Bishop, he has done what was told him to do, even till today—he had many failings, but his Motive was to do good.

He had taken the [Mormon] Tribune[30] till the Volume ~~w~~ run out, had attended one of their meetings—felt like a Cat in a strange garrat [attic]. He did not believe that either [William S.] Godbe or [Elias L. T.] Harrison had any special appointment or authority from God—never did—had read a few spiritualist tracts—had never been to witness any of their spiritual manifestations.

He had lost nearly all faith in miraculous power. Some of his brethren had hurt his feelings by circulating many things about him. Sometimes thought some of his members did ~~not~~ not rally round him to his assistance, as they ought to do. Had tried to do all the good he could—had been regular at all public meetings for 17 years—except when sickness had prevented. Had tried to bring up his family (3 wives and about

29. Cahoon had associated with William Godbe and would be excommunicated three-and-a-half years later on October 8, 1874.

30. A Godbeite publication that within the year would become the *Salt Lake Tribune*.

20 Children) loyal to this Kingdom. He hoped that this influence will cease—he had read the 1st volume of the [Mormon] Tribune, and several works on Spiritualism—the result lead him to investigate the Bible, Book of Mormon & Doctrine & Covenants and to institute one important question viz Is the religion of Andrew Cahoon true or false? that was the question he was seeking to solve. He holds to the priesthood and should he ^not^ do so ^all would be gone^. He had no sympathy with the Godbeites. He was in the habit of reading at home—he reprobated this spirit of persecution. He should never join any other Church, were he cut off from this. If he had acted unwisely was willing to be chastised. He had no desire to injure any body—but he wanted the Spirit of persecution to stop. He did wish there was an opportunity for the Elders to ask questions, and have them answered by the wisest men there was in the Church—he was told, that this was the very place.

Elder W[illia]m G. Young—said that there was a difficultys between B[isho]p Cahoon & his Councillors & Teachers—he heard the B[isho]p make a remark in a public meeting—that he did not believe all the bible, he did not believe in a Devil—at these remarks some of the brethren took exception, and talk[ed] about them, which he very much regretted.

Prest. Geo A. Smith said, after Conference, the 1st Presidency intended to visit B[isho]p A[ndrew] Cahoons ward, and investigate matters and things there. He hoped the brethren would shape themselves with their wives & children, so as to come to Conference with a prayerful heart—that we may have a good time—there was a good deal of apostacy abroad.

Elder Geo Q Cannon said the Cooperative Stock Herd is organized, and will soon be ready to receive stock.

Prest. B Young[:] Wanted the brethren to be prepared for ^an^ organization at Conference for the hauling of rock for the Temple. Bishops, ascertain what you can raise for the Emigrating fund from your wards—and report at Conference. He also recommended the use of Oxen instead of Horses or Mules.

In regard to B[isho]p Cahoon, if He did not know the religion of Jesus Christ was true, without sitting down to study it out now, he had better resign his office ^as^ Bishop. He requested the Bishop to spend a portion of his time in prayer, instead of reading, before the 1st

Presidency went down to visit him—and unless he finds out by that time, that the Gospel is true, he will certainly be dismissed from his Office and another appointed in ~~its~~ his stead.

School adjourned for two weeks at 1 o clock pm. Benediction by Prest. G[eorge] A. Smith.

April 15, 1871; Saturday

Theological Class met at the Tabernacle at one o clock pm. Present Prest. B[righam] Young presiding. Singing. Prayer by Elder Geo Q Cannon. Singing.

Donations to Emigration Fund[:]

Yans Rozengreen	1.00
Ann Maria Beck	1.00
Horace Drake ^12th Ward^	5.00

Elder John Sharp spoke of the building of the Temple, which was something new in this little world, although, we are the only ones who understands the object and purpose of them, and are required to build them as a preparatory work to accomplish the work of Salvation for the whole world. Not only for the living but also the dead. Said the brethren who had been accustomed to the quarrying of Rock, were perfectly willing to go ^at^ it again providing they can get something in exchange for their labour, hence Prest. Young requires some of us to pay our tithing in ~~ab~~ advance so that we can set them to work at once. The Only way of Salvation that he knew anything about was to do what we are told to by those who are over us.

Elder Geo Q Cannon refer'd to a Stock drive which was deemed advisable, owing to the establishment of a Cooperative Stock Herd, and many persons desirous of knowing what stock they had, so that they might determine what amount to put into the Stock herd. The subject was named here to learn the mind of the President and members of the School.

It was Motioned & Seconded That the Drive takes place.

Elder W[ilford] Woodruff suggested that the drive is conducted on a gratuitous principle, so as to avoid the usual cost of 2 or 3 dollars per head, as in former years.

Elder B[righam] Young [Jr] enquired what would be done with the stray~~s~~ animals, provided the owners could not possibly be present—as under such a circumstance, he lost 7 horses, and has never been heard from since.

Elder Geo Q Cannon said the best wisdom would be brought into requisition when the stock was brought here, in relation to the stray.

Elder G[eorge] B. Wallace suggested that what ever course we adopt in relation to the drive and strays, the importance of taking a strictly legal course, so as to avoid the possibility of a law suit by Apostates and Gentiles ~~for tak~~

Elder A M[ilton] Musser said [if we heard] the united voice of the Apostles, Bishops, and people North and South as to what should be done with the Strays—it would be, let them go towards emigrating the poor.

Elder A[mos] Fielding said that the usages of Nations becomes Law, and if the drive is conducted strictly according to law, neither ~~Jew~~ Gentile or Apostate can have any legal claim upon Strays that have never had any brand upon them.

Elder W Woodruff said, if we took ~~of~~ out of the Stock driven up, just what belonged to us, and turned the balance loose again—theives would certainly have fewer to pick from.

Prest. B Young said, if he owned cattle and could not take care of them, he would rather give them even to an enemy, than suffer them to perish on the range—was sorry that his brethren did not take care of theirs.

If a drive is determined upon, let due notice be given in the papers, and by Hand bills throughout this and adjoining Counties. There are no [such thing as] strays, every animal is owned by some of our people, and he was opposed to making any charge to any one who claims their own. [As to the] Temple, we wish~~ed~~ the tithing to go towards the building of the Temple—if the Quarrymen think well to go to work, we will try to have them hauled—and if ~~we~~ the Masons are willing to work, we will promise them bread to eat, a little Meat, some store pay.

He then gave some excellent council on domestic economy, and avoid expensive habits, this he especially intended for the Mechanics working on the Temple. Let us learn how to raise, what we need, we shall soon be able to ~~raise~~ supply New York Market with our fine potatoes &c. He said he had recommended to the Regents of the University to take the 13th 14 & 17th Wards ~~and~~ School Houses, and establish a gradation of Schools and he very much desired to see it attended to forthwith that the children of the City [be] properly classified.

Elder W Woodruff withdrew his Motion for a drive.

Prest. D[aniel] H. Wells Recommended every one to look well after their land titles. The Lord has kindly brought us ~~al~~ out, from what appeared to be an unavoidable collision. It clearly shows that we have been fighting on the line of law, and the decision of the Supreme Court, has ratified every Legislative enactment that was strictly legal, and no act of Congress can set them aside—the attempt, on the part of Judge [James B.] McKean &c was nothing short of trying to accomplish Judicial Murder, which was the most despicable of all Murderers. They undertook to fasten the stigma of Murder on himself, Prest. Young & others, and he for one would like to have all the testimony they have in their possession, to be brought before a proper tribunal—and when found insufficient, to plant a suit upon to have the same placed in ^the^ District Court Record as a testimony to future generations, that those who have been branded and dealt with as Murderors was nothing but a foul & wicked aim at the life of the servants of God.[31]

The School was adjourned for one week at one oclock pm. After singing Benediction by Elder B[righam] Young Jun[io]r.

April 22, 1871; Saturday

Theological Class met in the Tabernacle at One oclock pm. Present Prest. D[aniel] H. Wells presiding (Prest. B[righam] Young being absent at Provo). After singing Prayer by Elder L[orenzo] Snow. Singing.

Elder A[lbert] Carrington spoke of the necessity of each one of us, pushing forward the work on the Temple, many can supply either Clothing, provisions or other things that will be required by the Masons who daily toil there. This council coming from the first Presidency, should be responded to ^by^ us—by all latter day saints.

Also attend more strictly and correctly to our Tithes and Offerings for whatever extent of means we many have obtained by lawful

31. In March, Judge McKean had read instructions to a Third District court jury that claimed "several men in high positions in the [church] have been indicted for high crimes, some of them for murder," without alluding to who had been charged. He may have been foreshadowing his alliance with William Hickman. See Nov. 4, 1871, entry; "Judge McKean to the Grand and Petit Juries," *Deseret News*, Mar. 22, 1871; Turner, *Brigham Young*, 364–65.

~~means~~ effort, we are only stewards over it, and ^should^ spend it, for the building up of the Kingdom of God. The [Perpetual] emigration Fund should also be ~~should~~ strengthened by all the means we have in our power. Reprobated the practise of many of the brethren who have been helped here by the fund, and yet have been very careless about paying that amount back again to the fund &c. He then gave instructions to the Missionaries recently called.

Elder Jno [John] Taylor said that we who remain here, are also on Missions, and should be continually under the guidance and dictation of the Almighty—we should have our wills and passions under the controul of the spirit of the Lord. When going abroad on a Mission, we have no desire to have our own way, but are willing to do anything we are required to do. This should be our constant feeling while living here in these vallies. Spoke of the law of tithing and the importance of living up to it honestly—if we do, God will bless us, and fill our coffers to overflowing, if we neglect it, how easy it is for the Grasshoppers to come and devour the fruits of our toil. Let us cultivate the spirit of the Lord, and be honest, and full of integrity. God is regulated and amenable to Law a thousand times more than we are—and he cannot save any of his Children on any other principle than that of Law, and becoming subject to correct principles. We here are living under the living oracles of God, and however much we may feel ~~K~~ like venerating the Memory of ancient Prophets & Apostles, we should pay more particular heed to Inspired Men in our midst, who are teaching us the mind & will of God.

May God bless you and all Israel is my Prayer, and may his curse be upon her enemies.

Prest. D H Wells read a portion from 30th Chap[ter] 2nd Chronicles and 3rd Malaki—on the subject of tithing & offerings. He employed between 30 & 40 men, and only a very few desired a credit on the tithing books, there has also been quite a number working on the Public Works, and only a portion of them, think or care about paying their tithing—and yet each and every one are calculating on receiving their blessings in the House of the Lord. The saying of Prest. Young that not more than one tenth of the tenth of the increase ~~of~~ is paid into the tithing House. There are many blessings promised to the people of God who pay their tithes and offerings. Let us lay aside doing wrong, and attend to our duties. Tithing is one of the Celestial Laws—and we should observe it, and the Lord will rebuke the devourer for our sakes.

The School was adjourned for one week at one o clock pm. After singing Prayer by Elder G[eorge] Q. Cannon.

April 29, 1871; Saturday

Theological Class met at Tabernacle at One oclock pm. Present Prest. B[righam] Young presiding. After singing prayer by Elder B[righam] Young Jun[io]r. Singing.

Prest. Young said this was the place where questions of doctrine should be brought forward and settled.

Elder Geo Q Cannon then read the rules of the School. There was a unanimous assent to sustain them.

B[isho]p Andrew Cahoon said his religion were the acts of his life—his conduct as a Husband a Father, a Citizen. Many believed that Joseph [Smith] ~~the~~ was a Prophet, and that Brigham [Young] was his lawful successor, and yet were men that could lie, and were anything but good men, hence their religion was false, or their conduct would be better. He regretted that his remarks at a previous school had been misunderstood. He intended to be nearer to Prest. Young than he had been—he had kept too far aloof from him aforetime. He knew that he [Young] was a Father to this whole people, and to him also[;] he felt well in his presence.

Bro A M[ilton] Musser & other Elders had visited him in his ward, and some of his remarks, drew forth from Elder Musser the severest chastisement, which cut him more deeply than Prest. Young ever did but wherein he had failed beforetime he intended to do better in the future, Prest. Young could not drive him from him. He had perused spiritual writings, but had not embraced spiritualism. He had been unwise, and some of the members of his ward had been also, and he did not feel well ~~fo~~ towards them—for they had been handling him (their Bishop) like chopping up mince meat. He intended ^to^ adhere more ~~mo~~ closely to the councils of the servants of God. May God bless the first presidency, the twelve [apostles], and all good men in the Kingdom of God, was his constant prayer. There was something out of geer among the priesthood of his ward, the one appointed as head teacher had not been sustained, he had ~~expres~~ spoken to his councillor a few days ago very severely.

Elder Geo Q Cannon perceived quite an improvement in the spirit and testimony of B[isho]p A[ndrew] Cahoon, for the way he exprest himself a few weeks ago led most to believe that he was in the dark. But to day he bore testimony of the servants of God, and if he ^had^ done so aforetime instead of reading Spiritualist books, he never would have been in the dilemma that he had been in for some time past, if He hoped that He and the Teachers and other authorities in his ward, would meet together tomorrow, in the right spirit, and have all things rectified, was his prayer in the name of Jesus.

Elder John Taylor made a few encouraging remarks on the principle of acknowledging ~~God~~ the hand of God in all things, instancing Job, Abraham, & Jesus as samples. Many may be our troubles & trials, we have God to go to—~~he has a~~ though whomsoever he loveth, he chastens, but if we will only do right, He will defend us, and protect us and bring us off conquerors over every foe.

Elder A. M[ilton] Musser went last Sabbath by (invitation) with others to visit B[isho]p Andrew Cahoons Ward. In speaking after others had spoken, he could not but treat on the subject that others had spoken ^on^. He said he had travelled with Prest. Young and been considerably in his presence for many years—and yet would never offer that as an Apology for Apostacy. In his remarks he did not wish to wound his feelings, for he loved B[isho]p Cahoon and other Bishops, and had sought to benefit and bless them.

Prest. D[aniel] H. Wells said the City Council had contemplated the removal of the present meat Market [First South and Main Street] to a Temporary one, to be ~~re~~ erected on a lot the City had purchased from Bro John Van Cot[t], but the Butchers had petitioned the Council to remain where they are, until a permanent one can be built.

~~Br~~ Prest. Young Motioned. ^& was seconded^ That the city Council be requested to remove the present Market house to the lot lately owned by Bro Jno [John] Van Cott, that the House now used as a boarding House, be torn down, and a good fence put round the lot, after all the trees are cleared off—all to be done in 30 days from this date—Carried unanimously.

Elder [Benjamin] Hulse enjoyed a privelege to day that he had longed for many years past—viz—to live in the midst of the Servants of God. Wanted to live a life time in the service of God.

B[isho]p [Edward] Hunter made a few remarks, about hauling rock, paying tithes and offerings, and the general drive of loose stock on the range.

Moved & Carried. That a Committee of Five be appointed ^to appoint a place^ to receive and distribute the Stock—~~Col[onel] A[lbert] P Rockwood ^H. O. Spencer^, Peter Nebeker, and A Gardner & David Hilton & A H Raleigh &~~

A[lonzo] H. Raleigh—Chairman

A[rchibald] Gardner	Peter Nebeker
Tho[ma]s Jenkins	H[oward] O. Spencer
& David Hilton	

Moved & Carried That Rich[ar]d Morris act as Clerk.

Moved by A[lbert] P. Rockwood & carried That the following be ~~divided into~~ ^observed in the drive^ districts viz. 1st all the range north of the ~~Tooele~~ ^Island^ road[,] 2nd From ~~Tooele road~~ ^Island road^ to ~~Black Rock~~ ^Tooele road^[,] 3rd from ~~Coons~~ the Point of the West Mountain to Harkers springs—4th from Harkers spring to Bingham Kanyon[,] 5th from Bingham Kanyon to ~~Jordan River~~ ^Rose Kanyon^[,] 6th from ^Rose Kanyon to^ ~~Jordan~~ River[,] ^7th From Jordan River^ to South Cottonwood[,] 8th the south part of Davis County.[32]

Moved That	B[isho]p Raleigh take charge of	No 1
D[itt]o " "	J. Weiler " " "	No 2
" " " "	Tho[ma]s Jenkins—	" 3
"	B[isho]p Miller—	" 4
"	Sam[ue]l Bateman	5
"	B[isho]p A[ndrew] Cahoon—	6
"	I. M. Stewart—	7
"	B[isho]p J. Stoker—	8

Moved & Carried That the drive Committee be at their posts on Tuesday ~~evening~~ ready to start with their drive on Wednesday ^& Thursday^ ~~morning~~ and taken to ~~the~~ Jordan Bridge till further orders.

~~B[isho]p Hunter~~ Br[other] J[esse] C. Little said they wished the drive to be conducted in a very careful manner. Those interested in stock on the range are expected to go and when brought in, no charge to

32. Tooele and Harker's Canyon are west of Salt Lake City and south of the Great Salt Lake, so the proposed cattle-drive districts started southwest and moved east to Bingham and Rose Canyon, near Herriman, then to Cottonwood on the southeast bench of the Wasatch mountain range.

be made for driving—all that are not claimed to be carefully herded, and when the owners apply for them, they must pay the herd bill. It is distinctly understood that the above arrangements are entirely entered into, without the council or authority of Prest. Young, though he is willing to render them any assistance that ~~lies in his power~~ is necessary.

School adjourned for one week at one oclock pm. Benediction by Elder Geo Q Cannon.

May 6, 1871; Saturday

Theological Class met at Tabernacle at One oclock pm. Present Prest. B[righam] Young presiding. After singing Prayer by B[isho]p L[orenzo] Young. Singing.

B[isho]p [Edward] Hunter made a few remarks on the recent drive, that what Horses were not claimed, were turned over Jordan [River]. What Cattle were not claimed are taken and herded on good feed, and the owners can have them by paying a very moderate price.

Elder Geo Q Cannon said, that as there seems to be some difficulty in starting a Co-perative Herd here, and as one is already started in Davis County, those who desire it may patronize that Herd, if they cannot get up one here.

Elder Peter Nebeker mentioned several discouraging circumstances that had attended his efforts in starting a Cooperative Herd.

Elder H[oward] Spencer said if there was more union in the directors there would be no difficulty in starting a Cooperative Herd.

Prest. B Young said that one of the great objections he had to a general drive, was the opportunity it afforded thieves to take a full description of the unclaimed stock, so that they can make a full sweep ~~if after~~ of it when they are turned back again on the range. He then Moved and was carried That the Bishops of the Territory consider themselves a Committee to gather means for the Emigration of the poor. The Bishops are appointed to attend to the spiritual and Temporal affairs of their Wards—and their responsibilitys resting upon them are so great, that when the books are opened, and they are judged, they will be found to stand between the people and their duties. He then spoke of the importance of each one paying promptly their fast offerings. [He] illustrated the principle of Faith by several examples—time was an important element of wealth if rightly used.

They had commenced to labour on the railroad south [and] in a few days the Iron will be here, and will be laid down, and they calculated to keep on till they got through the Territory.[33] He then encouraged the people to raise Wool, but do not think of selling it to go out of the Territory. For the Provo Factory alone, they require over 700,000 lbs of wool for this year—and the quantity will not produce enough cloth to supply the County of Utah. Hence the necessity of more Wool and more factories.

Mining—The Lord has seen fit to open the Mines. Though the best has not yet been found, yet while the Money is somewhat easy, pay up for your land—secure every claim by forming a company and not become excited. Let us use our Means to gather the poor, to build factories, School Houses &c the time will come when the Machinery and other things that are being brought here to develope the Mines—will be dispose[d] of in a similar way to those at Camp Floyd[34]—and these ~~b~~ excitements will all pass away. He wanted to deal out the word of the Lord to the Elders at the school, but when organized found the spirit of apostacy, and had to withhold it—and apostacy was still here.

He then enquired how many of the County Court were present, & Judge [Elias] Smith, R[euben] Miller, B[isho]p I[saac] M. Steward & Bro [George A.] Neal stood up. He then asked them for the privelege of using the Street west of State road—for the Railway to run south, each one acquiesced and promised to grant a County right for that purpose.

He then recommended the brethren not to sell their Land to outsiders, ^nor^ ~~not~~ expose their families by taking strangers ~~as~~ in to board, but where families came along that needed board, if you have convenience, take them in, charge a good price, and make a good profit from them.

Bro [Welcome] Chapman gave some of his experience in raising 11 Wagon loads of provisions for the Temple ~~at~~ hands at Nauvou—and labouring on the Council House soon after ~~eo~~ he came in here in 1848—without any expectation of being remunerated for it.

---

33. This became the Utah Southern Railroad, acquired by Union Pacific in 1875. Despite the name, the line built by Mormons only extended south of present-day Santaquin, still in the northern part of the state. While it eventually reached Milford, no rail line to St. George and the more populous southern parts of the state was built. The Los Angeles Salt Lake Railroad line, completed in the early twentieth century, went west into Nevada and offered stage service to southern Utah.

34. When the army left in the early 1860s, equipment at Camp Floyd sold for pennies on the dollar.

B[isho]p John Sharp recognized the principle of chastisement as being of God, was thankful to experience it himself. Spoke of his recent visit East to purchase Iron &c for our new Southern Railroad. Much excitement and many questions he met with there.

Prest. Young made a few remarks in favour of a peace policy.

Meeting adjourned for one week at 1 pm. After singing Benediction by Elder B[righam] Young Jun[io]r.

May 13, 1871; Saturday

Theological Class met at the Tabernacle at One oclock pm. Present Prest. B[righam] Young presiding. After singing Prayer by Elder J[esse] C Little. Singing.

Prest. B Young in speaking on the authority of a Bishops ~~and his~~ Council, as to whether in the absence of a Bishop, his Council can take up the case of Membership and act upon it. He said, the law of God on this subject was very definite in the Book of Doctrine and Covenants and should be observed with the utmost exactness—or we will imperceptibly slide away from the thread of the Gospel law.

What makes a Bishop? Why, unless a literal descendant of Aarron can be found, we take a High Priest and Ordain and set him apart to act in the duties of the Lesser Priesthood.[35] If a Member of his, transgresses for lying, theft, Adultery &c that member is summoned before him, and his councilors. The facts of the case are then brought out by testimony—if the facts are sustained, the Bishop can cut them off, if the party accused is not satisfied, they can take an appeal to the High Council, and from there to the 1st Presidency and from there to the General Conference, all this is their right.

In the absence of a Bishop and his first Councillor the second Councillor has the right to call up before him and the authorities of the Ward, any member who ~~h~~is wicked—and sever him from the Church as far as their fellowship is concerned, that Councillor should then take the case before the High Council for their sanction.

A Question was then asked by B[isho]p Phineas Young as to ~~the aut~~ whether a Bishop has the right to take away a lot from one of his members who had two lots, and dispose of it to some one else, allowing that lot to be adjudicated by a committee as to its value.

35. This teaching regarding the calling of a bishop, and the rights of direct descendants of biblical Aaron to that office, comes from D&C 68:16–20.

Prest. Young said, has a Bishop the right to take away a Horse, a Cow, or a Wife, belonging to any one else, and give to another? He said Bishops as well as others do many things they should not do. And any member of their Ward thus agrieved, have recourse before the ^High^ Council, have all the facts of the case brought out, and righteously adjudicated upon.

He then spoke of the eternal variety there is in the appearance of the Human countenance and equally so in their experience after receiving the Gospel—and we must not expect every person to pass through precisely the same as ourselves.

He then spoke of the various gifts bestowed upon the saints of God, one has one gift, another has another, but a third may not have any great manifestation of the Spirit, and yet all may be equally good and acceptable in the sight of God. Many of these remarks were made in consequence of some stringent statements made by an Elder last Sunday Morning when preaching, (that all persons must find out and experience a Knowledge, that God loves us). We must not measure every one by our own half bushel.

~~The Question was then submitted whether the decissions of a Bishop without Councillors are strictly binding? and whether an appeal to the High Council would'nt be entertained without regard to the crime charged.~~

Elder James Leach gave a brief account of his [conversion] experience.

Elder Geo Q Cannon enjoyed much, the remarks made last Sunday Morning, and also those of Prest. Young to day—and rehearsed a portion of his [conversion] experience.

~~Prest. Young~~

Elder Geo Goddard gave a short account of his experience after receiving the Gospel.

Prest. Young made a few more remarks on the temptations of Satan, in his assails ~~towards~~ upon the Saints.

He then enquired for the Probate Judge of Davis Co[unty] and select men, and then asked them if they would grant the Utah Central R[ail] R[oad] Co[mpany] the privelege of a street from ~~Centerville~~ Centerville [to the train depot]—which was granted. He then complained of the City Corporations & County Court, who have never voted the first Dollar towards the building of the Railroad which enhances the value of property all around. They ought at least to vote $50,000 each—instead of allowing the Company to carry such a heavy burthen.

He then said that he thought of sending his Son Willard to West Point to get his Education, hitherto an outsider had always been sent—but if the school were willing he should like to send him, and a unanimous vote was given.

School was adjourned for one week at 1 oclock. After singing Benediction by B[righam] Young Jun[io]r.

May 20, 1871; Saturday

Theological Class met at the Tabernacle at One oclock PM. Present Prest. B[righam] Young presiding. After singing Prayer by Elder A[lbert] P Rockwood. Singing.

~~E~~ B[isho]p Levi Stewart exprest his gratitude at meeting again in the School of the Prophets, having been absent for about 12 Months on a Mission to the Kanab Country,[36] whither he had been sent to establish a settlement, spoke of the peaceable disposition of the Navajoe~~s~~ Indians, and other tribes. The Country is a fine Grazing place—better than for Farming. Heat not so oppressive as here, it was a Healthy climate—many of the settlers had commenced to plant out Orchards. He rejoiced in the principles of truth, and realized there was yet much to do in building up the Kingdom of God.

Prest. D[aniel] H. Wells spoke of the responsibilities resting upon us, inasmuch as God had marked out for us the way. There are great blessings laid up in store for the faithful, but in order to obtain them, we must not indulge in immoral acts ~~or let us~~ let no one suppose that secret sins can be indulged in with impunity, God and himself certainly knows of those sins, and we will come to a certain point in our experience when we will become our own accusers. For all secret sins, will be made manifest on the house tops. We are now living in a time of test, and God is trying us to see if we can endure without wavering, so that he can entrust us with the Kingdom. Spoke of the value and importance of ~~im~~ observing the Word of Wisdom, which many were neglecting. Let us strip ourselves of the ways of the World that ^are^ not congenial with the Spirit of the ~~world~~ Gospel—explained

36. Kanab is on the Utah–Arizona border, roughly halfway between St. George to the west and what is now Lake Powell to the east.

the correct principle of equality. God has the best Government on earth, and has visited his Saints himself, and sent his angels in different times, but are we prepared for those. We cannot steady the Ark[37]—but we can work with God and his servants and assist to establish his Kingdom.

The following Question was answered[:] Are the decisions of a Bishop~~s~~ without Councilors, strictly binding, and whether an appeal to the High Council, wouldn't be entertained without regard to the crime charged.

Elder Geo Q Cannon read several extracts on the subject out of the Doctrine & Covenants—showing that for a decision to be valid, a Bishop must have his Councillors, unless he be a literal descendant of Aarron.

Elder Elias Smith, Judge of Probate made a few remarks on the Location of the new line of railroad south, that the County are willing to pay a reasonable price for land through which the Railroad will go, owned by ~~prof~~ private individuals—but nothing exorbitant.

Prest. B Young said, any man who wants pay for the few ~~f~~ feet of land needed for the Railroad to pass through, is unfit to live in a decent community, and no desire to assist in building up the Country. If we dont mind, we shall never own a foot of land on the Earth—let us try, and look at things as they are—dont let us be blind, naked, foolish & covetous.

School adjourned for one week at One o clock. After singing Benediction by Elder G Q Cannon.

May 27, 1871; Saturday

Theological Class met at Tabernacle at One o clock pm. Present Prest. B[righam] Young presiding. After singing Prayer by B[isho]p Jno [John] Sharp. Singing.

Elder John Taylor, in all our acts, and in every relationship of life we should ever seek to be under the inspiration of the almighty, then we will never go estray. Most of the blunders we make through life is in consequence of not having the Counsels of the Lord.

A Bishop or High Councillor living under the influence of the Holy Ghost will always have the spirit of revelations to dictate, govern and decide upon every case that comes before them, so with every man holding the Holy Priesthood. A Teacher thus imbued is more honorable than an Apostle who does not magnify his calling—&c.

37. See 2 Samuel 6, when Uzzah is struck dead for steadying the Ark of the Covenant to prevent it from tipping over, a cautionary tale about overstepping one's authority.

Elder [Robert] Collins bore testimony to the value and blessing of enjoying the good spirit of the Lord and exprest his determination to a renewed ~~exer~~ observance of the Word of Wisdom.

Elder [blank][38] exprest a similar resolve—to renewed diligence in the work of the Lord.

B[isho]p Jno Sharp when men speak by the good spirit of the Lord, it was music to him, to listen to them. He then spoke of the great increase of Machinery that has been imported to this Territory for Manufacturing wool into cloth. There are parties now here offering our Wool growers 2 or 3 cents per lb more, than our Brethren are giving who have Factories, is it wisdom to sell wool to be sent off, and thus let our Machinery lie idle, and our hands idle also?

He suggested an extension of Cooperation, to take hold of, not only ~~in~~ the Manufacturing department, but also the Banking and Exchange business. The same cooperative principle had been suggested by Prest. Young in the different kinds of labour to be performed on the Temple. The only way we were ever taught in our early experience, to be saved, viz to do as we were told.

Elder [Emanuel M.] Murphy was a patron of home maufacture &c. ~~complained of a lack of water which some o were using on the bench~~

Elder Ja[me]s Cummings spoke on the subject of Machinery and the maufactory of Wool into Cloth. Complained of some large wool growers, who have acquired great wealth for their Mining claims who would rather send their wool East because they can get Money for it, rather than let our Manufacturers have it, in exchange for Cloth. Spoke of the remunerative business in the raising the wool, over that of the making Wool into cloth by Machinery & the importance of sustaining home manufactory.

Elder W[ilford] Woodruff, spoke on the same subject, shall we sustain our own Machinery and Manufactories, or shall we neglect it. We ought to study the interests of Zion, if we dont study its interests, we had better ~~g~~ leave and go to California. We had better cooperate in everything that will build up Zion. We have the power to build a Temple and occupy it—a privilege which the ancient apostles never had. We are

38. Joseph F. Smith noted that "two brethren unknown to me bore their testimony to the truth of Mormonism." JFSJ, May 27, 1871.

building a Zion here, though Earth & Hell are opposing us—whatever Council is given us, let us carry it out.

Prest. B Young said that by and bye, he expected water to be brought ~~from~~ along the [South Jordan River] Canal now in progress, and other Canals will be built to convey water along the base of the Eastern Mountains, and all the land between there and Mill Creek &c. also from Utah Lake to Davis County, and a portion along the base of the Western Mountains, as far as Tooele Co[unty].

Speaking of Wool, said those who have wool and must have money for it, he would pay them Money ~~for it~~ and as much as Eastern buyers are paying.

It was the intention of God to raise up a Kingdom of Priests, and from among this people—and He (Prest. B Y[oung]) felt it his duty to assist them in becoming such—but they are slow to learn, though they have Eyes but see not, have Ears but hear not, yet as a people we are a Wonder to the World, we have good peace, now, but shall have more, if the people will only do right. The Rock being hauled for the Temple must be hauled on labour Tithing alone, and if the Bishops cannot accomplish this, He will haul it all himself. Look after the Poor in their Wards, and not allow them to go near the Tithing Office.

Next Saturday & Sunday will be a two days meeting at Ogden. Rec[eive]d of Geo Anderson $2.50 for P[erpetual] E[migrating] F[und].

School adjourned for one week at one oclock. After singing Benediction by [blank].

June 3, 1871; Saturday

Theological Class met in Tabernacle at one oclock p.m. Present Elder Orson Pratt presiding. The first Presidency ~~being~~ and most of the twelve [apostles] being absent on a two days meeting—at Ogden. After singing prayer by Elder G[eorge] B. Wallace. Singing.

Elder O[rson] Pratt gave liberty to the School for either Business or remarks.

Elder John Taylor, would like to see a good degree of freedom manifested by the members of the school. We are all on one common level—and though he believed in Presidencies and position in the Kingdom of God, yet it was very common for the Holy Spirit to reveal some things to obscure individuals, that are not made Known to others, hence an exchange of ideas and reflections are profitable to all. We are all the children of God, and should try to overcome a bashfull feeling, and rise up to speak when anything rests upon the mind. Every man in his place should be respected and honored—and let us respect ourselves—this was the Prophet Joseph Smiths Council to the Elders in his day, Let us try to elevate ourselves mentally, morally & physically. Do unto others, as you would they should do to you. Let our word be our bond.

Elder [Daniel] Shearer had never spoken in the school, though he had been a member a long time. He deprecated the spirit of discontent which he had noticed in some—let us try to be contented and happy. Some continue in the Church for a long time, naturally smart and are humble, and are on a level with the body. But when they ~~as~~ get a little of this worlds goods, seem to cultivate the spirit of pride and ambition, and can hardly notice their poorer brethren, this was a dangerous condition to be in. He then adverted to the condition of the Jews, at the time when Jesus came—and that of the Gentiles when the Book of Mormon came ^forth^, it reveals to us the true mode of baptism and the unchristian method of sprinkling infants—which is a mockery to God.

Elder G[eorge] B. Wallace complained of many who come to him to seek council in his official capacity—and finding that in some cases—the decisions of men holding the priesthood do not agree with some holding a Civil capacity. Let the priesthood and officers in the Kingdom always act in concert, and the difficulties that so often arise would cease. He also complained of some of the Theatrical Officials enticing away his children to act as Supes [extras] without any consultation or consent of their parents.

Elder Orson Pratt we now occupy a position as a people very different to what we shall do in a day to come. In Jan[uar]y 2nd 1831—the Lord said, you shall be a free people and shall have no Laws but mine to govern you.[39] We now, are mixed up in our government and allied more or less with Civil Authority, it was so with the Jews—by their own special request—asking for a King—which God granted—in his displeasure, and more or less revealed to those Kings his mind and will through his Prophets. It was the same on this continent, and Nephi by ~~sp~~ universal request became their first King—and was a good and

39. A reference to God telling Joseph Smith that Zion would be prepared for the Saints. See D&C 38:22

righteous man—he entirely acquiesced in the remarks of Bro Wallace—viz the importance of the Civil and Ecclesiastical authorities being united and in strict harmony with each other. The day will come when Civil authority will mostly cease. Kings and Priests will hold their authority, and governed by revelations.

It is of the highest importance that the decisions of our High Councils and Bishops Courts should perfectly harmonize with the Laws to which we are amenable.

School was then adjourned for one week at one oclock pm. After singing Benediction by Elder J[ohn] Taylor.

June 10, 1871; Saturday

Theological Class met at the Tabernacle at One oclock pm. Present Prest. B[righam] Young presiding. After singing prayer by Elder J[esse] C Little. Singing.

Elder Geo Q Cannon read a notice pertaining to the Celebration of the 4th July.[40]

Elder J[ohn] R. Winder Chairman of [the July 4th celebration] Committee, stated the object of the Committee, which was, to have an expression of Mechanics & Artizans, as to whether they will turn out on that occasion by a general display of their several branches of labour, or simply be represented by banners &c.

B[isho]p A[lonzo] H. Raleigh & J[ohn] B. Maiben, exprest a hearty desire to have the day well and thoroughly celebrated—both by Military and Civilians.

Prest. B Young said, if a celebration be attempted, let it be done as it should be, he would suggest that a good Military display be introduced in the procession, Trades be represented also, and a universal turn out of Farmers, ^&^ Artisans, ^if^ School children are there let them be protected from the Sun.

Moved & Seconded & Carried, That ^a^ Committee from Farmers & Mechanics ^& others^ be Nominated now. The different Committees were then Nominated and can be found on separate sheets of paper.

40. The church planned to commemorate US Independence Day with celebrations, but clashed once again with federal authorities when they attempted to have the territorial militia march. Instead, children walked carrying flowers as part of a procession, with banners and decorations installed throughout the city, including in the Tabernacle at Temple Square. "Independence Day," *Deseret News*, July 5, 1871.

B[isho]p R[euben] Miller of Mill Creek sent a letter to Prest. Young, and was read to the School ~~was read~~ by Elder Geo Q Cannon requesting the privelege of having the Water of Big Cottonwood turned into the Canal so that it might be used by the farmers in Mill Creek Ward, whose crops were languishing for want of water.

In response to this, Prest. Young, the Members of the school and Members of the County Court gave their unanimous consent and a Note was sent to B[isho]p R Miller giving him the privilege.

School was adjourned for one week at One o clock pm. After singing Benediction by Elder B[righam] Young Jun[io]r.

June 17, 1871; Saturday

Theological Class met at the Tabernacle at one o clock pm. Present Prest. B[righam] Young presiding. After singing Prayer by Elder J[oseph] F. Smith. Singing.

By request of W[ilford] W. Woodruff[,] B[isho]p R[euben] Miller reported that some 80 Men and Boys turned out last Monday to dig a ditch to admit water from Big Cottonwood Creek to the Canal, and had succeeded, which had proved a great blessing to the people.

Elder [Samuel] Turnbow spoke of some 50 five acre lots that was in a parched and suffering condition for want of water. He then notified the owners of said lots to meet him on Monday to assist in letting more water into the Canal. A Note was addressed to Prest. Young by a Member of the School soliciting ~~ane~~ an explanation of the 10th Section in the Book of Doctrine & Covenants.[41]

Elder Geo Q Cannon & Prest. Young each gave an explanation. It was shown that a Glorified being had power to communicate to persons in any part of the earth, ~~and~~ he may also be sitting in this congregation, go home with any of us for supper and we supposing him to be a Brother from a distance.

Considerable explanation was given by Prest. Young to questions ~~by~~ put by several members of the School.[42]

41. Joseph Smith, after realizing the first 116 pages he had dictated from the Book of Mormon were lost, received a revelation that became D&C 10. It asserted that "wicked men" had altered the text to embarrass Smith and that he should continue the dictation without revisiting those earlier pages.

42. One of Young's answers explained that "Eloheim, Yahova, & Michael, were father, Son and grandson. They made this Earth & Michael became Adam." JFSJ, June 17, 1871.

Prest. B Young then spoke of the Camp Meeting now being ~~being~~ held by the Methodists, he was very sorry that some little interruption had taken place last evening by some one asking questions. This he was very sorry for, and made a particular request that some Teachers from each ward, be sent there to night, and prevent any disturbance.

Meeting was then adjourned for one week at one o clock pm. After singing Benediction by Elder G[eorge] Q Cannon.

June 24, 1871; Saturday

Theological Class met at the Tabernacle at One o clock pm. Prest. B[righam] Young presiding. After singing prayer by B[isho]p John Sharp. Singing.

Prest. D[aniel] H. Wells said we lived in an eventful period—and are going through a tuition [tutorial], how to aid and assist in the building up of the Kingdom of God. Hence we come to this school that we may be taught how to become one, and ~~become~~ better acquainted with those principles of righteousness that God has revealed. But the Enemy is on the alert and seeking in every possible way to ~~secure~~ seduce and draw away the Saints from the observance of those duties.

Complained of the negligence of the Saints in not going to meeting~~—going~~ ~~not~~ attending ward meetings, paying fast offerings &c. Spoke of the corroding influence of wealth among the Saints. We should live under the benign influence of the priesthood. If we felt right [with God], we should hasten to volunteer and be anxious to do whatever we are required to do. He said that he hoped every one among the Latter day saints will turn out and celebrate the birthday of our National Independence and thus sustain the efforts of our spirited Committee.

Elder Levi Richards adverted to the lack of attention that is paid to the sanitary condition of our City. Recommended the free use of dry earth which is the finest deodorizer in the world—deprecated ~~us~~ the use of Colouring matter in Cheese, Candy &c, also the poisonous influence of Mother Winslows Soothing Syrup,[43] Godfreys Cordial[44] &c,

43. Charlotte Winslow was a nurse who studied children's teething. Her product was marketed as Mrs. Winslow's syrup, first produced in 1849. Its ingredients contained morphine, sodium carbonate, spirits of foenicula (fennel), and aqua ammonia (ammonium hydroxide).

44. Godfrey's Cordial, named after Thomas Godfrey of Herefordshire, England, was

the base of which is Opium, and its effects on the infant system is most deleterious. Tobacco produced more positive injury ~~th~~ on the human intellect than all other poisons put together.

B[isho]p Phineas Young condemned the use of Walkers Vinegar Bitters[45]—which has ~~to~~ been freely taken by many in our midst, naming several instances of sudden death which occurred, he verily believed, from their use. He had used himself to chewing & smoking tobacco for many years—but at length became convinced of its baneful effects and has left it off entirely. ~~ane~~ He did not think that God would ever require anything of his people but what he would give them strength to perform it. Several other speakers denounced the use of Tobacco, Liquor &c.

Prest. D. H. Wells advocated the free use of dry earth to deodorize the effluvia [odor] arising from human execrence, stables, &c. when done it makes the best kind of fertilizing element.

Prest. B Young urged the City Council, the passing of stringent laws to enforce cleanliness throughout the City. A Vote was then taken and unanimously sustained, That the City Council take immediate~~ly~~ steps to purify and cleanse the City. He & Bro Geo A Smith were going up North for a few weeks. & hoped [blank].

Meeting was then adjourned for one week at one o clock pm. After singing Benediction by Elder G[eorge] Q. Cannon.

July 1, 1871; Saturday

The School met at One o clock pm in the Tabernacle. Present Prest. D[aniel] H. Wells presiding. (Prest. B[righam] Young, Geo A Smith and several of the twelve [apostles] having started last Monday Morning for Bear Lake &c for a few weeks.) After singing prayer by Elder Amos Fielding. Singing.

Prest. D. H. Wells gave liberty for any member of the School to speak.

Elder Geo Q Cannon said he was pleased with the prospects and surroundings of the Church and Kingdom of God. Though there are a

---

a patented medicine given to children to ease pain and help them to sleep. It contained sassafras, opium, brandy, caraway seed, and treacle (molasses).

45. Joseph Walker's vinegar bitters was called a "blood purifier" made entirely from alcohol and vegetables. The claim that it brought on "sudden death" was probably an exaggeration, though bad patent medicine could poison consumers.

great influx of strangers coming among us, and much opposition manifested towards us, by apostates &c, yet did not believe there is anything going to happen, but what will tend to our benefit, and the Glory of God enhanced by it.

Many coming here by Railway are actually fulfilling the prophecies, some of the most influential men of the Nation, visiting here express their astonishment at what they see and there never was a time when so many strangers had been brought under the sound of the Gospel. He earnestly desired that God would overrule the developement of our minerals, for the good of the saints and enhance the Glory of God. He lamented the practice of many of our young people who were learning to smoke, & drink—hoped the Elders of Israel would set before them a good example.

Rejoiced in the liberty that God has given us, and hoped that each would put on a bold front, and maintain~~ed~~ it, even at the risk of our lives, he despised a temporizing spirit—prayed that God would bless his people and enable us to do our duty.

B[isho]p A[lonzo] H. Raleigh spoke of the corruption of our Government, both Politically, Religiously, and Morally, as much so, perhaps as any Nation that was ever destroyed on account of its iniquities. Refer'd to the proclamation issued in this Mornings paper by the Acting Governor, Secretary [George A.] Black,[46] to prohibit ~~the~~ any ~~f~~ Military procession on July 4th—as announced ~~C~~ in programme, by the Committee.[47] He strongly recommended the quiet observance of the original programme, and leave the result in the hands of God, dont let us be afraid to take a firm stand, only let us know that we are right, then go ahead.

On Covenants, he said that no man can come here in this school and make a Covenant that he will Keep the Word of Wisdom, with a feeling in his heart that he will continue to break that Covenant, without losing the spirit of God, and sooner or later ^will^ apostatize from the Church. Every one alone is responsible to God for his conduct, each one is here on a Mission, and should act, not as eyeservants,[48] but with

46. George A. Black (1841–1914) was the secretary of the territory and acting governor until George L. Woods, the newly appointed governor, arrived in Utah. Woods would serve until 1875.

47. See also Nov. 26, 1870, entry.

48. That is, a person who obeys only when watched.

as much precision as if there was no other creature on the earth, but to do our duty naturally, because we ^are^ here for that purpose.

Elder [Robert H.] Collins was anxious to observe the Word of God from the Mouth of his prophet, and shake no blow or resistance ~~aga~~ till the prophet says Arise and thrash O ye Captive daughter of Zion.

Elder A[mos] Fielding advocated the strict observance of the word of wisdom, and not imitate the bad practises of the Gentiles.

A Governor that will violate his oath and trample under foot the Constitution, to bring trouble upon this people, God will curse, and he did not feel himself too good to curse him.

Prest. D. H. Wells said that two weeks ago, a Committee was appointed [to organize a July 4 celebration], and they issued a programme, all that are in favour of carrying it out, hold up their hands, and all lifted up their hands. He should not countermand his orders, for a portion of the Military to take part in the celebration of the Nations Birthday. If we are to be abridged of such a palpable right—we may expect that every other right and liberty will be swept away from us.

The School was adjourned for one week at one oclock pm. After singing Benediction by Elder Orson Pratt.

July 8, 1871; Saturday

Theological Class met at the Tabernacle at one oclock pm. Present Prest. D[aniel] H. Wells presiding. After singing Prayer by B[isho]p L[orenzo] Young. Singing.

Elder Orson Pratt said it was a source of joy to see so many of the Servants of God, meet here week after week, and learn so many things which they could not learn in our mixed assemblies—and which have a tendency to good amongst the people of this Territory. Spoke of the various organizations established in the outside world—such as Temperance Society's, Bible Societies &c. Woman Suffrage Society &c all of which are good there, but are not at all necessary among us. As the evils such societies are intended to correct do not exist to such an extent ^here^ as to ~~ne^e^dt~~ need them. There is one evil however indulged in here, that a Female organization might profitably be employed ^to correct^, viz patterning after the Gentile Fasheons, and teach that portion of Law which was given 40 years ago, for the Saints to wear garments of their own make and fasheon &c.

Another evil is indulged in here, that needs correcting. viz for a Young Man to undertake to keep company with a daughter without first asking the consent of her Parents. In this, there needs a reformation. The day will come when even young men will counsel their parents pertaining to their marriage associations. Before we as a people go back to Jackson Co[unty, Missouri], we have got to ~~bef~~ become a pure people~~—we~~ we must have a standard of our own, and discard foolish Gentile fasheons.

B[isho]p Lorenzo Young enquired if the Revelation refered to by Bro Pratt, pertaining to our garments being the workmanship of our own hands—had more reference to the time we returned to Jackson Co[unty] than it does at the present.

His religion was more precious to him to day than at any previous time—it was good to him by night and by day, had over come many old bad habits, such as drinking Tea, getting Angry, ^&c^. ~~wearing plain clothing &c and~~ He hoped to see the greatest men in Israel setting such examples as they wish us to follow—he wanted to see Bishops, Presidents and heads of families to set such a lead in fasheons, as ~~h~~ is becoming Latter Day Saints.

Elder Phineas Richards said that there is no subject of greater importance to talk about Than the word of Wisdom. Some exult in the observance of it by abstaining from Tea & Coffee, when those very ones will crowd their plates with meat, and perhaps take hot water which is as injurious as either tea or coffee. He then exposed some of the false methods of dealing with their children in their general government.

B[isho]p L[orenzo] Young spoke of the looseness of the reins that now hand upon Israel and the time being near by when the head will begin to draw the reins a little tighter.

Elder Geo B Wallace took another view of the subject of dress—Viz that some who meet in our public assemblies, are so filthy in their person, ~~and~~ clothing and habits as to be a disgrace to the rest. Some persons therefore have as much need to rise up a little higher in these things while it is the duty of others to come down & be more modest & retiring in their dress &c.

Prest. D. H. Wells said he supposed we all might ~~all~~ do a little better than we do, if we were to try. No one, two or three persons can rule the tide of fasheon. It is somewhat curbed in this community—and will be more and more. He would be glad if we could make our own Hats & Bonnets. Prest. [Brigham] Young has done more to make and wear home made clothing than any other family, except some in the Country who make nearly all their families wear. He did not approve of the fasheons of the day, but he did like to see neat and graceful attire. He hoped the remarks made to day would have a beneficial influence on our families.

School was adjourned for one week at One o clock pm. Benediction by Elder G[eorge] Q Cannon.

July 15, 1871; Saturday

Theological Class met at the Tabernacle at one o clock pm. Present Prest. D[aniel] H. Wells presiding. After singing Prayer by Elder E[dward] Stevenson. Singing.

Elder Jno [John] Taylor who had just returned from a visit to the East, spoke of the vague and indefinate notions of God and Eternity, entertained by the religious world. They dont know God, nor the plan of salvation, he felt thankful for his standing as a member of the Kingdom of God and then contrasted the value of a Knowledge of the Gospel as revealed from God, with the uncertain dogmas and theories of Man made systems. Refered to our Baptisms, Confirmations, officiating for our dead, Marriage for time & eternity, sealing Ordinances for our Wives and children, in all of these things, the world is totally ignorant of, and he felt so thankful for such inestimable blessings, that in returning to the bosom of the Church again, he felt like shouting Hallelujah.

Elder M[ilford] B. Shipp returned Missionary from England, esteemed it a great privelege to mingle again with his brethren in the tops of the Mountains. Was truly thankful to his Heavenly Father for his constant watchcare that had been around him since he left here, some two years ago. He considered the Religious world were fast drifting to a species of infidelity. He had much joy in his [missionary] labours.

The Elders sent from here, all felt well and ^when^ they occasionally met at the various Conferences, it was a time of great rejoicings. After making a few more remarks expressive of thankfulness & gratitude, he prayed that God would bless his people &c.

Elder Cha[rle]s Lambert had been on a Mission to England for the past 9 months. Had a good time while there, and very thankful to return he then related some of his experience when he arrived in Nauvou. He laid the last stone on the Nauvou Temple—came to these Mountains in 1849 and rejoiced in the work of God up to the present time.

Bishop [Thomas] Callister (Beaver [Utah]) felt it to be a great privelege to ~~H~~ come to this school. Ten years ago he was called on a [colonizing] Mission to Beaver, had taken much satisfaction in his labours. This school had accomplished a great amount of good throughout the Valley. So much has had been done in his sphere of action, was mostly attributable to the influence exerted through the instructions imparted in this school, he felt well in the testimony of his brethren, and calculated to use his influence to build up the Kingdom of God.

Elder Nephi Pratt said he believed it was necessary for a Young Man to go out into the world, to obtain a testimony of the truth of the Gospel, for the majority of young men that are reared up here, enjoy at times the spirit of the Lord. But when far away from friends and connexions, and having to rely ~~wholey~~ entirely on God and his promises and to open his Mouth in defense of the truth, then it is that the spirit of testimony comes upon him.

Elder Geo Q Cannon was always delighted to listen to the testimonies of our young Elders. Our united duty as Elders of Israel was at the present time to sustain and rally around the Priesthood—especially at the present time~~s~~ when at attempt was made to assail us at our Election.

New York City will yet be drenched with blood, notwithstanding their anxiety to bring trouble upon the Latter Day Saints. Let us be strong in the Lord our God, and we have nothing to fear. He will give us the supremacy in these Mountains.

Prest. D H Wells hoped every Man in Israel would be on hand at the day of Election and deposit his vote for the right men—and not go blindly at it, and vote haphazard as some good men did last Election, he warned his brethren against exposing themselves in the hot sun, lest they should receive a sun stroke, dont drink Liquor. He spoke of the good crop that we are about to be blest with, we should be firm, true & faithful and endeavour to conciliate each other when[49] any misunderstanding arises, and thus avoid angry passions, and unpleasant words. Let us be united in building up the Kingdom of God.

49. The remaining portion of this entry is written vertically, somewhat obscuring the horizontal text already recorded.

Meeting was adjourned for One ~~Month~~ Week at one oclock pm. Benediction by Elder Orson Pratt.

July 29, 1871; Saturday

Theological Class met at the Tabernacle at One oclock pm. Present Prest. B[righam] Young presiding. After singing Prayer by Elder W[ilford] Woodruff. Singing.

~~Prest. D[aniel] H. Wells, said it was~~ The School was resolved ^by unanimous vote^ into a Convention for the nomination of Officers for the coming Election.

Moved & Seconded That Paul A Schettler act as Secretary. Moved, seconded & Carried That Louis S Hills, John Vancott, & John Rowberry be nominated as Commissioners for locating lands for University [and] as Councillors to represent Salt Lake, Tooele, Summit.

Moved & Seconded & Carried That W Woodruff, Geo Q Cannon, W[illiam] Jennings—& Jos[ep]h A Young—Select Man[50] for Salt Lake County. ~~Reuben~~ Moved, Seconded, & Carried That Reuben Miller act as Select Man. Moved Seconded & Carried That Henry Rudy ~~act~~ act as Justice of the peace in Brighton precinct.

Moved Seconded & Carried [that] Solomon J. Despain ~~act~~ as Justice of the peace in Granite presinct and Joseph Snell as Constable for D[itt]o.

Moved, Seconded & Carried That A[lva] D. Heaton as Justice of the peace of Bingham presinct and John Hogan as Constable. Judge [Elias] Smith then gave some timely council pertaining to Elections &c. It was then Moved, Seconded & Carried That this Convention be dissolved.

A Question was asked ~~the~~ by Bro [Lucius] Peck as to the reason a discrepancy between the genealogy of Christ as given by Matthew & Luke. Answer[:] One gives the Male and the other Female ancestry.

Prest. Geo A Smith refered to ^the^ recent and sudden death of some of our leading Men who have plural families—hence the necessity of the heads of families making their wills, so as to prevent their property from being squandered among the Lawyers, and he strongly recommended Fathers & Husbands to reflect upon the subject as a wise and prudent step.

Prest. B Young said it was 5 weeks to day since he attended the school before, they took [railroad] cars to ~~Wasatch~~ ^Evanston^, then

50. Selectmen were governing officers of a town or county.

on to Bear Lake & Soda Springs the latter is a place of great interest and many curiosity's. They travell'd every day, remained 10 days in that vicinity, saw some beautiful hot springs. It was a very desirable place for this people to possess. And in 15 Months or 2 years, the railway will be completed, from Evanston to that place, towards Montana. The Atmosphere was bracing and delightful—they saw no spider, fly ^or^ lizard. He wanted to start a place there ~~for ourselves~~, by Capitolists to build boarding Houses &c for the accommodation of our own people, as well as parties from the East and West who will flock there by thousands as soon as the railway is completed. He wanted some good Mechanics to go—and the Capitolists to go, and take up the land, and build up a large place—it is in Idaho.

Many had been trying to wipe out Mormonism but had not succeeded, neither will they—all the powers of Earth and Hell are as much opposed to us to day as ever. In fulfillment of Prophecy great numbers are coming here as visitors, and while here the good Spirit that broods here hovers over them and they cannot help but speak ~~of~~ well of us. But when they get away they are surrounded by another spirit and influence, and then will speak all manner of evil against us.

He then read a blank form got up by Bro E[lias] Smit[h] Judge of Probate, setting forth the legal form of Making wills, and he particularly desired the brethren to obtain one when printed—and immediately make our wills, to avoid litigatory lawsuits after our decease about our property.

School adjourned for one week at one oclock pm. Benediction by Elder J[ohn] D. T. McAllister.

August 5, 1871; Saturday

Theological Class met at the Tabernacle at One O clock pm. Present Prest. B[righam] Young presiding. After singing Prayer by B[isho]p Sam[ue]l Woolley. Singing.

Prest. Geo A Smith spoke of the effort that was likely to be made on Monday (Election day) by our Enemies to secure one of their own class in Office.[51] He trusted however that the Bishops were alive to their

51. Smith need not have worried. For example, Apostle Lorenzo Snow was elected to the territorial legislature from Box Elder County with 1,369 votes; his two opponents received one vote each, presumably their own. "Local and Other Matters," *Deseret News*, Aug. 16, 1871. In Salt Lake City, the precinct totals for Mormon candidates were 3,853 to 345 for opposition candidates. "Election Returns," *Salt Lake Herald*, Aug. 8, 1871.

duty in this respect, and made every preparation for voting. I want every good man in Israel to make voting and the interest of the Poles [elections] his business, on Monday next. He then refered to the Legislature of the Territory which had been conducted on the most economized principle. The Territory was out of debt, and the taxes were very light.

Elder Geo Q Cannon spoke of the responsibility now resting upon the Bishops in attending to a thorough organization for looking after every legal voter, in their respective wards. Every precinct in the adjacent Counties should be well guarded and scoured by scrutinizing men, to see that every male and female voter cast their votes on Monday next.

Elder Geo Q Cannon, not only Bishops, but every American Citizen should feel under obligation to not only do their duty in voting ^themselves^ but should use their influence in inducing others to do theirs. Spoke of the slackness of many Bishops in endeavouring to settle difficulties between brethren and prevent cases from coming before the [Stake] High Council.

Elder John Pack, this land was given to the saints by the Almighty, not any portion of it was given to us by our enemies, and shall ~~b~~ we now yield it to them. No—none should neglect so important a duty as casting their vote for those of our own choice.

Elder W[ilford] Woodruff said we should watch and pray and especially deposit our votes on Monday next, and use every means to influence others [to] do the same.[52]

Prest. G[eorge] A. Smith urged every man in Israel who had a team to turn out and use it ^on^ Monday in carrying voters.

Elder Ja[me]s Leach felt independent to do right, no matter what others did.

Elder James Brown, from conversation with outsiders, said that many of them were seriously looking for us to be busted up as a people, hence the necessity of every one doing their duty. For should our enemies ever~~y~~ ^be^ allowed to run the election we shall be in a poor fix. But if we do our duty our majority will be so great, as to throw our enemies so far in the shade that will discourage them, only let them get one Officer in, it will strengthen them hands, and embolden them in

52. Woodruff also related a story, meant to emphasize the importance of every vote, that while in Nauvoo he cast the deciding ballot that elected Brigham Young and others to the city council. HOJ, Aug. 5, 1871.

their future crus[a]de against us. Let us therefore take a decided stand maintain our rights, and God will enable us to do so.

Prest. B[righam] Young urged upon the school to be alive to their duty. We have the priesthood of the son of God—and through this Priesthood the people are made acquainted with the mind and will of God. But the priesthood ~~ea~~ are under no obligation to force men and women to the Polls, this is an act of their own free will. There never was a time when opposition was greater, than at present, to the Kingdom of God, but our enemies were never weaker.

This is the City of Zion, set upon a Hill and we have nothing to fear, God has given us this Country, and we have nothing to fear, only let us do our duty by obeying the council of the Servants of God. The Capitolists are coming here with their wealth, and many of our brethren are getting it, he was glad of it—they will leave their means here to build Factories, Import Machinery &c &c.

Infidelity is fast increasing among the people. Even Ministers are mostly infidel, there are none who believe the ~~Gos~~ Bible as the [word of] God, but a latter day saint.

School was adjourned for one week at 1 oclock pm. Benediction by Geo A Smith.

August 12, 1871; Saturday

Theological Class met at 1 oclock PM. Pres[en]t Pres[ident] ~~D~~ B[righam] Young presiding. After singing Prayer by Elder H[orace] Eldredge. Singing.

A question was asked by a member of the school If it was right for the 13th Ward Coop[erative] Inst[itutio]n to rent the upper room of their premises for the printing of the "Salt Lake Review," a very rabid [anti-Mormon] paper.[53]

Elder Geo Goddard said as a Member of the Ward, he believed that Bro [James] Freeze who manages the store, rented the room without the knowledge of B[isho]p [Edwin D.] Woolley or any of the Directors, and that he rented it under a false representation supposing it was wanted for the publication of a decent paper. He knew that B[isho]p Woolley intended to give them notice, ^to leave^ should anything of

53. The newspaper was founded by Frank Kenyon, a non-Mormon who was also the editor of the *Corinne Reporter*. Both papers were critical of the LDS Church and its leaders.

a rabid character appear in their paper, and he had no doubt but the Bishop had already done so.

~~Th~~ Elder F[rederick] A. Mitchell, one of the Directors said, it had been done without his knowledge. He very much regretted what had been done but had no doubt, that B[isho]p Woolley had already given them notice to leave.

Prest. B Young said that inasmuch as the 13 Ward Store (Co op) had moved into the 14th Ward, he did not think the people of the 13th should be held accountable for what that institution does, neither were they under any obligation to trade there, especially while such a stink exists in the upper room, as the printing of such a dirty sheet as the "Salt Lake Review."

He then commented on the course recently adopted by the Salt Lake Herald, by replying to the falsities that so frequently appear in the "Tribune," which is altogether unworthy the attention of any one who has ^any^ regard for Truth and righteousness, and if the Herald did not cease to notice such trash, he should cease to patronize that paper.[54]

A Member of the School, on paper, stated that some of our Merchants were advertizing in the Tribune and Review, and that he should not patronize them himself, was it right? This was read to the School, and met with a unanimous confirmation. The names of [merchants] Cha[rle]s Bassett & Riggs & Lechenburg are among the number.[55]

Prest. B Young said he was determined not to sustain those who sustain our bitterest enemies, and all who felt like him, hold up your hands, and every hand was lifted up. It was his imperative ~~to~~ duty to sustain those who sustain the Kingdom of God.

Prest. Geo A Smith said there had been two or three preliminarys Meetings held in the City Hall, in relation to the establishment of a Utah Cooperative Bank ~~and I~~ and if it was the mind of the school that such an institution should be organized, he wished them to make it manifest by uplifted hands. There was a unanimous show of hands.

Elder Louis S Hills then read ~~a series of resolutions and bye laws~~ ^the Constitution^ [of the Utah Cooperative Bank] that had been prepared for presentation to the school.

---

54. The *Salt Lake Herald*, first printed in 1870, was a Mormon-owned newspaper edited by Edward L. Sloan, who had worked previously at the *Deseret News* and the *Millennial Star*.

55. See Aug. 19, 1871, entry for more.

Elder John Taylor said he perceived in the Countenances of the saints that the Spirit of the Lord prompted them to act in concert with the first presidency in everything which they brought forward. Cooperation in our midst had been a balance wheel in the regulation of our commercial affairs—and was a perfect success. Spoke of an effort being made by some to draw off from the Kingdom of God. There is no other place on the face of the earth, where we could get an answer pertaining to God or Godliness. The Railroad had accomplished wonders in our midst, and there had been a great financial engineering done by the President and his friends. And not only railroads, and Commerce, & Banking, and everything else that pertains to the rolling forth of the Kingdom of God.

Elder W[ilford] Woodruff felt thankful that he lived to see the commencement of a grand cooperative movement, which he had no doubt would continue until it circumscribed the whole of our temporal matters. We should learn to sustain ourselves—and leave off as fast as possible the patronage of our enemies—Let alone those who support our bitter enemies. He heartily endorsed this movement, and prayed that we might grow brighter and brighter. Motioned & Seconded, & Carried That the Constitution be accepted and the Books be opened for subscription.

~~W[illiam] Jennings Moved that the Books be left at the Bank of Hooper & Eldredges Bank for six days to receive subscriptions.~~

H[orace] S. Eldredge Moved, was Seconded & Carried That Prest. B Young, W[illiam] H. Hooper, H[orace] S. Eldredge, W[illiam] Jennings, Jno. [John] Sharp—F[eramorz] Little, L[ouis] S. Hills ^be Directors.^ Moved, Seconded & Carried That Prest. B Young be president of the Bank. That H[orace] S. Eldredge be Vice President That Louis S Hills be Cashier. That the Books be opened at Hooper & Eldredge Bank for subscription from 10 am to 3 pm—until a sufficiency be subscribed.[56]

School was adjourned for One week [at] one o clock pm. After singing Benediction by Elder Amos Fielding.

56. The company started with $100,000 in capital as Bank of Deseret. The next year it was chartered under the 1863 National Banking Act and became Deseret National Bank. Arrington, "Banking and Finance."

August 19, 1871; Saturday

Theological Class met at the Tabernacle at One oclock pm. Present Elder Orson Pratt presiding. (The first Presidency and most of the twelve [apostles] having gone to Provo], to hold a two days meeting.) After singing Prayer by Elder A M[ilton] Musser. Singing.

A Letter was read from [merchants] Riggs & Lechenburg explanatory of the reasons why their ~~n~~ advertisement appeared in the Tribune, which stated that, as they were under some obligation to take some pay on that office, and without much reflection agreed to take it in advertisements. After the reading of the letter[:]

Bro [Obadiah] Riggs arose, and stated that both he and his partners Bros Lechenbergh & Nebeker were anxious to abide in the Councils of the Servants of God, they had enlisted for life in the Kingdom of God. They had no sympathy for Outside or Apostate Papers. They had immediately, on hearing the sentiments of the School last Saturday withdrawn their advertizement from the Tribune, and wished to continue their allegiance to the Kingdom.

Elder Orson Pratt then took a sense of the school on the ~~school~~ subject, and a unanimous ~~vote~~ uplifted hands shown the entire satisfaction they felt towards the letter and explanatory sentiments expressed by Bro Riggs.

He also refered to the covenants we had made some two years ago, not to sustain our Enemies. He had observed that strictly himself, and thousands besides, hence the success of our cooperation, retaining the means accumulating as profit, amongst ourselves. He also spoke of the extreme, unnatural fasheons that are more or less indulged in by the Ladies, especially in their Bonnets &c—and some fashons might be improved ^on^ by the Gentlemen, in the style of ^their^ pants.

Encouraged the observance of the Word of Wisdom, having a tendency to prepare us for a renewal of our bodies, when the proper time comes.

Elder [William] Henry made a few remarks on honesty, economy, paying tithing, emigrating the poor, living the life of the righteous &c.

Elder Lot Smith as a returned Missionary [from Great Britain], exprest [h]is gratitude for the privelege of returning home safely after a two years absence. Much good is obtained by attending these school. Spoke of the blessings and responsibilities that accompany obedience to the laws and ordinances of the Gospel. He hoped that he will never grow lukewarm on his return—but continue to increase ^in^ a constant growth in his interest towards the Kingdom of God.

Compared the superior life giving power of the Son of God, ~~in~~ and the future glory & exaltation of ~~fa~~ the faithful—to the transient pleasures & gratifications of the world. The Kingdom of God will shortly come out & rise above the present difficulties that now appear to surround it.

Elder David M Steward also a returned Missionary—had nothing else to live for but the Kingdom of God. Came in at an early day—felt thankful to see & realize the advancement & growth of the Kingdom. Spoke of the rottenness of the world, the uneasy and dissatisfied state of the apostates whom he had the fortune to look ~~both~~ after, both at California & the East.

Elder Jos[ep]h F. Smith circumstances had kept him from attending the school for two months past,[57] was gratified to hear the testimonies of his brethren. The Lord had blest them while preaching the Gospel—the plainer duties of our Religion seem to be hardest to observe and live up to. the duty of cooperating ourselves together is one of the most difficult to carry out by many, selfishness steps in, and thwarts us in our path. He wanted that kind of religion, that exalts and happifys us not only here, but hereafter. We are not here to aggrandize to ourselves the wealth & means of this world. We are here to build up the Kingdom of God with whatever means may come within our reach. Men are not so apt to serve & love God in wealth as in poverty. The Lord is now trying us with wealth. Let us remember that we are only stewards as yet—over what we have. We can only say that it belongs to us, after we have been tryed & proven, and ~~exalted~~ become immortal &c.

B[isho]p Edw[ar]d Hunter called for some Men from B[isho]p [Reuben] Miller & B[isho]p [Andrew] Cahoons ward to do some work near little Cottonwood [Canyon]—to remember the vegetable Tithing &c.

A Question Is it right for us to buy lumber of the Truckee Lumber Co[mpany]—as the Co[mpany] was favorable refer'd to through the [Deseret] News?

Elder Orson Pratt answered, by saying that a favourable notice to outside Merchants was no guarrantee for us to sustain them. But rather

57. Smith and members of his family had been ill.

than patronize outsiders—let us leave our orders at the Cooperative store, and they can obtain what we want.

Elder [Daniel] Shearer made a few remarks.

The School was adjourned for one Week at one o clock. Benediction by Elder G[eorge] B. Wallace.

August 26, 1871; Saturday

Theological Class met at the Tabernacle at One o clock pm. Present Prest. B[righam] Young presiding. After singing Prayer by Elder Geo Goddard. Singing.

A Letter was read from Bro W[illia]m Spring, in which he stated that from letters he had lately rec[eive]d from his aged parents ~~there~~ in England they expressed a strong desire to see him, and they being far advanced in years had a strong desire to see them also, and respectfully submitted to the President, whether he might take a Mission to England, and have a privelege of getting ~~a~~ some means from his friends here, to assist him there.

A Question was then asked by L[ucius] W. Peck who the Shepherd, the stone of Israel was. Answer, By Prest. B[righam] Young, Jesus Christ. He said it ^was^ his doctrine, for any member of the school, who knew anything to communicate worth knowing, to get up, and state it, but do not hatch up something that can benefit neither themselves or any one else.

Elder Orson Pratt read a portion from the Doctrine & Covenants 8th Paragraph. in which Jesus declares that He ~~h~~is the good sheperd, and stone of Israel.[58] He will come to Zion as a Shepherd to turn away ungodliness from ~~Josef~~ Jacob.

Another Question Is it right to confer the priesthood on a Dead child [via proxy?] Answer No.

Question—Would it not be well for some one to be appointed to make out Wills for the brethren, and also a place of deposit.

The Question was very much appreciated by the school and a unanimous ^vote^ exprest, to attend to the business.

Prest. Geo A Smith said that Sydey [Sidney] Rigdon had sent a letter to Prest. Young and exprest a desire to come to Utah on a visit, in company with his Wife, Son &c. if ~~Prest. Young would furnish~~ means

58. See D&C 50:44.

^could be furnished^ for them to come.[59] The case was left with the School and no action taken.

Prest. Young said it would take about a thousand dollars to bring them out and send them back again—and if the school wished to entertain ~~the~~ it, they were at liberty to do so.

Prest. D[aniel] H. Wells & Amos Fielding testified to the lying and invective spirit of Sydney Rigdon, and having so many apostates here now, they had no desire to assist more to come.

Prest. B Young said, if it were possible to do the old Man any good by him coming here, he should be glad, for the injury sustained by his course, has been to himself and those who followed him. He had a desire to have Bro David Whitmer[60] here, ~~th~~ who was one of the three Witnesses to the Book of Mormon that he might be rebaptized, obtain his blessings and die in the faith.

~~He enjoyed t~~ Prest. Young said that the same spirit that rested upon the Prophet Joseph [Smith] rested upon him ever since he had been in the Church. He very much liked it, for it made him very happy, and taught him to comprehend much of this earth, without having ~~our~~ ^his^ affections placed upon any of its wealth. How slothful and sluggish we are as Elders of Israel and how unlike what God would have us be—how prone we are to slander and throw obstacles in the way of our brethren & Sisters.

Elder Anson Call said he heard S[idney] Rigdon tell his Vision about the battle of Gog & Magog which was a false and ~~he~~ lying Revelation, and led many astray.[61] He also testified that when he heard Prest. Young ^preach^ just after the death of Joseph [Smith], his Voice and appearance too, were those of the Prophet Joseph, or his ears and eyes both deceived him.[62]

---

59. Rigdon's church, which continued in Pittsburgh after Joseph Smith's death, flourished briefly before being reorganized by William Bickerton. Rigdon and his family moved from Pennsylvania to New York, where he would die in 1876 without visiting Utah. Van Wagoner, *Sidney Rigdon: Portrait.*

60. David Whitmer (1805–88), one of the original members of the church, became critical of Smith's leadership and was excommunicated in 1838. He was interviewed about his involvement with Mormonism numerous times and later wrote the pamphlet *An Address to All Believers in Christ.*

61. In Rigdon's last sermon in Nauvoo, he made several prophecies about the end of the world.

62. Some Mormons later stated that as they watched Brigham Young speak after

Elder Lorenzo Young spoke very mercifully towards the faults and failings of Sydney Ridgon and thought a visit to this place might do him good, many in our midst had backslidden more than he had.

Elder W[ilford] Woodruff said the nearer we get to the Lord, the more mercy we see displayed towards erring humanity. Hence it is that Prest. Young entertains the most merciful feelings towards those who have done wrong and would gladly assist towards reclaiming them—and he for one did not feel like saying anything to oppose it.

School was adjourned for One week at One oclock pm. After singing Benediction by Elder Geo Q Cannon.

September 2, 1871; Saturday[63]

Salt Lake City, Old Tabernacle. School of the Prophets met at 1 p.m. President B[righam] Young presiding. School sang hymn on the 66th page. Prayer by Elder B[righam] Young, junior. School sang hymn on the 132nd page.[64]

Prest. D[aniel] H. Wells Introduced the subject of every body making his own will, especially those, who have large families, on account of the peculiar position we are in as regards the laws of the Country and every Latter Day Saint ought to be interested in it. Read a notice from Bro Abinadi Pratt, in which he offered his services to write out wills, and guaranteed satisfaction.

Elder Tho[ma]s Ellerbeck. Said that men, who have large families, and whose property is in such a condition, that it cannot be well estimated and divided, should especially make out their wills. He then read the will of President B Young, leaving out names & figures.

Prest. B Young Two of these documents ought to be made out, one to be deposited at the Probate Court, and one to be kept by the party in a safe place.

Th[oma]s W. Ellerbeck spoke about the benefit of making Dry earth closets [outdoor toilets], as a sure preventive for typhod fever and summer complaint.

Joseph Smith's death, Young was transformed to look and sound as Smith. See Van Wagoner, "Making of a Mormon Myth."

63. Although unsigned, different handwriting and textual clues indicate the minutes for the next five meetings were kept by a different clerk than George Goddard.

64. The hymnal used was *Sacred Hymns and Spiritual Songs for the Church of Jesus Christ of Latter-day Saints*, published in Liverpool in 1869. Page sixty-six is "I'll Praise My Maker While I've Breath," and page 132 is "Sweet Is the Work, My God, My King."

Levi Richards Complained that many strangers were trespassing in his orchard, depositing their droppings under his trees, because there never were no public places provided by the City authorities.

Geo Q. Cannon Related his experience with the Earth closet during the last two years, and recommended, that the same be also introduced inside of the houses especially for the benefit of women and children in cold and stormy weather.

Ed[ward] Wheeler Made a few remarks upon the subject and recommended burning all offal.

Th[oma]s Fenton Spoke about the different kinds of manure, how they should be mixed & applied and was much opposed to burn any kind of offal.

Th[oma]s Winter Said he came from Bath [England], the cleanest town in the world, where all the priveys were washed out by water.

Geo B. Wallace Remarked that ~~wats~~ vaults could never be kept sweet, neither places where it was washed out by water, but that dry earth was a perfect deodoriser. Complained, that there were cowyards & hog pens in this City, that were more offensive than backhouses. A great deal of sickness ^in the City^ was caused, because we did not know, how to diet ourselves.

Elder [Richard] Britton Made some very appropriate remarks about the different kinds of manure, & how to apply them.

Prest. G[eorge] A. Smith Gave notice, that a lady lecturer was exhibiting some relics from Jerusalem at 4 p.m. and would also give a lecture at 7 pm to day and 5 p.m to morrow.[65]

School sang hym on 325th page ["Praise to the Man Who Commun'd with Jehovah"]. School was adjourned to next Saturday 1 pm. Benediction by Prest. Geo A. Smith.

September 9, 1871; Saturday

Salt Lake City, Old Tabernacle. School of the Prophets met at 1 p.m. President Dan[iel] H. Wells presiding. School sang hymn on the 154th page ["Behold the Savior of Mankind"]. Prayer by Elder Horace Eldredge. School sang hymn on the 257th page ["Come, All Ye Sons of Zion"].

65. Mrs. C. L. Whitman of London advertised that she would display images from Egypt and the Holy Land, as well as artifacts such as the "widow's mite," as part of her lecture tour through the United States. "Exhibition," *Salt Lake Herald*, Sep. 2, 1871.

Prest. Geo A. Smith Remarked that it had been resolved to build a temple at St. George of rough Stone, like the Kirtland Temple, and finished after the manner of the same, also some black rock and red sandstone shall be used, ~~and~~ which is only a few miles distant. He wanted about 50 masons to make preparations and get ready to go to St George, to spend the winter there in rushing up the temple.

Elder Orson Pratt. Read a letter from Sidney Rigdon to Prest. Brigham Young, asking for $100,000.00 in coin to be sent per Express, for counsel that would be given.

Prest. Geo A. Smith Said he pitied the old gentlemen, as he thought, he was crazy, and if he had kept faithful, he might have accomplished a great deal of good. Prest. B Young was still sick, but he had urged upon him to lay the matter of calling 50 masons for the St George temple, before this School.

Prest. Dan H. Wells. Remarked that Prest. Young desired this brethren not to forget to make their wills.

Elder George Groo. Gave a very interesting account of his mission to England, and the experience he has gained while away from home.

Elder George Noble. also gave an account of his experience ^while^ on his mission to England, and exhorted the brethren to be faithful in all things.

Elder Elias Smith Instructed the brethren about the importance of making out wills properly, and stating everything plain, so that there can be no misunderstanding.

Prest. D. H. Wells. Confirmed the statements of Judge [Elias] Smith, and warned the brethren to abstain from the sin of onanism [masturbation], as it would ruin every man who practises it. He was sure, that the young man, who killed himself lately, had done so in consequence of this practise.

J. C. Stewart [David M. Stuart], Said he had spoken here before about 2 weeks ago, and he felt very much interested in the remarks, that had been made by the returning Elders, also the valuable instructions, we had received here this afternoon. It was the pleasantest part of a mans life to be on a mission, provided he has the Spirit of the Lord. He had performed some very rough missions in California, also a very pleasant one to Scotland, but in the States he found it uphill business.

Elder Geo Q Cannon notified the School that blanks [templates] for wills can now be had at the Deseret News Office.

Prest. D H Wells adjourned the School till next Saturday at 1. pm. School sang the hymn on the 166th page ["Salem's Bright King, Jesus by Name"]. Benediction by Elder Orson Pratt.

September 16, 1871; Saturday

Salt Lake City, Old Tabernacle. School of the Prophets met at 1 p.m. President Geo A Smith presiding. (Prest. B[righam] Young came in at ½ past one.) School sang hymn on the 163 page ["Jesus, Mighty King in Zion"]. Prayer by Elder Tho[ma]s Jeremy. School sang hymn on the 71st page [Jehovah, God the Father, Bless"].

Prest. D[aniel] H. Wells. Asked the Bishops if they were ready, to report how many masons were willing to go to Dixie [southern Utah], and assist in the building of the [St. George] temple.[66]

B[isho]p [John] Stoker Reported of North Kanyon Ward the following stonelayers, Edward Simons, Henry J. Harrison [George] Burton, stonecutter.

B[isho]p [Alonzo H.] Raleigh James Smith, W[illiam] L. Perkins 19th Ward.

B[isho]p [Alexander] McRae Robert H. Swain.

B[isho]p J[ohn] Sharp Edw[ard] Brain.[67]

B[isho]p Edw[ard] Hunter. Reminded the brethren to pay their tithing, that the promised blessings might follow. His motto was always "Pay your tithing and be blessed.["] He gave his property to Brother Joseph [Smith] in Nauvoo, when he was poor, and needy of it, and Bro [Orson] Hyde pronounced blessings upon his head, that he had no idea, he would ever receive. Depriving the dead of their privileges, was cutting the very h[e]artstrings of our faith. Was very much pleased, how he got along with the Emigration, and that the new comers were so soon provided for. There were very liberal feelings manifested.

Elder Geo Q. Cannon We live according to my views in the most interesting time, that has ever been upon this earth, especially if we watch the different and continuous schemes, which our enemies are

66. The groundbreaking took place in November 1871, followed by six years of construction.

67. All the men nominated to work on the temple in St. George were either stone or brick masons. William Perkins was from Tennessee, the rest were from Great Britain.

planning against us. By all these we learn a good deal of experience, and our ennemies are doing all they can by their doings, to assist in the accomplishment of the great work, that is before us. Considered it a very great privilege to commence the building of another temple, and that it would be a great blessing for the people of our Dixie, and save them a good deal of travel and expense. Spoke of the great blessings, that the people could obtain by the building of tempels, and that he longed to see the time, when all marriages will be performed in temples only, where the Elders of Israel clothed in priestly robes, can administer the ordinances of the Holy Priesthood.

B[isho]p John Sharp Considered the call for the stonemasons a call on the people, because a good many men will have to be employed besides them to assist in that work, and these hands and their families will have to be provided with the necessaries of life. Reminded the brethren of the feelings they had when coming here, on board the ship and in other places, and that they had not come here to gather riches, but to build up the Kingdom, in building temples to administer for our dead, and that it was a very great privilege for us as a people.

Prest. Danl H. Wells Said, that if some of the brethren should be called upon to act as jurors, to accept it and serve because of duty, and because it was considered good policy, and in regard to military, if a posse should come round to our houses at midnight, we might expect, that they were after our lives, and should kill them if possible in defence of the same. Our enemies have not made many points yet, because the Lord has frustrated them in their designs, and we had to make our best efforts, and we have to be always ready, and keep our powder dry.

Elder Wilford Woodruff Gave out a notice of a ¼ Sec[tion] of land in the Pulsipher field,[68] and requested all landowners of that ¼ Section to meet at the close of the School, as something had to be done, or the land would be lost.

Elder Lorenzo Young Related, that he listened a little while ago at the Land Office to a conversation of G[eorge] [R.] Maxwell and a gentleman of Chicago in regard to those ¼ Sections, on which there were no houses or improvements, and that it seemed to him, that they were trying to make trouble, where parties had not conformed to the laws.

68. The field abutted the Jordan River, about three miles south of Temple Square and one and a half miles west.

Prest. Geo A Smith Exhorted the School to be very particular in complying with the laws, and rather live a year or two on a ¼ Section than loose it. He also stated that Prof[essor] [John] Park who intends going east to visit Universities, take a mission to preach the Gospel, also Br[other] [Leon] Bellevieue to preach the Gospel in Europe. Several hundred of the Elders who had relatives in the East should prepare themselves to go there during the winter, and preach the gospel to their friends. The masons for Dixie should take their teams & provisions along.

Prest. B Young Invited all, to go south with him and help to work, and survey the country a little. School was adjourned to next Saturday at 1 pm. After singing of hymn on the 28th page ["God Moves in a Mysterious Way"] dismissed by Elder G[eorge] Q Cannon.

September 23, 1871; Saturday

Salt Lake City, Old Tabernacle. School of the Prophets met at 1. p.m. Elder Orson Pratt presiding. School sang hymn on the 115th page ["Messiah, Fully Grace"]. Prayer by Elder Geo B. Wallace. School sang hymn on the 180th page ["Come, Humble Sinner"].

Elder Orson Pratt Called upon the Bishop's present, to report the name of masons, who were willing to go to Dixie to assist in the building of the Temple.

Bishop [Alexander] McRae reported [carpenter] Archibald Frame.

Elder Orson Pratt Remarked, how necessary it was for us as a people, that had grown so fast, and that lived in settlements, several hundred ~~feet~~ ^miles^ distant, to build more temples, and especially for the benefit of older people, to whom travelling a large distant is quite a anoyance. For the younger portion of the people, who desire to enter into matrimony, it was just as important, not to have to travel so far, to be sealed by the proper authority. Said the Brethren should be just as willing to go to Dixie, as to go on a Mission abroad. Said he would rather with his family be in deep poverty, that to refuse a mission, to which he has been called.

Elder [Christian] Tweede Said, he knew a man from Box Elder, that had apostatised, and still held his ticket for the School [of the Prophets], and he would like to see it taken from him.

Elder Orson Pratt. Remarked, that such a man, who refused to give up his ticket, had no honor left within him. Suggested for somebody to make some remarks about polygamy, and to prove that it was not a crime.

Elder Aurilius Miner. Spoke about the differences in law as regards to what is termed a crime, and that it depended on the authority of those, who declare certain acts as crimes. He had a right to be here and had certain duties to perform, and he had to stay here, till his work was done, and it was his privilege to defend himself in the execution of his duties. The law of individual right existed out of necessity, but when society is formed, other laws have to [be] framed to protect everyone in his right. He wanted to show the right the people had, to arrange their own affairs and if our administrators did not do their duty, we the people, had the right to change them. He wanted to live as a man, to maintain his rights, & hold, that polygamy is no crime, and that no human authority has a legal right, to declare it a crime. He wanted a vigilance committee, to guard the rights of the people, not a mob, but good substantial men, who can be depended upon. Thought it would be well, to call a big Mass meeting & appoint five Delegates to go to Washington [DC] and demand our rights, and the removal of the present Officers of the Government.[69]

Elder David Fuller Thought Bro Miner labored under a little misunderstanding in regard to the feelings of the people, as he & others were only waiting for the signals to be given, and he was ready.

Elder Levi Richards. Endorsed what had been said, and remarked that "vox populi" was "vox dei"[70]; was very much in favor of a Mass meeting to be held forthwith.

Elder B[urr] Frost. Felt like Brother Miner did, and considered it our duty, to back up those, who have been indicted, and carry them through safe, and call a Mass meeting soon.

Elder [Alexander] Findley Referred to the subject of polygamy and said, that from the nature of men and women alone we could know, that it was from God, and not a crime.

Elder J[ohn] D M Crockwell Spoke about his experience in vigilance matters, and endorsed what had been said.

Elder Orson Pratt Remarked, that we had a kind of a political school, and that things had come to light, that we did not know before,

69. The call for a mass meeting was in response to the recent polygamy raids in Provo which resulted in some arrests. Church leaders would spend the next months urging calm but also readiness to fight. "Raid at Provo," *Deseret News*, Sep. 20, 1871.

70. Latin for "the voice of the people was the voice of God."

namely that there was considerable feeling among the people. About the acts of the Court and Grand jury, and he was willing to wait, till the proper authority shall say, what should be done.

Elder D[imick] B. Huntington Referred to the taking away of our [city] charter in Nauvoo & other things, and thought we would have to pass through many trials yet. Counseled the brethren to keep qui[e]t, and let them listen to the watchmen on the towers of Zion.

School was adjourned to Saturday next 1 pm. After singing of the hymn on page 165 ["Salem's Bright Light"] Benediction by Elder [Albert P.] Rockwood.

September 30, 1871; Saturday

School of the Prophets met in the old Tabernacle at 1 oclock pm. Present Prest. Geo A Smith presiding. After singing Prayer by Elder W[ilford] W. Woodruff. Singing.

Prest. D[aniel] H Wells, said Prest. B[righam] Young was not very well or he would have been present,[71] he [Young] felt perfectly calm and resigned in regard to the present excitement that is now agitating the public mind, our enemies never anticipated that he would be willing to go into Court and meet the charges that have been made against him—by so doing, they were ~~being~~ met on their own ground, and were foiled in their attempts to destroy the Leaders of the people.[72]

He exhorted the Brethren to be quiet and not be excited, but do right, and also in a state of readiness in case of extreme emergency &c.

Elder Orson Pratt spoke of the two great Powers that are antagonistic to each other, viz of God and the evil one—which had existed during past generations—and was going on at the present time. Refered to the aggressions that we have been subjected to in a Territorial capacity, having one right after another torn away from us by the Government Officials who have exercized more authority than the whole people of the Territory have, it was very ^trying^ to be infringed upon to such an extent as we have been ~~subject to~~, but the time will come when we shall not be subject to these things, and that will be when we

71. Young spent several days with severe stomach pains and got little sleep. "President Young was up during last night 16 times with the diarrhea." HOJ, Oct. 2, 1871.

72. Young was indicted by a grand jury for "lascivious cohabitation," and on October 2 a warrant was issued for his arrest. He was allowed, because of his illness, to remain at home under the watch of deputies. Turner, *Brigham Young*, 365.

are prepared as a people to receive that great boon. Spoke of the great lack ~~of~~ in the observance of the Word of Wisdom by the saints ~~He did~~ and also the serious lack in attending Meetings. Such unfaithfulness existing, no wonder so many of our people are taken to the Cemetry, and the visitation of Grass hoppers [destroying crops]. Unless we Keep the commandments of God, we have no guarrantee for his blessings to rest upon us &c.

Elder W. W. Woodruff said, our success as a people depended on our faithfulness in Keeping the commandments of God. Neither the Ancient Saints, nor the Latter day Saints can obtain ^the^ blessings of God on any other principle. No principle was ever revealed to the Sons of Men, but what was intended for their observance.

He believed their was sufficient integrity however, ^among the saints^ who are doing their best in obeying the laws of God, to preserve us from the hands of the wicked. He had great faith in Prayer, and recommended the school to bear up continually before the Lord, the anointed of God. ~~told of~~ He once heard a simple, fervent prayer offered in [prayer] Circle by the Prophet Joseph when in deep trouble, and was answered in three days.

We should also pray for our enemies. For if ever any poor devils needed praying for, the Judges, Lawyers, &c in our midst needed it. Let us be valiant for the truth and stand up like men in the cause of Zion.

Moved, & Carried That Elder E[noch] B. Tripp, take a Mission to ~~England~~ the States.

Elder Lorenzo Young recommended Parents to look after their children and teach them to observe the Sabbath Day, and not allow them to range through the Kanyon, yelling, and hooting, and disturbing the public peace of those who live near by.

Adelbert D Harmon [in the] Kays[ville] Ward [assigned] for Dixey [to work on the St. George Temple] as Teamster &c.

Elder Geo Q Cannon said, those who do not train up their Children in the way of righteousness God is angry with such Parents. A Man who is faithful as an Elder in Israel and teaches by precept and example his family and they fail to follow in his footsteps, they will not attain to like blessings with him. A Father may be great in the Kingdom of God, but it is no guarrantee that his Children will also be great. In many instances, the sons of the Humble & meek, ~~will~~ by their virtues and good works, will entirely outstrip the sons of the great, ~~whose~~ ^though their^ advantages have been much greater. Spoke of the serene confidence that Prest. Young enjoyed, especially during the past two weeks of excitement, the trouble sought to be brought upon us as a people, will fall upon their own heads. He had full faith that God would bring down to hell those who are now harrassing and seeking to bring trouble and distress on the Anointed of God. It is right we should pray, and exercis~~ing~~e Faith in God. God is in the midst of this people and if we will only obey his Laws, & listen to his Councils. He will give us the Victory, which I prophecy in the Name of Jesus Christ—which was responded to by a hearty Amen by the school.

Pres[ident] Geo A Smith, was thankful to see so many here, and notwithstanding our many follies & failings, as a people, the Devil ~~&~~ & his agents are not inclined to befriend us.

Temples are built to observe religious ~~observanc~~ ceremonies, not only for the living but the dead and when any ^are^ being built, the Devil is mad—and trys to stir up strife. We do not really ~~enjoys~~ appreciate the blessings bestowed upon us. He spoke of the indifference of many in taking out their naturalization papers. Refered to the Prophet Joseph [Smith] who gave himself up into the hands of his enemies—this he did by the earnest entreaty of his wife and others, though he himself felt, that by so doing, He was going as a Lamb to the slaughter.[73] ~~H~~

The Republicans as a Political party, have had a rule for the last 10 years, and were pledged as a part of their platform, to ~~destory~~ ^abolish^ slavery, and destroy the Latter Day Saints—and would use every effort to accomplish it.

School was adjourned for two weeks[74] at 1 oclock pm. After singing Benediction by Elder Geo Q Cannon.

October 14, 1871; Saturday[75]

Theological Class met in the Tabernacle at One o clock pm. Present Prest. Geo A Smith presiding. After singing Prayer by Elder B[righam] Young Jun[io]r. Singing.

73. Joseph Smith fled Nauvoo in June 1844, but returned to submit to arrest and was subsequently killed at Carthage Jail.

74. The school did not meet on October 7 because of general conference.

75. Since the school had last met, Brigham Young, Daniel H. Wells, and George Q.

Elder C[harles] C. Rich gave a very favourable account of the labours of the brethren in Bear Lake Valley, ~~th~~ Health abounds generally, most of the Crops were destroyed by Grasshoppers. But hope for better prospects in the future, as there seems to be no eggs left this season. The School of the prophets is well attended in Paris [Idaho]. It is a great privelege to come to these schools, because here, correct principles are taught, and no Elder should ever attempt to teach, unless they know it is right. Hence the importance of coming here, to have our ideas tested. In every situation we occupy, we ^should^ strive to fill ^it^ most faithfully, and set the best kind of examples, so that our influence may be good among those we mingle with. If we strive lawfully to be Saints, God has pledged himself to provide for his Saints, and we have nothing to fear. We need faith and knowledge to meet, encounter, and overcome, every trial that comes in our path.

Elder B[righam] Young, Jun[io]r was thankful that nothing was ever reported abroad that was told in this school (this, of course he spoke ironically).[76] The hand of the Lord had been made very manifest of late—and although, according to the estimation of our enemies, all polygamist[s] will soon go under, ~~but~~ there is nothing to fear. Pres[iden]t [Brigham] Young had not lost one moments rest, on account of the Court doings—and were ^he^ to go to Camp Douglas, he would not be in the hands of his enemies. That place was not Carthage [Illinois]—Salt Lake City was not Illinois—but while we are harrassed internally, we must not loose our hold on those extreme Northern points, we are trying to settle, in and around Soda Springs, and along Bear River. There is a splendid stock raising country on the Black Foot & Bear River bottoms. Millions of tons of good Hay could be cut in those regions—they need more settlers on the Bear River, and he would be glad if some from this school would go and strengthen those settlements. Stock raising was a very profitable business which can be gone into, on the frontiers, if ~~pr~~ well taken care of.

Cannon had been arrested for cohabitation. All three leaders were released and allowed to attend general conference and otherwise go about church business. Other polygamists were also targeted and funds were raised for their bail while they awaited trial. Allen et al., *Story of the Latter-day Saints*, 345–47; Bigler, *Forgotten Kingdom*, 290–92; Turner, *Brigham Young*, 365–67.

76. Although the school had hundreds of members, secrecy was still expected to be observed.

Prest. B Young & D[aniel] H. Wells now came into the School.

Elder Peter Nebeker explained his terms for taking Cattle to Herd, viz—they charge for Cattle under 3 years old at 50 cents per head per month and insure their lives included. Young Colts on the same terms. Older Cows and Cattle $1.00 per head per month. Sheep, returns the old stock & adds 1 lamb ~~out of 4 raised~~ ^to every 4 ewes^ & give 1½ lbs Wool per head) will take Mares & raise Colts on the halves, and halter break them—Work Horses $2.00 per head insurance included.

Elder Geo Q. Cannon then read the following names as missionaries Rob[er]t Maxfield—James R Miller[,] W[illia]m Boyes[,] R[ichar]d Howe—Jonas Erickson—James Winchester—Simpson D Huffaker[77]—De Wit C Thompson—Tho[ma]s a Wheeler, W[illia]m B Kelley[,] Seth M. Lovendahl[,] Hy[rum] W. Brown.

A Vote was taken to sustain the above [missionaries] which was unanimous.

S. Van Dyk of Ogden was also sustained as a Missionary [to] Holland.

Dan[ie]l Weggeland D[itt]o D[itt]o for Scandinavia.

~~Elder~~ Prest. Geo A Smith said, that those ^who^ intended to go down to Dixie to ~~bi~~ help build the Temple, would be expected to bear their own expenses ^in going, while there, and returning^ and attend to it as a labour of Love. Regarding it simply as a Mission—there had been so little raised in the South this season, that those who go from here to work, need not expect assistance from that quarter.

School was than adjourned for one week at One oclock pm. After singing Benediction by Prest. Geo A Smith.

October 21, 1871; Saturday

Theological Class met ^in^ the old Tabernacle at 1 oclock pm. Present Prest. B[righam] Young presiding. After singing Prayer by Prest. D[aniel] H. Wells. Singing.

Prest. D. H. Wells spoke of the many tickets [of admission to the school] that are lost accidentally by the Members of the School, and the probabilaty of strangers who may find them, trying to palm themselves in, by those tickets. He wished the doorkeepers to be very particular, and not admit a stranger, without ascertaining that he is a good member of the Church.

77. Simpson D. Huffaker (1847–1903) was notable for being one of the first missionaries who was born in Utah Territory as a second-generation Mormon.

He then spoke of the ~~negligence, and~~ neglect of many duties, by those who profess to be the people of God in these vallies, our principles, and liberties are not assailed by those in Power and it is of the utmost importance that we stand by each other to sustain those principles that brought us hither. The warfare now waging is not against Brigham Young as an individual, but against our Holy Religion, and therefore we all as saints should make it our common cause, and be willing to share in the expenditure needful to carry on a successful defense which he ~~very~~ verily believed would be a success. It is now a legal fight or a money fight—these we'll try first in the courts here, and try to beat the devil on his own ground.

It was then moved and carried That J. C. Fackrell Bountiful [Utah] ~~and R[obert] S T. Fuller~~ take a Mission to the States to visit his friends &c.

~~P~~Elder David McKenzie said, from the position he occupied ^he^ had the privelege of seeing many Newspapers, and among them very few, who have the moral courage and manhood of saying anything that ~~it~~ is ^at^ all favourable to us, as a people. Dr. Miller,[78] however, Proprietor of the Omaha Herald stands preem~~fi~~nently as a bold and independant advocate of our rights, and as he publishes a good, useful family paper, ~~he would~~ all who feels to show~~s~~ their appreciation of his sraightforward course, will please hand in their names & means, as subscribers to his paper, at the close of the school.

Prest. Geo A Smith spoke of the united effort on the part of the latter day saints, that is now necessary in manfully resisting the illegal course now taken the US Officials, they will certainly be overtaken in their own snare.[79]

The following means was handed in towards defraying the Lawsuit expenses now pending[:]

Ansel Call	10.00	Nathan Meads	1.00

78. George L. Miller (1830–1920), a Democrat, founded the *Omaha Herald* in 1865. Like others who spoke in defense of Mormonism, he was uninterested in preserving polygamy but was opposed to government overreach and believed plural marriage would die out as the railroad brought a moderating influence to Utah.

79. Smith's prediction was not just bravado; the Mormons had a strong legal case against Judge McKean's actions and overreach. Charges against not just Young, Wells, and Cannon would be dismissed, but all Mormons imprisoned for adultery or cohabitation would be invalidated by the US Supreme Court in the April 1872 *Englebrecht* decision. Bigler, *Forgotten Kingdom*, 294–95. See also Apr. 20, 1872, entry.

Jos[ep]h Argyle	5.00	W[illia]m. Brown	3.00
Sam[ue]l McKay	3.00	Ja[me]s Wickens	1.00
John T. Gerber	2.00	N. Tuttle	1.00
Rob[er]t Parker	2.00		
[Total]			$28.00

22.00 rec[eive]d D[avid] Mckenzie

The rules of the School were then read and ^were^ unamously sustained by uplifted hands. Prest. Geo A Smith made a few appropriate remarks on the importance of observing them.

Elder [Robert] Collins made a few remarks on the necessity ~~ho~~ of every prophecy being fulfilled, that was spoken of by the Prophets, and though there may be a little friction on the surface, we need not fear, for God will not give ^up^ the work now, which he started with the Prophet Joseph Smith. The old Ship Zion had successfully sailed so far and will undoubtedly move along until she safely reaches harbor.

Elder Amos Fielding spoke of the similarity between the Judge, Lawyers & Jury in the days of Joseph [Smith], and those now in our midst engaged in these ungodly suits. Whatever measure they meet to the people of God, will most assuredly be measured back to them. Let us live so as to have power with God, for he only is our strength & shield.

Prest. Geo A. Smith suggested the wisdom of the brethren looking out some suitable place in a warm climate, for our wives and little ones could be sheltered, if we were driven to the wall, or put to such shifts as our enemies are determined to do, if possible. But God will defend us, if we do right. If the Latter day Saints should ever leave these Vallies, the property in them will not be worth a cent. The Mining interest also will be entirely destroyed. We stoop however, to conquer, and we'll rise also to conquer. When men are deprived of every right, ~~and~~ they are often driven to desperation—and who can help it.

Prest. B Young said he was in no way concerned about this people, if they will only live their religion. If we are driven to the necessity of being ~~driven~~ put to the test on a/c [account] of our religion, will you give it up, or fight for it (fight was the answer) yes, said he, many will fight that will not pray and do their duty. The Court is now probing us to see how much we will stand, and they may keep on pinching and pinching until we can endure it no longer, and should we be driven to that alternative, Mining and other interests will be a very poor business in these vallies. Some will tell what is now said ~~(will tell all they have heard~~ as soon as they get out of this school. Such ~~h~~ consummate hypocracy and false brethren are what we have to contend with all the day long—but all such will be damned. Let the Seventies, High Priests, Bishops &c call their Quorums, and all who feel to hand over their means to pay these lawsuits, all right.

School was adjourned for one week at one oclock pm. After singing Benediction by Prest. Geo A Smith.

It was also moved that R[obert] S. T. Fuller take a Mission but was overruled, by the testimony of Bro Anson Call, that he was dishonest, untruthful, and indolent.

October 28, 1871; Saturday

Theological Class met at the Tabernacle at One o clock pm. Present Prest. D[aniel] H. Wells presiding. After singing Prayer by Elder Lorenzo Snow. Singing.

Elder A[lbert] Carrington who had returned but a few days, from his Mission to England, was pleased to be present, and rejoiced in the providences of God, that had been over him to this time, he had acquired considerable influence over his natural petulent temper, and desired to exercise the utmost patience towards those who are engaged in harrassing and hunting after Prest. [Brigham] Young and other brethren for they are doing the work of their Father the Devil. Spoke of the lies and misrepresentations that are published in the Salt Lake ~~Herald~~ ^Tribune^ and Corrinne Reporter,[80] but when he remembered the source from whence it came, it did not disturb his feelings. He then gave his experience in trying to become a very patient man, and called upon the brethren to do the will of God, and live their religion, let us put aside every specie of Pride, Selfishness, Vanity &c, deprecated the habit of indulging in an exorbitant thirst after gain by Tradesmen who buy at the lowest price of the ~~consumer~~ ^producer^ and ~~lat~~ selling at the very highest price to the consumer, this practise did not become latter day saints.

Prest. D[aniel] H. Wells, said that Prests B Young & Geo A Smith had gone south for the benefit of his health, as was contemplated, his

80. The *Corinne Daily Reporter* ran from 1871 to 1873 in northern Utah. The town was midway between Ogden and the transcontinental railroad line at Promontory.

health had become feeble, the weather was fine, and went without any intention of evading the law. He calculated to meet his trial at the courts and fight them there, when the time comes. ~~the~~ We came here many years ago, and have as much right to walk these streets as any body else. Let us all receive ~~his~~ ^the^ providences of God like good and obedient children. We may have been a little remis[s] in our duties, and the Lord may see fit to chastise us, if so, let us receive it as from the hands of a Kind and indulgent Parent. Let us follow our File leaders, and not indulge in a revengeful spirit. He hoped they would not send their Posse Comitatus [conscripted deputies] after the~~ir~~ president during the winter so that he may rest their in peace until spring when he will be ready to meet his indictments fairly in the Court. Our enemies are filling up their cup of iniquity very fast. God will thwart their plans and purposes, if the Saints generally were not pretty near right, this persecuting spirit would not be after us—as it now is. May we rest our soul in patience—let us be obedient to the councils of Heaven.

Elder Orson Pratt spoke of various prophesies that have been uttered, in this school, one especially in reference to those who have been sustained and patronized in ~~mos~~ our midst, who are now wielding their influence and means to oppress and harrass our people. He believed in the experience of this people, that we should some time or other be brought under bondage, but in the due time of the Lord, would be delivered again. The mighty hand of God would be stretched out and m~~y~~iraculously deliver his people. He also quoted a passage in the ~~Doctrine & Covenants~~ ^107 Psalm^, referring to a time after we had been brought into the wilderness, viz. ~~They shall again be brought down very low~~ Again they are diminished and brought low through oppression, affliction and sorrow. The righteous can endure afflictions much easier than the half hearted. Let us give heed to the council given in this school and do right.

Elder [Robert] Collins made a few remarks on the final triumph of the righteous.

Elder A Carrington & B[isho]p [Edward] Hunter spoke in favour of encouraging ~~the~~ ^the^ Democrat Paper Edited by B Pomeroy, and also the Omaha Herald, and the Capitol, published at Washington [D.C.][81]—each of whom boldly advocated ~~Civil~~ the principles of Civil and religious liberty.

---

81. *Pomeroy's Democrat* was published by Mark "Brick" Pomeroy (1833–96) in New

B[isho]p Hunter also strongly recommended every one to look well after titles to their property.

Elder Abinadi Pratt ~~w~~ spoke a few words of warning to the Fathers in Israel, for not watching over more effectually their sons who have received their endowments, but who instead of honoring the priesthood by attending the Elders Quorum &c, instead of spending their time in Billiard Saloons and acquiring loose, and wicked habits.

The School was adjourned for one week at one oclock. After singing Benediction by Elder W[ilford] Woodruff.

[Subscription to the] (Omaha Herald) [by] (W[illia]m Lowe—2.00)

November 4, 1871; Saturday

Theological Class met at the Tabernacle at one oclock pm. Present Prest. D[aniel] H. Wells presiding. After singing Prayer by B[isho]p Lorenzo Young. Singing.

Henry Lewis paid $5.00 for Defence fund.[82]

Elder Geo Goddard made a few remarks on the obligations resting on Latter day ~~st~~ saints, and the importance of humbling themselves at the present time, ^keeping away from Billiard Saloons, etc^ attending to the duties required at their hands, and praying fervently for the Lord to avert the impending troubles.

Elder Jno [John] Picknell said that many Saints were in the habit of sustaining some of the Butchers in the Meat Market who are not in the Church.

Elder Orson Pratt gave some very timely council to the Elders of Israel pertaining to ^the^ ~~their~~ temporal government of their children—and dissuade them from visiting the various Billiard Saloons which are Kept by our bitterest enemies, and ^would^ have their hands imbrued in the blood of the anointed of God if they could.

It is equally wrong for our Children to visit the drinking places where there are no Billiards, but all sorts of wickedness carried on unless the children of the Latter day saints are checked by suitable parental

York from 1869 to 1889 as a weekly paper supporting populist causes. A column in the Washington *Capitol* of October 8, 1871, despite calling polygamy a "vile practice," was reprinted in the *Deseret News* for condemning Judge McKean's grand jury packing. "The Mormon Crisis," *Deseret News*, Oct. 25, 1871.

82. That is, the legal fund established to defend those arrested for cohabitation. See Oct. 21, 1871, entry.

restraint—but allowed to go on in there present course that many are indulging in. In a few years they will rise ^up^ and become the Murderers of their own parents. Let Parents then look after their sons, instruct them in their duties and warn them to Keep away from such Hell holes. He also called upon Parents to instruct their daughters to keep away from Gentile influences, no matter how polished in manners and in dress they may be, for there cannot be an alliance between a believer and unbeliever in Marriage, without entailing misery in this life, and that which is to come.

Elder Geo Q Cannon refer'd to the critical nature of our present position. Hence the necessity of the Saints being united and prayerful, prompt in their duties—& energetic, as Bishops, Teachers, Elders &c. We must however become famous, as a people, that is our destiny—and our enemies are now giving us widespread popularity. He then quoted the circumstances connected with Mordecai, the Jews and Haman—wherein the latter had laid a trap to destroy the two former, but humbling themselves in Sackcloth & ashes, & uniting in prayer to God for his deliverance. And the result was, that Haman who had provided a Gallows for Mordecai—was hung upon it himself.[83]

He felt confident in his faith that God would deliver us as a people, and we would come out of these trials brighter and better than we have ever been before. We should be ~~unsual~~ unusually vigilent in our duties—and the Lord will soften the hearts of our enemies from time to time, if we will only do right. He had no doubt the Judges, Lawyers &c who are opposing the principles of the Kingdom of God, are accomplishing a very useful and important work and their results, very beneficial to the Latter day Saints—especially to those who have been unkind to their wives.

Prest. D. H. Wells exprest great thankfulness to God and his brethren—to whom he felt indebted for his deliverance from Captivity, which took place last Saturday afternoon. And was liberated on Monday.[84] He had faith that this crusade would soon cease—if the Saints

83. The story of Haman, who plotted to wipe out the Jews, is recounted in Esther in the Old Testament.

84. Mormon gunslinger Bill Hickman had charged Wells, Hosea Stout, and William Kimball with being accessories to the 1857 murder of Richard Yates. Upon payment of $50,000 bail, Wells was released from the military prison at Camp Douglas. The charges were subsequently dropped. Bigler, *Forgotten Kingdom*, 291–92.

will only walk should[er] to shoulder in their duties. God will deliver his Servants. Let us live as we should do, and the Grasshoppers and other things will leave us. We should be wise and not talk too much even before our families, for we know not how the Devil may use them in future against us—should any of them turn away from the faith.

If we will only be faithful and true, the Lord will turn away the present crusade—and we'll continue to walk these streets, and maintain our rights in these mountains. Let parents take a wise and judicious course towards their children, not too rigid and tecknical, lest they brake loose, and get away from all restraint, but instil into their minds correct principles—and gently lead them along.

Spoke of Hosea Stout and W[illia]m Kimball[85] who are still in Captivity, by indictments of crime, in which they are entirely innocent. Wm Kimball had been cut off from the church on acc[oun]t of his drunkenness, he could not or would not live his religion, but he was the son of a Prophet and his father [had] felt much anxiety about him.[86]

He was thankful to be here to day, and last saturday too. And for ^what^ had happened since then—if his life had to be forfeited for the benefit of his people, all right, he was perfectly ready to live or to die. We have got power, influence and means and will find God to be on our side. Warned us against sustaining our enemies. Let us [be] wise, and maintain our holy faith, and finally be saved in the Kingdom of God.

School adjourned for one week at one o clock pm. After singing prayer by Elder Jos[ep]h F. Smith.

November 11, 1871; Saturday

Theological Class met at the Tabernacle at one o clock pm. Present Prest. D[aniel] H. Wells presiding. After singing Prayer by Elder B[righam] Young Jun[io]r. Singing.

Elder Edw[ar]d Stevenson, rejoiced at the present time in the blessings and priveleges that we enjoy—compared the present crisis of our Country, with the known facts that Farmers never put in their sickle to cut down their grain, until it is perfectly ripe—so also, the Lord never

85. William Henry Kimball (1826–1907), son of Heber C. Kimball and Vilate Murray, was a deputy US marshal and a captain of minutemen during early Utah Indian conflicts. He was a postmaster at Parley's Park and drove the mail between Salt Lake City and Park City from 1870 to 1885.

86. Heber C. Kimball died in 1868.

destroys any Nation, until it is ripe in iniquity, and sufficiently warned them by sending his inspired servants to tell them of coming Judgments, and invite them to flee from the wrath to come.

We as Elders, have more or less forgotten the Lord our God—and he is now feeling after us, should we ~~no~~ humble us, and turn unto the Lord, he will yet have mercy upon us—and deliver us from the hands of our enemies—as he did, the Nephites, when heavily burdened under the hands of their enemies.

Let us place our faith in God, humble ourselves before him, ~~an~~ Keep his commandments, and we will yet see deliverance come to Israel.

Elder Abinadi Pratt, said that nothing but humility and faithfulness ~~can~~ on the part of the Latter day can ever secure the interposition of the Almighty in their behalf, the time will come when prison house walls, however high, or however thick, will never contain the servants of God, &c.

Elder Geo Nebeker said seven years ago, he started on a Mission to the Sandwich Islands [Hawaii], they are a singular people, but he was satisfied they are a portion of the human family that are entitled to the Gospel of Jesus Christ, ~~and th~~ as has been ~~seen~~ so abundantly manifested, by the Gifts and blessings enjoyed by them. Much labour had been devoted among them by the Elders during the past 7 years. There had been a gradual increase of the Spirit of God among them—and more labourers are needed there. Their native habits are very low and degraded and it seemed desirable by the Elders to try and induce them to lay ~~old~~ aside their old customs, and adopt ~~them~~ others more in accordance with civilized live, but so far, the Elders have been able to offer them, but very small inducements, only ten dollars per Month [to work at the Laie plantation], without board, and yet even ^with^ that small remuneration, they are willing to labour and continue.

The Government are trying to hold out inducements to Capitolists, by offering several thousand dollars to any one who will build a Cotton or Woollen Factory, with a view of giving employment to men ~~or~~ Women & Children. On one of those Pacific Islands, some Native Elders have been preaching there, and raised up Churches of more than 2,000 members. The number of inhabitants on the Sandwich Islands are very numerous—and a field of labour is there before us, that could easily employ the labour of every Elder in Israel—&c.

Elder Geo B. Wallace was satisfied, that we as a people are the only friends that God has got on the face of the earth—and that will acknowledge his right to rule among the children of men. If we will only keep our eye on our file leader, he will lead us back into the presence of our Father and God. Let us keep our ears open, and listen to the voice of the good shepherd, let us realize that God has a head on the earth. God will defend us, and we will see his salvation. Some of us will have dreams and visions, and the future will be unfolded to our minds. Some have had visions pertaining to the truth of this great latter day work, years before coming into the church. The movements now going on in our midst through the Courts, are giving us a widespread popularity, and will eventually do us a great amount of good—since these troubles commenced, there are not a tithing [tenth] of complaints brought before the High Council, which he regarded as a very good sign.

Elder Geo Q Cannon said that Prest. [Brigham] Young and Geo A Smith [staying in southern Utah] were well and enjoying themselves, such he believed were the feelings of the brethren & sisters throughout the Territory. We are having a peace that the world can neither give nor take away—such is the legacy of all latter day saints. We should live so to have ^it^ at all times, and under all circumstances.

Was much interested in the remarks of Bro Nebeker—about the Sandwich Islands, especially as he himself had the pleasure of preaching the first Gospel Sermon in their Native tongue. The Native Elders were more devoted and valient in testimony, than the White converts. ~~He then~~ There is an excellent field of labour on those Islands for either native Elders or others who may be sent there. No man is allowed to marry on those Islands until they can both read and write.[87]

B[isho]p [Edward] Hunter gave notice that the last company of Saints [blank].

John Swenson paid $5.00 towards the defend fund.

School adjourned for one week at one o clock pm. Benediction by Elder J[oseph F.] Smith.[88]

87. For more on Cannon and the early Hawaiian missionaries, see Hammond, *Island Adventures*; GCQJ, 1850–54.

88. These last two paragraphs were written vertically on the page, somewhat obscuring the horizontal text already written.

November 18, 1871; Saturday

Theological Class met in the Tabernacle at One oclock pm. Present [blank] presiding [blank]. After singing Prayer by Elder John Pack. Singing.

Elder Geo Q. Cannon said, if we exercised our gifts as the servants of God, he believed we should be inspired to speak on occasions of this Kind, ~~we~~ on the circumstances that immediately concern us. It seems to me that just at the present critical condition that now surround us—we need a special endowment of the spirit of God that whatever we say, especially in a public manner we shall be perfectly satisfied with what we have said. He then spoke of the present crusade inaugurated by the Federal officers against the Latter Day Saints. No man or set of men can deliver us from the hands of the wicked, this is the work of God, and none but God can possibly rescue us, and place us on an established basis, beyond the reach of any earthly power; Let us cultivate the spirit of union and Love, that we may be able to ^exercise^ an influence, that the world so much dreads. The Co operative Movement has created a power commercially that no other policy could have accomplished, and had there been a universal response to this principle, our power and influence in the commercial world would have been much greater than it is to day. This, he regarded as a stepping stone to a more perfect order of things, even the "Order of Enoch"—and as it becomes more general, there will be less distinctions among Men, especially in the Kingdom of God, and there will be no poor in our midst.

The First Presidency [Daniel H. Wells] who have been indicted for Murder, never had the spirit of Murder within them, and no men who indulges in the thought that they have winked at or sanctioned the Murders that have been committed in this Territory, will sooner or later apostatize from the Church ^unless they repent^. Prayed that God would enable us to keep the faith.

Elder John Pack considered himself as one of the first beginers in Mormonism. Had experienced the Mobbing & driving from the days of Kirtland down to the present time, and in every instance, God had accomplished good to Israel. In the days of the Prophet Joseph [Smith] there was always some, ~~who~~ in the Church who really thought the Prophet did wrong, and ought to be brought to Justice, and consequently, perhaps not intentionally, ~~g~~ consented to the shedding of

Innocent blood, such, did the Law's[89] & Higbee's[90] &c. The spirit of murmuring still lingers in the bosom of many in the church, and should President Young ever be sent to Prison, he will go there by the spirit of persecution, and those who consented thereto among the saints had better look out, for Prest. Young was a Man of God, and would continue to be, whether he lived or died. We shall never be driven from this land, God in his mercy has given it to us, and God is on our side, he is our strength and shield, and he will deliver us.

Elder A [Milton] Musser said the feelings of the people in the country was much the same, as is experienced by us in the City in regard to the abridgment or our rights and priveleges. He had named the subject—of contributing to the Defense fund, to the people up North—and met with an anticipated response.

He heard a gentleman say while in the west, a few days ago, that Prest. Young was the greatest statesman either in Europe or America. He then said that he thought a general expression of feeling by the masses of the people, against the encrochments on our Municipal ordinances—&c [would be welcome].

Elder John Taylor was much pleased with the remarks of Bro Musser, except the last, and I would say "keep quiet. " Mind our own business, and let the clique wiggle away. Israel will be the Head and not the tail. It is for us to do right, and God will establish his Kingdom and, this I prophecy in the name of the Lord God of Israel. Let us cleave to the right, and we have nothing to fear, God will take care of his servant Brigham, and we need not worry ourselves about him. He did not expect our troubles to grow less but become greater, and God would gives us wisdom to cope with them.

Questions were sent up to Prest. [Daniel H.] Wells, as to whether it is right for Members of the School to rent there buildings for Meat Markets, Brothels, Gambling &c.[91]

89. Brothers William (1809–92) and Wilson Law (1807–77) were excommunicated in 1844 for opposing Joseph Smith. They published the *Nauvoo Expositor* in 1844, which Smith, as mayor, had destroyed, leading to his arrest and murder. As a result, the Laws were among those blamed by the Saints for the Smiths' deaths.

90. Brothers Francis M. Higbee (b.1820) and Chauncey L. Higbee (1821–84) had been officers in the Nauvoo Legion. Willard Richards, a witness to the murders of Joseph and Hyrum Smith, said the brothers were part of the mob that attacked the jail.

91. For a study of prostitution in Salt Lake City at the time, see Nichols, *Prostitution, Polygamy, and Power.*

Prest. D. H. Wells, said he did not think any member of the School would knowingly rent their Houses for any such purposes. He had been trying to day to enter the City [Hall], & had met with some hinderances from Maj[or] [Silas B.] Overton, but should try to accomplish it on Monday if possible.

Spoke of one of our City papers recommending the people pay no more Licenses to the City Treasury. The City Authorities had comply'd with the Law in publishing a Quarterly exibit in the Deseret News. He then enumerated many improvements in the City, which has cost a great many thousand Dollars &c.

School way adjourned for one week at One o clock pm. Benediction by Elder B[righam] Young Jun[ior].

November 25, 1871; Saturday

Theological Class met at the Tabernacle at one o clock pm. Present Prest. D[aniel] H. Wells presiding. After singing Prayer by Elder Geo Goddard. Singing.

Elder Jos[ep]h F Smith felt thankful for the knowledge and blessings of the Gospel. We are not living for this life alone—but are striving to lay a foundation for future ages. We should prize our priveleges—and endeavour to ~~try~~ cultivate our minds—and hold~~ing~~ sacred the covenants we have made with God. There is still a necessity for these things to be urged upon the members of this school. He regarded our present difficulties as a necessity—on account of our unfaithfulness—and unless we repent and do better, the chastising hand of our Heavenly Father will not be taken off us.

The Kingdom of God however, will triumph and be established on the face of the earth, of this he had a testimony, whether he himself stands faithful or not. The object of this school of the Prophets was to remind and instruct the Elders of Israel in the duties of their office and callings. Yet notwithstanding this, there are some who will reveal whatever they hear in this school, although repeatedly have lifted up their hands to observe secrecy. The time is fast hastening, when such individuals will be pointed out, and hoisted from the midst of their brethren. He then called upon the members of this school, to so live our religion, that the spirit of discernment and revelation may rest upon us, to that extent as to see and understand the spirit of our neighbours.

Many persons obtain blessings in this Kingdom that are entirely unworthy, through the recommendations of Bishops & other Elders. For the lack of instruction, many brethren and sisters come to receive their endowments without a due regard to cleanliness and decency. He then condemned the spirit of covetousness, but did not think he could handle riches to advantage at present. We should observe the word of wisdom, and not ~~ob~~ sustain our enemies.

A Question was asked on paper, as to whether drinking Tea & Coffee was in keeping with the Word of Wisdom, the school unanimously said no.

Elder Amos Fielding, advocated the "Word of Wisdom," and keep away from our enemies.

Elder Orson Pratt regarded what had been said, as being of the utmost importance. Much more so, than if some new doctrine had been unfolded to us. Revelations had been given to us pertaining to our duties from the begining. Rules of our life, the coming to these vallies, the organization of the school of the Prophets, the open^ing^ up of settlements &c were all given by the spirit of revelation. There are many things however, that we Know very little about, but if we are faithful, the Lord will in his own time reveal to us as a people those things. He very much regretted that so many should continue unfaithful in those small requirements of the Almighty, such as the "Word of Wisdom," abstaining from sustaining our enemies &c. Until we do strictly observe these things, God will not reveal the greater things that have got to come forth. The time will come when every faithful man and woman in the Kingdom of God, will be taught of God from on high.

Prest. D H Wells made a few remarks on the necessity of sanctifying & preparing ourselves. For enduring the presence of Holy Beings and finally the presence of God our Heavenly Father, the importance of keeping the "Word of Wisdom," that the blessings of God, promised therein, may be enjoyed by us. Nothing of a sinful nature can endure the presence of God. The Devil directs his mark at the Head, so as to injure the body. Israel is alive and active, and we have nothing to fear. He desired to live and build up the Kingdom of God.

School was adjourned for one week at One oclock pm. After singing Benediction by Elder ~~B[righam] Young~~ H[orace] S Eldredge.

December 2, 1871; Saturday

Theological Class met in the Tabernacle at One o clock pm. Present Elder Orson Pratt presiding. After singing Prayer by B[isho]p E[dwin] D. Woolley. Singing.

David Sorenson paid $2.00 towards defence fund.

Elder Orson Pratt gave permission for any business to be brought forward.

Elder A[lbert] P. Rockwood said he was in possession of a letter that originally was sent by the Governor of India, which letter came through the Government of Great Britain, to the United States Government, ~~an~~ from there to Gov[erno]r [George L.] Wood[s] of this Territory and finally to Bro Rockwood—enquiring by what process Land impregnated with salt can be subdued—and after several remarks it was finally resolved. That a Meeting of the board of the Agriculture & Manufacturing Society, be held at the Historians Office at the close of the School—with a view of obtaining the necessary information, and forwarding the same through Gov[erno]r Wood[s]—to its final destination.

Elder Geo B. Wallace gave a few methods of his own experience how to manage and bring under successful cultivation the above Kind of land.

Elder W[ilford] Woodruff gave a graphic account of his experience with a very severe Snow Storm, on his way from Randolph to Evanston, having to travel some 15 miles in the storm, and after a very providential opening, he reached Ogden, and finally to this City, in health and strength, for which he acknowledged the hand of the Lord.[92] It is our duty to trust in God, be diligent, and faithful & true in all our duties to God and each other, and the Kingdom will be established in spite of all the opposition that is now arrayed against it.

Elder Geo Q Cannon spoke of the necessity of the saints exercising Faith in God, in relation to Prest. [Brigham] Young whose trial [for unlawful cohabitation] is set for Monday next, when it would be a physical impossibility for his presence on that occasion, but it often happens that

92. Woodruff refused to abandon his team of horses for the train, writing that the spirit inspired people, including a bitter ex-Mormon, to help him. A local man "had ten Chinamen with him" whom he ordered to help dig Woodruff and his team through three feet of snow until he could put his horses on a freight train. WWJ, Nov. 27, 1871.

our enemies overstep the bounds of prudence to that extent as to defeat the object they seek to bring about. And it will be always the case, if we will only do our duties, and God will bring us off victorious in spite of all their venomous designs. The flagrant injustice that has been done us, by the Court no[t] sitting [local jurors], has won for us ~~such~~ a host of friends all over the universe, that no other circumstance could have accomplished. Let us continue our unabated faith and prayers to God for his blessing to rest upon his servants, and that he will thwart the plans and purposes of the Wicked & ungodly.

B[isho]p E[dwin] D. Woolley spoke on the subject of Faith, in the experience of a sick child, recently, when the Lord Kindly honored his faith, in its restoration. Let us humble ourselves before the Lord, and entreat him to thwart the plans of our enemies, He bore testimony to the truth of what Elder Cannon had said.

Elder Z[erubbabel] Snow. (Attorney) felt cheered at the remarks already made. He realized in part, some two years ago, the designs of our enemies in laying their plans, to bring about those things that we now see. They were trying to destroy the reputation of the Servants of God—their course was and would be, to convict under a show of Legality in Court, for sinning against mans ~~last~~ laws. The same Spirit that prompts the enemies of God in these days, is precisely the same ~~as~~ that prompted the death of the Saviour.

The $5000.00 bail [for Young and others], will never be paid by his Council, until it should be so decided by the Supreme Court at Washington [D.C.]. They began this game themselves and must risk the consequences. A lesson is being taught us, that no other circumstances could teach. There may be things that will be greivous to bear, but the Almighty will most assuredly bring us out all right at last. There are thousands of Millions ~~of~~ on the earth, that will have to acknowledge this great work—then let us never leave it.

Elder B[righam] Young Jun[io]r advocated the principle of Faith—which should commence at the family Alter, and by a constant attention to our duties to God, this will lay a foundation broad and deep for the exercise of Faith.

Elder Orson Pratt endorsed the sentiments of the previous speaker. Spoke of the imprisonment of his brother Parley [P. Pratt] in Missouri with three other brethren—and the power of Faith in delivering them—by the simplest imaginable means, but we must be willing to put works with our faith if we expect to succeed.

The school was adjourned for one week at one o clock pm. After singing Benediction by Elder J[ohn] Taylor.

December 9, 1871; Saturday

~~On Thursday~~ Theological Class met at the Tabernacle at One o clock pm. Present Prest. D[aniel] H. Wells presiding. After singing Prayer by Elder Geo Nebeker. Singing.

Elder W[illia]m Taylor 14th Ward paid in $15.00 for defence fund.

Elder Jos[ep]h Barfoot who had received a serious injury in his Eye, was administered to by several brethren on the stand. Elder John Taylor being mouth.

Elder J[ohn] D. T. McAllister made enquiry as to how property should be filed on which Meeting & School Houses were on, where a deed was never given for said property, but simply held as trust for such purposes?

Elder E[lias] Smith (Judge of Probate) said where there is no other claim ~~f~~ on lots where Meeting and School Houses stand, than is vested in the hands of School trustees who have been legally elected & qualified, he believed that the Bishops could file ^their declaration^ on those lands, this was simply his opinion, but our laws being very defective on that point, in all probability our Legislature may prepare something more definite on the subject. He also gave instructions pertaining to the fileing ^of^ a declaratory statement of property.

Prest. D[aniel] H. Wells warned the brethren against ^the employment of^ unprincipled Lawyers in getting out their declaratory statement many of whom are on the look out for such jobs—and stirring up strifes among the people, and defending Saloon keepers & brothel House Keepers, in opposing the City Ordinances &c. Bro[thers] [John R.] Winder, [William] Clayton and Jonason have printed forms, and are prepared to make out statements for the brethren, at a small rate of fees.

Elder Jno [John] Winder said the form he decided upon in making our declaratory statements, had been scrutinized and sanctioned by Judge [Elias] Smith.

Elder Jos[ep]h F. Smith said that some had exprest a desire to meet in a warmer room through the winter, he had named the Matter to Bro Wells, and he could not think of any other room so suitable as this, but the brethren should be well wrapp'd up and prepared for a cold room. He then made a few remarks on the laws of life and health. and spoke on the low sunken condition of the world of Mankind, who were as wicked as they had knowledge to become. Recommended well ventilated rooms to sleep in, we have but one life to live, in this probation, and we should try so to live, as to extend our existence to a good old age.

We have a guarrantee from the almighty that we shall never be driven from our homes in these vallies, but enjoy our rights, & priveleges undisturbed, provided on our part, we keep the commandments of God, but if we do not, we have no guarantee. He could not have believed two years ago, that in 1870 & 1871—We should have been deprived of such a constitutional right, as our Militia to Meet annually to Muster. This and many other infringements on our rights will not be taken off of us until we as a people repent and keep the commandments of God. There is scarcely any of the Moral laws of God but what we have lightly esteemed and more or less neglected. He condemned the practise of preaching one thing and practising another. There was much abuse indulged in under the law of Plurality of Wives. Many bring disrepute and disgrace upon that holy principle, by the improper course pursued by the Husbands who have more wives than one. He also spoke on tithing and the necessity of living up to that law. Also allowing Cattle to run loose in the Streets to do damage to fences and eat up their neighbours hay, and then refuse to pay for the damage. Let us do our duty, and we will triumph in the name of Jesus Amen.

Elder B[righam] Young Jun[io]r had learned enough this afternoon to pay him well for the time he had spent here to day. He strongly recommended abstinence from drink at our meals—he had experienced the beneficial effects of it himself. Those who practise it, will seldom or never have a headache, or need any pills or Cathartic [laxative] Medicine.

~~He~~ Prest. D. H. Wells bore testimony to the good things refer'd to this afternoon. God was dealing kindly and gently ^with~~to~~^ us, and causing the severity of his providences to pass by us. Let us then appreciate his mercies and turn round and do better, especially in those things wherein we have been negligent. Let us sustain each other—so that we may ~~be~~ have greater power with the almighty.

Last Saturday we were requested to unite our faith in God, that he would remove from us some of those obnoxious Officials—and as he now done it[93]—how thankful we ought to be, let us then wait upon the Lord and make known unto him our wants and situation. Let us be Fathers & Husbands instead of Masters—and treat them by the power of kindness so as to gain their confidence and affection. A good wife is a great blessing, and they ought to be prized. Let us cultivate the spirit of peace in our families and our neighbourhoods. The abuse of the polygamic principle had once to be laid aside in the days of Jacob on a/c [account] of the ~~dau~~ afflictions heaped upon the daughters of Zion. It is possible, that we as a people may be denied the principle of a plurality of wives—hereafter, for not honoring it thus far. The woman is the glory of the Man, and are to be eternal blessings, if we will only treat them right. If we do not honor this great principle, God will surely take it away from us.

School was adjourned for one week ~~at~~ at one o clock—Benediction by Elder O[rson] Pratt.

December 16, 1871; Saturday

Theological Class met in the Tabernacle at One O clock pm. Present Prest. D[aniel] H Wells presiding. After singing Prayer by Elder Geo Nebeker. Singing.

Elder [William] C Staines said this was the first time he had ever been called upon to speak at the School. He had enjoyed himself much while on his Mission East on the Emigration business, never had better health in ~~th~~ his life, which blessing had been promised him by Elder [Wilford] Woodruff before he started. Some prominent men east had told him that the Government was determined to put a stop to Plurality [of wives]. Since his return, he had occasion to go south [to St. George] on business, had met with Prest. [Brigham] Young who was well & his brethren who were with him. He was much pleased with the Southern Country. He met with many friends, and the best of treatment. There was a very calm quiet spirit throughout all the settlements in regard to the present difficulties, knowing that God would bring everything out all right.

He himself never ~~f~~ felt better in his life than at present—and a calm spirit rested down upon the saints. God has confered his ~~spirit~~ priesthood upon us—and he will stand by us and see us through. He will manifest his Power in our behalf—if we only do right. Whatever the

93. Territorial governor John W. Shaffer had died in office and the US attorney, Charles H. Hempstead, resigned.

servants of God dictate us in relation to our future course, let us to a man walk up and carry it out, and all will be right.

Elder Orson Pratt in speaking of the present crusade said he was well satisfied as to the final result being the certain triumph of truth over error, and that no power beneath the Celestial Kingdom will be able to annoy or perplex us. But how far the Lord is disposed to let us suffer persecution he did now know. He had reflected much and searched much in the Bible, Book of Mormon & Doctrine & Covenants, on the future destiny and glory of the saints. But the intervening circumstances were not revealed, they were hidden from us, and he oftentimes felt thankful that such was the case. We have got to be tried in all things, even unto death, many of the early saints in Missouri have been put to this test. We do not know what we would do in case we were severely tried, we all no doubt feel anxious to endure faithful even to the end, ~~to~~ & by the grace of God we will stand. We may see serious times of trials before we are entirely free from persecutions. God may soften the hearts of some of our bitterest enemies—and by the presentation of an enabling act wherein, our previous Wives & children shall be regarded as legitimate ^&^ provided we in the future shall lay aside the practise of Plurality ~~then you~~ ^we ~~may~~^ may be admitted into the Union as a State—but if we will only be diligent in keeping the ~~Keep~~ commandments of God, our future pathway will be as clear as the ~~das~~ noon day sun, as it will be marked out for us by the servants of god.

Elder John Taylor said the Lord introduced ~~by~~ the Polygamy question. He did not think he [God] would change his mind. The circumstances ~~cir~~ surrounding us are not of our seeking for God says, He will make the wrath of man to praise him, and the remainder he will restrain. He had no principle of religion to barter away. If we cannot get all the privileges we want let us enjoy all we can get. He had no~~t~~ disposition to fight, for 100,000 against 40 Million would be a very unequal combat. He had no fear about the issue. God would prove himself wiser than the devil. He his [is] ten thousand times more interested in the rolling forth of his work than we can possibly be.

He then Prophesied in the name of the Lord—That the work of God should continue to roll until all enemies are put under his feet. God bless Israel, and all ~~bl~~ who bless Israel.

Prest. D H Wells said Prest. [Brigham] Young might or might not be here—but God will deliver him,—and whether he comes or not, it will be all right. He himself had been deprived of his liberty for about 48 hours[94]—and through the faith and Kindness of his friends & blessing of God, he had again enjoyed his liberty. And no one can truly estimate this boon, only by contrast—and as to what we will do, or not do—it would not be policy to say—but this we will do—and that is just what God reveals for us to do. He told a gentleman, We would neither refuse nor obey, neither would we fight or run away. Our enemies will be caught in their own snare, but they are certainly making the most of their brief authority but God would bring us through, only let us do right. Both friends & foes in the states think we must certainly give up plurality, but God himself will reveal his will to us in the future, as he has done in the past just at the very time it is wanted. He looked for far more revelation than we have hitherto had. If there is one sin worse than another that man can commit, ~~is~~ it is the betryal of the servants of God. Therefore beware how any of you carry anything to our enemies from this school.

Though there are a great many of Meek, unpretending men in this Kingdom who would rather suffer at the stake, than forfeit their integrity. May God help us to live our religion and do right, and we will be preserved.

"Eternal Vigilence is the price of liberty" therefore you latter day saints be ready with your ~~guns~~ Arms and Ammunition. And keep them where you can put your hands upon them at a Moments notice—and be sure to have your powder dry.

School was adjourned for one week at one o clock pm. After singing Benediction by W[ilford] Woodruff.[95]

December 23, 1871; Saturday

Theological Class met at the Tabernacle at 1 o clock pm. Present Prest. D[aniel] H. Wells presiding. After singing Prayer by ~~E~~ B[isho]p J[esse] C. Little. Singing.

Elder Tho[ma]s Whittaker of Centerville paid $5.00 towards defence fund.

Elder B[righam] Young Jun[io]r never saw the hand of the Lord made more manifest than during the past three Months, especially in

94. See Nov. 4, 1871, entry for Wells's arrest for murder.
95. Woodruff's name was inserted in pencil later in different handwriting.

our surroundings, he had no doubt but we as a people would come out all right, if we only do right. That was a solemn and important consideration. In regard to the principle of Polygamy, he had been taught it from his youth up, and accordingly had practisedg it—and should not relinquish it, unless Prest. [Brigham] Young was to take the responsibility upon himself, by counselling us to lay it aside for the time being. Some had so signally failed in attempting to live polygamy, as to richly deserve being cut off from the Church, and therefore he did not at all wonder at being persecuted at the present time. He believed however that if the Federal Officers pressed us too hard, so as to be under the necessity of leaving here, we should send a Colony to build up Jackson Co[unty] M[iss]o[uri]. He then rehearsed a dream that he had, he was in an elevated position, so that he could see the entire Continent of America from the Atlantic to the Pacific Oceans. He could not discern one large city east ~~and~~ ^or^ West, nor one Railroad, but could distinctly see the Territory of Utah from St. George to this City. Also at a signal, the people collected here by thousands, a Call was then made for Volunteers to go East or West to establish Colonies, for the Country had become entirely depopulated. One after another rose up and volunteered, and the Clerk taking down their names.

Elder John Pack spoke of the good results likely to flow from the persecuting spirit now going on—but the time of our greatest trial, he believed, had not yet come. We have not yet been called upon to sacrifice a portion of our religion for the sake of peace.

He had seen closer times than these in the days of Joseph [Smith]. He believed that we as a people who trust in God, will stand through the fiery ordeal. Our enemies had accomplished nothing as yet, but there own shame. God will defend this people, and work out his purposes in his own way. Some may have to seal their testimony with their blood, besides Joseph and Hyrum [Smith]. If that should be the case all will be right. We have good peace even now—in comparison with the Ancient Apostles and Saints. He had a constant assurence that those [who] will live faithful will inherit Eternal exaltation.

~~Elder~~ Prest. D H Wells read a few lines from a letter just rec[eive]d from Prest. B Young, of a very consoling nature, in the shape of a dream. There was no danger of us having to surrender any portion of our Religion. But as to Polygamy, if anything ever caused that principle to be withheld from us, it will be in consequence of the God of Heaven being displeased with many who have gone into it. He for one should be thankful to become a State, and intended to use his influence to effect it.[96] Our enemies are seeking to deprive us of every Civil, and religious liberty. We can stand it, and go through it, and come off victorious. He was in favor of fighting our way through the courts, though it may cost us come liberty, and much money—he was glad it is no worse. He did hope however that every man in Isreal[97] will be in a state of readiness at a Moments notice to turn out to the rescue if needed. The power arrayed against us formidable, and they mean no good towards us.

B[isho]p E[dward] Hunter who had just returned from a visit East said he had rejoiced in the doctrine & practise of Celestial [plural] Marriage, regarded it as a greater blessing than anything else. Had noticed great changes in and around Philadelphia and among the people also, during his absence of 21 years. The people seemed to be entirely overshadowed with a careless and worldly spirit, they dont want religion. He cannot see how the Lord can permit them to go on much longer adding sin to sin.

Elder W[ilford] Woodruff warned the school against telling out of this house what is spoken here, but keep sacred, the covenant we have made.

School was adjourned for one week at 1 oclock pm. After singing Benediction by H[orace] S Eldredge.[98]

December 30, 1871; Saturday

Theological Class met in the Tabernacle at One o clock pm. Present Presiding [blank]. After singing Prayer by B[isho]p Alex[ande]r McRae. Singing.

In response to the question by Prest. [Daniel H.] Wells, If there was any business to bring before the School?

Elder Geo Dunford spoke of the necessities of those families whose Husbands & Father's have been incarcerated in Prison [for unlawful cohabitation] and thus deprived of the privelege of sustaining them [their

96. The territorial legislature would renew its bid for statehood in January 1872, dispatching George Q. Cannon and others to Washington, DC, to press Congress. For the fourth time, Congress denied the request.

97. The remainder of this entry is written vertically, somewhat obscuring the horizontal text already recorded.

98. Eldredge's name appears in a different handwriting as a later insertion.

families]. He suggested the idea of such families being cared for and their wants attended to, out of the general Defense fund instead of by private subscription.

Elder A M[ilton] Musser said he had been canvassing this very subject in the Country, and met with a liberal response. Every Elder in Israel should make it a personal consideration and give freely what we can. If a sacrifice was required of many lives, and much property to sustain the principles of our holy religion—what of it. We should cheerfully regard our priveleges as of far greater importance than gold, silver, or Houses. We must see, that no Family suffers for want of food or shelter. He did not believe that one principle of our holy Religion would ever be given up on any consideration. If it takes everything we possess to establish the Kingdom, we must not hold back. The Church is going through a partial trial at the present time, but all will come out right, to those who are true latter day saints or friends of God. Our enemies are envious, and seek to take advantage of this people. Our Leaders are anxious to have the Kingdom of God established in righteousness. Let us be willing to subscribe freely, to sustain the interests of the Kingdom of God—not only with our prayers, but with our means.

Elder John Taylor said that We as well as our enemies are after Means and influence, only they dont care how they get it, and we do. ~~ours~~ The time will come when the Saints will take the Kingdom and possess it. We are building our plans upon the Revelations of the Lord of Hosts, and will certainly prosper. ~~We~~ He believed all the operations of our Judges would fizzle, ~~and~~ out—and come to nought. This ^is^ not the cause of Prest. [Brigham] Young or Wells. It is the cause of truth and righteousness, it is the cause of the people, and each of us will sustain it by our Means. Israel shall triumph and the powers of darkness shall be put down. Let us follow the wisdom of God through his servants.

Prest. D H Wells said, if the people of this Territory, were aroused to a united action, they would be willing to sacrifice their property and their lives also—in the defense of Zion, and flee to the Mountains—but this is not the ~~b~~ present kind of warfare. We have to meet our enemies in the Courts. And means ~~are~~ ^was^ wanted to carry it on. Two men had been to Prest. D H Wells this week, who promised to clear our brethren who are now in Prison, if ~~they would~~ he would pay them for it. Only give our enemies rope enough—and they will hang themselves.

He would willingly sell his House & lot, if he could get as much for it, as would give us a State Government.

He expected Prest. Young & himself to ~~be~~ appear in Court on the 9th Jan[uar]y—and he particularly desired the Faith of the Latter day Saints—and hoped the brethren would be ready with Works also, without asking questions.

It was a Monstrous outrage that was being perpetrated upon this ~~time~~ people, at the present time. Have faith in God and keep your powder dry—and be ready at a moments notice. If necessity forced us to retire from these vallies, as a people we should do it cheerfully. The Latter day Saints are not so liable to go astray in times of War than in times of peace. Let us sustain our Cooperative Institution. Be liberal with our means—whatever we do to build up the Kingdom of God, we do it to build up ourselves.

The School was adjourned for one week at one o clock pm. After singing Benediction by A[lbert] O. Carrington.[99]

99. Carrington's name is a later insertion and in different handwriting.

CHAPTER FOUR

"THE GREAT PILLARS OF OUR SALVATION"

1872

January 6, 1872; Saturday

Theological Class met at the Tabernacle at One o clock pm. Present Prest. D[aniel] H. Wells presiding. After singing Prayer by Elder A M[ilton] Musser. Singing.

Elder Geo Q Cannon read a few lines address'd to the Prest. of the School, of the, suggesting that a special Prayer be offered to the Lord by the school, for the deliverance of Prest. B[righam] Young[,] Prest. D. H. Wells, ^George Q Cannon^ John L. Blythe, Tho[ma]s Hawkins W[illia]m Kimball, Hosea Stout, B[righam] Y. Hampton & James Thom[a]s, all of whom are now in bondage, and are shortly expecting to take their trials.[1]

It was then Motioned & Carried, That said Prayer should be offered and also That Elder Orson Pratt should be Mouth.

Elder O[rson] Pratt then offered a ~~suit~~ comprehensible prayer for the health, wisdom, & final deliverance ^and usefulness^ of Prest. Young and the others now under bonds, or in prison—and the speedy overthrow of all those who are in any way connected with the present persecutions.

Prest. D. H. Wells then suggested that inasmuch as the Legislature

1. Young was under house arrest, pending trial for cohabitation, and would not be able to preside over a school meeting until after the US Supreme Court's late-April ruling in *Englebrecht v. Clinton* (see Apr. 20, 1872), voiding recent jury indictments and sentences. Thomas Hawkins (1829–1903) was a Latter-day Saint being held in the territorial prison for polygamy. He had been the chief justice of the Utah Supreme Court for five years. When released, he would escape south to Arizona and eventually die in Mexico. Brigham Young Hampton (1836–1902) was the LDS deputy city marshal in Salt Lake City, in prison for murder. His biographer described him as a "thug" who, for instance, when released immediately arrested the witness against him. See Turner, *Brigham Young*, 367–68; Hughes, *Thomas Sunderland Hawkins*; Nichols, "In Defence of God's People," 345, 349–50. See also entries herein for Oct. 14, 21, 1871; May 25, 1872.

will meet on Monday, and the ~~possibly of~~ possibility of having conflicting circumstances to contend with—that a special Prayer be offered by Elder John Taylor in behalf of the legislative body. Motioned & Carried unanimously.

Elder John Taylor then Offered Prayer for and in behalf of the Legislative body who will be ^in^ session for some time on and after Monday next, that every Member of that body may be inspired by the almighty to legislate for the good of the saints of God, and not interrupted by arrests, or otherwise &c both of the above prayers were responded to by a unanimous Amen.

Elder Geo Q Cannon who had been absent four weeks[2] was again delighted to be in the midst of his brethren ~~a~~—and partake of the good spirit that reigns in this school. He fully believed that Prest. Young would be liberated from the hands of his enemies, and continue to lead the Saints as the Mouthpiece of God for years to come.

While East he conversed with prominent Men pertaining to the Government, but the best and most friendly disposed of them, suggests that we as a people should surrender that portion of our faith, which Congress has seen fit to stigmatize as evil[.] This surrender of Polygamy by the ~~Sain~~ latter day Saints, will prevent Congress from putting it down by main force, which they will most certainly do. But rather than ^the^ giving up of one principle of our holy religion, he was perfectly willing to stand by and see the fight between God and ^the^ wicked. Never let us yield one particle of our faith, but stand by and sustain every principle that God has revealed—even to the death if necessary. The enemies of God will most certainly be defeated—it is for us however to live humble, and devoted to the interests of the Kingdom of God.

Elder Isaac Laney, suggested the propriety of appointing a Committee of 2 or 3, to enquire into the circumstances of the families of Hosea Stout, W[illiam] Kimball, &c and if they require help, to assist them out of the general Defence fund.[3]

2. Cannon had been in Washington, DC, lobbying government officials to intercede in Utah on behalf of the church and those arrested for cohabitation.

3. Bill Hickman said that in 1857 Hosea Stout and William Kimball had accompanied him to Echo Station in the mountains east of Salt Lake City, that Stout had held a latern while Hickman "went to the tent where [Richard] Yates lay asleep and brained him with an axe." This was during the Utah War, and Mormons suspected Yates of being a government spy. Contrary to the accusation against him, Stout was in Salt Lake City

Elder W[ilford] Woodruff, said the secret of the present antagonism about Polygamy, was simply, because it was a command of God, and Lucifer was opposed to it. He did not believe in abandoning one principle of the Gospel to please this Nation or any other. We can afford to risk the issue and consequences of the present persecution—the controversary is between God and the Nation. Let us remember to Keep the commandments of God, to attend to our prayers and duties and God will deliver us. We shall certainly come off much better, by cleaving to our religion than by bartering any portion of it away for the sake of a State Government. Let us unite our prayers together.

The School was adjourned for one week at one o clock pm. After singing Benediction by Elder Jos[ep]h F. Smith.

January 13, 1872; Saturday

Theological Class met in the Tabernacle at One oclock pm. Present ~~Elder John Van Cott~~ ^President D[aniel] H. Wells^ presiding. After singing Prayer by Elder ^Jno [John]^ Van Cott. Singing.

Elder [Christian F. N.] Twede related a dream which he had on New Years Morning.

Elder Amos Fielding spoke on the present condition of affairs, repudiated the idea of relinquishing any portion of our religious views.

Elder [Robert H.] Collins related a vision which Joseph Smith gave to him about 4 Months after his death. He shown him the Saints leaving Nauvou in a body ~~leaving~~ crossing the great Mississippi [River], and travelling Westward. He then showed him a Mighty army going in the same direction, a much greater army than has ever been here before. But he did not see that it entered the valley. He believed the waves of persecution would run much higher than at present, ~~and~~ but that a chosen few would finally be picked up to return to Jackson County [Missouri].

Elder David Fulmer also related a dream, in which he noticed such an immense fortification that seemed to reach almost to heaven, and their artillery was let loose upon us, until the earth fairly trembled but the balls fell before reaching the City &c, he awoke feeling comforted, and ^he^ really believes that our enemies cannot really do us any harm.

Elder John Taylor realized that the great work in which we are

at the time of the murder, according to his diary. Stout, *Utah's Pioneer Statesman*, 250; Prince, *Hosea Stout*, 329–32.

engaged, God and Angels also are interested in, and have much more to do ~~work~~ with it than we, and whatever will best answer the purpose of moving it forward, will take place. God will not step out of his path, ~~for~~ either for Judges, Congress or Any one else. If it was necessary for the Captain of our Salvation to be made perfect through suffering, it is also necessary for his Saints to pass through the same ordeal. Spoke of the nature of the civilization that the Courts have introduced here. As a people, let us endeavour to do right, by following the Councils of those who are placed over us. God is wiser than the Children of Men. He manages to take care of them, and he also will controul us. No man can stop the work of God, but go on and increase—until the Knowledge of God shall cover the earth as the waters cover the mighty deep.

Elder [William] Miller spoke of ^a^ sign that was seen in the heavens about 9 feet long and 1 foot wide—seen some years not far from Prest. [Brigham] Youngs house—and two others, one in England, and the other passing through this ~~Valley~~ Territory, each of which he gave an explanation to, which had direct reference to the trials among Kings, and nations—and the Priesthood, and the Saints generally. He then related a dream which he had about 9 years ago. He dreamt that he stood in the presence of Uncle Sam who stood before him as a large well made man about 12 feet high—but quite naked,[4] and started back in a state of affright—at the sight of Elder Miller, who represented the latter day Saints. He noticed that Uncle Sam was much afflicted with the bad [sexually transmitted] disorder, which indicated the Moral condition of the Nation.

Elder A[lbert] Carrington urged the necessity of latter day Saints living humble and faithful, so that the Lord can work with us in bringing about his great purposes. Let us ask the Lord to bless us in ~~t~~ our labours, and also ask him for wisdom to use it for the building up of his Kingdom. Warned the school against the love of gain which is idolatry. We as a people have great power if faithful. God has been very kind to us. His hand has turned away one trial after ~~trial~~ another that should cause every lover of truth, to be very earnest and fervent, in our service ~~in~~ ^toward^ God our Heavenly Father. In our present or any future crusade that may be arrayed against us—if we continue faithful God will enable us to triumph over all our enemies &c.

4. Miller said that Uncle Sam's clothes had been "knawed off by rats, except rags round his neck." JSFJ, Jan. 13, 1872.

Elder John Winder related a dream.

Elder Geo Q. Cannon Moved & was carried Bro John H Standerfird take a Mission to the United States.

He then spoke of the many manifestations ~~of~~ and gifts of the Spirit, bestowed upon the ~~Spirit~~ Saints according to their faith—especially that of revelation which has rested upon Prest. Young to a Marvelous degree since the death of Joseph Smith—and the time will come when the universal verdict will be rendered him, as one of the greatest Prophets that ever lived upon the earth. He then rehearsed the great wisdom that God had displayed in the many deliverances that he had wrought for us his people. The Members of the leading Quorums of this church were never more united than at the present time,

School was adjourned for one week at one oclock. After singing Benediction by Elder B[righam] Young [Jr].

January 20, 1872; Saturday

Theological Class met at the Tabernacle at one o clock pm. Present Prest. D[aniel] H. Wells presiding. After singing Prayer by B[isho]p A[lonzo] H. Raleigh. Singing.

Elder O[rson] Pratt spoke of the remarkable progress that has been made in the Church and Kingdom of God during the past 40 years, especially in the laying aside of a great amount of our old traditions. When he first became acquainted with the Prophet Joseph [Smith], there was not more than between one and two hundred members of the Church in all the World. By the revelations of the Holy Ghost ~~He had it revealed~~ the Divinity of this work was made known to him, which is an all sufficient testimony to him for one probation.[5] The Kingdom is gradually ^growing^ in strength and power, ~~&~~ keeping pace with its advancing years. He hoped, that if we ever be admitted into the Union as a State, it would be ~~entitled~~ entirely on constitutional grounds, without the relinquishment of one principle of our holy faith—which he was personally very much opposed to—it would not be honest in us to do so. We should [not] be reducing ourselves to the level of the Christian World. He was highly in favour of maintaining our faith inviolate, and

5. In Mormon theology, "probation" is the equivalent of "mortality," the time between the pre-mortal existence and the afterlife, during which one learns right from wrong and is tested on knowing the difference (2 Ne. 9:27; Alma 12:24; Hel. 13:38; Morm. 9:28).

never barter away one principle for a little Political Power—and if a Convention [for statehood][6] should be held in this territory he for one would suggest that the Delegates appointed should be so instructed by the people, that they should not allow ~~one~~ the forfeiture of any Religious or Political right for the sake of being admitted into the Union.

Elder W[ilford] Woodruff strongly recommended the Elders of Israel to keep a Journal of the dealings of God with them. The Prophet Joseph used to urge this upon the Elders. ~~C~~ Bro Woodruff said he ~~co~~ kept a record of every sermon that he heard Joseph preach. He wished that a more correct account had been kept of the early doings of the early Elders of the Church, and the dealings of God with his people.[7] He has never neglected one day without writing something in his diary.

In regard to the Spirit of Prophecy, we are apt to look two [too] high, and except too much in the wrong direction. The still small voice of the spirit was what we should seek after and cultivate. [When] the Church [was] in its infancy when a Man was called to go on a Mission, the Lord had to be enquired of, and obtain from Him a Revelation. But now [through] Prest. [Brigham] Young living in the light of revelation hundreds are called to go on a Mission and have to start in a few hours. The Church has grown, and we are continually led by the spirit of revelation. We have much to be grateful for, the Kingdom is onward and upward. He then related several forewarnings of danger ^by the Spirit of God^ which he always listened to and acted upon. And himself, family & friends saved from sudden destruction.

Elder Geo Q Cannon said we had great cause for thankfulness, that we as a School can listen to the words of the servants of God pour out upon us the spirit of Prophecy and Revelation, and [especially] when we reflected how much peace we enjoy, and attending to the Ordinances of the Gospel, notwithstanding the unfavourable surroundings of our enemies. How humble and grateful we ought to be to our Heavenly Father. Neither imprisonment or death, can either give or take away that peace, which is the heritage of the Saints, if we ever expect to mingle and

6. A constitutional convention would be held between February 19 and March 2 in the City Hall on 100 South and State Street, but the resulting petition for statehood would be rejected by the US Congress.

7. Woodruff was echoing Pratt, who had said "he wished that there could be a small plain History of Joseph Smith written by some one who had a good Memory by some one who could remember the circumstances as they were." WWJ, Jan. 20, 1872.

associate with the ancient or Modern servants of God who have suffered Martyrdom for the truths sake, we much expect to travel the same road. I know this is the work of God, by the revelations of God. He hoped we would never swerve from the truth, nor relinquish one iota of those sacred principles that God has revealed, but endure steadfast to the end.

Elder A[lbert] Carrington had been much interested in what had been ~~said~~ heard this afternoon, of the testimony's of his brethren, and the kind handdealing of his Heavenly Father during the early infancy of the church. His feeling was, to [try to] be able to meet and attend to every requirement that God made upon him.

He knew ~~any~~ ^of no^ one following the dictates of the good spirit going astray, but are right all the time—but those who are to be fed all the while with outside manifestations, will sooner or later apostatize from the Church.

Elder G. Q. Cannon said as there was several Phreno[lo]gical Lectures going to be delivered in the City, he would just say that he did ^not^ believe much in that science, and hoped the Elders would not patronize them, especially in having charts of ^their^ own characters taken.[8] Several once prominent members of the church have had their charts taken, and it seemed to puff them up so, that they eventually apostatized, A[masa] Lyman[,] W[illiam] Shearman &c.

Elder A Carrington sanctioned the above suggestions—also Prest. D. H. Wells.

The School was adjourned for one week at one o clock pm. After singing Benediction by Elder C[harles] C Rich.

January 27, 1872; Saturday

Theological Class met at the Tabernacle at One oclock pm. Present Prest. D[aniel] H. Wells presiding. After singing Prayer by Elder I[saac] Groo. Singing.

Elder C[harles] C Rich was pleased to meet in the School of the Prophets. Here we can be corrected in Doctrine or in practise, it takes many years and even ~~in~~ a life ^time^ to learn, before we can attain perfection, but tis very encouraging to find that we are progressing. We have no fear to be discouraged on acc[oun]t of our enemies, they are in

8. Phrenology purported to tell a person's personality by the shape, contours and bumps of their skull.

the Lords hand, and he has pledged himself to provide for his Saints. We are Gods ministers and have many responsibilities lying upon us, individually & collectively. This is the work of the Lord and he will bear it off—~~his~~ Let us be cheerful, inasmuch as our labours are those of love which they will be if we enjoy the Spirit of the Lord.

Elder Wright, [from] Box Elder—experienced embarrassment in attempting to preach, but desired to conceal himself on some previous occasions to prevent being called upon, and was severely reproved for it—in his own mind and conscience. Salvation will come by strict obedience to his laws, ^&^ faithful service in his cause. ~~and we~~ The greatest blessing Men or women can enjoy in this life, is the Spirit of the Lord. Some persons are so organized that they are naturally honest. Others, ~~that they~~ are inclined to cover up, are deceptive, and will even steal &c—but these ~~at~~ must be overcome—or they may not have ~~power~~ ^any part^ or lot with the righteous. We have our Agency, and must use it to overcome every unrighteous and unhallowed appetite.

The enemies of God are doomed to utter des~~cription~~^struction^, and (~~He~~) he did not wish to hasten that awful time. Prest. [Brigham] Young was in the hands of an enemy—but he was happy, and God was with him. He was in constant communion with God—and acted as he was Moved upon by his Spirit. Whoever has that spirit, the world cannot take it away from him, it lives in him, and through him like fire in flint. Let us couple works with our faith if we wish to be saved, and may the blessing of God rest upon every member of the School.

Elder A[lbert] P. Rockwood said that Gov[ernor]r [George L.] Woods[9] had vetoed the bill recently passed by the Legislature ^to convene a convention^—but he was thankful, there was another way by which a Convention can be held[10]—and no doubt would be. From remarks made by the Governor he regarded as an insult not only to himself, but to the community, and being so far from truth, had made him righteously mad.

9. George L. Woods (1832–90) had been governor of Oregon from 1866 to 1870. A Republican, he had arrived on the coast with his parents when they moved there from Missouri when he was a teenager. He worked as a carpenter and attorney before he ran for office.

10. That is, the convention would be held without the governor's support. It was, of course, a doomed endeavor from the beginning to try to convince federal officials to ignore the opinion of the federally appointed executive.

Prest. D H Wells. Moved, & was unanimously Carried—That we hold a convention, ~~an~~ appoint officers, & Draft a Constitution for admission into the Union as a State. We will go right along without any regard to those who try to stand in our way, because they are possessed with a little brief authority. All the vexatous prosecutions they have commenced, are based on the trick of a Lawyer, and are illegal. Every step they take will only get their feet deeper in the mud.

If the saints do right, the Devil will be unable to hoist ^us^ at this time. He was satisfied that in a short time the efforts of our enemies ~~f~~ will fizzle out. He said that Prest. Young recently expressed his fear that some of the brethren are becoming selfish and worldly minded. Let every Man be honest with himself and the priesthood, and show our profession by our works. If we dont want to be latter day saints, let us cease to make pretensions and join something else.

The Glory of Zion is increasing day by day and will continue to increase—but let us cease finding fault, ~~an~~ or our minds will become darkened and we'll lose our faith.

School was adjourned for one week at one o clock pm. After singing Benediction by Elder Jos[ep]h F. Smith.

February 3, 1872; Saturday

Theological Class met in the old Tabernacle at one o clock pm. Present Prest. D[aniel] H. Wells present. Singing. Prayer by B[isho]p S[amuel] A. Woolley. Singing.

Elder George Goddard refere'd to the importance of the times in which we live, and the necessity of the Elders of Israel being united in keeping the commandments of God and standing shoulder to shoulder with the servants of God, in stem^m^ing the tide of corruption that has lately been pouring into our midst, that we may finally triumph over the wicked, and establish the Kingdom of God.

Elder Jos[ep]h F Smith spoke of the necessity of man submitting to the will of another, it is not natural for Man to submit to restraint. Was free to admit that as a people we are the best that can be found on the face of the each [earth], who are more or less restrained by the influence of the Spirit of God, were it not for this, how long would it be, before we should descend to the level of the most reckless.

We have put on [the badge of] Christ, and therefore ^are^ under the greatest responsibility to live the Gospel, and teach it by precept also. Unless we do this, we simply stand in the presence of God as Hypocrites, and shall be judged as such. He and all he had was in the Kingdom of God—and desired to continue therein all his life. He had laboured diligently on Missions and other ways for many years, not only for the Kingdom of God, but for his own Glory and exaltation, for the two are inseparable.

Elder Geo Q Cannon said that the City Election for our Officers will take place in a few days, and it beho[o]ved every man in Israel to be on the alert and wide awake in not only voting our selves, but encourage our Neighbours, unless we do this, we cannot reasonably expect to gain our future elections, as we have done in the past. And should we lose one of our City Elections—we shall see such a profligate use of our means that will bring us into a long and continued bondage.

After some suitable and timely remarks by Prest. D H Wells, & Orson Pratt The School was adjourned for One week at One o clock pm.[11] After singing Benediction by Elder W[ilford] Woodruff.

February 10, 1872; Saturday

Theological Class met at the Tabernacle at One o clock pm. Prest. D[aniel] H. Wells presiding. After singing Prayer by Elder B[righam] Young Jun[io]r. Singing.

Elder [Syvert] Ivarson 2nd Ward said he could prove from the Book of Mormon that Jesus Christ was God the Father ^& Creator^. page 521, 426, 175, 150, 523, Doc[trine] & Cov[enants] Sec[tion] 12/120 & 166 page. The above quotations were read with a view to establish the doctrine that God ^the Father^ and ~~G~~ Jesus Christ was the same identical person.

A written Question was then read by Prest. Wells, sent in by a member of the School. If a Sister is Sealed to an Elder for Time & all Eternity, can such Sister, if she is tired to live [tired of living] with her husband who is still in good standing in the Church, be sealed to another man for time and all eternity?

Prest. D. H. Wells said that a Sister who is sealed to a Man in the

11. In addition, "Elder O Pratt announced a course of lectures to be given by himself. Bro D. H. Wells spoke a few moments. . . . A committee of 7, including 2 women was chosen to celect nominees, also a like committee for the convention." JFSJ, Feb. 3, 1871.

Priesthood for time & all eternity, without sufficient cause, that sealing Ordinance can never be reversed.

In anser to Elder Ivarson, he said, that God the Father, and Jesus Christ, were two separate and distinct personages, that we are indebted to revelation in this our day, that God in Embryo was in every Man. There are three that bear record in Heaven, the Father, Son & Holy Ghost. Jesus was begotten by the Father in the spirit, and also in the flesh, ~~we~~

Elder Orson Pratt, said the last words of the Saviour while on the Cross, Into thy hands I commend my spirit—before Creation, the question was asked by the Father, whom shall I send, and Jesus said, Here am I, send me, proving that the Father & Son were two distinct and separate personages.[12]

Bro Ivarson said that he simply thought that Jesus Christ was the Father of our Spirits.

Elder Geo Q Cannon said the Doc[trine] & Cov[enants] makes this subject ~~wa~~ very plain & clear, that Jesus always owns and acknowledges the Glory & supremacy ~~to~~ ^of^ the Father—also in many places in the New Testament. It is through Jesus Christ, that all Revelations have ever come, either in Ancient or Modern times.

Elder O[smond] Shaw refer'd to the [fifth] Lecture on Faith by Joseph Smith wherein he speaks plainly & possitively, that there [are] two great governing powers. When once a man becomes a Father, he is an Eternal Father.

Elder Geo B. Wallace related a Dream that he had nearly 30 years ago, in answer to a prayer that ~~he~~ God would reveal to him as to whether Plural Marriages existed in the Church of Jesus Christ of latter day Saints, in his Dream he saw the Prophet Joseph, not as a Man but as God, he saw many Worlds, and the guide told him that those worlds were created and peopled by Joseph Smith because he had many wives.

Prest. D. H. Wells said, that Monday was the day of our City Election, and he was desirous that every legal voter should deposit his or her Vote, and that every care and vigilence should be used by the priesthood of each ward in securing Vehicles to carry the voters.

Elder Geo Q Cannon gave some timely instructions about the Election.

The School was adjourned for one week at One o clock pm. After singing Benediction by Elder Jos[ep]h F. Smith.

12. Pratt is quoting from Moses 4:1 in the LDS Pearl of Great Price.

February 17, 1872; Saturday

Theological Class met at the ~~Feb[ruary] 17th~~ Tabernacle at One o clock pm.[13] Pres[en]t Prest. D[aniel] H. Wells presiding. After singing Prayer by Elder Jno. [John] W. Young. Singing.

Elder C[harles] C. Rich exprest feelings of gratitude for the possession of correct principles, as revealed in the Gospel of Jesus Christ, and the many privileges he enjoys in connexion with it. It was our duty to learn what right is, and here in this school is the place where we can learn, and should seek to correct and improve our lives. Should any incorrect doctrine exist among the Elders of Israel, here, we can be correct[ed]. He felt proud to live in a dispensation, when he could do good, and disseminate correct principles among his fellow man. Let us overcome our own failings and imperfections and we will then be better prepared to combat errors outside of us.

The following Question was read[:] Is Death the effect of Adams transgression?

Elder Orson Pratt said the surest ~~test~~ ^evidence^ we have pertaining to the Creation, and the fall is from the Word of God as revealed in the Bible. The real cause of Death is sin—the scriptures abound in references to that subject.

Man was the first Creature that God placed on the earth, ~~so~~ then the other various Beasts and other animated creatures. So says the New Revelations ^or translations^ given to Joseph Smith the Prophet concerning. On the Morning of the 7th day in Creation, God placed Man on the Earth—the Beasts & the Fowls were then brought before him to receive their names. God created in Heaven the Beasts, Fowls, & all other animated Creatures, in spirit—but did not receive their bodies until after Man was created. ~~C~~ The original cause of Death and pain was Mans transgression, so says the old and New translation of the scriptures.

The World will continue to change until it becomes perfect. So with the Beasts spoken of in John's Revelations, they will be filled with the Knowledge of god, and fish & Fowls, all Creatures will praise the name of ~~G~~ the Lord, as well as Man, after the Millen[n]ium.

Pres D. H. Wells did not profess to understand Geology, Many had been driven to Infidelity by studying that Science. The Eternity of

13. Several members of the school, including Wilford Woodruff and Daniel H. Wells, had just spoken at the funeral of Bishop Abraham Hoagland of the Fourteenth Ward.

Matter was a principle that God revealed to His servant Joseph Smith. Let no one stumble on a/c [account] of a seeming contradiction between the researchers of developements of Geology and the Revelations of God. Our Religion reaches around and circumscribes all the Sciences of the day—and leaves them, hanging as it were in Mid air.

He hoped that either He himself, or his brethren would [n]ever get so much of this worlds Knowledge as to lose sight or neglect our Holy Religion. If we will keep and observe the Word of Wisdom, God has promised to give us treasures of Wisdom and Knowledge. There are sufficient sparks and gems of truth in the old Scriptures left us, that if we are only blest with the gift of the Holy Ghost, we will be able to confute the errors ^of^ scientific researches, or the dogmas of the Religious world.

Elder W[ilford] Woodruff recommended us to travel in ~~travel~~ shallow water, and not to trouble ourselves about the mysteries that are all around us. Spoke of the increase of infidelity among the Nations of the World. Let any one deny the Holy Ghost and the Atonement of Jesus Christ, then the Devil leads them to ~~lead~~ shed innocent blood—~~The~~[14]

He warned the School against a smattering of human Knowledge, that might injure their faith in God, but he would promise that if we will only live humble and be obedient in the Kingdom of God—their minds will expand, and a fountain of Knowlege should be opened to their understanding.

As a general rule Men who deem themselves Wise in this worlds Knowlege, seldom embrace the Gospel, they know too much and would not humble themselves to receive it. But those who dont Know so much, and pretend to know but little are the ones who are willing to be taught of God, and embrace the plan of Salvation. It were far better never to go to School at all, than to acquire ~~a little~~ Knowlege as to lose their faith. Some persons both young & old, seem[e]d to be naturally sceptical &c.

He then warned the brethren against indulging in hard thoughts against Prest. [Brigham] Young—and all those who continue to do so will assuredly apostatize. Many things are being talked of about him, as if he had taken advantage of some one in his deal, property having taken ~~advantage~~ a rise since he bought it, many are supposing he had taken

14. This paragraph was written vertically, somewhat obscuring the horizontal text already on the page.

advantage of those he obtained it from, but he, Pres Wells, testified that such insinuations were false and untrue.

The most union [being united] in Israel was never more manifest, than at the Election last week. Spoke of the union & prudence of the Sisters in Utah—and he would be willing ~~for~~ ^that^ the Vote of the Sisters should determine as to whether Polygamy should be in or left out, of the Constitution about to be drawn up by the Convention.[15]

School was adjourned for one week at One oclock pm. After singing Benediction by Elder C[harles] C Rich.

February 24, 1872; Saturday

Theological Class met in the Tabernacle at 1 o clock pm. Present Prest. D[aniel] H. Wells presiding. After singing Prayer by Elder Geo Goddard. Singing.

Elder Jos[ep]h F. Smith said we are passing through strange scenes just now, we are told ~~those~~ that "Those who live godly in Christ Jesus shall suffer persecution." And those who [do] not live godly in Christ Jesus will certainly suffer persecution. We can take it which ever way we please. There is less apostacy in the [rural] country than in the City—and much room for improvement in all of us. We must be what we profess to be, or God will reject us. God Almighty commenced this work through the Prophet Joseph [Smith], and still continues it. He was astonished, for any one to become lukewarm in this great work—yet all would be willing to exert themselves to make a dollar in money. And how many are become careless and indifferent in regard to their souls salvation[?] He wanted to have his children taught well in the principles of the Gospel, which in his estimation was of far more importance than to leave them means sufficient ~~wealth for them~~ to revel in folly and luxury, without them. Spoke impressively on the strength of family ties, that exist not only here, but will continue hereafter.

God will not desert us, unless we desert him—but his Eye is continually upon us. We are trying to frame a Constitution prior to us becoming

15. Two years earlier, some 5,000 LDS women had met in the Tabernacle and rallied in support of polygamy. They were rewarded by the territorial legislature the next month when it granted women the right to vote. Apparently the women had shown up at the polls in numbers in 1872 in order to draw this compliment from Woodruff. The influential *Woman's Exponent* newspaper was about to be launched and, in June, would begin a forty-two-year run.

a State,[16] but whether God will ever permit us to be admitted into the Union or not, he did not know, neither did he feel at all concerned in the Matter, but if ~~he~~ it would ^prove^ a blessing to Israel, he hoped we might be admitted, if not, he hoped we might continue to be as we are.

The people of these Vallies have mostly been governed by the laws of the Priesthood, and not the laws of the land. Let us act uprightly and justly with each other.

He then adverted to some of the blessings that a State Government would confer upon us. No people on the earth would have ever borne so patiently with the insults and abuse that our enemies have recently heaped upon us. God is guiding and governing this people. He was firmly of the belief, that our present difficulties and troubles, are brought upon us, on account of our unfaithfulness. Not one man is Israel, in one ~~Israel~~ thousand, would be willing to labour at home in Zion, for 3 or 4 years, and let the value of his labours go for the benefit of the Church, while they ~~would~~ might willingly go on a foreign Mission for that length of time, yet the principle is the same.

Elder John Pack, had been in the church for over 40 years, gathered with the Church in Ohio, had been with the saints through all their troubles, to the present time. He came into this Church for Eternal life. Had reared up many Sons and Daughters—who were an honour to him and the Church also. His Religion was dearer to him than life itself— and he could not barter off any portion of it, for any worldly consideration. He like many others around him, was in the decline of life—and was now as willing to have his ~~l~~ integrity towards God tested, as in the days of Missouri. He was ~~an~~ once dragged from his carriage ^while^ by the side of his wife, by a Mob of over 20, to kill him in the woods, but God delivered him out of their hands. He was altogether indifferent, as to whether we become a State Government. And as to renouncing any portion of his religion for any worldly consideration, he would rather be cut to pieces first.

He then very excitingly reviewed the 5th Section that partially passed yesterday at the Convention, condemning in unmeasured terms the Gentile [non-Mormon] element, elected as a portion of the Convention.[17]

16. "The Convention for the framing of a Constitution has set in the City Hall during the week but not adva[nce]d far." WWJ, Feb. 24, 1872.

17. Section 5 prevented the US Congress from imposing "unconstitutional" conditions on the proposed state, including the abolition of polygamy. The "gentile element"

Elder Jno. [John] Taylor admitted the strange circumstances that we are now passing through—but we must not forget that this is the Kingdom of God—and when he wishes to change things, he will do it. We must expect to be jostled and jolted occasionally, but what of it. We are not going to barter off our rights or our Religion. Neither are our boys or girls getting further off from Polygamy, than formerly, our girls are more willing to day, to go into the family of a good man than previously. Let us then keep the commandments of God, and do right, cleave to the truth, and God will bring us off victoriously.

Prest. D. H. Wells reprobated [disapproved of] a course of violence towards our enemies. He much prefer'd a wiser policy, though it might cost much money and what of it, God has given us the Money, and if some of it he uses in paying Lawyers to help us in the courts, how much better, than to use violence. He then spoke very favourably of a State Government, in which condition we should have far less contact with the General Govenment Officers, than we necessarily have now to do with them as a Territory. The Majority of this people are for God and his Kingdom. As to how soon our victory and deliverance may be achieved, depends very much on our faithfulness. But he considered that[18] it would be a grand advance for us to become a State Government, and should use his faith and prayers for that convention to form such a constitution as would meet with the approbation of Congress. The Convention are made up of some of our best men, and will doub[t]less guard the interests that are so dear to all Latter day saints. False brethren are what are ha[n]ging on these malicious suits, and he always regretted to see any one leaving this church. He hoped that the brethren would be faithful and pray that God would break the rod of the oppressor, and deliver us from their hands.

School was adjourned for one week at one oclock pm. After singing Benediction by E[lder] W[ilford] Woodruff.

Prest. Wells was grieved that so many of the brethren had set at naught the council of the servants of God, by not sustaining and patronizing the

probably referred to Brigham Young's attorney, Thomas Fitch, who was sympathetic to Mormons but called on the church to give up polygamy in exchange for statehood. "Territorial Convention," *Deseret News*, Feb. 28, 1872; "The Constitutional Convention," *Salt Lake Herald*, Feb. 24, 1872; "That Speech," *Salt Lake Tribune*, Feb. 24, 1872.

18. From here to the end of this date's entry, the scribe wrote vertically over the top of existing text.

principle of cooperation, these were more opposed to Israel [the church], than those outside the Church.

March 2, 1872; Saturday

Theological Class met at the Tabernacle at One o clock pm. Present Prest. D[aniel] H. Wells presiding. After singing Prayer by Elder Sam[ue]l Evans. Singing.

Elder Orson Pratt felt very thankful for the many blessings, the Lord had bestowed upon us as a people. Contrasting the present political power and influence we possess—with ~~their~~ ^our^ past, while in Kirtland Ohio. About 41 years ago, a prophecy was given that we should be able to organize ourselves in such a way, that our enemies should not have power over us. He then rehearsed the experience of the saints, in connexion with the gradual developement of political power, as we were driven from place to place. We have now lived 20 years as a Territorial Government, which is a very oppressive one, and which Congress has no right to impose on any of her subjects. He then spoke of the Convention which had been sitting for the past two weeks, for the purpose of drafting a Constitution to present to Congress for our admission into the union. The delegates had worked faithfully during the time of their sitting.

If Congress should refuse us admission, He should be in favour of a Monster petition being got up throughout the Territory, asking for a State Government, outside of the union[.][19] The Constitution they had framed, was more liberal, than any other upon which all previous states are founded. He then spoke of a few benefits, and advanced political influence that we shall gain, in the event of our becoming a State.

Elder W[ilford] Woodruff spoke of ^the^ immutability of the word of God. He could see the hand of God, as he leads and guides the destinys of this people. A dark cloud had been over us, for some months past. And yet, the spirit of calmness & composure has rested upon his Servants. Let us do right, have faith in God—and nothing can checque the onward course of this Church. During the past 40 years the Lord has been giving us an experience, and preparing us to accomplish his

19. Pratt was suggesting secession from the Union. His reference to a monster petition was to a document that would be signed by as many people as possible and delivered either piled up in stacks or pasted together into a scroll and unraveled upon presentation.

purposes. All that fight against Zion will certainly ^be^ put to shame and confusion, as past experience proves.

If it's the will of the Lord to give us a State Government, we shall certainly have less to do with the Government, than we have now in a Territorial capacity, then, we can elect our own Governor, Judges &c whereas now, those officers are forced upon us without our consent.

The acts of the wicked will fall upon their own head, and the righteous will be delivered. It is our privelege to ask the Lord for a State Government; and if its his will, he will grant it, by raising up friends to urge our petition through both Houses of Congress. Do not forget our prayers, nor fail in any of our duties and God will establish Zion in these Mountains.

The School was adjourned for One week at One o clock p[m]. After singing Benediction by Elder J[oseph] F. Smith.

March 9, 1872; Saturday

Theological Class met at the Tabernacle at One o clock pm.[20] Present Prest. D[aniel] H. Wells—presiding. After singing Prayer by B[isho]p E[dwin] D. Woolley. Singing.

Elder Geo Goddard made a few encouraging remarks to faithful men of God, holding the Priesthood.

B[isho]p John Sharp said Men of truth were men of courage, the opposite were cowards and hypocrites. And after several other remarks, he mentioned that the Agent of a Coal Company in Wyoming, exprest to him a desire to hire some 90 men of our own community to go and work their Mine, to whom they would give steady employment and fair wages, besides furnishing houses for their families.

Elder Daniel Jones, who had just returned from a trip among the Indians—said they were very susceptable of true impressions. ~~they~~ We have got to take a wise course towards them, feed them, and be kind to them. ~~they told Bro Jones they were willing~~ He had been to Uinta Valley to meet them and after much conversation with them. Had accomplished more than he expected, he particularly enjoined kind treatment

20. Several of the members had just come from the funeral of William W. Phelps, a prominent church writer, printer, and hymnist, whom Woodruff called "a vary Peculiar Man in many respects." Phelps wrote the words to "If You Could Hie to Kolob," "Now Let Us Rejoice," and "The Spirit of God Like a Fire Is Burning," among other hymns. WWJ, Mar. 9, 1872.

towards them, and they ^will^ prove to be true friends, and we may see the time, when we shall appreciate their friendship.

Elder John Taylor entirely concurred in the sentiments exprest by Bro Jones about the Indians. They are of the House of Israel, and will sooner or later receive the Gospel, the same that we have received[.] The very lands that we occupy and have our farms upon—rightly belongs to them, and yet we purchase ^of^ and pay to the United States for, ~~Our Lands~~ and they bought it of the Mexicans, but the Mexicans never paid the rightful owners, (the Indians) for it. The time will come when everything that is now wrong will be put right. The Ephraimites[21] will by and bye inhabit this land—according to the predictions made thousands of years ago [in the Book of Mormon]. The Indians will obey the Gospel and with them a "Nation will be born in a day." Let us therefore carry~~ed~~ out the Council given us by Bro Jones. He was much pleased with the preference given to our people by the Union Pacific R[ail] R[oad] for workmen. This was only a beginning of what would be—the Gentiles have lost confidence in each other, and will have to enquire for good latter day saints to transac~~tion~~ their business, and look ~~for~~ ^to^ them for council.

Elder [Robert H.] Collins related a dream, that He was in the mountains with President [Brigham] Young, and a short distance from them was a band of well drest Indians, though a fence separated them, at length a fine portly Chief, on a large Horse, rode up, ~~to Prest. Young~~ opened the Gate and approached Prest. Young, and after a short conversation agreed to abide the dictatorship ~~of P~~ and all his men of Prest. Young. At this Moment, Prest. Young saw in the distance a small band of Latter Day saints on Horses, and Prest. Young called upon them to come along quick, and they did so at full speed. On their arrival, the Indian Chief asked him if it was not right, for "one hand to wash another," the President conceded that point. And ~~they~~ then gave orders for them to go down to Missouri and burn them [Missourians] up.[22]

Prest. D. H. Wells made mention of the desire of the U[nion] P[acific] R[ail] R[oad] Co[mpany] to obtain Mormon labour, and put it to

21. The Book of Mormon forefather of the American Indians was from the tribe of Manasseh (Alma 10:3), but Orson Pratt asserted in a missionary pamphlet that Lehi's daughters-in-law were from the tribe of Ephraim. Pratt, *Divine Authenticity*.

22. It was believed that Native Americans would help reclaim lost property in Missouri, and this "redemption of Zion" (Missouri being Zion) would preface the building of a New Jerusalem in America prior to the Millennium (D&C 105:9; 3 Ne. 21:23–25).

the school which was unanimously sustained. Inasmuch as the project met with the sanction of the school, when a sufficient number of men was obtained it ~~was~~ would be necessary to appoint a Bishop and have a regular Organization there for their benefit.

The School was then adjourned for One week at one oclock pm—After singing Benediction by Elder W[ilford] Woodruff.[23]

March 16, 1872; Saturday

Theological Class met at the Tabernacle at one o clock pm. Present Prest. D[aniel] H. Wells presiding. After singing Prayer by B[isho]p A[lonzo] H. Raleigh. Singing.

Elder Demick Huntingdon complained that our present Indian Agent had not, during the winter, distributed the Blankets as he ought to have done, and the Indians felt bad, He hoped the brethren would be kind to them and feed them, when they come to your houses.

Let us acknowledge God in all things[.] Whatever is now going on, we may rest assured will all be for the best, we have a Moses to lead us, let us uphold his hands, and do right, tis true, the reins have been loosely down for some time, and when taken up again, will be ~~to~~ held tighter than heretofore.

Prest. Geo A Smith said owing to sickness, he had not been to school for some time, felt thankful that many had been prompt in this duty, and hoped that the brethren were governed by principles of integrity in all their daily transactions. He also urged the importance of every man and woman, being duly naturalized [as US citizens], so as to strengthen our political hands. We need not fear that Zion was going to be bartered off, or cheated out of her rights, the enemies of the Kingdom of God will ~~b~~ come to grief and be put to shame.

Elder A[lbert] Carrington admitted that he was a conservative radical, radical by nature, conservative by strict schooling. Refer'd to the fair and zealous discharge of the duties performed by the members of the [statehood] convention—who brought forth one of the best, if not, the very best of any Constitution now extant. He then explained and gave reasons, why a certain ordinance was embodied in the Constitution. He should be much pleased, if the people would turn out en masse to

23. Immediately afterward, members nominated candidates for the US Senate and Congress, in case the application for statehood was accepted. JFSJ, Mar. 9, 1872.

the polls on Monday next—and vote for the Constitution, and those Senators and representatives whose names are now before the public. Without a scratch [replacement candidate] on any ticket—he had full confidence in those f outsiders whose names are on the ticket, that they would labour diligently for the good of Israel [the church].

He entertained a very strong impression that Utah would be admitted into the Union, this Session. God will put hooks into the Jaws of the wicked just in proportion as Israel will do right.

Prest. D. H. Wells spoke of a convention to be held in the City Hall F on the 5th of April, at which two delegates can be appointed to attend a [Republican Party] Convention at Philadelphia for the Nomination of President of U.S.[24] He then spoke of the infamous wrongs and ungodly crusade that had been perpetrated against us as a people, the tables will turn before long if the Saints will only do right. If we can only be admitted into the Union, it will give us another lease of at least 20 years[.] We have everything to hope for, and live for, there has been a very steady and rapid progress with us during the past. The establishment of the Zion of God upon the earth is the great Moving ambition and desire of the Elders of Israel.

Let us ratify the Constitution by our vote on Monday next. After which, even should it be received by Congress, will be sent back here again, for another ratification of the people, before we can go into the Union.

A letter was then read in which the Assessor ~~of~~ and Collector of City Taxes complains of over 800 delinquent tax payers, and hoped the Bishops will urge upon the Members of their wards to come up and settle them, to avoid the necessity of adopting stringent Measures to enforce their payment.

Bishop [Edward] Hunter urged on the Bishops and Councillors to carry out the council they had received pertaining to the Election on Monday. Also let us see that we all get proper titles to our property, it will form one of the strongest holds against ours enemies. He also recommended a kind and generous treatment towards the Indians, the Church had given them tons of food, and intended to feed. He then spoke of the efforts made by outsiders to allure and entice

24. Wells's interest in seeing two delegates sent to Philadelphia was not out of love for the Republican Party, but in order to vote against the nomination of Ulysses S. Grant for re-election. See the entries for June 1, 22, 1872.

away our Children. He wished the brethren would ~~a~~ encourage our own Sabbath Schools.

The Meeting was adjourned for one week at one o clock pm. After singing Benediction by Elder W[ilford] Woodruff.

March 23, 1872; Saturday

Theological School met at the Tabernacle at 1 o clock. Present Prest. D[aniel] H. Wells presiding. After singing Prayer by Elder S[amuel] Richards. Singing.

The Clerk then read the rules of the school, and Prest. D. H. Wells desired all those who intended to strictly observe the rules to manifest it with uplifted hands. All hands appeared to be raised. He then complained of a ~~loose~~ ^careless^ habit in losing their tickets, and hoped they would be more careful hereafter and that each one will endeavour to observe the rules of the school, that a good and healthy influence may be exerted by every member.

Elder J[oseph] B[ates] Nobles was very thankful to return home again, after a four months visit to the [United] States, among his relatives and old friends. He had tried to do good, by sowing the good seed wherever he had an opportunity[.] He endeavoured to show the difference between their positions as religionists, and ours. The Lord blest him in speaking to ~~making~~ many public gatherings, and allaying much prejudice. We must keep our covenants, or we will be chastised, God chastened us when we were only a handful, and he will most assuredly Chasten us now, until we are brought to observe the golden rule, and live, so as to enjoy the spirit of the Lord.

Prest. D. H. Wells desired the Southern [Salt Lake Valley] Bishops to have some more rock hauled from the Quarry to the Railroad, so that the men on the [Salt Lake] Temple block may be kept at work on the Temple.

He also wished the brethren to remember the defense fund,[25] and sustain it by their means, as the present Crusade [against the church] is a very expensive one, let us be united, and try by our good works, to avoid an actual collision. He knew that many would be perfectly willing to fight for our rights, but wisdom dictated a milder and more pacific course.

He then spoke of the indignities that some of our brethren have

25. That is, the legal fund for those charged with unlawful cohabitation (polygamy).

been subjected to who have been held as prisoners, and hoped that the funds of the defense may be replenished by those who are still at large, for not one of us can tell who may be the next victim.

We want to go on with the building of the Temple rapidly through the summer, and also to raise means for Emigrating the poor. To pay our Tithing [on time] in the time and season thereof. If we do not, God will bring us to account, and any one who permits his wealth to stand between himself and his God, will surely be sifted as wheat, and go over the dam.

God has planted our feet in these vallies of the Mountains, and we calculate to abide here, let us be valient thereof on the side of ~~t~~ truth and righteousness, and we will finally triumph. Do not let us patronize our enemies, but maintain the house of Israel, and build up the Kingdom of God. Let the Mass of latter day saints dry up from patronizing them, and the effect would soon be felt.

School was adjourned for one week at 1 o clock pm. After singing Benediction by Elder Orson Pratt.

March 30, 1872; Saturday

Theological Class met at the Tabernacle at One oclock pm. Present Prest. D[aniel] H. Wells presiding. After singing Prayer by Elder W[illia]m Folsom. Singing.

Elder W[ilford] Woodruff hoped to live long enough to see pleasant [tribe of] Ephraim enjoy all the blessings, that were long since, enjoyed by their forefathers. He then spoke of the Elders of Israel who held the destinies of the Nations in their hands, and the necessity of them living worthy of their high and holy calling. He then related a dream that he had while on a Mission ~~to~~ in England—pertaining to the Lamanites [Native Americans]. He saw a beautiful Temple rerected [erected] on the Mountains of Israel, he went in, and while there, a large number of Lamanites came in and seated themselves in a place by themselves, by and bye, they began to work [perform ordinances], and they seemed to accomplish more in two hours than others could do in a day. But a strict account was kept of ^all^ the labour that was performed by every one in that house. And they appeared to have been inspired by some Prophet to enter that Temple, and enter upon those blessings promised by their forefathers.

We are a branch of Ephraim, and received the Gospel first—and should treat the poor degraded Indian with kindness, for they fell through unbelief. We should also be anxious to build this [Salt Lake] Temple here, and that in St. George. He then spoke of the persecution that was pressing upon us by the heads of this Nation, by unlawfully keeping in bondage, our Brethren. As Latter day Saints, we should seek the blessing of God ~~of~~ upon the Saints, and his displeasure upon his enemies. The Leaders of this people have stood the test, and been proved for many years, hence, we should hold up their hands, and exercise faith for them, these honours and labours that God has put upon our brethren, should stimulate us [to] follow in their footsteps. A faithful humble follower of Jesus Christ, is in a far more exalted position, than can be confer'd upon men by the world. Let us be faithful to God and each other, and endure to the end, that we may be saved for Jesus Sake. Amen.

Elder Jos[ep]h F. Smith said it was a glorious thing for us to have such a hope, and ~~glor~~ prospects, as lies before us, if we continue faithful. We read of the good and wise men who lived in Ancient times who were instructed by God, Jesus Christ, and Angels, also in our day of God and Angels conversing with the prophet Joseph Smith. Are these things true or false—have the eyes of Men been opened to see the future condition of Men, in his exalted and saved condition, also, of the Damned. And have these things been revealed for the benefit of Mankind, and us especially who have embraced the Gospel. And do we believe in these revelations, if so, can we lie, cheat, steal, or take the name of God in vain, if we do these things, we are either under the most fearful condemnation, or we must be wo[e]fully ignorant, and more the objects of pity, than we are perhaps willing to admit. The Gospel is as much intended for the Indians, as the Jews or Gentiles—and the responsibility rests upon us, to carry the Gospel to each of the above. We embraced the Gospel of our own free agency, we continue in the church on ~~a~~ the same principle, No one either entered the kingdom by force or are retained in it by the same.

How many of us to day are fooling away our time in folly, fasheon, and nonsense. Is there one Merchant who ha~~a~~s been one any length of time, but have apostatized from the Church. Most of them have become infidel, and denied all revelations from God. If [we see] those who accum[ul]ate riches so fast, and so much faster than other people—[it] is almost a sure indication of obtaining them by a dishonest course. No person who really believes the Gospel can take such a course. Let us learn our duties and then do them.

He was thankful that he knew who he was, who his father was, and ~~wh~~ the object for which he came upon the earth. He once had a vision of the Celestial Kingdom,—its order and its unity—and by dreams had his way marked out for him. [He] was once very poor, ragged and dirty, went 4 days without food—had a loathsome disease occasioned by almost starvation—was only between 16 & 17 years old—and felt low spirited. Under those circumstances, he had a dream which proved a very great comfort to him. ~~before~~ Because he had a delightful introduction to the Prophet Joseph [Smith], his Father [Hyrum Smith] and all his old friends and acquaintances, who moved, and spoke, with the utmost order, and it filled him with such joy and satisfaction that nothing on the earth had ever done before.

Elder J[oseph] F. Smith [continued], We have got to redeem Zion—to redeem the Earth—and make it blossom as the rose. This is the land of Joseph, and must be cleansed from sin—and prepared for the Millen[n]ium, God has decreed these things, and must come to pass. The Remnant of these Lamanites, must become a white and delightsome people. They have been sought after, and destroyed, as much so, as the Woff [wolf] or the Bear. But a remnant of them will be left, to be a thorn in the side of the wicked, and a battle axe in the hands of the Almighty. And those who are now fighting and oppressing this people, will be broken to pieces by the Almighty in his own due time.

We are only tenants at will, at the present time but the time will come by the bye, when the Earth will be owned, ~~by~~ and enjoyed by the saints of the Most High. Bill Hickman[26] should never have been tolerated among this people, since he was known to have been a dishonest man. No matter how dishonest, and black hearted a man may be, we have tolerated them, and fellowshipped them, on a/c [account] of being cousin to some one of good standing. But he [Smith] hoped the time

26. William A. Hickman (1815–83) converted to Mormonism in 1838. In 1854 the Utah legislature created Green River County—later divided into nine separate counties—and Hickman became county sheriff, legislative representative, and tax collector. He became a spy for the federal government and was excommunicated after he published *Brigham's Destroying Angel*, in which he claimed in 1872 that he had killed individuals marked by Young for elimination.

would come, that such men would be branded on the forehead, and on the back, and cast out from the midst of Israel.

School was adjourned for two weeks at ~~6~~ One o clock pm. owing to [general] Conference falling on next Saturday at 10 o clock am. Benediction by Elder O[rson] Pratt.

April 13, 1872; Saturday

Theological Class met in the Tabernacle at One o clock pm. Present [blank] Presiding [blank].[27] After singing Prayer by Elder [Zebedee] Coltrin. Singing.

Elder H[orace] Eldredge realized that it was good to meet in the school of the Prophets, where ideas may be exchanged to our mutual profit. We need to be instructed, and it was very essential for all of us to have a knowledge of the truth of this work. We should so live before the Lord, as to enjoy his holy spirit. We should strictly keep our covenants with each other, and observe the Word of Wisdom, which we have often covenanted to do. If we lived as we should do, there would be no ^need for^ Bishops ~~trials~~ or High Council trials.

Elder L[orenzo] Snow said that most of our time was devoted to temporal concerns. It seems to be almost inevitable for little differences to arise between brethren, but he was happy to say that very few ever came to a Bishops or High Council trial. The vast majority are settled by the parties themselves, we have fewer difficulties [in Brigham City] than exists in any other community. He then dwelt on the great variety that exists in human nature, refer'd us to the pinching and teasing [taxing] of the ~~of the~~ English Government towards the Colonies of this Nation, produced this great republic, so a constant teasing us with a Vorhees Bill[28] or some other bill. We know not how soon ~~w~~ the Lord may urge us on, until we become the Head, instead of being where we now are. We must rally around our Head, and the Almighty will be pleased to bring us up.

Elder W[ilford] Woodruff said ever since he was a little boy, he never could think there was anybody on the earth that loved the Lord, unless [who could not see] there was a Head and body of the Church, which

27. Wilford Woodruff was the senior-most leader at the meeting and likely presided.

28. The bill from Indiana Congressman Daniel W. Voorhees would have barred Mormons from jury service, but it failed to pass Congress. "Review of Affairs in Utah," *Latter-day Saints Millennial Star*, July 9, 1872; Maxwell, *Robert Newton Baskin*, 119–20.

is so beautifully exprest by the Apostle Paul. He had observed a great many cripples in his life, some lacking one limb and some another—but he never ~~say~~ ^saw^ any without a Head. So with the Christian world, having no Head, are without life, just as much as a Natural body, without ~~a Head~~ one. He was not at all surprised at the persecution we are receiving, he was astonished that we did not have move [more], but God will bring us off victorious. Since we had openly come out with the principle of Polygamy, God had thrown a shield around us, and protected us. The Nation we live in, has become corrupt with Whoredoms, Thieving, & every foul crime that will shortly sink it to perdition. It may be that the highest tribunal in the land, viz The Supreme Court—may also be induced to turn against us. The President has tried his hand, and perhaps Congress may legislate against us—but the Lord will bring us off victorious—and this Nation will fill up the measure of their iniquity.

Elder E[dward] Stevenson, borne testimony to the above. Related many sayings of the Prophet Joseph [Smith]—^one was, that wherever the records were, there was the true Church & head^. And also that a little over a year ago when holding a two days meeting in Provo Prest. [Brigham] Young said, we shall build a Temple in St. George, and the Government will send soldiers there to watch us, we will build fifty in this Territory, and I wonder whether they will send Soldiers to every place, ~~but~~ for the Devil is after us. He then spoke on the Word & [of] Wisdom, it being a revelation from God—and if we live for it, we can have a living vital spirit of inspiration with us continually.

Elder Amos Fielding said, another proof of where the true Church was, can be found by the persecution which will always attend it. Apostates were not persecuted. The Nation is nearly full of crime and corruption, and nearly ripe for destruction.

School was adjourned for one week at One oclock pm. After singing Benediction by Elder A M[ilton] Musser.

April 20, 1872; Saturday

Theological Class met at the Tabernacle at One o clock pm. Prest. D[aniel] H. Wells presiding. After singing Prayer by Elder E Morris. Singing.

Elder L[orenzo] Snow refered to the recent dispatch from Washington [DC], being the decision of the Supreme Court in the case of

Englebredt & the City Council, which had been decided against the City, by the District and Supreme Court of Utah. The case was appealed to the Supreme Court at Washington and by a unanimous decision, ^they^ reversed the decision of the two lower Courts and in favour of the City, which far exceeded the speakers expectation.[29] Indeed, the benefit that will acrue to this community, ~~is of~~ will be most incalculable, 500 times more than it has cost in means and Anxiety. It secures to us, all the rights and priveleges gauarranteed to us, by the ^City^ Charter, that was Signed ~~th~~ by [US] Prest. [Franklin] Pierce. He then spoke of the effects produced, by the Almighty introducing the Book of Mormon, and the necessity of all people receiving it, being gathered together, for the strength and unity to maintain ~~to maintain~~ the principles contained therein.

Elder Orson Pratt felt truly thankful for the decision recently come in from Washington. Yet at the same time, it was possible for Congress to enact Laws pertaining to the fundamental principles of the Bible viz. [outlawing] a plurality of Wives, which they did in 1862 [with the Morrill Act], and it may be that Judges may be sent here to enforce them, and if so, will not, the benefits resulting from the recent decision, be nullified. Just so long as we continue under a territorial form of Government, so long will the Devil have power to harrass and perplex the people of God. But God will sooner or later, give us an entire victory over all our enemies. We all feel freear, and we can express our joy and gratitude to God, while in a school capacity—but should refrain from doing so in a mixed assembly. It is wisdom to be silent while in the presence of our enemies—lest it should kindle a bitter, persecuting spirit. He wished to enquire whether the recent decisions would afford us any relief in the future pertaining to the Polygamic suits.

Elder L[orenzo] Snow said, as that principle [of plural marriage] was not involved in the question before the Supreme Court—he could not tell that it would. Let them send us some decent, well informed Judicial Men, and we are not afraid to meet them. He never did believe that Congress had any right to legislate in matters of religion.

29. The issue was whether territorial Chief Justice James B. McKean could bypass the territorial marshal, who was Mormon, and have a US marshal empanel a jury of non-Mormons in order to convict men for illicit cohabitation. The ruling resulted in some 130 people being freed. Bigler, *Forgotten Kingdom*, 294–95; Turner, *Brigham Young*, 367–69.

Elder John Taylor said the Government can just exercise as much power as the Lord lets them. We are now in about as good a position as we could ask for. The Lord has done well for us. We are under his direction & controul, so is his servant Brigham [Young]. Narrow and contracted notions he was always opposed to—such as the Methodist Republicanism that had been made manifest towards us lately. Let us lean upon, and trust in God, he will bless us, and bring us off triumphantly. And his blessing be extended to all Israel.

B[isho]p A[lonzo] H. Raleigh made mention of some further explanations that the Supreme Court had decided upon not only sustained the City in destroying the Liquor in the Englebredt case, but ~~always~~ also in reference to the drawing of jurors.

B[isho]p L[orenzo] Young rejoiced to notice an increase of self controul among the Latter day Saints, at the recent good news that the Lord had brought about, he thought it was a good omen, that much secret prayer had been offered up before the Lord. Let us acknowledge the hand of the Lord in this deliverance.

Prest. D. H. Wells said the news from Washington made him feel good all over. He always thought that such a subject, being a legitimate law of legislation, viz of the drawing of Juries—would meet with just such a decision as was given. He entirely approved of our efforts in endeavouring to gain admission as a state. Let us try to stave off unfriendly legislation ~~by~~.

The Juries must hereafter be selected according to the laws [from among men] of the Polygamy [persuasion]—this much, is certainly an advantage we have, in future cases of Polygamy. This is a dispensation of gathering, to secure a power and strength, that an isolated condition, we could never attain to. Let us be united and Zealous in building up the Kingdom of God. If we handle means let us pay our tithing. How few rich men can stand in this Kingdom. He wished we could always realize that all our blessings come from God. He expected in a few days, that Prest. Young & the other brethren will be released, as soon as a certified Copy of the decision reaches the City, and the Court sit, and order their release.

School was adjourned for one week at one o clock pm. Benediction by Elder W[ilford] Woodruff.

April 27, 1872; Saturday

School of the Prophets met in the Tabernacle at One oclock pm. Present Prest. B[righam] Young presiding.[30] After singing Prayer by Elder A[lbert] P. Rockwood, singing.

Prest. B[righam] Young, after an absence of some months from the school, said he felt well, enquired after the health of the brethren, the efforts of our enemies have fizzled out, as he said they would when the [investigation] commenced against him. The illegal proceedings had cost much money, but it had only exchanged hands, it had not gone out of the world. He had had quite a good winters rest, and his whole system had been recuperated. The Government could not secure any credit, without discharging every United States Official that was here. The Almighty had commenced to scourge this Nation, the withering hand of God had already commenced in Chicago, Illinois, the very place [Illinois] where the persecuting plot started from towards the saints. We need not indulge ^in^ any feeling of revenge towards our enemies, they are in the hands of God, he had enjoyed the good spirit of God, the truth of God. He expected the other Brethren would be liberated during this afternoon, by our Prosecuting Attorney [Zerubbabel Snow]—who had been deprived of standing in his lot and place, and executing his official duties, for many months.[31] He also expected to commence proceedings against those parties who have illegally convicted & deprived him of his liberty, and also that of his brethren. And have them tested by the laws of the land, which they have so outrageously trodden under their feet.

He also hoped and expected to meet at Conference to morrow, and talk to the people. God bless you my brethren is my prayer—in the Name of Jesus Christ.

Prest. Geo A Smith, felt thankful for the privelege of being at School. He also felt grateful that our President was liberated under a Writ of Habeus Corpus, issued by our Probate Judge [Elias Smith]—whose

30. "I attend[e]d the school of the prophets & for the first time for months all the Presidency were there. President Young had been liberat[e]d from his Confinement on a writ of Habeus Corpus by the Probate Judge Elias Smith." WWJ, Apr. 27, 1872.

31. Zerubbabel Snow (1809–1888) was elected territorial attorney general in 1869. A Mormon convert from Vermont, he had been a member of the First Quorum of Seventy since 1835 and was himself a polygamist.

right, to issue it, he was perfectly satisfied would be sanctioned by the Supreme Court.

He refered to ^the^ effects that the Decision of the Court will have in many cases, that [h]as been unlawfully conducted during the reign of Judge [James B.] McKean. Let us do right, be honest towards God and each other, and God will certainly fight our battles and Zion will triumph &c.

Elder [Henry G.] Boyle, a return'd Missionary, of 14 Months absence. Felt joyful, and thankful, had been kept well posted, while away, by telegraph, and letter. Realized that the most consummate wisdom had been displayed by the leaders of Israel, and that the utmost patience and forbearance [had been] evinced by the people—[while] in every part of the Country, Utah and the Mormons was the topic of conversation. He had been labouring in Virginia, where the Gospel had never before been introduced, and had a hard time. Every conceivable lie and falsehood was freely circulated, and had to face much opposition. He also travelled & preached in Tennesee where every facility was granted them to preach by having every Meeting House open to them by asking for. Had baptized about a dozen in Tennesee and about twenty in Virginia—a good field is now open in both of the above States. And good faithful Elders sent there might do a good work. He had taught the first principles of the Gospel, the necessity of Authority to preach & administer it. Had also taught them the principle of Plural Marriage, and almost invariably ~~their~~ ^his^ teaching was received with good results. In the Southern Country, the pure Negro stock, and the White population, are both fast running out—and a mixed race springing up, of a Mongrel breed. He bore testimony to the truth of the Gospel, God was at the Helm—and we need not fear. He directs and controuls our Leaders &c.

Elder Daniels, a returned Missionary, said he was exceedingly thankful to be here, for here are the people of God. If they are not here, He has none upon the earth. God hears and answers his prayers, his spirit has been a companion to him while away, and may God help us to keep his spirit to guide and lead ^us^ into all truth.

Elder John Taylor, was pleased to see Prest. Young with us again. As he said, it was all right for the Saints to [be] persecuted, and in bondage, and it was ^all right^ for them to be liberated. Judge McKean and others who had taken such a prominent part, had become a stink and byeword in the estimation of all good men throughout the Nation. God is at the Helm, and Zion will triumph, and may we all fear God and keep his commandment.

May 4, 1872; Saturday

Theological Class met in the Tabernacle at One oclock pm. Present Prest. B[righam] Young presiding. After singing Prayer by Elder A M[ilton] Musser. Singing.

Elder [Syvert] Iverson, bore the following testimony viz that Jesus Christ was no other personage than God the Eternal Father, the Maker of all things, the creator of the Heavens and the Earth—he then read several passages out of the Book of Mormon, which he regarded as unanswerable proof.

Prest. D[aniel] H. Wells said that God the Father, the Father of our Spirits, and Jesus Christ, were not one and the same identical person; but any one who attains to Celestial honour and Glory, necessarily becomes an Eternal Father.[32]

A Question was then read, That as Jesus said, John the Baptist was the greatest of all Prophets, yet he who was least in the Kingdom of God, was greater than he. An explanation was asked for.

Prest. D. H. Wells said, that Joseph Smith, explained that Jesus meant himself when he said that He who is least in the Kingdom of God is greater than he.

Elder W[ilford] Woodruff said the Lord never fails in any promise that he gives to the children of men. He deals with Men ~~in~~ on the most broad democratic principles. The Law that God has revealed to us in this day, is easily understood by the most illiterate. This law of the Gospel was given that Man might be brought back into his presence, and exalted in the Celestial Kingdom, but the human family must abide the Law, ~~as~~ or they cannot gain the promise. He felt to rejoice that Prest. Young was here with us again. When he was first arrested, he said that all their efforts would turn out a great fizzle. The Prayers of the Servants of God have prevailed, and God has delivered those ^who^ were in

32. Iverson made the same point three months earlier (see the Feb. 10, 1872, entry) and was answered by the same respondent, Daniel H. Wells, as well as by Orson Pratt and George Q. Cannon. He may have wanted to pose the question with Brigham Young present. If so, the church president's silence seems to have signaled his approval of what Wells said.

bonds. We should never lose sight of the promises, and so live, that we can lawfully claim them.

When Prest. Young first set foot on this [Salt Lake] temple block, he put down his cane upon it and said, Here the greater Temple of God will be built. No man who has ~~I~~ ever lifted up his hand against this Kingdom, [h]as ever prospered. No weapon that ~~was~~ ^is^ formed against Zion can prosper. This prophecy has been most remarkably fulfilled. We shall prosper if we keep the commandments of God—the Hand of God has been over us as a people.

Elder Jos[ep]h F. Smith said the Lord had delivered his servants ~~as~~ in answer to prayer. Our Enemies are still as bitter and revengeful as ever—but it is for us to keep the commandments of God, and He will fight our battles. We should not only thank God, but give thanks to the Supreme Court for doing their duty. Judge [James B.] McKean however, is down, and defeated, and many of his old friends can now turn round and abuse~~d~~ and kick him—such is the nature of the friendship of this world. But not ~~us~~ so with God, let us then do right and secure the confidence of God, and it will endure. He was astonished that such a universal dislike should exist towards us, seeing that we do not premeditate evil towards any of the human family.

Prest. B[righam] Young spoke of the destitution that existed among this people some 20 and 25 years ago—especially in the way of clothing, hence the anxiety to raise sheep, and Import Machinery so that we could make our own Clothing. But to day we have lots of men in our midst with Greenbacks[33] in their hands wanting to buy ~~it u~~ up all the wool, and send it out of the Country. For our brethren to dispose of their wool for this purpose, simply because they could realize two cents a lb more of an outsider[,] he did not think it was right[.] We shall feel better by sustaining ourselves and the people, rather than crave after what is made by the Gentiles. The Devil will not admit us into his nest, the Kingdom of God will be an independent Kingdom. The kingdoms of this world will crumble and decay. The Merchants will yet say, no one will buy our merchandize. Let us pay attention to our farming business, and live our Religion, and let mining alone. These items about wool &c

33. Paper money was first issued by the US government about ten years earlier during the Civil War.

was made partly for the Home Missionaries to preach about among the wool growing community.

He then refered to a charge that Willard Richards Jun[io]r ^& Bros^ made to him a short time ago, that hundreds of Elders had told them ~~as a Family~~ that He had robbed the [Richards] family of what righteully belonged to them.[34] ~~He~~ Prest. Young then enquired if any member of the school had ever made such a statement, but no one responded. He then explained his connexion with Willard Richards ~~f~~ and his family for a great many years. He had always been a friend to them, and the charge was as cruel and as uncalled for as could be. He then spoke of the order & beauty that will exist in the House of God, when his kingdom is organized according to the mind & will of God. It would happyfy and bless the whole community, every man would be in his place, and all would be contented and happy.

Elder Geo A Smith bore testimony to the truth of Prest. Youngs remarks in reference to his conduct towards Willard Richards & his family. That the boys, when a little more age creeps over them, ~~they~~ will weep and howl for the course they have taken towards Prest. Young.

Elder W[ilford] Woodruff, bore testimony to the same facts, woe be to that man who had made such statements about Prest. Young.[35]

Elder Rob[er]t L. Campbell spoke with much respect to ^toward^ Elder W[illard] Richards. He had lived with him as a clerk and received chastisement from him whenever needed. Let us as Elders entertain the kindest and most charitable feelings toward his boys, that they may honorably bear and honour their Fathers name.

Elder Jos[ep]h F. Smith & Levi Richards bore testimony to the kindly feeling of Pres[ident] Young towards [Levi's brother] Willard & his family. In conversing with [his nephew] Heber John Richards, he exprest a desire & belief that he would yet occupy a portion of his Fathers land—& Levi told him He hoped that no unrighteous means would be resorted to. Levi was thankful this thing had come before the

34. When apostle Willard Richards died in 1854, his oldest son, Heber J., was thirteen years old. Apparently Brigham Young managed their father's business property in their behalf and had not yet transferred it to the sons until the newspaper questioned it in 1872. By then, the sons—Calvin Willard, Heber John, Joseph Smith, Willard Brigham, Stephen Longstroth, and others—were in their twenties and thirties. "Widows and Orphans Claiming Their Rights," *Salt Lake Tribune*, Mar. 11, 1872.

35. The rest of the entry was written vertically over the top of existing writing.

School that Prest. Young be entirely exonerated from thought or act he had ever done towards that family.

School was adjourned for one week at 1 oclock. After singing Benediction by Prest. Geo A Smith.

May 11, 1872; Saturday

Theological Class met at the Tabernacle at One o clock pm. Present Elder Orson Pratt presiding.[36] After singing Prayer by Elder Amos Fielding. Singing.

Elder Orson Pratt said, as the school was now open, if there was any business to bring before it, there was an opportunity, though ~~it~~ he did not think it wisdom to investigate or decide upon any particular doctrine, especially in the absence of the first Presidency.

Elder Jno. [John] W. Young bore testimony to the truth of the Gospel, and the necessity of seeking first the Kingdom of God. This probation was one of test and trial, and it behooves us to realize and act upon this fact. God has not forsaken us, the dawn of prosperity is dawning upon us, he was very thankful for the reappearance ~~of~~ and freedom of our friends and brethren, who have lately been liberated from bondage.

If there were any in this school whom he had offended, he would be thankful if they would call and make the same known to him, and he would endeavour to rectify it. His faith and all [he had] was in the kingdom of God. He had been engaged for some time past in building a Railroad through the Northern Settlements.[37] He had been partly successful in obtaining outside Capitol to invest in our lines of railroad, and yet we ~~remain~~ have the controuling power. We have the bone and sinew in our midst, which the outside Capitalists require—and which is so essential an element in the construction of great enterprizes. May God bless you Amen.

Elder Geo B Wallace spoke of every man in Israel being prophets or should be. The spirit of the living God is within us, if we live as we

36. Brigham Young and George A. Smith were in Provo.

37. John W. Young, a son of Brigham Young, had been a principal subcontractor for the Union Pacific railroad. Afterward he raised capital to build lines from Brigham City north into Idaho, south from Ogden to Salt Lake City (later as far as Santaquin), and from Salt Lake City east into the mining district around Park City. Adkins, "History of John W. Young's Utah Railroads," 8–10.

should do then whatever is said to us by the Servants of God we can tell whether it is the mind and will of God or not. It is our privelege to have dreams and visions, and be forewarned. This is the place to be corrected or confirmed in any doctrine we entertain, and which we sometimes advance in Ward Meetings or country Settlements [towns].

Himself and Bro J[ohn] W. Young being members of the ~~God~~ [Salt Lake Stake] High Council, had many difficult cases to decide upon, and said how necessary it was to hear both sides of the testimony before Judging between them.

He believed that God and Angels were pleased with us as a people, as imperfect as we are. If we were only ready, God was willing to give us a Government that would entirely free us from the yoke of bondage that we have been subjected to, and he would also pour the wealth of the world into our hands. Let us be faithful and may God bless us.

Elder Demick Huntington gave an interesting account of the Ute Indians, One of the Chiefs had sent out [Mormon] Missionaries of their own tribe, among the [other] Indians, to testify that Joseph [Smith] the Prophet and Hyrum [Smith] his brother had been murdered by the white Gentiles &c. The spirit of God was working with them [Native Americans], and we should pray for the Lord to visit them by Dreams and Visions. He then related a vision, of a personage appearing to an old Indian Chief, who revealed to him, that the Mormons were the only ~~t~~ friends, the Indians had on earth, and they must be united with them, not steal—nor kill them &c. ^A great many tribes are about to meet in Conference and spend a month with each other, not far from here, with a view of becoming better acquainted—and be of mutual benefit to each other.^

Elder Orson Pratt said, there were more promises made in the book of Mormon to the Lamanites [Native Americans] than to the Gentiles—and before ever we can return to Jackson Country [Missouri] to build up the great City of Zion, many of the Lamanites will have to be civilized and Christianized in the true sense of the word. Jesus said to the forefathers of the Lamanites, that as many of the Gentiles who would repent and turn to the Lord, they shall assist the remnants of the House of Jacob in building up the City of the New Jerusalem [in Missouri].

The Indians will have to leave of their wandering habits, have ~~they~~ their wants supplied, and the Gospel preached to them. When the City of the New Jerusalem shall have been built, a great Mission will be given, to gather in from Patagonia [South America] & Chili, Peru, Esquimaux [Eskimos] &c all the remnants of the house of Jacob. The Saviour will ~~then~~ come, when all the tribes of the Lamanites will be gathered together. He then quoted several prophesies pertaining to the future glory of Zion, and the benefits that will acrue to those who observed the Word of Wisdom.

Elder [blank] ~~said~~ related a vision, of a personage appearing to him one night, and told him to leave off the use of swines [pig] flesh, and keep the Word of Wisdom.

Judge [Elias] Smith said that many of the brethren owning property in the City had not yet filed their [land] claims [with the federal government], and only 11 days was remaining, for the privelege of doing so.

Elder W[ilford] Woodruff, warned the brethren against a careless indifference about properly & legally securing their property. There are many outsiders who are watching every chance to take any advantage they can of our carelessness.

School was adjourned for one week at 1 o clock. After singing Benediction by [blank].

May 18, 1872; Saturday

Theological School met in the Tabernacle at One o clock pm. Present Prest. B[righam] Young presiding. After singing Prayer by Elder A[mos] Fielding. Singing.

B[isho]p Edw[ar]d Hunter contrasted the present with the past, dealing of God with his people, and the necessity of the Elders mangifying both Priesthoods, that they become the sons of Moses and Aarron, and the elect of God, and thus be prepared to meet all the wiles of the adversary. He then spoke of the high and holy calling of a Teacher in Israel. No other officer in ^the^ Kingdom has the right to preside in his house, but a Teacher, and he always honored them by calling his family together, and submit to their teaching.

B[isho]p E[lijah] F. Sheets who had just returned from a visit to Sanpete [Utah], attended two days meetings there, found them a good, faithful people. In Fort Ephraim during the past eight months, the saints resolved to put away what Eggs were laid on Sundays, for the benefit of the Emigration fund, the Eggs amounted to eight hundred dollars. He did not think the brethren in the City paid their tithing so well, as in the Country, we should take a more lively interest in the duties of to day, that by doing them each day in their time and season, we not only receive a present blessing, but we shall be ~~pleased~~ prepared for those great blessings that are in store for the faithful in the future.

Prest. D[aniel] H. Wells made a few encouraging remarks on the subject of tithing—and the necessity of all wool growers to sell their wool to those owning Factories, and not dispose of it to outsiders because they can get Cash for it. This policy is so suicidal that no Man of God will do it.

He strongly commended the practise of attending to the small but constant effort to build up Zion, as in the case of putting away sundays Eggs for the Emigration. There are very few of the Rich brethren who think they can afford to pay up their Tithing as honestly as a poor man. The Lord never blesses the Elders with means for any other ~~means~~ purpose than to build up Zion—and not to build up the Devils Kingdom with [means]. Let us then sustain what is right, and will immediately benefit and bless the institutions of Zion.

Elder W[illiam] Willis deprecated the too common practise of patronizing light literature, which prevails to a great extent among the Latter day Saints. He much prefered truth to fiction.

Elder A M[ilton] Musser said, those who did not enter their declaratory statements of their City property—before Friday next, will certainly risk, if not entirely forfeit it. If the brethren did not pay for and obtain titles to the land they had preempted, they would ~~run~~ most certainly lose it. He complained of some who paid their tithes in articles almost valueless. If we as latter day saints do our duty, our Leaders would have more confidence in us. All those brethren who are Missionaries ought most certainly to pay promptly their tithes & offerings, and attend to all the requirements of the Kingdom of God, in order to faithfully preach and exhort others to do so ~~it~~ too.

Elder Lorenzo Young said, we had no right to squander away our time or any other talent. Novel reading was attended with no good result. The practise of Card playing he also condemned, ~~not~~ a lack of confidence existed also to a great extent, so that we cannot consistently call upon each other to combine our faith together in laying hands on our sick, for the blessing of God to be bestowed upon them. He recommended Parents to occasionally teach ~~our~~ ^their^ wives and children the duties & obligations that rest upon them towards God & each other.

Elder Geo Goddard made a few remarks on the importance of being actively employed in doing all the good we can, by sustaining every institution of the Kingdom of God.

Elder James Leach sanctioned the above remarks—felt well in acting in the capacity of a teacher.

Elder [blank] felt well, & happy in being at the school. Had witnessed the power of God in healing the sick, in calming the winds, and waves of the Ocean. Had a strong desire to visit his friends in Scotland, to bear testimony of the truth—&c

Elder Edw[ar]d Stevenson spoke of the difference between the theory and practise of our religion—especially in regard to the Word of Wisdom. The time to serve the Lord is in fair weather, so that when the storm comes, we shall be ready to meet it, and look to the Lord for strength and succour. If we have done our duty our confidence in God will never fail us. The Lord giveth and the Lord taketh away—let us then be faithful, to overcome our weakness &c.

The School was adjourned for one week at one oclock pm. After singing Benediction by Elder G[eorge] B Wallace.

May 25, 1872; Saturday

Theological Class met at the Tabernacle at One oclock pm. Present Prest. Geo B. Wallace presiding.[38] After singing Prayer by Elder Geo Goddard. Singing.

A Question was asked, When the land preempted over [on the west side of the] Jordan [River] had to be paid for.

Judge E[lias] Smith said all the land declared for in 1870 or before that date, must be paid for in July next.

Elder [Thomas] Hawkins who had been confined in Camp Douglas for many months past, as a prisoner ^on a false charge^ for Lacivious Coabitation. Felt truly thankful for the privilege of again being at liberty to bear testimony to the truth. While a prisoner he had been well treated ^by the Officers^, his companions were Murderers, Whore

38. George Wallace, first counselor in the Salt Lake Stake, was presiding in the absence of the First Presidency and several apostles who had traveled to a two-day church conference in Ogden. WWJ, May 25, 1872.

Masters and Thieves. He answered many questions ^while in prison^ was a very firm believer in the principles of the Gospel. His Heavenly Father had been exceedingly kind to him during his confinement. He had the kindest feelings towards his first wife, who would have persecuted him to the death if she could [over polygamy]. She has had ill advisers, she has contracted a debt, that will take a long while to pay—but he ~~a~~ intended to be a friend to her, and time will tell that he is her best friend, but not as a Husband. He then expressed a fervent desire for all to be faithful and true to God and his servants to the end.

Elder J[esse] C. Little had been very much pleased with the remarks of Bro Hawkins, ~~he~~ ^who^ had been afflicted, and imprisoned, for his religion, and ~~he~~ had borne his afflictions with much patience and fortitude. He ^J[esse] C.^ was a believer in Polygamy. God Almighty had revealed it, and whether a man had trouble with it or not, no matter, if we enter into it in good faith, ~~he was~~ ^we are^ bound to be benefited by it. He was in the habit of talking very plain to his guests, and advocated Polygamy as the revealed will of God. Let us all do the best we can, keep the faith, and endure to the end.

Prest. Elias Smith said he was a practical man, but not much of a preacher. Had endeavoured to keep within the sphere he had been called to. His labours had been more of a temporal than spiritual nature. He was sorry that so many brethren had been so dilatory ~~about~~ as to lose their land, which they had preempted, but not legally secured. Much valuable land had gone into the hands of our enemies in consequence of the indifference of the brethren.

He had the utmost confidence, in the ultimate triumph of the great work of God. God reigns, and his Kingdom will grow and increase, in his own due time. He expected to work his way into the Kingdom, and to get into it on no other principle.

(Elder [J.C.M.] Crockwell)—said when a man entered his declaratory intention to preempt land, within 30 days of said declaration, the law required him to build a good ~~pr~~ permanent house, and live in it at least 6 Mo[nths]—himself ^& family^. If such arrangements are not strictly complied with, no man need expect to secure their land. He then made some very valuable remarks on the law of Homestead & Mining law &c. A second wife can preempt land by strictly conforming to the law. If any one fails to make improvements on land that he filed upon, within the specified time—rather than lose it, let him legally surrender~~ed~~ it, and let his second wife preempt it.

Elder Geo B. Wallace spoke of the time when it was council for us to live in forts, then in Towns and ~~seill~~ Citys. Now that it is safe for us ^to^ live on our farms, ~~made~~ many had failed to comply, such was the waywardness of some of our brethren. We have had many instructions on the land question to day.

The School was adjourned for one week at one oclock pm. After singing Benediction by Elder [Thomas] Hawkins.

June 1, 1872; Saturday

Theological Class met at the Tabernacle at One o clock pm. Present Prest. D[aniel] H Wells presiding. After singing Prayer by Elder Amos Fielding. Singing.

B[isho]p E[dward] Hunter felt impressed with the great importance of every Elder in Israel to magnify their calling in the priesthood, he himself could not reasonably expect to be much longer here, being far advanced in age. Felt thankful he had such good health. Spoke somewhat of his early experience in the Church, the necessity of paying promptly our tithes and offerings—which duties should be performed as a great privelege. We may as well try to do without daily food, as to live without the Spirit of the Lord.

Elder A M[ilton] Musser spoke of the universal failings and short-comings of Man—and the tendency of each to scan [examine] and scrutinize the other. Let us fortify, and keep well guarded, the faith of the gospel that is within us—and not destroy it by indulging in anything antagonistic to the requirements of the priesthood. He felt convicted of one fact, and that is, that we in the City, are not so faithful as those who live in the Country settlements—not only in the payment of tithing, but in many other things. He felt grieved that some were renting their property to unvirtuous persons for unlawful purposes. This was not right and every Elder ought to set their faces against all such things. He also regretted that so many were patronizing the Butchers & others, who were trading without license and setting the city authorities at defiance.

Elder Geo Goddard refered to the anniversary of the Birthday of Prest. B[righam] Young who was 71 years of age to day. He then offered up a prayer for him, and blest him in the name of the Lord Jesus—and all the members of the school said Amen.

Elder Geo B. Wallace said the greatest blessing we can confer upon Prest. Young, will be for each one of us to live our religion—and every faithful latter day saint never omits to pray for Prest. Young, his counsellors, the Bishops & all the Saints. When he first drank at the Gospel fountain, it was so sweet and precious to him, that he thought all his Brothers & Sisters who [he contacted would] rejoice to receive and enjoy the same, but in this, he was mistaken, but he continued to pray for his relatives—&c.

Elder A[mos] Fielding felt blest in all he had listened to, spoke of the power and influence that Jacob had obtained over Esau. He had prevailed by praying to the Lord during the night, and had the assurance of an Angel that his prayer had prevailed with God. We hold the same priesthood as Jacob, and if we only live as it is our privelege to live, we also can have Power with God, even as He.

Prest. D[aniel] H. Wells regretted that any of the brethren should either patronize apostate Butchers or those who are doing business without a license, and trampling municipal authority under their feet.

He said, a Republican Convention will convene on the 5th June for the purpose of Nominating U[lysses] S. Grant as the next President of the U[nited] states. This same Grant once said that he would not do Prest. Young the honour of shooting him, but would hang him. Now let all Israel be united in prayer & supplication to God that he may not even receive a nomination by his friends, but if so, that he may be defeated at the Election.[39] And all the school said Amen.

Gave good council to the school, about selling Wool, and patronizing Friends instead of foes in business, let us be all united in sustaining Israel, and be wise in all our actions. He hoped to see the same when an Elder abroad will be known by their abstinence from Smoking, tea drinking &c

The School was adjourned for one week at One ~~week~~ ^oclock^ pm. After singing Benediction by Elder O[smond] Shaw.

39. There is no evidence Grant said he would rather hang Brigham Young than shoot him. He exceeded his predecessors' efforts in enforcing anti-cohabitation laws, however. He traveled to Utah in 1875 and he and his wife, Julia, met with Young. Alexander, "Conflict of Perceptions."

June 8, 1872; Saturday

Theological Class met in the Tabernacle at One o clock pm. Present Elder Orson Pratt presiding.[40] After singing Prayer by Elder Geo B Wallace. Singing.

Elder O[rson] Pratt, said we have a Temporal and also a spiritual work to perform on the earth, and during the past years of our experience in these vallies a vast amount of labour has been performed by the latter day saints—and in the future no one can tell what lies before us. The Lord has greatly blest us since we came here, not only by increasing the quantity of rain, but by removing the Grasshoppers in answer to our prayers. He then spoke of the abundance of Iron Ore which abounds in this Territory, but owing to ~~a~~ ^not^ strictly carrying out the council of the servants of God, it has not been developed to that extent as it might have done—and unless some of our Capitolists will take hold of this, it may fall into the hands of Foreigners.[41] From them we shall have to purchase [the iron], and thus we must become more or less subject to them, though he really thought the Lord would rather the saints enjoyed these blessings, than go into the hands of outsiders. No council was ~~g~~ ever given more faithfully to this people, than not to trade with our enemies, and yet, if that council had been carried out, we would not now see so many outside Merchants who will sign any petition that has a tendency to bring down upon us the pressure of Government, to deprive us of our rights, and bring trouble and calamity upon us. He hoped however we would learn wisdom, even though it should be by the things that we suffer.

Elder Crosby[42] from St. George, had been there [in St. George] for the last 10 years, he was formerly a resident of this City, helped build it up from the stump. They were putting out many apple trees in Dixey [southern Utah]. This spring he had visited the Country on the Sevier

40. Brigham Young was traveling in the northern part of the territory.

41. In 1850 Young sent apostle George A. Smith and about 170 colonists to settle what became Parowan, Utah, and the Iron Mission. It was a difficult area to settle, and the settlers were able to produce pig iron to be freighted elsewhere for smelting but not in a financially viable manner.

42. Jesse W. Crosby (1820–93) was a convert from 1838, a frequent missionary to Canada, and one of the first pioneers to the Salt Lake Valley in 1847. In 1861 his was among 300 families called to southern Utah, in his case because he had experience making molasses from beets, turnips, and carrots. He also became a freighter, transporting goods to and from California. Crosby, *Traveling in the Ministry*, 1:66, 75–81.

[River], where the brethren were putting in thousands of acres of Grain, and where ^there^ is plenty more vacant land for any one who ~~wh~~ wants to go there and live. The Iron Ore in the Southern Country is there in such abundance, that would supply ~~all~~ the United States with all the Iron ware they needed, but for the want of more Capitol they cannot accomplish much. The Iron Ore contains 90 per cent of the pure Metal. The Mining districts were opening up in all directions, and a Market was ~~of~~ open for all the surplus Grain, Fruit & Vegetables south of Provo.

The Southern Mission had been of a very forbidding character—at on[e] time serious thoughts were entertained of abandoning it, but for the encouraging words of Prest. [Brigham] Young. Prospects however were brightening for the saints in that Country. The culture of Lucerne [hay] was gone into ~~with~~ extensively, and by another season they hoped to have a great quantity for sale at Pioche and other Mining Camps, where now, the poorest kind of Hay was selling $80.00 per ton. The "Sevier [River] Bridge" was in a very rickety and unsafe condition, and considering the immense travel over it, there should be a better and safer bridge.

Elder C[hristopher] Merkley ~~had heard from some ^one^ f~~ was told the other day that they had been ^doing^ quite a good business in the Manufacture of Iron, and that if more Capitol could be invested, they would do much more.

Elder Geo B. Wallace spoke of the signing of the petition lately, to prevent Utah from ever becoming a ~~school~~ State. Many signed it who never for one Moment expected to see there names published—but he was glad of the exposure.[43] The Apostates were enemies to God and his servants and were linked in with the Official [federal] ring. He believed that God had shown Prest. Young by Vision where to lay out St. George, and many of his purposes also pertaining to that Mission, and however forbidding it may have been, he had no doubt there was something rich in store for those who faithfully abide there. He never knew Prest. Young to give wrong council—~~We~~

Prest. Orson Pratt said all outsiders had a perfect right to sign any

43. The petitioners objected to the imposition of Mormon theocracy and the practice of polygamy, also arguing that taxes would be raised if they became a state. The *Deseret News* published the names of the signers, but the *Salt Lake Tribune* observed that the large number of signers "gives the lie" to "the idea that there existed in this country but a small 'ring' opposed to the Church." "Memorial," *Deseret News*, June 12, 1872; "The Right of Petition," *Salt Lake Tribune*, June 7, 1872.

petition they please, but [not] when any one in the Church desiring to keep this people in a state of vassalage [signed such a petition.] ^He^ enquired, if that was right. The first Presidency, twelve [apostles], and all the leading men in Israel have repeatedly signed Petitions, for a State Government, and no one knowingly could possibly sign an opposite one that deserved a standing in the Church. And if they did not repent, he hoped to see the time when every one of them would be severed from the Church. All Merchants whose names ~~was~~ ^were^ found on that petition, he hoped they would be known and ~~utterly~~ entirely left alone by the saints.

The School was adjourned for one week at One oclock pm. After singing Benediction by Elder A[mos] Fielding.

June 15, 1872; Saturday

Theological Class met at the Tabernacle at One o clock pm. Present Prest. D[aniel] H. Wells Presiding. After singing Prayer by B[isho]p E[dwin] D. Woolley. Singing.

Elder Geo Goddard expressed a very strong appreciation of an Ordinance recently passed by the City Council to close up all Sunday trading, he was satisfied that the majority of the Elders of Israel would gladly sign a monster petitions to sanction and sustain the Council in their effort to improve the Morals of the people. He also advocated the necessity and desirableness of inaugorating a system of early closing, that our young men may have an opportunity of being more useful in their respective wards.

Elder Amos Fielding, said in Manchester, England, the Wholesale trade for many years past, have always closed at six o clock pm. Was in favour of not only closing up all general business at an early hour, but all liquor & ice cream saloons.

Elder Geo B. Wallace considered [that] the subject desired the utmost consideration, and whether the closing of Stores earlier would remedy the evil complained of, was a question, for young men, ~~to~~ being engaged from early morning till between 9 and 10 at night, will soon wear out the strongest constitution. If every one would only live their religion, all would be right, our Wives, Daughters & Sons need much instruction. God is blessing us as a people, he has rebuked the devourer for our sakes—and there is every human prospect of a bountiful harvest.

The prosperity of any community, depends upon the success of its producers. Spoke of the remarkable prophecies of Heber C. Kimball which have been literally fulfilled, some of them remain to be fulfilled, one being, that a Bushel of grain will be worth a bushel of gold,[44] this as all others ~~b~~ will be brought about upon Natural principles.

Elder John Pack felt good to be here, has just returned from a visit to the [United] States. Was not ashamed to own that he was a latter day saint. Our enemies are outwitted, and they know not what to do or say. Had been introduced to some of the leading men in "Springfield" Illinois, the political feeling in and around there are in favour of [Horace] Greeley,[45] and not [Ulysses S.] Grant for President. No matter who succeeds, God is at the helm, and will make all things subservient to his purposes. In regard to the word of Wisdom, it was no virtue in him, not to take liquor or smoke or chew Tobacco. He did not care much for the inducements of evil, set before us in this City[,] [only insofar] as it gave every one an Opportunity to resist the same. And happy is that man who has a natural thirst for drink, and overcomes it. Let us keep the commandments of God.

Elder Levi Richards spoke of existing evils, we are placed here to be tried. Human excrecense [excrement] exposed, is the greatest source of the Typhoyd Fever. And yet, a little dry earth is the most thorough deodorizer than can be found anywhere, and consequently this evil can easily be remedied. Condemned in unmeasured terms the use of "Winslows Soothing Syrup."[46] Also the practise of sending our Cows from 4 to 6 Miles on the prairie with very poor feed, and which produces milk of a very unhealthy quality.

Elder [Robert H.] Collins believed, that the leading men of Israel would move on the cause of Zion as fast as they can. The more

---

44. Kimball reportedly said this in 1849 when Mormons speculated that travelers returning with gold from California would pay dearly for food. Brown, *Life of a Pioneer*, 149.

45. Horace Greeley (1811–72) was the founding editor of the *New York Tribune*. After losing the Republican nomination in May 1872, he ran as a Democrat and won the nomination in July, then lost the election in November. He died a few weeks after the election.

46. Mrs. Winslow's Soothing Syrup, a morphine-and-alcohol tonic, was marketed to nursing mothers and teething infants. Invented in 1845, it was selling 1.5 million bottles annually by 1868, according to the Wood Library–Museum of Anesthesiology. An endorsement in 1861 promised that if customers "open the door for her, Mrs. Winslow will prove the American Florence Nightingale of the nursery." *New York Times*, Oct. 5, 1861.

knowledge we can get, the stronger our faith will be. If we can only keep up side by side with the authorities we are doing very ~~l~~ well.

Prest. D. H. Wells said we ought to try to purify the Atmosphere and everything around us, especially as the means of doing it, is within the reach of every person in the community. No person allowing a [public] Nuisense to grow up even in their own yard, can do so, without being liable to a fine. He urged all present to keep down all impure effluvia [waste], and try to remedy every evil that presents itself. Let us try to raise a little Lucerne [alfalfa], and feed well, our Cows, we must do so, or we cannot ensure good and wholesome Milk. Treat all animals kindly and righteously that they may be more useful to us. We must cooperate, all can do something both Men, Women & children. It was against the Law for persons to expose themselves to bathe, either in City Creek, or in the Slough.[47] The City Authorities were trying to carry out the most salutary and wholesome laws, and the people ought to aid and assist them in carrying them out. Let us be diligent in trying to carry out every sanitary and healthful rule around our homes, persons &c. Let us keep our boys out of the street, many accidents occur th^r^ough the foolhardy habits of rude boys. It is the duty of the Elders to encourage each other to come to this school. ~~and all~~ God will most certainly accomplish his purposes, upon the earth, either by us ~~us~~ or some others whom he will raise up.

This Territory is now the head center of Zion, by and bye, Missouri will be—and it is our privelege to live so as to set an example, worthy of being followed by the outside world. No man has any right with any more wealth than what he can take proper care of.

School adjourned for one week at one oclock. After singing Benediction by Elder Crockwell.

June 22, 1872; Saturday

Theological Class met in the Tabernacle at One o clock pm. Present Prest. B[righam] Young presiding. After singing Prayer by Elder B[righam] Young Jun[io]r Singing.

Elder W[illiam] H. Hooper, Delegate to Congress, had been anxiously waiting for the privilege he now enjoyed of mingling with his friends in

47. There were marshy areas along the Jordan River that would now be called wetlands but at the time were seen as swamps or sloughs.

Utah[.] ^For^ nearly 8 Months past he had been incessant in his duties as a Delegate to Congress. Taking our past 18 Months experience, and looking at it from mans standpoint, it seemed at times, as though our enemies were going to have it their own way, and jeopadize both the lives, property & political rights of the people of Utah. The [Englebrecht] decision of the Supreme Court, had been arrived at by the members thereof ^by^ looking at things far above the Partizan or the Bigot.

He then spoke of the late persecution by the United States Officials, and the return of Prest. Young from Dixie [southern Utah], which act at the time, he (W. H. H.) very much doubted the Wisdom of,[48] but ~~in~~ in the providence of God, it turned out to be the very thing that was wanted to secure the sympathy and good will of the American People.

After the decision of the Supreme Court, Judge McKean ~~wa~~ had been indefatigable in trying to pass some special legislative enactment, that would partially neutralize the decision of the Supreme Court—but did not succeed.

It seemed absolutely needful for us as a People to be placed in very critical circumstances, in order to brighten us up—and wake us from our apathy and laziness, and fulfil the old adage—that "Necessity was the Mother of Invention".

[The US Senate chaplain] Dr. [J. P.] Newman, who came here to destroy Mormonism,[49] but went away again maddened with rage under a sense of defeat—had done all he could against this people, but he's down. [US vice president] Schuylor Colfax also who made his brag, that who came here, ~~that~~ he bearded the "Lion in his den"[50] had done all he could injure and destroy this people—but he also was politically dead.[51]

48. Young had been indicted for polygamy in October 1871. After posting bail, he traveled south to dedicate the site of the St. George Temple, missing his court date. The evidence indicates that he was considering going into hiding, but that he decided to return and stand trial under an arrangement with Chief Justice James B. McKean that included house arrest beginning January 2, 1872. Turner, *Brigham Young*, 365–68.

49. Newman was the minister of the Metropolitan Methodist Church of Washington, DC. In 1870 he visited Utah and engaged in a public debate with Orson Pratt in the Tabernacle regarding the question, "Does the Bible sanction polygamy?" Tullidge, *Life of Brigham Young*, 403–06.

50. In nineteenth-century America, "to beard someone" meant "to oppose to the face; to set at defiance." Webster, *American Dictionary*, 1828.

51. After Colfax was found to have taken bribes as part of the Crédit Mobilier scandal, he never held office again. The vice president, on President Grant's re-election, was Henry Wilson.

And may God grant the [that] He who now sits in the Presidential chair [Ulysses S. Grant], may go down into oblivion and rise no more.

He then passed a very high eulogy on the Character of Horace Greeley, and hoped he would be the successful ~~com~~ Candidate for the Presidential chair.

Elder Geo Q Cannon felt truly thankful for the privelege of returning home again, after an absence of some weeks to the States—refering to the results recently brought about through the "Decision of the Supreme Court." He felt to give God all the Glory, it is for us as latter day saints to see and recognize the hand of God in all things. His labours, in connexion with Capt[ai]n [Willam H.] Hooper were of a very pleasant and agreable character—had been treated with much kindness by Members of Congress. The [proposed state] Constitution, with which he was entrusted, ~~were~~ was printed by order of Congress[.] The most influential men in the House, recommended them not to urge the constitution for a state government this session, but wait until after the Presidential Election. They had several interviews with ~~the~~ President ^Grant^ who seemed to be proof against any favourable impression towards the people of Utah. He Geo Q was now fully satisfied that He [President Grant] was the prime mover of Judge McKeans course.

~~He viewed at the halls~~ He spoke of the bold and indefatigable labours of our Delegate W[illiam] H. Hooper.

Elder W. H. Hooper spoke of the high and noble Character of Mr Willis Drummond, the head of the land department.[52] It gave him peculiar pleasure to bear such a testimony of that great and good man.

Prest. B Young, in speaking of those who deny the faith, they become a stink to every one in Heaven, Earth or Hell. Whenever we conclude to barter off ~~any~~ ^one^ principle of the Gospel for any consideration whatever, we also shall become a stink and reproach in the eyes of Heaven and Earth. God overrules and dictates in all matters pertaining to his Kingdom.

If ever we go into the family of States, we will go in without purse or scrip. So in any future trials He would go also on the same principle. He had tried what money would do, and he was satisfied that Lawyers were

52. Willis Drummond (1823–88) was a Union major during the Civil War. On appointment by President Ulysses S. Grant, he served as Comissioner of the General Land Office for three years. He would later be elected to the US Congress from Iowa.

of very little account. The Priests are the ones who persecute in every age, they seek our destruction.

Polygamy was ^one of^ the great pillars of our salvation, the sealing power was that by which man & man & woman would become united in the link of priesthood—and the man who boldly avows his faith in that doctrine in the world, he will be more respected than those who prevaricate. God will ~~finally~~ give his saints, the Gold & the Silver and the wealth of this world, just as soon as they are prepared to use it for the building up of the Kingdom of God, and not before. In the development of the Mines, so far, has only shown the lower grades of Ore. It is necessary for us to undergo all the changes of circumstances that surround us. Only let us live our religion and all will be well. God will bring us off victorious.

A letter was read from Elder W. J. Silver, Machinest, asking a question Whether it was right for the saints to ^Employ^ a Plumber & Glazier or any other outsider who had signed the Anti State Petition, as did Mr. Lyon,[53] and who is now being employed by several of the Brethren.

Prest. Young said in reply, that no such man, as would sign a Petition [that] in its provisions would tend to the destruction of the saints, should never ~~would~~ ^work^ about his premises, and if such an one was there, should be dismissed forthwith—& all who feel as I do, hold up your right hands, and all hands responded.

The School was adjourned for ~~a~~ One week at One oclock pm. After singing Benediction by Elder W[ilford] Woodruff.

June 29, 1872; Saturday

Theological Class met at the Tabernacle at One o clock pm. Present Prest. B[righam] Young—presiding. After singing Prayer by Elder T[homas] W. Winter~~s~~. Singing.

Prest. Young enquired how many members of the School have paid anything into the Emigrating Fund this Year? A few held up their right hands. He then made a particular request of every Member to pay in something immediately, so as to emigrate the poor from their distressed situation. He also desired them to bring in their old tickets [of

53. Two men named Lyon signed the petition against statehood, one of whom listed his occupation as "teamster" and another who identified himself as a "miner." "Memorial," *Deseret News*, June 12, 1872.

membership] to the Secretary, and have them exchange for new ones. He also requested the Elders when preaching in the Tabernacle to direct their attention to the congregation instead of doing it to the strangers.

Elder Jno. [John] Taylor said the text he had to preach about was Salvation, and then contrasted the infidelity of the world, with the faithful recognition of God our Heavenly Father by the Elders of Israel. Refered to the many privileges enjoyed by the people of God, ~~which~~ and the necessary obligations that accompany them. Many deliverances the Lord has wrought out for us, and will continue to do the same, if we only put our trust in him. Spoke of Revelation, to it we are indebted for the first principles of the Gospel, and also ^for^ the guidance of the people of God, we cannot get along individually or collectively without it. Predicted the final & universal triumph of the Kingdom of God. He felt comforted under these considerations. He also intended to carry ^out^ the suggestions of Prest. Young.

Elder W[illiam] H. Hooper felt happy in the privilege of mingling his Spirit with his brethren in this school. Spoke of the over ruling providence of God, that is constantly over us if we keep the commandments of God.

He also stated ~~o~~ that in all [US] congressional districts, Government permitted one pupil to West Point, and another one to the institutions of ~~Ino~~ Annopolis, but owing ^to^ circumstances in our past experience, only one had availed ~~themselves~~ himself of this privilege, viz Willard Young Son of Prest. B Young who was sent to ~~so~~ West Point, who was nobly acquitting himself in his graduating studies in a short time. He ^W[illiam] H[ooper]^ expected to be notified of a vacancy in the institution at Indianopolis [Annapolis], when a young Man between 17 & 20 would have to be selected, who was well developed physically, of good moral character, with a good sound English Education.

Prest. D. H. Wells enquired for the names of young Men who might be deemed suitable ~~for~~ to make a selection from, for graduate at the Indianopolis [Annapolis] Institution [US Naval Academy]. The following names were handed in[:]

Anson P Call's grandson, Bountiful
Josh. Toronto Junr. 20th Ward
John T. Caine Junr. D[itt]o
R. P. Morris. 19th D[itt]o

Wm. H. Branch Junr. St. George
Andrew S Johnson. 15th Ward
Bruce Taylor. 14th [Ward]
Chas. Carrington. 17th W[ard]
Cummings. 14th [Ward]
Chas. Burton. 15th [Ward]
Hammond Brinton. Big Cottonwood
Jas. Walter Eardley Junr. 3rd Ward

Elder W[ilford] Woodruff spoke with gratitude to God, for the prospect of a bountiful Harvest.[54] He ~~wa~~ [God] had also commenced to favour Zion, to build it up, gather the poor, would bless the leaders of Israel with the light of Revelation—~~and~~ &c.

School was adjourned for one week at One o clock pm. After singing Benediction by Elder Amos Fielding.

July 6, 1872; Saturday

Theological Class met at the Tabernacle at One o clock pm. Present. ~~Prest.~~ Elder Orson Pratt presiding. After singing Prayer by Elder W[ilford] Woodruff. Singing.

Prest. O Pratt reminded the Members of the School, that in the exchange of old tickets [of admission] for new ones and to avoid confusion next Saturday, it is expected that every Member shall have a ^new^ recommendation from the Bishops of their respective wards, and those ^members^ who reside in the City, can obtain a new ticket by calling upon Elder Geo Goddard on Friday next, and those living in the Country can get them on Saturday from 9 am till 1 pm by applying to Bro Geo Goddard. Elder Pratt said this new restrictive measure may be the begining ~~th~~ of that time when men will be chosen for the ~~enjor~~ enjoyment of those privileges that are intended for the faithful.

Elder Geo Goddard stated that in order to obtain a new ticket from him, ~~it would~~ they must come with a recommendation from their respective Bishops.

Elder Geo Q. Cannon spoke of the necessity for a stricter rule being observed towards the membership of the School. He also adverted to the evils and contaminating influences now in our midst—and hoped

54. Woodruff and others, such as Joseph F. Smith, had been absent for some time attending to their crops.

that by coming in contact with them we may be able to resist and entirely overcome them, ~~and~~ that we may become strong and mighty in the cause of truth. He made particular ~~attention~~ mention of the principle of Polygamy, no person that speaks lightly of it without endangering their salvation. He acknowledged the providences of God, in keeping up a continual assault by our enemies, because they had a tendency to keep capitol out of the Country, which was all right.

B[isho]p David Brinton, just returned from a Mission to England, he felt truly thankful for the experience he had gained during his labours. He never spent two happier years in his life, had enjoyed good health, many friends greeted him everywhere, was never home sick. Left his family in the hands of the Lord, and on his return found them well. Some of his fellow labourers had fallen through small pox—which he regretted, though many were afflicted with a still more fearful disease, viz. Home sickness. He owned an overruling providence [of good health] that had been over him. Two infant children died between here and Omaha, probably from the use of Ice water,[55] Prayed that all present might keep the faith and endure to the end.

Elder [Edward] Shoenfeld also a returned Missionary, felt truly thankful for the privilege of going on a Mission, gave an interesting account of some circumstances connected with it. The world do not possess the principles of life and exaltation, they may have many things that are not yet here, but they are only a question of time and Means.

B[isho]p A[lonzo] H. Raleigh spoke of the responsibility resting on the Bishops in recommending persons to this school. Refered to certain landmarks [criteria] for their guidance in the rules of the school, in regard to attending meetings, payment of tithing and Offerings &c &c. Those who fail to go to meeting, shew great ^want of^ respect towards the priesthood, and for information he wished to know, how far these landmarks should be observed by the Bishops, in recommending persons to this school.

Elder Geo Q Cannon regretted the ~~observ~~ absence of the first presidency,[56] ~~to~~ for a full answer to the above question, such flagrant

55. In fact, the girls may have died from the ice water. In the nineteenth century, ice obtained from polluted water sources could carry typhoid. Only gradually did the ice companies learn to harvest their product from lakes located away from population centers. Weightman, *Frozen-Water Trade*, 10.

56. The three primary members of the First Presidency were Brigham Young, who was ill; George A. Smith, who was traveling and would arrive back that evening; and

cases named by B[isho]p Raleigh, he Geo Q. would not like to recommend such ones.

The school was adjourned for One week at one o clock pm. After singing Benediction by Elder H[orace] S. Eldredge.

July 13, 1872; Saturday

Theological Class met in the Tabernacle at One o clock pm. Present Elder Orson Pratt presiding.[57] After singing Prayer by Elder Amos Fielding. Singing.

Elder O[rson] Pratt said there were many subjects that might be talked over here, and when practised faithfully by the members of the school, would wield an immense influence among the people for good. Many evil practises have been introduced here by outsiders, and most of the older ones of our brethren have withstood such things in other countries, but our young people, to whom those practises are new, may be overcome to some extent, and therefore needed the constant watch care of the Parents.

Spoke of the swift judgment that overto^o^~~ken~~ two persons ~~is~~ in ancient Israel, who endeavoured to introduce whoredoms in their midst, Phineas, the Grandson of Aarron thrust a Javelyn through a Man & Woman who were guilty of it, and this righteous act of Phinehas was rewarded by the Almighty, by conferring the priesthood of Aarron upon him for ever and ever [Num 25:6–13]. He then denounced the practise ~~of~~ ^and^ indulgence in Fasheons, and foolery, ~~or~~ ^and if not checked^ we will bring down the wrath and indignation of Almighty God upon us.

Elder Amos Fielding reprobated the use of stimulating liquors, which was largely impregnated with poisonous substances—and total abstinence was the only safe and effectual remedy for intemperance. God had promised great and precious blessings to those who observed the word of wisdom.

Elder [Robert] Dickson said he was sent by the Prophet Joseph [Smith] on a Mission to Novo Scotia [Canada]—accompanied by Jesse

---

Daniel H. Wells, who may have been absent from this meeting. George Q. Cannon was himself a member of the presidency since June, as were Albert Carrington, Joseph F. Smith, Lorenzo Snow, Brigham Young Jr., and John Willard Young.

57. Brigham Young, George A. Smith, Daniel H. Wells, and George Q. Cannon were attending the dedication of the new Third Ward meeting house. Class would ajourn early so members could attend political caucuses. HOJ, July 13, 1872.

Crosby—and stated some very interesting items in his experience that occurred some thirty three or four years ago—and also during a recent Mission just completed.[58]

The School was then adjourned for one week at one o clock pm. It was closed some time earlier than usual on account of a [political] Caucaus Meeting being held, previously announced. After singing Benediction by Elder Geo B. Wallace.

July 20, 1872; Saturday

Theological Class met at the Tabernacle at one o clock pm. Present Prest. D[aniel] H. Wells presiding. After singing Prayer by Elder A M[ilton] Musser. Singing.

Elder Ja[me]s S Brown who had just returned from a short mission east, ~~and~~ felt truly thankful to be present again in the school of the Prophets, had preached a few times [in the East], but no particular beneficial results appeared manifest, further than interesting conversations with various individuals, until ~~their~~ ^his^ means was about exhausted and then returned home.

Elder A M[ilton] Musser had many times thought when hearing ^from^ or reading letters written by Missionaries in the united states, that He could accomplish some good there as a Missionary, having so much Knowle^d^ge of the habits & customs of our people. There are many speculators in our midst who are expecting to become rich and wealthy, by gobbling up our salt mountains, coal beds &c. He felt particularly grateful for the abundant crops that abound everywhere—and refered to other local topics of interest in our territory.

Prest. D[aniel] H. Wells said so long as an Elder has faithfully borne a testimony while on a Mission, to larger or smaller congregations, he should not be discouraged or indulge in the thought that he had done no good. He has sown good seed, and God alone can give the increase. Spoke of regret and chagrin by the Elders of Israel, ^of the course^ ~~at t~~ that the sons of Joseph [Smith] the Prophet were taking, the Devil was

58. Robert Dickson's original mission to Canada was in 1843. He went back in 1871 but was "attacked with heart disease" and became convinced he would die. However, after administering a blessing to himself, he was granted a vision that convinced him he would "arise from my sick bed and get home." Dickson, "Report of a Mission," Aug. 6, 1872.

using them, to cause many to turn away from the truth, and subvert the Kingdom of God, but they will not succeed.[59]

Grain was going to be plentiful, and cheap, and will ^be^ a splendid good time for us ^all^ to lay up a large supply. Notwithstanding we are contiguous to other countries, and we ^may^ not possibly see grain so high as it has been, yet the judgements of God may come upon the Nation, and they may have to send here for breadstuffs—therefore I council you to lay up a good supply. He then warned the brethren against two [too] much exposure in the sun while the weather was so hot, the thermomitor being 100 in the shade, we should all be temperate in our habits, and endeavour to preserve our lives, for the sake of the Kingdom—for God had not two [too] many good men to carry on his work.

Elder John Pack explained how to build a Grainery so as to entirely exclude mice or other vermin.

The Meeting was adjourned for one week ~~for a~~ at One o clock pm. Benediction by Elder Orson Pratt.

July 27, 1872; Saturday

Theological Class met in the Tabernacle at One o clock pm. Present Prest. ~~D[aniel] H. Wells~~ ^B[righam] Young^ presiding. Singing. Prayer by Elder A. M[ilton] Musser. Singing.

Elder O[rson] Pratt spoke of the audacity and hardihood of ~~of~~ one of the Prophet Joseph [Smith]'s sons, who has been publicaly declaring that his Father not only never taught, but positively denounced everything connected with the [temple] Endowments—whereas He himself O P was a living witness, besides hundreds of others, that had ocular demonstration that Joseph taught the Endowments in Nauvou, and saw Emma ^his wife^ with the Temple clothing on. Her influence over the children was very great—and also Apostates had done what they could to blind their eyes. The habits of Drinking, Whoreing, Profanity & Fasheons were gaining ground in our midst among our young people, and if they are not checked, the prophecy could never be fulfilled where it says, let your garments be the workmanship of your own hands &c. [D&C 42:40].

59. In April the oldest Smith son, Joseph III, had publicly opposed Utah statehood because of polygamy. In early July the youngest son, David, arrived in Utah to conduct proselytizing activities. Joseph Smith III, "Affairs in Utah, *Saints' Herald*, Apr. 1, 1872; Scherer, *Journey of a People*, 1:288–89.

Prest. B Young enquired how many had their endowments while Joseph Smith the prophet lived, four brethren only were present at the School, viz. Prest. B[righam] Young, Orson Pratt, Levi Richards & John M. Bernhisell, who received them in a brick store—six besides Joseph received them first, then five afterwards. In a very few years, there will not be a man living on the earth who knew Joseph in the flesh. Spoke of the spirit of division that is creeping over the Elders of Israel, and how the enemy is seeking every opportunity to create discord and confusion.

He then enquired how many members of this school had signed a petition ^to the City Council^ to have the Telegraph Poles removed from the centre of the street, not one admitted the fact, he then said that H[orace] S. Eldredge, John T. Caine, ^~~&~~^ Louis S. Hills ^& W[illiam] C. Dunbar^ had signed it, neither of these were present, and very seldom were, but allowed every trifling excuse to keep ^them[selves]^ away from the school. If such do not repent, they will certainly apostatize. Our Gentile enemies had made use of H. J. Faust[60] as a tool to go round among the Elders of Israel to get signers, to ~~remove th~~ ^the^ petition to present to the ~~petition~~ City Council, to have the poles removed. He then complained of the slackness of the Elders of Israel in paying their tithing, and donating means towards the emigrating fund. We are drifting into a fearful state of worldly mindedness and in ten years from now we won't get a farthing for tithing nor for ^the^ P[erpetual] E[migrating] Fund ^at the rate we have been going on for the last 10 years^. Many of our new comers are unwilling to work except at the very highest wages. No person can trifle with or deviate from the words of the leader of Israel, with impunity. If the people in the days of Joseph had been of one heart and one mind, every plan or scheme of his would have been successful. He then related a portion of his own experience many years ago, acknowledging the hand of God in blessing him with temporal as well as spiritual things—saying that he knew, that the Prophet Joseph was equally able to controul in temporal things, as he was in Spiritual.

60. Henry J. Faust (1834–1904), a German immigrant, passed through Utah on his way to the California gold mines, married a Mormon woman, and joined the LDS Church. As superintendent of the cattle association, he and "seventy others" petitioned the city council to remove the poles that had been erected in May because they posed a danger to animals when there was a runaway wagon or carriage. "Council Proceedings," *Salt Lake Herald*, May 23, 24, June 4, July 24, 1872.

Prest. D[aniel] H. Wells spoke of the Election shortly to take place. He wished it to be well guarded, by wise and judicious persons being appointed ~~to~~ to prevent, if possible, the ballot from being stuffed with illegal votes. Four precincts needed a good ^deal^ of watching viz Bingham, Silver Creek, Little Cottonwood & Granite. Sam[ue]l Bateman, Rob[er]t J. Golding [were assinged to monitor] ^Bingham^ [Canyon][;] Albert Dewey [and] Nathan Tanner [the town of] Granite. ^S[outh] Cottonwood^ Bro E[dward] F M Guest[,] D[itt]o. Henry Brown[,] D[itt]o.[61]

The above named persons w~~h~~ere selected and desired to attend to it.

Judge E[lias] Smith gave some very useful information in regard to the general management of the Election.

School was then adjourned for one week at one o clock pm. Benediction by Elder J[oseph] F. Smith.

August 3, 1872; Saturday

Theological Class met in the Tabernacle at One o clock pm. Present Prest. B[righam] Young presiding. After singing Prayer by Elder John Taylor.

Prest. B Young gave Union as a text for the brethren to speak upon this afternoon, it was necessary for the former day saints [in the New Testament] to be one, it is also expected of the latter day saints to become one, and as yet, we have made but little progress.

He then spoke of the ~~under~~ unusual amount of temporal prosperity that is attending the latter day saints, and the growing worldly mindedness and careless indifference that is manifest among the wealthy Elders of Israel—instead of building up the Kingdom of God. He also condemned the secret and stealthy way of doing business in the world, and also among the saints, we should be open and free in all our business transactions.

He then enquired how long it would be before we could lay down our means, time and ability, to be dictated by the priesthood, that we may become a happy and joyous people, for as Jesus said Except ye are one, ye are not mine.

Prest. Geo A Smith said the Church had been organized for over 40 years, and during that time had been trying to become one. Next

61. The concern about a close election was premature. For instance, in the case of George Q. Cannon running for the position of Congressional delegate against George R. Maxwell, the vote in Davis County was 1,181 to 3. "Election Returns," *Deseret Evening News*, Aug. 9, 1872.

Monday was the election day, and he felt anxious for every good man & woman that was qualified, to come forward punctually and cast their votes, we should be willing to use every lawful and constitutional means in our power to defend the rights of Israel. Every mean and despicable plot will be resorted to, to deprive us of our rights, and we should therefore wake up to our duties and our privileges.

Elder John Winder explained the law governing the place of voting, viz in the presinct where the voter resides, and no where else.

Elder Geo Q. Cannon endorsed fully the sentiments advanced by Prest. Young, especially in reference to the sordid and growing ~~indifference~~ worldly mindedness, apparant among many of the elders of Israel, and then instanced the experience of the ancient Nephites and Lamanites, when they became rich, and proud, and fell into transgression, then the judgements of God overtook them and wasted them away.

Elder John Taylor said we are the Elders of Israel, the anointed of God, and what ~~ten~~ ever tends to build up, and establish the trust reposed in us—we should use all our means to carry out—and whatever has a tendency to divide and scatter, we should oppose it. God has placed principles in our hands and we should be prepared to defend them.

He repudiated all connection with political organizations, for corruption and rottenness were rampant in all such—and he would never be identified with any ~~such~~ ^of them^.

~~Prest. B[righam] Young then arose and dissolved the School of the Prophets for the time being until further notice.~~

After singing Benediction by Prest. Geo A Smith.

Prest. B[righam] Young arose and said it was a busy time, ~~and~~ the brethren anxious to get at their work ^and^ the weather was very hot. He had done his best to establish the School of the Prophets and the third ^meeting^ had not passed, before the Devil showed himself in their midst—and taking all circumstances into consideration, he should not adjourn this school, but dissolve it until further notice, and of course all other schools [of the prophets] throughout the Territory will also be dissolved.[62]

62. The reason seemed to be two-fold. Too many of the members were being careless about their tickets and were losing them, creating fear among school leaders that the tickets might be found and used by non-members. Another reason was dwindling attendance. Young was so frustrated, he had some members, including George Reynolds and Wilford Woodruff, list which meetings they had attended and sign their names to their statements in the presence of the other members. Patrick, "School of the Prophets," 29–30; SotP, bx 1, fd 2.

November 4, 1872; Monday

A Meeting of the First Presidency, several of the Twelve Apostles, the Presiding Bishops, Presidents ~~Jos~~ of the Seventies, of the High Priests' Quorum and of the Bishops and their Councilors of this City, was held at the City Hall, at 7 p.m.

President B[righam] Young stated that the object of the meeting was to take steps for the organization of the School of the Prophets. He wanted those who were to be members of that School to be men who loved the Lord and did not have Babylon in their hearts, but were determined to keep the commandments of the Lord. He did not want any to be members of that School who were not willing to enter into the Order of Enoch and to build up a city upon that principle, to hold all that they have subject to the dictation of the Holy Priesthood.[63] If there were any present who could not subscribe to that principle, he wished them to withdraw. With other remarks of this character he continued for a short space, then ceased and gave others the privilege of speaking, adding, however, that rules would be drawn up for the School.

President [Daniel H.] Wells said that it would not be any harder for him, he thought, to live up to this Order than what he had been called upon to do.

President Joseph Young, Sen., felt to endorse what had been said by Bro's. Brigham and Wells. He gloried in the idea whatever the result might be to him personally.

President B Young then said: All that feel to take right hold and show their good will to be what they profess to be, let them raise their right hands.

All hands were raised. He then asked: Shall we organize now? All hands were raised.

Geo Q. Cannon motioned that President B Young be President of the School. Unanimously carried.

D. H. Wells motioned that Geo Q. Cannon be Secretary of the School.[64] Carried unanimously.

President B[righam] Young motioned that Wilford Woodruff be Treasurer. Carried.

---

63. The roll book lists 310 names, suggesting that Young significantly curtailed membership.

64. Cannon kept the minutes for this meeting, but George Goddard would resume his former responsibility as record keeper on November 18.

The President then said: The School now being organized, let us join in prayer. He then prayed.

President Young then made remarks similar to those made at the opening of the meeting, as Bro O[rson] Pratt had come in since the opening, stating among other things that if matters that were conversed upon in the School were told outside of the School, as they had been in the case of the other School, he would dismiss the School until the person who did so ~~were~~ ^should be^ found out. There was nothing that he was afraid of all men hearing. There had never been anything taught in the School that he should have any objection to all the world hearing. But it was not right for the members to do as some had done, as the Spirit which prompted them to do so was not of God.

The names of those who had been selected to share in this meeting was then called by the Secretary. (See Roll.)

The Meeting was then adjourned until next Monday ^evening^ Nov 11th, 1872, at half past Six at this place.

President Wells made the closing prayer.

November 11, 1872; Monday

The School of the Prophets met according to appointment at the City Hall at half past six o'clock p.m. Roll was called by the Secretary, Geo Q. Cannon (See Roll). Prayer was offered, ~~by~~ ^at the^ request of President B[righam] Young, by President [Daniel] H. Wells.

President B Young said that at the last meeting he had done the most of the speaking, at this meeting he desired others to speak. The object of the School was set before them, and he wished them to occupy the time.

President D. H. Wells alluded to the organization of the School in this room. At one of the first meetings President Young was filled with the power of God and spoke under its influence; but he was checked, the Spirit of God was grieved, and from that time those precious things were withheld. There was unbelief, apostacy and hardness of heart in the breasts of members of the School. Matters that were talked of in the School were published on the street. The President had felt to discontinue the Schools, and ^he had done so; but this School^ ~~it~~ was now reorganized, and he (the speaker) hoped that the members would do everything required of them and not sift their ways to strangers by giving the means that God had given to Babylon, to the enemies of His Kingdom. This is God's Kingdom, His Government and we must sustain it. We must seek for His Spirit and be filled with it. God has let loose the floods of corruption, and opened the mines, to test his people and to prove whether they will be true to him when these floods surround them or not.

President B Young ^said:^ To change our tactics[,] to do the will of God and take delight in it, is what is required of us. The contrary of this is what has been done in too many instances—to desire to do the will of God; but not do it. If we can get brethren together in a School, (for however many meetings there are there is but one School) to keep the Sabbath day and do other things required of them, to do the will of God and take delight in it. Whether we shall organize a branch, as he alluded to at Conference, or not, we should be willing to do so. When we get ready we shall organize. We have said all the time that we delight in receiving revelations; but he often thought in the days of Joseph [Smith] that if the people did not obey the revelations, he [God] would not give them—^what^ a King to give laws and not have them obeyed! He [Young] could fellowship a man a thousand times better who would take a chew of tobacco in a modest, decent manner, than a man who would abuse his family or cheat his neighbor. The man who chews tobacco hurts himself; but not so with the other man. If he were to feel as tired when he got home as when he came here, and he were to take brandy sling,[65] the Lord would bless it to him. Yet he [Young] did not drink brandy, coffee or tea. The Word of Wisdom consists in taking that which his system required when it is needed. If we would learn Wisdom and follow ^it^ then we would be all right; but who understands the Word of Wisdom?

President Wells bore testimony to the remarks of President Young respecting the Word of Wisdom. He alluded to the case of Bro [Ira] Ames of [Wellsville] Cache [Valley]. He had been in the habit of unwisely drinking strong coffee and other beverages; but he ceased when the School started, and in consequence of stopping so suddenly, he sickened and died. This was not wisdom. He related an instance where he had a dreadful fall. A strong drink of brandy was given him; it would

65. A brandy sling was equal parts brandy and water, with sweetener. Webster, *American Dictionary*, 1828, s.v. "sling."

have made him drunk at any other time; but ^it^ had no effect on him of that character. He recovered from the fall and experienced no ill effects from it. This was medicine. Yet these are not for the common use of man; when thus used, they cease to be beneficial. The violation of the Word of Wisdom is not a matter of fellowship and will not clip a man in his glory; but he will not have the blessings which are promised.

President Young said how many are there here to-night who are fond of these things [alcohol and coffee] who will take advantage of what has been said here to-night. Those who ^would^ do so would be unworthy of a place in this School. If the brethren did not wish to speak or take an interest in the things before us, we would adjourn.

Bishop L[orenzo] D[ow] Young did take an interest in the School. Had the remarks made here to-night been made in public meeting, or in Conference, advantage would have been taken of them. But ^he felt that^ it was not his privilege to take advantage of such teachings. Yet the Lord required of no man what he is not able to perform. He spoke at some length, bearing testimony and exhorting.

Bishop E[dwin] D. Woolley had not sat silent because he was not interested, but because he thought it was the privilege ^of others^ to speak before him. He endorsed what had been said by President Young. He alluded to the organization of the School and its dismissal and described his feelings respecting it.

Geo Q. Cannon stated his feelings in relation to the re-organization of the School and his thankfulness in view of the object to be accomplished.

Wilford Woodruff made remarks of a similar character. This work cannot stand still, it must go forward or go backward.

Orson Pratt rejoiced in what he had heard last Monday evening and this evening, in the re-organization of the School and in the prospect of a more perfect organization of the people ~~with~~ which must be entered into when the centre stake of Zion ^is built up.^ There seems to have been three laws given to the people. The first, the more perfect law, given in 1831; the second, the Order of Enoch; the third, the law of Tithing.[66] He should be pleased to see the Order of Enoch entered into if it was

66. In 1831 the law of consecration (D&C 42:30–39) required Mormons to dedicate their money and property to the church, in return for stewardship (not ownership) over as much as they could manage. By contrast, the United Order, as practiced in Utah, granted each member an ownership percentage based on how much he contributed, and dividends were distributed accordingly.

the will of the Lord that it should be commenced. This we could do here; but the other ^(the higher law)^ we are forbidden to enter into until we go back to the land of our inheritance [Missouri].

President B Young said here was a good opportunity for the Bishops to commence in the Wards and elsewhere.

It was motioned by Pres[ident] D. H. Wells that we adjourn until next Monday at 6½ p.m.

President B[righam] Young said here was the place to propose the names of new members, and not to mention it elsewhere. He proposed to have Bro Geo Goddard invited here that he may keep our records. He was good at this. He did not want to confine Bro Cannon to it any longer than was necessary.

Bishop Edw[ar]d Hunter made the closing prayer.

November 18, 1872; Monday

The School of the Prophets met at the City Hall at ½ past 6 oclock pm as per adjournment. Present Prest. B[righam] Young presiding. Roll was called by the Secretary, Geo Q Cannon, see ^roll^. Prayer by Elder Orson Pratt.

Prest. ^B[righam]^ Young said this was the place for the brethren to speak and open their minds freely, especially on matters of doctrine; He thought it might be wisdom for doctrines of the Gospel ~~migh~~ to be introduced here for their united consideration, Celestial Marriage &c. It would also be good to ~~cons~~ examine and become better acquainted with the Catechism[67] and Compendium.[68] Much had been revealed about Consecration, and he ~~ho~~ did ^not^ know a better time than the present ^to go into it^, and could easily draw up a deed, that no Judge could invalidate. We might commence to cooperate in various settlements, and be conducted by those appointed for that purpose, whether Bishops, or others and have the people instructed in doctrine &c. We should study the Book of Doctrine & Covenants for in reality, it was our Bible, as much so, as the Old Testament is the Bible of the Jews.

67. John Jaques's *Catechism for Children*, published by the church in Liverpool, was a question-and-answer approach to theology, with cross-references to scriptures. It went through seven English editions and additional foreign translations. Jaques (1827–1900) later edited the *Millennial Star*. In 1873 he became Assistant Church Historian.

68. The *Compendium of the Faith and Doctrines of the Church* was compiled by apostle Franklin D. Richards in Liverpool in 1857 while serving as president of the European Mission.

Shall we enter into a solemn ~~po~~ compact, that our property shall be placed in the hands of the Trustee in trust, for the building up of the Kingdom of God, there never will be a better time to do it, than the present.

Prest. D. H. Wells was much pleased with the items that had been advanced, not one of which could be discussed without profit. By taking up points of doctrine and [having them] freely talked over he had no doubt [the school] would be attended with the most beneficial results. In regard to consecration, he had no other desire than for himself and what he controuled, ~~should~~ ^to^ be used for the building up of the Kingdom of God. The Lord never would reveal anything but what would benefit and bless his people, if carried out according to his design.

None but the carnally minded would ever find fault with what God reveals. Those who cannot cont[r]oul their passions are in bondage. He heartilly endorsed every sentiment that was advanced by Prest. Young, and was prepared to enter into them heart and soul.

Those who should be our protectors are seeking to deprive us of our rights, and all we ask of them, is are the common rights that are due to all citizens.

Elder Orson Pratt was much pleased to hear the subject ~~broached, of the law~~ of Consecration ^broached^ which he had much considered for the last 40 years, if it could be so managed that property ~~o~~ consecrated, could not ^be^ frustrated by any technicality of Law, he should be thankful to see it gone into. It was a great subject, and an important one. He thought one of the first things to consider, was how to make the deed binding, so that property once consecrated, could not henceforth be controuled by those who consecrated it, but entirely ~~used and~~ controuled by the Authorities of the Church for the building up of the Kingdom of God.

He was thankful also for the privilege of discussing points of doctrine in this school, there were thousands of items in the bible and Doctrine & Covenants that he did not understand, and should be pleased to be instructed in them, if it ^was^ wisdom for him to know them.

Prest. Young then made some very interesting remarks on the subject of light. He ~~then~~ ^also^ ~~a~~ made special request of all present to pray with their families, each one testified with uplifted hands that they did so.

Elder John Taylor had noticed the channel that the Mind of Prest. Young had been led, one thing was, The consecration of our property, he did not much care about property, but he did care about being a good faithful latter day saints, and whatever was suggested by Prest. Young he was perfectly willing to abide it, because he knew that he [Young] was Gods Mouths piece. It was our duty to carry out whatever he suggests. He would like to know upon what principle the law of consecration was to be carried out. The Order of Enoch [joint stock company], or having all things common [no private ownership] as in the days of the Apostles, ~~or the 1st principles the~~ ^he would like to see^ [the] establishment of those principles that neither the laws of the land, nor apostacy can upset, Whatever God wished to introduce for the benefit of his people through his servant Brigham, he was heartily in favour of &c.

Prest. B Young said it was the duty of the Latter day Saints to live their religion, and pay no attention to the doings of Government, nor the [political] Rings that are here, for they cannot do anything to injure the Kingdom of God. Let us do right and go right along, and leave the result in the hands of God. So sure as we agree to cooperate in the establishment of the Order of Enoch, so sure we shall be able to go along without any hinderance from our enemies. Only let a number of Families thus unite, and appoint their trustees to controul and council and direct, each man operating in the department of labour he is ~~me~~ best adapted for, and in a very short time they would become exceedingly wealthy, build Temples and gather around them every Mechanical improvement, so that they will be able to export a great deal, and import but little. Elders Pratt & [Wilford] Woodruff were appointed to speak on doctrine at next meeting. ^Meeting was adjourned for one week at ½ past 6 pm.^ Benediction by B[isho]p E[dwin] D. Woolley.

Motioned That ^Bros^ Isaac Brockbank, Theodore McKean, W[illia]m Asper[,] Hy[rum] Arnold, Elias Morris, F. A. Mitchell, A C Pyper, Rob[er]t L. Campbell, Rob[er]t Campbell, Harrison Sperry[,] Geo B. Wallace, Ja[me]s P. Freeze, Rob[er]t Neslen, Andrew Burt, & N[athaniel] H. Felt, be [re]admitted as members of the school.

The Clerk was instructed to direct a note of invitation to each of the above.

The subject of tithing was talked over, and Prest. B Young distinctly stated that all tithing money should be paid into the hands of B[isho]p [Edward] Hunter who should hold it, subject to Prest. Youngs dictation, or it may be paid to Tho[mas] Ellerbeck if Prest. Young directs him to receive it, [and] that Horace Whitney[69] had never been appointed to receive Cash tithing. That B[isho]p Hunter should have his Office and Clerk to attend to this business.

November 25, 1872; Monday

The School of the Prophets met in the City Hall at ½ past 6 oclock pm. Present Prest. B[righam] Young presiding. Prayer by Elder Wilford Woodruff.

Elder Geo Q. Cannon then read (by request) the rules of the school, and Prest. B Young enquired if each member of the school were living in strict accordance with the rules of the school. And after repeating them one by one before the school, asking them if they strictly observed each rule. several replyed in the negative, ~~as~~ such as strictly attending Meeting, Fast meeting, paying fast offerings, keeping the word of wisdom, ^paying tithing^ & praying regularly in their families, each giving what they deemed sufficient reasons for such neglect.

B[isho]p R[obert] T. Burton enquired what should be done with those having a standing in the Church, who possitively refuses to pay tithing.

Prest. B Young said, let all such be cut off from the church, and if they have had their ~~tithin~~ endowments, let their names be blotted out from the church records.

Elder Orson Pratt entirely coincided with the above council, it being strictly ~~strictly~~ in accordance with the Law as revealed in the Doctrine & Covenants~~—see page 256~~.

Prest. Young said, he did not want any man to work either on the Railroad or in the Co operative Institution, unless they paid their tithing.

B[isho]p L[orenzo] D[ow] Young enquired if a man, who in every other respect was a good man, but did not pay his tithing, should be rigidly dealt with, or should they be laboured with by the Bishop or Teachers before taking that step.

Bishop E[dward] Hunter alluded to the extensive blessings, that the Lord had promised to those who strictly observed the Law of tithing.

~~Bish~~ Prest. B Young speaking on the subject of tithing said he did not believe there was any of us in this school that had paid an honest

69. Horace K. Whitney (1823–84) clerked in the General Tithing Office. His first wife, Helen Mar Kimball, had been a plural wife of Joseph Smith. He had two plural wives and twenty children, including apostle Orson F. Whitney and Horace G. Whitney, manager of the Salt Lake Opera Comapny.

tithing, and that he should ascertain how much each one had paid, whose names were now enrolled as Members in this New School.

Elder Geo B Wallace said he had recently read the revelation wherein it distinctly stated that those who should cease to pay tithing, their names should be erased from all the church records. He wished to enquire who the proper persons were to carry it into effect, for instance, W[illiam] S. Godbe, E[lias] L. T. Harrison ^&c^, who had been cut off, by the highest authority of the church, had their names been erased from the books[?]

B[isho]p E[dwin] D. Woolley named a similar case to that of L[orenzo] D. Young['s] [telling].

B[isho]p John Sharp plead for a month to try to labour who those in his ward who had lost the spirit of the Gospel, and consequently refused to pay tithing.

Prest. Young said if any man refused to pay tithing, this is optional with him, and we have an equal right to refuse him our fellowship. Where men neglect that duty, they generally fail in others, and such persons should be dealt with for Apostacy. He said also in reply to Bro Geo B. Wallace that those cases, [regarding] whose names should be erased from the books, should be left to the discretion of the first Presidency. No one should be allowed to have their endowments unless they have paid their tithing.

B[isho]p E[lijah] F. Sheets spoke of some who were willing to be charged up with their tithing, year after year, but dont pay any until it becomes a large sum, What shall be done with them. Prest. Young said, you know the law.

Elder W[ilford] Woodruff spoke of the necessity of pruning ~~the tree~~ off the dead branches from the tree, and those who would not pay their tithing, did not deserve the fellowship of the saints, and ought to be cut off.

~~Elde~~ Prest. B Young said, that all those who failed to attend meetings, pay tithing, &c. their names should be blotted out from the books of the church, and with draw from them the fellowship of the Saints.

Elder Orson Pratt spoke of the extreme leniency exercised towards transgressors, ^now^ ~~to~~ in comparison to what was practised among ancient Israel.

Elder Geo Q Cannon felt thankful that the law of God was about to be enforced more rigidly than formerly—the ^choosing^ time seems to have come and he would be glad for every member of this new School to be thoroughly scann'd [examined], especially on the subject of tithing.

Prest. Young again said, the dead branches must be cut off, or the tree will die, that was his mind. If the Bishops would only look well after the collection of the tithing there would be an immense amount more collected than there is now, but the misfortune is, very few of the Bishops pay their own tithing, hence, they are careless about others. ^They ought to collect monthly where salaries are worked for^— and paid monthly.

Elder W Woodruff said the best time for Farmers to pay their tithing was at the time they raise their produce, before they put it away in their bins and cellars.

Prest. D[aniel] H. Wells said he wished it understood that when any one is cut off ~~for not paying tithing~~, it should not be for not paying tithing, but for apostacy, for nothing ~~should~~ could present a stronger proof of apostacy, than a neglect in payment of tithing.

School was adjourned for one week at ½ past 6 pm. Benediction by B[isho]p L[eonard] W. Hardy.

December 2, 1872; Monday

The School of the Prophets met in the City Hall at ½ past 6 o clock pm. Present Elder Orson Pratt presiding. ^Prest. D[aniel] H. Wells came in about ½ past 7.^ (the [rest of the] first Presidency being absent) ^Prest. B[righam] Young sick.^ Prayer by Edward Hunter.

Elder Orson Pratt said, in the absence of the first presidency, he would suggest that a portion ~~t~~ of the Doctrine & Covenants be read, for the purpose of our Mutual improvement.

Elder Rob[er]t L. Campbell then read Section 1 page 65.[70]

Elder Orson Pratt, made a few remarks on the power of the priesthood refer'd to, ~~by sealing~~ ^to seal^ up the rebellious & unbelieving [for condemnation] on the earth and [damnation] in heaven.

Elder W[ilford] Woodruff enquired if the [sealing] power refer'd to was that conferd upon Elders, Priests, Teachers & Deacons, ~~as preachers~~ ^of the Gospel^.

Elder O Pratt thought that each of the above branches of priesthood

---

70. The first section of the Doctrine and Covenants began on page 65, preceded by the Lectures on Faith, which would not be removed from church canon until 1921.

might hold that power, but wisdom may dictate the time when it would be right to exercise.

Elder Woodruff mentioned an instance in his experience while with Elder [David W.] Patten, who on one occasion, where the people had rejected their testimony—washed their feet, as a testimony against them; he did know that God backed up and sustained the testimony of the lessor priesthood, but the power spoken of in the section just read, he though[t] was of a more special character, than that commonly held by ^all^ Elders who go forth to preach the gospel.

Prest. D. H. Wells who had recently come in, said it was ~~b~~ much better to bless, than to curse, though the power to curse existed in the Priesthood and where it was exercised in righteousness it would stick—but not otherwise. When the Lord chooses to turn the Keys against any Nation or people, then it will be right. Elders should be careful who go forth to preach the Gospel, how they deal ~~with~~ in curses against their fellow beings—lest peradventure their victim might have done some good to one of the least of Christs disciples.

Elder W Woodruff bore testimony to the truth of Prest. Wells remarks—and named an instance of bearing testimony to a number of individuals, especially one who had once held the priesthood &c—and apostatized. He was constrained by the spirit to go and warn him three times, the man was coming toward him, and fell dead at his feet.

Another Section or two [of the Doctrine and Covenants] was then read and remarks made by Elders Pratt, A[lonzo] H. Raleigh, D[imick] B. Huntingdon & Geo B. Wallace. That when the Kingdom of God is fully established, different sects will be protected under it by being subject to its civil law and rule.

Elder W Woodruff said it was very plain, that the judgments of God commences upon the inhabitants of this wicked world after the introduction of the Gospel—especially this and other civilized or ^Christian^ Nations. This is according to all the revelations we have on the subject.

Bishop A[lexander] McRae enquired if a Bishop & his council can cut a man off from the Church who has received his endowments.

& Prest. D. H. Wells enquired if there ^was^ any man in the Kingdom who could not be ~~hand~~ dealt with by a Bishop.

Elder Geo B. Wallace said one Bishop could not be cut off by another.

B[isho]p E Hunter, said the first Presidency could only be tried by a B[isho]p with 12 high priests.

Elder O Pratt, in answer to Bro McRaes question said there was no revelations that forbid the action of a B[isho]ps Court towards one who had rec[eive]d his endowments.

Prest. D H Wells said a Bishop was a common Judge in Israel, and could cut off any man in his Ward. But a Bishop could only be tried by a High Council with the 1st Presidency at their head. A Bishop who is not a literal descendent of Aarron, requires two councillors, to make his court a legal one. No one can act as a Bishop without holding the high priesthood.

Elder W Woodruff enquired if there was any members present who had not heard the rules of the school—and whether it was right for any member to reveal to any one that there was such a thing as a School of the Prophets.

Two brethren replyed, that they had not heard them read.

Prest. D. H. Wells said the rules were similar to what were read in the other school. It ought to be distinctly understood by every one ~~that~~ one that comes here, that they should not reveal to any one that a school was in existence, or anything pertaining to it.[71]

The school was adjourned for one week at ½ past 6 pm. Benediction by Elder A[lbert] P. Rockwood.

December 9, 1872; Monday

The School of the Prophets met at the City Hall at ½ past 6 pm. Present Prest. D[aniel] H Wells presiding.[72] Prayer by Elder Jos[eph] F. Smith.

Elder Orson Pratt made a few opening remarks, and enquired if the members of the school had any special subject on their minds, they wished investigated, if not, he proposed the reading of Revelations, as suggested by Prest. Brigham Young. Section 2nd. Paragraph 1st [of the Doctrine and Covenants].[73] Several interesting remarks were made

71. From this date on, many of the diarists stopped recording details about the proceedings, and the same was true of the Historian's Office Journal.

72. Brigham Young was in St. George for the winter. George A. Smith, who was visiting the Holy Land, would not return until the following summer. This left Wells to preside over the meetings for the next few months, assisted by apostle Orson Pratt.

73. The sections here correspond to the Liverpool edition of 1845, reprinted through 1869. In 1876 the order and numbering of the sections would change from topical to

by Elders Orson Pratt & John Taylor on Chronology. The time of the organization of the Church was, according to the Vulgar [common calendar] or Incorrect Era—1830 years [and four months] since the birth of Christ. But according to the true Era it was exactly 1830 years.

Paragraph 2nd. The Prophet Joseph [Smith']s sins were remitted before baptism—and the enemies of this kingdom sometimes uses that fact against the doctrine of Baptism for the remission of sins, but God has a right when he sees fit, to depart from any fixed rule or order, but this does not invalidate the general doctrine as taught in the Testament & Book of Mormon that Man is required to observe water baptism as the only means of securing ~~of~~ a ~~forgiveness~~ ^remission^ of sins.

Paragraph 3. The Judges of this Generations will be the faithful Elders who have borne testimony to the truth of this work, and baptized many into the Church, and otherwise administered in the Ordinances of the Gospel[.] Though those Elders may finally apostatize, their testimonies will Judge the people, and all their administrations will be valid, which were performed while they were in good standing.

Paragraph 4. God is unchangeable. Sometimes he gives a command to kill, and at other times he gives an opposite one.

Elder Jos[eph] F. Smith said God is unchangeable, and whatever the nature of his edicts may be, however ^apparantly^ conflicting they may appear to us, are in the strictest conformity with the unchangeableness of his character, and purposes, ~~and~~ ^for^ his commands vary according to the circumstances & condition of things. The Personal and Official acts of God the Father, God the Son and God the Holy Ghost—there will never be a confliction of acts between any of those personages.

Paragraph 5. The Son coming in the Meridian of time, meaning half way between the begining and the end of time. There are about 200 Chrono^lo^gists professing to give the exact time from the begining to the birth of Christ, and yet they all differ. There being no definite revelation on the subject it was impossible to come to a correct understanding ~~to~~ of that time, and was a matter of so little importance, that we need not trouble our minds about.

Joseph the Prophet in writing the Doctrine & ~~Revelations~~ Covenants, received the ideas from God, ~~as~~ but clothed those ideas with such words as

---

chronological order, making section 2 section 20. Where the paragraphs had been numbered, they would be divided into verses, so that in 1876 paragraph 1 became four verses.

came to his mind—but in translating the book of Mormon by the use of the Urim and Thumin, God not only revealed the ideas but the words also.

Prest. D H Wells remarked, that God revealed such words in translating the Book of Mormon as Joseph understood, and had that been done through Orson Pratt, or John Taylor, ^probably^ different words would have been used by each one ^to convey the same meaning^. The records from which the Book of Mormon was translated, was in the reformed Egyptian.

School was adjourned for one week at ½ past 6 o clock pm. Benediction by Elder Jos[ep]h F. Smith.

December 16, 1872; Monday

The School of the Prophets met in the City Hall at ½ past 6 oclock pm. Present Prest. D[aniel] H. Wells presiding. Opening prayer by Elder J[esse] C. Little. Minutes of last meeting were read and approved.

Prest. D H Wells asked the following question. Suppose a person who had received the blessings of the Gospel, and continued in good standing until he had attended to the ordinances of the Gospel for his dead friends, ~~after which~~ which was duly recorded, after this, he apostatizes, and his name is blotted out from all the records of the Church, will his apostacy render his official acts for the dead null and void, or not?

Elder Orson Pratt did not think his apostacy would invalidate those acts, but as to whether it would be the same in regard to any sealing ordinance in the marriage relation he was not so clear upon.

Elder Jos[ep]h F. Smith sustained the same views in regard to the baptisms for the dead, as the record would shew that the act was duly performed, and out of the records the dead will be judged. But as to ^his^ being sealed to a dead woman, after his apostacy, that woman would have to be sealed to another one in good standing, or she would be without a Husband in the resurrection.

B[isho]p A[lonzo] H. Raleigh said, if a man who administers for the dead and then apostatizes, if his name is blotted out from all the records of the church, of course it would be erased from the baptismal record also, and if so, ~~how could it~~ the books would not shew that such persons had ever been baptized for.

Elder Jos[eph] F Smith did not think the apostates name would ever be blotted out from that record, but remain intact so as to agree ^with^

the records in Heaven, but his name would be blotted ^out from the book of life^.

Prest. D. H. Wells said, his feelings had been pretty well answered, he also believed ~~his~~ ^~~the~~^ his [the apostate's previous] administration ^~~of the apostate~~^ would stand, because they were performed while he was in good standing, but his own former sins would all come back again ^up^ on this own head, all that he had ever administered for would stand, but all ^the blessings^ that had ever been confered upon himself would be forfeited, he would also lose his wives and children. By and bye an A^n^gel will come and reveal who has received the gospel in the spirit world who have been baptized for by the living.

Elder Geo B Wallace. Those who received the Gospel in the spirit world, are they entitled to a Celestial Glory in the 1st. resurrection equal to those of the living who obey the celestial law[?]

Prest. D H Wells said that such will come forth in the first resurrection, and enter a Kingdom of glory, but what kind of glory[,] it was ^not^ for him to say.

Elder Orson Pratt said he thought that, from those in the spirit world, some would attain to a Celestial Glory, some inherit a Terrestrial and others a Telestial [D&C 76], according to their works in the spirit world, as well as while they were in the flesh.

Elder Geo B. Wallace said that he thought, all those in the spirit world who received the fulness of the Gospel, and continued faithful till the 1st Resurrection, would ~~confer~~ come forth and enjoy a celestial Kingdom.

Elder Jos[eph] F. Smith said whatever blessings were confered on the living, or on the dead, each would be sure to receive the same if they continue faithful. He then spoke of some, upon whose heads were confered the greatest blessings that God ~~tha~~ can bestow, and sealed up by those having authority, [and who, it is said,] can commit all kinds of ~~ig iniquity~~ sin with impunity, so long as they do not commit the unpardonable sin. He did not believe any such doctrine, but no matter what a man is promised by the servants of God—if he sins, he must repent, or he will never come forth in the first resurrection.

Prest. D. H. Wells said, all men will be judged according to the deeds done in the body. God ~~can~~ will forgive sins, but on general principles, no man can be forgiven, except by repentance, ~~th~~ which is the only way for any one, he must become amenable to the law of the Gospel through Jesus

Christ. This work is one of progress, those in the Celestial [level of heaven] can administer to the Terrestrial and the Terrestrial to the Telestial.

Elder N[athaniel] H Felt in speaking of those inhabiting different Glories, he enquired whether they would be all on one planet and Mingle more or less together, as ~~things are~~ ^we do^ now, here, or whether they will each be entirely distinct and apart—he rather inclined to the former view.

Prest. D. H. Wells, said where God and Christ was, those who did not obey the Gospel could never come.

Elder D[imick] B. Huntington enquired if the Lamanites would do their work [of building the New Jerusalem], before, or after they received the Gospel.

Prest. D H Wells ~~said~~ & Elder Orson Pratt did not think they [Lamanites/Native Americans] would obey the Gospel first—a portion of [a] revelation was read to that effect.[74]

School was adjourned for one week at ½ past 6 pm. Benediction by Elder Rob[er]t F. Neslen.

December 23, 1872; Monday

The school of the Prophets met in the City Hall ^at ½ past 6. Present Elder Orson Pratt presiding.^[75] After the roll was called, Prayer was offered by A[lbert] P. Rockwood.

Elder Geo Goddard mentioned that about 10 years ago Prest. H[eber] ^C.^ Kimball in speaking of the Ordination of the Prophet Joseph [Smith] said Peter & James came in the spirit and John in the flesh. ~~he~~ G[eorge] G[oddard] enquired if that was a generally understood fact by the Elders.[76]

Elder Jno. [John] D. T. McAllister, thought that Peter & John must have received their resurrection, as he could not see how a spirit could place their hands on the head of a person perceptably [to convey priesthood authority].

---

74. See, e.g., 3 Ne. 21:23–26, explaining that Lamanites (Native Americans) and righteous gentiles would "build a city, which shall be called the New Jerusalem … and then shall the work of the Father commence at that day, even when this gospel shall be preached among the remanant of this people," meaning the Indians.

75. Wells was "confined to his room, having symptoms of Inflammatory Rheumatism," leaving Pratt to preside. GQCJ, Dec. 21, 1872.

76. What Heber C. Kimball said on June 19, 1862, was that when heavenly personages came to earth, they did so in the flesh, "as did Peter, James, and John when they appeared to Joseph Smith." JD 9:152.

Elder Geo B. Wallace was glad this subject was brought up, that some light might be thrown upon it. ~~Elder~~ B[isho]p A[lonzo] H. Raleigh made a few remarks.

Elder N[athaniel] H Felt Could see no inconsistancy in Peter, James & John, ~~too~~ all three continuing in the flesh from the days of Christ, in order to fulfill their work.

Elder Orson Pratt said from the testimony of the Book of Mormon & Doctrine & Covenants, many were resurrected about the time of the Saviours resurrection. That John the beloved disciple had the promise of the Saviour that he should tarry on the earth without tasting of death. He believed that Peter & ~~Joh~~ James came in the Spirit and placed their hands on the head of Joseph [Smith] in connexion with John in the flesh, John being mouth. This was simply his opinion and did not advance it as correct doctrine. Peter & James though in the spirit still retained their apostleship. He then spoke of an A^n^gel ^who^ appeared to our Father Adam, to give him instruction about the meaning of the sacrifices that Adam was offering, viz that they were typical of the Sacrifice of our Saviour. That this Angel had never lived on this earth, but [1½ lines blank].

Elder N[athaniel] H Felt did not see the consistancy of one being in the flesh & two in the spirit. As in the 1st Presidency it took three to constitute a constitutional quorum, ~~the~~ &c.

Elder Geo B Wallace, if one holds the Keys of power, he thought he could administer without the aid of councillors when necessary—but when the authority is held conjointly as in the case of Peter James & John it required the three to ~~ordain~~ confer that authority.

B[isho]p A[lonzo] H Raleigh. Whether any one holding the Me^l^chisadec Priesthood can administer in [the temple ordinances of] washings, anointing, &c singly.

Elder O Pratt said they held the power, but that power may be limited, and have to act in connexion with others—but he cited several cases that took place in ^the^ early rise of the Church where the High Priesthood single handed ~~set apart~~ ordained others to the same priesthood.

Elder Geo B Wallace confirmed the above view by reference to his own experience.

Elder N H Felt did not think that such an event of ~~such~~ so great importance as the ushering in of a new dispensation, ~~would~~ could be bro[ugh]t in by an inefficient quorum, which one in the flesh & two in the spirit seemed to be, in his opinion. By reference to the practise and usage of the Prophet Joseph & Prest. B[righam] Young, expressed by Elders ~~by~~ Rob[er]t L Campbell and J[ohn] D. T. McAllistor it was shown that the Ordination of the prophet Joseph was ~~va~~ correct and valid.

Elder Rob[er]t L Campbell then read from the Doctrine & Covenants Section 7. Par[agraph] 6. The baptism of fire & the Holy Ghost.[77]

Elder O Pratt speaking of the baptism of fire, as ~~having~~ being the light of the Holy Ghost, or spirit of light, made manifest to the natural eye, instancing several cases in the Scriptures & Book of Mormon. Resurrected beings having flesh & bones have the power of hiding or making manifest their glory.

In [Pratt's] reading about meetings being led by the Holy Ghost [blank].[78] [Question:] Why do we always begin our [sacrament] meetings with singing—then speaking—would we do so, if there was no strangers ~~B[isho]p Raleigh~~ present[?] Have we learned it [the format] from Sectarians[?]

[Discussed] teachers being required to see that there is no iniquity or hardness in the Church. [Does this rule out punitive measures?]

B[isho]p Raleigh did not think the language was so imperative in its meaning, as ~~an~~ the same language [might be] used to [describe an employer's relationship to] a hired man, because in the former it was used in connexion with others having their agency.

B[isho]p Hunter spoke of a Teacher as particularly adapted by the spirit of his calling, in the settlement of difficulties &c.

B[isho]p [Alexander] McRae, thought a Teacher can call and persuade but can never force men to do their duty, and for those who persist in their wickedness can only be dealt with by cutting them off from the church. Many valuable remarks were made on the subject and labours of the Teachers by B[isho]p [Robert T.] Burton and Elders Geo B. Wallace.

Elder Geo Goddard said that between 3[00] and 400 teachers are employed in this city [where crime and vice occurs], most of whom hold the Melchisadic Priesthood, and yet act in the lessor priesthood, he thought if those teachers would meet~~ing~~ the president of that Quorum

77. The section cited by Campbell is now 88:25–32.

78. They will discuss whether there should be a set format for worship services, given the direction to be led by the Spirit, implying spontaneity.

and receive instruction from the Head, the evil now complained of would cease to exist~~—and th~~ and that if the Teachers did their duty, many Bishops and High Council trials would certainly be avoided.

School was then adjourned for one week at ½ past 6 pm. The name ^of Tho[ma]s Taylor^ was suggested [for membership] by J[ohn] D. T. McAllister by the request of Prest. D[aniel] H. Wells—and was unanimously voted in. Benediction by B[isho]p A[lonzo] H. Raleigh.

December 30, 1872; Monday

The School of the Prophets met in the City Hall at ½ past 6 pm. ^Present Elder Orson Pratt presiding.^ After the roll was called the Meeting was opened by Prayer by Elder Jno. [John] Taylor.

Elder R[obert] L. Campbell then read the Revelation on Tithing from [section 107] page 324.[79]

Prest. Pratt particularly desired the views of Bishops especially on this subject as they are the ones who have a great deal to do with tithing.

B[isho]p L. W. Hardy enquired, that if a person earned one year, Ten thousand dollars, ~~one year~~, and pays One thousand tithing—the next year he earns nothing, how much tithing ought he to pay?

B[isho]p A[lexander] McRae said if a person earns nothing, there is nothing due.

B[isho]p Tho[ma]s Taylor said the Revelation did not say anything about it being paid yearly. If a man only earned as much as sustained his family, he thought he ought to pay his tithing on whatever it costs to keep his family.

B[isho]p E[dward] Hunter believed that if the people ^paid^ an honest tithing on their interest or increase, there would be sufficient to sustain the priesthood and the poor. The poor Man to pay One tenth of their time, if these things are attended to, there will be an ample revenue for all purpose, of Priesthood, Poor, Temples &c.

B[isho]p A[lonzo] H Raleigh gave some reasonable views on the ~~tithing~~ revelation pertaining to the surplus property to ~~g~~ be given in as tithing, after which one tenth of our increase according to the honest convictions of an honest man. The people for the past 7 or 8 years have been dwindling in their feelings & spirit, in reference to tithing, meetings

79. Section 107 (now 119) calls for surplus property to be "put into the hands of the bishop of my church of Zion" (v. 1).

&c &c—but visible signs of improvement are apparant to him—and to most other Bishops, &c.

The Law of the Lord is ^given in^ general terms, and cannot be dealt out to us in detail—this of necessity must be left to the B[isho]p and the individual himself.

B[isho]p F[rederick] Kesler wanted to find out what the surplus property meant, in the revelation—he had never met with a Man who had any surplus property. He was very anxious for every Bishop to thoroughly understand the law of tithing alike so that they could teach it alike.

Elder Geo B. Wallace said the law of tithing was an eternal law. Throughout the various revelations of God every item may be gathered that is necessary in regard to the payment of tithing.

Elder Orson Pratt spoke of the time in Jackson County [Missouri] when the law of full consecration came from the Lord it required a full surrender of all our propertys' to the Bishop, and then receive as his inheritance [ration] whatever Newel K Whitney, the common judge in Israel might see wisdom to give him.

The surplus property spoken of, any man coming in the Church from abroad, he considered it was the Bishop and his Councillors duty, to find out what property they had, and then ~~say to~~ ^tell^ him, what they deemed surplus property, if he refused to pay it, let him go his own way. He was satisfied that the law of tithing had not been lived up to since 1838—but before we could ever return to Jackson County, he believed we should have to honour this lesser law.

B[isho]p A McRae said, those who first coming in the Church, cheerfully pay their honest tithing generally abide in the faith, ~~an~~ while others who refused or neglected to observe that law are far more likely to ~~apologize~~ ^apostatize^.

B[isho]p E Hunter said in 1852 Prest. [Brigham] Young called on the Bishops to collect another tithing and the people generally responded. If we only act our part, he believed that ~~things~~ ^we^ will gradually get ~~into~~ ^to observe^ a more perfect law.

He believed in Men being recognized in their labours while engaged in preaching the Gospel, so that a chain of character can be preserved in such cases. Let the books show it, as men are to [be] judged out of the books.

Elder John Taylor felt that it rested entirely with Prest. Young, as to the proper adjustment and regulation of this matter. The revelation on tithing was plain enough, and if any further information is required, let Prest. Young be applied to, there has been no regular plan adopted in regard to tithing, and untill the Lord makes known something definite to us as a people, let us go on and do the best we can.

Elder Geo Q. Cannon believed everything on the earth was created for our good and use, yet there is a law of consecration, of tithing &c. all of which are intended to remind us of God the real ownership, and we as stewards—that we are his Children, that all our faculties, time means &c, are his[.] To prepare us for our destiny, he must engender within us a true feeling of his ownership[.] If we have faith to pay a tenth, it is well, if enough faith to consecrate all, full better. While we have the living oracles among us, tithing and other things may be altered according to wisdom in their administration.

He had just returned from Washington [DC] because he could spend a few days at home cheaper than remain ~~here~~ there.

Himself and Bro [William H.] Hooper had met with general good feelings and respect—Prest. [Ulysses S.] Grant was very vindictive in his feelings, but Congress are very conservative, and full of enquiry about the affairs of Utah.[80]

School was adjourned for one week at ½ past 6 pm. Benediction by Elder Geo Q Cannon.

80. Cannon was in Washington, DC, for only two weeks and did not meet with President Grant. When he visited members of the House of Representatives, he was "surprised at the cordiality shown to myself." GQCJ, Dec. 3–21, 1872.

CHAPTER FIVE

"AN ETERNITY OF KNOWLEDGE"

1873

January 6, 1873; Monday

The School of the Prophets met at the City Hall at ½ past 6 pm. Present Jos[ep]h F. Smith presiding. Prayer by B[isho]p L[eonard] W. Hardy. The roll was then called, and Elder Rob[er]t L. Campbell was requested to read in the Doctrine & Covenants Sect[ion] 2 par[agraph] 13, &c.[1]

Par[agraph] 17—Every president of the high priesthood, or presiding Elder, Bishop, High Councillor, and High Priest is to be ordained by the direction of a high council or general Conference.[2] This gave rise to a Question as to the non compliance with the above, at the present time. Several instances were quoted where the first Presidency had called and ordained men to the Bishopric &c—and the prevailing opinion among the members was that the living Oracle [prophet] had a perfect right to deviate from the Letter of instructions as given in the Doctrine & Covenants, according to circumstances in the growth and developments of the Church.

Elder Jos[ep]h F Smith thought Prest [Brigham] Young strictly conformed to the printed instructions in the Doctrine & Covenants whenever it was practicable—only deviating, when circumstances required. It was a common practise for men to be sent to get their endowments before being ordained Elders, he thought the Bishops should get their wards together and get the voice of the people, and if

1. This portion of the Doctrine and Covenants discusses the roles of certain priesthood holders—elders, priests, teachers—and how they are to be called and ordained. What was D&C 2:13–25 at the time is now D&C 20:64–83.

2. Paragraph 16 also requires that anyone "ordained to any office" first receive "the vote of" the home congregation. The following discussion questions whether such directives were requirements or guidelines suited to the 1830s church before it became more populous.

the Brethren are deemed worthy, for them to then ordain~~ed~~ them to the ~~Mechel~~ Melchisadeck Priesthood, so that they may be ready for their endowments, without troubling the brethren at the endowment house to ordain them.

B[isho]p F[rederick] Kesler enquired, whether a Bishop should ordain young men to the priesthood, or whether he should call his ward together, and if nothing objectionable is known of the party, he should send the individual to the Prest of the Quorum he wished to be attached to.

Elder Jos[ep]h F. Smith said in an organized body in the Church like a ward, and in the absence of a regular organized quorum of Elders, he thought the Bishop ~~as a president~~ holding the High priesthood ^as President^ should attend to those ordinations. *see end[3]

Elder Rob[er]t F. Neslen enquired if it would be right for a Father whose sons life was in jeopady by sickness, to ordain him to the high priesthood.

Elder Jos[ep]h F. Smith said ^he supposed^ a Father had a right to bless & ordain his child with all the priesthood he has himself.

B[isho]p L. W. Hardy spoke of some difficulties in carrying out the ~~written~~ letter of instruction in the Doctrine & Covenants in ordaining Men to the priesthood. He also believed that a Father could bless & ordain his children, and those ordinations would stand to all eternity.

Elder Geo B Wallace said we had got to have our ears open to what comes from the living oracles—so as not to clash with the letter of the Doctrine & Covenants—for circumstances have much to do with Ordaining Elders &c.

Elder N[athaniel] H. Felt deemed it wisdom to honour every branch of Priesthood, so that in ordaining Elders, he did think that Bishops should respect and honour the Prest of the Elders Quorum ^by^ recommending them to him for that purpose.

Elder Jos[eph] F. Smith said ^in^ the Gospel there was a perfect plan instituted through every branch of the priesthood, but that perfect order had not been carried out as yet.

Elder J[ohn] D. T. McAllistor complained of having men being sent

3. At the end of this entry, secretary George Goddard added the note that "Bishops should attend to the ordinations themselves, after observing the order in ~~connexion with~~ the Doctrine & Covenants."

to the Endowment House before being rebaptized.[4] And many also who are married [civilly] before going there, and whose children are not legal heirs to the priesthood, but they would have to [be spiritually] adopted to their parents.[5]

B[isho]ps Kesler, McRae, S[amuel] A. Woolley, & A[lonzo] H Raleigh made several remarks on the subject of Marrying persons before they had their ~~priesthood~~ endowments. Many things had been done by permission. Whatever the Lord ordains for a specific purpose that and that only is the ~~only~~ object for which he does ordain.

The School was then adjourned for one week at ½ past 6 pm. Benediction by Elder J[esse] C. Little.

January 13, 1873; Monday

The School of the Prophets met in the City Hall at ½ past 6 pm. Present Prest D[aniel] H. Wells presiding. Prayer by Elder Geo Q Cannon.

Minutes of last meeting were read and laid over for amendments.

A letter was then read by Elder Geo Q Cannon from Prest B[righam] Young, wherein he suggests an expedition to the south of the [Little] Colorado [River][6] ^in Arizonia^ on the South side of the [San Francisco] Mountains;[7] composed of 100 Men, Agriculturalists, Blacksmiths, & other Mechanics, Shoemakers, Tailors, &c. to take with them Tools, Seeds, Ammunition &c, to establish a Colony on a Cooperative plan.[8]

Prest D. H. Wells desired the Members of the school to furnish him with the names of the Brethren suitable for such a Mission, at an early date.

Elder John W Young who had left his Father [Brigham Young] on Wednesday last, said he never saw him look better, ^nor in better health^ except a pain in his stomach. It was his Fathers intention, after ~~his~~ the above settlement was established, ~~he purposed~~ to have other

4. Anyone who received the ordinance of the endowment was expected to be rebaptized first.

5. Those who had been civilly married, rather than married/sealed first in the temple, needed to have their children sealed to them. Children of couples married in the temple were considered automatically sealed to their parents, or born in the covenant.

6. The Little Colorado River flows from New Mexico through eastern Arizona and empties into the Colorado about seventy miles south of present-day Lake Powell.

7. Goddard mistakenly wrote "California Mountains." For more on the location, see the entry for Mar. 3, 1873, below.

8. The initial attempt in 1873 was unsuccessful, but in 1876 colonizers established the towns of Holbrook, St. Joseph (now Joseph City), and Sunset (now Winslow). See Peterson, *Take Up Your Mission*.

settlements started in quick succession, so as to take up and occupy those important points of Country, ~~where t~~ all of which to be conducted on the Cooperative ~~plan~~ principle. The climate of that country was beautiful, and he (J. W. Y.) himself was perfectly willing to make [himself] one [of the colonizers], ~~for~~ to go there.

Elder Geo Q. Cannon did not think it would be wisdom for brethren called on this mission to sell out their entire property, especially at a sacrifice, to go there. But a portion of them might be young men fitted out by their Parents or others, with every thing necessary for such an expedition. Prest Young had his mind much impressed of late towards the Indians in the southern Country. Men of Wisdom and experience will be required in connexion with younger ones to carry out the plan proposed by the President. He sincerely hoped the time was near by when we as a people will be drawn closer together in a temporal point of view. He observed with much regret that with the growth of wealth among our people, there was an increase of Selfishness &c.

Elder W[ilford] Woodruff, said, all the outside world were united in fighting against Zion—and the great work of the Almighty God, had to be carried out by the handful of people in these vallies. And if we have not faith enough as yet, to enter into the Order of Enock, we surely have sufficient to enter upon an effort of co operation, like the one suggested. We are too anxious to get rich as a people, and get Railroad stock, or Bank Stock &c.

Elder D[imick] B Huntingdon testifyed that Prest Young was guided and inspired by the same spirit as Joseph [Smith] the Prophet—in the selection of ^the^ Salt Lake ~~Citu~~ Country and Arizona as resting places for the Saints.

Prest D H Wells said Mormonism was bound to rise, and ^the saints will^ have the controuling power along the entire range of these rock[y] Mountains, Notwithstanding the outside pressure ~~they~~ that might be brought to bear against us.

He was decidedly in favour of establishing this post alluded to, it would become a tower of strength to Zion, he saw wisdom in extending our ~~stren ground~~ Territory—and refer'd to the hellish designs now contemplated ~~an~~ by Prest [Ulysses S.] Grant—shewing himself to be a poor contemptable coward.[9]

9. In his Fourth Annual Message to Congress, delivered a month earlier on December 2, 1872, President Ulysses S. Grant called for Congress to take action against Utah

We however will hold these Mountains, in spite of all they can do. The Majority of our children will stand faithful & true to carry on the work, when we are gone. He himself felt to rejoice in the great work of God—and would be thankful to ~~devote a~~ do a thousand times more than he now does for its advancement. The only object any individual should have, in seeking after the wealth of this World, should be to extend their sphere of usefulness, and hold it for God and his Kingdom. It is our duty to hold ourselves in readiness to be used by him who leads us. He then spoke of the Monied interest of the outsiders now in these mines &c that will operate as a check to Prest Grants movements.

Elder Geo Q. Cannon requested the prayers of the Members of the school, and the [prayer] circles &c—for the Lord to bless him in his labours as a Delegate from this people to Congress.

Meeting was adjourned for one week at ½ past 6 pm. Benediction by Elder Jos[ep]h F. Smith.

January 20, 1873; Monday

The School of the Prophets met at the City Hall at ½ past 6 pm. Present Elder Orson Pratt presiding. Prayer by B[isho]p A[lonzo] H. Raleigh.

Elder R[obert] L. Campbell was requested to read from the book ~~from th~~ of Doctrine and Covenants. Par[agraph] 18. Section 2 to 22 Par[agraph] where children should be brought before the church to be blest.

Is it right for ~~Paren~~ a Father to bless his children at home?

Elder O Pratt, did not think it was, where there is a branch of the church, the order in the revelation should be comply'd with.

Q[uestion:] Who are the Elders refer'd to?

A[nswer:] A B[isho]p, as a High Priest can bless children.

B[isho]p A H Raleigh had made it a custom for many years to bless his own children when 8 days old, recorded their blessings verbatim. He had also blest Children at fast meetings, either of these modes [public or private], he deemed it in strict conformity with the spirit of the revelation. Every Father is a Patriarch to his own family.

Elder Geo B Wallace had pursued the same course as B[isho]p Raleigh, regarding it as a right that a Father had.

Territory, where "the policy of the [territorial] legislature" had been to "hold a position in hostility to" the federal government. Grant wanted to see the territory brought to heel, including the "ultimate extinguishment of polygamy." Richardson, *Compilation of Messages and Papers,* vol. 7, part 1.

Elder O Pratt did not question the right of a Father being a Patriarch over his own house, neither in blessing their own children, but that does not exonerate us from observing the order of the Church.

Prest D[aniel] H. Wells has just come in.

Elder R[obert] L Campbell, had made it a practise to bless his children, and have sent them to the fast meeting to ^be^ blest there also.

Q[uestion:] Is the revelation explicit as to the age of a child being 8 years old ^before baptism^. It was universally thought [by the school] w[h]ere children ~~were~~ ^are^ capable of repentance at ~~6 or~~ an earlier age, it would be right to baptize them.

If Parents neglect to teach their children the principles of ~~their~~ the Gospel, they will have to answer for such neglect. B[isho]p Raleigh thought if a parent properly instructed them, and admonished them—it was then optional with the children whether they accept or reject baptism.

Elder N[athaniel] H. Felt did think it the bounden duty of Parents to baptize ^their^ children at 8 years old.

Sect[ion] 22 Par[agraph] 4[10] was then read, where it expressly teaches that Children ~~in~~ of the saints should be baptized when they are 8 years old, or the ~~sain~~ sin of neglect lies on the Parent.

Q[uestion:] Is the partaking of the sacrament an ordinance that remits sins, if partaken worthily. Some said yes.

Prest D. H. Wells remarked, that according to the revelation it was the imperative duty ~~to see an~~ of Parents to see that their children were baptized ~~f~~ when 8 years old. ~~T~~ When any one sins, the best way to have them forgiven, was to sincerely repent of those sins, and be baptized for their remission. We ought to be careful and not use harsh words so as give offence and wound the feelings of others. He then mentioned a case where one brother had been called a thief &c by another, and had frequently sought ~~to heal up the breach~~ for a reconciliation, but the other refused. The injured party had refused the Sacrament, and Prest Wells had told him that inasmuch as he had sought a reconciliation and was refused, he had better partake of the sacrament, and let the sin rest upon the head of the obstinate one.

Elder J[oseph] F. Smith refering to the revelation pertaining to the partaking of the Sacrament, where it ~~spea~~ teaches the Elders &

10. This is now D&C 68:25.

Congregation to kneel while observing ^it^,[11] it would much accord with his feeling, for it to [be] attended [to this way] by Saints alone, and not in mixed [faith] congregations. He did think it ^a^ most sacred ordinance.

Elder G. B. Wallace, thought if we acted in this, ^or anything else^ in accordance with the mind of the living oracles that we have in our midst, we cannot go estray.

Q[uestion:] Should Children before baptism receive the sacrament?

Elder O[rson] Pratt did not think they should. When he had seen it offered to them ~~by others, he thought O Fool~~ ^he felt that it was wrong^ that while they are subjects of the Kingdom of God, ~~but~~ they are not members of the Church of Christ for whose benefit the Ordinances of the Gospel were instituted. He should much like to see the Sacrament administered in a more exclusive way ^than we do^—where persons not in the Church are not present.

Elder N H Felt highly appreciated the practise of kneeling while partaking the sacrament, but did not object to outsiders being present, but in this as in everything else, the living oracles being here, the spirit [of the law] giveth life, while the letter [of the law] killeth.

Prest D H Wells said that Children who are willing to partake of the Sacrament, he should never refuse them, he loved to see them partake of it, and they are just as much members of the Kingdom of God, before baptism as after.

Elder A[ngus] M Angus [Cannon], said he had taught his children to partake of the Sacrament, and always thought he was doing ~~a~~ right—and felt comforted by the remarks of Prest Wells.

Elder N H Felt entertained the same views, and had taught his children the same.

Several interesting remarks were made on the subject of [the law of] adoption.[12]

Q[uestion:] Is it right to wait for ^a^ [spiritual] testimony ^of willingness^ from our dead friends, before we are baptized for them. Answer. No, It is our duty to be baptized for them. We baptize, lay on hands, & seal at the present time by [general] permission, and in due time of the Lord, [all] the ordinations will be attended to. The Fount [font] at the Endowment House was dedicated for baptisms for the

11. D&C 20:76, formerly 2:22.

12. See Jan. 20, 1868, entry.

dead, ~~and to~~ though they did not refuse to baptize for health or for remission for sins, but he ~~wishe~~ much prefer'd a cold-run^n^ing stream ~~for those~~ purposes.

Meeting was adjourned for one week at ½ past 6. Benediction by Elder A. M. Cannon.[13]

January 27, 1873; Monday

The School of the Prophets met in the City Hall at ½ past 6 pm. Present Elder Orson Pratt presiding. ^Prest D[aniel] H. Wells came in a few minutes after the roll was called.^ Prayer by Elder Elias Smith.

Elder Rob[er]t L. Campbell then read Sec[tion] 2 Par[agraphs] 2[2–23] in doc[trine] & Cov[enants].[14] The prayer used in the blessing of the bread & water at the Sacrament, being read.

Elder J[oseph] F. Smith thought the [exact] words as in the Doc[trine] & Cov[enants] should be used.

Elder Jno. [John] Taylor took the same view of it, we cannot be too particular in strictly adhering to the inspired form, not only at the Sacrament, but the words to be used at Baptism, he considered it a dangerous practise to commence a departure from the written revelations, refering to the Apostacy as an illustration of ^what a^ gradual departure from the ancient order may lead to.

Bishops [Alexander] McRae, S[amuel] A. Woolley, F[rederick] Kesler & ~~R~~ [Alonzo H.] Raleigh well remember, that Prest [Brigham] Young distinctly stated that he wished the words to be used, as in the book.

<u>Elder N[athaniel] H Felt</u> urged the same.

<u>Prest D H Wells</u> said there cannot be more beautiful language used, than what we find in the form [given in the Doctrine and Covenants]. In reference to kneeling while ~~at~~ praying at the Sacrament, it had never been practised at head quarters either at Nauvou or here, by the Church at large in mixed congregations.

<u>Elder Jno [John] Taylor</u> spoke of the early usage among the first Elders while on Missions, they instructed the people to adhere to the strict letter of the law, in administering the sacrament.

<u>Elder O Pratt</u> considered it perfectly right for the first Elders to be

13. This paragraph is written vertically, somewhat obscuring the horizontal text already written.

14. Now D&C 20:77, 79.

very particular to have the written formula strictly adhered to, and it was equally right in the growth of the church for the first Presidency to change the form, and allow the congregation to sit.

Elder Jno. [John] Taylor made some excellent remarks on the various ~~on~~ Men of God in different dispensations[15] holding the priesthood—and from whom the surrounding Pagans learned many principle and correct ideas of God—shewing that whatever truth may be found among the pagans, they obtained it from the true priesthood.

Elder N ^H^ Felt, said, that some even among us, suppose that the Israelites when they came out of Egypt strictly conformed to the rites & ceremonies, as practised by the Egyptians, and from whom they learned those rites.

Elder O Pratt refer'd to ancient history, which rebutted the above idea [espoused by Nathaniel H. Felt].

Par[agraph] 24 [of section two was read]. If any member of the Church transgresses &c to be dealt with according to the scrip[tur]es.

Elder O Pratt enquired whether this was strictly attended to at the present time.

Elder J. F. Smith said it was partially done, and much left undone. He knew of one or two, and had no doubt but there was many more who ought not to [be] held in fellowship.

Elder A[ngus] M Cannon spoke of some whose conduct would not bear investigation, according to the testimony of one of our night watchman, who saw and heard a great deal more than he would like to reveal. Bro Angus did not approve of iniquity being thus tampered with and winked at [approved of].

In answer to a Question What is [considered] scripture. It was stated that it was Ancient & Modern revelation.

Prest D H Wells said in the various Wards there is a combination of local authority, and they are the ones who are best calculated to either bear with, or dig around, those who are delinquent in many duties. They are to be ~~Elder N H~~ judged by the Scriptures of divine truth.

Elder Ja[me]s Leach spoke favourably of two brethren whose names he had submitted for the Mission south.

15. LDS theology divides scriptural history into seven dispensations named after Adam, Enoch, Noah, Abraham, Moses, Jesus, and Joseph Smith. Courtney J. Lassetter, "Dispensations of the Gospel," in Ludlow, ed., *Encyclopedia of Mormonism.*

Par[agraph] 25 [of section two was read].[16] Elder O[rson] Pratt enquired if there was a general Church record kept in which all the names of the Church Members were enrolled.

Prest D H Wells said wherever there was a branch of the Church there was a record kept, but no general record that he knew of.

Elder R[obert] F Neslen. There were many hundred pound weight of records [books] in London alone.

B[isho]p A H Raleigh enquired what it meant by a members name being blotted from the records, after expulsion.

Elder J F. Smith & Prest D H Wells, said, ~~all th~~ by an entry of each expelled ~~per~~ member being made in the record, but certainly by not expunging their original entry, for all the official [priesthood and temple] acts of such an one while in good standing was perfectly legal.

The School was adjourned for one week at ½ past 6 pm. Benediction by Elder W[ilford] Woodruff.

February 3, 1873; Monday

The School of the Prophets met in the City Hall at ½ past 6 pm. Present ^Elder Orson Pratt presiding. Prest D[aniel] H. Wells came in ½ past 7.^ Roll called. Prayer by N. Davis.

By permission Elder F[rederick] A. Mitchell enquired, when the kingdom of God is fully established,[17] will there be in it Methodists, Baptists, Catholics &c.

D[imick] B. Huntington stated the views of the Prophet Joseph [Smith] on that subject, viz that Heathen and all others outside of the Church, will be fully protected in their rights.

B[isho]p A[lonzo] H Raleigh said whatever sects of religion might exist when the Kingdom was established, there would [be] neither Methodists ^or^ Baptists, for they will have tapered off long before then, and will only be known in history.

Elder G[eorge] B. Wallace said for the last 25 years, he has always understood that others besides Latter day saints, will be on the earth when the Kingdom is established, and all will be protected in their rights.

16. The revelation required that the list of names of all church members be updated at each general conference.

17. That is, the theocratic kingdom of God on earth. For more on this, see Grow et al., *Joseph Smith Papers: Administrative Records*; Rogers, *Council of Fifty*; Grow and Smith, eds., *Council of Fifty*.

Elders S[amuel] A. Woolley & R[obert] F. Neslen exprest similar views.

Elder Elias Smith, did always considered there was quite a difference between the Kingdom and the subjects of a Kingdom—and that on ^no^ one outside of the Church will ever have anything to do with the making or administering of the laws, but be subject to him.

Elder N[athaniel] H. Felt said the Church of Jesus Christ of latter day saints would constitute the heart of the Kingdom of God.

Elder Orson Pratt then read from Doc[trine] & Cov[enants] that the Lord would cut his work short in righteousness and that those who remain from the least to the greatest shall be filled with the knowledge of the Lord.

Elder Rob[er]t Campbell thought there was a difference between being members of the M Kingdom and subjects of the Kingdom, and illustrated the idea by reference to the those outsiders now in our midst who are w amenable to our Municipal laws &c, and therefore are subject to them but cannot be deemed members.

Elder N. H. Felt, thought the difference considered consisted in either being Members of the Church, or not, and those who are not will be subjects of the Kingdom.

~~Elder D. B. Huntington, Said~~

Elder D B Huntington expreSt similar views.

Elder R[obert] F. Neslen. When the Kingdom is established, Christ will come and reign over it, and that there will be others beside saints living then and will be protected under it.

Elder Orson Pratt never could see a difference between the Kingdom of God & the Church of God—but after the setting up of the Kingdom, there will be all kinds of religious sects & Heathen, ^&^ even until after it is established when Zion shall issue her laws for the government of all other denominations. But when Jesus Christ comes in the clouds of Heaven he will take vengeance on them that no know not God, and have not obeyed the Gospel. But to suppose that after Jesus takes full dominion over the earth in his resurrected body, together with his Apostles in their resurrected bodys, with the Myriads of those he brings with him, & that at that time there will be Baptists, Methodists &c on the earth, he never did, nor ever expected to believe any thing of the kind.

Elder N F Felt thought the Saviour will ^would^ come to Zion, long

~~before~~ & exercise rule & issue laws, for a long time while other sects are on the earth, beside latter day saints.

Elder F. A. Mitchell always did believe that those living on the earth after the kingdom was established, who are not saints, would be free to exercise their agency either to accept or reject the Gospel.

Elder G. B. Wallace. There will be many by and bye, who will not have faith enough to embrace doctrines of Christ, but enough to observe the laws of the Kingdom of God.

Elder S. A. Wallace entertained the same views as G[eorge] B. W[allace]—that there was quite a difference between the Church of Jesus Christ and the Kingdom of God. According to [Old Testament prophet] Zecheriah, during the Millenium there will be others besides saints, and be subject to the laws of the Kingdom.

Elder D[avid] McKenzie. When the Saviour comes, the Jews will have been gathered, and the Nations gone up to Jerusalem to fight. Many would be destroyed, and that others besides saints would be on the earth besides saints.

Elder Jos[eph] F. Smith, God is the author of the Kingdom and also of the Church of Jesus Christ, because the subjects ~~are~~ of the last are ^also^ the subjects of the first. He endorsed the sentiments of Elder Orson Pratt. May not the leading men of this church become Governors, ~~&~~ Rulers & law Makers, over and among the various sects & parties of other denominations. ~~some of these lawmakers may not be members of the Church~~ The Kingdom of God & the Church of God are one and the same thing, that during the Milleneum, there will be a mighty labour to perform by the Elders of Israel in attending to the ordination of the Gospel for their dead.

Elder George Morris said the Church had grown from 6 members to a Territory—where we now exercise considerable rule and dominion, and will continue to increase until it circumscribe all that are good on the face of the earth.

Elder N Felt did think that in the future government of the Nations, there would be representatives from Hottentots [South African natives] and other heathen, would ~~there~~ be there in the great congress of Nations, to assist in making Laws suitable to their various peculiar conditions and circumstances.

Prest D H Wells said we see this matter pretty much alike but express ourselves differently. Men in this probationary [mortal] state, have their volition, and can either reject or accept the Gospel, [but] except a man be born of water & the spirit [he] can never obtain a celestial glory. There is an organization in the Kingdom of God, and there is an organization of the Church of Jesus Christ of latter day saints. When God reigns, his servants will be sent to govern the different Nations of the earth, and adapt the laws suitable to their degraded condition. When we speak of exaltation, we speak of those whom [that which] but few will attain, even to become Gods, and sons of God, holding the controuling power. The great ^eternal^ plan of Salvation was devised long before this earth was brought into existence.

The School was adjourned for one week at ½ past 6 pm. Benediction by F[rederick] A. Mitchell.

Some interesting remarks were made by Prest Wells and Orson Pratt, on the subject of ^the^ Sealing ordinances. The first one who will receive their resurrection in this dispensation will be Joseph Smith and he will give the keys [of the ordinance of resurrection] to others.[18]

February 10, 1873; Monday

The School of the Prophets met in the City Hall. Present Elder Orson Pratt presiding. (Prest D[aniel] H Wells came in at 8 pm.) After the role was called Prayer by Elias Morris.

~~Elder Geo~~ B[isho]p A[lonzo] H. Raleigh suggested that 21 par[agraph] 4 page be examined. It reads thus. And Joshua in the sight of all Israel, bade the Sun and Moon to stand still and it was done.[19]

Elder Orson Pratt said it was a common way of expression, as among us at the present time, when we say The Sun sets, and rises—on that principle we can easily see and account for the mode of expression as above.

Elder Geo B Wallace said that Bro W[illia]m Clayton taught last evening in the 17 Ward that no man who has only One wife in this probation can ever enter the Celestial Kingdom. Also That no one who receives the Gospel in the spirit world can ever enter into the Celestial Kingdom. Bro Wallace desired to know whether the above doctrines were correct?

18. This last paragraph appeared on the reverse of the loose sheets used by Goddard to keep the minutes.

19. This is from the first Lecture on Faith in the Liverpool edition of the Doctrine and Covenants, preceding the revelations.

Elder Rob[er]t F Neslen thought it very timely for these subjects to ^be^ thoroughly ventilated, for they have been taught for years past by the same individual.

Elder W[ilford] Woodruff said he did not believe either ^in^ one or the other of those doctrines. But he did believe that many who [died without the gospel] went in the spirit world, who will receive the gospel and [will] enter into the Celestial Kingdom. And moreover, that those who have had one wife sealed to them over the alter, and should die before they had a chance to obtain a second, would certainly be entitled to a Celestial Glory.

Elder N[athaniel] H. Felt sustained the above views.

B[isho]p S[amuel] A. Woolley refered to the opinion expressed by Prest [Brigham] Young, some time ago in the Tabernacle, viz That some persons being contented with one wife here, while others that are more ambitious have many, [it is] so with some [that] ^they^ are perfectly satisfied with a City lot, others strive for more &c, each ~~can~~ are entitled to a Celestial Glory, though varied in capacity. Prest Young also told him that though [his] [i.e.,] B[isho]p Woolley's[,] son had died without a wife, he [the son] could have some sealed to him, and he would lose nothing by dying prematurely.[20]

Elder John Taylor sustained the same views, believing that those who heartily endorse the Doctrine of Plurality, and should die before he has more than one wife sealed to him, [will have the opportunity in heaven]. He did not believe in the views advanced by Bro W[illia]m Clayton.

Elder W[ilford] Woodruff made some excellent remarks on the same subject.

Elder Rob[er]t Campbell said that Bro Clayton had preached 4 times lately in the 12[th] ward, he said that the 144,000 spoken off [of] in the Revelations would be Gods, and be entitled to ^all^ the Women that ever lived on the earth—and those who had only ~~only~~ one wife in the flesh, sealed over the alter, may go into the celestial Kingdom [as] angels, but would have no increase, while in the Terestrial and Telestial Kingdoms there will be no females at all.

Elder Orson Pratt quoted the words of Joseph [Smith] the Prophet, that God had revealed to him that some who had died before the Book

20. Samuel H. Woolley (1847–70) died at age twenty-two without having married. He had four brothers or stepbrothers who died after 1873 without marrying.

of Mormon came forth—were in the Celestial Kingdom. ~~Th~~ Any person who has been personally commanded to take more wives by the Almighty through his servants, and should refuse—they would be damned.

Elder Jos[eph] F. Smith who had administered so long at the endowment house, could not do so with any pleasure unless he fully believed that those for whom they administered the ordinances, were entitled to a Celestial Glory. He thought that many women would be sealed to those who attain to the highest glory. He heard Prest Young say, that a Man fully believing in the doctrine of Plurality, though he had but one wife, would be entitled to a Celestial glory. He (J[oseph] F. S[mith]) felt that he was a polygamist child—and always believed in the doctrine,[21] and should he have died before marriage, he could have had wives sealed to him, and enjoy celestial Glory. He believed that the doctrine taught by Bro W[illia]m Clayton was wicked and incorrect.

Elder D[imick] B Huntington mentioned ~~to~~ a private conversation he had with Bro Joseph, the Prophet, ~~that~~ on the subject of Polygamy, he [Joseph] told him that God had commanded it to be observed, and if he himself [Dimick] did not comply with it he should be damned. ^Spoke of Prest Young councilling the brethren some time ago, to use Oxen instead of Horses—let us live by the words of our prophet—^

Elder A M[ilton] Musser, queried, whether a Bishop had not the right to correct erroneous doctrines when they heard them advanced.

Elder W[ilford] Woodruff heard Bro Clayton express those doctrines [mentioned by George Wallace above] over a year ago, in the 17 ward, after which he Bro W W warned the people against such a doctrine.

Elder R. F. Neslen named a case where a good worthy brother in Farmington [Utah] had been much depressed in his feelings in consequence of Bro Claytons doctrine, but was much rejoiced when B[isho]p [Reuben] Miller the other day advocated the opposite views. ~~He~~ Bro R[obert] F. N[eslen] fully believed the views expressed by the brethren to night.

Elder G. B. Wallace once had a dream, after an earnest prayer to God to reveal to him about the doctrine of polygamy, [in which] a personage

21. When his wife died in 1837, Hyrum Smith married Mary Fielding, who bore Joseph F. Smith the next year. Five years later Hyrum acquired another four wives. After Hyrum's death in 1844, Mary became a plural wife of Heber C. Kimball. See Smith, *Nauvoo Polygamy*, 620–21.

took him away, and shown to him Joseph the Prophet as a God, and he also saw many worlds, and was told that Joseph had many wives [on earth], and therefore had many wives [in heaven].

B[isho]p A[lonzo] H Raleigh said he had learned by observation, that many who had been favoured with a close and intimate acquaintance with Joseph, unless they continued to walk in the spirit side by side with the servants of God that still lived, they stood in great danger of being tripped up.

Prest D. H. Wells thought it would be a good thing, if the Elders would preach publicly, would preach the Gospel according to Brigham. How timely he gave the council to use Oxen, they cost less to keep, travel nearly as fast with a load as Horses or Mules. He wished the Elders to urge upon the people the necessity of raising oxen. He would prefer that Oxen be taken on the southern Mission. Speaking of Bro Clayton, said he [William Clayton] had enjoyed extraordinary privileges with Bro Joseph,[22] and that most things he had pretty correct, though he may have erred in that spoken of to night, but he never heard him, himself. The Elders going round as Missionaries should correct any wrong doctrine they may come in contact with.

He did not think that Plurality [of wives] was intended ^for^ many, few there be that will find the way of the [etermal] lives. Some ~~of~~ ^have^ gone into polygamy to satisfy a selfish and lustful desire. The principle was revealed for the purpose of raising up a righteous and holy seed, and polygamous children will yet stand boldly forward and honourably defend it.

School was adjourned for one week at ½ past 6 pm. Benediction by B[isho]p F[rederick] Kesler.

February 17, 1873; Monday

The School of the Prophets met in the City Hall at ½ past 6 pm. Present Elder W[ilford] Woodruff presiding. ^Prest D[aniel] H. Wells came in about 7.^ After the roll was called Prayer was offered by Elder George Morris.

Prest Woodruff enquired if any members of the school had any business, and none being presented He said that he did not feel like

22. As Smith's secretary in Nauvoo, Clayton had special access to the prophet and an intimate glimpse into his life and teachings.

following our usual mode of reading out of Doc[trine] & Cov[enants] but he would prefer learning the minds of the brethren upon the signs of the times, the signs of the second coming of the Son of Man &c.

A portion of ~~the~~ a letter was then read from Bro Geo Q Cannon in which he refer'd to the antagonistic spirit of Prest [Ulysses S.] Grant, [William] Cl[a]ggett, and the rest of the members of the Congress.[23]

Bro Woodruff said it ^was^ his mind that instead of buying up Members of Congress with Money, he would rather leave them in the hands of God &c.[24]

Elder Geo B. Wallace was thankfull that we had file leaders, and it was for us to follow their council. He felt that the Nation was fast filling up the cup of their iniquity, and would soon totter and fall, exhibited the rottenness of their condition by reference to a dream by a brother.

Elder Angus M Cannon related a dream that he had last night in which he saw Prest Grant perfectly naked, and in a filthy condition, and in that state was about to start to Rock Island [Illinois].

Elder I[saac] Groo, spoke of the importance of this Dispensation, and of the times in which we live. If we will only keep the commandments of God, we have nothing at all to fear, the government of this Nation is one Mass of corruption from Prest Grant down to the lowest paid officer. He was perfectly willing to aid and assist the Almighty in any way that was required.

B[isho]p Tho[ma]s Taylor felt that all was right, the Kingdom will be victorious, and when he heard some things in this City, he felt like Bro H[oward] Spencer, that he was ready to help the Lord. There is nothing to fear, if we will only do right, he would like to be saved in this Kingdom, and his family also.

B[isho]p E[lijah] F Sheets testified that this was the work of God, had known it for many years, and most of ~~th~~ his lifetime had been spent

23. Most of Cannon's letter recounted a speech by Utah territorial delegate to the US Congress, William H. Hooper, and an antagonistic response by William H. Clagett (1838–1901), territorial delegate from Montana. It had to do with a bill to grant Colorado statehood and Hooper's suggestion that it be amended to include Utah. Cannon, who would replace Hooper as territorial delegate beginning in March, reported that President Grant called for Congressional committees to draft "legislation against Utah." Cannon to Young, Feb. 5, 1873, in General Correspondence, Incoming, Young Office Files, CHL.

24. Money was nevertheless paid at various times to politicians, reporters, and other influence-peddlers. See, for instance, Cannon, *Candid Insights of a Mormon Apostle*, 392–93n9, 430.

in this Kingdom, and this Nation is now arrayed against one Man and a mere handfull of people, he prayed for strength to endure to the end, the Kingdom of God must stand, and the Kingdoms of this world must be subject to it.

B[isho]p A[lonzo] H. Raleigh had no doubt but every one in the kingdom of God, would be tested and tried to the core, and before Uncle Sam gives us a rub, that there will be a sifting and dividing ^time^ among ourselves, those who are faithful will be called out from among those who are less so. Every Man who has done his duty, he had no doubt would be ~~only~~ able to stand. He rather questioned the policy of establishing our Bank, being the most prominent of our financial affairs, on the same basis as Banks in the world—viz on Government Bonds which have to run for many years before they are redeemable, it seemed to him that the present rotton condition of the Nation, indicated that their end was drawing very near, and that the currency will be found in many pockets, that will be utterly worthless.

Elder N[athaniel] H Felt, said what was now taking place, was an additional testimony to him, that this is the Kingdom of God, [but] there is many [a] slip between the cup and the lip,[25] he reviewed our past experience, and the wonderfull interpositions of providence, which would be as signally manifest in the future, as in the past.

B[isho]p A[lexander] McRae felt willing to do whatever Prest Young or Wells required of him—this ^is^ Gods Kingdom, and will stand, and he himself was ready for anything that came along.

Elder Henry Arnold felt thankful to be in the midst of the friends of God, had been in the church 32 years, he knew of no other way of demonstrating his faith, but by his works, and hoped to continue faithful to the end.

Elder Geo B Wallace spoke of the immense army of Grasshoppers that came out of the Kanyon [one year], and eat [ate] every green thing—and leaving the ground bare, it was a trying time then, and though it was trying time to day let us trust in God and do our duty, and all will be well. He had no fear, let us obey the Voice of God through his servants, and he would risk it. [He] was not afraid to die, the sting had been taken away.

25. This is an aphorism, "There's many a slip twixt cup and lip," meaning that anything can go wrong.

Prest Elias Smith had long since been a Member of the Church, and felt thankful for being preserved through ^so^ many trying scenes and circumstances, when death at times seemed inevitable. He used to be a warm politician in days that are past, but of late had realized that this was Gods Kingdom, and did not care whether Grant or anyone else occupied the Presidential Chair.[26] Was willing to do what was required of him, and that God would do his work without waiting for any one.

B[isho]p W[illia]m Thorne, felt to rejoice, that what was now transpiring, was proof that the Kingdom was advancing, our strength lies in our union, and confidence in God, from what we have learned about the present rotten condition of the Nation, was proof of its speedy destruction. Prayed that we might continue faithful to the end.

<u>B[isho]p James Leach</u> never felt better than to night, if we are subject to those who are over us, we gain the victory every time. Felt thankful for such a man as Prest Young, and he desired to put his trust in God, he knew that Israel would rise, and the Nation will fall, and the blow will fall heavier on the enemies of Gods Kingdom, than on the saints.

<u>Elder Elias Morris</u>, learned lessons from the past, to put his confidence in God, and knew that it would be well with the saints, they [outsiders] were aiming their shafts at our head, but God will frustrate the designs of the wicked, was willing to act his part in the Kingdom.

B[isho]p W[illia]m Hickenlooper had always felt to obey council, we have a prophet and leader, he felt himself no better than any one else, and willing to die if necessary, we have the truth, and whether we live or die it will be well with us.

<u>Elder J[ohn] Winder</u>, said, if he was asked whether he loved the Lord ~~whether~~ while in this comfortable room, he should say like Peter of ~~him~~ old, Yea Lord, thou knowest that I love thee, but how it would be under other circumstances, he does not know how it would be, he prayed that he might be ready for whatever might come. ^At his late fire, all his guns and ammunition were burnt up, and tomorrow morning, he intended to buy another [horse and wagon] outfit.^[27]

Elder W[ilford] Woodruff much enjoyed the present meeting, and

26. In the early 1850s, Smith had chaired the commission that wrote the legal code for the State of Deseret. The Code Commission provided the initial framework for the legislature to add to and subtract from. In 1873 he was a probate judge.

27. Winder's wagon house, located behind his new home, caught fire in December 1872. "Fire Last Night," *Salt Lake Herald*, Dec. 19, 1872.

he felt to prophecy that Bro Winder should never apostatize, that he never should desert his post. He never felt like councilling his file leaders, whatever the Lord dictated Prest Young, it would be right, the Lord will avenge the blood of his people, and vengeance is mine saith the Lord. We have a wicked set of men in our midst and they are bent on the death of our leaders, was pleased with the feelings expressed to night.

Prest D H Wells refer[re]d to the efforts now being made by the [US] President & Congress to subjugate us to the most humiliating position. The reason that no one had a word to say in favour of Zion in Congress—was because they were not bought, he thought it would be well for the brethren to rub up their fire arms and keep their powder dry, and trust in God; he had no doubt the [US] President intended to move the troops [overseeing Reconstruction] from the South, and station them somewhere within a days march of Utah. He was not at all concerned at what the Prest could do against us. The brethren here to night, feel just the same in spirit as Bro Geo Q. Cannon,[28] a peaceful quiet spirit. A ~~Memorial~~ ^protest^ had been got up, and signed by some of our leading Attorneys & Merchants, against the Memorial recently sent from here [by anti-Mormons] to hag[29] on the President & Congress to use us up, and was telegraphed yesterday, to be in time to get it before the committee early this week. Many of our rude young men, in a time of trouble would doubtless ~~pri~~ prove their integrity while many of our pious friends would fail. Any ~~integrity inter~~ attempt to root out plurality [polygamy] from our midst, will only cause it to take deeper root than ever—every effort based on falsehood to injure us, will always fail. We may safely follow the lead of Prest Young, he is led right. Though he is fast aging, his interest for the Kingdom does not abate. ~~He~~ Works and faith should always go hand in hand, our means is given us for the building up of the Kingdom of God. The Government of this Nation[30] is so rotton, that it will sooner or later fall by the weight of its own corruption. Let us be ready with our means, time and talents, always on hand to build up the Kingdom of God. In his own feelings,

28. Cannon had closed his letter to Brigham Young saying that "these threats and movements fail to excite or disturb me. … I feel an abiding conviction that the plots of the wicked will fail." Cannon to Young, Feb. 5, 1873.

29. Hag meant "to harass; to torment." Webster, *American Dictionary*, 1828.

30. The remainder of this entry is written vertically over the horizontal text already written.

he would avoid an open rupture with the government as long as he possibly could, we must cling most tenaciously to the Constitution of the United States.

School was adjourned for one week at ½ past 6 pm. Benediction ~~for~~ by George Goddard.

February 24, 1874; Monday

The School of the Prophets met in the City Hall at ½ past 6 pm. Present B[isho]p Edw[ar]d Hunter, was unanimously voted to take the chair and open the meeting. Opened by Prayer by Elder Geo Riser.

During prayer Prest D[aniel] H. Wells and Elder W[ilford] Woodruff came in and Elder A[ngus] Cannon was called upon to read on the 74th page of the ~~Cov~~ Doc[trine] & Cov[enants].[31] Question, When did the ^high^ [Melchizedek] priesthood leave the earth anciently? Ans[wer:] When Moses died. Though some held the high priesthood even until Jesus came yet in a very adulterated [inchoate] form.

B[isho]p E[dward] Hunter spoke of the great privelege granted in this dispensation of being ordained to the Melchisadec Priesthood, and acting in the lessor priesthood at the same time, and by magnifying both, we become the sons of Moses and Aarron, the seed of Abraham and elect of God.

Prest D H Wells, said a Man may be a Prophet, yet not necessarily an Apostle. If there was ^a^ High Priest on the earth during the time from Moses to Christ, he did not know it.

<u>Elder W Woodruff</u> said that while he acted under the Aaronic priesthood, as a Priest, God manifested his power quite as much as since he held the Apostleship, he gave him dreams and visions &c. No matter what priesthood a man may hold, if he magnified it, God would own and bless him under it.

<u>B[isho]p Hunter</u> spoke of the peculiar blessings that is connected with the lessor priesthood, especially in the settlement of difficulties, their being a special power and influence given to those acting in that priesthood.

<u>Elder W Woodruff</u> ^said^ that he did not think it wisdom to have

---

31. Section 3 (now 107) has to do with the Melchizedek and Aaronic priesthoods. For information on the development of these two separate priesthoods, see Prince, *Power from on High*.

our minds exercised about any matter that revelation was silent upon, and as to whether or not, the high priesthood was enjoyed between the time of Moses and the Saviour, did not really concern us, as we had many pressing duties that should engage our attention in preference.

(Page 77) Is the Council in Zion, the same as the high council in the Stakes of Zion?[32] Ans[wer:] The Councils refered to are equal in authority in their decisions, both being equal to the first presidency's decisions, that is, when there is a unanimous decision agreed to by every member.

B[isho]p Hunter spoke of the Agency given to every man, whereby he has the power to settle his own difficulties on the principle of reconciliation, but when an individual permits his case to be taken to the High Council, he forfeits his own Agency, and has to submit to and abide the decisions of others, whether it suits him or not.

Elder Jos[eph] F. Smith entertained the idea that, though in the Doc[trine] & Cov[enants] it is stated the decisions of the High Councils were equal to the decisions of the first presidency, yet he did think, there was a higher authority vested in the first presidency, by virtue of their position.

Elder Geo B. Wallace sustained the same views.

Prest D. H. Wells, ~~th~~ said the first presidency exercised the presidency over every High Council throughout all the stakes of Zion.

Prest D H Wells said the priesthood in this Church constituted the most complete system of government that ever existed on the face of the earth, suited to any and every emergency that may arise among the people. An Elder is an appendage ~~t~~ to, and ~~are~~ ^is^ a part of the high priesthood, ~~an~~ though they cannot officiate in many offices, until they are ordained to the high priesthood.

Elder Geo B. Wallace related a very encouraging dream.

B[isho]p Hunter related one also, and the interpretation to each was plainly manifest, viz To resist the Devil and he will flee from us. We should be encouraged to put our trust ^in the Lord.^

The School was adjourned for one week at ½ past 6 pm. Benediction by B[isho]p Thomas Taylor.

---

32. They are discussing Doctrine and Covenants 3:15 (now 107:37):"The high council in Zion, forms a quorum equal in authority, in the affairs of the church, in all their decisions, to the councils of the twelve at the stakes of Zion." In later editions, the word "twelve" became capitalized.

Prest Wells related a Dream that Elder Geo Q Cannon recently had, wherein he saw the brethren ~~arrayed~~ arrayed in front of an immense army supplied with all the implements of war, and just at the very moment when they expected to be annialated, all in an instant the whole army vanished in ~~an instant~~ a moment.[33]

March 3, 1873; Monday

The School of the Prophets met in the City Hall at ½ past 6 pm. Present Elder Orson Pratt presiding. Roll Called. Prayer by B[isho]p F[rederick] Kesler.

Question. Elders generally when baptising, use the words, "for the remission of thy sins,["] yet the order in the Doc[trine] & Cov[enants], those words are not included. Which is right?[34]

Elder Pratt said in first baptisms, we should use the form as given in the Doc[trine] & Cov[enants], but in the 2nd baptisms[35] we should use the words, "for the remission of thy sins."

Elder Geo B Wallace refer'd to ^the^ subject of last Monday evening as to whether the Melchizadeck Priesthood was taken away at the time of Moses and not restored until the Saviour came. A Revelation was then read on the 84th page ^Doc[trine] & Cov[enants]^ which states that the Melchisadeck priesthood was taken away from the children of Israel on account of their stiffneckedness.[36]

Elder Orson Pratt named several instances in the old testament that clearly proved that the high priesthood existed among some of the tribes of Israel, long after the days of Moses.

Elder John Taylor entertained the same views as Bro Pratt. It was very evident to him, that the high priesthood was enjoyed by Prophets and others on this continent, as well as those on the Eastern Continents.

33. This paragraph was inserted by George Goddard at the end of the minutes.

34. The wording in the Doctrine and Covenants is: "Having been commissioned of Jesus Christ, I baptize you in the name of the Father, and of the Son, and of the Holy Ghost. Amen" (originally D&C 2:21; now 20:73). However, the next section (the one under discussion) refers to "the baptism of repentance for the remission of sins" (3:10; now 107:20).

35. It was common in nineteenth-century Utah to be re-baptized for a variety of reasons, all of which were different than baptism in order to make a confession of faith and receive admission into the church. One study notes that "the practice of rebaptism for rededication, renewal, reformation, health, and preparation for temple ordinances continued throughout the nineteenth century." Quinn, "Practice of Rebaptism at Nauvoo," 232.

36. D&C 4:4; now 84:24.

The Egyptians also had that priesthood, as shewn by the doings of [biblical] Joseph, who sold Corn (during the famine) in exchange for Money, ~~C~~ Cattle, Land and the people themselves, the only exception in the sale of lands by the Egyptians, was the Priests, whose lands were reserved for themselves [Gen. 47:26]. He instanced the case of Elisha & Elijah to prove that the high priesthood was had by them.

President B[righam] Young who had been absent from the school for over 3 months, on a visit to St. George, came in, accompanied by Prest D[aniel] H Wells—and by Prest Youngs request Elder David McKenzie read two letters from Bro L[orenzo] W. Roundy[37] ~~g~~ in which he sets forth a descriptive view of the country on the little Colorado [River], in the neighbourhood of the San francisco Mountains in Arizona.

Prest Young express a desire to start a Mission in that Country, and endeavour to convert the Moqutch [Hopi] Indians who are very industrious and tractable people. He wished those who went there, both old and young, to enter ^into^ a combination ~~for~~ to labour for the good of the community, on a cooperative principle. We have got to build up Zion, to gather Israel, and extend the Kingdom of God on the earth. If we have any other business on hand, we are falling short of what we have been called to.

Prest D H Wells stated the leading objects of that Mission and ^that^ between 3[000] and 4000.00 dollars have been subscribed towards the purchase of Machinery, Mills &c by some of our Moneyed Men. Many who had been called, ~~wh~~ were told to be getting into a state of readiness, so that when it was wisdom for them to go, there might be but little or no delay, and they all understand the plan upon which the Mission is to be carried out.

Prest Young enquired, shall we make up a Company and send? And who will volunteer?

Elder Orson Pratt, B[isho]p [Alexander] McRae, ^&^ D Day each expressed their willingness to go if required.

In relation to the School Books, ^he [Young] said^ we are getting to be a strong people, and the cost of school Books ^from the States^ must exceed over twenty thousand (20,000.00) dollars ^per Annum for the Territory^ and the seeds of Infidelity are being sown [and] broadcast

37. Lorenzo W. Roundy (1819–76) was baptized in 1837. He drowned three years after this entry in the Colorado River at Lee's Ferry, on the border of Arizona and Utah.

in those books, and it was his mind that Bro Orson Pratt & Sister Eliza R. Snow[38] be employed by the Church to make our books, ^in the [phonetic] deseret alphabet^ ~~and that~~ as long as they lives~~.~~It is our duty to build up our Cities, and pay no attention whatever to those who are Mining here. Gold is not wealth, but only a representative of wealth by the Gentiles. We have every facility for building up Zion and ourselves. We should always employ our own people to teach our children, the influence of Gentile Teachers tends to infidelity, and sour[s] the minds of the children against the gospel. ([The school] left off [reading] in the Doc[trine] & Cov[enants] Sec[tion] 3. Par[agraph] 18.)[39]

The School was adjourned for one week at ½ past 6 pm. Benediction by Orson Pratt.

March 10, 1873; Monday

The School of the Prophets met in the City Hall at ½ past 6 pm. Present Elder Orson Pratt presiding. After roll call Prayer was offered by Elder John VanCott.

Elder W[ilford] Woodruff suggested that if Prest [Brigham] Young should pay us a visit to night, the whole school rise on their feet, as a respectful salutation, at his entrance.

Elder Orson Pratt said he had no~~t~~ doubt but every member of the school would be thankful to observe any rule that may be made known to us, but while he himself was acting as a President, he should be sorry to introduce anything that might be deem[ed] an innovation.

It was then Moved by Elder Geo B Wallace & Seconded by Elder Orson Pratt, That on Prest Youngs entrance, the school should rise on their feet. (Carried)

Elder Rob[er]t L. Campbell then read Section 3rd. Par[agraph] 18.

Elder W[ilford] Woodruff enquired if any present remembered hearing the Prophet Joseph [Smith] say how old Adam was when he died:—No one reply'd.

38. Eliza Roxcy Snow (1804–87) was baptized in 1835. Known as "Zion's Poetess," her poems appearing in church and city newspapers, she was appointed secretary of the newly formed Female Relief Society in 1842, the same year she married Joseph Smith as a plural wife. After his death, she married Brigham Young. In 1866 she was called to help reorganize the Relief Society in Utah. After leading the organization unofficially for fourteen years, she was officially appointed president in 1880.

39. Currently D&C 107:40.

Elders D[imick] B. Huntington, John Taylor & [Alexander] McRae—testified that while they were in Adam Ondi Ahmon [Missouri] with the Prophet Joseph, ^they^ heard him say that on that spot was the place where Adam offered sacrifice, ^pointing with his stick to the very alter itself^ and where he blessed his posterity.[40]

The Question was asked whether any one present ever heard Joseph say, that any portion of Missouri was the place ~~the~~ where the garden of Eden was. No one answered.

Elder Orson Pratt remarked that Nephi [of the Book of Mormon] was the descendant of Manassah and not of Ephraim, though we have an idea exprest in a hymn, thus, "I wance was pleasant Ephraim".[41]

Prest D[aniel] H. Wells derived his impression that Missouri was the place were Adam blest his posterity, and offered sacrifice, from the Prophet Joseph himself; and he also thought the same fact can be found in some of our publications.

Elder Jos[eph] F Smith remarked that on the 118 page of the book of Mormon in the book of Jacob, where the Lord prohibited the practise of Polygamy and Concubines, ~~He~~ he J[oseph] F. S[mith] enquired if the reason for this revelation was given in those ^116 pages of^ Manuscripts which was stolen and lost.[42] He said the words Polygamy and whoredom were synonimous in their meaning according to every dictionary that he had ever seen. And was sorry that ever such a word should have been recognized by us as a people in reference to our plural marriage, because Polygamy means a plurality of Wives or a plurality of husbands.

Elder John Taylor said that though the above may be sustained by many of our Lexicographers, yet by usage and custom the word Polygamy is regarded only as a plurality of wives.

Elder Geo B Wallace thought that whenever the Gospel of the son

40. The name given in 1838 to this Missouri town, Adam-ondi-ahman, came from an 1835 revelation stating that "three years previous to the death of Adam, he called Seth, Enos, Cainan, Mahalaleel, Jared, Enoch, and Methuselah, who were all high priests, with the residue of his posterity who were righteous, into the valley of Adam-ondi-ahman, and there bestowed upon them his last blessing" (D&C 3:28; now 107:53).

41. He was probably continuing the discussion of Joseph of Egypt from the previous meeting, held March 3, 1873. Ephraim and Manasseh were sons of biblical Joseph.

42. Jacob 2:27–28 reads: "Wherefore, my brethren, hear me, and hearken to the word of the Lord: for there shall not any man among you have save it be one wife; and concubines he shall have none; for I, the Lord God, delight in the chastity of women. And whoredoms are an abomination before me; thus saith the Lord of Hosts." For the lost 116 pages of dictation, see the entry for June 17, 1871.

of God was on the earth in its fulness, the law of Celestial Marriage was also preached and practised.

Prest D H Wells said there would be more plural marriages performed now, if it were not for the spirit of Babylon that rests upon the people, who fancy they cannot afford to keep more than one wife, ~~there would~~ the word P^ol^ygamy was a correct word to be used by us, to designate a plurality of wives. The only legitimate Government ~~of God~~ upon the face of the earth, is the Government of God, the sectarian world have no more right to solemnize marriages, than to administer baptism, neither of which is recognized by God, nor are valid in his sight.

The reason why Jacob denounced Polygamy among the Nephites, was because of their wickedness and abominations—but the principle of Plural or Celestial Marriage was righteous and holy.

We should all try to carry out in our influence and in our lives, that this is the Government of God—and is the only legitimate Government there is on the face of the earth. Gods revelation pertaining to the law of Marriage is binding on all those to whom it is revealed, and he will hold us accountable for its observance—but let us be warned by what we read in the Book of Mormon, against the abuses of that doctrine.

He believed our young girls ~~are~~ were not so much opposed to plural Marriage as many suppose, let them meet with a Man they love, and they will be willing to follow him to the ends of the earth, or abide on a farm, or do anything else that a good husband might require.

He much regretted the prevailing habit of profanity that was growing amongst our young men, especially those who are hauling [goods] to Pioche [Nevada] &c for Gentiles. The insidious growth of such evil practises were much more to be dreaded than an open enemy, and it would be far better for brethren who have sons thus inclined ~~had far better~~ ^to^ pull up stakes, and go into some outside settlements to get away from such influences.

There are many applications for more wives who do not at all deserve it, but cannot be denied without endangering your throats and mine, and therefore for the time being such things were permitted, while Israel was growing.

He also urged the importance of Bishops making some provisions for employing & feeding the poor & destitute, carrying out the Deseret Alphabet &c.

School was adjourned for one week at ½ past 6 pm. Benediction by Elder John Taylor. Read in Doc[trine] & Cov[enants] to par[agraph] 30. Sec[tion] 3.[43]

March 17, 1873; Monday

The School of the Prophets met in the City Hall at ½ past 6 PM. Present Prest B[righam] Young Presiding. Roll called. Prayer by Elder B[righam] Young Jun[io]r.

Elder Rob[er]t L. Campbell was requested to read in the Doc[trine] & Cov[enants] to par[agraph] 30. Sect[ion] 3. where it refers to the Quorums of the lessor priesthood viz The Prest over the ~~priests~~ ^Deacons^ [with multiples of] 12 in a quorum. Priests 48. Teachers 24. A Question was asked whether those had ^ever^ been in existence or would be hereafter according to their respective numbers.

B[isho]p E[dward] Hunter answered in the negative, but would be glad to see them full.

Elder O[rson] Pratt said those revelations were given at different times and before the [temple] endowments were made know[n]. At the Conference in Amhurst, Lorraine Co[unty] Ohio He was called to preside over ~~96 Elders~~ the Elders, ^though^ there ~~no~~ was not a full quorum of 96—A few days after Conference the Prophet Joseph [Smith] Ordained him to the High Priesthood.

Prest D[aniel] H. Wells said he thought those Quorums ought to be kept full according to the pattern [of twelve], and when any of them are taken to the higher priesthood, let others be called to fill their places.

B[isho]p Edw[ar]d Hunter said from henceforth, the quorums of the lesser priesthood, shall be kept full according to the requirement of the Lord, if it is thought best.

B[isho]ps A[lexander] McRae & James Leach made a few remarks on the local working of the lesser priesthood.

B[isho]p E[dwin] D. Woolley said he always regarded the quorums of the lesser priesthood, as found in the Doc[trine] & Cov[enants][,] [to be general models]. These he considered a different class of quorums to those ~~Teache~~ who are usually called and used by the Bishops of the various wards, who are mostly men holding ~~to~~ the higher priesthood.

Prest D H Wells said he considered the duty of ^the Presidents of^

43. D&C 107:58.

those various quorums was, to meet each quorum ~~according~~ and instruct them in their duties.

Elder O Pratt, said ^he^ thought those called to act as Presidents over the Quorums of the lesser priesthood, at our general conference, that they preside over all the Priests of the whole church, so with the Teachers & Deacons.

Prest D H Wells, did not think the Presidency of these quorums as sustained in our general Conference, ~~did not~~ extended beyond the bounderey of this stake of Zion.

B[isho]p A[lonzo] H. Raleigh suggested the propriety of giving the members of those quorums ~~a~~ practical duties to perform according to their particular priesthood, so that B[isho]p Hunter & Council, ~~instead~~ & other Bishops may have time to reflect instead of attending to the breaking of bread &c at the sacrament.

Elder John Taylor thought the number of quorums might be multiplied adfinitum, but reserve the number of 12, 24, 36 & 96.

Elder Geo Q Cannon who had but a day or two since returned from Washington [DC], said the past Session of Congress had been one of the most interesting, as regarded Utah. [Montana territorial delegate] William H.] Claggett made a speech against Utah, which was full of misrepresentations and slanders. [Utah territorial delegate] W[illiam] H. Hooper reply'd the following day and answered all the main features of his lying antagonist. [Idaho territorial delegate] [Samuel A.] Merritt[44] & several others made a special visit to President [Ulysses S.] Grant to try to obtain his influence against Utah, by urging special legislation, [but] this obnoxious interference of these pettifoggers had the very opposite effect, to what they themselves expected. Sen^n^ator [William] Windham [of Minnesota][45] & [Senator] [John A.] Logan[46] of

44. Samuel A. Merritt (1827–1910) had introduced legislation to curtail polygamy and strip the LDS Church of its power. Born in Virginia, he moved to California during the Gold Rush, and after losing re-election in Idaho, he moved to Salt Lake City to work as an attorney, remaining to his death in 1910. See GCQJ, Feb. 5, 1873.

45. William Windom (1827–1891), originally from Ohio but having moved to Minnesota in 1855 when he was in his mid-thirties, won election to the US House of Representatives in 1859 and to the Senate in 1870. He would later become US Secretary of the Treasury.

46. John A. Logan (1826–86) represented Illinois in the US Senate for thirteen years. In 1860 he sponsored an amendment to a bill that would have divided Utah Territory in two. In 1873 he introduced his own bill, the topic of Cannon's remarks, that would

Illinois were very bitter [against Utah]. Claggett had the floor twice in speaking against Utah and in favour of the [Logan] Bill, but both times were choked off by another member bringing forward something else. The day previous to adjournment [Speaker of the House] [James G.] Blaine[47] said he thought the calender [had business] previous to that of Utah. [Congressman] Ben Butler [of Massachusetts] came in with a case of impeachment and bro[ugh]t it forward, and absorbed about an hour,[48] the house then adjourned till Morning, then when introduced and the Utah bill came up, a Member said a bill of such importance ought not to pass so hastily, especially as there was not a quorum in the house, and moved that the bill be laid aside, which was done.

The majority of the ^members of^ Congress are very friendly towards us, especially those who have paid us a visit, and while here, had fallen in good hands. He spoke of the indefatigable labours of Bro W[illiam] H. Hooper. God had blest ~~both~~ both of them while in Washington with his Holy ~~Ghost~~ ^spirit^ and had never enjoyed a Mission better in his life.

School was adjourned for One Week at ~~½ past 6~~ ^7 oclock^ pm. Benediction by Elder L[orenzo] D[ow] Young.

March 24, 1873; Monday

The School of the Prophets met at the City Hall at 7 oclock pm. Present Prest B[righam] Young presiding. After Roll was called Prayer was offered by Elder Martin H Peck.

Prest D[aniel] H. Wells said there were some things of momentous interest pertaining to the Kingdom of God, that by watching the whisperings of the spirit, we may be le~~a~~d to know what our duties are from time to time. The present ^is a very^ opportune time to try and civilize the Indians, inasmuch as the President of the U[nited] States has

have eliminated the Utah offices of attorney general and marshal. It passed the Senate and moved on to the House of Representatives, where it was tabled. See, for instance, Jones, "John A. Logan," 107–08.

47. James G. Blaine (1830–93) was US Congressman from Maine from 1863 to 1876 and Speaker of the House in 1873. Later he would be elected to the Senate, serve as US Secretary of State, and run unsuccessfully against Grover Cleveland for US president in 1884.

48. Federal judge Mark W. Delahay (1828–79) of Kansas would be impeached for alcoholism and resign from office in December rather than stand trial. See GQCJ, Mar. 3, 1873.

inclined towards a Peace policy, it seems a good time for us to use what influence we can to ~~br~~ lead them to learn useful arts and industrious habits, prior to them becoming citizens of the United States.

Another thing was the making of our type, our paper, and print ~~out~~ our own matter for school Books &c.

Prest B Young said he knew what the Lord wanted of this people, and what was now required, was just as much the mind and will of the Lord, as anything that had ever been revealed to the children of men. What had recently been done by the Government in freeing the African Race, laid the foundation for the Lamanites [Native Americans] to become Citizens, entitled to land as others—and can demand of Government ~~the~~ ^a reasonable^ price of the land they had taken away from them.[49]

We are a distinct and separate people, and must become an independant people, and self sustaining, it is our duty to build up Zion instead of building up Babylon. ~~th~~ Let us encourage everything pertaining to our home manufacture. We are in this County [Salt Lake County] perfectly able to build our ^own^ Temple. They are equally able in Cache County, in Utah County, Sanpete &c to build one in theirs; and instead of having our eyes on these Kanyons, ^after gold^ we should make it our business to Gather Israel, Build Temples, and establish Zion.

Elder John Taylor fully endorsed the sentiments of Prest Young, and could clearly discern the hand of providence in operating on the mind of President [Ulysses S.] Grant to be peaceably inclined towards the Lamanites, who have got to take a prominent part in this great Latter day work. It is our bounden duty to have our hearts entirely set on the performance of those things that are indicated to us by our Leader, Prest Young, and should possess the same spirit.

We are nominally connected with the United States Government—but virtually ~~that~~ they are our deadly enemies, and whenever they meet together and legislate for us, their only aim seems to destroy & uproot us. We should certainly try to become self sustaining and independent—then whatever becomes of the United States, we shall be

49. Not until passage of the Indian Citizenship Act of 1924 were Native Americans born within the United States accepted as US subjects based solely on birth. Prior to that time, they were only considered for naturalization if they had served in the military, married a white person, or paid taxes on land they owned.

able to make what we need and supply our own wants. Let us feel that we are for the Kingdom of God, and are willing to devote ourselves to the establishment of Zion—and may God enable us to do this in the name of Jesus.

Elder Geo Q. Cannon, said in almost everything that is said by the President, and done by Congress, has a direct tendency to make us a separate and independent people. God in his providences were all pointing in that direction. It is also of the utmost importance that we should foster the establishment of home industries, especially the Manufacture of Iron, the growth of wool, the Making of paper, all of which were essential to our existence as an independent people.

He instanced, the remarkably persevering efforts that were used to educate the public sentiment in favour of abolishing slavery until the time came for it ^to^ take place, and He did not ^think^ the time was far distant when the public mind might be so influenced as to bring it to be as much in favour of Polygamy as ~~they are~~ ^it is^ now opposed to it.

He then spoke much in favour of our young men and women learning some branch of business to prevent them from fostering evil in their hearts and practises &c

Elder Brigham ^Young^ Jun[io]r said, our Salvation depended on our carrying out the Council of the Servants of God given to us this night. He had a good opportunity of seeing many young men who were very wild in their habits, and about Sixty of them he had called, and sent them on a home Mission and were doing remarkably well. He also recommended the same course through this valley, and urged emphatically the establishment of home Manufacture. &c.

Elder Joseph F. Smith, said he had many ~~of~~ enquiries of brethren going on the Southern [Utah exploration] Mission, which he had not the ability to answer, and suggested that the Bishops of each ward should collect together those in their Wards and council them. He was gratified to listen to the projects suggested this evening, for the building up of Zion.

We should make our own Iron, our Shovels, Spades &c. In looking over those articles used in his own house, ^he noticed^ most of them were imported from abroad. The Lord aid the President and the people in carrying out these things.

There was a vast amount of Gentileism in our youth that ~~are~~ have received their education from Morgans College,[50] University [of Deseret][51] &c for they had learned to smoke & other evil habits but he did not ^charge this upon the Teachers^ and he did not want his children to grow up in any such ways.

The School was then adjourned for one week at 7 oclock pm. After singing Benediciton by Prest B Young.

March 31, 1873; Monday

The School of the Prophets met in the City Hall at 7 oclock ^pm^. Present Prest B[righam] Young presiding. After singing Roll called. Prayer by B[isho]p L[orenzo] D[ow] Young.

Elder J[oseph] F. Smith said he had received ~~one~~ ^a^ report ^from^ West Jordan Ward that 15 Men and one woman had left that Ward for the Arizona Mission, with everything necessary for self preservation, and the opening up of a new country.

Prest B Young said it was his intention to offer his resignation ~~of~~ as Trustee in trust [of the Church], and should urge its acceptance, at Conference, [at which] it would be necessary for another one to act in that capacity, and he suggested that eight others be appointed ~~to~~ as his assistants, each of whom would have to give security according to the laws of our Territory. He then suggested the following ~~m~~ [:] John L. Smith,[52] Legrand Young, Elijah F. Sheets John Sharp, Jos[ep]h W. Young, Moses Thatcher,[53] ^&^ Jos[ep]h F. Smith; Moved by Prest

50. Morgan Commercial College, founded in Salt Lake City in 1867 by John H. Morgan (1842–94) and serving as many as 900 students, inspired the rejuvenation of the moribund University of Deseret. Unable to compete with Deseret, Morgan closed his school in 1874. He thereafter served in the Utah legislature and was called as president of the Southern States mission and then named to the presidency of the Seventy. Richardson, *Life and Ministry of John Morgan*.

51. The University of Deseret held classes in the downtown Council House and would not move up the hill to its current location (changing its name to University of Utah in 1892) until 1900.

52. John L. Smith (1828–98) was an attorney who had been president of the Swiss Mission, 1855–57, and Italian Mission, 1860–64, and had worked in the LDS Historian's Office. His older brother, George A. Smith, was first counselor in the First Presidency and would become the new trustee-in-trust on his return from a mission to the Holy Land.

53. Apostle Moses Thatcher (1842–1909) had arrived in Utah as a child. He founded Thatcher Brothers' Bank, Thatcher & Son general store in Logan, and other establishments, while serving as superintendent of Utah Northern Railroad. In 1896 he refused to submit to First Presidency oversight in politics and was dropped from the Quorum of the Twelve.

D[aniel] H. Wells, and Seconded by Elder Geo Q. Cannon That those names be accepted.

Prest D. H. Wells made a few remarks on the present being a suitable time for Prest Youngs resignation, both on account of his advanced age, and the accumulated cares of the Church.

Prest B Young said he wanted to throw off his business cares, connected with the Bank, Co operative Inst[itutio]n, Railroads, and as Trustee in trust, [and] when liberated from these responsibilities he expected to be just as much engaged in giving council to the brethren, as he has ~~done~~ been heretofore.

Elder Geo Q Cannon said he felt really pleased, and was satisfied it was the mind and will of God, that Prest B Young should take the course he ^had^ now determined on, for he was well aware that one chief design of all the Bills that they have tried to pass ^through^ Congress ^were intended^ ~~was~~ to entangle Prest Young with vexatious law suits, and if possible to strip him of all he possesses and ~~if possible~~ ^also^ to get a haul from [from taxes on] back tithing.

Prest Young then asked the School to suggest 6 more names [as assistants to the trustee-in-trust].

Elder Rob[er]t L. Campbell made a few remarks of sanction to the present movement.

~~The names of Horace S. Eldredge & A[braham] O Smoot, were named by Bro R[obert] L Campbell & Jos[ep]h S. Smith & John Van Cott, ^President J D T M[cAllister] and A M[ilton] Musser.~~

Elder Geo Q Cannon much prefered leaving the entire choice to Prest Young.

B[isho]p E[dwin] D. Woolley fully endorsed bro Geo Q Cannon's suggestion, and also of Prest Youngs resignations being a wise and timely circumstance.

Prest B Young ~~Mo[ved]~~ spoke of the necessity of having a Clerk appointed to act ~~as~~ at our General Conference—and he Moved and was Seconded That George Goddard be presented ~~at~~ before the Conference for that purpose.

Prest Young suggested the proposition that Himself, & family his Sons and Son in laws, retire to a place by themselves and establish a stake of Zion, and shew the people how to live as one family, he wished the brethren to think it over by next meeting.

The School was adjourned for two weeks ~~to~~ at the old Tabernacle at 4 o clock pm.[54] Benediction by ^Elder^ Brigham Young Jun[io]r.

D[aniel] McArthur,[55] Tho[ma]s Taylor, F[rederick] A. Mitchell, Ja[me]s P. Freeze John Van Cott, and A M[ilton] Musser were also suggested as assistants to the Trustee in trust.

April 14, 1873; Monday

The School of the Prophets met in the Old Tabernacle at 4 o clock pm, as per adjournment. Present Prest B[righam] Young presiding. After singing Prayer by Elder D[imick] B. Huntington. Roll called.

Prest B Young spoke with much encouragement on the present condition of the Kingdom of God, & we should be very humble and grateful to our Heavenly Father, and live our religion. He really believed also that the Lamanites [Native Americans] would shortly receive the Gospel, and that while the Government will seek to destroy them, our hands ~~by them~~ will be strengthened. Last summer a Gentlemen from Mexico called on him, and told him of ^the^ real feelings of the Indians in that Country, and said they were utterly tired of and disgusted with the Catholic Faith, and that he had come here to get acquainted with this people &c.

Prest B Young refer'd to the effect that the 14th Amendment act will be likely to have towards the Lamanites, in not only giving them the right of Citizenship, but give them also a legal power to obtain from Government a just and equitable price for all the Land they have ever taken away from them.

Elder D[imick] B. Huntington gave an interesting account of some of the Lamanites, who are looking for the judgements of God to come upon this wicked nation, and were willing to do anything or go anywhere Prest Young might say. He begged of the brethren to pray for the Lamanites that they might come to a Knowledge of the truth. That God would visit them with dreams and visions.

B[isho]p E[dward] Hunter spoke of the kind and good feelings of the Indians, whom he ^had^ taken much pleasure in supplying their wants according to the wishes of Prest Young. They possessed noble

54. April 7 was general conference, so no meeting would be held.

55. Daniel D. McArthur (1820–1908) was the presiding bishop in southern Utah, later president of the St. George Stake for three years before losing his eyesight and being released.

feelings of friendship and independence of Character, and he believed that God approved of a kind and generous treatment towards them.

School was adjourned for one week at 4 pm at the old Tabernacle. After singing Benediction by Elder John Van Cott.

April 21, 1873; Monday

The School of the Prophets met in the Old Tabernacle at 4 pm. Present Prest B[righam] Young presiding. After singing Prayer by Elder Henry Groo. Roll was called.

Elder B[righam] Young Jun[io]r suggested that some of the most particular friends and who are best posted with the country & particular location where Joseph [Smith] the Prophet received the first revelation, ^should^ ~~and then~~ trace on Map from there through his future travels in connexion with the early incidents of his History, which to him would be very interesting.[56]

The brethren did not seem to be prepared to speak on the subject.

Elder Angus Cannon said he understood that the U[nion] P[acific] R[ail] R[oad] was bringing the Rocky Mountain Coal [in Colorado] cheaper than they will bring coal from Weber [Davis County] and that our own line sustains them and works with them in that Monopoly, and that if that is not corrected, our brethren will certainly have to abandon their labour, and that our mines will soon be in ~~th~~ hands of outside Capitolists.

Prest B Young, said, that time and circumstances alone can rectify what Bro Angus complains of [railroad fares]—they could not entertain the subject here. He said he had no objection for some one to go back and search out the early locations where Joseph commenced ~~his~~ the latter day work. He also expressed a strong desire to make some change in the education of our children, that some good solid reading might be placed in their hands that will strengthen their faith in the truth, ~~rathern than~~

He also spoke of the sin and ruinous consequences of unlawful intercourse with the sexes. Also the importance of carrying out his councils given at conference in reference to our becoming self sustaining.

Elder Orson Pratt, very much regretted the loose morals among many portions of our youth. He thought much good might be done by

56. A map of church history sites, in other words.

the teachers, who should not be stereotyped in their questions but endeavour to find out the real condition of every family, and instruct them in their duties. In some wards there are many families who are seldom if ever visited by Teachers. He also spoke of much ignorance existing in the country settlements on the principle of Plurality. He was however pleased with the general display of home made clothing among the brethren & Sisters.

He felt much interested of late, in reading the Book of Mormon, in relation to the near approach of the time when the Lamanites will take hold of this latter day work,—for they are the ones, who are to build the New Jerusalem in Jackson Co[unty] [Missouri].

Elder R[obert] L. Campbell said almost 20 years ago, he wrote a letter to Prest Young in reference to inculcating the principles of the Gospel in our ordinary routine of educational studies. He was willing to labour night or day in this great work. When visiting schools, he often asked the children if they prayed &c. He also informed the Bishops that the Deseret University were willing to educate from one to two from each ward—gratuitously to prepare them to operate as Teachers.

Elder G[eorge] Q. Cannon in speaking of the immense amount of labour & responsibilities that are forcing themselves upon the Elders of Israel, seemed to him, to demand a classification of labour so as to render our efforts more effective. He lamented the great neglect of Teachers in visiting Families, and the loose habits observable in our young people, their proneness to read light and trifling lit~~t~~erara~~g~~ture, using obscene language, &c. He prayed that God would inspire our hearts to attend more fully to look after these things &c.

~~Benedic~~ Meeting adjourned for one week at 4 pm. Benediction by Elder E[lias] Smith.

April 28, 1873; Monday

The School of the Prophets met in the old Tabernacle as per adjournment, at 4 o clock pm. Present Prest B[righam] Young presiding.

Elder Geo Q Cannon spoke on the subject of starting a family organization, as suggested by Prest Young some weeks ago, who desired the Elders to reflect upon it, And then express their views as to his commencing the Order of Enoch with his own family. ~~H~~ Elder G. Q. then spoke of the success that attended the Nephites in living under that Order for nearly 200 years, during that period, they were prospered exceedingly, and the blessing of the Lord rested upon them, but afterwards they gradually fell into Classes, many grew very rich, and became proud, gradually sinking into sin and wickedness. Our present situation is getting into a similar condition, ~~we are g~~ some ~~of~~ are becoming rich, and as a consequence, look down upon the poor, ^&c^ ~~some are~~, hence we are falling into distinct classes, according to the temporal circumstances & position of each. There are almost every kind of evil practises thrust upon us, and many of our people are being entangled by them—and unless something is done, we will become a fearful prey to the pressure of surrounding circumstances. He therefore hailed the day when we could ^enter^ into the holy order of God, and thus become one [cooperative] in Temporal things, when such was the case, God our Heavenly Father would signally display his power in our behalf, selfishness would die out, and the principles of the Kingdom of God would triumph over the narrow ^&^ contracted views of the world.

Elder John Taylor refered to the peculiar spirit of the age when the ^order of^ Enoch was entered into by the people spoken of by Bro Geo Q Cannon, ours is a very different time, and the ~~s~~ present Spirit of the times is altogether different to theirs. What ^ever^ the Lord requires at the hands of this people, he believed that a great many of them ~~people~~ would respond ^to^ it. We expect to be guided and dictated by him, not only in our Spiritual but our Temporal concerns. We are his people, and we must be subject to him in all of our affairs. He did not believe it possible to establish a perfect Government, amongst a mixed and corrupt people, hence the necessity of doing what God requires—~~the~~ and whatever he makes ~~makes~~ manifest through his ~~servants~~ servants, will ~~result~~ ^terminate^ in the most happyfying and glorious results to the Saints of the most High, and the building up of the Kingdom of God. He prophesyed this in the name of Jesus Christ.

Elder Orson Pratt had reflected much on this subject for many years, if the time had come when we as a people are to enter into our stewardships, ^he asked^ who are the persons to be appointed to receive our consecrations? He thought the Bishops would be the ones, as being compatible with the revelation on the subject. When this order is carried out fully, there will doubtless be some idlers, but the Lord has provided what should be done with such. This order existed ~~on~~ on North and South America amongst Millions of people for 167 years.[57] He then suggested a modus operandi for this order to be commenced and carried out, according to the plan that was to be carried out in Jackson Co[unty] M[iss]o[uri]. We never can build up Zion, nor convert the Lamanites, until we become united Temporally in all our property. He thought it would require a commencement in some new place, ~~&~~ instead of any old ~~place~~ ^Settlement.^

Prest B Young, said ^can^ we establish Zion until we learn how—but [if we begin,] we may learn to live as the inhabitants of Zion. He thought it would never do for this principle to be commenced in a family capacity—such a plan would lead to covetousness & separation—but by a Mixture ^of^ persons and Nationalities. We want to pattern after the heavenly order, if we can, God has not the least objection for us to try. One of the strongest proofs of ~~t~~ us being the friends of God is the hatred that the world have towards us. When once we begin this order, he wanted to organize it, so that we would never more be the subject to be interfered with by Lawyers. Should ~~we~~ any ever apostatize, they will not take anything with them; We must enter into an everlasting Covenant with each other, that cannot be broken, to serve God and keep his commandments, such a people would be his people, they would be his Fathers, his Mothers, his Brothers & his sisters, and if any of his Family would not go with him, among such a people and for such a purpose, they might go there own way.

The School was adjourned~~nt~~ for one week at 4 o clock pm. Benediction by Prest Elias Smith.

May 5, 1873; Monday

The School of the Prophets met at 4 oclock pm. Present Prest B[righam] Young presiding. After singing Prayer by Elder W[illiam] Thorne. Singing.

Elder Geo Q. Cannon said the [general] Conference closed before a further selection of High Councillors being [had been] appointed, [so] there are more needed, in order to obtain a full quorum whenever needed. He also stated that a number of aged Brethren was needed

57. Pratt is referring to Book of Mormon times, probably the span from 34 CE to 201 CE (3 Ne. 26:19; 4 Ne. 1:24).

throughout the Territory to act as Patriarchs. The following names were presented & sustained,

as High Councillors

Thos. Williams	Geo Nebeker	Milando Pratt
John R. Winder	Angus M Cannon	Geo J Taylor
A[lexander] C Pyper	Joseph Horne	John Sharp Junr.
C[harles] R Savage	Hy[ram] T Richards	Robt. F. Neslen
& Geo B Spencer		

for Patriarchs

W[illia]m Hyde	Joseph L. Heywood
Geo Lake	Phineas Richards
W[illia]m Budge	Erastus Bingham
Elias Smith	Prest. Jos[ep]h Young Sen
Aaron Johnson	D[imick] B. Huntington
Lorenzo W Young	Evan M. Greene
Thos Kington	Lorenzo H. Hatch
Ezra Chase	Thos. Callister
James Rawlins	Edwd. Hunter
Jonathan Pugmire	Gardner Snow
Levi Jackman	Father [Anson] Call
Levi Richards	Father ^Beryl^ Covington
David W Rogers	Father [Chauncey] Loveland
David Cluff Senr	Father [Samuel] Alger
Eleazer Miller	Father [William] Alford
Jesse N. Perkins	Absalom P Free
Lyman A Shurtliff	Lyman Leonard

Elder W[ilford] Woodruff felt very thankful for the changes that are now being made, especially in the Temporal affairs of the Kingdom of God, a vast amount of responsibilities had been upon the shoulders of Prest Young for a long time as the leading Spirit of all the great enterprizes in our midst, such as the Railroad, Zions Co ope[rativ]e Mercantile Inst[itutio]n. The Bank &c. He felt that the Kingdom of God was moving onward at a very rapid ^rate^ hence the necessity of new offices, and more good men being called into active service, not only in Temporal but spiritual things. Was much pleased with the Patriarchal Ordination being extended to others, to meet the growing wants of the people.

Elder John Taylor fully endorsed the above sentiments, could see great wisdom in what the Lord was doing through his servant, Brigham, it was his privelege as our Prophet, Seer & Revelator to ~~look~~ hold communion with, and ~~hold~~ receive revelations from God, and it was also our privelege, who hold the Priesthood, to receive the same spirit, he spoke very encouragingly on the future glory and destiny of this people, and prayed that God would bless continually his servant Brigham.

B[isho]p E[dward] Hunter spoke of his early experience with much pleasure.

The following names were also added as Patriarcks

Daniel Shearer
Benjn. Brown
Albert Merrill
Wm Burgess
Geo A Neal
Henry Herriman
Ezra Oakly

John Vance
Jas. Turnbull
Charles Edwards
Jeremiah Woodbury
Jesse P. Harmon
Wm. Stewart
David Fullmer

John Doolittle
Geo Bundy
Horace Gibbs
Saml. Merrill
Levi Hancock
~~Benjn. Brown~~

The School was adjourned for one week at 4 oclock pm. Benediction by B[isho]p N Davis.

May 12, 1873; Monday

The School of the Prophets met in the old Tabernacle at 4 o clock pm. Present Prest B[righam] Young presiding. After singing Prayer by Elder J[ohn] R Winder. Singing. Roll was called.

Prest Elias Smith admitted having a natural timidity in discharging religious duties, but felt that he was pretty faithful in temporal affairs. He felt honored in being a member of this school, had endeavoured to observe the rule of secrecy as to what transpires here, and shown from his own experience the necessity of being very cautious in answering questions, especially when any legal point is involved. He had no doubts in regards to the Gospel, but [had] all the trials that he could possibly get along with. He always tried to think twice before he spoke once. Nothing was so precious to him as Salvation, and while a young man had any amount of Religion offered him from the various sects of the day, but could not embrace it, there was too much inconsisten~~t~~cy about their doctrines, but had a strong desire to learn truth before he died, that appertained to this life and a future state. About this time he embraced the Gospel, and hoped to live long enough to finish the work he came here to do. He had a great dislike to sit in Judgment between two brethren who had a difficulty. When^ever^ he heard any one say that I have served the church long enough, I shall now work for and serve myself, ^he deemed such an one on the high road to apostacy.^ He hoped the Order of Enock would soon be introduced to destroy the principle of selfishness that so distressingly makes itself manifest, in members of the same family where a few dollars are involved.

Elder A M[ilton] Musser said these meetings had a stimulating influence on the minds of the Elders. God our heavenly Father, like a good earthly parent gives many and frequent lessons to his children. He deprecated the idea of ^Parents^ leaving property to children unless the wills were so arranged as to finally come into the P[erpetual] E[migrating] Fund or some other of our public institutions. There are but few children that can duly appreciate something for nothing, or to use property aright, that they had no hand in producing. He hoped these schools would be kept up, for the benefit of the Elders.

Elder Orson Pratt approved fully of the sentiments expressed by the previous speakers. The Doctrine and Covenants teaches that Parents who have property[,] [who are] in the Church, should leave and will that to the Church instead of to their children, and for the Children to receive their inheritance from the Church, the same as their parents, and let them go to and improve the same. If there was any way of making our property safe for the use of the Church, without lawyers being able to get ^it^ by the instigation of the children, he should be glad.

Prest D[aniel] H Wells esteemed the law of Inheritance as one of the strongest laws of God. The early disciples could not or did not succeed in carrying out the law they tried to establish in their day, by having all things common. In our day, at the present time, we have not been able to see and comprehend the law sufficiently, as to give it a practical shape, we are living in a ~~world~~ wicked world, and have many evil influences to contend with. We should combine our interests for the general good, but whether it would not curtail individual enterprize, by having all things ^in^ common, ~~or by each individual labour and efforts~~ ^was to him a serious question.^

Our own best interests are enhanced, while we are seeking with our might to establish and build up the Kingdom of God. Even [Every]

Man ~~should~~ in Israel should be put where his labours will be the most useful and subserve the most good in the Kingdom of God. If every man is rewarded according to his works, this very principle brings all men on [i]nequality[;] some will necessarily receive more than others, and some less. He did not believe there was any Law ~~necessarily~~ that would prevent a rich man from entering into the Kingdom of Heaven. ^The more means a good man has, the more gigantic enterprizes he can take hold of and accomplish.^ We have no right to use our means for anything but what tends to build up the Kingdom of God.

For every man to have accorded unto him, ~~that~~ ^what^ he can use for building up Zion, this is what I regard equality. Our children have got to act out their agency, ~~and~~ ^they^ have minds of their own, and must meet the evils and temptations that are in the world. Who could not but rejoice to see their children rise up, in their might and strength, to enhance the stability of their fathers house.

School was adjourned for one week at 4 o clock pm. Benediction by B[isho]p F[rederick] Kesler.

May 19, 1873; Monday

On ~~Satur~~ The School of the Prophets met in the old Tabernacle at 4 o clock pm. Present Prest B[righam] Young presiding. Prayer by B[isho]p A[lexander] McRae. Roll called.

Prest B Young suggested to the school that a number of young men be sent as Missionaries to the Sandwich [Hawaiian] Islands, and if any of the brethren had Sons suitable for such a Mission he wished them to report the same. One of his boys [Brigham Morris Young], also [a boy] of Judge [Elias] Smiths were going.[58]

He then ~~mentioned~~ ^made^ enquiry of some of the brethren, as to how they understood the remarks made at the previous school by Bro D[aniel] H Wells and Orson Pratt on the subject of the Order of Enock.

Elders Geo Goddard, & Geo B. Wallace remarked that they [Wells and Pratt] expressed different views on the subject, according to their understanding. The Clerk was then requested to read the minutes of said Meeting.

Prest Young said in speaking on a subject of such importance, no two

58. The seven missionaries called in 1873 included Brigham Young's son Brigham M., John Taylor's son Richard, and Edwin D. Woolley's son Hyrum, but no son of Elias Smith.

could express themselves in precisely the same words, yet their meaning and ideas of ~~the subject~~ ^it^ might be identical, he so regarded and understood Bros Wells & Pratt at our last meeting.

Elder Z[erubbabel] Snow then came in the school by letter of invitation—and Prest Young ^said^ that an unpleasant altercation had taken place between himself and Bro Snow at the Court House, and wished to have the case laid before the school. He said that a difficulty existed between B[isho]p [Frederick] Kesler and Wife about the division of property, and he sent him to Z[erubbabel] Snow, attorney with a request that he would conduct the case in Court for ~~for~~ him, as she had taken it before the District Court. Bro Kesler went to him and stated his case, wishing him to act for him, but Bro Snow refused. He then told him he was sent by Prest Young, whose council ~~it~~ was for Z[erubbabel] Snow to conduct the case. Bro Snow, then said as long as he himself acted under Prest Youngs Council, he had always been a poor man, but when I declared my manhood, and acted without his council, I have prospered.

The above was stated to me [Brigham Young] by Bro Kesler. A few days after[,] I saw Bro Snow at the Court House, and asked him if he made use of those words to him, and he said, If I did say so, every word of it is true, and I told him every word of it was false. I then reminded him of the assistance the church had rendered him, and Bro Snow possitively denied that he had received ^even as much^ as a Meal of Victuals from the church.

Bro Z[erubbabel] Snow admitted that he had spoken very rashly and improperly to Prest Young, while in a violent passion and at the spur of the moment, and on future reflection had occasioned [in] ^him^ very unpleasant feelings, he also admitted that what he said while in a passion, would soon be forgotten by him as to what he did say, and after expressing regret at his conduct, he asked forgiveness of Prest Young, which was freely granted, by extending to him the right hand of fellowship, hoping he would in the future be more guarded. An example was thus set by the President of the ~~School~~ Church, to the members of the school, of Stooping to Conquer, or extending forgiveness to one who has trespassed, which spoke in unmistakable language to all present, that under similar circumstances, Go and do thou likewise.

After singing, Benediction by Elder Geo C. Riser.

May 26, 1873; Monday

The School of the Prophets met in the old Tabernacle at 4 o clock pm, as per adjournment. Present Prest D[aniel] H Wells presiding. After singing Prayer by Elder James Leach.

Elder D[imick] B Huntington gave an interesting account of several tribes of Indians, who are getting exceeding angry, towards the Government, and the Government Officials for deceiving them so many times, he was satisfied that Zions redemption was near at hand, and Prophesied that the House of Israel would soon come in by hundreds and thousands to be taught of the Lord, and he hoped therefore that the Brethren would speak ^kindly^ to the Indians, and feed them. He wished the Church or the City would build a room on his lot that he could accommodate them with lodgings when they come in, which they often do, by 20, 30 or 40 at a time.

Elder W[ilford] Woodruff spoke of the drivings and fightings of the Indians by the Government, the hand of the Lord was over that people, there is a great work for them to do, in building up Zion & the New Jerusalem, they will certainly be inspired, and ^receive^ revelations from God, and we who have come into the Gospel a little before them, ~~and we~~ should exercise faith for them, and pray for them. A few days ~~or~~ after they came into the Vallies, they saw a few Indians who came to their camp, and they gave them some bread[.] Since that time, we have grown and the Lord has blest us, and the Indians are better fed and clothed than they were. We have many duties to perform towards the Indians. God alone is our friend, and the Lamanites around us, had they ~~h~~ not been a portion of the House ~~Indians~~ of Israel they would have been cut off root and branch long ago. They are of the seed of Joseph, and God requires us to look after their salvation. He prophesied in the name of the ~~name of the~~ Lord Jesus Christ that this Government ^or Nation^ was nearly ripe for the Damnation of Hell. He spoke of the first Elders of the Church who had been taken away [to heaven], for a wise purpose, [because] it was necessary for an organization in this dispensation [to exist] behind the vail—he believed that Joseph [Smith] had lived his time out and done his work. Let us do right, build up Zion, and establish the Kingdom, keep the commandments of God, and no earthly power can drive us from these vallies.

D[imick] B. Huntington said some two or three hundred of the

Indians had been baptized, ~~an~~ up North by Bro Hill,[59] some 30 or 40 came down to see Prest [Brigham] Young, and Bro Demick ordained two of the Chiefs as Elders of the Church of Jesus Christ of Latter day Saints, and while his hands were upon their head he felt that the prophesy~~s~~ was being fulfilled, when a Nation should be born in a day.

Prest D H Wells hoped the brethren would preserve the rule of this school by keeping secret what transpires here—and he hoped that Demick would not implicate himself of this people by untimely council that could be used in a Court against us, let us do the Indians all the good we can, but be wise in what we say or do. The work of the Lord will go on in their midst, and will shew them that we are their friends, and that He is their friend.

The Dominion will pass from the Gentiles into the hands of the House of Israel, and no power can prevent it. Let us be careful how we act, this will be a gradual work, and God will carry it on, we can baptize and Ordain the Indians, preach the Gospel and the Lord will carry out his purposes. The blessing of the Lord rests upon us, and none can see the kingdom except the few that subscribe to & accept the terms the Lord has made down.

The School was adjourned for one week at 4 o clock pm. After singing Benediction by Henry Grow.

June 2, 1873; Monday

The School of the Prophets met in the Old Tabernacle at 4 o clock pm. Present Prest D[aniel] H Wells presiding. After singing Prayer by Elder Sam[ue]l L. Evans. Roll called.

Elder Levi Richards, enquired if ^it^ was justifiable for us to introduc~~ing~~e ~~foreign~~ ^artificial^ diseases into our system. Small pox, for instance by Vaccination, the practise of which he very much deprecated, and was more to be dreaded than the small pox itself. Small pox taken naturally was not so dangerous in its consequences as the Measles. We ought as a people to understand about these things, and not send for a Doctor for every ailment that overtakes us.

---

59. George Washington Hill (1822–91), an early settler of Ogden, came into contact with Shoshone Indians and learned some of their language. This was probably why he was chosen in 1855 to accompany two dozen other men on a mission to the Indians in the Salmon River area of Idaho, where they established Fort Limhi. Brown, "Life and Missionary Labors of George Washington Hill," 30–31.

B[isho]p A[lonzo] H. Raleigh, said he was appointed to wait upon several Doctors some time ago, learned from them that all the injury ~~that~~ liable to acrue from Vaccination was a skin disease.

Elders Tho[ma]s Taylor, Geo Goddard, N[athaniel] H Felt, ^&^ Isaac Groo, spoke on the subject, most of whom believed that Vaccination partially warded off the severe form of small pox.

Elder Levi Richards condemned in unmeasured terms the use of Poisons as Medicine, and advocated the Thompsonian practise[60] as being equal to every ~~spe~~ kind of disease.

Elder Isaac Groo said his Father when about 40, died under the Thompsonian treatment, and ^he^ had consequently a very great aversion to that practise.

Elder S[amuel] L Evans gave some of his experience in relation to sickness, had to do with the old school practise, as well as more simple remedies, but could not condemn either.

Elder Levi Richards again advocated natural remedial agents for the cure of all diseases.

School was adjourned for one week at 4 o clock pm. After singing Benediction by Elder D[imick] B. Huntington.

June 9, 1873; Monday

The School of the Prophets met in the Old Tabernacle at 4 o'clock p.m. Present Prest Brigham Young, Presiding. Prayer by William Hickenlooper. Roll called.

Prest D[aniel] H. Wells remarked that Prest Young touched on certain principles and doctrine yesterday,[61] and particularly that doctrine pertaining to Adam being our Father & our God, and thought this was a proper place to call for the minds of the brethren and learn whether we as a school endorse the doctrine.[62]

He bore a powerful testimony to the truth of the doctrine, remarking that if ever he had received a testimony of any doctrine in this Church he had of the truth of this. The Endowments plainly teach it and the Bible & other revelations are fully of it.

The ~~principle~~ doctrine was approved or endorsed by Henry Grow,

60. Samuel Thomson (1769–1843) advocated that people should be their own doctors and use common herbs and plants, especially lobelia, although it was itself an emetic poison.

61. See Van Wagoner, *Complete Discourses of Brigham Young*, 5:2968–74.

62. See Jan. 24, 1868, entry.

D[imick] B. Huntingdon, & Joseph F. Smith. The latter read a portion of a revelation given to the Church, ^page 2[01] Doc. & Cov.^ affirming that Michael or Adam is the Father of all—the Prince of all, and stated that the enunciation of that doctrine, gave him great joy.[63] A[lonzo] H. Raleigh said he had never heard any one dispute the doctrine, to him it was perfectly natural, as was every other principle of the Gospel when understood.[64]

Prest Young queried whether the brethren thought he was too liberal in launching out on this doctrine before the Gentiles. He was positive on the truth of the doctrine, but thought we should be cautious about preaching on doctrines unless we fully understand them by the power of the Spirit, then they commend themselves to the hearts of our hearers. Spoke of the vain theories of men[65] with regard to the Great first Cause. Said there were many revelations given to him that he did not receive from the Prophet Joseph [Smith]. He did not receive them through the Urim and Thummim as Joseph did but when he did receive them he knew of their truth as much as it was possible for ~~them~~ him to do of any truth. He thought it advisable to adjourn the School, as it was a busy time and only about one third of the brethren present.[66]

John Lyon fully endorsed the ~~princip~~ doctrine, but asked explanation why the Scriptures seemed to put Jesus Christ on an equal footing with the Father.

Prest Young replied that the writers of those scriptures wrote according to their best language and understanding.

Geo B. Wallace endorsed the doctrine—& narrated a dream he received in answer to prayer, shewing that many worlds were made to God because he had many wives.

Joseph F. Smith said ~~he did not believe~~ "a man could ~~enter~~ ^not attain^ unto ~~the~~ ^a^ fullness of ^the^ glory ^of the Father^, who did not take to himself more than one wife."

---

63. The wording "Michael, or Adam, the father of all, the prince of all, the ancient of days" comes from 50:2 of the Liverpool Doctrine and Covenants (now 27:11).

64. In the top margin of the next page, the words "delineate upon them" are written, without any noticeable connection to any other text.

65. In addition to "the vain theories of men," Young may have had the theology of Orson Pratt in mind. Pratt objected to Young's teaching about Adam. See Bergera, *Conflict in the Quorum.*

66. The school would adjourn for a month and reconvene on July 7, 1873.

School adjourned until the first Monday in July at 4 p.m. at this place.[67]

July 7, 1873; Monday

The School of the Prophets met in the old Tabernacle at 4 oclock pm as per adjournment on June 9th. Present Prest B[righam] Young presiding. After singing Prayer by B[isho]p E[lijah] F. Sheets. Singing.

Prest Young said he had talked a good deal lately to the Bishops and at other places on the principles of tithing, he would now like to hear remarks from his brethren on the same subject.

Elder Geo Q Cannon felt that God was moving upon his servant Brigham in reference to tithing, for unless something was done to wake up the people on that subject, we are as a people exposed to the anger and indignation of the Almighty. He would far rather turn over all his property to the Church than be subjected to the influence of Mobocracy. We cannot trifle with God, with impunity, he will not be mocked. We are menaced at the present time by the greatest of dangers, and unless we take the warning that is now given us, nothing but trouble is ahead of us Unless we as Bishops & Apostles & Elders catch and reecho the warning notes as they proceed from his Servant Brigham, and ~~close~~

Elder John Taylor did not regard the law of tithing as simply having to do with Dollars and Cents—but also as a test of our Faith, it being one of many other duties required at our hands as professed latter day saints. If we neglect our duty God will chastise us. He would much rather ^we should^ so live before the Lord, that we can have confidence in God. If we have laws and dont keep them something must be done either to turn us out, or be chastised until we do. He feels that his Servant Brigham is right and ought to be sustained.

Prest B Young said one of the commandments of God was to keep the Sabbath day holy, and meet often to look after the Widow & the Fatherless—and pay our Tithing, which is One tenth of our property, and then one tenth of our income. We ought to get from our ~~Mechanics~~ City ~~or~~ brethren at least $2000.00 daily. He felt that the Words of the Lord through his mouth spoken to the Bishops two weeks last Thursday [were as gentle burdens] dropp'd at their feet, as the words of an old song.[68] A portion of the law of God is for us to build Temples we have

67. The entry is unsigned but written in a different hand than George Goddard's.

68. One verse of "How Gentle God's Commands" reads: "His goodness stands approved, / Unchanged from day to day; / I'll drop my burden at his feet / And bear a song away."

got either to put them up ourselves, or assist with our Means, to pay those who are willing to do the work.

~~Prest.~~ School was adjourned for one week at 4 o clock pm. Elder Henry Grow Dismissed the Meeting.

July 14, 1873; Monday

The School of the Prophets met in the old Tabernacle at 4 o clock pm. Present Prest B[righam] Young presiding. Roll called. After Singing Prayer by S[amuel] A. Woolley.

Prest ~~Geo A S~~ B Young read a Circular recently issued by B[isho]p [Edward] Hunter & Council to the B[isho]ps throughout the Territory, and much objected to the use of his own name being used therein so prominently, which placed him in the eyes of the world as a Target to shoot at.[69]

B[isho]p E[dward] Hunter much regretted that he had ^not^ first presented a Copy before it was printed, to Prest Young, and he unterly repudiated the idea of injuring Prest Young by using his name in it.

Prest Young did not doubt for a moment the integrity of B[isho]p Hunter, or his Councillors, but regarded it as ^a^ serious lack of wisdom.

Elder Geo Goddard testified to the earnest and zealous feelings of B[isho]p Hunter & J[esse] C. Little in getting up that circular, desiring to act promptly in waking up the people to the payment of their tithing. Elder A M[ilton] Musser fully endorsed the above sentiments of the last speaker.

Prest Geo A Smith Motioned and John Sharp seconded That what Circulars have been sent out, should be recalled and another one issued as just read by Elder D[avid] McKenzie. "Carried unanimously."

Prest Geo A Smith made several remarks on the coming Election which comes off on the 4th August, and desired the brethren to be wide awake in the important duty of voting for whoever might be Nominated.

B[isho]p A[lonzo] H Raleigh recommended every Man occupying a prominent position, assuming the responsibility, that the spirit of his calling will [be] naturally suggest[ed] to him if he lives in the line of his duty.

69. The circular divulged that the church had amassed a debt of $30,000 toward the Salt Lake Temple, which was still twenty years away from completion. It alerted non-tithe-payers that they would no longer be allowed to partake of the sacrament. Hunter, Hardy, and Little to LDS bishops, July 8, 1873.

The School was adjourned for one week at 4 o clock pm. Benediction by Elder Martin H. Peck.

July 21, 1873; Monday

The School of the Prophets met in the Old Tabernacle at 4 o clock pm. Present Prest B[righam] Young presiding. Roll called. Prayer by J[ohn] D. T. McAllister.

Elder Geo Q Cannon read on the subject of Tithing from 8th [verse of] Malachi and and ~~17 or~~ 27th Ch[apter] from 3. Nehemiah.

Elder W[ilford] Woodruff felt satisfied that very many of our people do not pay their tithing, he kept an account of his money receipts and the products of the earth, and paid a tenth of each. The law of tithing was of God, and none can negelect it without suffering loss, it has never been annulled, and has been in existence ever since the days of Adam, we shall prosper by keeping the commandments of God, and Visa Versa.

Elder Orson Pratt said tithing is a law, and if so, there must be a penalty attached for its non observance. It takes effect here by excommunication, but like many other laws, we have been very careless and indifferent about them. Church discipline in his opinion has been too lax, and if the workers of iniquity were dealt with according to the laws of the Church, by excommunication, it would have a good effect by dividing the righteous from the wicked.

Elder Geo Q Cannon. Unless the law of God is executed upon transgressors, there is danger of ^many^ being overcome by the Wicked practises that seem to be gaining ground at the present. The tone of the people is being lowered, and indifference to many duties is sadly on the increase. Our hearts should be free from the love of the world, and pay our tithing. Those who are determined not to work righteousness ~~th~~ should be dealt with by the Bishops, and let a dividing ^line be^ drawn. There is a class growing up in our midst, by the influence of Money, that God is not pleased with, by such inequality as now exists and as Bishops. Apostles &c we must be stirred up to use our influence—in obtaining the same spirit as Prest Young possesses.

Elder D[imick] B Huntington, bore testimony to the truth of the Gospel, and longed for the time when an entire consecration is required, to get rid of this eternal growl about paying our tithing.

Elder Geo B Wallace, thought we should do more, if we knew more.

He had been at the Bishops meeting, when tithing was discussed, and they were divided in their judgments on the subject, how then can the people be taught aright—some Wards are run by a ring, composed of some of the worst men. Complained of the slackness and indifference of Teachers in teaching the laws of God among the people.

Elder D[avid] McKenzie fully endorsed the sentiments of Bro Geo Q Cannon. ~~it w~~ Believed that tithing was a law, unless we observe it we shall be burned. Refered to the visitation of Grasshoppers as being under the direction of the Almighty.[70] The object of 9/10 of the people came here to get away from the foolish, vain, and wicked practise of the world, and it beho[o]ves us to set our faces against the first encroachments of the enemy.

Elder R[obert] L Campbell spoke more favourably of the saints in the Country, attending meetings, than those in the City. Recommended good council to be given to our young—much regretted the thin attendance at the Tabernacle, had been much exercised about tithing lately, especially about his sons tithing.

Prest B Young proposed holding two days meeting in the Tabernacle ~~a w~~ two weeks from next Saturday & Sunday, Aug[us]t 9 & 10th—he requested the brethren to make it public and come themselves.

[On the] Arizona [exploration] Mission, most of those who went there are returning. After Conference he contemplated calling 2 to 3 hundred good substantial men to accompany him, he thought of making for himself a home for a year or two, and establish a Colony. Most of the Merchants ~~as~~ will apostatize—he said it many years ago, and he did not feel to take back one word of it. No man can oppose the first Presidency and enjoy the Spirit of the Lord—and no one ~~th~~ can disregard their councils, and prosper in the things of God. ~~F~~ Most of the Sectarian Priests will be damned for their dishonesty and corruption.

Our Bishops and leading men seem blinded to the real condition of the ~~leading~~ people, they do not teach them about their duties, and neglect many duties themselves, and fail to properly instruct their people. How easy it is to see the providences of God—unless we wake up and

70. If the grasshoppers were sent as punishment for not paying tithing, it probably refers to a time of prosperity and complacency many years after the 1848 incident that later, after relying on late reminiscences, came to be known as the miracle of the seagulls. For more on that event and problems with the accounts, see Hartley, "Mormons, Crickets, and Gulls."

do our duty God will permit the wicked to find Gold, they have already found Silver & Lead, the earth is the Lords, and fulness thereof, and by and bye he will give it into the hands of the saints.

Let us then pay up our tithing, keep the Word of wisdom, go to meeting, & whatsoever we are ~~called~~ counciled to attend to. Unless we want to pay our tithing, let us unite in a co-operative capacity and sign a legal document that will bind us together as one family, ~~and~~.

School was adjourned for one week at 4 oclock pm. After singing Benediction by Bro Geo Morris.[71]

July 28, 1873; Monday

The School of the Prophets met in the Tabernacle at 4 o clock pm. Present Prest B[righam] Young presiding. Roll called. After singing Prayer by B[isho]p Tho[ma]s Jenkins.

Elder Joseph F. Smith said, in his remarks which he made at Tooele yesterday, that there was no necessity of the Holy Ghost being given to the disciples while Jesus was with them, but after He left them, the Holy Ghost was to be given them ^to be^ in the stead of Jesus Christ. He was led to make those remarks without any previous reflection, and he did not now know whether they are strictly correct or not—on reading a few passages from the New testament he thought they were correct.[72]

Elder O[rson] Pratt, read on page 45. D[octrine] [and] C[ovenants][73] showing the Father to be a personage of Spirit, and the Son a personage of tabernacle, being filled with the spirit of the Father. No man on earth can act in the name of the Father and the Son, only as they were filled by the spirit of God.

Elder A[ngus] M Cannon always had an idea that the disciples when sent out ~~to~~ by Jesus to preach & heal the sick &c, received the Holy Ghost and acted under the influence of that spirit.

Elder Geo Q Cannon refer'd to the case of the Prophet Alma [Book of Mormon] where the Holy Ghost was freely bestowed upon his

71. Just below the final words of this entry, two lines of text were erased, but some of the words can still be made out: "He wanted to introduce [illegible] the [illegible] in the church."

72. Joseph F. Smith had traveled to a conference in Tooele with Brigham Young, George Q. Cannon, and George A. Smith (*Salt Lake Daily Herald*, Aug. 3, 1873).

73. This is from the fifth Lecture on Faith in the Liverpool edition of the Doctrine and Covenants.

brethren from under his hands, and from other quotations, he thought the Holy Ghost must have been enjoyed by the servants of God before Jesus came as well as after he left.

Elder O Pratt quoted from the Book of Mormon and the pearl of great price, shewing that the Holy Ghost had been enjoyed by the people of God since the days of Adam.

Elder John W. Young, fully endorsed the remarks of Geo Q Cannon, and he also considered that it was necessary for even Jesus himself to have the Holy Ghost, as shown by what took place at his baptism.

Elder Joseph F. Smith also endorsed the same views, yet while Jesus was here, and He being greater ~~than~~ in point of Presidency & position [in the godhead], might he not perform the duties of the Holy Ghost towards his disciples. He always considered the Holy Ghost was a distinct personage in the Godhead, as much so, as either the Father or the Son. He also believed that the Holy Ghost had been enjoyed by the servants of God in all ages of the world.

Elder N[athaniel] H Felt, did not consider the Holy Ghost to be a personage ~~of~~.

Prest D[aniel] H Wells, quoted the words of John, there is one coming who is mightier than I. He shall baptize with Fire and the Holy Ghost. He always ^believed^ the Holy Ghost was a personage of Spirit that before Jesus come in the flesh, he had a body of Spirit of his ^own^ that the Father also has a spirit of his own.

Elder O Pratt, said, in a printed discourse of the Prophet Joseph [Smith], he said that the Holy Ghost was a personage of Spirit. During the personal ministry of Jesus, it was not clear to him that the personage of the Holy Ghost was given during the Saviours Ministry.

Prest B[righam] Young. The Saviour could not be preached ^as Christ crucified^ before he came in the flesh and ~~was crucified~~ ^performed his mission^. The Holy Ghost was Gods Minister, and had a tabernacle of Spirit. ~~and ministers~~ The Spirit that revealed to Peter ^that Jesus was the Christ^ came from God. In the new translation ^of the Bible^ the dove that rested upon the head of Jesus, ~~is~~ ^was^ a token or sign that he had received the Holy Ghost, and the Father was pleased with what he had done—but ^not^ until Jesus came and finished his work, ~~did~~ ^was^ the Holy Ghost ~~commenced~~ ^dispensed to all ~~t~~^ to help the Saviour in building up the Kingdom of God. ~~The spirit~~

~~proceeding from Jesus convicts men of the truth of this work, this fact makes the wicked mad, and want to fight against it~~

The Spirit of Christ rested upon the disciples when they went forth to preach and heal the sick, but the Holy Ghost was not given until Jesus ascended.[74]

The School was adjourned for two weeks at 4 pm. After singing Benediction by Elder H[oward] O Spencer.

August 11, 1873; Monday

The School of the Prophets met in the old Tabernacle at 4 oclock pm. Present Prest Geo A Smith presiding. After singing Prayer by Elder F[ranklin] D. Richards. Roll called. Prest Geo A Smith requested Bro [blank]

Elder Orson Pratt ~~wished~~ to have the subject of Carnal commandments spoken upon to day, it being touched upon by Prest [Brigham] Young yesterday.[75] The Dispensation of Moses, which contained many strict laws to the children of Israel, the breaking of which, subjected them to the penalty ^of death.^ Even breaking the Sabbath day, and disobedience to parents, subjected them to Death penalty, before [after] the law of Carnal Commandments were given.

^The following instances are under the law [:]^ Death was the penalty of Whoredom, as in the case of Tamar. Onan was also slain for spilling his seed [birth control]. Ex[odus] 19 ^ch[apter]^–12 & 13 v[erse] [states that] whoever should touch the Mountain on a certain occasion should either be shot or otherwise Killed. D[itt]o [Exodus] ^ch[apter]^ 21:12 [regarding] children smiting either Father or Mother or Cursing them where [they were] liable to [receive] death penalty. [Exodus] 30 ^ch[apter]^ [15–]20 v[erses]. To Minister befor the Alter, unless the administrator wash their hands and feet, death was the penalty. The Use of Oil for anointing purposes must not be used for any other thing else. Over 3000 were slain in one day, for worshiping the ~~35 2~~ Golden Calf.

---

74. For more on the evolution of beliefs regarding the physical characteristics of the Holy Ghost, see Bartholomew, "Textual Development of D&C 130:22"; Swanson, "Development of the Concept of a Holy Ghost."

75. According to the *Deseret News*, Young's wide-ranging sermon addressed the mission to Arizona, obedience to church leaders, and the "condition of the nations of the earth, politically, socially and religiously." Van Wagoner, *Complete Discourses of Brigham Young*, 5:2989.

Death was the penalty for breaking the Sabbath day. Priests who did not stay 7 days in the ~~temple~~ [erased] ^Tabernacle^ ~~while ministering there~~ ^who ~~had been~~ are being consecrated & set apart^ were subject to death. Death to Aarron if he came near the Mercy seat.[76] The eating of blood was forbidden on penalty of death also for eating any of the Sacrifices on the 3rd day. [Death also] for blaspheming the name of the Lord. Some of the Levites were not permitted to go into the Temple to examine the sacrifices ^covering up of the altar & sacred things^—all of those and many others are sufficient to prove the strictness of the law given to the Children of Israel through Moses.

Elder W[ilford] Woodruff said there was a great contrast between the laws refered to and the Celestial law as given through the Gospel. If the eyes of the people of this City were opened, the[y] would be more alive to their duties, and would hunger and thirst after righteousness. We are living under great privileges, and have had many keys and principles pertaining to the living and the dead. He denounced the fashions of the [people of] Babylon which are so eagerly sought after by our Wives and Daughters. We have a great amount of preaching and are more or less responsible for this privelege. Many of the Elders are giving way to smoking & Drinking &c which he was sorry to see.

Prest Jos[ep]h Young had been deprived of many meetings through sickness, was thankful to be here, did not feel really satisfied with himself, though his spirit ~~was~~ ^felt^ mighty, proving its Divinity. Did not want to abuse his family, nor ^see^ any elder in Israel abuse each other, wanted to see a people, and to be one himself, that were governed by the law of Doing to others as we would wish others to do unto us. From the Head to the foot, he wanted to see all public or private abuses cease. He wanted to see the Mayor, Councillors, Policemen act on a principle of right towards the public, and not act from selfish purposes. Was thankful for the many blessings he rec[eive]d from the hands of God. He wanted to see this Temple built. There are big things ahead of it, and we'll see them by and bye.

Elder Geo Q. Cannon [cited] 22 ^ch[apter]^ Ezekiel—threatened heavy judgments on a/c [account] of many sins comitted in Jerusalem. The penalties to be inflicted upon us for the violation of the Celestial

76. The mercy seat was part of the Ark of the Covenant, intended for God rather than for man (Ex. 25:18–22).

Law ~~he believed will be much more severe than under the Law of Carnal commandments~~. God does not require of us to be a blood shedding people, and consequently has thrown around us—a set of circumstances that would make ^it^ very impolitic to take away life.

Prest Geo A Smith desired this subject to be further investigated by the next school.

School was adjourned for one week at 4 o clock pm. After singing Benediction by B[isho]p ~~Elder~~ F[rederick] Kesler.

August 18, 1873; Monday

The School of the Prophets met in the old Tabernacle at 4 o clock pm. Present Prest D[aniel] H. Wells presiding. After singing Prayer by E[dwin] D. Woolley. Roll called.

Prest D. H. Wells said he knew it was Prest [Brigham] Youngs desire to have the subject of "The Carnal Commandments" discussed in this school, in their bearing on the Laws of the Land ~~as at present,~~ and the higher Law of the Gospel, ~~which is written on the heart~~. He also refer'd to the sins of the Fathers being visited on their Children to the 3rd and 4th generation. We believe that God is just, and ~~as to~~ ^upon^ what principle such a law can be borne out in our understanding of justice he would like to find out.

Elder Orson Pratt said there was a penalty attached to every law that God had given. There are severe penalties connected with the higher law of the Gospel, which we are all acquainted with, but those penalties may not be inflicted immediately upon the transgressor, ~~but reserved~~

He thought that God dealt with ~~the~~ his children according to the light and Knowledge they possess. The Jews who crucified the Saviour had an offer of Salvation, ^to take effect^ some 2000 years after they comply'd with the conditions of the Gospel ~~in this probation.~~ baptism excepted. He also spoke of [King] David whose sin of Murder ~~&~~ or the shedding of Innocent Blood &c, subjected him to being sent to Hell, and remain there for a long while, and probably the forfeiture of his Exaltation.[77] He refer'd also to several other instances in the Bible & Book of Mormon, which seemed to indicate that God dealt with the people according to the light and Knowledge they possessed in regard to the laws they had transgressed. There are some Laws that God has given,

77. See 2 Sam. 11–12.

that he can change according to the circumstances of the people—and there are other laws which are eternal and admits of no change.

A[lonzo] H. Raleigh said Man ^may have^ ~~has~~ been an accountable being before coming here, and consent~~ed~~^ing^ to a certain crime there, may account for the principle of visiting the sins of a Father upon ~~this~~ his Children unto the 3rd & 4th generation.[78] He also deemed the laws of God to be eternal and unchangeable, and no matter who transgresses them, whether David or Himself, the penalty would be the same.

He thought the ^Law of^ Carnal Commandments was well suited to the stiffnecked race to whom they were given—and thought they would be equally well adapted to the present generation. While Men have their free agency, they will have the chance of apostatizing a thousand years hence—as well as now &c.

B[isho]p L[orenzo] D[ow] Young did not think that God would punish a transgressor of his Law, when done in ignorance to the same extent, as when a Knowledge of that Law was well understood.

Elder Jos[ep]h F. Smith said where there is no law, there is no condemnation. So the Indian, or the Heathen who committed Murder, would not be adjudged as having committed that crime, because they dont know it to be a crime. He made a few remarks on the liberty of the Gospel, which by the righteous~~ly~~ observance of correct principles ~~they~~ ^we ~~were~~^ were ~~en~~ living in the enjoyment of the liberty of the Gospel. ~~The~~, and therefore free from sin, and under no condemnation.

Prest D. H. Wells made a few remarks, ~~on th~~ on the above subjects, and concluded that whatever God did in any dispensation was right, for he is the standard of right and had his reasons for whatever he did. He had no doubt, ~~but~~ that God mercifully ^withheld^ the Gospel from those who ~~h~~ never had it offered to them—all men have got to comply with the conditions of ^the^ Gospel either here, or hereafter. He did not know of any plan of salvation that had been ~~relieved~~ revealed to redeem a rank Apostate, who had tasted of the powers of the world to come, or the Murderers of Jesus—though~~t~~ he thought it would be better for such to repent and be converted, and do better.

78. Raleigh seems to be thinking of the pre-mortal existence and why people are born under different circumstances, implying that it could be the result of sins committed before entry into mortality.

The School was adjourned for one week at 4 o clock pm. Benediction by Ja[me]s Leach.

August 25, 1873; Monday

The School of the Prophets met in the old Tabernacle at 4 o clock pm. Present Prest D[aniel] H. Wells presiding. Prests B[righam] Young & Geo A Smith being absent on a Missionary trip to Bear Lake, Cache Valley &c. After singing Prayer by Elder Isaac Groo. Singing. Roll called. The Minutes of last school was read.

Elder O[rson] Pratt speaking of the crime of Murder, said God would inflict a penalty according to the light and Knowledge that people had of that crime, for instance, an Indian would be far less severely dealt by, than those who had embraced the Gospel, received the Holy Ghost, and tasted of the good word of God, [and] such could not be forgiven in this life, nor in the world to come—[this is] Gods dealing with his subjects, as Moral Agents, [and] it is clearly taught in the Book of Mormon, that the more enlightened ^people are^ upon the laws of God, the greater the penalty will be upon such, when they transgress—Satan[,] whose object was to destroy the Agency of Man[,] proposed to the Father, to save all the Human family, he afterwards rebelled, and one third of our brethren [in the pre-existence] fell with him.

B[isho]p [Alonzo H.] Raleigh enquired if God ~~if~~ even gave a law in any dispensation where there was any variation in the penalty by whomsoever transgressed.

Elder O Pratt said in every dispensation there are some who do not embrace it, or enter into it, therefore all such are not amenable to ^the^ revealed laws of God.

Prest D. H. Wells refered to the apostacy of those who have tasted of the powers of the world to come and ^enjoyed^ the Holy Ghost, then denying the same, [which] placed them in an awful condition, ~~had e~~ and the plan of Salvation that would take hold of such characters had never been revealed, to his knowledge. They had accepted the Atonement of Christ, and then rejected it, ~~and~~ they had exhausted therefore, the present plan of salvation, and could not repent. He thought they would become Angels to the Devil, they could ^not^ enjoy a Terra Firma Glory—but probably cast out into outer darkness ~~which~~ where no ray of light can penetrate, and which condition is fearful to contemplate.

No being could ever have ^a^ capacity to become a God without possessing Knowledge sufficient to qualify him to become a Devil. It was according to a predetermined plan devised by the Gods, that Jesus should come in the Me^ri^dian of time, and become the Saviour of the World. And as he came through Virgin Mary, ^he had to^ forget~~ting~~ his previous glory—and prove his integrity before his Father. So with us, when we came here all Knowledge of our previous existence was forgotten. Had we not have Kept our first estate, we should not have been permitted to come forth and take tabernacles [of flesh].

Let us endeavour to make our calling and Election sure, for straight is the gate and narrow is the way that leadeth to the lives, and few there be that find it. He then warned the brethren against gradual innovations of the strict plan of Salvation, which was the way the present distracted condition of the Christian world was brought about, by discarding one principle after another, until scarcely a vestige of the true order ^of the Gospel^ is traceable among them.

The ~~C~~ Law of Carnal Commandments is what all Criminal Codes in every civilized communities are based upon.

School was then adjourned for one week at 4 o clock pm. After singing Benediction by B[isho]p Tho[ma]s Jenkins.

September 1, 1873; Monday

The School of the Prophets met in the old Tabernacle at 4 pm. Present Prest D[aniel] H. Wells presiding. After singing Prayer by ^Elder^ ~~J D T McAllister~~ ^Isaac Groo.^

Elder D[imick] B. Huntington gave a very interesting account of the various tribes of Indians, where located, and their general feeling and dispositions, towards us as a people, and also towards Americans generally. Many of them are expected to come in at Conference to be baptized; quite a number were in the habit of calling upon him, when they came into the City to have a talk, and make known their wants and grievencies, he had often given them orders on B[isho]p [Edward] Hunters [storehouse] for provisions, and being short of house accommodation, the Church had Kindly permitted him to build one, especially for their use & comfort which they much appreciated.

B[isho]p [Edward] Hunter said he had ~~taken much pleas hon~~ paid Bro Demicks orders [out of the bishop's storehouse] for Flour, Butter,

&c. and sometimes meat [to Natives] and was often struck with the respect they entertained towards themselves, never feeling themselves inferior to any one they are talking to, some of them in person and features bespeak a superiority over the Chinese or Japanese, the latter he did not think were capable of receiving so great an exaltation as the Indian. ~~He~~ Saw Little Soldier[79] to day and told him he was getting old, and so am I, and when I go away, shall see [apostle] Peter an old favourite of yours and mine. He seemed to understand me, ~~and had a~~ as refering to an hereafter.

Elder Orson Pratt spoke of the exalted position the ancestors of these poor degraded people ^once^ occupied—and towards whom many prophecies had been made and fulfilled, while many others would have their accomplishment in these latter days. They are certainly destined to take an important part in the establishment of this great latter day Kingdom. Many promises and blessings were now resting on the heads of the present generation of Indians, the Lord was evidently begining to move upon many of them by his spirit, and they would soon be prepared to receive and obey the Gospel, the Arizona Mission was partly intended to bring us into a closer contact with them for that purpose.

Prest D. H. Wells recited some of his experience with the Indians many years ago, also a dream, which fully confirmed him in the correctness of the peace policy of Prest [Brigham] Young, the Arizona Mission is expected to accomplish a beneficial result among the Tribes in that region.

School was adjourned for one week at 4 pm. After singing Benediction by B[isho]p Tho[ma]s Jenkins ~~Elder Isaac Groo~~.

September 8, 1873; Monday

On ~~Thu~~ The School of the Prophets met in the Old Tabernacle at 4 o clock pm—Prest Prest Geo A Smith presiding. After singing Prayer by Elder Geo Goddard. Roll Called and Minutes of last school were read.

Prest Geo A. Smith gave an interesting account of Prest B[righam] Young and partys visit to Cache Co[unty], Bear Lake &c. There was several intricate subjects discussed from the Old Testament, such as Judah's [sexual] connexion with his daughter in law Tamar, God's connexion with ^the Virgin^ Mary ~~the~~ who was betrothed to Joseph. ~~The~~

79. Little Soldier was a prominent Shoshone chief from north of Salt Lake City in present-day Davis County.

Lots connexion with his daughters. The slaying of 70,000 in the days of David for numbering the ~~peo~~ children of Israel &c.

Meeting was adjourned for one week at 4 oclock pm. After singing Benediction by B[isho]p W. Hickenlooper.

B[isho]p L[orenzo] D[ow] Young, gave an account of a vision that ^his son^ Joseph W Young had before his death, in which he was deeply impressed with the necessity of more strictly observing the word of wisdom.[80]

Elder Geo Q. Cannon very much regretted to find a growing tendency in some of the Elders, in the use of ardent spirits & Tobacco, their breath exposed them.

September 15, 1873; Monday

The School of the Prophets met in the old Tabernacle at 4 o clock pm. Present Prest B[righam] Young presiding. After singing Prayer by Elder Isaac Brockbank. Singing. Roll called & Minutes of last Meeting were read ~~&~~ Which occasioned quite a number of remarks being made on the difficulty of any one taking Minutes by the ordinary method of long hand, so as to correctly represent the ideas of a rapid speaker.[81]

A few remarks were also made on the necessity of our public speakers in the New Tabernacle[82] raising their voice to a pitch sufficient for all to hear, which had not been the case with some, for a long time past.

No special subject or business being brought before the School, it was adjourned for one week at 4 o clock pm. ~~O~~ Benediction by B[isho]p W[illia]m Thorn.

September 22, 1873; Monday

The School of the Prophets met in the Old Tabernacle at 4 o clock pm. Pres[en]t President B[righam] Young presiding also Prest D[aniel] H. Wells, 3 of the twelve~~s~~ [apostles] and about 40 members. Singing.

80. Joseph W. Young had died three months earlier on June 7, 1873. While supervising the St. George Temple and other construction projects, he had suffered heat stroke, and before dying, he said he was visited by a spirit messenger looking for a man of "purity of life … for the ministry in the Spirit World; [but] that he (Joseph) had one blemish. He had … always used tea." His last words reportedly were, "Brethren, be careful on that temple wall, and don't let the chisel fall." See Young, *Memoirs of John R. Young*.

81. For the next several meetings, George Goddard's minutes are considerably shorter.

82. The current Salt Lake Tabernacle was completed in 1867. The Old Salt Lake Tabernacle, completed in 1852, remained on Temple Square until 1877, when it was replaced by the Assembly Hall.

Prayer by Elder A [Milton] Musser. Singing. Minutes of last meeting were read and accepted.

B[righam] Young Jun[io]r gave an interesting account of the faith and enterprize of the Saints in Cache Co[unty] ~~Oxford[,] [Idaho][,] being an exception, being nearly one half ^of the people being^ apostate~~

B[isho]p L[orenzo] D[ow] Young felt thankful to be here, regreted the growing tendency among the Elders to send ^for^ a Doctor when their Wives and children were sick, instead of exercizing faith in the ordinance of anointing with oil & prayer.

Elder Jos[ep]h F. Smith said, when called upon to administer to the sick, he sometimes felt that he had so much to do, that he could scarcely find time to ~~to~~ go. Is not this hurrying way of attending to that ordinance, one reason why many families are tempted to send for a Doctor[?] He believed however, that if more time & faith was devoted to this, God would honour ~~to~~ that ordinance far more frequently than he now does.

Elder Orson Pratt made a few very interesting remarks on the same subject citing instances [of blessing the sick] from the Book of Mormon, New Testament, and his own experience, ^said^ ^~~may not~~^ much of the failure refer'd to, may arise from the neglect of ~~the~~ observing the word of wisdom, or some other ~~other~~ important duty.

Meeting was adjourned for one week at 4 pm. Benediction by Elder John R Winder.

September 29, 1873; Monday

The School of the Prophets met in the old Tabernacle at 4 pm. Present Prest B[righam] Young presiding also Prest G[eorge] A. Smith. After singing Prayer by Prest Geo A Smith. Singing.

Prest B Young ^in reference to laying hands on the sick^ recommended the Elders and saints generally to order their lives, so that they can have confidence in their own prayers, to try to exercise faith for the sick, rebuke disease and command it to depart, and to stay & converse with them or not[,] just as the Spirit of the Lord may direct at the time. He then spoke of Co operation which was a principle that belongs to the Latter day Saints, it was ^the^ first stepping stones to the order of Enock. And unless the brethren take hold ^of it^ more fervently, than they have done, they will dwindle ~~ago as~~ away, and go into the spirit of the world. He then gave an interesting recital of ^his^ own experience in the early times of the church when he had to leave every thing the Lord had blest him with, and he never once repined at it or mourned over it. He came into these vallies poor, ~~but~~ ^&^ the Lord has blest him with much wealth, but his heart ~~is~~ ^was^ not placed upon it.[83] He wished his brethren the Bishops to stand staunch & firm in their sustaining the Co Operative Institutions, but we are agents to ourselves and we can either establish the righteousness & power of the Kingdom of God, or not, just as we please. He said to the credit of his Councillors and the twelve [apostles], that no requirement could be made of them, but what would be cheerfully ~~complyed~~ performed, no matter at what sacrifice. ~~but~~ We should sustain our own [member-owned] stores, or we transgress against the law of right and righteousness. We want to enter into cooperation in our Manufacturing, and farming, and everything else that we ~~can~~ possibly can.

Prest Geo A Smith bore testimony to the truth and valuable instruction of Prest Young.

School was adjourned for two weeks at the City Hall at 7 pm.[84] Benediction by B[isho]p E[dwin] D. Woolley.

October 13, 1873; Monday[85]

The School of the Prophets met in the City Hall at 7 pm as per adjournment. Present Elder Orson Pratt presiding. Prest D[aniel] H. Wells came in a short time after the school opened. Singing. Prayer by Elder Theodore McKean. Singing. Minutes of previous meeting were read and accepted. Roll called.[86]

1st Question asked. Is it right for children to be ordained should they die before they are baptized:[87]

Many instances were mentioned ~~we~~ w[h]ere infants had been ordained when only a few days old, by the Patriarch John Smith. There was

83. At Young's death in four years, his estate would be valued at $1.6 million, a huge sum in that day. Allen and Leonard, *Story of the Latter-day Saints*, 379–80.

84. No meeting was held October 6 due to the church's general conference.

85. From here on out, there are two sets of minutes for some meetings. I will use the final version but add some details to the notes from the rough draft.

86. The rough draft points out that there were twenty-four members present.

87. As noted in the rough draft, Orson Pratt had "enquired if any member of the school had any particular question or subject to present—and the following questions were submitted," including whether it was "legal" to "ordain unbaptized children whose parents suppose them to be dying."

no revelation given requiring that to be done, though some Elders had done so besides Father John Smith.

2nd Question. A child dying ~~ju~~ a short time before being 8 years old, ^and unbaptized^ being disobedient and had acquired many bad and wicked ways, Would such an one need a proxy to be baptized for ~~them~~ ^him^ for the remission of ~~their~~ ^his^ sins[?]

It was generally thought that He would not, for though he might have done many things that he knew was wrong, yet he might not ~~be~~ fully understand the consequences of ~~their~~ ^his^ conduct.

Several remarks were ^further^ made on the subject of juvenile Ordinations [in general], and though some children had been ordained to the high priesthood, yet had to be reordained again before admitted into the Quorum

Prest Wells ^said^ some had ordained children when thought they would die—this had been a comfort to some parents, though there was no law or revelation given for or against it, consequently he could not see any harm or wrong in ~~it~~ having it done, neither could he think there was any particular virtue in it. Infantile Children are subjects of blessing and exaltation, he thought they would attain to ~~all~~ just as much, as though~~t~~ they had been ordained. He also made some excellent remarks on the subject of Baptism.

Elder O[rson] Pratt ~~did did not think that~~ ^thought^ [a] Spirit that ~~came~~ ^came^ from the eternal worlds, ~~had~~ arrived to maturity in size, as well as intelligence, before coming here, and after entering an infantile tabernacle, and dying, he thought such would continue to grow until they ~~are~~ ar^r^ived to the full statue of a Man.

Prest Wells did not think it [the questions][88] ~~th~~ essential to the happiness and exaltation [of the child].[89]

October 20, 1873; Monday

The School of the Prophets met in the City Hall at 7 pm. Present Prest D[aniel] H. Wells presiding. After singing Prayer by Elder E[rastus] Snow. Singing. Roll called and 32 members responded. Minutes of last meeting were read and passed.

88. More specifically, as stated in the rough draft, "the above questions and others growing out of them [which] occupied the evening till nearly 9 oclock."

89. "The school was adjourned for one week at 7 oclock pm.," notes the rough draft. "Benediction by B[ishop]p A[lexander] McRae."

Prest Wells then proposed the following question. Is it right for an Elder or Bishop to express sentiments publicaly in a ward meeting, to a mixed audience, precisely opposite to those advanced by Prest [Brigham] Young at our late Conference?

The following members exprest their unqualified disapproval of such a right, and that no one could indulge in such a course, without sacrificing the fellowship of the saints. A[lonzo] H. Raleigh, A[lexander] McRae, D[imick] B. Huntington, Tho[ma]s Taylor, Geo B. Wallace, Orson Pratt, and D[aniel] H. Wells.

After some interesting conversation on the subject of obedience to the Head [of the church,] three paragraphs of Section 7. on page 97. Doc[trine] & Cov[enants] were ^then^ read and commented upon by Elder Orson Pratt and Prest D[aniel] H. Wells.[90]

School was then adjourned for One ^week^ at 7 o clock pm. Benediction by Elder H[enr]y Arnold.

October 27, 1873; Monday

The School of the Prophets met in the City Hall at 7 pm. Present Prest B[righam] Young presiding. After singing Prayer by Elder W[illiam] Asper. Singing. Roll Called and 36 Members answered to your names. Minutes of last meeting were read and [blank].

Elder Geo Q Cannon who was expecting to go to Washington [DC] in a few days, as our Delegate to Congress, exprest his fullest conviction that his seat there will not be denied him, because of his being a Polygamist, although many faint hearted Mormons had exprest there doubts on the subject. He desired the faith and prayers of his brethren while away, and he had no doubts whatever as to the result, for Zion was Onward and upward.[91]

Elder W[ilford] Woodruff entertained the strongest confidence that God would stand by and sustain us, just in proportion as we sustain and uphold those principles that he has revealed.

Elder Jos[eph] F. Smith said we ought to be proud to assert our

---

90. This is the Olive Leaf revelation "concerning the upbuilding of Zion" (current D&C 88).

91. Cannon was seated by Congress and served for eight years until the anti-polygamy legislation of the 1880s forced Utah to give up its territorial seat. For more on his tenure, see Bitton, *George Q. Cannon*, 183–213.

principles boldly and unflinchingly and never be afraid ^to^ do so, for they were God given and were good.

Elder Orson Pratt was thankful that Bro Cannon was elected as our Delegate, for it was a duty we owe to God and to ourselves, and leave the result in the hands of God, for it ~~would~~ ^will^ be right whether they receive him or not.

Elder Geo B. Wallace said a Polygamous Elder with a large family will carry more influence and respect than any one who has not entered into that order, Mentioned a dream that he had in which he saw Prest [Ulysses S.] Grant in a very humiliating and ignomineous condition.

Elder Angus M. Cannon was pleased and satisfied with the Choice of his Bro as Delegate, and had no doubt the result would be good for Israel [LDS Church], he also related a dream somewhat similar to the one above.

B[isho]p A[lonzo] H. Raleigh endorsed the sentiments previously expressed.

Elder B[righam] Young Jun[io]r said his feelings were in union with his brethren, deemed it wisdom to lay aside all fear towards our Government, felt thankful in the choice of our Delegate, and ^satisfied that^ every interest in Utah will be properly represented.

B[isho]ps E[dwin] D. Woolley ~~&~~ A[lexander] McRae ^& Judge [Elias] Smith^ said the feelings and sentiments already expressed, were in exact accordance with their own.

Prest Geo A Smith spoke of the respect and priveleges ~~an~~ shown him, at Washington on the floor ~~at~~ of Congress ~~about a year ago,~~ ^on the 4th June last^ being there as a known Polygamist.[92] He particularly desired the brethren to think, feel and pray for Bro Cannon during his absence, that he may have power and influence in Congress so as to fasten himself entirely upon them[93] ~~so as~~ to secure their respect. &c.

School was adjourned for one week at 7 o clock pm. ^Benediction by Prest Geo A Smith.^

92. He had been refused admittance to the Republican National Convention in Philadelphia because of polygamy and "was averse to making a contest of their decision. He spent some time in the east visiting friends and took no part in politics." Dunford, "Contributions of George A. Smith," 175–76.

93. This meant "to unite closely in any manner and by any means" (Webster, *American Dictionary*, 1828).

November 3, 1873; Monday

The School of the Prophets met in the City Hall at 7 pm. Present[,] Prest B[righam] Young presiding[;] also Geo A Smith C[ounselo]r and 4 of the twelve [apostles]. After singing Prayer by Elder Rob[er]t Campbell. Roll Called and 43 members responded. Minutes of previous meeting were read and approved.

Elder Geo Q. Cannon, mentioned a case in the 7th Ward where one of our brethren had sold a portion of his land to an outsider [non-Mormon], which he [Cannon] considered as a breach of faith, and did not deserve the fellowship of the saints for so doing.

B[isho]p W[illia]m Thorne, said there were many Apostates in the 7th Ward who had bought property there, and quite a number of our old members who had sold property to them.

Prest B Young, said the property refered ~~ref~~ to by Bro Cannon was in reality owned by some heirs now living in California, and he did not think those who had bought it would occupy it very long before it was disputed, by the rightful heirs. ^At least he would not want anything to do with it.^ He recommended ~~Bp W Thorn~~ that a friend be raised, to put ~~put~~ up a number of houses there for rental by our brethren so as ^to^ retain the balance of [electoral] power in that ward. ~~though he fully believed the Gentiles~~ He also made some important remarks on the subject of selling property to outsiders.

Elder Elias Smith[:] As the Probate Judge[,] [he] was ~~th~~ well conversant with the history of the ownership of the lot spoken of in the 7th ward, and he did not think the original heirs had a particle of claim upon it.

He said he had given Council to the School Trustees of that Ward and several others, to have the deeds of their ~~school &~~ Meeting house lots to be deeded to the B[isho]ps of said Wards & their successors in office, for the use and benefit of the Members of the Church of Jesus Christ of Latter day Saints. He wished to know if that Council was correct.

Prest B Young answered in the affirmative.

Prest Geo A. Smith who the day previous had attended the funeral of Bro Isaac Laney whose Coffin was very plain and unadorned by his own special request, was led to speak on the growing tendency to extravagance and costly expenditure in the burial, and Monuments over our departed friends, ~~which amounted almost to Idolatry, in this, he co we were following the f practise of the Gentile world, and thought it~~

~~high time for the saints to~~ which often proved very embarrassing for the surviving family to liquidate. This was not right, and neither ancient nor modern scripture justified or encouraged it.

B[isho]p [Edward] Hunter and several others spoke on the subject and Prest B[righam] Young requested every Member of the school to express their wishes in writing ~~and~~ as to the manner and style they would like their family and friends to carry out at their burial, these he wished to be presented ^at the^ next meeting, as he intended to have them recorded in a Book.

School was adjourned for one week at 6 o clock pm. After singing Benediction by Prest B Young.

November 10, 1873; Monday

The School of the Prophets met in the City Hall at 6 pm. Present Prest B[righam] Young presiding. Geo A Smith & D[aniel] H. Wells C[ounselo]rs. Also 6 of ^the^ Quorum of the Twelve [Apostles.] After singing Prayer by Elder Lorenzo Snow. Singing. Roll called and 51 members answered to their names.

^Prest Young introduced Henry Dinwoody, W[illia]m Clayton, Horace K. Whitney & Paul A Shettler who were unamously admitted as members of the school. He also extended an invitation to the members of the High Council through Bro [George B.] Wallace to be present next meeting.^

Prest Young ~~desired~~ ^called on^ the members of the School to hand in their papers, expressive of their views and desires in relation to the manner of having ~~of~~ their funeral ^services & interment^ conducted &c. 19 were handed in & Elder Geo Q. Cannon read them before the school, those members who failed to respond, promised to have them at our next meeting.

Prest Young then desired Elder Geo Q Cannon to ^read^ a printed form of a will which he deemed the best legal form he had ever seen, it had been carefully got up with a view of preventing the estates of the Elders from going into the Courts and swindled by the Lawyers. In answer to a question as to where those forms could be obtained Prest Young said he intended to have some printed, and those Elders who desired to use one for their own wills could obtain one ^through him^ but not for public exposure.

He ~~introduced~~ mentioned Elder Wm Clayton as the most capable man in the community to make out Wills in strict conformity to law and recommended the brethren to avail themselves of his services.

He next ^called^ attention to an article published in our papers a few days ago, issued by ~~the Te~~ a Committee of the Teachers institute, and entitled An Appeal on Public Schools, containing also a part of a petition to our next Legislature for the raising of Funds out of our Taxes ~~and~~ Fines &c for school purposes, and which petition they intend to circulate throughout the Territory, to obtain signers ~~thereto,~~ to such an extent as to secure legislation in their favour.

The above ^article^ was read by Elder Geo Q Cannon—which ^caused^ considerable discussion on the main features of it, and was unqualifiedly condemned by every Member of the school, as calculated to work diametrically opposite to the principles of improvement, ~~besides placing a large amount of means at in the hands~~ by introducing a species of pauperism in the community.[94]

Elder Elias Smith expressed his entire satisfaction in most of ~~the~~ ^our^ laws regulating the Public Schools, and his unqualified disapproval of the course recent taken by the Teachers Association deeming the Article just read as a direct insult to Prest Young and the whole community.

Prest B Young entirely concurred in the sentiments expressed by Judge Smith.

Prest D. H. Wells said he had more or less mingled with ^the Teachers^ and ~~C~~ listened to their addresses on several occasions, and ^had^ also spoken himself on the subject of education—but they never submitted to him a Copy of their appeal, Petition &c before publishing the article refered to.

The following Motion was then made & carried unanimously That all present use their influence to induce the people not to sign their Petition.

94. The appeal originated with Mormon educator Karl G. Maeser. The comment about pauperism implied that taxes (there were only flat taxes in that day) would have to be paid whether or not someone could afford it. More importantly, though, the church did not want government-run secular schools replacing the existing church schools. Until 1890 students were instructed in LDS Church buildings by LDS teachers, overseen by three-member school boards made up of ward volunteers. "Public Schools, an Appeal," *Salt Lake Herald*, Nov. 8, 1873; Buchanan, *Culture Clash and Accommodation*, 1, 6–8, 11–12, 14.

Meeting adjourned for one week at 6 pm. Benediction by Elder F[ranklin] D. Richards.[95]

November 17, 1873; Monday

The School of the Prophets met in the City Hall at 6 o clock pm. Present Prest B[righam] Young presiding. Geo A Smith & Dan[ie]l H. Wells C[ounselo]rs and 5 of the twelve [apostles also present]. After singing Prayer by Elder Geo B Wallace. Singing. Rolls called & 68 Members responded. Minutes of last meeting were read and accepted.

The Clerk then read 15 papers handed in by the brethren pertaining to manner they desired their funeral ceremonies conducted.

He also read a Telegraphic ~~Disp~~ communication sent [from] Prest Geo A Smith to Prest E[rastus] Snow at St. George—Asking several questions respecting the Temple, how far ~~it~~ advanced, what material on hand, what facilities for further progress, and what kind of aid they most needed from the North in Men, Teams, Forage or provisions. The Answer from Prest E Snow was also read in which he suggested that ^from^ 50 to 100 ~~men~~ able bodied men including 10 masons, with teams sufficient to take them down, some Groceries, dried fruit, Pork & Butter.

Prest B Young then laid the matter before the school and desired the Members to express their minds upon it.

~~P~~ Elder John Taylor expressed his entire concurrence in what ever had a direct tendency to build up the kingdom of God and had no doubt that what was needed to aid and assist them in ~~St George~~ building the Temple in St. George where ordinances for the living and the dead could be administered, would be freely responded to.

Prest D. H. Wells said he would furnish a Team and Teamsters all fitted up, to haul provisions for those who go there to work.

Prest ^B^ Young said he expected to spend the winter in the south and render considerable help towards the temple with his Teams &c. And he wished the Bishops to enquire of the Masons in their wards, if they wished to go there and help to prepare for the ordinances of the Gospel to be administered, he did not want [them] to go, unless they felt ~~anxious and~~ perfectly willing, and would rather go than not,

95. Richards and Lorenzo Snow had traveled by train from Brigham City so they could accompany Young and other leaders the next day to Farmington. FDRJ, Nov. 10–11, 1873.

so that they may have a credit on the [tithing] books. He thought they had better call on Sanpete and Beaver Counties [to the south] for the labourers. ^He also requested the Bishops to gather up what Groceries, Dried Fruit—provisions, &c. they could, and send them down without making any public stir about it.^

Prest Geo A Smith also urged on the brethren to make a united effort to accomplish what was required.

Prest B Young then said he wanted to see a community of Elders in this City or elsewhere willing to be one in Temporal things, or in other words, enter into the Order of Enock, conducted by a Committee or Trustees, who should have charge of the company, ^&^ those who were not willing to observe their council he did not want there. We would raise our own fruits, Grain, Fowls, Butter, Cheese, Beef, Mutton, Pork &c. Manufacture our own Clothing & wear it, abandon the use and wear of all unnecessary imported articles. The means raised by our united labours, put to usury in doing good, not fooled away in folly and extravagance, all things controuled by the Trustees. ~~kee and nothing kept secret from the Members~~ If the Elders will only take a right course in handling the things of this world, the Lord will pour untold wealth into our hands.

Elder David McKenzie was then requested to read an article published in a small sheet ~~pu~~ edited by Messrs ^J. D.^ Young & ^John^ Riter, which was a scurrilous and lying reflection on the doings of the City Council, ^making special mention of Councilor [Henry] G[row] & Alderman [Isaac] G[roo]^[,] and several of the Council being present bore united testimony to its being a tissue of lies from begining to end.[96]

~~C[ounselo]r Hy Grow~~ Prest Young said he supposed that Councillor was here, meaning C[ounselo]r Hy Grow, who immediately rose, and said he thought that publication might have originated from a conversation ^he had^ with a man who severely commented on the doings of the City Council, ~~and cast~~ ^in reference [deference] to^ Prest Youngs wishes.

The question was then asked ~~who~~ ^what^ the name of the individual was. Bro Grow said it was Bro D. L. Davis,[97] one of the employees

96. A sheet called *The Circular* claimed the city council forgave mayor Daniel H. Wells a debt of $50,000. There was apparently nothing to this rumor. "Arrant Falsehood," *Salt Lake Herald*, Nov. 18, 1873.

97. David Lazarus Davis (1841–1926) was born in Wales and migrated to Utah in 1861. He founded the Great Salt Lake Yacht Club in 1877.

of Z.C.M.I. Several members of the school ~~expr~~ spoke in the highest terms of Bro Davis as a Business man, courteous to customers, and universally respected, and were much astonished at the remarks he was charged with having made in conversation with Bro Grow.

After ~~several~~ some ^further^ conversation on the subject, and also in relation to raising Men and Means towards the Temple in St. George. ^The Wards were then called over and it was ascertained the Bishops of the 1st & 3rd Wards had not been notified to attend the School [of the Prophets]. Prest Young said all the City Bishops and Councillors were invited or should have been when first organized, He then instructed the clerk to notify those who had been omitted.^

The School was adjourned for one week at 6 oclock pm. ~~After s~~ Benediction by Elder Sam[ue]l L. Evans.

November 24, 1873; Monday

The School of the Prophets met in the City Hall at 6 pm. Present Prest B[righam] Young presiding[,] ^Geo A Smith & D[aniel] H Wells C[ounselo]rs & 3 of the twelve [apostles].^ After Singing Prayer by Elder A[lbert] Carrington. Singing. The Minutes of the last meeting were read & accepted. Roll Called and 74 Members answered to their ^names.^

^The Clerk read^ 12 more papers ^which^ were handed in ^by the brethren^ pertaining to the ~~order~~ manner they desired their burial services conducted. Several partial reports were also read from 1st. 2nd, 7th, 14th ^16th^ and 19th wards, amounting in Cash, & Store pay ^to^ over $600.00 besides some provisions, one mason, ^& other^ and two labourers, to aid and assist in the building of the Temple in St. George.

Prest Geo A Smith said if any of the brethren present felt like volunteering themselves as willing to enter into the order ^approaching that^ of Enock, he would like them to report themselves. He also spoke with much satisfaction of the progress of the Narrow Guage railroad between Ogden and Brigham City.[98]

Prest B Young asked the brethren if they wished to contemplate the plan of the Order of Enock, according to ~~what the order~~ ^what^

98. On November 17 the narrow-gauge Utah Northern Railroad reached Smithfield in Cache Valley, northeast of Brigham City. In Ogden the line linked up with the Utah Central line to Salt Lake City and, beyond there, the Utah Southern line—all constructed after the Transcontinental Railroad bypassed Salt Lake City in 1869 in favor of the Ogden–Brigham City–Lucin–Oasis route. See Strack, *Ogden Rails*.

he had on his mind to carry out, he would prefer to commence such an organization with good, honest, but poor men, and he had faith to believe that he could dictate such a company, so as to make it a success. He also believed ^such^ a system of Cooperation could be ~~atten~~ entered into by a number of brethren, so as not to run any risk of interference by the law of the land in case of an occasional apostacy, which is sure to take place more or less, and if the brethren chose to offer themselves to enter into this order, He would dictate them himself until they were perfectly organized.

~~Y~~ One of ^the^ principal objects to be accomplished by this order is to ~~bring~~ make the people one in their acts.

Prest Young said what the Bishops wished to do for the Temple in St. George must be done quick, and report to B[isho]p [Edward] Hunter at latest by Thursday next.

He desired the brethren to reflect on the subject he had laid before them about the order of Enock, and report themselves at his office to Bro Carrington who would be left in charge ^at his office^ during his absence ~~at St George~~ as he expected to leave in a few days for St. George to spend the winter there.

In the absence of further business The School was adjourned for one week at 6 o clock pm. Benediction by B[isho]p E[lijah] F. Sheets.

December 1, 1873; Monday

The School of the Prophets met in the City Hall at 6 oclock pm. Present Prest D[aniel] H. Wells presiding also 3 of the Quorum of the twelve [apostles]. After singing Prayer by Elder R[obert] L. Campbell. Singing. Roll called and 68 members were present. Minutes of last meeting were read and approved. The Clerk then read one paper on the subject of [the writer's preference for his] burial services.[99]

Elder O[rson] Pratt suggested that all future papers on the same subject, should pass without reading them before the school.

B[isho]p E[dward] Hunter and Geo Goddard gave a report of what means had been donated towards the Temple at St George by the various wards of this City, over $900.00 in Cash was reported, besides Store pay, Tithing Orders, Flour, Dried fruit &c.

99. See Nov. 3, 1873, entry.

B[isho]p E[lijah] F. Sheets then stated that the above means had been expended in Steel, Iron,[100] Groceries, Dry Goods, Boots, Shoes &c, which was sufficient for two teams, and would [be] ready to start for St George in the morning.

Elder Jno [John] VanCott reported as one of the Missionaries [sent] south to raise Labourers and ~~Teams~~ Masons to assist on the Temple in St. George, ~~T~~ that 80 men were promised in Sanpete Co[unty] including 10 Masons. B[isho]p Tho[ma]s Taylor accompanied Bro Van Cott.

B[isho]p E. F. Sheets spoke with much pleasure of the liberality [of the donations] of the Saints in Sanpete and Cache Co[untie]s.

Prest D. H. Wells said he had received a Telegra~~ph~~^m^ from Prest [Brigham] Young, who left here on Friday Morning last, ^stating that he^ held meeting in Payson the same ~~day~~ evening, on Sunday at Nephi, at Gunnison to day, and on Saturday & Sunday, expected to be at Richfield, Sevier Co[unty].[101]

Prest D. H. Wells contrasted the liberality of the Saints [mostly Scandinavian emigrants] at Sanpete Co[unty], where in Manti alone, 800 Dollars was raised in about ½ an hour, while in this ^whole^ City not more than $2000.00 will be probably raised, by an effort of from 2 to 3 weeks. This may be partly accounted for, by the existence of more expensive and Babyloneon fasheons that prevail in the City, than in the more remote settlements of the Territory, hence those who live in a more frugal and primitive style, are in reality more wealthy than those who live and luxuriate in the foolish and vain fasheons of the world. He then called on the school to express their views on the subject.

Elder John Van Cott, said the saints in Sanpete were proverbial for their industry, frugality and liberality.

B[isho]p E[dward] Hunter exprest much satisfaction with the Spirit of paying labour tithing in this City, ^much means was now being expended^ Over $400.00 a day was paid towards our Temple.

Elder R[obert] F. Neslen, thought the ball room was the place where

100. Nineteenth-century building technology included wrought-iron floor beams, cast-iron columns, and in the case of the St. George Temple 1¼-inch steel rods to support the upper floor joists and a cast-iron baptismal font. "Building Materials," *Dictionary of American History*; Welch, "Early Mormon Woodworking," 17, 37, 49, 90.

101. On Tuesday, November 25, Young and others rode the train to Provo to celebrate completion of the railroad to that point. They continued on to St. George by wagon.

very expensive habits were acquired,[102] by our young people, and the place where there was a wide field for the wise and judicious watchcare of Parents & those of Mature years, with a view to the correction of the evil refered to.

B[isho]p A[lonzo] H Raleigh thought a lack of fully appreciating our religion, and its claims upon us, was one important reason why our City donations do not come up to ~~th~~ those of the Country above refer'd to, he ^was^ rather ~~condemned the~~ opposed to [social] parties in a ward ~~expected~~ except for Latter day saints, and he found it very difficult to get a sufficient number of that class to ~~get~~ ^make^ up a party.

B[isho]p S[amuel] A Woolley recommended every ward to be closed for Parties on a/c [account] of the almost utter impossibility of having one, without the annoyance of some miserable whore master getting in by the introduction of some would[-]be good brother. If Parties are to be had, let them all be at the Social Hall, where Gentiles ^would be afraid to crowd themselves in.^

C[ounselo]r Jno [John] R. Winder, did not approve of depriving our young people of a reasonable amount of recreation. Let them have it, or they may be driven to more objectionable places to obtain it where no judicious controul can be exercised over them, he strongly recommended that our parties should commence earlier, have no recess, and close at latest ½ past 12.

B[isho]p Taylor sustained the same views as the last speaker, urging also the necessity of Parents mingling with their children in the dance, and also encourage them to go to meeting, and instil into their minds at home the principles of the Gospel, and [blank].

Elder O Pratt did not attribute all the blame to our youth for following after the fasheons of Babylon. He thought the Merchants was mostly at fault for importing all that class of goods to the almost utter exclusion of our own manufactured ware, and giving them a prominence in their establishments then when the people went to buy, they had to purchase those or nothing.

He also made a few remarks on the Order of Enock or more properly the order of Joseph Smith, which was attempted in the early history

102. In July the *Deseret News* had criticized the expensive attire worn at the city's ball rooms. "Fashionable Extravagance," *Deseret Evening News*, July 29, 1873.

of the church, some ^12 or^ 15 being designated by revelation to enter into it, but through covetousness could not then be established.

Elder Sam[ue]l L Evans suggested as an incentive to effect a reasonable retrenchment in their families, for the Head of a Family to allow each member a certain amount of means ^and encourage them^ to put ^it^ into Zions Trust Co[mpany] for laying aside some of the expensive habits complained of.

Elder Angus M Cannon mentioned that some very disreputable parties were being held in Ballo's Hall,[103] where whisky was freely indulged in, bad language &c and many sons and daughters of our prominent citizens attend them. It was astertained that they were conducted by some not in the church, and the Mayor promised to have some Policemen there to check improper doings.

The School was adjourned for one week at 6 pm. Benediction by ~~Sam~~ Elder Sam[ue]l L Evans.

December 8, 1873; Monday

The School of the Prophets met in the City Hall at 6 o clock pm. Present Prest D[aniel] H. Wells presiding. 3 of the quorum of the twelve [apostles present]. After singing Prayer by Elder Andrew Burt. Singing. Roll Called and 62 members responded. Minutes of last meeting were read and accepted. The Clerk read 5 more papers on the subject of burial rites.

Prest D. H. Wells reported that Prest [Brigham] Young had visited several of the Sanpete Settlements, held 14 meetings, preached himself 6 times, ~~an~~ company all well, snow [in the county] from 6 to 8 inches deep.

A Question was asked whether it would be a benefit to the Latter day Saints in this Territory by having a [federal] Branch Mint established [to produce coins].

Elder O[rson] Pratt thought the mere advantage ~~of~~ to us as a people by having some Government Buildings erected, here, was very trifling, in comparision to the disadvantages that would accrue to the community, by necessitating an extra batch of Government officials, most of

103. The music hall was founded in 1855 by Sicilian convert to Mormonism Dominico Ballo (1805–61). His band included eight clarinets, four "bass horns" (tubas), three cornets, two piccolos, a trombone, and drums. He had previously played with the Royal Guard in Palermo and had taught music at West Point. Cook, "Pioneer Bands," 22–25.

whom having rendered themselves very obnoxious to this people. He therefore would prefer having no Branch Mint.[104]

He then refered to the Mournful subject suggested by the perusal of those papers sent in by the brethren viz Death ^& Burial^.[105] He therefore thought it might be pleasant and agreeable to our feelings, to change the subject of conversation, ~~being~~ ^to one^ so closely connected with it in its nature, and yet more cheerful to contemplate viz the Resurrection. Which he made a few remarks upon, refering to the Book of Mormon, Doctrine & Covenants & the Bible.

~~Elder Geo B. Wallace~~ He [Orson Pratt] thought however the Resurrection was very near at hand.

Elder Geo B. Wallace heard Prest Young say, ~~no one~~ Joseph Smith would be the first in this dispensation to receive a resurrection, and would then hold the Keys, and that no man in the flesh would ever hold the Keys.

B[isho]p A[lonzo] H. Raleigh always thought the resurrection, like the generation of Men, would be brought about by the most natural and simple principles, and that cannot be understood except by actual experience. Some things he has heard on the subject have always been puzzling to his mind.

Elder A[ngus] M. Cannon confessed ignorance of the subject, so far as the Scriptures explained it, but if the Lord had revealed anything ~~on the subj~~ pertaining to it, he should very much like to know it.

Elder Geo B. Wallace spoke of some remarks Prest Young made at the funeral of the Wife of Bro Jos[ep]h Young, that they would come forth with the ^same^ clothing, and scars on their body,[106] ~~instancing~~

104. "The coming of the railroad in 1869 and the discovery of silver in 1873 attracted" so many outsiders that by the end of the decade "some 20 percent of the population" of Salt Lake City was non-Mormon, according to the census. Buchanan, *Culture Clash and Accommodation*, 11–12. "In 1880 a visiting journalist described Utah as one large mining camp with Salt Lake City as its Main Street." McCormick and Peterson, *Silver in the Beehive State*.

105. The members of the school had prepared statements for their families indicating their funeral and burial wishes. See Nov. 3, 1873, entry.

106. Joseph W. Young's first wife, Mary Ann, died while traveling to Utah in 1853. The next year Brigham Young speculated on what it meant that when Jesus resurrected he still had the nail scars in his hands and feet (Van Wagoner, *Complete Discourses of Brigham Young*, 2:762), and the church president had probably addressed the same topic at the funeral. Joseph Young himself died in June 1873, a few months before this School of the Prophets meeting.

~~the case of the~~ he also related a vision or dream that Bro Jos[ep]h W. Young had respecting his wifes resurrection.

Judge Elias Smith, attended that funeral, and heard those sentiments made by Prest Young, who instanced the case of the Saviour who still retains the scars he received while in the flesh. Elder Young[107] who was also present heard those remarks made.

Elder O[rson] Pratt made a few more remarks on the subject of the resurrection in regard to the same identical parts of the body being brought forth ~~in the~~ and resurrected.

Elder Rob[er]t Campbell refered to the subject of transformation that is to take place with some who are to be changed in the twinkling of an eye.[108]

Elder N[athaniel] H Felt refered to some explanation that Heber C Kimball once gave on the subject of the resurrection.

Elder D[avid] McKenzie—said in the absence of revelation on the subject of the resurrection, he did not think it profitable to theorize too much until something definite was made Known which he did not think would be very soon.

Elders Woodbury & [James] Leach related some sentiments they heard from the Prophet Joseph Smith on the resurrection—subject.[109]

Elder Jos[eph] F. Smith expected to be resurrected precisely in the same way as Jesus was, and no other.

Elder Millen Atwood heard Prest Young say that when the doctrine of the resurrection was made Known we should be astonished at the simplicity of the process.

Bp. L[eonard] W. Hardy who was with Bro Jedediah M Grant[110] during his sickness, ~~and while h~~ said, for a considerable times his Spirit left his body, and on its return, said he saw his wife and child, each

107. This might be Lorenzo Dow Young, one of the few members of the school with the Young surname who would have been old enough in 1853 to remember the contents of the sermon.

108. That is, resurrected in an instant when Christ returns to the earth.

109. At the next meeting, the following was written and then crossed out: "It was suggested that the testimony of Elder James Leach be added to the minutes, what he heard the prophet Joseph [Smith] say in regard to the Resurrection. Prest Wells said he did not for a moment question the honest motive and intention of Bro Leach, but he very much doubted the possibility of any ones memory retaining the exact sayings of any public speaker after the lapse of so many years, especially when it had reference to doctrine."

110. Grant died of pneumonia in 1856.

having a ^perfect &^ beautiful body although his child had been eaten by wolves on the plains. The child however had not grown in size, but was more inteligent ~~which proved to his satisfaction that as our bodi~~.

Elder O[rson] Pratt briefly adverted to the perfection of a glorified body, pertaining to eating, & sleeping.

Elder A[ngus] M. Cannon had reflected much on this subject ~~and~~ but could not come to any conclusion as to what Kind of food could be partaken without producing death.

Elder Jos[eph] F. Smith thought as we needed to eat and drink here, so we should there, that things here, are typical of what will be hereafter, only in a more perfect state. He knew nothing however about these things, and cared less—all he wanted, was to know his duty, so as to bring him to a Knowledge of God, and obtain eternal life.

Elder W[illard] G. Young had been much edified by what he had listened to, but wished to suggest what had proved a blessing to the young men who had become rowdy and reckless in their manners, Himself and a few prominent members of the ward got up a few parties, at which they ^complimentary^ invited these boys, and the ~~principal~~ leading men of the surrounding country, thus bring^ing^ into close contact the two extreme elements, and which had a most beneficial effect on the youth, by placing immediately before them an example worthy of their imitation.

School was adjourned for one week at 6 o clock pm. Benediction by Elder J[ohn] D. T. McAllister.

When he rec[eive]d the keys he should go to the Graves of the saints,[111] and the first one he might go to, he might command him to come forth in the name of the Lord Jesus and he would come forth, the next one he expressed the same command to [blank].

December 15, 1873; Monday

The School of the Prophets met in the City Hall at 6 pm. Present Prest D[aniel] H. Wells presiding also~~n~~ 3 of the twelve [apostles]. After singing Prayer by Elder W[illia]m C. Staines. Singing. Roll called and 64 members were present.

Pres[iden]t D[aniel] H. Wells ~~in refering to the subject of the Resurrection ^made a few remarks on the subject of the resurrection^~~,

111. This last paragraph was added below the minutes.

~~which was the subject one of our last meetings conversation said, there was a certain portion of element in the natural body of man that will never perish, it being immortal in its nature, and that is what will be resurrected, the great bulk of the human body being of the earth, earthy will of course perish and decompose. The Order of the resurrection not having been revealed, of but little could be said about it, but there was no doubt it would be entirely controuled by the Holy order of the priesthood. Pres[iden]t [Brigham] Young once said, that those who had been faithful in this dispensation would be resurrected first, and they would be instructed to go forth and resurrect those who have been slumbering for a longer period, carryingout the saying of the scripture, The first shall be Last, and the last first. & He then~~ briefly alluded to some of the ordinances that will be administered as soon as we have got our Temples finished, which will continue during the thousand years of the Millenial reign of Christ on the earth, and while the work of the first resurrection is going on.

~~He had often heard it said, that we should obtain no greater blessing that what we earned in this probation, he did not however think that correct, He could not imagine whatever we could do to earn so great and precious a blessing as Eternal life which was the greatest gift that God could bestow upon his children, we shall reveive that exaltation because we are of the lineage of the Gods, and not because as a compensation for anything we can do to earn it.~~

~~*It was suggested that the testimony of Elder B[isho]p James Leach be added to the minutes, what he heard the prophet Joseph [Smith] say in regard to the Resurrection.~~

~~Pres[iden]t Wells said he did not for a moment question the honest motive and intention of Bro[ther] Leach, but he very much doubted the possibility of any ones memory retaining the exact sayings of any public speaker after the lapse of so many years, especially when it had reference to doctrine.~~

Elder W[ilford] Woodruff ~~also adverted to the unreliability of memory expecially after a great lapse of time since the sayings had been las made~~ [said] he himself had written a great many sayings and sermons of Joseph Smith, but when once written they invariably left his memory. ~~The Lord led and instructed the Prophet Joseph like a child, and many things he was taught he had but a very imperfect understanding~~

~~of at first, his views on the resurrection changed somewhat prior to his death.~~ He then traced the principle of progress in the dealings of God with his people, since the rise of the Church especially in reference to Baptisms for the dead, The calling of Elders to preach the Gospel &c.

Elder Demick Huntington related the circumstance of a Liberty Pole[112] in ~~Nauvou~~ ^Far West [Missouri]^ being struck by lightning, and many of the shivers of the pole lying around, the Prophet Joseph deliberately said, as the Lord lives, as this Pole has been shivered to pieces, so shall the Nation of these United States be.

Elder Jno [John] Taylor said there was but little made known to us, in regard to the resurrection of the Body, and as in that, so with everything else pertaining to the things of God, in the absence of Revelation, we are ignorant and know nothing. Joseph Smith knew nothing, even of the first principles of the Gospel, until God revealed them to him &c.

Elder Orson Pratt said there was an eternity of knowledge that we did not understand, and there was a great deal that had been revealed, which was the privelege of the Elders to comprehend, if sought after by Faith and diligence. God revealed much to the Brother of Jared, and other faithful servants of God, and he did not ^think^ there was a single member of this school, but what could enjoy the same great blessings, those ancient servants of God enjoyed. He thought the school of the prophets was organized to assist each other in the things of God, and the Spirit of prophecy and revelation should be here, so that we can reach after things that will be profitable and useful for us to know.

Elder N[athaniel] H Felt made enquiry respecting some passage in the Doctrine & Covenants, which elicited a number of remarks from Elders W Woodruff, Pratt, ^John^ Taylor & Prest D H Wells.

Elder George Goddard submitted the following subjects for the consideration of the school viz 1st—Whether some plan could not be devised to find employment for the poor who are willing to work but cannot find any to do, and thus keep down feelings of desperation that hunger and starvation are very apt to engender.

2nd. That with a view of exercising a wise and judicious controul over the recreations of our youth, more especially in our dancing parties,

112. A liberty pole was a wooden flagstaff on which a flag was hung bearing the image of a pine tree and the words "An appeal to heaven." The overall symbolism of the liberty pole during the American and French revolutions was defiance of government.

would it not be a good policy for the Bishops ~~of~~ throughout the City to unite upon a reasonable hour for closing them, so as to avoid the necessity for recess, and check a moral & physical evil, that late hours are apt to entail.

After some further conversation on the subjects of the resurrection, the Holy Priesthood, ~~Ordin~~ Fore Ordination &c. and owing to the lateness of the hour.

The Questions ^previously^ submitted ~~by Elder Geo Goddard~~ were laid over until next meeting.

School was adjourned for one week at 6 o clock pm. Benediction by Elder Isaac Groo.

December 22, 1873; Monday

The School of the Prophets met in the City Hall at 6 pm. Present Prest D[aniel] H. Wells presiding[,] also 4 of the twelve [apostles]. After singing Prayer by Elder Rob[er]t F. Neslen. Singing. Roll called and 55 members were present. Minutes of last meeting were read and ^after^ considerable curtailment were received.

~~The following subjects were then brie~~

The Resurrection and Restitution were ~~again~~ subjects that elicited some interesting remarks upon by Elder Jos[eph] F Smith, Prest [Daniel H.]Wells, Elder Orson Pratt & others.

Employment for the poor was next refered to which brought ^out^ the following suggestion. That if they would be willing to work for ~~a~~ low wages or even their board, during the heavy pressure of the times, many would employ them.

<u>Dancing Parties</u> and the late hours they are usually kept up elicited some appropriate remarks from Prest Wells and others, with a recommendation to the Bishops to have them closed at an earlier hour ranging from 12 and not later than 1, avoiding the necessity of recess, and but a moderate indulgence in round dances.[113]

<u>Elder Jos[eph] F. Smith</u> spoke of Ex Bishop Andrew Cahoon, who he understood was exerting a very baneful influence among the people of his neighbourhood by teaching false doctrines, that he himself denied or ridiculed the fundamental Doctrines of the Gospel.[114] It

113. "Round dancing" described how ballroom dancers held each other and spun round and round the dance floor doing the waltz or some similar dance step.

114. See Apr. 1, 1871, entry. Cahoon was excommunicated the following year.

was suggested that the proper ~~would~~ way to proceed would be for the Bishop to send the Teachers to him, and if they found cause of complaint, to cite him before the Bishop or High Council. Let the order of the Church as laid down in the Doctrine & Covenants be strictly observed in his case.

Prest Wells called the attention of the school to the various bills now ^pending^ before Congress which are intended to deprive the citizens of Utah of every Constitutional right, and with a view of strengthening the hands of our Delegate Bro [George Q.] Cannon, he invited the ~~mes~~ cooperation of the school in taking up item by item [the content] of these obnoxious Bills and get up some briefs to expose their unconstitutionality.

Elder John Taylor made some stirring remarks on the same subject, ~~and rehearsed some~~

School was adjourned for one week at 6 o clock pm. Benediction by Elder George Goddard.

December 29, 1873; Monday[115]

School met in the City Hall at 6 p.m. Prest D[aniel] H Wells presiding. Also 4 of the twelve [apostles present]. After singing prayer by Elder Nathaniel H Felt. Roll called and 61 members were present. Minutes of last meeting were read and accepted.

A communication from Elder N[athaniel] H. Felt addressed to Prest D H Wells was read suggesting that addresses to all the different Governors of the States, & the Senators & Representatives of the same[—]remonstrating against the passage of the infamous [anti-polygamy] bills ~~against Utah~~ designed to affect Utah, and signed by their former constituents [who had immigrated to Utah][—]be gotten up & forwarded without delay.[116]

Elder A[lbert] P. Rockwood suggested the propriety of a [voter] registration law, in place of the present system of numbering tickets making

115. The rough draft of the minutes summarized the discussion as "one of unusual interest to all present, [that] called forth many remarks and suggestions as to the best and wisest way of meeting the vile attempt now being made to rob us of our civil and religious rights[,] [during which] ~~nearly~~ ^many^ of the leading members of the school spoke on the subject, and which finally resulted in the suggestion that all the Members of the School act ^as^ a committee of the whole to prepare briefs containing rebutting facts and statistics, ~~to~~ and submit them to a special Committee."

116. See Mar. 17, 1873, entry.

it penal to place any mark upon a ticket by which the voter would be known, and ~~extend~~ ^apply^ the same in the Municipal Elections as well.

Elder Angus M. Cannon asked how it would do to adopt the Civil and Criminal Codes of California, he thought if this were done our friends in Congress might use the fact advantageously in gagging our foes.[117]

Elder Geo Wallace was of the opinion that we ought to meet our enemies face to face in Congress, ^right^ square, ~~on the issue,~~ and trust to no side issues.

Elder Orson Pratt said he had been very busy since last meeting and had no time to devote to the subjects alluded to. But he was not in favor of adopting the California Codes without close scrutiny.

Elder Hosea Stout said he was in favor of the measures suggested by Bro Felt. As to the bills now before Congress affecting Utah, were [Illinois Senator John A.] Logan's bill to become law, there wouldn't be sufficient liberty left us to thank God for. What he thought ~~was~~ ^is^ required was good ~~requiren~~ ^sound, Constitutional^ arguments from Utah to put in the mouths of our friends in Washington [DC], who would help us if we give them the power. There are some of our laws that might be improved. For instance a County Court is required to put 50 names in the jury box, from which 15 are ~~selected~~ ^drawn^ for a grand jury, and 24 for 2 traverse juries. He would change this so that every eligible voter in the County should have a chance to be drawn. He endorsed the suggestion of Br[other] Rockwood ~~respecting~~ ^to^ abolishing the system of marking ballots also of having the candidates attend the counting of the votes. And advised the brethren to see what they could do towards helping our friends in Congress.

Bro Felt ~~thought~~ said that the suggestion he had made was not original with him, it was simply the plan the Lord had ~~himself~~ instructed their Saints to pursue, and he believed it would be productive of good.

Elder Orson Pratt said if the Governors did no more for us than they had when appealed to on a similar occasion it would amount to but very little.[118]

Elder John Taylor thought it wisdom to use every exertion in our

117. In other words, it could be argued that Mormons were not passing theocratic legislation.

118. The Council of Fifty had drafted a letter to each state governor, excluding Missouri, in March 1845, asking for help. Almost no one responded. See Grow et al., *Council of Fifty Minutes*, 312–18.

power to stay those proceedings, and it was absolutely our duty to do so, as men of God holding the Holy Priesthood. He thought it was not practicable to apply to the governors for lack of time, but that the plan might be successfully pursued of appealing to the Senators and Representatives. He endorsed ^Brother Rockwood and^ Bro [Hosea] Stout's suggestions about the jury law. He said the authorities east wanted to destroy Mormonism, but in the name of God every step they took in that direction would fall upon their own heads, and would lay the axe at the root of the tree in their own destruction. We will conquer if they pass their ~~suggestions~~ bills, but we should use every means in our power, and then leave the result with the Lord.

Bishop A[lonzo] H. Raleigh ~~then~~ said ~~our~~ ^the^ adoption of any particular code was only following the practise of other States and Territories, and there was no particular harm in it unless we should therein adopt some particular law inimical to ourselves, which however need not be embodied in ~~the~~ ^our^ code.

Elder [George B.] Wallace again spoke. Also Elder [Hosea] Stout, exhorting the brethren to meet the issue square in the face, and advance our Constitutional arguments immediately to help Bro [George Q.] Cannon in Washington. The latter [Hosea Stout] recommended a Statute of limitations in criminal cases, and shewed wherein the U.S. Statute of Limitations [was] affected by the Polygamy bill.

Elder Geo J. Taylor endorsed the ~~applications~~ ^appeal^ to Senators & Representatives and spoke about the treaty [of Guadalupe Hidalgo in 1848] with Mexico as also did Elder David McKenzie.

Elder Joseph F. Smith said it occurred to him that ~~so far~~ as we had hitherto petitioned ^&^ memorialized Congress ^&^ inso much as there was another crusade against us it behoved us to repeat them. He approved the suggestion about the jury law, but thought that if we attempted to please our enemies about the ballots ^system^ ~~we would it~~ still they would howl about us.

Elder Rob[er]t F. Neslen—thought we should use the press freely to disseminate our views, and there were many papers ^abroad^ that would be willing to publish for us.

Elder Franklin W. Young thought it would be well to have a committee appointed to act in the matter and thus avoid unnecessary delay.

Elder Joseph F. Smith said there was one ^powerful^ engine ^not^

yet alluded to, the use of money, to procure admission to the columns of newspapers.

Elder Angus ^M.^ Cannon. ~~Felt. suggested~~ & Felt again spoke.

Prest Wells said we needed a working committee to get up a protest against the provisions of those bills now before Congress and also to answer the memorial now in circulation. He asked why did not Congress pass a clean law against Polygamy and leave the franchise of the people and their political rights undisturbed. It was because the [Federal] ring in Utah wanted their fingers in the peoples' purses and in the treasuries. What we want is to have some material ~~for~~ rebutting facts and statistics. All of the School [of the Prophets] should work as a Committee of the whole and prepare their briefs and submit them to a special committee[,] and [Wells therefore] suggested that ~~a~~ ^such^ committee be appointed[,] which was accordingly done. Prest D[aniel] H. Wells, Elias Smith. Zerrubabel Snow, Hosea Stout, D[avid] McKenzie [and] John R. Winder [were appointed to the committee].

Meeting was adjourned until Monday Jan[uary] 1873 [1874] at 6. Benediction by William C. Staines.

CHAPTER SIX

"WE HAVE NOTHING TO FEAR"

1874

January 5, 1874; Monday[1]

The School of the Prophets met in the City Hall at 6 pm. Present Prest D[aniel] H. Wells presiding[,] [also] 5 of the twelve [apostles]. After singing Prayer by Elder Theodore McKean. Singing. Roll called and 57 members were present. Minutes of last meeting were read and accepted.

Prest D. H. Wells, as Chairman of Committee appointed last meeting,[2] reported that several documents had been prepared, and to avoid unnecessary delay, and that Bro [George Q.] Cannon might receive them in time to be of service to him [in Washington, DC], had been forwarded as fast as Bro David McKenzie could ~~write~~ get them ^compiled &^ written, so that there was nothing to read before the school as the result of the Committee's labours. ^The report of the committee was accepted and they were requested to continue their labours.^

Elder D McKenzie said the Documents forwarded contained rebutting items in opposition to special legislation, such as refering to the conduct of our Judges, and the Jury system as resorted to by them, also refered to the opinions of some prominent Senators as expressed during last session of Congress when opposing the passage of the Frelinghuyson Bill &c.[3]

Elder Orson Pratt then read a lengthy communication on Crime and Polygamy, which he had prepared for publication, drawing most of

1. The CHL has rough drafts of the minutes through February 16, which I have occasionally drawn from in the footnotes to augment the polished versions.

2. See Dec. 29, 1873, entry.

3. US Senator Frederick T. Frelinghuysen (R–New Jersey) had introduced a bill to enforce bigamy laws in Utah Territory, with support in the House of Representatives from Luke P. Poland (R–Vermont) and George C. McKee (R–Mississippi). Senator Oliver P. Morton (R–Indiana) spoke against the legislation. See GQCJ, Jan. 31, 1874.

his arguments from the Old Testament, and the code of criminal laws of the united States, It was suggested that it be forwarded to Bro Geo Q. Cannon for him to use it in any way he thought best.[4]

Suggestions from any Members of the school were solicited, and Elders O Pratt, John Taylor, Albert Carrington, Elias Smith, J[ohn] R. Winder, & D McKenzie made a few remarks on ~~the~~ some of the leading points that these obnoxious bills sought to abolish—such as our present Jury system, voting at Elections &c.

Prest D. H. Wells said he had received a Telegram from Prest [Brigham] Young, who with his Councillor Geo A. Smith send their greetings to the Members of the School, and wish them a Happy New Year.

Elder John Taylor then made the following Motion which was Seconded & Carried That we reciprocate in the expression of good wishes, by sending the following telegram[:]

> Prest B[righam] Young and Geo A Smith. The Assembly on Monday evening feel much obliged to you, for your kind remembrances and congratulations, and while they hear with pleasure the success of your arduous undertakings in the progress of the [St. George] Temple, join in returning the compliments of the Season, and wish you a Happy New Year, and ten thousand more.

School was adjourned for one week at 6 o clock pm. Benediction by Elder Isaac Brockbank.

January 12, 1874; Monday

The School of the Prophets met in the City Hall at 6 oclock pm. Present of the ^1st Presidency^ Prest D[aniel] H. Wells presiding also A[lbert] Carrington [and] 3 of the twelve [apostles]. After singing Prayer by Elder Henry Arnold. Singing. Roll called and 67 members were present. Minutes of last meeting were read and accepted.

Prest Wells requested the Clerk to read a letter just received from our Delegate at Washington [DC] Elder George Q Cannon, in which he said there was now five Bills before Congress, all seeking for special Legislation for Utah, any one of which if passed and became law, would

---

4. This was Pratt's *The Bible and Polygamy: Does the Bible Sanction Polygamy?* published by the Deseret News in 1874, reproducing the 1870 debate between Pratt and the reverend John P. Newman (see Aug. 13, 1870, entry) and quoting LDS Church leaders on the topic.

prostrate us as a people at the feet of our enemies, and our lives and liberties would be at the disposal of men in power in our midst. He also expressed the most implicit faith and unshaken confidence in God, that he would not suffer any yoke to be fastened upon us, or permit us to be brought into bondage, unless it be on account of our own misconduct.

Elder D[avid] McKenzie by request of Prest Wells, said the committee had continued their labours, and every night since ^last meeting^ they had mailed documents to our Delegate [Cannon] as fast as prepared. He himself had devoted his entire time to the subject since its commencement. He then read a synopsis of the chief topics, that the Committee had based their communications upon.

Prest Wells then gave liberty for remarks from any member of the school, and the subjects of our Jury Law, mode of selecting our Juries, our Law pertaining to the Prosecuting District Attorneys &c were freely discussed by Prest Wells ~~F~~ Albert Carrington, Orson Pratt, W[ilford] Woodruff, Joseph F. Smith, A[lonzo] H. Raleigh, Hosea Stout &c., these subjects occupied most of the evenings discussion, ~~and~~ some advocating the necessity of amendments to the same ~~durin~~ by our present Legislative assembly.

Elder Angus M. Cannon said there was ^considerable^ talk outside of this room, that some important changes were needed in our City Council, that the minority of our Citizens should be represented there by some not of our faith, that Nomination of Officers should not be made by our leaders, but left to the choice of the people, both as to Nomination and Election also.

Prest Wells said as this school represented the interests of all the people in this city, it would be a good place to talk over and decide upon whom should be nominated for office at a forth coming convention. He himself had been requested to allow his name ^to be^ put for nomination as Mayor of the City, and if his friends wished him reelected, he would accept of it.[5]

Elder O[rson] Pratt spoke in favour of not only retaining Prest Wells, as Mayor [of Salt Lake City], but every other Officer who had been faithful to their trust[.] As proof that our City Council had done their duty, the City was out of debt.

5. Wells had been mayor since 1866 and would continue in office to 1876.

Prest Wells said the city was not only out of debt, but having loaned the Gas Co[mpany] $50,000.00, the interest of that money actually provides the City with Gas from over 100 lamp posts which was a great benefit to the community and he regarded it as ^a^ good financial success.[6]

He also intimated that the establishment of the Water Works would receive early attention, and have everything pertaining to them so thoroughly done, and the pipes &c so large, and of the very best material, as to ensure entire satisfaction. By having large Cast Iron pipes, with plenty of Hydrants, Water could be thrown over the highest building in the City.[7] They might have to borrow some Money on a short loan, but the tax charged to those who used the water, though small, would amount to more than the interest on the money borrowed.[8]

Elder Joseph F Smith regretted that any one connected with this School should so far betray the confidence of ~~their~~ his brethren, as to associate with and encourage outside faultfinders, especially in reference to some of our City Officers. He hated Hypocracy, but admired moral courage and Manhood to unbosom our feelings here if we have any. He also charged the same member [Hosea Stout] with the habit of using profane and vulgar language, with such conduct he had no fellowship neither with those who indulged in it. ^The above remarks were based upon rumor, and he wished to know if they were correct.^

Elder W[ilford] Woodroof endorsed ~~of~~ ^the^ sentiments just expressed.

Prest Wells would much prefer that all grievances be settled here instead of talking outside.

Elder Angus M. Cannon said that some who were most active in talking and conniving with apostates and others, are members of this school.

Elder Hosea Stout, (who Elder J. F. Smith had special reference to in his remarks) said that owing to the lateness of the evening, he would ^waive^ his reply until next Monday evening.

School was then adjourned for one week ^6^ pm. Benediction by Elder Theo[dore] McKean.

---

6. Natural gas was used to light public streets and some buildings but not yet private residences. Salt Lake City began the shift to electrical power in 1881, again primarily for street lights and public buildings. McCormick, "Electrical Development in Utah."

7. At first culinary water was brought to customers from City Creek through coated wooden pipes. The city would begin installing pressurized cast-iron pipes in 1875. Hooten, "Salt Lake City Old Water Conveyance Systems."

8. The rough draft shows that Wells complained that, through taxation, federal officials were trying to "get their hands into our treasury."

January 19, 1874; Monday

The School of the Prophets met in the City Hall at 6 pm. Present of the 1st presidency ~~Prest~~ D[aniel] H. Wells presiding, also Lorenzo Snow,[9] Brigham Young Jun[io]r & A[lbert] Carrington and 5 of the twelve [apostles]. After singing Prayer by Elder John Sharp. Singing. Roll called and 86 members were present. The Minutes of last meeting were read and approved.

Elder Hosea Stout in his reply to the statements made by Elder Joseph F Smith at the last meeting said there was a wide ^spread^ dissatisfaction among the people from Bear Lake to St. George, ^and in the City particularly^ toward the Members of our [Salt Lake] City Council—and they wanted a change, when they complained to him about them, he invariably told them to go and lay their grievances before the authorities of the Church.

He admitted the habit of using rough language, especially when excited, had tried to controul and overcome it, but did not take the name of God in vain to the best of his recollection.

A short time ago there was a universal feeling of discontent in reference to the Co op[erative] Institution [ZCMI]. He would be thankful and much prefer, that if any Brother either knew or thought he knew anything wrong against him, if he would come to him as a friend, privately and remind him of his faults, instead of publicly exposing him. He would like to see a more open, free and frank spirit among us, instead of shyness and distrust.

Elder Orson Pratt asked Bro Stout what changes he thought was necessary in the City Council. Elder Hosea Stout, said, anything that would unite the people ^together on a ticket^ would suit him, for he wanted to see union.

Prest B[righam] Young Jun[io]r testified to the confidence and good feeling that existed in Bear Lake and Cache Counties towards the City Council & the Authorities of the Church.

Elder W[ilford] Woodruff spoke of the opposing element to the priesthood [church dissidents] from the days of Joseph [Smith] until now, the many excellent traits of character in Prest [Brigham] Young, as evinced by his works, the necessity of wise legislation, by good men, to

9. Snow rarely attended because he lived in Brigham City and presided over a School of the Prophets in that vicinity. He was in town for the annual legislative session.

be of courage, do right, be faithful and united, then Congress and her many [anti-polygamy] bills cannot hurt us.

Prest Wells enquired of the Legislative Brethren [who had traveled] from a distance, whether the spirit of dissatisfaction prevailed among the people or not.

Prest L Snow, and Elders F[ranklin] D. Richards, A[braham] O. Smoot, Geo Peacock,[10] Jesse N Smith,[11] W[illiam] W. Cluff, & W[illard] G. Smith, all testified to the ~~go~~ confidence and good feeling generally entertained by the people, not only towards Prest Young & the Authorities of the church, but towards the admirable course pursued by our City Council.

Prest Wells said, faultfinders were to be found mostly among, Gamblers, Whores & others, but not among Latter day Saints. The City Council wanted to build up and sustain the Kingdom, and had to fight iniquity in every form, hence the hue & cry of dissatisfaction. He also spoke on many other important items.

Prest Jos[ep]h Young Sen[io]r said, if we are in danger, it is because we ourselves are wrong, we lack union, we are comparative strangers to each other. Called on the Bishops to hunt out the poor then, feed, clothe, & warm them. Regretted the course that his son John[12] was taking in publishing falsehoods and misrepresentations about the Authorities & City Council, he [wished he] would stop it.[13] ^Scolding will never unite the people.^

~~Elder Elias Smith~~ [President Joseph Young] asked Prest Wells if he would relinquish his position as Mayor provided he was satisfied that a majority of the voters prefered some one else.

---

10. George D. Peacock (1822–78) wore several hats in Sanpete County. He was the Manti postmaster, constable, probate judge, and a member of the territorial legislature.

11. Jesse N. Smith (1834–1906) presided twice over the Scandinavian mission. He also helped to settle the southern Utah town of Parowan and would later be sent to colonize Arizona. His father, Silas Smith, was Joseph Smith Sr.'s brother, making him a cousin to Joseph Smith Jr.

12. John C. Young (1851–1910) wrote pseudonymous critiques of church leaders for the *Salt Lake Tribune*. Some thirty years later the paper would reveal his identity after he was safely ensconced in Oregon, where he eventually became the postmaster of Portland. "Utah, Its Evils and Their Remedy," *Saints Herald*, Jan. 15, 1887, 45; "Ginx Writes of Mormonism," *Salt Lake Tribune*, Oct. 16, 1904; "Postmaster J. C. Young's Busy Life Is ended by Death," *Oregon Daily Journal*, May 30, 1910.

13. Young is recorded in the rough draft to have said he wanted to throw his son's "type out of the window."

Prest Wells said yes, but should council with Prest Young if so directed.

Elder Elias Smith, John Taylor & Jos[eph] F Smith each made remarks on the above subjects.[14]

School adjourned for one week at 6 oclock pm. Benediction by Elder W[illia]m Asper.

January 26, 1874; Monday

The School of the Prophets met in the City Hall at 6 oclock pm. Present of the 1st Presidency D[aniel] H. Wells, presiding also Lorenzo Snow, B[righam] Young Jun[io]r, A[lbert] Carrington and 7 of the twelve [apostles]. After singing Prayer by Elder James P Freeze. Singing. ^Roll called & 88 members were present.^ Minutes of last meeting were read and accepted.

Elder R[obert] Campbell said he understood that a printed ticket was already out for Mayor & City Council ~~it~~ to present at our forthcoming election, and that his name was on it, he ~~disclaimed~~ knew nothing of it, and was put there without his knowledge or consent. Several other Members of the School whose names were also on the ticket, each disavowed all knowlege of anything connected with it.

Elder Geo Spencer[15] said that Dr. Benedict[16] had been canvassing in favour of the ticket among the clerks of Z.C.M.I. ^&^ stating that Elders Carrington, Tho[ma]s Taylor, & A[lexander] McRae approved of the names of [William] Jennings[17] being on for Mayor in lieu of D H Wells &c.

---

14. The rough draft records that the Smiths and Taylor all praised Daniel H. Wells's governance of Salt Lake City.

15. George B. Spencer (1840–1924) was a son of Orson Spencer, president of the University of Deseret (University of Utah). He helped to settle the Muddy River area of Nevada, near Las Vegas Springs, and then the Bear Lake region of Idaho where he became the LDS bishop, sheriff, and probate judge. He would also serve a mission to Switzerland.

16. Dissatisfied with Salt Lake City leadership, Joseph M. Benedict (1844–96) decided to run for city alderman on an opposition ticket, albeit unsuccessfully. As a surgeon, he became a founder of the Catholic-affiliated Holy Cross Hospital in Salt Lake City. *Biographical Record of Salt Lake City*, 417–18; "The Election To Morrow," "Municipal Election," *Salt Lake Herald*, Feb. 8, 10, 1874.

17. William Jennings (1823–86) would not win the mayoral election in 1874, but he would eight years later. In alignment with Angus Cannon and Hosea Stout (see entries for Jan. 12, 19, 1874), he felt a change was needed in the city's leadership. The Liberal Party decided that year to run Mormon candidates. Jennings was an English emigrant, Mormon polygamist, owner of the large Eagle Emporium retail store, and president of the Utah Southern Railroad. Whitney, *History of Utah*, 741–43.

Elder Sam[ue]l L Evans said he heard Dr Benedict say that W[illiam C. Staines [blank]. Each of above brethren repelled the insinuation of the Dr. as a direct and wilful falsehood.

Elder W[ilford] Woodruff, suggested that he [Benedict], as a member of the church, be dealt with by the Teachers for lying about his brethren. He also suggested the propriety of getting up a ticket here to night, and Elder O[rson] Pratt seconded it, and was carried Unanimously—the following names were then presented, as named ~~by Prest [Brigham] Young before leaving for South,~~ ^as approved^ viz For Mayor, D. H. Wells, For Aldermen 1st. Ward, Isaac Groo, 2nd Geo Crisman 3rd Jeter Clinton, 4th A[lexander] C Pyper, 5th. For Council, B Young [Jr.], Theodore McKean, Albert Carrington, John R Winder, Henry Grow, Nathaniel H Felt, David MKenzie, Hyrum B Clawson, Tho[ma]s Williams. Treasurer. Paul A Schettler, Recorder, Rob[er]t Campbell, Marshal J[ohn] D. T. McAllister.

Before the above were put to the meeting Elder D[avid] McKenzie suggested that all present go into a committee of the whole and each one use his influence to have the above ticket voted entire, every name being ~~se suggested by Prest. Young himself before leaving the City,~~ ^approved by this body^ and as we are menaced on all sides by open and avowed enemies, let us rally around our head, and make manifest by our Union, that we will sustain our Leader, rather than to follow after any factious or disaffected Spirits.

Prest D H Wells said he had never sought any position in this Church, but when Prest Young and his brethren placed him in any responsible ~~pl~~ situation, he ^was^ willing to do his best, and calculated never to shrink from any duty that was legally imposed upon him. He thought it best to have a convention called, and some of this School act as a Committee with a few Sisters, and carry the matter through.

Elder Jno. [John] Wayman made a few remarks, about a privelege being granted the members of each Ward to ~~sele~~ nominate those of their own choice.

~~Elder~~ ^B[ishop]^ Jno. [John] Sharp said a hint to the wise was sufficient, that if Mormonism was represented on the street corners, we might well fear the result, but he thanked God that Latter day saints generally minded their own business and would vote for their own ticket.

~~Elder~~ ^[B[isho]p^ Ja[me]s Leach spoke well of the Members of his ward, who he knew would carry out the Council of the Authorities, He also expressed the most implicit confidence in Prest Wells.

Elder Geo B Wallace did not believe a ticket could be got up, to suit everybodys fancy, but fully anticipated the one now presented would be as unanimously elected, as any previous one.

Elder Orson Pratt Moved That we adopt the entire ticket and use our influence to get every name upon it elected. Seconded by Elder Jos[eph] F. Smith and Carried Unanimously.

A few remarks were then made by B[isho]p A[lonzo] ~~H~~ Raleigh & Prest Wells, ~~&~~ A Carrington, ^& J. F. Smith^ respecting one of the Alderman who had officiated for many years in that office.

It was then Motioned & Carried That a Convention be held in the Old Tabernacle on Saturday 31st at 2 PM. It was also Motioned that the above Convention be published in the [*Deseret*] News & [*Salt Lake*] Herald.

Prest Wells recommended Latter day Saints acting on their own Agency & responsibility, instead of throwing on Prest Young for him to receive all the shafts of the Wicked. Instead of B[isho]ps urging these election matters before a mixed audience at their Ward Meetings, let it be done through their Teachers, and learn to be wise as Serpents, and avoid as much as possible the assaults of the enemy.

Meeting was adjourned for the week at 6 pm. Benediction by Elder L[orenzo] Snow.

February 2, 1874; Monday

The School of the Prophets met in the City Hall at 6 pm. Present of the 1st Presidency, Dan[ie]l H Wells presiding. Also A[lbert] Carrington, and Elders O[rson] Pratt & John Taylor of the twelve [apostles]. After singing Prayer by Elder David McKenzie. Singing. ^Roll was called [and] 67 members answered.^ Minutes of last meeting were read and approved.

Prest Wells, said he owed no apology to this school for himself being under the continual dictation of Prest [Brigham] Young ~~who is~~ the leader of this church, and ~~he~~ ^who^ is led and guided by the spirit of the Almighty, therefore the world may continue to throw their filth and foul insinuations as long as they please, he heeded them not, but simply and most earnestly desired to magnify any and every calling he had to fill as a Servant of the Almighty for this was his Kingdom.

The Secretary then read several letters of Elder Geo Q Cannon written to different Brethren, which breathed the spirit ^of^ deep gratitude towards God, the most unshaken faith in his wise and overruling providences, and promises, and thankfulness for the Prayers, labours, and faith of the Saints in Zion, of which he had the most undeniable proof, by realizing the wonderful influences they were producing all around him.

~~Several~~ Elder A[lbert] Carrington then read a telegram from Prest Young in which he expresses deep and anxious desires towards our Legislative Assembly, that they may not alter or amend any of our existing laws, so as to entangle around our feet, a network of financial or other difficulty.

Several extracts were then read from a small circular published & Printed by ~~the sons of Prest Jos[eph] Young & Elder Levi Riter~~ ^John C Young & John D Riter^,[18] in which was couched the most unblushing insinuations towards the Servants of God, and holding up to ridicule and contempt ~~those~~ the principle of obedience to the Priesthood of the Son of God, rank ^and avowed^ apostacy breathed through every sentiment.[19]

Elder John Taylor fully endorsed the sentiments of Prest [Daniel H.] Wells, ~~in his~~ deeming it an honor to be a servant of the living God, ~~which~~ whose Kingdom is now on the earth, and no power in Congress, or throughout the wide world can overthrow it. He therefore felt perfectly reconciled to the providences of God, as he well knew the truth and correct principles would finally prevail, and all that was wanted, was for the Saints & Servants of God to do right, and leave the results in the hands of God. He then made a few remarks on the labours of the Members of the Legislature, believing that it was their chief aim to do nothing but what would be for the best good of Israel, referring to the Ballot. Registration Law &c.

18. John Dilworth Riter (1850–1925) had recently been a student at the University of Deseret. He and Young were both in their early twenties. Riter's father was well educated, with a library of "some three hundred books," and prominent in the mining industry. *Third Annual Catalogue*, 7; Evans, "History of the Public Library Movement," 5.

19. The tone no doubt was similar to John C. Young's weekly column in the *Salt Lake Tribune* that ran under such headings as "Harem News," written as humorous letters from an observer named "Ginx" who reports to "Dear Brig" on the goings-on in the Lion House and elsewhere. See, e.g., *Salt Lake Tribune*, May 23, 1876.

Elder Orson Pratt made a few remarks on several bills now before our present Legislature.

Elder A[lbert] Carrington fully approved of our present mode of voting, viz naming [those who voted] and numbering the votes. Pensylvania had lately resorted to the same, and Ohio was expecting to come to it, having tried almost every other way. He considered this the most effectual way of cleansing the ballot box [of fraud]. He was opposed to the operations of a Registry Law.[20]

Prest Wells said the great hue & cry against our mode of voting, was not raised so much from a legal objection, as from the pretended fear that many would vote differently but from being exposed to the priesthood[,] [who would know they voted for opposition candidates].

B[isho]p F[rederick] Kesler made a few remarks about a Free School[21] being started at South Cottonwood.

Elder J[ohn] Taylor made some striking contrasts between our situation here, and the old settled Countries, showing that while ^the^ free School system might continue & do tolerably well, in the one, where large legacies were bequeathed for that purpose & other favourable circumstances existed, it never could be sustained here by direct taxation, for he knew that those who now clamour most in its favour would refuse to pay the taxes when assessed. He was also himself opposed to it on several grounds one being the pauperizing tendencies it had, in destroying that self sustaining principle which constitutes the great Motive power to honorable attainments.

^Elder^ ~~Judge~~ Elias Smith made a few remarks on the same subject and in the same direction.

Prest Wells hoped we would continue our Faith, Prayers & efforts, in behalf of Bro Cannon, the God of Heaven had heard our prayers, and will do, if we keep faithful. We shall never be routed from this place, for the majority of this people are for God & his Kingdom, and he felt thankful to know it. Made a few remarks on the [political] ticket recently nominated at the convention, we should sustain it entire, He felt

20. Until 1878 voters presented themselves at the polls and stated their eligibility, then wrote down their preferences on a scrap of paper (there were not yet government-prepared ballots) and presented it to the election judge, who numbered it and recorded the voter's name and ballot number. Davis Bitton, "The Secret Ballot Comes to Utah (1878)," *Meridian* online magazine, 2004.

21. That is, a public school sustained by taxes rather than tuition.

that our Leader [Brigham Young] both sees, hears, & speaks the mind & will of God, hence he always waived his own private feelings.

Free Schools could not be carried on here. The outsiders would never pay taxes to sustain them.

Meeting adjourned for one week at 6 pm. Benediction by Elder A Carrington.

February 9, 1874; Monday

The School of the Prophets met in the City Hall at 6 pm. Present Elder Orson Pratt presiding[,] also of the ^c[ounselo]rs of the^ first Presidency Lorenzo Snow, ^B Young [Jr.], &^ Albert Carrington & ~~B[righam] Young Jun[io]r~~ also John Taylor & Wilford Woodruff ~~ofth~~ of the twelve [apostles]. After singing Prayer by Elder Henry Grow. The Clerk being absent on Election Duties, the roll was not called nor the Minutes of the previous meeting read.

The Municipal Election ~~having~~ ^being^ just closed and much excitement manifested, by W[illia]m Jennings name as Mayor being on the opposition ~~Tithe~~ Ticket, in contradiction to that of D. H. Wells which headed the Peoples ticket, and ^the^ fact that ~~all~~ Gentiles, Apostates, Gamblers, Whores, and ~~th~~ disaffected Mormons all concentrated on the opposition, the days proceedings formed the chief topic of remark from various members of the school.

Elders W[ilford] Woodruff, G[eorge] B. Wallace, John Taylor, Orson Pratt ~~&c being the principle speakers~~ A M[ilton] Musser, Elias Smith and John Sharp being the principal speakers.[22]

A Memorial written by Bishop ^Edw[ar]d^ Hunter to the Hon[orable] Washington Townsend MC [Member of Congress] of Penn[sylvania], ~~was read to the school and approved~~ and signed by some former residents of that state, asking his aid and that of his Colleagues to prevent special [anti-polygamy] legislation for Utah, was read and approved by the School.

Elder F[eramorz] Little explained that he had taken steps to have his name stricken off the opposition ticket, and expected it would so have appeared in the Salt Lake Herald on Sunday Morning.

^Elder Carrington explained why it did not appear.^ Elders Woodruff

22. Woodruff, notes the rough draft, "gave his views about" church members who ran for office on the opposition ballot to be "voted for by our enemies."

& Carrington spoke highly of the unanimity of the Sisters in their voting [for Mormon candidates] to day.

Elder Carrington stated that at his request W[illia]m Jennings had been invited, ~~to~~ (by a Brother) to withdraw his name from the opposition ticket, but he refused to do so.

Elder Sam[ue]l Evans suggested that one or more active men be appointed in each ward to find out every legal ~~and~~ voter, so that every illegal votes may be challenged at our next election. ~~he~~ Aliens [immigrants] should look after their naturalization Papers.

School adjourned for one week at 6 pm. Benediction by Elder Jno [John] Sharp. [Minutes by] D[avid] McKenzie Clerk pro tem.

February 16, 1874; Monday

The School of the Prophets met in the City Hall at 6 pm. Present Prest D[aniel] H. Wells of the First presidency A[lbert] Carrington ^Ass[istan]t^ to D[itt]o also Orson Pratt, W[ilford] Woodruff, John Taylor & F[ranklin] D. Richards of the twelve [apostles]. After singing Pray[er] by Elder A M[ilton] Musser. Singing. Roll called and 76 members were present. Minutes of two previous meetings were read and approved.

Elder A[lbert] Carrington, said that from a Telegraphic communication from Prest [Brigham] Young, the [St. George] Temple was progressing finely, at two ^days^ meeting just held Prest Young spoke ~~3 times~~ ^3^ times and a unanimous vote was given to enter into the [cooperative] Order of Enock.

Elder Orson Pratt said ^by request^ he had hitherto taken charge of the school when the first Presidency were absent, and he thought when any of the C[ounselo]rs to the first Presidency were present, they should preside instead of one of the twelve [apostles], he having no ~~preside~~ desire to transcend his duties, but render honor to whom honor was due.

Prest D. H. Wells said that as Bro Pratt had simply acted by request of the first Presidency, he had done perfectly right, but when any of the Ass[istan]t C[ounselo]rs were present; ~~by~~ they should preside, by virtue of their new appointment.

Elder Geo Goddard enquired the name of the Angel who first appeared to the Prophet Joseph [Smith], as ~~the~~ Nephi is given in the Pearl of Great Price and Times & Seasons, and Moroni in other of our publications.

Elder Orson Pratt said for many years his mind had not been directed to that circumstance and consequently his memory was not clear on that point.

Prest D. H. Wells said he should give a preference to that published in the Doc[trine] & Cov[enants], viz ^Moroni^ that book having passed under review of the Prophet last.[23]

Elder D[imick] B. Huntington mentioned a case in the 16th ward where a good Brother refuses to take the Sacrament, because another receives it who is much given to lying and who is a very bad man.

Prest Wells did not think it wise for any one to deprive themselves of that privilege, because some unworthy one partakes of it.[24]

Elder W Woodruff sustained the same view of the case.

Elder L[orenzo] D[ow] Young enquired ~~if it~~ ^whether^ was ~~not right~~ ^necessary^ for those who ^receive, and also^ administer the Sacrament to kneel with the congregation, as per Doc[trine] & Cov[enants].

Prest D H Wells said since that book was published, the Church had grown, and instructions given in an early day when all the members could meet in a small room, were not always suited to its after growth, so that we must not regard them as being binding under all circumstances. Even Joseph [Smith] before his death blessed the Sacrament in a standing position, and the members meeting in a Grove, where it would not be wisdom to kneel.

Elder E[lias] Morris enquired if it was not right for any member doing wrong such as getting drunk, to make a public confession of that wrong before partaking of the Sacrament.

Prest Wells said it would not be wisdom especially in a mixed audience,

---

23. Oliver Cowdery was the first to name the angel when in April 1834 he referred to it in the *Messenger and Advocate* as Moroni. That same year E. D. Howe published his book, *Mormonism Unvailed*, in which early Mormon convert Leman Copley said he asked Smith to confirm a story he had heard from Joseph Knight, which Smith did. Copley said that "an old man dressed in ordinary gray apparel, sitting upon a log … was Moroni," who had returned once again with the gold plates (Howe, *Mormonism Unvailed*, 276–77). In 1835 the name appeared in the Doctrine and Covenants (10:2; now 27:5) as an addition to a revelation that had been published previously without mentioning the name. Joseph Smith called the personage Moroni in a question-and-answer session published three years later in the July 1838 *Elder's Journal*. The confusion aluded to above came about because in 1838 Smith also called the angel Nephi in the draft of his official history, which was published in the *Times and Seasons* in 1842 without correction.

24. In this day's entry, the clerk jumbled the order of speakers and topics; I have reordered them to maintain the continuity of the discussion.

as it would do more harm than good, but if a man sin let him be dealt with according to the law of the Church.

B[isho]p A[lonzo] H. Raleigh made a few remarks on the necessity and right of the Elders, Bishops, High Councillors &c to have the spirit of Revelation within them, so as not to be under the necessity of judging entirely by the sight of the eye or hearing of the ear.

Elder John Taylor had always considered it a duty and privilege of the servants of God in any calling, if living their religion, to enjoy the spirit of Revelation, yet at the same time, ^~~in dealing with~~^ any one ~~being~~ dealt with, whose fellowship was at stake, we must be guided by the testimony adduced.

Elder Hosea Stout said he felt it was the duty of a Bishop, or a High Councillor to see, that they had the spirit of judgment upon them at the time of dissecting testimony, or they will suffer the consequences. He named a case where Joseph [Smith] the Prophet had a revelation from God pertaining to the sin of an individual, but could not introduce that as testimony before the High Council.

Elder John Sharp named a similar instance where Prest Young had a revelation of a persons guilt, and the guilty one subsequently admitted it himself.

Elder Geo B Wallace made a few remarks on the same subject, backed by his own lengthy experience of nearly 20 years, in connexion with High Council trials. He regarded the voters of the opposition ticket at our Municipal Election (those who did it with their eyes open) as ^much^ guilty of rebellion to the priesthood, as if done at one of our public Conferences.

B[isho]p F[rederick] Kesler mentioned the outline of several cases of difficulty in his ward, which he was handling with all the wisdom he could get.

B[isho]p S[amuel] A. Woolley enquired if testimony [accusation] of an outsider could be taken against a brother in good standing. ^He was aware what it said in Doc[trine] & Cov[enants].^

Elder Geo B. Wallace said, if a charge was brought before him against a brother by an outsider, he should consult the highest authority at hand, and if told to entertain it he should do so. But where the fellowship of a member was at stake, they would not like it.

Prest D. H. Wells said the counsel of the Almighty was in the bosom of ~~the Alm~~ his servants, and they sometimes acted on the impulse of the Moment, at other times when a man's fellowship is pending they acted according to the law and testimony, and when there is any doubt always lean on the side of Mercy, the time will come, when the servants of God will have to judge the world.

School was adjourned for One week at 6 oclock pm. Benediction by Elder Elias Morris.

February 23, 1874; Monday

The School of the Prophets met in the City Hall at 6 pm. Present Prest D[aniel] H Wells presiding[,] also Alb[ert] Carrington Ass[istan]t co[unsellor] & Orson Pratt, W[ilford] Woodruff, John Taylor & Jos[eph] F. Smith of the twelve [apostles]. After singing Prayer by Elder E. Snelgrove. Singing. Roll called and 66 Members answered. Minutes of last meeting were read and approved.

The Clerk read a Memorial recently sent to Senator ^Cha[rle]s^ Sumner,[25] Member [of the Senate] from Mass[achusetts] soliciting his aid and influence against the passage of any bills containing proscriptive measures for Utah.

A Letter was also read from our Delegate Geo Q Cannon to Prest D. H. Wells. Prest Wells said a Memorial had been presented in Congress from a Committee of Gentiles & Apostates in this City, urging Special Legislation.[26]

It was then Moved and Carried That a Committee be appointed to draw up a Counter Memorial to the above, with a view of checkmating the same. Prest Wells appointed the following as the Committee[:] Elders Orson Pratt, John Taylor, ^A[lbert] Carrington,^ D[avid] McKenzie & A. M[ilton] Musser.

Elder E[lijah] F. Sheets, gave a brief report of his visit to Sanpete [County]. In Company with Elder Tho[ma]s Taylor, they found Grain rather scarce, but a good feeling among the people, united in everything required at their hands.

Elder Jos[eph] F. Smith who expected to leave in a few days on a Mission to England, said he hoped to have the prayers of the brethren while absent, that he might be kept in the faith, and do good, be

25. Unfortunately, Senator Sumner died sixteen days later on March 11.
26. See June 8, 1872, entry.

faithful and true from this time forth & for ever. A unanimous ~~Vote was~~ ^Amen^ responded.

<u>Elder John Taylor</u> spoke of ^the^ great struggle ~~g~~ that always existed between the powers of Light and the powers of darkness, and that as the Kingdom of God grows, and our powers of resistance increases, so will it be called into requisition. The Devil would like to destroy the kingdom of God. ^if he could^ ~~He expected~~ and ^Elder Taylor said^ his business while on this earth was to fight the Devils, He had nothing else to do. He then traced the opposition to this latter day work from a small neighbourhood, to the present effort now being made in Congress with the President at their head, to crush the Kingdom of God, but if we do right, there is no power on earth can harm us. If the storms blow, and the powers of Hell should be let loose upon us,[27] we have nothing to fear. God is moving and all is right. Everything that can be shaken will be shaken, if we can only have clean hands and pure hearts, he was perfectly willing to leave the balance.

Prest D. H. Wells, made a special request of the Bishops to look well after the poor, and find employment for thsoe who are out of work, as much as possible. He felt like keeping up a full quota of Temple hands, in preparing rock for the Temple, as they had found it difficult~~y~~ a time back to get men, and although there may be but a moderate supply of Bread stuff on hand, let us exercise Faith in God, and put in plenty of seed, we having nothing to fear, he felt encouraged, and if the Devil gets more mad then he is, no matter.

Let us, in this School only be thoroughly united in favour of the Kingdom of God, in our Faith, Prayers & good works, and the influence of our union will be felt by our Delegate. No man who has the testimony of Jesus in his heart, will ever be found to oppose Israel[,] [meaning the church].

B[isho]p L[eonard] W Hardy said the poor in the 12th ward were well cared for and lived as well as he did.

B[isho]p A[lonzo] H Raleigh suggested, that the City Council revive and enforce the City Dog Law, for they are becoming so numerous as to be~~come~~ an intolerable nuisance.

27. The scribe repeated twice "If the storms blow, and the powers of Hell should be let loose upon us."

The School was then adjourned for one week at 6 pm. Benediction by Elder R[obert] L. Campbell.

March 2, 1874; Monday

The School of the Prophets met in the City Hall at 6 pm. Present Prest D[aniel] H. Wells presiding[,] A[lbert] Carrington Ass[istan]t C[ounselo]r. After singing Prayer by Elder Tho[ma]s Taylor. Singing. Roll called and 50 members responded. The Minutes of last meeting were read and approved.

Prest Wells wished the Clerk to read a Telegram ~~which had been~~ ^just^ received from Prest B[righam] Young and Geo A Smith, stating that in several settlements in Dixie, the people had been organized into the Order of Enock, and in other places they were ready and anxious for organization, which was a source of much joy to the Presidency, and hoped the brethren in Salt Lake City would be equally so, and those [interested] to hand in their names to ~~Prest Wells,~~ ^Elder A Carrington^. They also expressed a wish for the Brethren to meet and adjourn the [general] Conference until 1st ^Thursday in^ May.

Prest Wells then requested the Clerk to read from the Doc[trine] & Cov[enants] what the Lord had revealed through the Prophet Joseph [Smith] concerning the order of Enock—and he read a long revelation commencing on page 284.[28]

Prest Wells said, when the Kingdom of God was fully set up, the ways of the world would be turned upside down, Society as now organized possessed no uniting or cementing element, it was therefore absolutely necessary for God to interpose, and introduce an order of things in which he could be recognized as the rightful owner of earthly things, and dispense the same ^through his priesthood^ to a people who were willing to receive them ~~as st~~ and handle them as Stewards, according to the order of God as revealed through the living oracles.

Elder Geo B Wallace said from his first initiation into the church he had looked for and expected the God of Heaven to organize his people in Temporal matters, he ^believed he^ was ready now, as he ever would be, to enter the order, when required.

28. The revelation from April 1834 became D&C 99 in the Liverpool edition and D&C 104 in the current version. It used code names for various church leaders: Pelagoram for Sidney Rigdon, Zombre for John Johnson, and so on.

Elder L[orenzo] D[ow] Young made a few remarks on the cultivation of kind and encouraging feelings towards each other, especially towards ^those^ who experience a sudden change of position and circumstances, he deprecated the practise of the world, of kicking a man when he's down. He also prayed that god would prepare us for his order of Government.

Prest D H Wells ~~contrasted~~ ^spoke of^ the present maxims and ways of the world especially in the acquisition ~~of~~ of wealth, how uneven and unfair they operated in society, by raising some to affluence, and keeping others in abject poverty, hence as a natural consequence, a constant war is waging between Capitol & Labour. God is left out of the question, He is not acknowledged, but all goes to build up the Devils Kingdom. He rejoiced to know that God was about to usher in a state of things that would correct these evils.

Elder L[orenzo] D[ow] Young made a few remarks on the right and wrong way of acquiring wealth.

Elder E[dwin] D Woolley made a few favourable allusions to the character and ability of our late Sup[erintenden]t of the Co op[erative] Institution [William H. Hooper].

Elder A[lonzo] H. Raleigh said [he agreed with George B. Wallace, that] since his first introduction into the Church, he had been looking for and expecting the time would come when his time and means would be under the dictation of the servants of God, whenever that order was introduced here, he wished to be apprized of it, that he might be on hand, as he expected to be.

Elder Tho[ma]s Taylor could not endorse a habit too often indulged in, by the Elders of ~~casting~~ directing their insinuations against Merchants as a Class, instead of confining them to those individuals who are known to do wrong. An honest man cannot be anything but an Honest Man let him be found in the Mechanic Shop or behind a counter, and a Dishonest Man was very hard to convert into anything else.

Elder Geo B Wallace had full confidence in the living oracles, the letter of the book killeth, while the Spirit giveth life. When the order of God is introduced, we would hear no more about ^individual^ tithing, High Council trials, or unpleasant feelings about dollars and cents.

Elder Ja[me]s Leach desired to be one with his brethren. Elder S[amuel] A. Woolley hoped to be willing when the proper time came, to do what was required of him.

Prest Wells spoke of the recent financial crisis,[29] and its partial effect on our Co op[erative] Institution, was pleased to learn it was in a healthy and sound condition notwithstanding, hoped the brethren would not offer or sell their stock below par, as the Institution was on a good solid basis, and ~~could p~~ all past indebtedness was paid up, ^that was due^ and they were prepared to pay as fast as their debts ~~fell~~ ^became^ due.

Elder R[obert] F Neslen spoke highly of the Coop[erative] Enterprize, it had done a great amount of good, was a stepping stone to a more advanced order, hoped the brethren would use their influence to hold it up in public estimation, &c.

Elder A[lbert] Carrington, briefly ~~and closely scanned the~~ ^reviewed^ the general Character of Merchants, Lawyers, Doctors & Parsons, ~~based on his~~ ^from a standpoint of his^ own experience with the same. He also expressed full confidence in the present condition of our Co op[erative] Institution, knowing it to be in a solvent and thriving state.

School was adjourned for one week at 6 pm. Benediction by Elder Rob[er]t Campbell.

March 9, 1874; Monday

The School of the Prophets met in the City Hall at 6 pm. Present Prest D[aniel] H. Wells presiding[,] [with] A[lbert] Carrington Ass[istan]t C[ounselo]r and Elders W[ilford] Woodruff, Orson Pratt & John Taylor of the twelve [apostles]. After singing Prayer by Tho[ma]s E. Jeremy. Singing. Roll called and 69 members were present. Minutes of previous meeting were read and approved.

The subject of Special Legislation ^for Utah^ was refered to by Prest Wells, also the Memorial got up and signed by ~~many of our~~ ^26^ Lawyers a few days ago, ~~and~~ the general activity and strenuous exertion of our enemies, that are being made, to induce Congress to pass one of those obnoxious bills, which would utterly deprive us of every civil and Religious right. And with a view of counteracting the above, He desired the brethren [who had emigrated] from the various states of the Union, to draw up Memorials of remonstrance and appeal, get them signed by old citizens of each State, and forwarded to Senators and ~~Congressmen~~ ^Rep[resentatives] who^ represent their several States.

29. The Panic of 1873 started with a stock market crash in Vienna that cascaded across Europe and the Atlantic, leading to a four-year economic downturn referred to at the time as the Great Depression. White, *Republic for Which It Stands*, 260–87.

Elder Hosea Stout said he had ~~discovered~~ ^been reflecting upon^ a law ~~in Section 7~~ which provided and authorized the holding of a ~~district~~ ^US^ Court in a County, if the expenses of said court were paid by the County ~~court,~~ and there were cases sufficient to justify it. He suggested that an appeal be got up, setting forth the ^Law &^ facts in the case, duly signed, and sent to Judge [James B.] McKean, if he complyed & held court, it would demonstrate that legal courts could be held here, and if he refused, we will have additional arguments to use, against special legislation. This subject occupied considerable time and finally resulted in the appointment of Hosea Stout & Albert Carrington, a Committee to draw up said petition, signed ^by our best Lawyers &c^ presented to Judge McKean, and also published in the papers.

It was then ascertained from what States in the Union the brethren of the school hailed from, and arrangements made for Memorials to be immediately drawn up, ~~a~~ signed and forwarded.

A telegram was then read from Dixie [southern Utah] containing some particulars of the plan of organization, and the progress that Prest B[righam] Young & Geo A Smith were making, in getting the brethren to enter into it. Two letters were also read from our Delegate ~~School~~ Elder Geo Q Cannon. One [letter] announced the receipt of a Memorial from B[isho]p [Edward] Hunter & ~~others~~, the other, his experience in connexion with the McKeis and other bills before the Ter[ritorial] Com[mission].[30]

The School was then adjourned for one week at 6 pm. Benediction by Elder Geo B Wallace.

March 16, 1874; Monday

The School of the Prophets met in the City Hall at 6 pm. Present Prest D[aniel] H. Wells presiding. A[lbert] Carrington Ass[istan]t C[ounselo]r & Elders W[ilford] Woodruff, ^&^ John Taylor of the twelve [apostles also present]. Minutes of last meeting were read and approved. After singing Prayer by Elder John H. Rumell. Singing. Roll called and 61 members responded.

A number of very interesting telegrams were read to the school received a few days ^ago^ from Prests B[righam] Young & Geo A Smith

30. As chair of the House Committee on Territories, George C. McKee (R–Illinois) had introduced a bill to disenfranchise women in Utah and grant more power to federal officials in the territory. GQCJ, Feb. 25–26, 1874.

on the subject of the Order of Enock, and wishing the twelve [apostles] to visit the wards of the City to ~~labour~~ lay the matter before the saints, and give them an opportunity to hand in their names to the Bishops, both Male and female, who desire to enter the order.[31]

Prest D. H. Wells said he visited, and preached in the 20th ward yesterday, on the subject, and Elder W Woodruff said he had done the same in the 16th ward. It was ^then^ announced that several Memorials had been drawn up, signed and forwarded to the ~~Reps~~ Members of Congress representing several states in the Union.

The Clerk read a letter from Judge [James B.] McKean ^as Published^ in the Deseret News, in which he declines to hold a ~~Co~~ District Court in Salt Lake County as per request of many Memorialists.[32]

~~A law passed by the Legislature and vetoed by the Governor giving a Months extension for persons to file on their property, who had failed to do so within the specified time granted by Congress. was the subject of many remarks~~.

Prest Wells then made a few remarks on the order of Enock as far as he viewed and comprehended it and desired to hear from the members of the School their minds and feelings on the same subject, especially as the twelve [apostles] had been called upon by Prests Young & Geo A Smith to visit and preach to the Members of the various wards of the City.

Elders John Taylor & W Woodruff ventilated the subject at considerable length. showing the absolute necessity ~~of~~ ^for^ a change in our Temporal matters, in order to unite and bind us together as a community, or we will never have power among the Nations. This Dispensation comprizes in it every good principle that existed in all past dispensation. Celestial Law & Baptism for the dead were revealed just at the right time, so the Order of Enock comes along when circumstances that now surround us, demand a change in our social policy.

Elders Geo B. Wallace, John Sharp, Jos[eph] Pollard. Howard Spencer & Tho[ma]s Taylor also shown some of the advantages that would

31. The telegrams back and forth between Young in St. George and leaders in Salt Lake City discussed farming, making clothes for the United Order, and progress on construction of the Salt Lake Temple. See telegrams in Young, Office Files, box 46, fd. 8, CHL.

32. McKean explained that the district court had a backlog of cases in several counties, not just one, and that many of the cases involved the US government, which by statute could not be tried in a county court. McKean, "Judge McKean and the County Court," *Salt Lake Tribune*, Mar. 15, 1874.

acrue from a proper classification of labour, ^or^ a well conducted cooperative system, by having suitable men appointed to take charge of, and superintend the various departments, such an order as contemplated will not only, find employment for the people, (instead of pauperizing them by Charity as at present) but it will develope our own manufacturing resources, they each hoped to be ready to respond to what was required, when they could get a proper understanding of it.

School was adjourned for one week at 6 o clock pm. Benediction by Elder J[ames] P. Freeze.

March 23, 1874; Monday

The School of the Prophets met in the City Hall at 6 pm. Present Prest D[aniel] H. Wells presiding [and] Elder W[ilford] Woodruff & John Taylor of the twelve [apostles]. After singing Prayer by Elder Levi Richards. Roll called and 69 members were present. Minutes of last meeting were read and approved.

<u>Prest Wells</u> gave a privilege to the school for the presentation of any subject for consideration and <u>Elder Geo B Wallace</u> propounded the following question. Whether it was right for one Brother to sue another Brother to secure a [payment of] debt to prevent its being outlawed by the statute of limitations?

The subject being one of considerable interest, elicited a great many remarks, and [was] illustrated by many cases recently brought before various authorities of the church[.] Many expressed decided opinions on the questions, which resulted in the following, as being the unanimous conclusions of those present—Viz

That where a Brother ^is^ owing a debt by Note or Book account, and refuses either to pay or renew his obligation to prevent its being outlawed, the proper course to pursue, ~~wi~~ would be to labour with him by the priesthood, according to the Order of the Church, should this fail, then a Brother would be entirely justified in obtaining it by a Legal process.

The question was also asked, Whether a Note endorsed by an interest payment, (if the word interest was not specified) would not renew its obligation.[33]

33. Before there was paper currency, people exchanged promissory notes and recorded payments on the back side of the notes. Utah's territorial legislature had passed the Civil Practice Act of 1870 four years earlier limiting debt collection to four years, so the first notes to fall under this statute's jurisdiction were just coming due. Not that the

The Answer as given by Elder Elias Smith & others, was that it would not. And the only safe way to prevent its being outlawed was by having a New Note, renewed within a period of every 4 years, that being the ~~period~~ ^time^ of limitation that a Note can be collected by law. Neither would an endorsement of any kind secure its renewal. All [store] Book accounts contracted since the passage of the Law of limitation can run two years ~~since~~ from the date of the last entry before being outlawed.

Prest Wells & Elder Woodruff ~~each bore testimony to the remarkable quality of our soil, especially adapted to the growth of wheat, having rested for a thousand years and received the washings from these mountains,~~ each gave some timely council to the cultivators of the soil—shewing the necessity of replenishing it with manure to prevent its entire exhaustion of the Wheat element, as was the case in some countries, where Wheat used to be grown in great quantities, now they cannot grow a bushel. We have in this Territory some of the choicest Virgin soil in the world, ~~but~~ and need care and culture to preserve it.

School ~~was~~ adjourned for one week at 6 pm. Benediction by Elder R[obert] F. Neslen.

March 30, 1874; Monday

The School of the Prophets met in the City Hall at 6 pm. Present Prest D[aniel] H Wells presiding [and] Orson Pratt, W[ilford] Woodruff & John Taylor of the twelve [apostles]. After singing Prayer by Elder Miner G Atwood. Singing. Roll called Sixty Members present. Minutes of last meeting were read and approved.

The Clerk then read a letter from Elder Geo Q Cannon our "Delegate" addressed to A M[ilton] Musser.

A Telegram was also read from Prest Geo A Smith, requesting some Dry Goods and Groceries to be sent down to St George for the workmen on the Temple to the amount of about $1600.00.

Prest Wells said that whoever would assist in raising that amount, they should be allowed the same on their Cash Tithing [account], and the ~~following names and amounts were called out~~ sum of $1125.00 was

legislature had singled it out as a topic of particular concern, however. The territory had simply copied a lengthy statute from the New York Code that included the limitation on collections. The states of California and Nevada had also copied the New York statute. *Hubbell's Legal Directory*, 372.

promised, all of which to be paid by the 1st May, by different members of the school, and a few of the Policemen whose names and amounts were obtained by Andrew Burt, while the school was in session.

The question, as to whether Bishops should, or should not give receipts for Cash tithing to the members of their wards was freely discussed, and B[isho]ps E[dwin] D. Woolley, N[athan] Davis, F[rederick] Kesler, J[ames] Leach, W[illiam] Thorn ^A[lexander] McRae^ & several others were unanimous in their feelings, that they should not, but continue as heretofore, to keep a strict account of all money tithing paid into their hands in a book kept for that purpose, of the name, and amount paid. And when these small sums accumulated, to take it to B[isho]p [Edward] Hunters Office and get ~~one receipt~~ ^an order^ for the whole amount, and each individuals name and amount endorsed on the back.[34]

The subjects of consecration ~~and~~ Order of Enock, and United Order, occupied the remainder of the evening, and as no one was fully posted in detail with the system now being inaugurated by Prests B[righam] Young and Geo A Smith in St. George [Utah] and other settlements in the south, a great variety of ideas were advanced by different members of the school.

Prest Wells & Elder John Taylor spoke at length upon the present condition of Society ^in the world^ as now organized commercially ^& Politically^ & its influence on the morals, ~~producing~~ producing dishonesty, and destroying confidence among the people, and we ~~as a people~~ to a great extent have copied after them ~~world~~ and as a natural consequence, confidence in each other is almost extinct, hence the necessity for the Lord to interpose, with some plan to unite us, in our Temporal concerns, and ~~so~~ classify, and utilize our labour, ~~as to produce far more beneficial results~~ ^foster home industries, & create work for the^ unemployed, until we can raise among ourselves, everything we need to eat, drink, or wear, under such a wise and economical arrangement where no one calls anything [h]is own. God can handle us to much better advantage in the building up of his Kingdom.

34. After bundling small IOUs into a single note at the Bishop's Storehouse, a local bishop could use the note at a church facility or almost anywhere else in the city as currency. Similarly, printed tithing scrip was used to pay church employees, feed the poor, and compensate individuals for donating goods in excess of tithing.

Meeting was adjourned for one week at 6 pm. Benediction by Elder Andrew Burt.

April 6, 1874; Monday

The School of the Prophets met in the City Hall at 6 pm. Present Prest D[aniel] H. Wells presiding [and] Orson Pratt, W[ilford] Woodruff & John Taylor of the twelve [apostles]. After singing Prayer by Elder Harrison Sperry. Singing. Roll called and 65 members responded. Minutes of previous meeting were read and approved.

B[isho]p A[lonzo] H. Raleigh proposed a question on the subject of tithing, and whether a Bishop held the right either to remit tithing, or deviate from the letter of the law which requires one tenth of our increases.

It was suggested that ^the^ circumstances surrounding the saints at the time that law was given were very different to what they are now, and some laws would not bear the same rigid interpretation at one time, as when first given, hence the necessity and safety of leaving the execution of those laws to the wisdom of the living Oracles. Several brethren bore testimony to the fact, that the people as a whole paid a fair tithing, ~~some thought, that taking the Territory throughout, a little over 2/3 of a full tithing was paid. B[isho]p A. H. Raleigh this agreed with~~ the testimony ^of the bishops from^ ~~of~~ the tithing report, received by B[isho]p [Edward] Hunter from all the Counties in the Territory, ^was that 2/3 of the tithing was paid.^ ~~B[isho]p A H Raleigh did not think there was over a tenth of the real tithing of the people paid.~~

~~The subjects of consecration and the United Order were next conversed upon~~ ^by Elder John Taylor & Prest Wells &c^ ~~shewing~~ ^said^ that what property we controul is not ours but Gods, and as such should hold it for the building up of his Kingdom. We should be careful not to sustain our enemies who use their means to secure special legislation, and keep up the opposition [news]papers in our midst. ~~it was not deemed prudent to cut a man off from the church for not paying his tithing~~ We should be united in our prayers in behalf of Bro [George Q.] Cannon for a strong effort was being made to unseat him if possible, and also to get one of those obnoxious bills passed which would plunge the Territory into a state of anarchy, the prayers of a faithful people avail~~able~~eth much &c

Elder John Taylor spoke of the willingness of the Elders of Israel to accomplish whatever is required of them, instancing the raising of 500 teams to fetch the saints from the Missouri River,[35] their cheerful response to ~~fulfill~~ [serve at the] start on any kind of a Mission, and other labours which he adverted to, which was an unmistaken^a^ble proof that God had a good people here.

School was adjourned for one week at 6 o clock pm. Benediction by ^Elder^ Elias Morris.

April 13, 1874; Monday

The School of the Prophets met in the City Hall at 6 pm. Present Prest D[aniel] H. Wells presiding [and] Orson Pratt, ^&^ W[ilford] Woodruff, of the Twelve [Apostles]. After singing Prayer by Elder W[illiam] Eddington. Singing. Roll called and 62 Members were present. Minutes of previous meeting were read and approved.

After a few remarks being made on the subject of tithing. The following questions were submitted in writing by a member of the school[:]

1st. Whether it would ^not^ be appropriate as a token of respect, for those Members of the school who might ^desire^ it to meet Prest [Brigham] Young & Co[mpany] ~~at Provo~~, at Provo on their arrival, ~~there~~, if so what day and hour should they start?

2. What would be the probable cost of ~~such~~ the trip [by rail]?

3. What has been done in the various wards, in reference to the united Order?

2nd Elder F[eramorz] Little, Sup[erinteden]t of S[outhern] R[ail] R[oad] Co[mpany] in answer to the 2nd question, kindly offered a gratuitous rider [ticket] per Rail to any or all Members of the School ~~who~~ who wished to shew their respect to Prest Young.

1st. Prest D H Wells, in reply to the 1st question, said there would be no impropriety for any one who wished it, to go and meet Prest Young, on his arrival at Provo. He himself intended to do so. Time of starting from here would depend upon when ^Prest Young & Co[mpany] reached there.^

The 3rd question was answered by the following[:]

35. A reference to the 1834 Army of Israel (also known as Zion's Camp), a paramilitary march led by Joseph Smith and others from Ohio to Missouri in support of church members driven from their homes across the Missouri River from Jackson County into Clay County. The march was unsuccessful.

B[isho]p F[rederick] Kesler reported that about 50 names had been enrolled in the 16 ward.

C[ouncilo]r E[lias] Morris " 50 " 15 ".

B[isho]p [Alexander]McRae " 32 " 11 ".

B[isho]p L[orenzo] D[ow] Young made some enquiry pertaining to the [United] order.

Prest Wells said all he knew about it [enrollment in the United Order] was what he had received by telegrams from Prest Young, and they had all been read ~~at~~ ^before^ the School. He had visited several wards and spoke to them on the subject, and the more he thought ~~upon~~ ^of^ and ~~upon~~ spoke upon it, the more his mind expanded, and he could see that God was inspiring his servant Brigham to lay it before the people, to bring us closer together, into a more solid compact, to classify labour, to create employment for the people, by opening ^up^ new industries, be a check on extravagance in dress &c, encourage home Manufactures, inspire those now dependent to become more comfortable & self sustaining. In this order there will be no abridgement of enterprise, but rather encourage and increase it. Wealth in itself will not damn any one, but the improper use made ^of^ it, constitutes the evil. True Charity ~~is~~ consists not so much in giving means to help the needy, as putting them in a way to sustain themselves by their own industry. ~~Being dictated by the priesthood in our temporal affairs, all these things can be more successfully carried~~. Music, education and other necessary accomplishments will be taught and rendered available other side*[36]

Elder F Little made a few excellent remarks on the same subject. Expressed his gratitude to God for blessing his efforts in trying to get a comfortable home, and other surrounding ~~com~~ conveniences and improvements, had always worked hard both Mentally & Physically, and from the nature of his organization, he took peculiar pleasure in finding employment for others.[37]

B[isho]p L D Young gave a short epitome [summary] of his experience from the time he embraced the Gospel, did not ^receive it on its

36. The sentence is followed by a gap to the end of the page.

37. Little is defending his capitalistic ventures as a co-owner of five lumber mills, a gristmill, a saloon, and a contracting business that had helped build the railroads, irrigation canals, telegraph lines, and public buildings. In the next meeting, he will nevertheless give his name as a volunteer to live the United Order. In two years he will be elected mayor of Salt Lake City.

first presentation, but^ ~~do so, without~~ pondered[38] well the step he was about he was about to take. ~~was~~ ^He acted with^ caution~~s~~ then, ~~had been ever since~~ ^had always been known since, as slow and cautious^ and expected ever to be, ~~would b~~ had ~~always worked hard~~, ^been a hard worker^ his life had been threatened several times for the Gospel sake, and yet by the blessing of God, he was now enjoying good health. & hoped to endure faithful to the end.

Prest Wells ^then^ said all those who wished to be dictated by the Priesthood in their temporal affairs, might call out their names, and gave his own first. Others also were given in as follows[:]

D. H. Wells
W Woodruff
Orson Pratt
Amos M Musser
D[imick] B Huntington
~~B[isho]p~~ A McRae
Geo B Wallace
George Goddard
Abinidi Pratt
A[lonzo] H Raleigh
Howard O Spencer
Jno [John] R Winder
Andrew Burt
W[illia]m Thorn
W L N Allen
N[athaniel] H Felt
Daniel Corbett
James Leach
E[lijah] F. Sheets
F[rederick] Kesler
W[illia]m Asper
J[ohn] D. T. McAllister
Elias Morris
Geo Nebeker
Levi Richards
Theo[dore] McKean
Jos[eph] Washington
Jesse W. Fox
Edw[ar]d Hunter

School adjourned for one week at 6 pm. Benediction by Elder N[athaniel] H. Felt.

April 20, 1874; Monday

^(Prest [Brigham] Young & party arrived in the City at 4 oclock this afternoon).^ The School of the Prophets met in the City Hall at 6 pm. Present Elder Orson Pratt presiding [and] Elders W[ilford] Woodruff & John Taylor of the twelve [apostles][;] the latter was not present at last school. After singing Prayer by Elder W[illia]m H Folsom. Singing. ^Roll called and [blank] members answered to their names.^ Minutes of previous meeting were read and approved after which Prest Pratt gave a privelege ~~for any~~ ^to those^ Members to give in their names as willing to enter the united order, who did not do so at the last meeting[:]

John Taylor
John Van Cott
David McKenzie
George C. Riser
Paul A Schettler
Henry Grow

38. "Pondered" was written over the word "pondering."

Sam[ue]l L Evans	Isaac Brockbank	A W. Winberg
Henry Arnold	Jos[eph] Bean	F. W. Young
Miner G Atwood	Milando Pratt	George Hoggan
Mark Barnes	Jos[eph] Pollard	M[artin] H Peck
Jos[eph] Booth	F[eramorz] Little	Alex[ande]r Steel

Several members of the school having gone down to Nephi[39] to Meet Prest Young & party there, and holding a two days Meeting, ~~the~~ afforded them an opportunity of listening to many remarks from Prest Young and others, on the subject of the United Order that so many had recently entered into in the South,[40] wherever the subject had been fairly laid before the People, and were now called upon to report to the school what they had heard, as Prest Young and party were too much fatigued to be present this evening, having laboured incessantly from the time they started [home] from St. George. Consequently the entire evening from the time of opening until near 9 oclock was occupied by Elders John Taylor, F[eramorz] Little, E[lijah] F. Sheets, Prest O Pratt[,] & Elias Smith, the three former ~~enumerating~~ ^rehearsing^ what they could remember having heard at Nephi respecting the nature and object of uniting the people together in a Cooperative organization, as contemplated by this New or United Order. The Main features of which seemed to be, for each organization to be governed by a President, ^2^ vice presidents, Secretary, Treasurer & a board of directors, under a Constitution ^& bye laws^ so thoroughly in accord with our civil laws that no legal tribunal or lawyer can render it inoperative or void. That the leading objects aimed at will be the classification of labour, the utilization of time and means, the encouragement of home industries, to benefit and bless the worthy and industrious poor, to blend the interests of the people in one direction, in contradistinction to the clashing and conflicting interests now existing, ~~the encour~~ to

39. The train only reached as far as Provo, so those who met Young's party in Nephi would have had to travel the remaining forty miles by carriage, wagon, or on horse.

40. On Sunday, April 19, Young's sermon was transcribed and published in the *Journal of Discourses* 17:47–50. He proposed that the cooperative movement should be adapted to each community, "perhaps the order of Enoch" in one case, "and perhaps an all-things-in-common order" in whatever way was determined best by the local authorities. That was, in fact, what happened. Some of the organizations were structured like joint-stock ventures, others like trade associations, and some were communal—about 200 separate organizations in all. L. Dwight Israelsen, "United Orders."

check the growing pride ^folly^ and extravagance in our midst, and encourage economy in dress &c. To cease sustaining our enemies—and with the surplus means that will naturally accumulate, under such a God like order, to be used to gather the poor, the building of Temples, or the purchase of the centre Stake of Zion. Missionaries Families ~~to~~ to be provided for, children educated &c &c. ~~T~~

Prest Orson Pratt greatly rejoiced to know that the time had now arrived for the fulfillment of those things that he had so many years been preaching ^about^ and publishing, and only regretted, that he had not some thousands of dollars to put into this united order. He fully endorsed the wisdom of having the organization so arranged as not to clash with our Civil laws, we could not enter into the perfect order of God, until we ^were^ free from ^all connexion with^ any civil Government. He then enumerated many advantages that will accrue, by the carrying out of this new order, such as the purchase of land, the building of the New Jerusalem, to be done mainly by the Lamanites [Native Americans], who will have to be instructed in the Gospel, in Arts, Mechanics, Agriculture &c. If we enter heart and soul in this matter, God will soon prepare us to go back and build up the waste places &c.

Elder Elias Smith, highly appreciated the remarks he had heard, he knew they were correct, though there was something about his [physical and mental] organization that rendered him very slow and cautious in all his movements, and having occupied so many years an official position, it had always afforded him peculiar pleasure to ~~t~~ see the end from the begining in anything he undertook. Was one with the priesthood and always expected to be, but had not yet given in his name, hoped his brethren would not attribute that to any lack of appreciation on his part, to the plan now being inaugurated, or any want of confidence in the servants of God, it was neither, all he wanted, was a little more time for reflection, to obtain a fuller comprehension of the subject, which he hoped the brethren would grant him etc.

The School was then adjourned for one week at 6 pm. Benediction by Elder David McKenzie.

April 27, 1874; Monday

The School of the Prophets met in the City Hall at 6 o clock pm. Present Prest Orson Pratt presiding[;] [also present] John Taylor, of the twelve [apostles]. After singing Prayer by Elder Abinidi Pratt. Singing. Roll called and 75 members were present. Minutes of previous Meeting were read and accepted.

Two letters from Elder Geo Q Cannon, our Delegate at Washington [DC] were read to the School by the Clerk.

Elder Soren Iverson of the 2nd Ward, said as a Member of the School of the Prophets, ~~he in com~~ and as God doeth nothing but what he reveals to his servants the Prophets, he in common with the rest of the School was entitled to receive revelation, and he desired to bear testimony to that School, that God had revealed to him that Jesus Christ was the very Eternal Father, and Creator of the heavens and the earth and that he was the only Personage of Tabernacle in the Godhead, and that he ^himself^ never worshiped any other God but Jesus Christ, for he was king of Kings and Lord of Lords, that when the Father and the Son was ~~refered to~~ ^spoken of^, it has reference to the Spirit and tabernacle of Jesus Christ. To prove this, he gave many quotations from the Book of Mormon, Doc[trine] & Cov[enants] & the Bible. ~~He expressed a particular desire to be saved in the Kingdom of God, that~~ ^He said^ he advocated the same doctrine ^as above^ some two years ago in the school, but was not reply'd to by sound argument, and the only way he could satisfy his conscience and ease himself of the burthen that pressed upon him, was by bearing another final testimony to his brethren whose patience had enabled him to do, and thanked them for the same. ^He expressed a particular desire to be saved in the Kingdom of God.^

~~Elder Prest Orson~~ Prest D[aniel] H. Wells, Ass[istan]t C[ounselo]r Carrington & others came into the School in time to hear a few of his closing remarks.

Elder Orson Pratt said that although ~~in~~ many passages of ^scriptures^ taken in an unconnected sense, would seem to favor the ~~al~~ ideas advanced by Bro Iverson, but such views were in direct opposition to many new revelations given through the Prophet Joseph Smith, one when he was only 15 years of age where the personages of both the Father and the son appeared to him, and whom he not only saw, but heard them speak separate and distinct, he also refered to several other instances, equally conclusive on the subject.

Elder Geo B Wallace said, that though we were a school of Prophets, that School had a head, and through that channel we had to be taught, and no member can receive a revelation that conflicts with those already given by the Servants of God.

B[isho]p James Leach bore testimony to the honest character and faithfulness of Bro Iverson who was a member of his ward, but he was in error, and unless he repented, he would have cause to regret it.

Prest D H Wells names several instances w[h]ere the Father and the Son appeared in that relationship, and which clearly [had] shown the sheer absurdity of the ideas advanced by Bro Iverson, and he never wanted him to introduce the subject again before the School.

He said Prest [Brigham] Young was anxious for the organization of the brethren in this City, who desired to enter into the united Order, and those members of the school who wished to have their names put down, and who did not do so at the last meeting, had now an opportunity, the following were called out[:]

Albt Carrington, John Sharp, A[lbert] P. Rockwood, Tho[ma]s E Jeremy, H[enry] Dinwoody, W[illiam] G. Young, Rob[er]t Campbell, W[illiam] Hickenlooper W[illia]m Eddington[,] Lorenzo ^D[ow]^ Young, Thomas Taylor[,] W[illia]m McLachlin[,] Tho[ma]s H. Woodbury, W[illiam] A. Rosetter, R[onal]d Brimley, J[ames] P. Freeze, H[amilton] G. Park, E Snelgrove[,] F[ranklin] D. Richards, Soren Iverson, Millen Atwood, & George Crisman ~~Fred[eric]k Kesler~~.

Elder H[enry] Dinwoody said one reason why he had his name put down, was because he had long since felt the necessity of consolidating and utilizing our labour, by the aid of Machinery and apprentices, so as to successfully compete with imported articles in price and quality and which can only be brought about by a union of effort, as contemplated by the Order now being inaugurated.

Prest D H Wells said when the inspiration of the Almighty comes upon his Servants, to unite the people, it was our duty to listen and obey—and act unitedly with the head. If we accept it, all will be well, it was the word of the Lord to this people and all the ~~people~~ world, And those who unheed it will be damned. If we dont consecrate to the Lord, we must to the Devil.

Adjourned for two weeks at 6 o clock pm.[41] Benediction by Elder E Snelgrove.

41. The school did not meet the following week due to general conference.

May 11, 1874; Monday

The School of the Prophets met in the City Hall at 6 oclock pm. Present Prest B[righam] Young presiding, ^C[ounselo]r^ D[aniel] H Wells [and] Assistant C[ounselo]rs Brigham Young Jun[io]r[,] Jos[eph] A Young & A[lbert] Carrington besides Orson Pratt & John Taylor of the twelve [apostles]. After Singing Prayer by Elder Milando Pratt. Singing. Roll called and 68 Members answered to their names. Minutes of last meeting were read and approved.

Prest Young enquired if any members of the School held the same views as expressed by Bro Iverson, ^at the last meeting^ if so, He wished them to raise their hands. No on responded. He then said All those who do not believe in them, hold up your hands. The show of hands was unanimous.

Prest Young then wished to know how many Members of the school were ready and willing to go into this united order with all they have. All hands were raised, with very few exceptions. He then made enquiry of the Bishops, if their wards were ready to be organized, commencing with the 1st, and continued to the 20th.

Most of the Bishops gave a very favorable report of the good feeling that prevails among the Members of their wards, and as being ready for organization when required. The 20th Ward having been already organized, and the Carpenters over 20 in number had met and appointed their foreman, some other branches of industry were too few in number represented as to form an organized board.

Elder W[illiam] G. Young ~~refre~~ from South Cottonwood gave a very encouraging report of that Ward, having had a meeting and nearly 100 gave in their names as being both ready and willing for organization. B[isho]p Jacob Weiler & his councillor John Wayman had not ^yet^ given in their names, they desired to have a better understanding of what was wanted before doing so.

Prest Young said their was no particular hurry about the matter, only that those who were ready should be immediately organized, and commence operations, and those who are now faltering in their feelings would soon fall into line, when they saw the benefits that will arise from its practical working.

B[isho]p S[amuel] A. Woolley mentioned the peculiar situation in which he was placed with his family, with a view of receiving council, prior to ~~his~~ putting down his name, as a member of the Order.

Prest Young, ~~h~~ said ~~he was willing~~ if his wives or children were willing to enter into the United Order, he was willing to ~~apportion~~ ^appropriate to^ them a certain portion of his property, so that they might have it entered in their own name, but if they wanted to go to California or anywhere else, they should not have any of his property to take with them.

In reply to a question about Children, He said those who were willing to have their names entered as Members, to do so, and those too young to express a choice, the parents should choose for them, but any child, however young, who objected, pass them by, and honor their agency. Mechanics, if not enough in one ward to organize and operate profitably, let several wards unite together. We must all observe the strictest economy in our dress and manner of living, and not use up the entire value of our labour, by this means a fund can be raised to purchase what Machinery may be needed or build Railroads, Temples &c.

He wished those who understood the Manufacture of Wooden solid shoes to commence business immediately; Relief Societies should commence to organize and make our Hats, Bonnets, Clothes, Shoes &c. Bishops should organize their wards, get the Tannery Establishments opened up, stop immediately all further exportation of [animal] hydes, and get the business started, also shoe factories, to stop importations from abroad. All surplus Wagons, Thrashers, Mowers &c should be got together, and preserved from injury by exposure, until wanted. If [these items were] sold at half price [they] would raise a fund of over a Million dollars. Farming must be done by oxen instead of Horses that require Harness, this would be an immense saving. All [live] stock owned by the people to be kept up during the winter & properly fed & cared for, instead of being driven on to the prairies to the mercy of the elements. Mustard, Sugar Cane, Dye stuff &c must be raised in sufficient quantities to supply our wants. Our grain &c will all be sold or exchanged by officers in the Order appointed for that purpose, and not by private individuals, so that fair remunerative prices may be obtained.

By Motion of Elder A[ngus] M Cannon, J[oseph] C Young and Jno [John] D. Riter were cut off from the Church by a unanimous vote for Apostacy.

Adjourned for one week at 7 oclock pm. Benediction by A[ngus] M. Cannon.

May 18, 1874; Monday

The School of the Prophets met in the City Hall at 7 oclock pm. Present ^D[aniel] H Wells^ [and] Prest George A Smith presiding. After Singing Prayer by Elder H[enry] Dinwoody. Singing. Roll called and 70 members answered. Minutes of last meeting were read and approved.

Prest Geo A Smith enquired how many Wards had been Organized [in the United Order] since last Meeting, the 7th and 14th wards responded [while] the ^1st^ 5 & 8^ 11 12 & 16 intended to organize during the ~~do~~ week, and the rest of the Wards within a few days after.

He said Prest [Brigham] Young had been down to Provo a few days to attend to a little business and have a rest. The former was done but the latter he failed to secure, had taken cold, which caused his absence to night. Himself and Elder [David] McKenzie held a large Meeting in Provo, at which they both spoke.

B[isho]p N[athan] Davis said the Iron business in which he was engaged was a very important one, and with an additional Capitol, he might just as well have 200 employed as the few already, many of whom could be boys, whose labour could be made profitable, and they ^also^ being prepared as Mechanics, of different grades—this important branch of business he thought should be among the first to have attention, as it formed the chief basis of all other branches. And now was a very opportune time as one of the leading Foundrys had just collapsed for want of funds.

The question was then raised as to whether the people should be instructed to put in a small portion of their property at first, until by its practical working, their Faith and Confidence should inspire them to put in the balance, or whether a full consecration should be placed before them.

B[isho]p Tho[ma]s Taylor said he never preached a full consecration to the 14th Ward, and they were not organized on that basis, neither did he think them prepared for it, and yet, he believed he had carried out Prest Youngs mind, as far as he could comprehend it.

Elder Geo B Wallace said he believed that God wanted us to become as one United family, and anything short of this, is simply trying to patch up an old garment, and smacks very much of sectarianism. The Lord wants men to come into this order heart and soul, not half hearted. If he was worth a hundred thousand, he would put every dollar of it in, and be willing to work at anything the servants of God might choose to set him to.

B[isho]p Tho[ma]s Taylor thought when the present effort was once started with a general determination to foster and encourage home manufacture, that it will work so well, that the Majority will want to put in all they have for the building up of the Kingdom of God.

Elder W[illia]m H Folsom made a few remarks on the same subject.

B[isho]p[s] E[dwin] D. and S[amuel] A. Woolley also spoke on the subjects of the United Order in connection with home Manufactures, and the necessity of ourselves and families practising what we preach, or things will move very slow.

B[isho]p E[dwin] D. Woolley, says it may be some time before the people see eye to eye, but there are some things that he thought required prompt attention over $5000.00 worth of [animal] Hydes & Skins are exported weekly from this City, and in a short time are sent back again at an advanced price of 200 per cent. The Tanning and Dressing business can easily be gone into, also Iron and Wool. If these branches [of industry] are not soon taken hold of, with a sufficient amount of Capitol to carry them ~~out~~ ^on^, the Gentiles will certain step in and do it.

B[isho]p L[orenzo] D[ow] Young said he should like to see the Wool growers of this Country so far consecrate their wool, as not to sell one pound more of it to outsiders, but let it all be kept for our own factorys to work up.

Prest Geo A Smith advised the rest of the wards to organize as quickly as possible. He also advised that no half way business be recommended to their wards but whoever enters into this United order, to do so, with all they have got, and with one heart and one mind, and for anyone to sell their wool to go out of the Country [territory] is a wicked act, and no one doing it, can look a Man of God in the face without a sense of conviction. Unless any one is ready to go with all they have into this order, let him wait until he gets ready but if such only gets the Spirit of the Holy Gospel, with ~~with~~ which the servants of God are inspired[,] they will not desire to hold anything back.

Elder E[lias] Morris urged the necessity of every ward organizing as quickly as possible, at which time some further steps will be revealed that will be right for us to take.

Elder H Dinwoody suggested that instead of forming separate

boards of Mechanics in each ward, ~~each branch~~ every Mechanic ^of each branch^ throughout the City should be organized, and their labour consolidated under one Foreman, with all needful[42] Appliances of Machinery and Apprentices, so as to successfully compete with imported articles.

Meeting adjourned for one week at 7 oclock pm. Benediction by Elder A[ngus] M. Cannon.

May 25, 1874; Monday

The School of the Prophets met in the City Hall at 7 oclock pm. Present Prest B[righam] Young presiding. [Also present:] C[ounselo]r D[aniel] H Wells [and] Ass[istan]t C[ounselo]r A[lbert] Carrington. After singing Prayer by Elder Paul A Schettler. Singing. Roll called and 63 members were present. Minutes of last Meeting were read and accepted.

Prest B Young said, those who have put down their names to this United Order should bear in mind that they have covenanted to have their heart, soul, and affection in it, as well as their time dictated by the priesthood, and if we enter into it in this way, we shall very soon want our means there to. He ^himself^ intended to put into it all he had.

In answer to enquiries it was ascertained that the 1st, 5, & 6, 7, 8, 11, 12, 15, 16, 19, ^&^ 20 ^wards^ had been organized [in the United Order], and the 2nd,^ 3, 9, 10, 13, & 17[43] intended to do during the week.

In answer to a question by B[isho]p Tho[ma]s Jenkins[,] Prest Young said that as the 4th Ward ^was^ too small for a separate~~ion~~ organization, they had better unite with the 7th.

B[isho]p S[amuel] A. Woolley enquired if it was the intention for the Officers of the Order to dictate the time of the Members, if so, some of his ward would never submit to it, as they said it would reduce them to mere serfs, make slaves of them, and utterly destroy their agency.

Prest B Young said the Heavenly host were all governed on the same principle, and so with us when we first received the Gospel, we in the exercise of our Agency listed[44] to obey God through his servants, and while we enjoyed the spirit of the Gospel, our joy was full by keeping the

42. The remainder of the entry is written vertically, somewhat obscuring the text already written.

43. I have added commas between the ward numbers for readability.

44. An archaic definition of the verb "to list" was "to lean, incline, advance or stretch toward," as in "the wind bloweth where it listeth" (John 3:8).

commandments of God as they were revealed or dictated to us by his servants, but for a long time past we have pursued a wayward course. He also wished the Officers of the [United] Order in the different wards of the City to be notified to meet with us in this school on Monday next at 7 o clock pm at which time The School was adjourned.

Benediction by B[isho]p Tho[ma]s Taylor.

June 1, 1874; Monday

The School of the Prophets met in the City Hall at 7 oclock pm. Present Prest D[aniel] H Wells presiding. [Also present] Ass[istan]t C[ounselo]r A[lbert] Carrington, John Taylor[,] Orson Pratt. After singing Prayer by Elder A[lexander] C Pyper. Singing. Roll called and 149 Members were present.

Prest D H Wells said he had hoped Prest [Brigham] Young would have been present this evening, but having travelled from Cache Valley perhaps he might ^not^ feel able to be here,[45] but as the evening is short and insufficient time to do much in the way ^of^ deciding upon any definite plan of operation, ~~as~~ he thought it would be necessary to adjourn this meeting to the Old Tabernacle ~~till~~ till Tomorrow afternoon, but as Bro[thers] Taylor & Orson Pratt had been devoting considerable time and travelling in connexion with the subject ^of the United Order^, He called upon them to make a few remarks.

Elder Jno. [John] Taylor gave a short account of his visit with Elder Orson Pratt through Sanpete [County] &c said they ~~and~~ organized the ^people into^ [the] United Order in every place, and being a subject entirely new to them, they did not all fall in with it at once but when they got through, they thought at least there was one half the entire population that joined.

They also appointed ~~P~~ Elder Orson Hyde as the general President of Sanpete, and Canute Peterson[46] [of] Ephraim and ^B[isho]p^

45. Brigham Young had traveled to Franklin, Idaho, to celebrate the railroad reaching that far. However, when the train ran off the track, Young and others, including Erastus Snow, were taken back to Logan by wagon. Peterson, *History of Cache County*, 73.

46. Norwegian emigrant Canute Peterson (1824–1902) would later become the stake president himself. He had just returned from two years as president of the Scandinavian Mission. One of his daughters, Sarah (Canute Peterson had four wives and twenty-one children), was married to future apostle Anthon H. Lund.

W[illia]m Seeley[47] [of] Mt Pleasant as his Councillors. They gave general instructions to Bishops and others but not ~~into~~ details. They deemed it wisdom for them to go rather slow, and not rush and drive things. The Officers should not act as Masters but be kind, and easy. There was a good feeling among the people [of Sanpete County] generally.

Prest Geo A Smith then came into the meeting.

Elder Orson Pratt said that while at Mt. Pleasant they received instructions from Prest Young, that they should organize the people in Sanpete on the principle of Cooperation agreeable with the laws of our Country, owing to a difference in our laws we could not carry out the same ^order^ as revealed ~~in the days~~ when living in Jackson Co[unty]. But the difference of this order and the [Zion's Cooperative] Mercantile Institution, is about as follows[:] persons could put in a portion of their means into ^that^ and receive dividend when declared ~~what it is,~~ but in this Order it is expected that we put in all we have, and when a dividend is declared, we ~~do~~ are not to draw it out, but to be added to the Capitol Stock.

He refered to a revelation which said that one man should not possess more than another [D&C 49:20] & again, ~~unifess~~ unless we are made equal in the bonds of temporal things, how can we become equal in Heavenly things. He did not think we could ever go back to Jackson Co[unty] and built up Zion, on any other principle than that of becoming united in temporal things.

Prest Geo A Smith gave a brief history of his visit with Prest B Young to Cache Co[unty]. ~~He~~ They visited Prest Youngs Farm of 13000 acres stocked with some choice Cattle &c, which he intended putting into the United Order.[48] They left here last Thursday and returned to day about 1 pm, they had a good rest, and enjoyed themselves much—prospect good for crops.

He hoped the brethren would ponder well what they were about

47. William S. Seeley (1812–95) was born in Upper Canada (Ontario). He was the first bishop of Mount Pleasant, serving thirty years in that capacity, and the first mayor, remaining in that office for seven years. The peace treaty ending the Black Hawk War was signed in his house.

48. This was the Church Farm, originally called Elkhorn Ranch, not a private farm—although this indicates how easily Young and others mixed the church's assets with his own. It should not be confused with his personal 600-acre cattle ranch south of Salt Lake City.

to do, it had been suggested to carry out a kind of Co operation. It would be necessary to commence as soon as we can with safety, in this City, and find employment, we must deliberate, council & determine by what means this can be accomplished. We must adopt a legal form of agreement, and our associations accordingly. He felt happy that so many of the brethren are being waked ^up^ ~~to~~ in their reflections & prayers upon this important subject.

Prest D H Wells ~~said~~ Motioned to adjourn ^the meeting^ till To-morrow in the Old Tabernacle at 2 o clock pm. He said We might commence to manufacture Hats, Bonnets, Shoes—~~Tanner~~ open Tannerys, [mills for] knitting Stockings, &c so as to stop further importations on these and other articles—so as ^to^ give employment to our own people instead of Importing so many Articles which might be just as well made here ~~by the labour of our~~. The object proposed by this united order will bring more comfort and union among the people—and by ~~having~~ ^commencing^ a little organization we might find employment for those who are now idle.

Benediction by Elder Levi Richards.[49]

49. For the second half of the year, the members quit meeting as the School of the Prophets and devoted themselves entirely to the new economic system, calling themselves the United Order of Salt Lake City (see appendix 3 herein). The gathering on June 1, 1874, was therefore the last, at least in practical terms, except that in nine years the school would meet again briefly, thus marking the actual end of the school.

CHAPTER SEVEN

"THE ROLLING FORTH OF ZION"

1883

August 2, 1883; Thursday

The following instructions form part of a Revelation received by President John Taylor, in Salt Lake City, April 28th, 1883:[1]

"These things belong to my Priesthood; but more properly to the School of the Prophets, who should be made acquainted with my laws. Let the School of the Prophets be organized, even all such as are worthy, but if they are found unworthy they shall not have a place in my school, for I will be honored by my Priesthood; and let my laws be made known unto them as may be deemed expedient."

In order to carry out the word and will of the Lord, as above expressed, President John Taylor at a meeting of the First Presidency and Council of the [Twelve] Apostles, held at the Endowment House, Wednesday, July 25th, 1883, appointed Elders Geo Q. Cannon and Geo Reynolds to get together all papers and information that they could obtain relating to the former Schools of the Prophets that were organized under the direction of Presidents Joseph Smith and Brigham Young, so that the School might be properly organized in accordance with the designs of the Almighty.

Minutes of a meeting of the [First] Presidency and Twelve, held in President Taylor's Office, on the afternoon of Thursday the 2d day of August, 1883. There were present: Presidents John Taylor and George Q. Cannon, of the First Presidency; and President W[ilford] Woodruff,

1. The 1883 School of the Prophets minute book opens with this excerpt from an extra-canonical revelation to John Taylor in which he is told to revive the School of the Prophets, followed by two introductory paragraphs and a presentation on the School of the Prophets to the First Presidency and Quorum of the Twelve by apostle George Q. Cannon, and then Taylor's reaction to it. For information on the revelation, see Holzapfel and Jones, "John the Revelator," 273–308.

Albert Carrington, F[ranklin] D. Richards, and F[rancis] M. Lyman of the Twelve [Apostles]; Elders L. John Nuttal[l] and George Reynolds, Secretaries[,] and John Irvine, Reporter.[2] President Joseph F. Smith and Counselor Daniel H. Wells came in toward the close of the meeting.

President George Q. Cannon in opening the proceedings of the meeting said: Mr. President [Taylor], in accordance with your appointment [assignment][,] Brother Reynolds and myself have examined the records as far as we can procure them, of the School of the Prophets, and everything we have pertaining to its organization in Kirtland, and also the organization of the School here by President Young. The school in Kirtland was organized after the revelation which was given in December 1832. That revelation will be found in Sec[tion] 88 of the Book of Doctrine and Covenants[3] in which the Lord said:

"And again, the order of the house prepared for the presidency of the school of the prophets, established for their instruction in all things that are expedient for them, even for all the officers of the church, or in other words, those who are called to the ministry in the church, beginning at the high Priests, even down to the deacons: and this shall be the order of the house of the presidency of the school: He that is appointed to be president, or teacher, shall be found standing in his place, in the house which shall be prepared for him. Therefore, he shall be first in the house of God, in a place that the congregation in the house may hear his words carefully and distinctly, not with loud speech. And when he cometh into the house of God, (for he should be first in the house; behold, this is beautiful, that he may be an example.) Let him offer himself in prayer upon his knees before God, in token or remembrance of the everlasting covenant, and when any shall come in after him, let the teacher arise, and, with uplifted hands to heaven; yea, even directly, salute his brother or brethren with these words: Art thou a brother or

2. John Irvine (1848–1909) was a Scottish stenographer who arrived in Utah in 1879 and became a clerk in the First Presidency's office. Irvine's transcriptions of sermons appeared in the *Deseret Evening News* and *Journal of Discourses*. However, in 1888 he was released due to "persistent drunkenness." Rogers, *In the President's Office*, xxxiv.

3. Members were using the 1880 edition of the Doctrine and Covenants, with the same numbering as the current LDS edition. The December 1832 revelation calling for an edifice that would house the School of the Prophets was followed by another revelation five months later on June 1, 1833, that expanded the definition of the house to be one where God would "endow those whom I have chosen with power from on high." See D&C 88:119; 95:8. The House of the Lord was completed and dedicated in March 1836.

brethren? I salute you in the name of the Lord Jesus Christ, in token or remembrance of the everlastin[g] covenant, in which covenant I receive you to fellowship, in a determination that is fixed, immovable, and unchangeable, to be your friend and brother through the grace of God, in the bonds of love to walk in all the commandments of God blameless, in thanksgiving, forever and ever. Amen. And he that is found unworthy of this salutation, shall not have place among you; for ye shall not suffer that mine house shall be polluted by him. And he that cometh in and is faithful before me, and is a brother, or if they be brethren, they shall salute the president or teacher with uplifted hands to heaven, with this same prayer and covenant, or by saying Amen, in token of the same. Behold, verily, I say unto you, this is a sample unto you for a salutation to one another in the house of God, in the school of the prophets. And ye are called to do this by prayer and thanksgiving as the Spirit shall give uttering in all your doings in the house of the Lord, in the school of the prophets, that it may become a sanctuary, a tabernacle of the Holy Spirit to your edification. And ye shall not receive any among you into this school save he is clean from the blood of this generation; and he shall be received by the ordinance of the washing of feet, for unto this end was the ordinance of the washing of feet instituted. And again, the ordinance of washing feet is to be administered by the President, or Presiding elder of the church. It is to be commenced with prayer ^and^ after partaking of bread and wine, he is to gird himself according to the pattern given in the thirteenth chapter of John's testimony concerning me. Amen" [D&C 88:127–41].

I will also read (continued Prest. Cannon) a description of this ordinance as administered by the Savior contained in the 13th Chapter of St. John's Gospel:

"Now before the feast of the passover, when Jesus knew that his hour was come that he should depart out of this world unto the Father, having loved his own which were in the world, he loved them unto the end. And supper being ended, the devil having now put into the heart of Judas Iscariot, Simon's son, to betray him; Jesus knowing that the Father had given all things into his hands, and that he was come from God, and went to God; he riseth from supper, and laid aside his garments; and took a towel, and girded himself. After that he poureth water into a bason, and began to wash the disciples' feet, and to wipe them with the towel wherewith he was girded. Then cometh he to Simon Peter; and Peter saith unto him, Lord, dost thou wash my feet? Jesus answered and said unto him, What I do thou knowest not now; but thou shalt know hereafter. Peter saith unto him, Thou shalt never wash my feet. Jesus answered him, If I wash thee not thou hast no part with me. Simon Peter saith unto him, Lord, not my feet only, but also my hands and my head. Jesus saith to him, He that is washed needeth not save to wash his feet, but is clean every whit: and ye are clean, but not all. For he knew who should betray him; therefore said he, Ye are not all clean. So after he had washed their feet, and had taken his garments, and was set down again, he said unto them, Know ye what I have done to you? Ye call me Master and Lord; and ye say well; for so I am. If I then, your Lord and Master, have washed your feet; ye also ought to wash one another's feet. For I have given you an example, that ye should do as I have done to you" [John 13:1–15].

One month after receiving this revelation—Sec[tion] 88—(continued President Cannon) the Prophet [Joseph Smith] called together a few of the brethren consisting of himself, Sidney Rigdon, Frederick G. Williams, Newel K. Whitney,[4] Hyrum Smith, Zebedee Coltrin, Joseph Smith, Senior; Samuel H. Smith, John Murdock, Lyman Johnson, Orson Hyde, Ezra Thayer, Levi Hancock and William Smith.[5] They were assembled on the 22d of January 1833 in conference and the Spirit of the Lord was greatly poured out upon them, speaking in tongues, &c. On the 23d of January they again assembled. It is not stated whether there were any others present besides those named on the previous day or not; I suppose ^these^ were precisely the same persons present. They are all dead with the exception of Brother Coltrin and William Smith, the Prophet's brother, the latter [blank] is out of the Church. On that day the history says:[6]

4. Newel K. Whitney owned the mercantile business in Kirtland, Ohio, in which the School of the Prophets met. He and his wife, Elizabeth, also housed Joseph and Emma Smith in their home when the Smiths arrived in Kirtland in February 1831.

5. Of those in attendance, Frederick G. Williams would become a member of the church presidency in February 1833 and Lyman E. Johnson would become a member of the Quorum of Twelve two years after that. In mid-1833 Ezra Thayer would be the one to purchase the site on which the Kirtland Temple was eventually built, acting as the church's agent. Joseph Smith's father and three brothers were also present, along with others previously identified.

6. Cannon is quoting from the manuscript history of the church, written about ten years after the fact in 1842 and published in the church newspaper in 1844. It would become the official *History of the Church* in 1902. See Church Historian's Office, History of the Church, Jan. 22–23, 1833; Smith, *History of the Church*, 1:323–24.

"We again assembled in Conference, when, after much speaking, singing, praying, and praising God, all in tongues, we proceeded to the washing of feet (according to the practice recorded in the 13th chap[ter] of John's Gospel) as commanded of the Lord. Each Elder washed his own feet first, after which I [Joseph Smith] girded myself with a towel, and washed the feet of all of them all, wiping them with the towel with which I was girded

I then said to the Elders, As I have done so do ye: wash ye, therefore, one another's feet; and by the power of the Holy Ghost I pronounced them all clean from the blood of this generation; but if any of them should sin wilfully after they were thus cleansed, and sealed up unto life eternal, they should be given over unto the buffetings of Satan until the day of redemption."

There are other revelations (continued President Cannon) connected with this that were given about that same time; but we have found nothing relating particularly to method of managing the school. The Lord says in a revelation (sec[tion] 95 of the Book of Doctrine and Covenants): "Nevertheless, my servants sinned a very grievous sin, and contention arose in the school of the prophets; which was very grievous unto me, saith your Lord; therefore I sent them forth to be chastened. Verily, I say unto you, it is my will that you should build an house. If you keep my commandments, you shall have power to build it, if you keep not my commandments, the love of the Father shall not continue with you, therefore you shall walk in darkness. Now here is wisdom, and the mind of the Lord; let the house be built, not after the manner of the world, for I give not unto you that ye shall live after the manner of the world; therefore, let it be built after the manner which I shall show unto ^the^ three of you,"—(Hyrum Smith, Reynolds Cahoon, and Jared Carter[7] were the three that were afterwards appointed—)"whom ye shall appoint and ordain unto this power. And the size thereof shall be fifty and five feet in width, and let it be sixty-five feet in length, in the inner court thereof; and let the lower part of the inner court be

7. Cahoon was a member of the Kirtland bishopric, and Carter would soon become a high priest. Five months after the original revelation was given to build a school, the Lord reminded his followers that he had given "unto you a commandment that you should build a house," and now the instructions had been modified slightly so that the upper floor would be the school (95:17), while the lower floor would be devoted to "your sacrament offering, and for your preaching, and your fasting, and your praying."

dedicated unto me for your sacrament offering, and for your preaching, and your fasting, and your praying and the offering up your most holy desires unto me, saith your Lord. And let the higher part of the inner court be dedicated unto me, for the school of mine apostles," (You will notice that is called here "school of mine apostles" instead of Prophets—)["]saith Son Ahman; or, in other words, Alphus; or, in other words, Omegus; even Jesus Christ your Lord. Amen" [D&C 95:10–17]. Not only was there a school in Kirtland, but also in Zion [Missouri], as will be seen from Section 97 of the Book of Doctrine and Covenants, viz.:

"Behold, I say unto you, concerning the school in Zion, I the Lord am well pleased that ^there^ should be a school in Zion, and also with my servant Parley P. Pratt,[8] for he abideth in me; And inasmuch as he continueth to abide in me; he shall continue to preside over the school in the land of Zion, until I shall give unto him other commandments; and I will bless him with a multiplicity of blessings, in expounding all ~~ex~~ scriptures and mysteries to the edification of the school, and of the church in Zion; and to the residue of the school, I, the Lord, am willing to show mercy; nevertheless, there are those that must needs be chastened, and their works shall be made known" [D&C 97:3–6].

Bro. Reynolds had selected these extracts before I [George Q. Cannon] took hold of the matter; and these appear to cover all the revelations given upon the subject that are published.

It seems that the school met and continued to meet in Kirtland before the Temple was built. I have not examined the history with any care after the completion of the Temple to know whether it was confined after that. Probably Bro. Woodruff and some of the brethren will remember whether that is the case. But the revelation contemplated the holding of the school in an upper room of the Temple when completed. It seems, however, that Joseph [Smith] in anticipation of the completion of the Temple, met with the school during the winter—that is, from January until April 1833—and then the school seems to have been discontinued. The Missouri troubles came on after that, and I have no

8. Parley P. Pratt (1807–57), a member of the Quorum of the Twelve from 1835, would become known for his defense of Mormon doctrine, authoring missionary tracts and books, and writing the lyrics to half a dozen popular hymns.

distinct recollection though I have not examined the history carefully—of their meeting after the month of April.[9]

They met according to the order given in this revelation (Sec[tion] 88). Those who were admitted to the School were admitted by the partaking of the Lord's supper first and then the washing of the feet afterwards.

When President [Brigham] Young started the [Salt Lake] school on the 9th of December, 1867, the first meeting was held in the City Hall. The Elders were invited there, in [which] the revelation contained in Section 88 was read, and also was read at a number of subsequent meetings; but there was nothing done by the President, so far as I recollect—and I am now speaking from memory in regard to carrying out the particular form given in this revelation. He called it a theological class—though it was also called the School of the Prophets; still he looked upon it more as a theological class, and his mind did not lead him to carry out the order laid down in the revelation. The brethren were admitted by his selection to begin with. He selected from the leading Elders—the First Presidency, the Twelve, presiding Authorities of this [Salt Lake City] stake of Zion—President of the Stake, the High Council, leading Bishops and leading men—and then as the School became larger they were admitted by recommendations from their Bishops, and each man received a card by which he was admitted to the School. We cannot find any minutes of these meetings. It is a very singular thing that they cannot be found, and we cannot account for it. Brother Reynolds and myself have done all we can by way of enquiry and search to find these minutes, but have failed. We cannot find the minutes of the first two years, which, of course, containing as they will a record of the organization of the school, are ^of^ the most importance. Brother George Goddard, who was clerk of the School, maintains we will find them here. We can find the roll book which was used in the beginning, but which was afterwards dispensed with, owing to the members becoming so numerous that it was found inconvenient to call the roll; but we can find no minute book from 1867 to the end of 1869.

August, 1872, the President [Brigham Young] became dissatisfied with the School and thought he would break it up. There was so much

9. The School of the Prophets met for four months, January through April 1833, then suspended operations until it was revived the next year as the Elders' School.

leakage and so many things being told outside of the school that he deemed this to be the best course to pursue.

This is all we have been able to learn respecting the school as it was organized in Kirtland, and as it was organized here. Of course, as to whether the School now proposed to be established should meet according to the pattern laid down in the revelation, or after the manner of a theological class, we suppose that you [President Taylor] will decide upon that Sir, as you feel led. We do not presume to say anything upon that point. I would say, however, before sitting down, that if we do organize such a School, I am decidedly in favor of being very choice in our selection of who shall be members. And I would like to see a School organized where, even if we did not give each other the salutation that is provided in this revelation, that at least we will act up to the spirit of it; so that we may be able to meet with those who will be worthy of the salutation; for if they are not persons of that character, I think it would detract exceedingly from the value of the meeting also from that union which I think should prevail in such meetings. We have taken the liberty of putting down a number of names whom we thought would be eligible for membership in this School. We have done this merely to give our views, so that, in the event of this matter being taken into consideration and something being done respecting it, you would have some names before you. I believe that is all we have to report.

Prest. Taylor. There are some things associated with this matter that will demand our serious consideration. The School of the Prophets was organized at a time when the Church was in its incipiency. The revelation which we have heard read was given in December 1832. And my impression is that the introduction to this School—by the washing of feet and by salutation—would be proper if it has not already been attended to. There were certain things attended to in Kirtland such as the washing of feet, that are very similar to this, that is, in what was then called Endowments. Afterwards fuller Endowments were given in Nauvoo, and it may have been in view of these, that President Young considered it[s] repetition of these matters unnecessary. How that is, of course, I am not prepared to say. I do not know how or why President Young arrived at the conclusion he did. Ordinarily, outside of that we would feel as we do in regard to some of the first principles of the Gospel of Christ, namely, that it is necessary to observe all the formulae associated therewith. Of course it is not for me to say anything else to Prest. Young's administrations in these matters, nor as to what led him to the conclusions he arrived at.

There is one thing however in connection with the administration of the ordinance in Kirtland—it was given, of course, by revelation. When we received greater Endowments[,] that ordinance seemed to have been dispensed with, that is the former one. I have myself however, had very many misgivings about the departure from any of those ordinances that have been introduced by the Lord. And I must say, too, that I have had serious misgivings about conferring all the blessings and powers of the Priesthood as we do in our endowments at the present time, upon everybody indiscriminately that is recommended to us as worthy by men sometimes, who themselves are unworthy and who do not comprehend their position; I say I have had serious misgivings as to whether it is proper to confer these blessings on so great a number of people who do not seem to comprehend them and who are not prepared to carry them out. And if we could only arrive at some form whereby a smaller degree or a portion of the endowment could be given to parties first; and whether or not that first thing was not the thing that here might be intended I am not [at] present prepared to state. But I will state that I have frequently in reflecting upon this, thought that the sacred things of God have been handled too loosely and too carelessly, and that they have been made too common. We do not seem to comprehend their value. Men may make mistakes and apostatize, and that they have always done it, and that there has always been confusion and difficulty arising from these things, we all know. The History of the Church is full of examples of this kind. I have been, as I have stated, of the opinion that if our endowments could be given only in part instead of as a whole, it would be much better and much safer, and we should thus avoid placing upon the heads of the incompetent people that which they are not prepared to receive and which they seldom live up to. It has seemed to me always to be tampering with sacred things to thus indiscriminately bestow all the blessings of the Priesthood upon all that come along.

I thought I would mention this among other things, and yet our marriage ceremony itself almost forces us, when a man and a woman get married, to confer these blessings upon them. Now, whether that ceremony should be performed in another way, and allow people to undergo a probationary state until they were considered worthy to enter into this everlasting covenant, would be a question for us to consider. This covenant has been entered into very extensively. Indeed many people have entered into this marriage covenant and taken upon themselves responsibilities that have brought a curse and destruction upon them. Therefore, it appears to me these are rather serious questions, and they are at least worthy of our consideration. Among the ancient Jews they had in their assemblages what they called a Gentile court. The Gentiles were not permitted to enter into the inner court of the Temple and partake with what were considered faithful Israelites. There were certain classes like we have among us that would receive certain portions of the law, say the first five books of Moses, the pentatuech. There were others that would receive everything and were prepared to do everything ^that the Law of God required.^

Now, we have folks in our midst that can only receive a portion of the Gospel and never profess anything else, yet they have gone through these things and entered into sacred covenants. There seems to have been distinctions made at all times. There will be distinctions hereafter in regard to the celestial, terrestrial, telestial and other Kingdoms. Why are these distinctions made? Because if a man cannot obey a celestial law he cannot inherit a celestial glory; if a man cannot obey a terrestrial law he cannot abide the terrestrial glory; if a man cannot obey [a] telestial law he can[not] enter into a Telestial glory. And the question in my mind arises whether we ought not to have these kind of distinctions among us. Certain it is we know that they exist, and that there are certain classes among us that never pretend to fulfill the law of the Gospel. Some will not even pay tithing. There are some that do not think they are obligated to listen to counsel. Brother Cannon has remarked on several occasions and remarked very correctly—we have people who profess to be Church people—that is—a class of men that will abide by counsel, that will live their religion, and keep—the commandments of God. We have another class that will only keep a part of the commandments and reject what part they think proper—a class that will follow their own counsels and pursue their own course. They are not what you would call Latter-day Saints. They are not fulfilling the law of the Gospel, nor those principles which were laid down for us to be governed by. These are serious matters all of them.

Now, the question arises, what are we to do with them? We have already re-trenched a little upon some of these things and prevented people who are not considered worthy to be married, or to receive a full recommend to go to the house of the Lord—we have already decided that they may be married by our Bishops, which, I think, is very proper. This, in my estimation, might be carried very much further. Instead of taking those that would be considered almost outcasts, instead of taking a great many of those that call themselves "Mormons" and are not—like men who used to call themselves Jews—for it was said, all are not Israel who are of Israel; and at the present, all are not Latter day Saints who are called that name. There are certain men heirs according to the promise. There are certain men who do not have the spirit of the Gospel, and who do not live, and never have lived, and never will, in accordance therewith. There are many who will never get into the Celestial Kingdom of God, if I understand things aright.

Well, now, these are things that demand serious consideration; and while we are desirous of carrying out the will and the word and law of God, and not stand in the way of any men, or prevent them in anywise from obtaining all the exaltation they are prepared to receive; still the question is, whether it is not necessary for us to tighten up on some of these points, and not place upon people—who may be otherwise good in many respects—responsibilities they do not comprehend, and which they are not prepared to carry out. Allow them, of course, all the advantages connected with the lesser law, but do not permit them to partake of the greater until they show themselves worthy.

The law of God is very strict and very rigid when we come to this higher order, and which is never lived up to. Now, that is saying a good deal, is it not? What is the meaning of those signs and the explanation given of them that we receive in the house of the Lord associated with endowments? Are they carried out? When I say, [some people have] never lived up to [them], where have they been? Now, there is something very serious associated with many of those matters. We read in the Book of Doctrine and Covenants that if a man does so and so after entering into this covenant, he shall be destroyed &c. As has been read in our hearing, Joseph Smith stated that, "if any of them should sin wilfully after they were thus cleansed, and sealed up unto life eternal, they should be given over to the buffetings of satan, until the day of redemption." I speak of the importance of these things, and in doing so there is a big field opens before me. I can see the thing very distinctly. "Now are ye the Sons of God, and it doth not yet appear what we shall be; but we know that, when he shall appear, we shall be like him; for we shall see him as he is" [John 3:2]. Then, we are the Sons of God. What else? Heirs of God. What is it to be an heir of God? Why, to be an inheritor of his possessions, is it not? Can you make anything else of it? I cannot. "Heirs of God and joint heirs with Jesus Christ" [Rom. 8:17]. In the Book of Doctrine and Covenants we have a confirmation of what is written in the Scriptures.

"And also all they who receive this priesthood receive me, saith the Lord, for he that receiveth my servants receiveth me; and he that receiveth me receiveth my Father; and he that receiveth my father receiveth my Father's kingdom; therefore all that my Father hath shall be given unto him; and this is according to the oath and covenant which belongeth to the Priesthood. Therefore all those who receive the priesthood, receive this oath and covenant of my Father, which he cannot break neither can it be moved; but whoso breaketh this covenant after he hath received it and altogether turneth therefrom, shall not have forgiveness of sins in this world nor in the world to come" [D&C 84:35–41].

It will be observed from the above that a covenant is entered into. It takes two parties to make a covenant. In this case one is our Heavenly Father, the other, those who enter into this Priesthood. It is said God's covenant cannot be broken; it is also said that ours cannot be broken without incurring certain liabilities. We may talk about being heirs of God and joint heirs with Jesus Christ, we may talk about all the Father hath is given to us, but if we violate this covenant we shall not have ["]forgiveness of sins in this world or in the world to come." We are aiming at a high exaltation and to move on an elevated plain; but that very exaltation implies great responsibilities and while we plume ourselves as being heirs of God and inheritors of all things, it is expected of us that we fulfill His law, and keep sacredly our covenants, and that God has as much right to demand of us the fulfillment of our covenants as we have to demand of him that he will fulfill his; and if we expect to derive from the Almighty those great and inestimable blessings He expects us and demands of us that we yield implicit obedience to Him, and to his law in all things, temporal and spiritual, and seek to do His will on earth as it is done in Heaven.

Very well, if we are heirs of God and joint heirs with Jesus Christ, and are allowed to partake of ordinances that are sacred—such as the God's [Gods] have partaken of—then, must we after that go to work and join in the follies of the world, and take our own way, and run recklessly and carelessly along and commit all kinds of follies? We are not prepared to do anything of the kind. We must not do it; we are placed upon another platform; and God will expect us to walk according to the revelations He has given. If not, shall we be prepared to associate with those parties? And if we are not prepared, shall we be excused if we having the power to bind on earth and it shall be bound in heaven, to seal on earth and it shall be sealed in heaven, to loose on earth and it shall be loosed in heaven [D&C 128:8]—shall we be excused under those circumstances when we go before God our Heavenly Father and find hundreds and thousands perhaps that cannot pass by the angels and the Gods, hundreds and thousands that the guard will not permit to enter into this higher society—the heirs of God and joint heirs with Jesus Christ[?] How foolish we shall look if we see a train of people standing in this position. The question will then arise, who conferred certain blessings upon this wretch and upon the other? I think we would feel a little ashamed if we were to hear a great number of them get the order; "Depart from me, ye accursed; I never knew you" [Matt. 25:41]. We should feel ashamed. We should be considered loose, the same as we consider men loose here who tamper with the ordinances of the house of God, or who tamper with the law, whether the law of the land, or the common law of God, or the law of the celestial kingdom of God.

Now, I feel that there is a very great responsibility resting upon us in regard to all these matters; and if we are aiming to join in the church of the First-Born, whose names are written in heaven, and to associate with the Gods and participate with them in the exaltations and glories of the celestial kingdom, are we going to drag a lot of unworthy people in with us? They cannot go, and they will not go. It seems to me, therefore, I have a strong feeling of that kind—that we ought to begin to straighten up and get things into shape. While there is a feeling around among a great many to keep the law of God and to do all that is required of them, yet there are those who do not want to step forward, or to do much more than they have done. They want to take the world easy and say, "Good Lord, and good devil, we do not know into whose hand we shall fall; for we have not much faith in God nor in the ordinances of the Priesthood." Then, again, there is a class of men who would seek the counsel of the Priesthood all the day long if there can be anything made by it—any money in it—they are on the alert and very anxious for the welfare of Israel; but the moment you come to talk about obedience to the Priesthood they are ready to turn around and say, "No, I am an independent man; and I do not propose to be placed in bondage." There is a class of men who have this kind of spirit. You know it. It is understood very well. Now, then, the question is, if we are trying to get into closer communion with God—which we ought to be—we want to elevate with us a class of men in whom we have confidence—men that when you set them down you will know where to pick them up—instead of elevating men who are all the time catering to the devil, who are covetous and stooping to every kind of meanness and corruption.

Perhaps I have said enough upon this subject. I could talk for hours upon it. The field opens up as I go along; but these are some few ideas that may be sufficient for the present to lead us to the conclusion that we ought to be very particular as to those we receive into this order. And then the question arises, whether we shall follow the order laid down in the revelation—the order of salutation &c. My impression is that if you say to a man as he comes in, Art thou a brother? and thus and so, I salute you—would not that have a tendency to cause people to reflect a little? The question is, whether it would not be better to follow that form, and see if we cannot get back to first principles and carry them out, and then carry out other things? When many of the laws of the Kingdom were first introduced they were, of course, the word and will and law of God; but the lack of knowledge, integrity and fidelity among the saints rendered them for some time inoperative and impracticable; for instance, as was the building of the Temple in Jackson County [Missouri], the carrying into effect the United Order, and other principles; but these were, nevertheless, the eternal truths of God, and were not mistakes made by the Almighty, but were calculated to be, ultimately carried out to their fullest extent, and it is for us to approach this consummation as far and as fast as circumstances here permit and the Lord shall indicate.

The matter now referred to is one of those things which requires our more serious consideration. We should not be justified in changing the form of the sacrament; we would not be justified in changing the form of baptism, nor of the laying on of hands. Other people thought they were justified in doing so and have done it. That has landed Christianity where it is. They have a form—and it is almost false to say that—but it is not the form nor the power. And while I would not wish myself to be hypercritical and too technical—I do not believe in technicalities—yet I do believe in the law of God and in the order of God.

President W Woodruff. I desire to make a few remarks, with the President's permission. The ordinance of washing of feet was introduced by Joseph associated with the School of the Prophets; there was also a washing of feet connected with the endowments given in the Kirtland Temple which was continued until the time the Saints left there. In Nauvoo he introduced the endowments we are receiving to-day.

I agree with President Taylor's views with regard to our giving endowments. I do think we should be more cautious and careful who we receive into our Endowment House to give them full endowments. With regard to giving a portion thereof, and then letting candidates prove themselves worthy before receiving the rest, that of course is a matter to be left to Prest. Taylor. I do not believe, however, that a man should be allowed to go into that house who does not pay tithing, and who drinks and curses and swears.

President Taylor. And breaks the Sabbath day.

President Woodruff Yes, sir; a man who breaks the Sabbath day has no business there.

President Taylor. There is one thing I desire to mention. There was very little said about these ordinances in early days. It was almost impossible to say anything. At the time these endowments were given by Joseph, in Nauvoo, or soon after that, there was the greatest commotion imaginable. There was not an opportunity to enter into those things, nor to teach them. And in referring to this school that was established here, I do not wish to reflect upon President Young; I have no such idea in my mind; but I like to look at things as they are and judge of results. After Joseph was killed things were done in a great hurry. We worked day and night, giving these ordinances, and many people were administered to in private houses—some right in my own house—when the work in the Temple was shut down.

President George Q. Cannon. At the time that this washing of feet was performed by the Savior; it was after the transfiguration upon the mount, when, according to our teachings, Peter, James and John received the authority to preside—received the keys of the Kingdom [Matt. 17:2]. The Savior had been visited by Moses and Elias, and Peter was so delighted, and also the other Apostles, that he proposed to erect three tabernacles, one for the Savior, and one for Moses, and one for Elias. We have been told that not only were the keys of the Kingdom given, but there was an endowment given also. How full it was of course there is nothing written to show. But it seems, even after that, that Jesus washed his disciples' feet. Now, whether the washing of feet was superseded by the endowment or not is a question in my mind, and probably, in all our minds. But it seems to me clear that after Peter, at least, had received an uncommon bestowal of power at the Transfiguration, that the Savior even after that washed his feet and the feet of the rest and commanded them that as they had seen him do[,] so should they do to one another. It was one of the last ordinances that He performed in their midst. Brother [L. John] Nuttall {[10]whispers to me a thing with which you are no doubt all familiar; that in the washing that takes place in the first endowment, they are washed that they might become clean from the blood of this generation—that is, I suppose, in the same way they are ordained to be Kings and Priests—that is, that ordinance does not make them clean from the blood of this generation anymore than it makes them Kings and Priests. It requires another ordinance to make them Kings and Priests. If faithful they receive of another endowment, a fulness of that power, and the promises are fulfilled in the bestowal of the power upon} them. This, however, is a question for you, Sir [President Taylor], holding the keys, to decide upon.

The Lord will reveal to you whether there is any propriety in the washing of the feet—whether it has been superseded by the fuller endowments we have received.

Now, with regard to President Young, I have no doubt the Spirit let him do as he did, and there were no doubt good reasons for establishing

10. I have placed material within braces {sometimes called curly brackets} for portions of the minutes that were redacted from the scans, obtained from Merle H. Graffam's typescript at BYU's Harold B. Lee Library, as well as from D. Michael Quinn's partial typescript at the Beinecke Library at Yale University. Quinn's version matches Graffam's except for a few variances that do not affect the meaning.

the school in the way he did establish it. I do not think the time had then come [blank] for the establishment of any such order as is laid down in the revelation.

In regard to your [Taylor's] remarks respecting the giving of endowments, I am fully in accord with them. It is a matter I have thought a great deal about. Bro. George A. Smith and myself had several conversations with President Young upon this subject. It was very strongly urged then that there should be a division in the endowments, and I have no doubt that the Lord will yet through you reveal to us what shall be done about that matter. It is as clear to me as the light of the Sun that there is a necessity for such a division. We have been carrying things on in a very crude manner for many years. Joseph in his haste to give the Apostles and other Elders their endowments bestowed everything he had received upon them. Being pushed, as it were by the spirit and the exigencies of the times, he bestowed these things in their fulness upon the men whom he selected.

In like manner, when the Temple at Nauvoo was completed, the Apostles (being in a hurry and the mob crowding upon us, and having to leave Nauvoo very quickly) bestowed in like manner upon the people everything that had been received from the Lord. What has been the result? Why, we see that things of God have become too common. Our endowments have become lowered to an extent that, to a man who appreciates their solemnity and importance, must look at it with pangs of sorrow to see the lightness with which these matter are treated. Men go into the Endowment House and come out of it as if it were some place of amusement. Now, there is nothing to my mind more clear than this: when you bestow blessings, however great they are, and make them easy to be obtained, and make them common, you reduce their value in the eyes of the people. They are easily obtained and therefore are to be considered of trifling importance. A man gains the favor of his Bishop, and without any previous trial, without going through any test, he is permitted to go into the house of the Lord and receive his endowments, {and in many instances, men receive their Second Endowment in the same way}.[11]

Now, I do not know, by my experience of human nature, and as a

11. As is alluded to in the text, the second anointing, which was practiced more frequently in the nineteenth century, confirms the promises offered in the temple endowment. See Buerger, "Fulness of the Priesthood."

human being that anything of that kind treated in that way does not have the effect upon men's minds that it should have. It seems to me that there should be something for the people to live for, there should be something to struggle for, and that something must be kept before them. But you bestow everything upon them to begin with and the human mind is gratified and satiety ensues; there is not that incentive to faithfulness in the future; there is not that reward to look forward ^to^; the incentive is taken away by the whole blessing having been bestowed too soon. I could cite many instances of that kind.

I remember my own case. I came home from a 5 years' mission on the Sandwich Islands. I had been as faithful as I knew how, I was engaged to a young lady and expected to get married. I was anxious of course that I should be married for time and eternity in order that my offspring might be born under the covenant. I got home and spoke to President Young on the subject. I asked him if he had any objection to my taking a wife. He asked me who I was going to marry; and upon his offering no objection, I stated that it would give me pleasure if he would perform the ceremony. "Well, George," said he, "I shall only marry you for time." I felt as though I would like it the other way; but I did not feel to question the decision of a Prophet of God. Well, he married me for time. I had had my endowments; my wife had not, and I suppose that was the reason.

Now, what was the effect this had upon me? The effect it had was to drive me to the Lord. I had not attained to the blessings that I wanted and therefore I felt to contend for them. When the Endowment House was completed I then had my wife sealed to me for time and eternity. I appreciated that blessing then—after living in the other condition for five months—as I would not have done in the beginning. I placed a value upon it, struggled for it, plead for it. {And in like manner I exercised faith that I might receive my Second Endowments}.

Well, understanding this in my own life is a living proof to me of the value of having something to look forward to, something in reserve.

This difficulty of a division of the endowments presented itself, as I have said[,] to President Young and President George A. Smith, and I think the Lord will reveal a way that will make this plain. By giving the {Lesser Priesthood the first key, and then let him magnify his position until he received the second key, and so on until he received the third key, I believe it would lead to the} happiest results. Here are men who [in some instances] have received a fulness of the Priesthood, men who, for some reason or other, are not obedient to the Priesthood; they do not care anything about the Priesthood, and the result is that in all our counsels and in all our places of deliberation we have a class of men, if the strict letter of the law were carried out, would not have any place in our counsels. The Priesthood has been made too common in that respect.

But if the Priesthood were conferred only upon men according to their faithfulness; if it were shown that there were keys and blessings that were in reserve for them that could only be attained to by faithfully keeping the commandments of God, I believe it would have the happiest effect upon our people, and especially in the organization of the School of the Prophets if it should be organized. There is this, too, you would admit a certain number of men, and if you are not careful you will admit a man, it may be [one] whom represents a class of men; and if he is admitted there will be others who will think they ought to be admitted because he has been to the school. There is need for discrimination to be used in the beginning, it seems to me, to prevent a reoccurrence of these things. And for one, I would not lift up my hand, if I had any voice, to admit any man to the school of the Prophets who would not be perfectly obedient to the Priesthood, and who would not be willing to consecrate all he had under the direction of the Priesthood. A man who cannot do that is not fit, according to my view of the School, to be a member, and I do not think such a man should think himself injured by my voting to keep him out, if he has not that faith. I hope and pray that God will inspire Prest. Taylor about these matters, that he will enable us to establish a correct order of things in relation to them. I feel that God is with us in this matter, and I feel, too, that it is no longer the mind and will of God that we should bestow full endowments indiscrim[in]ately, as we have been doing, and that in our temples we should institute a different order of things entirely.

<u>Elder Franklin D. Richards.</u> I do not feel that it would be wise to take up any further time in consideration of this matter. I want simply to say, however, that the feelings of my heart attest the truth of the sentiments expressed by President Taylor and President Cannon. And in regard to this matter of giving ordinances, blessings, and endowments and such, I guess the brethren have heard me speak in my public discourses of

how lavish the Lord has been in bestowing ordinances and blessings upon the people of His Church. I have felt, however, and have expressed my feelings in President Taylor's hearing that before long it would be necessary to give endowments in the lesser Priesthood in some such a way as the manner suggested. I feel that in this there is a very powerful means, and I think we will find out a very powerful helper, to inspire those who get the lesser endowment[,] [the Aaronic portion] only[,] at a time [of their initiation][,] to [continue in] faithfulness so as to be counted worthy to get their further endowments.

This is a principle that exists in the Gospel. Even our Master Jesus had respect to the recompense ^of reward^. It is natural, beginning with our little children, when we require something done in conformity with our will to hold the hope of receiving a reward; and I do believe that the time is near when the Lord will make it manifest to be the proper way to give a measure of the Endowments first, leading the people to attain the spirit and power of that measure before other Endowments are conferred. There is such a thing, as has been stated, as being in too great a hurry. Brother Joseph, however, in the exigencies of the times, was compelled to be in a hurry in regard to these things, for the Church was being driven into the wilderness, and he hastened to confer these endowments, even a fulness thereof, upon all whom he considered worthy. That some separation was intended would almost appear from the revelation which the Prophet Joseph gave concerning the City of the New Jerusalem. We will find there is designated a Temple for the Melchisedek Priesthood and a temple for the Aaronic Priesthood, so that special provision is made for this special thing—this separation[—]and it would not be difficult now—if the President felt the moving of the Spirit so to do—to make this distinction by making one temple for the Aaronic Priesthood, and another, say the one at Manti, for the Melchizedek Priesthood.

President Taylor. Oh no; these Temples are built for the administration of both priesthoods at the same time.

Elder F. D. Richards. In that case the Aaronic Priesthood could be administered in one portion of the temple, and the Melchizedek in another. Of course I merely make this suggestion, and do not contemplate that anything will be done in the matter unless the Lord manifest that it is His mind and will so to do. I have for some time past felt another thing, and particularly since the passage of this [1882 anti-polygamy] Edmunds bill. That bill has had this effect: to pick out and sever the brethren who believe in the Celestial order ^of marriage^ from those who do not ^and who are slow to practice it^, and it seems to me that this is the Lord's preparation to bring those brethren to a higher platform. I expect, however, that the day is not far distant when the Lord will manifest through our President his mind and will concerning all these matters. My mind is prepared for it. I think it would be consistent with the spirit and genius of our work; and I look for it in the due time of the Lord.

President Cannon. Respecting some men I will tell you my own feelings. If I am in the way, if I am unworthy, if it was thought I did not magnify my priesthood as I should do; with my present feelings if it were said to me: "We cannot permit you to enter the school of the Prophets," I would prefer it, rather than that I should be admitted, and then feel that I had been too leniently dealt with, and admitted where I should not have been. I would rather stay out of any place I am not fitted for, and strive for the help of God to qualify myself for it, I think every good Latter-day Saint should have the same feeling. I would like to feel myself so perfectly free and unrestricted, that if a man, even though he were an Apostle was said not to live up to his calling as he should do—that that man, if I objected to his name being put down as a member, would not put me down as his enemy; because if such an objection were given against me, I would, with my present feelings, submit and strive for the blessing.

President Taylor. A good many principles have been spoken of here today that ~~lay~~ ^lie^ right at the root of our religion. And our safety is abiding by the law and word and will and ordinances of God. I do not believe in departing from any of them, that is, so far as they are applicable to us.

The meeting then adjourned. Benediction by President Joseph F. Smith. John Irvine, Reporter.[12]

September 22, 1883; Saturday

The above report [of August 2, 1883,] was read in the President's Office, in the presence and hearing of the First Presidency—John Taylor,

12. Franklin D. Richards wrote after the meeting that "Prest. Taylor evidently aims at a high & higher moral standard in the organization of another school than has been heretofore attained." FDRJ, Aug. 2, 1883.

George Q. Cannon and Joseph F. Smith—and while it was being read, Bros Wilford Woodruff and Brigham Young [Jr.] of the Twelve Apostles came in. The report was, after its perusal, accepted by all the above-named brethren.

The question of who should be members of the School of the Prophets when again organized having been introduced, the following brethren were separately nominated and accepted by unanimous vote, as members of that School: the First Presidency[:] John Taylor, George Q. Cannon, Joseph F. Smith.

President Taylor instructed President Woodruff to call the Twelve Apostles and their Counselors to a meeting to be held at the President's Office, at 3 o'clock, on Thursday afternoon next, to consider their standing individually, before receiving them as members to the School. Geo Reynolds. Clerk.

September 27, 1883; Thursday

As per action of the meeting held Sept 22nd 1883. The First Presidency and Apostles met at the Office of President John Taylor at 3, o'clock P.M. Present: Presidents John Taylor, George Q. Cannon [and] apostles W[ilford] Woodruff, L[orenzo] Snow, E[rastus] Snow, F[ranklin] D. Richards, A[lbert] Carrington, B[righam] Young [Jr.], M[oses] Thatcher and H[eber] J. Grant. Secretaries L. John Nuttall and George Reynolds.

President John Taylor stated the object of the meeting to be, to give further consideration of the organization of the School of the Prophets.

The minutes of the meeting held on Thursday August 2nd 1883, also on Saturday September 22nd 1883, were read by Secretary Nuttall. During the reading of the minutes, President Joseph F. Smith and Councilor Daniel H. Wells came in.

At the close of the reading President Taylor asked the brethren to make such remarks as they felt to do on the subject before the meeting, and Elder John Irvine was invited in to fully report the remarks made by the brethren.

President Wilford Woodruff, I want to ask one or two questions of Brother Erastus Snow. He has been listening to the remarks which have been made here, and I believe he is the only man in this room who was in the Temple in Kirtland at the introduction of the first Endowment.

I want to ask Brother Snow if he was present on that occasion. Apostle Erastus Snow answered in the affirmative.

President Woodruff: That is one question I desired to ask. Then again I wanted to ask with regard to the principle of the washing of feet, whether he has any recollection of any special teachings by Brother Joseph Smith upon that subject. They commenced introducing the washing, as I understood, in the School of the Prophets, and it was continued through all our Endowments the following year, in fact as long as we were received in companies.[13] That is the question that I wanted to ask if it could be answered in a few words.

Apostle Erastus Snow: Before the main room of the Kirtland Temple was completed, while the carpenter work was being finished and painted, and the veils being put in place—some weeks previous to this a room for the school was finished—a west room of the attic, which was dedicated for the meeting of the Elders that should be invited by the Presidency of the church, in which to receive special councils and instructions, and in this room the rules and regulations governing the house were presented and formally accepted and adopted. It was in this west room of the attic that the Prophet first introduced and administered the ordinance of anointing the head. I was not present at the time. I was only a youth and had only been enrolled in the Elders quorum; but I learned that Joseph first anointed his councillors and they anointed him; the Presidency anointed the Twelve [Apostles], and they the first Seven Presidents of the Seventies, which latter were instructed to anoint the members of their quorum, there being at that time only one quorum of Seventies.

This I think was in the latter part of February, 1836, and was continued throughout the month of March; but of this I could not be certain without referring to the record or Journal. In that west room of the attic those to whom I have refered received the anointing of the head, and that anointing was sealed upon them by the laying on of hands. The President

13. Woodruff probably has in mind the washing of feet in late 1835 in preparation for the Kirtland Temple's completion, followed in January 1836 by a "purification" ritual involving full-body washings (Oliver Cowdery's Sketch Book, Jan. 16, 1836, postscript, MS 3429, CHL) and within the temple itself a few days later when the men were anointed with oil (Jessee et al., *Joseph Smith Papers*, 174, for Jan. 28, 1836), as Erastus Snow confirms in the next paragraph. However, the first washing of feet occurred three years earlier in conjunction with the School of the Prophets in January 1833.

of the High Priests quorum (Brother Don Carlos Smith) and the President of the Elders quorum (Bro. Alva Beaman)[14] and their councillors were also anointed, and they were instructed to anoint the members of their respective quorums. These quorums met in turns in that room, and the work was continued until each quorum was organized. All this, as I have said, took place, to the best of my recollection, during the later part of February and the month of March; the work seemed to continue for a month or six weeks before the main room of the Temple was dedicated, which took place on the 27th of March 1836.

President Woodruff: What I want to get at is when the ordinance of the washing of feet was first introduced.

Apostle E Snow: The introduction of the washing of feet in that Temple, so far as I have any knowledge, was after the dedication of the main room of the Temple. To the best of my knowledge it was not introduced in the west room of the attic when the quorums were organized and the members thereof received their anointings, but after the dedication of the main room the Priesthood was were called together in the main room, and the Prophet introduced the ordinances of the washing of feet. The pulpit erected for the Melchizedek Priesthood was in the west end of that building; the pulpit for the Aaronic Priesthood was in the east end. The vails were suspended from the ceiling of the main building and let down by means of ropes and pullies—made to be let down or rolled up, from the ceiling down to the floor. These vails divided the room into four parts. Then in addition to these there were small vails that could be let down to encircle each pulpit by itself. First a vail for the upper pulpit for the First Presidency; then another for the next three seats, and then a third; thus dividing the Presidency of each Quorum by themselves when they ^met^ in prayer or in consultation. But when the Priesthood generally were called togather in a Public Capacity, one vail could be let down crossways in the center, separating those of the lesser Priesthood from the Melchizedec. At the time we were all invited togather to receive the ordinance of the washing of feet, (my present recollection is that) the four principal vails were let down dividing the room into four parts, but this was for convenience rather

14. Don Carlos Smith was Joseph Smith's youngest brother. Alva Beaman was an early friend of Joseph Smith, whose daughter, Louisa, became Joseph Smith's first documented plural wife.

than to separate the Priesthood. The ordinance of the washing of feet was performed in each one of these compartments. In each compartment tubs ^were^ provided. The Prophet first gave general instructions and then the vails were let down, and the ordinance proceeded quietly in all the four compartments.

President Cannon: This ordinance was administered to the Priesthood only?

Erastus Snow: Yes, to the Priesthood only; there were no sisters present. The Prophet proceeded to wash the feet of his brethren, then he instructed the different leading elders to proceed to wash the feet of their brethren, and thus they washed each others feet.

President Woodruff: This ordinance appears to have been in connection with the giving of endowments rather than as an introduction to the school of the Prophets. I would like to ask Brother Snow if there ever was any change in the ordinance, whether there was an ordinance of the washing of the feet as an Endowment, and another as an introduction to the school of the Prophets?

Apostle Erastus Snow: I did not understand that this ordinance was an introduction to the school of the Prophets.[15] The salutation contained in the revelation was not made use of. The Priesthood was called in by a general invitation, and they came in promiscuously [without regard to rank]. After receiving general instructions they proceeded according to instructions given by the Prophet. The Prophet himself was in the room when I received my washing of feet, and I was present most of the day. The Prophet went from one room to another while the washing of feet was going on; and when they all got through the tubs were removed and everything cleaned up. Then the Prophet blessed the Elders and told them to speak and prophesy and speak in tongues as they felt moved upon by the Holy Ghost. It was after the washing of feet that the spirit of prophecy seemed to rest upon the Elders to a considerable extent, and a great many things were spoken by the Elders that appeared marvelous at the time.

President Woodruff: What I desire to get at is, whether there was any change in this ordinance during the two years it was carried on?

15. As Snow later explains, he had never personally attended the School of the Prophets in Kirtland. The initiation into the school on January 23, 1833, by the washing of the feet is described by Joseph Smith in *History of the Church*, 1:322–23.

Whether there was an ordinance of washing of the feet in the giving of Endowments, and another for admission to the school of the Prophets? I made some remarks, at a previous meeting that appear to conflict somewhat with the washing of feet as described by Brother Snow, and I do not desire them to so appear.

President Cannon: Here is the point, I see quite a distinction. I made use of some remarks as to whether the washing of feet in the giving of Endowments superseded the other ordinance. I do not believe it did. But to clear the point up, let us ask Brother Snow: Did you not understand that the washing of feet as a preparatory ordinance to admission to the School of the Prophets was an entirely distinct thing, and in no way connected with the Endowments?

Apostle Erastus Snow: I so understood. I did not understand it to be a preparatory work either. I understood it rather as a finishing work, and the words used in most cases, according to the best of my recollection, were: "I wash you and pronounce you clean from the blood of this generation."

President Taylor: Were you in the school of the Prophets?

Erastus Snow: I do not know that I ever attended anything that was called the School of the Prophets until I attended the school established by President Brigham Young in Salt Lake City.

President Taylor: The thing is here, Bro. Snow. There were two things apparently designated, one in relation to the Endowments, and another in relation to the School of the Prophets. You received your Endowments in that Temple, didn't you?

Apostle Erastus Snow: I received the same Endowment I understood, that was given to the Elders; which is a preparatory Endowment, but the ordinance of the general washing of the body, which was afterwards introduced in Nauvoo, was not attended to in the Kertland Temple.[16]

President Taylor: No. I understood that, I received my Endowment also in that house [Joseph Smith's Red Brick Store],[17] at the time

16. According to Oliver Cowdery, the washing was conducted in the Smith home just north of the Kirtland Temple: "And after pure water was prepared, [we] called upon the Lord and proceeded to wash each other's bodies, and bathe the same with whiskey, perfumed with cinnamon. This we did that we might be clean before the Lord for the Sabbath, confessing our sins and covenanting to be faithful to God. While performing this washing with solemnity, our minds were filled with many reflections upon the propriety of the same, and how the priests anciently used to wash always before ministering before the Lord" (see note 13 above).

17. See Historian's Office, History of the Church, May 3, 1842.

^when^ the Twelve were on their way to England. The ordinance that was attended to was precisely that of which you speak—that is, the anointing of the head and the washing of ^the^ feet, and the pronunciation of being clean from the blood of this generation. But there seems to be another ordinance associated with the School of the Prophets. You will remember, however, that soon after these things were introduced in Kertland, a great amount of confusion began to prevail[;] a spirit of apostasy, to a very great extent, prevailed among the people, consequently a great many of these things had necessarily to be dispensed with.[18] Furthermore, there were things revealed very frequently—not in their fulness, but still strictly in accordance with the word, and will, and law of God, which were only temporarily entered in to, and they were unable to perfect those things because of the weakness, and covetousness, and the wickedness of the people. But those things like other ordinances that were introduced by Joseph—say before the Temple was finished in Nauvoo[—]were perfect in themselves, and were calculated to be administered to all who were prepared to receive them, but not to everybody, and that is where the thing comes in. Now, then, as regards to the question t[o]uched upon here, pertaining to the washing of feet and the anointing of the head, and in the Endowments—the Endowments certainly were not the School of the Prophets; the School of the Prophets was not the Endowment; the order was different. You did not, when you had your feet washed, partake of the sacrament did you, Bro. Snow?

Apostle Erastus Snow: To the best of my recollection we partook of the Sacrament in the evening [in the Kirtland temple], and none but the Elders were present; but whether it was in the evening before the washing of feet or the evening after I am not prepared to say. I think it was the evening after we had got through with the washing of feet. That there was not a school organized according to the revelation, and which met during this period and afterwards, I am not prepared to say, because as I have said I was a mere boy at the time. The fact of I never having attending any such school is no evidence it did not exist.[19]

18. For more on the challenges to Joseph Smith's leadership during the Kirtland era, see Staker, *Hearken, O Ye People*.

19. For an account from someone who was there, see the remarks of Zebedee Coltrin on October 3, 1883, below.

President Taylor: There was a School of the Prophets in Kertland. There was also one in Jackson County, Missouri.[20] We are not told precisely who presided over the one in Kertland, but the impression is that Joseph presided over it, and that Elder Parley P. Pratt presided over the School in Jackson County.

Apostle Erastus Snow: I understand, President Taylor, that the School of the Prophets had been in existence two or three years before we received this washing of feet [in the Kirtland Temple] to which I have alluded. I had heard of it and had read the revelation, and understood such an order existed, but I never attended any meetings of the school until I attended the one established in Salt Lake. I did not understand that this washing of feet [in the temple] was identically the same with the ordinance for admission to the School of the Prophets. I understood it to be something extra. I did not understand this washing of feet as an introduction to the School of the Prophets.

President Cannon: That is the point we wanted to draw out.

President Taylor: When you received this washing and anointing it was as an Endowment, was it not?

Apostle Erastus Snow: Yes, as a portion of the Endowments; and that is what I meant by saying it was a finnishing work, because it was the last.

Apostle F. D. Richards: The fact that the School of the Prophets was organized in 1833, would lead us to pre-suppose that this ordinance [in the temple], of which Bro. Erastus has spoken, was not intended as a preparetory ordinance for admission to the school. The School had been established about three years before this Endowment was given.

President Joseph F. Smith: There are some remarks by the Prophet [Joseph Smith] in relation to this subject to be found in the 15th Vol[ume] ^of the^ Millennial Star. I think it would be well to have these remarks read.

The 15th Vol[ume] of the Star having been procured, Bro. George Reynolds read the remarks refered to. They are to be found [in the July 2, 1853, issue] on page 423,[21] and are as follows:

"You want to know many things that are before you, that you may know how to prepare yourselves for the great things that God is about

20. The school in Missouri was commended in a revelation that became section 97 of the Doctrine and Covenants.

21. See Historian's Office, History of the Church, Nov. 12, 1835.

to bring to pass. But there is one great deficiency or obstruction in the way, that deprives us of the greater blessings; and in order to make the foundation of this church complete and permanent, we must remove this obstruction, which is, to attend to certain duties that we have not as yet been attended to. I supposed I had established this church on a permanent foundation when I went to Missouri, and indeed I did so, for if I had been taken away, it would have been enough, but I yet live, and therefore God requires more at my hands. The item to which I wish the more particularly to call your attention tonight, is the ordinance of washing of feet. This we have not done as yet, but it is necessary now, as much as it was in the days of the Savior; and we must have a place prepared, that we may attend to this ordinance aside from the world.

["]We have not desired much from the hand of the Lord with that faith and obedience that we ought, yet we have enjoyed great blessings, and we are not so sensible of this as we should be. When or where has God suffered one of the witnesses or first Elders of this church to fall? Never, nor nowhere. Amidst all the calamities and judgments that have befallen the inhabitants of the earth, His almighty arm has sustained us, men and devils have raged, and spent their malice in vain. We must have all things prepared, and call our solemn assembly as the Lord has commanded us, that we may be able to accomplish His great work, and it must be done in God's own way. The house of the Lord must be prepared, and the solemn assembly called and organized in it, according to the order of the house of God; and in it we must attend to the ordinance of washing of feet. It was never intended for any but official members. It is calculated to unite our hearts, that we may be one in feeling and sentiment, and that our faith may be strong, so that Satan cannot overthrow us, nor have any power over us.

["]The endowment you are so anxious about, you cannot comprehend now, nor could Gabriel explain it to the understanding of your dark minds; but strive to be prepared in your hearts, be faithful in all things, that when we meet in the solemn assembly, that is, when such as God shall name out of all the official members will meet, we must be clean every whit. Let us be faithful and silent, brethren, and if God gives you a manifestation, keep it to yourselves; be watchful and prayerful, and you shall have a prelude of those joys that God will pour out on that day. Do not watch for iniquity in each other, if you do you will not get an endowment, for God will not bestow it on such. But if we are faithful, and live by every word that proceeds forth from the mouth of God, I will venture to prophesy that we shall get a blessing that will be worth remembering, if we should live as long as John the Revelator; our blessings will be such as we have not realized before, nor in this generation. The order of the house of God has been, and ever will be, the same, even after Christ comes; and after the termination of the thousand years it will be the same; and we shall finally roll into the celestial Kingdom of God, and enjoy it forever."

President Taylor: There is an important item. Read the last two or three sentences over again.

Brother Reynolds read: "The order of the house of God has been, and ever will be, the same, even after Christ comes; and after the termination of the thousand years it will be the same; and we shall finally enter into the celestial Kingdom of God, and enjoy it forever.

["]You need an endowment, brethren, in order that you may be prepared and able to overcome all things; and those that reject your testimony will be damned. The sick will be healed, the lame made to walk, the deaf to hear, and the blind to see, through your instrumentality. But let me tell you, that you will not have power, after the endowment, to heal those that have not faith, nor to benefit them, for you might as well expect to benefit a devil in hell as such who are possessed of his [the devil's] spirit, and are willing to keep it: for they are habitations for devils, and only fit for his society. But when you are endowed and prepared to preach the Gospel to all nations, kindreds, and tongues, in their own languages, you must faithfully warn all, and bind up the testimony, and seal up the law, and the destroying angel will follow close at your heels, and exercise his tremendous mission upon the children of disobedience, and destroy the workers of iniquity, while the Saints will be gathered out from among them, and stand in holy places ready to meet the Bridegroom when he comes."

President Taylor: The Prophet speaks there as if the then Twelve [Apostles] were to bind up the testimony and seal up the law, etc. whereas, they are nearly all dead.[22] But that was not to be done by them, for the

22. Two of the original Twelve were still alive: John Boynton and William Smith, although neither was still affiliated with the Utah church. William Smith was somewhat prominent in the Reorganized LDS movement in the Midwest.

time had not come; but it has to be done by the same priesthood, when the time does come. I will tell you another thing that I have had come to me very often while I have been preaching. In speaking about the prosperity of the work of God and the rolling forth of Zion, I have been led to say, "woe! woe! to them that fight against Zion." That is, in strict conformity with what has first been read. The Lord will handle them by and by.

After some further conversation on this matter, President Taylor said: We have met now to talk about the School of the Prophets. We have taken certain preliminary ^steps^ in relation to it, and if any of the Twelve have any remarks to make, or any light to throw upon the subject, there is now full opportunity to speak, so that we may come to some action in relation to this matter.

President Woodruff: I wanted to make some remarks at the proper time in regard to myself—my standing and position and to enquire if there was any objection to my being a member of this School.

President Cannon: thought it would be better to first accept the minutes which had been read, and then as members were proposed and accepted, they could be recorded as the acceptance of the First Presidency had been.

President Taylor enquired if they were prepared to vote on the acceptance of the minutes and the principles contained therein.

Apostles F. D. Richards was quite prepared to vote but would humbly ask that, before the question was put another word might be inserted in his remarks for the word "Polygamy." That was a Gentile word, and he would rather have another word inserted—say Patriarchal or celestial marriage.

President Taylor said that the alteration would be made as requested.

Counselor Daniel H. Wells was ready to vote on the acceptance of the minutes as a report of the meeting; but as to the change in the giving of Endowments, was that to be accepted without further discussion?

President Taylor: What is contained in the minutes in regard to that is simply an expression of opinion.

Coun[selor] Wells: What I wanted to get at, was that in accepting these minutes we do not vote to accept a change in the plan of giving Endowments.

President Taylor: There is no change of plan contemplated at all, further than to give a portion of Endowments at one time, and another at another time. But we have not arrived at that point yet. The question is merely as to accepting the minutes as far as we have gone.

Coun. Wells: There is this difficulty which presents itself to my mind. Persons do not get sealed until they are ordained to the Melchisedek Priesthood. But persons getting the lesser priesthood might want to take a wife. Now, in that case, would they be entitled to the sealing ordinances?

President Taylor: They would not have the privelage at first.

Coun. Wells: Bro. Cannon has stated in his remarks that he was first married for time. But there is this objection arises in my mind. A person who is not sealed according to the order of the Holy Priesthood, his children are not legal heirs to the Priesthood. Hence, where people are only married for time, I do not understand that their children would be legal heirs to the Priesthood, and consequently would have to be adopted.

President Taylor: That is correct. We understand these things.

Coun. Wells: Pres. Young thought probably the time would come when the first Endowment could be given to the lesser Priesthood in a garden where there would be trees, and then let those receiving this first Endowment go on and prove themselves for a while; but this question of marriage and sealing for time and eternity, and the heirship of children always came in as an objection to separating the Endowments.

President Taylor: Yet you know, and I know, and we all know that there are very great many of our people who are not living and probably never will live in a way to secure celestial exaltation. It is not because they are Latter-day-Saints that they are going into the Celestial Kingdom. It is not every one that saith "Lord, Lord," that is going into the kingdom of heaven. We find a great many incompetent people in our midst, and I suppose it is proper there should be for the time being; we are told the tares have to grow with the wheat until the harvest. At the same time we should ^not^ be very anxious for the tares to be mixed up with the wheat, especially if we want to accomplish any special purpose. And concerning these things I will mention an incident that will throw a little light on this subject.

One of our brethren—a very good man, (I won't mention his name)—wanted to know if his son, a very good boy—could have his Endowments. I replied that under the circumstances I would not want my children to have their Endowments. Why not? Because they would have to take upon themselves obligations and responsibilities which they might not be prepared to fill. Why not? I will show you one reason. Our youth are all the time subject to temptation and liable to be led astray. If they should commit adultery or fornication as it may be called, what would be the result? The result would be that they would have to make an acknowledgement before the Church and ask the forgiveness of the church, and if they were forgiven, after making their confession, they would pass, say for the first time; but for the second offense they must be cast out. That is the way I look upon people who have not entered into this covenant. When they have entered into the marriage covenant and commit adultery it is said they shall be destroyed. Now, I would not like to place my children in that position, under these circumstances. I would much rather they had a chance under the first arrangement of overcoming their weakness, and have a standing in the Church.

I now speak of the laws of God being carried out ^and we are supposed to carry them out^. I cannot feel in the least to have people who commit adultery continued members of this Church—that is[,] people who have entered into these sacred covenants. If there is any way for their redemption it is not made manifest to me. Furthermore, the [scriptural] law says they shall be destroyed. I would not want to place responsibilities upon people until their minds and character were matured, to enable them to act wisely, prudently, and intelligent, and to magnify their calling. What is meant then—I am among men who understand these matters—by the passage in the revelation where it says that "they that are sealed by the Holy spirit of promise, according to mine appointment, and he or she shall commit any sin or transgression of the new and everlasting covenant whatever, and all manner of blasphemies, and if they commit no murder, wherein they shed innocent blood—yet they shall come forth in the first resurrection and enter into their exaltation; but they shall be destroyed in the flesh, and shall be delivered unto the buffetings of Satan unto the day of redemption" [D&C 132:26]? Well, it is just on the same principle Peter spoke of, to people in his day. He said, "Repent ye therefore, and be converted, that your sins may be blotted out, when the times of refreshing shall come from the presence of the Lord; and he shall send Jesus Christ which before was preached unto you [Acts 3:19]." Now, what would be the law of God if carried out?— What is it to be destroyed in the flesh? What does that mean? {Sign of the Priesthood.}[23] You all know. What does that mean {Another sign of the Priesthood.} You all know. Now if that was carried out.

Coun. Wells: Is that what is meant by being destroyed in the flesh?

President Taylor: I think it would be pretty near.

Coun. Wells: Well, cutting [someone] off [from] the church don't pay the penalty.

Prest. Taylor: Leave them in the hands of God, or in the hands of the devil.

Prest. Cannon: I have some views on this subject which I would like to give expression to at the proper time. It is a matter in which I am deeply interested. I think there is not that harmony of views among us—I do not mean among the Twelve [Apostles], but among the Priesthood, that there should be, and probably this is because of our not understanding each another. Sometimes when it is convenient to Prest. Taylor I would like this subject talked over. I find a division of views of prominent men in the Priesthood upon this subject.

Prest. Taylor: Well, what is the School of the Prophets for?

Prest. Cannon: Just the thing.

Prest. Taylor: I will mention another case which will serve to throw a little light upon both points that have been discussed. There was the case of a young woman who had committed adultery. When she went through the Endowment House she was about 16 or 17 years of age and did not comprehend the nature of the obligations into which she was entering, which is the position of a great many. Well, she committed adultery. The man who committed this act with her stood in another position. He was more aged and ought to have understood things better, and to know what he was doing. That man cannot be forgiven. The other would be considered as of non-age. That is the way I have looked at that case. She had not arrived at the years of maturity; he had. In some of these cases there may be perhaps a change in relation to these matters; but it is a thing.

Coun. Wells: The man would be held more responsible, anyhow.

---

23. Taylor made a penalty sign usually reserved for the endowment ceremony. The signs, meant to symbolize punishment for betraying one's covenants made in the temple, were removed from the ceremony in 1990. "Comments on Temple Changes Elicit Church Discipline," *Sunstone*, June 1990, 59–61.

Prest. Taylor: It is a thing we should be very careful about. But I did not make that revelation. I cannot change it. I am not authorized to change it. The law says they [adulterers] shall be destroyed; I cannot say they shall not.[24] Unless the Lord manifests something to me about things of that sort, I do not feal authorized to go contrary to the word of God on these subjects. They are very important. As it is said, in times of men's ignorance God winked at it. Now He calls upon all people everywhere to repent. I look upon it that we are called upon to carry out the law and will and word of God, and we have no right to change either. Formerly we are told there were placed in the church Apostles, prophets, etc. for the perfecting of the Saints and the edifying of the body of Christ. But if these laws are not put into execution how is the church to be perfected. If drunkards, sabbath-breakers, whoremongers, are allowed to carry on their wickedness, how is the church to be purified? And who will be responsible for these things? Those who permit them. The church ought to be purified; we ought to be stepping forward in purity; and seeking to do the will of God on earth as it is done in Heaven.

Upon the question of accepting the minutes of the two previous meetings as read, being presented by Prest. Taylor, all the brethren present voted to approve and accept them.

On motion the meeting adjourned until 10 oclock A.M. tomorrow at the Presidents office.

September 28, 1883; Friday

The First Presidency and Apostles met as per yesterdays adjournement at the Presidents Office at 10 oclock A.M. Present Presidents John Taylor, George Q. Cannon, and Joseph F. Smith[,] [also] apostles W[ilford] Woodruff, L[orenzo] Snow, F[ranklin] D. Richards, A[lbert] Carrington, B[righam] Young [Jr.], M[oses] Thatcher and H[eber] J. Grant. Councilors John W. Young and Daniel H. Wells, and Secretaries L. John Nuttall and George Reynolds.

President John Taylor said: It has been thought proper in having people enter the School of the Prophets that their standing in the church and suitability for membership therein should first be thoroughly

24. He is referring to the promise of section 132 of the Doctrine and Covenants that such people will be "destroyed in the flesh, and shall be delivered unto the buffetings of Satan." See also D&C 42:24.

understood, and due precaution is very necessary in all these matters. The First Presidency have met and upon due consideration have passed upon their own names—and it would be well for the Twelve [Apostles] to take the same course; afterwards as other names are presented, they can be canvassed and properly accepted. Formerly the sacrament was administered, and afterwards the washing of feet was attended to, and they who were thus washed were pronounced clean from the blood and sins of this generation. We are now moving on a higher plane, and are being ^thus^ properly organized [this] will put us more in accord with our profession as Latter day Saints.

In reflecting upon these matters I have often had impressions that we should have these [School of the Prophets] organizations in the several stakes, and have proper persons appointed to carry them on, as Bro. Parley P. Pratt was called in an early day [in Missouri], and labored under the direction of the Prophet Joseph Smith. If we so decide, we can then have these matters properly carried out through the whole church in all its stakes.

In talking of the Kingdom of God being established upon the earth, [and the] will of God being done on ^the^ earth as it is done in heaven—as I understand it, if the Kingdom of God is established we must commence among ourselves.

When President Brigham Young organized the School of the Prophets, he called it a theological class, which was in effect the School of the Prophets, and after running the same for a season, he was compelled—for causes well known to us all—to discontinue them. Now the question is, shall we commence aright, according to the pattern laid down, and then continue right along without any failures? For we have a legitimate claim upon our Heavenly Father for his guidance and direction in all our doings; and by calling upon Him we will be enabled to carry out the mind and the will and law of God.

I am called a Prophet of God, also a seer and Revelator. My Councilors are also sustained as Prophets, Seers and Revelators, as also the Twelve and their Councilors.[25] Is this a fiction or reality? Joseph fixed these matters in his day, and they are no fiction.

The Presidents of Stakes are placed in the same position as the Church

25. The office of Counselor to the Twelve existed for fourteen years to 1891. See Quinn, *Mormon Hierarchy: Wealth and Corporate Power*, 10.

in Kirtland [Ohio] was, when the Prophet Joseph presided over it. The Presidents of Stakes and their Councilors stand in the same relationship to the Stakes, that Joseph Smith and his Councilors stood to the Stake in Kirtland, with this difference that their authority extends only to the Stake, while that of Joseph Smith and his Councilors extended to the whole world. That being the case they would be quite as competent to manage their affairs as we are to manage ours, and they could select that class of men to associate with them, as we have with us, for they have the right to know the mind and will of God in their behalf.

In regard to this School we read that the authority was to extend from the High Priest to the Deacon. This would embrace all the faithful in Zion.[26]

If these Presidents of Stakes shall be directed to thus organize, and if they had access to the First Presidency or to the Twelve, there would be a connecting link among all the presiding authority of the church and Kingdom of God on the earth, then they could extend the information received, so far as practicable among all their people.

There are many things which belong properly to the School of the Prophets and which concern the School of the Prophets and none others, and we should fully understand these matters as they are.

Now in our investigations as to each other [we] do not want to have any ill feelings engendered, and in considering the character of our brethren [we should] do what we do in the spirit of kindness and generosity toward each other, doing all that we do in the fear of the Lord. Thus we can introduce an order whereby the faithful saints can understand the mind and will of God and then be able to do it.

If you brethren of the Apostles will talk among yourselves and fully consider these matters, all right. We do not wish to be present unless you so desire, but when you want to meet with us, we shall be pleased to meet with you. You can have this office to meet in, or the Social Hall as you may wish.

Bro. W. Woodruff asked what course it would be expected for them to pursue in their talking together.

---

26. Taylor probably meant to imply that membership would be available to all faithful adult males, keeping in mind that deacons in those days were mostly adult men, rather than the young boys who today are ordained at age twelve. Hartley, "Men to Boys," 80–136.

Prest. Taylor: Just as you may think best among yourselves. I do not wish to propose any cast iron rules, but leave that matter with you for your own action.

The meeting adjourned and the apostles reti[r]ed.

At 4:30 P.M. President Wilford Woodruff with his brethren of the Twelve Apostles came to the President's Office and wished to meet with the First Presidency upon which a meeting was held. All [were] present as at this morning's meeting, also Elder Erastus Snow.

President W. Woodruff: I want to say to the First Presidency that we have been togather as a quorum since this mornings meeting except for one hour. We have had a free and full talk upon our individual affairs—upon our family matters, upon the word of wisdom, the duties and responsibilities that devolve upon us as Apostles, etc. And we have come to the conclusion that we will more fully observe the word of wisdom, as we have all more or less been negligent upon that point—that we will conduct our personal lives and the affairs of our families in a more Christian manner in the future, and in conformity with our calling and high profession as Apostles of the Lord Jesus Christ. We have examined into the reported criminality of Brother Carrington while in England, and have had a full explanation from him of these matters, and find there is no criminality to be attached to him, yet he was very unwise and imprudent in his course while abroad, which might have given cause for grave suspicions. Brother Carrington is also convinced that his conduct was not consistent with his calling as an Apostle.[27]

Brother John W. Young has also expressed his desires to more fully live up to the requirements of his religion, and to magnify his calling. Hence we have passed upon and accepted each of the members of our quorum who have been with us today and now present, and submit ourselves and our action for the consideration of the First Presidency.

Prest. John Taylor: As a body of Apostles you have the right to examine into the lives, conduct and character of each of your members, and if, upon your investigation you are and can be satisfied with each other, I am sure I ought to be. For you are competent to investigate and

27. More information would soon emerge about apostle Albert Carrington's sexual misconduct a year earlier with Sarah Kirkman, a housekeeper at the British Mission headquarters, and with several other women beginning in the 1870s, resulting in Carrington's 1885 excommunication. Bergera, "Transgressions in the LDS Community—Part 1."

adjudicate as between yourselves. I am satisfied with your action today and your report as I feel assured my Councilors will also be.

So far as Brother Carrington is concerned, I had received a letter from Brother John Henry Smith pertaining to some matters which I considered more a matter of imprudence and indiscretion rather than criminal. Yet I felt it proper to have the matter referred to you brethren of his quorum for such consideration as you might think proper, and handed the letter to Bro. F[ranklin] D. Richards that you might see what the charges were.

Elder E. Snow stated that the quorum had not seen the letter refered to, but that President Woodruff had made a statement in which he refered to the matters said to be contained in said letter, and upon which Bro. Carrington had made explanations.

Elder Woodruff: He did not have the letter read but had fully explained its contents so far as he knew them, as he had also received a letter from Bro. John H. Smith.

President Joseph F. Smith stated that some time ago Bro. F[rancis] M. Lyman had been informed by one of the brethren returning from his mission to England that there was some missconduct between Brother Carrington and a certain Sister while they were at Liverpool, which was very derogatory to the character and position of an Apostle while in charge of such an important mission. And he thought in justice to Brother Carrington that [a] full investigation should be held, especially as he cla[i]ms there was no criminality on his part.

Brother John Henry Smith's letter, also an accompanying document pertaining thereto, was read by Elder Nuttall. Upon which by request Elder Carrington said: ["]These statements are very much mixed—Sister [Sarah] Kirkman was an orphan girl and a resident of Bolton [near Manchester]. We needed an assistant house-keeper at 42 [Islington Road in Liverpool][28] and as she appeared a suitable person we had her come to 42 as an assistant house-keeper. She was not very strong and we soon found that cooking did not agree with her, hence she did the work about the house—and when she was not so engaged, I gave her the privelage of the prayer room whenever she pleased, and at her leisure to knit, sew, read, etc. ^and^ when it did not interfere with the

28. The reference is to the headquarters of the British Mission and editorial offices of the *Millennial Star*. Watt and Godfrey, "Old 42."

business of the office. She was a woman very free to chat and talk and make herself agreeable, as English women are; but as I thought gave no cause for any suspicion as to her conduct.

["]As to the statement that Sister K[irkman] was seen lying on my body, while I was on the lounge in the prayer room, I do not know of any such an occurrence, as there was none. Such a report may possibly have arisen from her free manner in coming into the room at times, and she may have sat down on the foot of the lounge at the same time that Sister Norman came into the room. There could have been no other cause. As regards the London trip—as Sister Kirkham was about to emigrate and she had not seen much of the country, and never been to London—I asked her if she would like to go to London and she accepted the invitation. I wrote to a Sister where I generally stay when there, enquiring if a room could be provided for her use and found it could—we went to London and while there I asked Brother West to take her around and show her the sights, and I never accompanied her to any place while there.

["]In relation to my accompanying Sister Kirkman to make purchases, etc. There had been some complaints as to some of the parties who had been furnishing 42 with supplies, and I went once with Sister K[irkham] to the baker as his bread had been somewhat lumpy with pieces of flour, also to the man who furnished the butter, and to the fish monger once.

["]The Cabin story is all false, and made out of whole cloth, for I do not know that I saw her at any time on the steamer more than to say good-by. The writing to me and addressing me as My Dear Pa, I do not know of receiving but one letter from her, and that was while I was at Glasgow. She asked me about when I would be at 42. She may have addressed me as Pa for I am old enough to be her grandfather. The Evanston matter was also made out of whole cloth.

["]Now as to my course I must admit that others might have had suspicions as to my conduct, as Sister Kirkman was very free and talkative, and which was to say the least very unwise, and imprudent, but there was no intuition of wrong by me or by her in these matters, yet I now see that others might think so.

["]I can say that I have never in my life, had any connection with any female other than my wives either at home or abroad, the Lord has preserved me from anything of that kind.["]

After hearing the statements of Bro. Carrington, the President asked the brethren present if they ^were^ still willing to accept and approve Bro. Carrington, to which they assented. President Taylor called a vote on the question. Are the Twelve and their Councilors willing to receive and approve of the First Presidency and of the quorum of the Twelve and their Councilors now present; and the First Presidency to receive and approve of the members of the Twelve Apostles and their Councilors present. All voted in the affirmative. Adjourned.[29]

October 2, 1883; Tuesday

Meeting of the First Presidency and Apostles 3 P.M. at President Taylor's Office.

Present: Presidents John Taylor, George Q. Cannon, and Joseph F. Smith[;] [also] apostles Wilford Woodruff, Lorenzo Snow, Erastus Snow, F[ranklin] D. Richards, Brigham Young [Jr.], Albert Carrington, Moses Thatcher, Francis M. Lyman, ^and^ Heber J. Grant, and Elders [L. John] Nuttall and [George] Reynolds.

Prest. Taylor instructed Brother Lyman what had been done toward organizing the School of the Prophets during the last two meetings (he being then absent) "We have thought that it was proper to fill a class of people who would adhere strictly to the laws of God; on that basis the School would be organized. He afterward refer^r^ed to the law of the Lord concerning adultry as contained in the Book of Doctrine and Covenants, both with regard to those who had not and those who had received their endowments; which laws he felt neither he nor any other person had a right to change nor alter. Regarding the School, the First Presidency had a full and free discussion and were in entire harmony, so with the Twelve. At the last meeting the First Presidency had voted to accept the Twelve, and the Twelve had voted to accept the First Presidency [as members of the school]. I think according to the leadings of the spirit we might introduce others; and organize the school as it was first intended. It may be well also to organize other Schools in the Stakes, under the direction of the Presidency of the Stakes, and the question is whether it would not be better for them, at any rate for a

29. Heber J. Grant recorded that "all of the brethren present confessed their faults and failings ... a number of the brethren confessed to breaking the Words of Wisdom—I was thankful that I was not one of the number that had to confess." Grant diary, Sep. 28–29, 1883.

time, to submit the names of those proposed for membership for supervision and acceptance.[”]

Prest. Woodruff thought it would be well, in the beginning, if the First Presidency could not meet to organize these schools, that some of the Twelve should.

Prest. Cannon drew attention to the enquiry whether members or branch schools could be admitted to the school in this city, also drew attention to ^differences in the^ Presidents of Stakes as to the standard they would insist upon with regard to those they admitted, some would require a higher standard than others. He thought something should be done to insure uniformity.

Brother Richards thought the Presidents of Stakes should first belong to the school here.

Prest. Cannon spoke of the revelation given about a year ago, regarding fulfilling the word of the Lord.[30] Some of the brethren in high positions had, so far as he knew not fulfilled that law.

Brother Lyman stated that he being absent when the vote was taken wished to be passed upon. Prest. Woodruff asked him some questions with regard to his life, which questions being satisfactory[i]ly answered, Brother Woodruff moved he be accepted. Carried unanimously.

Bro. Lyman said that he accepted all his brethren of the council with all his heart. He also accepted the minutes of the meeting as the rest of the brethren had previously done.

In answer to the question from Bro. Jos[eph] F. Smith Prest. Taylor said that at present it would be well to confine the School to official members of the church, and extend gradually. There might ultimately be more than one school in a Stake, if circumstances made it desirable.

October 3, 1883; Wednesday

Prests. John Taylor and George Q. Cannon, Apostles Erastus Snow,

---

30. The revelation of April 28, 1883, telling Taylor to reorganize the School of the Prophets, called on church leaders to be “diligent and act in their several positions, … and magnify the same, and honor and obey me, the Lord their God, and respect and obey the counsels of my holy Priesthood.” A few months previously, on October 13, 1882, a revelation called George Teasdale and Heber J. Grant to the Quorum of the Twelve and challenged all priesthood holders to “repent of all their sins and shortcomings, of their covetousness and pride and self-will, and of all their iniquities wherein they sin against me.” Holzapfel and Jones, “John the Revelator,” 273–308; Roberts, *Life of John Taylor*, 349–50.

Brigham Young [Jr.], Francis M. Lyman, ^and^ Heber J. Grant, and Elders L. John Nuttall and Zebedee Coltrin present.

Bro. Zebedee Coltrin said: I believe I am the only living man now in the church who was connected with the School of the Prophets when it was organized in 1833, the year before we went up in Zions Camp [from Ohio to Missouri].

Prest. Taylor: How many were then connected with the School at that time?

Bro. Coltrin: When the Word of Wisdom was first presented by the Prophet Joseph [Smith] (as he came out of the translating room) and was read to the School, there were twenty out of the twenty-one who used tobacco and they all immediately threw their tobacco and pipes into the fire.

There were members as follows: Joseph Smith, Hyrum Smith, William Smith, Fred[e]rick G. Williams, Orson Hyde, (^who^ had the charge of the school), Zebedee Coltrin, Sylvester Smith,[31] Joseph Smith Sen., Levi Hancock, Martin Harris, Sidney Rigdon, Newell K. Whitney, Samuel H. Smith, John Murdock, Lyman Johnson and Ezra Thayer.

The salutation, as written in the Doctrine and Covenants was carried out at that time, and at every meeting, and the washing of feet was attended to, the Sacrament was also administered at times when Joseph appointed, after the ancient order; that is, warm bread to break easy was provided, and broken into pieces as large as my fist, and each person had a glass of wine and sat and ate the bread and drank the wine; and Joseph said that was the way that Jesus and his disciples partook of the bread and wine; and this was the order of the church anciently, and until the church went into darkness. Every time we were called together to ^attend to^ any business, we came together in the morning about sunrise, fasting and partook of the Sacrament each time; and before going to school we washed ourselves and put on clean linen. At one of these meetings after the organization of the school, on the 23rd January, 1833, when we were all together, Joseph having given instructions, and while engaged in silent prayer, kneeling, with our hands uplifted each one praying in silence, no one whispered above his breath, a personage walked through

31. All except one of these men, Sylvester Smith, have been previously identified. Smith had been a member four years when he became one of the presidents of the Quorum of Seventy in 1835. He served on the high council in Kirtland, as well, but had left the church by 1838.

the room from East to west, and Joseph asked if we saw him. I saw him and suppose the others did, and Joseph answered, that is Jesus, the Son of God, our elder brother. ^Afterward^ Joseph told us to resume our former position in prayer, which we did. Another person came through; He was surrounded as with a flame of fire. He (Bro. C[oltrin]) experienced a sensation that it might destroy the [physical] tabernacle [or body] as it was of consuming fire of great brightness. The Prophet Joseph said this was the Father of our Lord Jesus Christ. I saw Him.

When asked about the kind of clothing the Father had on, Bro. Coltrin said: I did not discover His clothing for He was surrounded as with a flame of fire, which was so brilliant that I could not discover anything else but His person. I saw His hands, His legs, his feet, his eyes, nose, mouth, head and body in the shape and form of a perfect man. He sat in a chair as a man would sit in a chair, but His appearance was so grand and overwhelming that it seemed I should melt down in His presence, and the sensation was so powerful that it thrilled through my whole system and I felt it in the marrow of my bones. The Prophet Joseph said: Brethren, now you are prepared to be the Apostles of Jesus Christ, for you have seen both the Father and the Son, and know that They exist and that They are two separate Personages.

This appearance occured about two or three weeks after the opening of the school. After the Father had passed through, Joseph told us to again take our positions in prayer. We did so, and in a very short time he drew our attention and said to us that Bro. Reynolds Cahoon was about to leave us—and told us to look at him. He (Bro. Cahoon) was on his knees, and his arms were extended, his hands and wrists, head, face and neck down to his shoulders were as a piece of amber, clear and transparent, his blood having apparently left his veins. Upon the attention of the brethren being thus called to Bro. Cahoon, the change seemed to pass away and Joseph said that in a few minutes more Bro. Cahoon would have left us; but he came to himself again.

The school room was in the upper room of [Newel K.] Whitney's store.

October 10, 1883; Wednesday

Meeting of the First Presidency, the Apostles and the Presidents of Stakes at the Endowment House, at 5 P.M.

Present: Presidents [John] Taylor, [George Q.] Cannon and [Joseph

F.] Smith, Apostles W[ilford] Woodruff, L[orenzo] Snow, E[rastus] Snow, F[ranklin] D. Richards, B[righam] Young [Jr.], A[lbert] Carrington, M[oses] Thatcher, F[rancis] M. Lyman, Geo Teasdale and H[eber] J. Grant[,] [as well as] councilor D[aniel] H. Wells, and Presidents W[ilia]m Budge, William B. Preston, A[braham] O. Smoot, L. John Nuttall, J[ohn] D. T. McAlister, Abram Hatch, W[illiam] W. Cluff, Ira W. Hinckley, John B. Murdock, Thomas J. James, Christopher Layton, Hugh S. Gowans, Angus M. Cannon, Silas S. Smith, Lewis W. Shurtliff, W[illia]m R. Smith, C[hristian] G. Larsen, Jesse W. Crosby Jr.[,] [and] Willard G. Smith, also Elders Henry Eyring and Geo Reynolds.

President Taylor refer^r^ed to the first organization of the School of the Prophets by the Prophet ^Joseph Smith^, also to the Theological class organized by President Brigham Young.

The First Presidency and Twelve have held some meetings in regard to these matters, and it has been thought proper to have such schools in the several Stakes. The members thereof must be true men and faithful members of the church. No leakage of any kind can be permitted, not even to our wives, our children or to any body else. Not that there are any secrets in these matters, but because they do not belong to others. Bro. Nuttall will read our record as made, thus far. We do not wish anyone to be in a hurry, but to remain as long as shall be necessary. He then requested Bro. Nuttall to read the minutes of the meetings held August 2nd 1883, and September 22d 1883, which having been done Prest. Taylor said: It appeared that these things were to be presented to all the bodies of the Priesthood, but on the other hand it was only to reach those who were worthy. The first school, so far as we can learn, only comprised a small body of men, about twenty or twenty-one.

We have now thought that it would be well to have these things [local schools] established amongst the Stakes: carefully, advisedly and with due consideration. The First Presidency and Twelve Apostles feel that they are on the earth to do the will of our Heavenly Father, and to see that the Saints keep His commandments. I was a little surprised to find that there were so few belonging to the first school. Brother Zebedee Coltrin informs me that when the Word of Wisdom was read to the school there were twenty-one present, twenty of whom used tobacco, all these immediately, without demur, threw their pipes and tobacco away.

I will have Bro. Coltrin present at our next meeting, and we will meet at the Presidents Office tomorrow morning at 10 oclock.

It is expected that all who are admited will take a straight course, and do the will of God in its completeness. Nobody will be forced, but it is expected that those who do become members will have their conduct scrutinized; for if we are to pass by the angels and the Gods hereafter we must be willing to submit to a little scrutiny now.

Adjourned to meet at President John Taylor's Office, tomorrow morning at 10 oclock. Dismissed by Coun[selor] D. H. Wells.

October 11, 1883; Thursday

Adjourned to meeting of the Presidents of Stakes, in regard to the School of the Prophets, held at President John Taylor's Office, at 10 oclock A.M.

Present: Presidents John Taylor, George Q. Cannon, (and before the close of the meeting Joseph F. Smith), Apostles W[ilford] Woodruff, L[orenzo] Snow, E[rastus] Snow, F[ranklin] D. Richards, B[righam] Young [Jr.], A[lbert] Carrington, M[oses] Thatcher, F[rancis] M. Lyman, Geo Teasdale and H[eber] J. Grant. Stake Presidents W[illia]m Budge, J[ohn] R. Murdock, W[illiam] B. Preston, W[illiam] R. Smith, C[hristian] G. Larson, W[illia]m Paxman, L. J[ohn] Nuttall, Ira W. Hinckley, Willard G. Smith, Jesse W. Crosby Jr., Thomas J. Jones, A[n-gus] M. Cannon, J[ohn] D. T. McAllister, W[illiam] W. Cluff, H[ugh] S. Gowans, A[braham] O. Smoot, Abram Hatch, L[ewis] W. Shurtliff, S[ilas] S. Smith and C[hristopher] Layton. Elders Zebedee Coltrin, George Reynolds and Henry Eyring.

Prest. Taylor said: You will observe in the minutes read yesterday, (wherein there was a commandment given to organize the School of the Prophets,) a statement that "these things" more properly belong to the School; without entering into details I will say "these things" refer to temporal matters.

We are starting in to build up a kingdom, also a church, and a Zion. To do this will require wisdom and intelligence, which God, as the fountain of all intelligence, can alone impart or reveal. As it took the revelations and wisdom of God to start this work, so it requires the same wisdom to carry it forward. I ascribe our deliverances wholy to the Lord.

The intelligences [spirits] in the Heavens are associated with those on the earth, so also with the Priesthood, and though the communications be sometimes dim or slow, yet we without them can not be made perfect; nor indeed, can they without us, as we are operating, building Temples, administering ordinances, etc. and both are acting togather for our common humanity. In this respect we occupy a very peculiar and very honorable position. God was the friend of Abraham and Abraham was the friend of God; so also should we tell that we are friends of God, and He expects us to be true and faithful, and grow into His likeness, that we may see Him. And while here on the earth we should be one with Him, and let all our lives, hopes and acts be in conformity with His law. If we are one with Him, in all things, then we are heirs with Him, and joint heirs with Jesus Christ, and we shall inherit what he possesses. "All that the Father hath, hath He given unto you," says recent [1832] revelation [D&C 84:38]. He places everything in our hands and we are expected to place ourselves in His hands, and to operate with an eye single to the glory of God; and the quicker we get at it the more pleasing will it be to Him. The Divine requirement is "Son give me thy heart [Prov. 23:26]"; and surely if the Lord can trust us we ought to be willing to trust Him. (Prest. Taylor also referred to the young man who came to Jesus, and who the Savior told to sell all that he had and take up his cross and follow Him [Matt. 19:21].) There are a great many things to do in the building up of the Kingdom of God. We may have stiffer things to pass through than we have yet had. We shall require union of faith, and also the interposition of God to bring us through. It is written "for brass I will bring gold, and for iron I will bring silver, and [for] wood brass, and for stones iron [Isa. 60:17]." This will be predicated upon the principles of justice and righteousness; not on fraud or checanery. "Violence shall no more be heard in thy land, wasting nor destruction within thy borders; but thou shalt call thy walls salvation, and thy gates praise [Isa. 60:18]"

That is the feeling. In other words: "Thy will be done [Matt. 6:10]." Everything that we can control has to be held for the glory of God; every thing that is not right is carnal, every thing that is of God is true and right. There is a great deal of carnality in the world regarding riches; cliques, rings, corners, monopolies are organized by which millions are filched from the pockets of the people of the United States, every year; just as fraudulently as the Edmunds bill is fraudulent towards us, and our rights and liberties. Again women are destroyed by millions—these are carnal, sensual and devilish things. But because these things are wrong, is it wrong for men and women to marry [in polygamy] and fulfill the laws of Nature? No. So it is with regard to gold, and so forth. But the time is hastening when these things will be controlled in righteousness, and we shall take a course which will be accepted of God. Why was it said, "For brass I will bring gold," etc.? What was said regarding Joseph and Ephraim? "Blessed of the Lord be His plan, for the precious things of heaven, for the dew, and for the deep that croucheth beneath, and for the precious fruits brought forth by the sun, and for the precious things put forth by the moon, etc. [Deut. 33:13–14]." To what do these refer? To grain, to flowers, to gold, to silver, to precious stones. Was it a blessing to have these? Yes, but not as they are handled by the Gentiles.

I have had a number of manifestations about these things. At first I did not like them. I think, however, that the course we have been pursuing has been right, but, by and by there will be a further development in these matters. These will be some of the begin^n^ings [nearby], [but] the end will be that North and South America will be the Zion of God. We, as leaders in Israel will have to operate in these things. Not for our own aggrandizement, but to act with God.

I read a portion of the revelation to show that the school was to be organized. What class of men will belong to it? If God has a mind to call us to honorable stations, we ought to be as honorable as He is, to act also in the interest of Zion, which must be built up under the guidance and direction of the Lord, as was the Zion of Enoch.

We must begin to study on these matters, for this reason I wanted to meet the brethren and talk them over. We are the representatives of God, and He expects to dictate [to] us, that the will of God may be done on earth as it is in heaven. Where else can this begin if not with us? This school is a kind of initiatory step, to aid people to carry out the word, the will and the law of God. And if people think they cannot live up to these things they had better quit. If they cannot live the celestial, let them live some other law, and we will help them all we can. If we can be worthy to have the approbation of God, and Him for our friend and the riches of eternal life, we should have that peace that passeth all understanding, and Zion also will, by our industry and Gods blessing, be the richest of all people.

Apostle L. Snow asked: Is it the object to authorize the Presidents of Stakes to establish schools in their Stakes?

Prest. Taylor: That depends upon circumstances. I feel like going rather slow. I have called the Presidents of Stakes as leading men to lay these matters before them.

Prest. W. Woodruff endorsed the teachings of Prest. Taylor. Felt a change was coming on the church and on the world. Spoke of the greatness of coming events for which a people had to be prepared, and that revelation would be given to fit us for the work, and to stand in the midst of the judgments or else we go down with the rest of the world. We ought to wake up, and set our hearts upon the building up of the Kingdom of God. Then there would be no lack of means. Felt like Prest. Taylor[,] there would have to be a change in the giving of endowments. Referred to the prayer of Joseph [Smith] and the answer thereto, to be found in the Book of Doctrine and Covenants, with its complete fulfillment, He continued I believe that ^this^ priesthood has power with the heavens, some call us slaves—why do we submit to our leaders? Because we know they are controlled of God and empowered by Him; we are no more slaves, than it could be consistently said that Gabriel, Michael, and other angels are slaves to God. The Priesthood will prevail, as the world will find out. God has not stopped giving revelations. Revelations regarding work in the Temples for our dead, etc. When Israel rises up and lives their religion, then we shall not have trouble about grogshops,[32] etc.

Apostle L. Snow—Felt pleased with the Spirit which was manifesting itself to Prest. Taylor for us to be and to do a little better. If we are not holy, it is our duty, at any rate, to try to become so. I presume each and all can see principles in which they have been negligent, and by this we can determine to be more strict in those things in which we have been lax. I believe as Prest. Taylor or Bro. Jos[eph] F. Smith has said, regarding the Word of Wisdom, when I discover that my act of taking a little tea or coffee is injurious to my brethren, I will make the little sacrifice and leave it, though I may think that owing to my peculiar bodily condition it did me good. Men see the word of God fulfilled in those who live up to the Word of Wisdom by long life etc. God will be honored in them by the fulfillment of His promises.

32. Grog shops were saloons, "grog" being literally "a mixture of spirit and water not sweetened." Webster, *American Dictionary*, 1828.

When Prest. Taylor authorizes brethren to organize schools of the Prophets as I suppose he will, I would not reject men because they did not observe every law of God, but I would want every person to engage to be better and to observe the instructions given in the school.

Prest. J[ohn] D. T. McAllister—Spoke of his pleasure at being present. He fully accepted the teachings and endorsed them, and had a greater desire to be a help in building up the Kingdom of God. Had had many sweet associations by day and night, or in dreams, both with the living and dead. He loved tobacco and liquor but had given them up. Continued to express his feelings and desires in order that if deemed worthy he might be worthy to be accepted as a member of the school. Spoke of a vision he had had showing how the church was nourished by the Priesthood.

Asked forgiveness for ought he had said or done that might have offended his brethren. He asked if in a ward there were only 3 High Priests, as was the case in his Stake, and some were absent what should be done in a [church court] case coming before the Bishop, should a Seventy or Elder be taken temporarily or what should be done?

Prest. Taylor said it would be best to ordain some good men to be High Priests.

Elder E. Snow—referred to a revelation where Elders were spoken of in this regard.

Prest. Taylor said that could be done in the case of an emergency, but he advised the ordination of some of the Elders, of whom there were so many, to be High Priests, Young men with vim and intelligence. If a High Priest were needed[,] take a faithful Elder and make him a High Priest.

Prest. A. M. Cannon explained the course taken in the Salt Lake Stake of Zion when a Councilor was absent.

Prest. Taylor said there might be alternates where necessary, as in the High Council. It were better for the Twelve [Apostles] to ordain High Priests, but, if necessary the Prest. of the Stake could do so.

Apostle George Teasdale—said he had not been present with his Quorum for six months, as he had been on a mission. He felt like expressing his feelings this morning. Spoke of progress through faithfulness and righteousness, the love of God stifled out the love of the world. Spoke of giving recom^m^ends to the unfaithful [to attend closed services in the Endowment House], that if it were known that recommends were only given to those who lived the higher life, the people would live for that privilage. I have labored much amongst the endowments and reflected thereon, and would esteem a man my friend who would say don't you go to the House until you have determined to live righteously. Spoke of tithing as a key to a man's standing, as shown in the word of the Lord. Again regarding recommends, if a Bishop had not the backbone to decline to give an unworthy person a recommend, surely fifteen men, in a High Council could do so.

Prest. Taylor asked Bro. Zebedee Coltrin if he was present when the School of the Prophets was first organized by the Prophet Joseph Smith?

Bro. Coltrin: Yes Sir.

A number of questions and answers then passed between the brethren and Bro. Coltrin, [e]liciting the following information: Those who gave up using tobacco eased off on licorice root, but there was no easing off on Tea and Coffee; these they had to give up straight off or their fellowship was jeopardised. He never saw the Prophet Joseph drink tea or coffee again until at Dixon [Illinois] about ten years after.

He did not remember the washing of feet at the opening of the school, but could not say it was not so. (Prest. George Q. Cannon said the "History of Joseph Smith["] said they were washed on the 23d [of] January, 1833.) Elder Orson Hyde was the teacher and saluted the brethren with uplifted hands, and they also answered with uplifted hands. Spoke of the administeration of the Sacrament of the Lords Supper. The brethren always went fasting; they went in the morning, remained until about four oclock in the afternoon, when each had a glass of wine and a piece of bread, after the ancient pattern.

Joseph was the president and appointed Elder Orson Hyde teacher, as the school was not only revelations and doctrine but also for learning English grammar, etc. The teacher saluted the brethren (one or more) as they came in. This salutation was given every morning when they met. Bro. Sidney Rigdon lectured on grammer sometimes. It was in a larger school on the hill[33] afterwards, where Sidney presided[,] that the lectures on faith that appear in the Book of Doctrine and Covenants

33. In 1834 a two-story building was constructed for the church's editorial offices and printing press, and the Elders' School met on the ground level. In 1838 an arsonist destroyed the building. "Printing Office, Kirtland Township, Ohio," *The Joseph Smith Papers*, www.josephsmithpapers.org.

were given. Once Joseph gave notice to the school for all to get up before sunrise, then wash themselves and put on clean clothing and be at ^the^ school by sunrise, as it would be a day of revelation and vision. They opened with prayer. Joseph then gave instructions to prepare their minds. He told them to kneel and pray with uplifted hands. (Bro. Coltrin then gave an account of the appearance of the Father and Son as given in the Minutes of the Meeting of the 3d inst.)[34] Jesus was clothed in modern clothing, apparently of gray cloth. When he saw Him in the Kirtland Temple, on the cross[,] His hand[s] were spiked to the wood, and he had around him what appeared like a sheet. He had seen Joseph giving revelation when he [Coltrin] could not look on his face, so full was he (Joseph) of the glory of God, and the house was full of the same glory. About the time the school was first organized some wished to see an angel, and a number joined in the circle, and prayed. When the vision came, two of the brethren shrank and called for the vision to close or they would perish, these were Bros. [Levi] Hancock and [Solomon] Humphries. When the Prophet came in they told him what they had done and he said the angel was no further off than the roof of the house, and a moment more he would have been in their midst.

Once after returning from a mission, he [Coltrin] met Bro. Joseph in Kirtland, who asked him if he did not wish to go with him to a conference at New Portage [Ohio]. The party consisted of Prests. Joseph Smith, Sidney Rigdon, Oliver Cowd[e]ry[35] and myself. Next morning at New Portage, he noticed that Joseph seemed to have a far off look in his eyes, or was looking at a distance, and presently he, Joseph, stepped between Brothers Cowd[e]ry, and Coltrin and taking them by the arm, said, "lets take a walk." They went to a place where there was some beautiful grass, and grapevines and swampbeech interlaced. President Joseph Smith than said, "Let us pray." They all three prayed in turn—Joseph, Oliver and Zebedee. Bro. Joseph than said, "now brethren we will see some visions." Joseph lay down on the ground on his back and stre^t^ched out his arms and the two brethren lay on them. The heavens

34. That is, the minutes of October 3, 1883, when Coltrin related the details of the vision of God and Jesus during the meeting of the School of the Prophets.

35. Oliver Cowdery (1806–50) was Joseph Smith's scribe for the Book of Mormon dictation in 1829, one of the Three Witnesses whose collective endorsement appears in every edition of the Book of Mormon, and the second person (after Smith) ordained an elder in the church. He became the assistant church president in 1834.

gradually opened, and they saw a golden throne, on a circular foundation, something like a light house, and on the throne were two aged personages, having white hair, and clothed in white garments. They were the two most beautiful and perfect specimens of mankind he ever saw. Joseph said, They are our first parents, Adam and Eve. Adam was a large broadshouldered man, and Eve as a woman, was as large in proportion. (Bro. Coltrin was born September 7th, 1804, and was baptized into the church on the 9th [of] January 1831.)

Meeting adjourned until 3 oclock this afternoon. Benediction by Apostle F. D. Richards.[36]

Presidents Office, Thursday Afternoon 3.15 o.clock. Meeting [re]convened persuant to adjournment. Roll called—Present as in the morning. Meeting opened with prayer by Apostle Moses Thatcher.

Prest. Taylor: I should like to hear the Presidents of Stakes express their feelings on the subjects that have been discussed at these meetings. The Presidency and Twelve [Apostles] have already done so. We should now be glad to hear you, and trust you will be very frank and if you have any doubts let us hear them. We are your friends met togather for the up-building of the Kingdom of God.

(Bro. John Irvine came into the meeting to report the remarks of the brethren.)

Prest. William Budge of Bear Lake Stake expressed the pleasure he had experienced in attending the meetings which had been held during the conference; and the subsequent meetings, such as the present. He had enjoyed the instructions which had been given, and felt a desire to carry them out, and magnify his calling. He wished to live worthy before God, and to use all the influence and power he had to the building up of the Kingdom of God. This had been his object in life, and it was his object today. He felt firmly attached to the church, and desired more and more to do right.

Prest. John R. Murdock of Beaver Stake, felt thankful for the privelage of associating with this body of the Priesthood of God—the

36. Franklin D. Richards wrote that Coltrin "related visions of Father & the Son" and of having seen "Adam & Eve on a glorious throne." Wilford Woodruff recorded Coltrin's account of having seen "a personage" who "passed through the room dressed in usual Clothing," who was said to be "the Savior," and a vision of "a Man sitting upon a Throne … & a woman sitting beside of him," who were "Adam & Eve." FDRJ and WWJ, Oct. 11, 1883.

First Presidency, the Twelve and the Presidents of Stakes—and fully endorsed all the instructions, that had been given. It was his determination to make his acts conform with his expressions. He felt to keep the Word of Wisdom himself so that he might be in a possition to teach it to those who were placed under his charge. He felt built up in his faith by the teachings he had heard, and desired to press forward in the great work in which they were all engaged.

Prest. William B. Preston of Cache Stake, had enjoyed the conference and the meetings that had been held since, and endorsed the instructions which had been given. He had not fully kept the Word of Wisdom in the past, but by the help of the Lord he would try and do better in the future, not only in the better observance of that law, but in being a better husband, a better father—in short, a better Latter day Saint. It behoved them to square their lives according to the principles of the Gosple, and thus he felt to do. He desired to magnify the position in which he was called to act; that he might be counted worthy to enjoy the blessings promised to the faithful.

Prest. William R. Smith of Davis Stake, felt to carry out the instructions that had been given. He depricated some growing evils in the midst of the people, and advocated the keeping of the word of Wisdom. He bore testimony to the truth of the work in which they were engaged, and d[e]sired to magnify his position as a servant of God.

Prest. C. G. Larsen of Emery Stake, rejoiced in the privelage and opportunity he had enjoyed in meeting with and being instructed by the servants of the most high God. He desired to act in unison with his brethren. He felt to keep the word of wisdom, and to be an example in all respects to those placed under his care. He knew he was engaged in the work of the Lord, and he desired to live by every word that proceeded from the mouth of His servants.

Prest. William Paxman of Juab Stake, felt that (while Bro. Paxman was speaking Prest. Joseph F. Smith entered and took his seat) he had had a time of great rejoicing during the last seven or eight days, especial[ly] in these councils, and endorsed all that had been presented. He realized that the time had come when it was necessary for them to straighten up and to overcome their weaknesses. He desired to be fully devoted to the cause of God upon the earth, and to do all he could to build it up. He also desired to live in accordance with the Word of Wisdom. He had endeavored to do so for years, and had seen the fruits of it in his family. He felt to be humble and to be an instrument in the hands of God of accomplishing all the good he could. He was pleased to think that the organization of the School of the Prophets was again under consideration, and if he should be counted worthy he would be glad to be a member of that school. He rejoiced in the spirit that had been made manifest in these meetings. He could bear testimony that the power of God had been abundantly poured out upon His servants, and that they had imparted the bread of life to all who had sat in these councils. He hoped this good influence would go with them to their homes and that it might be defused throughout all the congregations of the Saints.

Prest. L. John Nuttall of Kanab Stake said: I rejoice in having this privelage to express my feelings on this occasion. I have had great pleasure in these meetings with the First Presidency of the church, as also the Apostles, for the consideration of the subjects which have been presented before us. I know that the spirit of the Lord has been made manifest to his servants, that the revelations of His will have been made known to them. I have had many manifestations of this whilst I have met with them and heard them speak in regard to these matters; and the only fear I have is should this school that is in contemplation be organized, am I worthy to become a member? I have felt in my heart that if I could not be considered worthy—if any of my brethren who are acqua[i]nted with me know anything that would make me unworthy, I would not desire to have my name placed upon the roll; but I desire to know the mind and will of the Lord through His servants in regard to these matters, that wherein I fail I might make myself competent to become a member [of the school]. My desires are to be a servant of the Lord, to serve Him to the best of my ability—that my time, my labors, and all that the Lord has blessed me with may be devoted to His service. I have made this resolve many years ago, and with the help of the Lord I desire to continue in this resolve while I shall live upon the earth. I fully endorse all that has been said by the First Presidency and by the brethren who have spoken in our meetings in regard to the subjects which have been presented before us. I accept them in every sense of the word, without any reservation. My desire is to be faithful and true to the responsibilities that may be placed upon me in this church and Kingdom. I have no other desire; and my labors among the people are to the end that I may do them good. So far as the Word of Wisdom is concerned, as it has been presented before us, I have endeavored to observe it for a number of years. I was in the habit of using tea and coffee, but have not done so for a number of years. I have endeavored to abstain from all these things that my example to my family and to those with whom I have associated might be worthy. Not that I am any better than my brethren; but I am striving as far as the Lord gives me strength to be His servant, to learn His mind and will, and then do it. I am gratified to know that the Lord has made Himself so manifest through His servant recently; for I have felt sometimes the great necessity of something being done—as my brethren have mentioned—in regard to these matters in the midst of the people; and I feel assured that ^what^ the Lord has made manifest will be taken up by my brethren, the Presidents of Stakes, and disseminated amongst the people in the various Stakes. My desire is that we shall prosper in the work in which we are engaged, as I know we will be; for the Lord is on our side; and that the blessings of the Lord may attend us in all our labors is my desire and prayer in the name of Jesus, Amen.

Prest. Ira W. Hinckley of Millard Stake, felt his weaknesses to a considerable extent. He could see that the reigns were being tightened, and that they were called upon to be better Latter Day Saints. His desires ever since he came to Utah were to labor in the cause of Zion, and he felt to heartily endorse all that he had heard during these meetings, and by the help of the Allmighty he would endeavor to carry them out.

Prest. W. G. Smith of Morgan Stake, bore testimony to the truth of the work in which they were engaged, and gave expression to his faith therein[;] with regard to the word of wisdom, he saw the necessity of keeping it and had resolved to do so. He felt to honor the Priesthood and to magnify the calling to which he had been called.

Prest. J. W Crosby Jr. Panguitch Stake, endorsed the teachings they had received, and trusted he might have strength to carry them out. While the brethren were speaking in regard to the organization of the school of the Prophets in his mind he canvassed the Panquitch Stake, and he could not think of men enough to organize a school of that kind—that is, men who had proven themselves worthy of what he understood to be necessary in a school of that mature. The great evil was that many of the Bishops and their councilors would not keep their own council. Things were told that should not be told. When people came for recommends for plural wives, in many cases the bishop told his wife, the wife told somebody else, and in this way the thing got spread all over the neighborhood. He had plead with the bishops in his Stake in regard to these matters, and councilled to act wisely and prudently in their office and calling. If I [he] should be seen fit by the servents of God to admit him a member of the contemplated school he would try his best to be a worthy member. He observed the word of wisdom; testified of its good effects, and by the preaching of the brethren who recently visited the Stake he thought the people were seeking to observe it with more strictness.

Prest. Thomas J. Jones of Parawan Stake had felt to rejoice in the meetings that had been held during this conference, and in the subsequent counsels, and he was satisfied that the teachings they had received were from the Lord. He realized the responsibilities resting upon the Presidents of Stakes. He often felt to question himself as to whether he was worthy of the position he held, and the question now presented itself, was he worthy to be admited as a member of the School of the Prophets? He desired however to do right, to fulfil the duties devolving upon him, and to keep the commandments of the Lord, even in the matter of the word of wisdom. (While Bro. Jones was speaking, Elder John B. Maiben entered and was told to remain by Prest. Taylor.)

Prest. A. M. Cannon of Salt Lake Stake, felt to rejoice in the recent conference, and in the meetings which had been held since its adjournment. He rejoiced that the Lord had moved upon ^the hearts of^ his servants to call the Presidents of Stakes to account. For one he had felt to examine his own heart and to lay it open before the Lord. He had always endeavored to keep the word of wisdom, and to bear testimony of the work of God under any circumstances and before any people. He felt the responsibility of his position, but he had ever sought to magnify his calling, to sustain those who were called to preside over him, and to be resigned to the will of the Lord in all things. He trusted he might be able to overcome his weaknesses. He was conscious of his failings, but he tried to labor with himself all the time, so that he might do his duty and be acceptable unto the Lord, whose blessings he implored upon all.

Prest. W. W. Cluff of Summit Stake, realized the responsibility resting upon Presidents of Stakes, and knew that it required a great effort on their part to live so that they might have the spirit and power of their office and calling—that they might magnify that calling that Priesthood which had been bestowed upon them. His desire was to serve the Lord, and to help to roll forth His great work in the earth. He bore testimony to the truth of the work. He believed in the revelations of Jesus Christ; he believed that the church was constantly led by revelation through His servants. He believed in the principle of celestial [plural] marriage, although he had never practiced that principle, and in this respect he realized that he was behind his brethren. He did not know what apology to offer or what reason he could give to excuse himself. He could not account for it only on one principle, and that was, that they were not all constituted alike, and that some did not attach the same importance that others did. There were a great many things that he had been very jealous and very tenacious over pertaining to the Gospel, and he found other men that he had associated with tenacious on other subjects and principles, etc. But notwithstanding he had been backward in carrying out this principle, yet he felt interested in this great work, and he had no desire whatever only to promote its interests and to serve the Lord. He hoped to take a course that would meet with the approval of his brethren, and that he might continue to labor in this great work. This was the desire of his heart.

Prest. H. S. Gowans of Tooele Stake, felt to endorse the teachings that had been given during conference and in the meetings that had been held since. He desired to sustain those who had been called to guide and direct the affairs of the Kingdom of God, and to live up to the requirements made by them from time to time. He spoke of the importance of setting a good example, and advocated that a man should practice what he preached. He strove to keep the word of wisdom to the best of his ability; had done so for a number of years. He spoke of the good results to be attained by the observance of this law, and expressed his desire to continue faithful in the work of God.

Prest. A. Hatch of Wasatch Stake, felt pleased with the privelage of attending conference and the meetings which had been held since. He desired to be in the line of his duty in every sense of the word. He desired to be in fellowship with his brethren. He was not perfect by any means; but he had been able to overcome some things and he hoped yet to be able to overcome all things which he ought to overcome. He endorsed the teachings which had been given in regard to the word of wisdom, and said he had endeavored to set such an example before the people in his charge that they could follow. He had never preached anything but what he had practiced. But there were some things he had not said much about. He was a most firm believer in the celestial order of marriage. Thought of all the principles of the church that was the most glorious. It seemed to him so[,] if properly carried out. But he had always been a little careful and a little fearful to assume the responsibility. Thought it might possibly wreck him. Had seen many a wreck along the road, and he did not know but that ^God^ had made him somewhat timid. Be that as it may, he felt to acknowledge the hand of God in preserving and guiding his life up to the present time in every particular. And he had a desire, and no other on the earth, to assist in building up the Kingdom of God, and to be associated with his brethren, and he hoped he would be able to meet their wishes and requirements. With the help of God he intended to do so. He hoped to be found worthy to retain his position and his association with his brethren; but rather than retard the work in the least degree, although it would be against his own feelings and his ambition, he would rather step down and out.

Prest. L. W. Shurtliff of Weber Stake, felt the responsibility of the position he occupied. But he desired to live up to all the requirements of the Gospel. He endeavored to keep the word of wisdom. If he were permitted to become a member of the School of the Prophets he would be thankful. His only desire was to magnify his calling, and to live worthy before the Lord.

Prest. Silas S. Smith of San Louis Stake, expressed the pleasure he had experienced in attending [general] conference and the subsiquent meetings. He felt heartily in accord with the instructions that had been given, and had a desire to carry them out. Gave a short account as to how matters were progressing in the San Louis Stake, and stated some of the difficulties which had to be met with. As to the work in which they were engaged, he firmly believed in its ultimate triumph.

Prest. Christopher Layton of St. Joseph [Arizona] Stake, felt thankful that he had been counted worthy to preside over one of the Stakes of Zion, and he was endeavoring to do the best he could. Had not strictly observed the word of wisdom, but would try to do so for example sake.

Prest. John Taylor: Brethren, we havc had a talk all around. I now want to know if the Presidents of Stakes, after having the expressions which have been made, are ready to sanction one another and have full confidence and fellowship in one another. If this is your feelings, signify by holding up the right hand. (The vote was unanimous.) Now I will ask the Twelve if they can receive into fellowship and confidence these brethren in the School of the Prophets, and if they can do so I wish them to signify by holding up the right hand. (The vote was unanimous.) Now, then, I wish to ask the First Presidency if they can receive these brethren into fellowship, and if they can to signify it by holding up the right hand. (The vote was unanimous.) Now, then, I want to ask the Presidents of Stakes if they feel to sustain the Twelve in their ministry and to operate with them in their several Stakes for the building up of the Zion of our God. If you can, make it manifest by holding up the right hand. (The vote was unanimous.) Now, then, I want to ask the Twelve and Presidents of Stakes if they have confidence in the First Presidency and feel to carry out their instructions and operate with them in building up the Church, the Kingdom, and the Zion of Our God. If you feel to do this, make it manifest by holding up the right hand. (The vote was unanimous.) .) ~~Now, then, I want to ask the Twelve and Presidents of Stakes if they have confidence in the First Presidency and feel to carry out their instructions and operate with them in building up the church, the kingdom, and the Zion of our God. If you feel to do this, make it manifest by holding up the right hand. (The vote was unanimous.)~~ Now, all who feel like sustaining the council of the First Presidency and the Twelve Apostles, make it manifest by holding up their right hand. (The vote was unanimous.) The councilors to the Twelve were also sustained by a unanimous vote. Elders Henry Eyring, John B. Maiben and George Reynolds then expressed their feelings and were, by separate votes admitted as members of the School of the Prophets.

Prest. Taylor ^invited^ Bro. Zebedee Coltrin to be present at tomorrows meeting. The appointment was made to meet at the Endowment House, fasting, tomorrow morning at 9 o'clock—8 o'clock for those who take their bath at the house.[37]

37. The Endowment House was on the northwest corner of Temple Square. Its tubs, which were supplied with water from City Creek and heated by means of a cast-iron stove, could be used apparently by anyone entering the building. In 1877 people were advised to "wash themselves all over perfectly clean" before entering the ordinance areas. Brown, "Temple Pro Tempore," 39; Anderson, *Development of LDS Temple Worship*, 39.

Meeting closed by singing "Praise God from whom all blessings flow." And the benediction by Apostle F. D. Richards.

October 12, 1883; Friday

Meeting of the First Presidency and [Twelve] Apostles, also the Presidents of Stakes, at the Endowment House, Salt Lake City, as per appointment last evening, at 9 oclock A.M.

Present: Prests John Taylor, George Q. Cannon, and Joseph F. Smith. Apostles W[ilford] Woodruff, L[orenzo] Snow, E[rastus] Snow, F[ranklin] D. Richards, B[righam] Young [Jr.], A[lbert] Carrington, M[oses] Thatcher, F[rancis] M. Lyman, George Teasdale, Heber J. Grant and Counsellor D[aniel] H. Wells. Stake Presidents: W[illia]m Budge, W[illia]m B. Preston, L. J[ohn] Nuttall, W[illia]m Paxman, C[hristian] G. Larson, Willard G. Smith, Thomas J. Jones, John R. Murdock, Abram Hatch, Silas S. Smith, Hugh S. Gowans, W[illiam] W. Cluff, J[ohn] D. T. McAllister, Jesse W. Crosby Jr., Ira W. Hinckley, A[ngus] M. Cannon, Christopher Layton, W[illia]m R. Smith, L[ewis] W. Shurtliff and A[braham] O. Smoot. Councilors Henry Eyring and John B. Maiben. Elders Zebedee Coltrin and George Reynolds.

Opened by singing: "Now let us rejoice in the day of salvation."

Bro. Coltrin, in answer to Prest. Taylor, stated he could conscienciously say before God and the brethren that he had kept his covenants made when Joseph [Smith] washed him, and that he had associated with no women but his wives. On motion Bro. Zebedee Coltrin was unanimously received into the School.

Prest. Joseph F. Smith said he did not think we could consistently ask the people to do better than we were doing ourselves, and he was thankful that the Lord had led President Taylor to take this step and begin at the head. He trusted we should have strength, wisdom and power given to us to live ^the^ lives of purity we now undertook, and to live by the resolutions we now made, from this time hence forth and forever. He had the utmost confidence in the motives and intents of the brethren composing this school, he believed them to be good men. He refered to brethren who said they kept the word of wisdom "in the Spirit and meaning thereof" and under this excuse took tea, coffee, etc. and claiming it was wisdom in them to do so. As well might men claim it wisdom to takes spirits, opium etc. If it is wisdom for me to take tea or coffee once a day, it can be said by others who have become accustomed to such practices it is wisdom to use narcotics and liquors. I believe this, that if the Almighty has said it is good to do a certain thing it is right for us to observe it, and leave the consequences with Him. At the same time perhaps it would be better not [to expect people][,]for those who had been for many years addicted to any habit[,] to leave it off too suddenly. But never let others see us infringe upon a law of God lest they take license at our acts.

He refer^r^ed to Patriarch John Smith's absence. Said it was because as he thought John had not lived his religeon, therefore he (Jos. F. Smith) had not asked that he (John Smith) be admitted, though he held the position of Patriarch to the church. He smoked and, though having two wives, he lived entirely with one. It became a question to his mind, if under these circumstances, if he was ^not^ worthy to belong to this School, was he worthy to be Patriarch? He asked the brethren to use their influence that Bro. John Smith might become a man. With regard to himself he said, that so far as he was concerned he had kept the covenants which he made in the house of the Lord, he had never known any women except the wives given him of God. When a youth he had used tobacco, and he loved liquor, but he let it alone, and he believed everyone who wished to could do the same as many had greater will power than he had.

Apostle F. M. Lyman, said he had visited nearly every part of the Territory in his labors, and had felt strongly impressed to become acquainted with the leading brethren, and had endeavored to bring about a reformation in what are deemed by some [as] small matters. If he had been more Zealous in teaching the Word of Wisdom than any other law of God he did not intend to be so. He felt the importance of all God's laws. But he had seen the most injury done in Israel amongst our youth, through the sin [of] intemperance, and knew fully that when men in position took any particular course the seeds they sowed would remain long after they had reformed, if their course had been improper. He knew of no law of God which was so largely disregarded as the Word of Wisdom, and the young justified themselves in their wrong doing because men in responsible positions did not keep it. Felt too, that if we regarded that part regarding the eating of meats we should be more blessed in the direction of health.

He had been guarded in his actions to women, he had never sinned in this direction, but had kept his covenants, he had not been tempted as some had.

Hymn sung—"Praise to the man who communed with Jehovah." Prest. Taylor called on Bro. A. O. Smoot to express his feelings.

Prest. A. O. Smoot of Utah Stake, expressed the deep feelings of gratitude he had in associating with the brethren present. Spoke of his like for coffee, and in former days of his use of tobacco. A year more ago he quit taking snuff. So far as the daughters of Eve were concerned he had not violated his covenants. He had avoided from his youth up all evil in that direction. He rejoiced in the move now being made, as so many faithful men on account of surroundings and influence have given way, here and there, until they seem to loose their appreciation of their standing in the church. Saw that much good, especially to the young, would arise from this movement, and felt to rejoice exceedingly. He must plead guilty to signing recommends when the spirit within him forbad it. Recently he had refused several whom he did not deem worthy. He prayed that God would help us to be wise and influential. Amen.

On motion Elder A[braham] O. Smoot was admitted a member by unanimous vote. Bro. Smoot expressed himself as in full fellowship with all the brethren. As did also Counselor D[aniel] H. Wells.

Prest. Taylor asked of Brothers Smoot and Wells if they could sustain the First Presidency and the Twelve [Apostles] in their councils, etc. They both answered in the affirmative. Prest. Taylor refer^r^ed to the great necessity of punctuality in meetings in those who presided, the First Presidency, Twelve, Presidents of Stakes, etc. Read the salutations on page 320 of the Doctrine and Covenants [D&C 88:133],[38] to show the necessity of the President or Teacher being first at the School. With Presidents of Stakes, if circumstances occured that they could not be punctual, they should send some one immediately to take their place and not keep the meeting waiting. God is a God of order, all nature acts upon laws, and we must not introduce disorder into our assemblages. The causes that brought about the delay this morning were unavoidable, but should teach us of a lesson of punctuality. Also there should be order in meetings, brethren should not talk in

38. See also the Aug. 2, 1883, entry below.

meeting, read books or newspapers, as he had occasionally seen some do. This set a bad example to the people. Again we meet together to transact business, and brethren come up and desire to be excused, often for trivial circumstances. He never had any thing to do but to keep the commandments of God, and to conform to the rules and requirements of God. Did not wish to destroy the order of the meeting, or be excused from any responsibilities placed upon him unless under very stringent circumstances. Too many had not time to attend to matters pertaining to the Church, they were always too full of personal affairs. Likewise when ordinances were performed, blessing the oil, administering to the sick, there should be quiet, order and peace. There was no need to do these things in the presence of outsiders, or in confusion of a departing congregation, but those attending to these matters should retire to a place where there was no confusion and where they would not be interrupted.

Prayer [by] Prest. Taylor. [Everyone] sang the Hymn: "This earth was once a garden place."

The First Presidency then proceeded down stairs to examine the preparations made for the washing of feet. On their return foot baths were brought in to the celestial room, where the meeting was being held. President Taylor removed his coat and vest (in the sealing room). Bro. Zebedee Coltrin removed his coat and hose [socks]: Prest. Taylor girded himself with a towel, and proceeded to wash the feet of Bro. Zebedee Coltrin, explaining that he did so because Bro. Coltrin was a very aged member of the Church and had belonged to the school instituted by Joseph [Smith], and had had his feet washed by the Prophet. Before washing his feet Prest. Taylor took Bro. Coltrin by the right hand and said unto him that because he had kept his covenants and kept himself pure he proceeded to wash his feet, and as President of the Church of Jesus Christ of Later Day Saints said, Thy sins be forgiven thee. He then washed his feet and again told him his sins were forgiven him. Bro. Coltrin then girded himself with a towel and washed Prest. Taylor's feet. He said that as a link connecting the old school with the present he washed President's feet and pronounced him clean from the blood of this generation, and sealed by the authority of the holy Priesthood many blessings upon him and washed his feet as a testimony thereof.

Prest. Taylor then washed the feet of:

Prest.	George Q. Cannon.
"	Joseph F. Smith.
Apostle	Wilford Woodruff.
"	Lorenzo Snow.
"	Erastus Snow.
"	Franklin D. Richards.
"	Brigham Young [Jr.].
"	Albert Carrington.
"	Moses Thatcher.
"	Francis M. Lyman.
"	George Teasdale.
"	Heber J. Grant.
Coun.	Daniel H. Wells.
Elder	Abra[ha]m Owen Smoot.
"	Christopher Layton.
"	William R. Smith.
"	John Riggs Murdock.
"	John D. T. McAllister.
"	John Bray Maiben.
"	Willard Gilbert Smith.

While more water was being fetched the brethren sang "Let us pray, gladly pray."

Prest Taylor then continued the washing of feet in the following order:

Elder	William Budge.
"	Ira Nathaniel Hinckley.
"	Christian Grace Larson.
"	Abram Hatch.
"	Silas Sanford Smith.
"	William Booker Preston.
"	Hugh Sibley Gowans.
"	William Wallace Cluff.
"	Angus Munn Cannon.
Elder	Leonard John Nuttall.
"	Henry Eyring.
"	Lewis Warren Shurtliff.
"	William Paxman.
"	Thomas Jefferson Jones.
"	George Reynolds.
"	Jesse Wentworth Crosby Jr.

Prests. Angus M. Cannon[,] L. John Nuttall and others assisted in bringing the water to the President, and in removing the bath as each Elder had his feet washed; fresh water being used in every case. All the brethren, (after the Twelve and their Councilors [and] Brother Wells) were washed according to seniority. Roll was then called, 38 present including Bro. Zebedee Coltrin.

The following is the form of ceremony used by Prest. Taylor:

Brother (giving name) in the name of the Lord Jesus Christ and by virtue of the Holy Priesthood I wash thy feet in accordance with the order instituted by God in his church and as practised by our Lord and Savior Jesus Christ when in the flesh upon his Apostles and deciples, and also observed by his servant Joseph Smith the Prophet as an introductory ordinance into the school of the prophets. I pronounce thee clean from the blood of this generation, and confer upon thee all the rights, blessings, powers and privelages associated with this holy ordinance, and I do it by virtue of the Holy Priesthood and in the name of the Lord Jesus Christ. Amen.

Occasionally he inserted "And I say unto thee thy sins are forgiven thee."

The administration of the sacrament was than proceeded with. Bread and wine being introduced and spread upon a table. The First Presidency broke the bread. The brethren all knelt and Prest. Taylor asked a blessing on the bread. Prests. Cannon and Smith handed the bread around to the brethren. (It was broken in large pieces after the ancient order about the size of a moderate sized man's fist.) Elder L. J[ohn] Nuttall handed the bread to Bros. Cannon and Smith.

Prest. Taylor said: There is a great deal of carelessness regarding the taking of the Lords supper. People should always remember Him and his at~~t~~onement when they do so. It was instituted that He might be brought to the rememberance of His Saints. The tokens, sacrifices, etc., of the ancient church were emblemitical of the atonement; it is the one thing running through the whole of the Scriptures. Men offered up the blood of animals, doves, etc. God offered up his own son. A blessing was then asked upon the wine by Prest. Taylor.

Prest. Taylor said, Jesus had promised He would no more drink of the fruit of the vine until he drank it new in His Fathers kingdom. The washing of feet is not the same ordinance associated with this as attended to ^in^ ~~the~~ administrations ~~of~~ endowments in the Kertland

Temple. There were some introductory endowments attended in that building, and the washing of feet was connected with the endowments. This is a distinct thing and is introductory to the School of the Prophets. The other was an endowment. It has become quite a serious thought if initiatory ordinances had not better be given first on account of the lightness with which the ordinances were now treated by many; and when persons had proven themselves worthy, give them another step in advance[ment]. The reason why things are in the shape they are is because Joseph felt called upon to confer all ordinances connected with the Priesthood. He felt in a hurry on account of [a] certain premonition that he had concerning his death, and was very desirous to empart the endowments and all the ordinances thereof to the Priesthood during his lifetime, and it would seem to be necessary that there should be more care taken in the administration of the ordinances to the Saints, in order that those who had not proven themselves worthy might not partake of the fullness of the anointings until they had proven themselves worthy thereof, by being faithful to the initiatory principles; as great carelessness and a lack of appreciation had been manifested by many who had partaken of those sacred ordinances. Had Joseph Smith lived he would have had much more to say on many of those points which he was prevented from doing by his death. It remains for us to look after and enquire into these matters, that perfect order may exist in the Church of God and that persons may not be put in possession of rights and privelages, and receive blessings, promises and endowments of which they are unworthy and can not enjoy.

We have an instance of that [exclusivity] in Section 88 verses 133–4 of the Doctrine and Covenants[:] "Art thou a brother or brethren? I salute you in the name of the Lord Jesus Christ, in token or remembrance of the everlasting covenant, in which covenant I receive you to fellowship, in a determination that is fixed, immovable and unchangeable, to be your friend and brother through the grace of God, in the bonds of love, to walk in all the commandments of God blameless, in thanksgiving, forever and ever. Amen. And he that is found unworthy of this salutation, shall not have place among you: for ye shall not suffer that mine house shall be polluted by him."

And verse 138: "And ye shall not receive any among you into this school save he is clean from the blood of this generation:" And if this principle would hold good in regard to the school of the Prophets, would it not more emphatically do so as associated with the endowments[?]

It is further said [in] Section 121 verses 36–8: "That the rights of the Priesthood are inseparably connected with the powers of heaven, and that the powers of heaven cannot be controlled nor handled only upon the principles of righteousness.

["]That they may be confer^r^ed upon us, it is true; but when we undertake to cover our sins, or to gratify our pride, our vain ambition, or to exercise control, or dominion, or compulsion upon the souls of the children of men, in any degree of unrighteousness, behold, the heavens withdraw themselves; and when it is withdrawn, Amen to the priesthood, or the authority of that man.

["]Behold! ere he is aware, he is left unto himself, to kick against the pricks; to persecute the Saints, and to fight against God."

It was almost impossible, for people rushed through as they were in the Nauvoo temple[,] to comprehend the blessings they received.[39] Hence it is a good deal like the saying of Jesus, "Give not that which is Holy to the dogs [Matt. 7:6]." The rich things pertaining to the kingdom of God are not to be trifled with. We must straighten up in regard to these matters. Though there is a freedom in the Gospel, and we do not wish to have too much law, there is a freedom belonging to man that he [Taylor] always felt very delicate of interfering with, especially among the Elders of Israel; yet the Gospel does not allow us the freedom of violating the law of God. He was pleased to see the zeal of the brethren regarding the Word of Wisdom, and according to the words of Prest. Brigham Young, it had now become a law unto us. Some ask what right had Prest. Young to do this? Just as much right as Joseph had to give a portion of a revelation at one time and then add to it afterwards.[40] There are some prominent leading principles in the church and kingdom of God that we cannot ignore, adultry is one of them and it appears necessary that some steps be taken to do away with this damning evil. If we take steps to do away with sabbath breaking, lying, covetousness, slandering, evils of all kinds, masturbation, etc. We

39. The temple was only in operation for two months, December 1845 through February 1846, until the evacuation of the city began. For more, see Anderson and Bergera, *Nauvoo Endowment Companies*.

40. Smith revised some of his revelations, for instance Doctrine and Covenants 27, in which he first introduced a bifurcated priesthood. Prince, *Power from on High*.

are doing a great work for all by doing this and having a class of men and women who are willing to be led and guided by the spirit of God, a[nd] different kind[s] of things will be ina^u^gurated. There is one thing which must be observed, that is, that the powers of the priesthood must be maintained as set forth in the Doctrine and Covenants. (Elder Reynolds read the latter portion of the 121st Section.[41])

President Taylor continued: There is something very beautiful in those sentiments, by the principle of this power all things can be controlled. We are told that the Glory of God is intelligence—we want to draw nearer to God and gain intelligence from all good books. We have no right to present any of our relations, children or friends to any of these plans or to receive any ordinances of the church who are not worthy from their acts. Just the same as Brother Joseph F. expressed himself in regard to his brother John, who does not and has not lived [up] to the privelages he might enjoy. (Refered to the affair of the divorce of Bro. Cahoon and his two wives a short time ago.)[42] We are the truest friends that the world has today, and if they would let us we would befriend them. There is a spirit of defiance to the Priesthood of God and some of our Elders are sometimes inclined in that direction.

I feel grateful today and feel to glorify God for his Spirit that has been manifest in our midst today, among the leading men of the church and kingdom of God on the earth; and when you bow the knee in prayer I ask you brethren remember me and the br^e^ethren my councilors, for we need your prayers and the blessings of God upon us and our labors. Then our peace will flow as a river and righteousness as the waves of the sea. Our dependency is in the Lord; the nearer we approach to God, ~~and~~ the greater our responsibilities are. Joseph once said that in attending to the ordinances, as we have today, that if we violate our covenants we shall be delivered over to the buffetings of Satan until the day of redemption. Prest Taylor then spoke of the signs in the Endowments and asked what they meant, have thought that the

41. "No power or influence can or ought to be maintained by virtue of the priesthood, only by persuasion, by long-suffering, by gentleness and meekness, and by love unfeignned" (121:41).

42. Alvira Cahoon of Ogden accused her husband, Thomas, of cruelty, profanity, and adultery when she sued for divorce in 1880. The two had lived separately for several months, but the bill of divorce was denied. "The Cahoon Case," *Salt Lake Tribune*, Aug. 1, 1880; "The Recent Divorce Suit," *Ogden Junction*, Aug. 4, 1880.

ancient Japanese understood something in regard to these matters in the Hari Kari.[43] We do not interfere with the lives of men, those who violate their covenants, we leave them in the hands of God, and in many instances that you know he has visited signal judgements upon transgressors. In the cases of whoredom, harlots who engage in those matters do not live to exceed five years, so the statistics say. Whoremongers and adulterers God will judge. It is a fearful thing to fall into the hands of the living God, it requires the greatest care to properly control ourselves and those associated with us. We will now have the cerimony attended to of the salutation that we may know all pertaining to these matters.

Sang: "This earth was once a garden place."

Prest. Taylor continued: It will not be wisdom for you to start these Schools hurriedly, we want them thoroughly supervised, only introduce honorable, God-fearing Latter Day Saints. We don't want sabbath breakers, profaners, those who do not keep the Word of Wisdom. We must get our High Councils and Bishops instructed. Teach them as we teach you, that they may become examples among their flocks. Those here, who have an idea of entering into these things, do so only carefully, let us know of your proceedings before entering into any of these organizations; be exceedingly careful whom you admit. We want to know their names and see their credentials, and we will send some of the Twelve to aid you organize or write to you. We must keep the things of this school sacredly; must not talk about them, they may be misconstrued. Hoped we should be able to keep our own counsel. Spoke of the reason why he required all recommends to be signed and countersigned. The brethren then retired previous to the organization of the school.

After a while the brethren came back to the room and found Prest. Taylor in his place—whereupon he saluted the brethren with uplifted hands as follows: "Art thou Brethren? I salute you in the name of the Lord Jesus Christ, in token or remembrance of the everlasting covenant, in which covenant, I receive you to fellowship, in a determination that is fixed, immovable, and unchangeable, to be your friend and brother through the grace of God, in the bonds of love, to walk in all the commandments of God, blameless, in thanksgiving, forever and ever, Amen." Prest. George Q. Cannon also with uplifted hands, as also each one of the members saluted the President and each member responded Amen.

43. See note 23.

Prest. John Taylor said: It will be proper to have a teacher appointed to this school. I will act in that capacity and in my absence Bro. George Q. Cannon, and in his absence Brother Joseph F. Smith. All who are in favor of this measure for the present will make it manifest. All raised their right hand.

Prest. Cannon said: There is a practice grown up among us when administering to the sick, or in praying together, that is in [people] whispering the words that are being uttered by the brethren in their prayer. This, as I understand, is not necessary or proper. It is very annoying to me and disturbes the chain of thought. I do not know with whom this practice originated. We can carry the words in our minds without repeating the words and thus enable those who are being administered to, to hear the words that are pronounced upon them.

Elder E. Snow corroborated the remarks of Prest. Cannon. Some think there is no healing of the sick without oil, that that is essential or appears so. In the examples of the Savior I have not found any account of his using oil. James says if any are sick among you call in the Elders and by the anointing of oil and the prayer of faith the sick shall be healed [James 5:14–15], etc. There are times in extreme cases when the anointing of oil is proper and essential, but, as I have understood it from the Prophet Joseph, not essential in all cases.

Prest. Taylor: It will be proper to use the oil when you have it, but when you do not have the oil, the prayer of faith is all sufficient.

Prest. Smith: When a person is sick of a fever or other serious disease, it is not necessary for each of the Elders who is called on to administer, to anoint with oil. But as a person has been anointed once or twice a day, other elders can lay on hands and pray for the sick.

Elder E. Snow: I do not want the brethren to get into a stereotyped way of administering to the sick.

Prest. Joseph F. Smith refer^r^ed to the passage in James, and had always looked upon that as a pattern for us to follow.

Prest. Taylor, related the healing of Bro. Elijah Fordham by the Prophet Joseph, and afterwards of Bro. [Joseph Bates] Noble.[44] Also

44. Joseph Bates Noble was one of several people Joseph Smith was said to have healed of malaria in 1839. Wilford Woodruff said Smith blessed a red handkerchief and gave to him to wipe the faces of children with, and by that means the children were healed. Historian's Office, Histories of the Twelve, Wilford Woodruff autobiography, 1857–58, box 1, fd. 22, CHL.

said: God bless you, brethren. God bless your wives and Children, that you may be enable[ed] to keep your covenants and to maintain your integrity, and save yourselves, your wives ~~wives~~ and children in the celestial kingdom of God.

Benediction by Prest. George Q. Cannon.

Prest. Taylor: Brethren if you will go to the Lord in humility and place your trust in him, He will direct you how to act in all things and at all times.

Adjourned Sine Die.[45]

45. "Sine die," literally "without day," means without scheduling a future meeting.

PHOTOGRAPHS

An aging Brigham Young oversaw the Salt Lake School of the Prophets when health permitted and when he was not wintering in St. George or avoiding arrest by federal authorities. *Photo by Charles R. Savage, ca. 1874*

Daniel H. Wells, counselor to Brigham Young in the LDS First Presidency, was mayor of Salt Lake City in the late 1860s and early 1870s. He usually presided over the School of the Prophets in Young's absence. *Photo by C. R. Savage Art Bazar, ca 1875*

Orson Pratt of the church's Quorum of Twelve Apostles presided over the school when the First Presidency was away. He liked to lecture at length on theology and astronomy. *Photo by Charles W. Carter, ca. 1880*

As the school's secretary, George M. Goddard called the roll, kept the minutes, and prepared reports and correspondence. *Photo by Savage and Ottinger, ca. 1870*

Businessman and journalist George Q. Cannon was an influential member of the School of the Prophets. He was elected in 1873 to be the territory's non-voting delegate to the US Congress and spent much of the next ten years in Washington trying to prevent the passage of anti-polygamy legislation. *Photo by C. R. Savage Art Bazar, ca. 1875*

When the third president of the LDS Church, John Taylor, tried to resurrect the School of the Prophets in 1883, he wanted to mirror Joseph Smith's original school in Kirtland, Ohio. *Photo by C. R. Savage Art Bazar, ca. 1880*

Apostles Joseph F. Smith (*left*) and Wilford Woodruff (*right*) recorded in their diaries details about the school and the discussions that took place. They stood and spoke their minds frequently, according to the minutes. *Photos by George Edward Anderson, ca. 1887, and Charles W. Carter, ca. 1877*

William S. Godbe (*left*) and Elias L. T. Harrison (*right*) led the mercantile revolution against Brigham Young's cooperative vision. Both were members of the School of the Prophets. *Engravings by H. B. Hall & Sons, published in Edward W. Tullidge's* History of Salt Lake City, *1886*

As chief justice of the Utah Territorial Supreme Court, James B. McKean, a native of New York, former US Congressman, and Civil War veteran, empaneled all-non-Mormon juries to try cases of polygamy, but this approach was condemned by the US Supreme Court. *Photo by Patrick H. McKernon, Saratoga Springs, New York, ca. 1870*

Zebedee Coltrin was the only surviving member of the original 1833 School of the Prophets who was still active in the LDS Church. He regaled members with stories of God and Jesus Christ that early participants in the school shared. *Charcoal drawing by an unknown artist*

Prest. D. H. Wells recommended every one to look well after their land titles — The Lord has kindly brought us out, from what appeared to be an unavoidable collision — it clearly shows that we have been fighting on the line of law and the decision of the Supreme Court, has ratified every Legislative enactment that was strictly legal and no act of Congress can set them aside — the attempt, on the part of Judge Mc Kean &c was nothing short of trying to accomplish judicial Murder, which was the most despicable of all murderers —

They undertook to fasten the stigma of Murder on himself, Prest. Young & others, and he for one would like to have all the testimony they have in their possession, to be brought before a proper tribunal — And when found insufficient, to plant a suit upon — to have the same placed in the District Court record, as a testimony to future generations, that those who have been branded and dealt with as murderers, was nothing but a foul & wicked aim at the life of the servants of God —

The School was adjourned for one week at one oclock p m

After singing Benediction by Elder B. Young Junr

G. Goddard Sect

Minutes for April 15, 1871. The recording secretary typically added his name and position: "G. Goddard Sect."

The Old Tabernacle on Temple Square was the scene of many of the school's meetings. *Photo by David A. Burr, ca. 1858*

The new tabernacle, still standing in Salt Lake City, was finished in 1867. After the school struggled to find a permanent home, it most frequently met there. *Photo by C. R. Savage, ca. 1885*

The ZCMI building on Main Street, constructed in the 1870s (the façade came later), was the centerpiece of Brigham Young's cooperative movement and his effort to run non-Mormon merchants out of town. *Photo by C. R. Savage, ca. 1890*

APPENDIX ONE

RULES TO BE OBSERVED BY THE MEMBERS OF THE FIRST CLASS OF THE SCHOOL OF THE PROPHETS.[1]

1. All members must be at the school punctually at the hour appointed, unless excused by the President, or can afterwards show good and sufficient reasons for their absence.
2. They must not take the name of the Deity in vain, nor speak lightly of His character.
3. They must observe and keep the word of wisdom according to the spirit and meaning thereof.
4. They must pray with their families evening and morning, and also attend to secret prayer.
5. They must provide for their families and not abuse them, nor be quarrelsome with or speak evil of each other, or their neighbors.
6. They are required to observe personal cleanliness, and must preserve themselves in all chastity by refraining from adultery, whoredom and lust.
7. They must not go after hay, go to the cañ[y]ons, nor hunt their animals, nor perform any other labor on the Sabbath day, but must rest and attend meeting in the Tabernacle, in their wards, and the fast day meetings, and observe the fast days, and make their offering to the poor on those days.
8. They must pay their Tithing.
9. If any member of this School has any difficulty with another member, he must go and be reconciled with him before attending the School.

1. The rules were written in February 1868, two months after the school was formed. There are rough drafts with variations in wording, a polished draft, and a final fair copy (transcribed here) in SotP, bx 1, fds 4–5, CHL.

10. They must not find fault with, nor rebuke any of the members of the School, this being the province of the President only.

11. In all matters, their dealings should be as much as possible with those in full fellowship in the Church of Jesus Christ of Latter-day Saints, but they must not deal with their enemies, and in all their deal[ings], conduct and conversation they must strive to do as they should be done by.

12. They should not hereafter incur debt beyond their means for paying as they agree, and must honestly pay their debts already incurred if they have the means wherewith to do so.

13. That which is not their own they must not take.

14. That which they borrow they must return according to promise and that which they find they must not appropriate to their own use, but seek to return it to its lawful owner, and if the owner cannot be found it must be deposited in the place designated for lost property.

15. They must not let down their bars, open their gate, nor make gaps in their fences, through which their animals can pass to the injury of their neighbor, neither must they let down his bars, or fence, or open his gate, to let their animals trespass upon him, and in all cases they must pay for the damage done by their animals.

16. No member of this School has the privilege of inviting his friends to attend without being permitted to do so by the President.

17. Whatever passes in the School must be preserved inviolate.

APPENDIX TWO

THE TRIAL OF WILLIAM S. GODBE AND ELIAS L T HARRISON, 1869

This transcript was taken from a photocopy of the original minutes in the Leonard J. Arrington Papers at Utah State University. The trial was public because Brigham Young "wanted no hint of secrecy." For more on the trial, see Walker, Wayward Saints, *152–66.*

Geo Cannon vs. William S Godbe & E[lias] L T Harrison

~~City Hall Salt Lake City Oct 25th 1869. 10 A.M. Roll called. Members present[:] Presdts. Brigham Young & Geo. A Smith, Orson Pratt, Wilford Woodruff, [Stake] Presdts Geo B Wallace & John T Caine, [and High] Co[uncilor]s W[illia]m Eddington, W[illia]m H. Folsom, E[manuel] M Murphy, Jos[eph] S Barfoot, John S Blythe, John Squires, Tho[ma]s E Jeremy, John H Rumell, S[amuel] W. Richards, W[illia]m Thorne, N[athaniel] H Felt, M[iner] G. Atwood, and Theo[dore] McKean. Prayer by John Squires.~~

Charge

Salt Lake City Oct. 23rd 1869
To the President & Members of the High Council of Salt Lake City
Brethren[:]

I hereby prefer a charge against Brothers W[illia]m S Godbe and E L T Harrison for harboring the spirtit of apostacy, and ask an early consideration of this matter.

Your Brother in the Gospel
Geo Q Cannon

[Minutes]

On motions two speakers were appointed on each side.
W[illia]m Eddington & S[amuel] W Richards for Plaintiff.
John S Blythe & M[iner] G Atwood [for] Defendants.

George Q. Cannon[:] Mr President & Members of the High Council, the duty devolves upon me as pros[e]cutor in this case to lay before you in brief my reasons for prefering the charge which is now before the council against Bros. W[illia]m S Godbe and E[lias] L T Harrison. I do not know that I shall be able to give you all the details as perfectly & with that minuteness which they require but still most of you are sufficiently farmiliar with them to supply any defects in detail ~~that~~ that my statement may contain. You are all well acquainted doubtless with the Establishment of what is known as the Utah Magazine.

In that work of late have appeared a series of articles which probally can best be com[m]un[ic]ated from a correspondence that appears in the last number which I will take the liberty of reading. They are entitled, "Steadying the Ark;" "Our Workmans Wages"; "The real representative of the Most High"; "The true developement of the Territory"; "Justifiable Obedience"; & in this last number an article called "Over governing," & another, "We are nothing if not spiritual." These writings contain sentiments so directly antagonistic to the teachings of the 1st Presidency & 12 [apostles] & to the general policy which has been enforced upon the attention of our people now for months & years that to my mind they clearly manifest an intention to destroy as far as possible and as far as the influence of the Magazine goes the teachings & the influence of the 1st Presidency—among the people.

As an individual in consequence of these articles I have felt that these brethren were giving way to a spirit of apostacy whether they themselves know it or not. Monday last the Bishop of the 13th Ward was requested to send two [block] teachers [George Goddard and John B. Maiben] to visit these brethren with several others whose names were not mentioned. They called on bros. Godbe & Harrison & reasoned with them upon the course they were persuing but at the conclusion of the interview they still maintained the same ideas as they did before. [At this, Cannon yielded the floor to George Goddard.]

Bro. George Goddard Stated that he & bro. John B Maiben in connection with Elders Orson Pratt & Wilford Woodruff called upon bros. Wm S Godbe & E L T Harrison last Monday afternoon as teachers & that Bro Godbe said talk about a man being cut off from the Church for not attending the School [of the Prophets] is all nonsense, also that if Bro Harrison is deep in the mud I am just as deep in the mire. Bro Goddard stated that he asked bro Godbe if he observed the word of

Wisdom in his family. He said he did according to his understanding of it. Asked him if he used Tea & Coffee & also asked him if he taught his family to observe the word of Wisdom. Asked him whether he felt to sustain the authorities of the Church. Asked him (supposing the case) if he was called upon to go to some remote part of the territory to build it up if he would do so; he said that would depend upon the circumstances and the position of life he happened to be in at the time.

John B Maiben, Stated that they met bros Godbe & Harrison at Bro Godbe's cottage house at ½ past 2 Oclock in the afternoon. The result of the questioning of Bro Godbe & Harrison was to the effect that they considered it their preveledge to have their own ideas and notions in relation to the doctrines, ordinances & institutions of the Kingdom of God and that they were responsible to the light of the spirit that was within them and not to the authorities of this Kingdom. He asked Bro Harrison how many times the spirit prompted him to pray for the President of the Church of Jesus Christ of L. D. Saints at which he felt insulted, he stated that he did not believe in appointed & set times for prayer but that he believed in praying to God as he was led by the spirit. He [Maiben] stated that the general spirit manifested by those brethren was to ignore the authority of the priesthood to a very great extent more especially in the case of Bro Harrison, [and] said [in conclusion] that [this] was the impression made on his feelings.

Bro Harrison Stated that he told bro Maiben that he did pray for President Young, which was acknowledge[d] by Bro Maiben.

Orson Pratt = I would state to the council that I was requested in connextion with Bros Cannon and Woodruff to meet with those Brethren (Wm S Godbe & E L T Harrison,) and talk with them not particularly in the capacity of teachers but to hear what was said on both sides as also to give such council & Instruction as might occur to our minds on the occasion = I heard all of the questions that were asked by the teachers both [of] bro Goddard & bro Maiben & the testimony that they have given here is correct, and I heard the replys of both Bro Harrison & Godbe to the various questions = The main thing that I saw on that occasion in relation to the feelings of those brethren was that same spirit that is manifested in the Utah Magazine, to ignore in some measure the authority of or the right of the [First] presidency, of this Church & the authorities therof, to council and dictate in all matters whether they be temporal or Spiritual = I saw that disposition manifested & after having heard all these things I took the opportunity to speak to the brethren as I always esteemed them much & especially bro Godbe whom I have esteemed as one of the best of men up to the present time and I felt sorry to see the influence that seemed to be over his mind, to lead him from what I considered the truth of heaven = I took the opportunity of mentioning that it always had been a principle in this Church for the members to receive the Councils & instructions of the authorities of the Church and to abide by their decisions in all things = It was mentioned by bro Godbe in the course of his remarks about some councils that had been imparted in relation to property[,] the property that was placed in the Colorado [River] Storehouse if I reccollect right[,] and the [distribution of goods to] Montan[a] concern. I took the occasion to remark that it was far better for us to loose our property and our wealth & have it all swept from us by obeying council than it was to disobey that council & retain our property: for the Lord might move on his servants to council us in relation to our property and we might not see the why's & the wherefores, but the Lord might have an object in view and would have the right to move on his servants to council us in relation to these matters and this very loss of our property might be in the [~~eyes~~] mind of God one means of our Salvation.

I considered that bro Godbe in yielding to that council had done an excellent thing. I brought up many reasons and testimonies from the scriptures and the book of [Doctrine and] covenants in relation to some other points[.] One was in regard to having certain stated seasons of prayer which bro Harrison seemed to think unnecessary. I quoted some revalations showing that God required the inhabitants of Zion to have their prayers in the season thereof & if they did not do it that they would be brought before the Bishop of the church. I also showed that the book of Mormon refered to stated seasons of prayer Morning & Evening & in one place even at Mid-day and thereof having remarked upon all these subjects and finding that there was still a spirit or feeling in the hearts of those brethren not to accept our councils and that they prefered to be ["]guided by light that was in them" = I felt that we had faithfully discharged our duty in relation to the matter =

W[illia]m S Godbe. Did you understand bro Pratt, that the reason why I mentioned about the Colorado Warehouse [and] the [Utah] Produce Co. [created to sell farm goods to Montana miners] was in order that you might know that I had responded to those requirements.

Orson Pratt = That is all correct yet bro Godbe in his remarks said he had heretofore been willing to make these sacrifices as he termed them, for the sake of unity [and] at the same time said that it was contrary to his judgement and the light that ^he^ seemed to have on the subject =

Wilford Woodruff: Corroborated the testimony given by Bro Pratt and stated that the spirit manifested by bro Harrison was very bitter and entirely opposed to the order of the Kingdom of God. Stated that bro Maiben asked bro Harrison how often he prayed in his family and he answered that he prayed whenever the Lord dictated him to pray or when the spirit revealed to him it was his duty to pray[,] and that he considered for a man to pray at stated times was idolatry & not required of him. He did so some times for the sake of his family but did not consider a man was in duty bound to pray night & morning. Spoke to him with regard to fellowship being withdrawn from him[.] Bro Harrison did not consider that President Young or the authorities of the Church had any right to withdraw fellowship from him until he was ^brought up and^ tried ^it was like hanging a man before he was tried^ & when the question was brought up with regard to the authorities of the church how far they had a right to dictate, Harrison said the priesthood was placed on the earth to teach, not to dictate, force or coerce =

That was about the idea of it = In fact he said that God Almighty nor Jesus Christ, nor any one else had power right or authority to force any man into the Kingdom of Heaven. Bro Woodruff remarked that the Lord Almighty did not force any one, but he condem[n]ed the world if they did not obey his Laws. Stated that the spirit bro Harrison manifested was not in favor of the priesthood governing or controlling or correcting, in temporal matters = he believed that the priesthood had a right to preach and teach the people. The spirit manifested by him was the same as that contained in the Utah Magazine, in those pieces that have been published in regard to this Church & Kingdom in dealing with temporal matters =

Geo Q Cannon: I have one question to ask the witness[es] present = What was the impression left on your minds by this interview &

conversation with these brethren? Was it that they were harboring the spirit of apostacy or not?

Geo Goddard: Stated that his opinion was that they were giving way to the spirit of apostacy =

Orson Pratt, That was the conclusion to which I came as an individual that they were opposed in their hearts to this Church guiding & dictating in all matters, and that they were bordering apostacy if not already entirely apostatized =

Wilford Woodruff: I can say the same as bro Pratt, the spirit manifested by those brethren especially bro Harrison, was entir^e^ly in opposition to all the dealings & Government of this church & Kingdom.

S[amuel] W. Richards: I would like to ask the brethren whether at the termination of their interview they discovered any change of feeling.

W[ilford] Woodruff: I did not[,] that I know of.

Orson Pratt: I could not discover any.

Geo Q. Cannon then read lengthy extracts from the articles that appeared in the Utah Magazine innumerated in his charge & commented strongly & forcibly on them. He also proved that they contained sentiments pandering to outside influences & directly opposed to the teachings and councils of the Presidency & authorities of the Church and that they had a tendency to darken the minds of the people and create opposition: he then submitted his case to the defence.=

W[illia]m S Godbe: Mr President & Members of the High Council: I do not propose on the present occasion to detain you by any lengthy remarks. The course that has been persued by bro Cannon has been so full: he has read so many extracts from the Magazine expressing sentiments that I do endorse & I am thankful to say that there are scarcely any points on which we can differ as to the ground taken in this case = I wish first to reciprocate most heartily the very kind sentiments expressed in my favor by Bro Cannon particularly = I wish to state in response to them that I have nothing but the kindest & most friendly feelings towards those gentlemen not only towards them but towards all men present today =

If I have an unkind feeling in my heart towards any man here to day I am innocent of the knowledge of it = What I have said privately & publicly [and] what I have endorsed in the [Utah] Magazine are sentiments that I have honestly entertained not only today but yesterday &

years ago. If it is apostacy to have such sentiments it cannot possibly be any constriction of language [to] be so in my case because I have always entertained them.

If the sentiments are incompatible with the Gospel my judgement is at fault = as I said on a previous occasion when this matter was called up I embraced the principles of the Gospel many years ago when but a boy because they appealed to my reason as being true. I know of no higher test by which to try them = they seemed to me to be true. Any amount of people told me they were false—men for whom I have deepest affection = My mother told me so—My nearest relatives told me they were wrong, & the testimony of the whole christian world told me that if I persisted in my course I should go to destruction.= They pictured to me the awful precipice over which I should fall, into irretrievable ruin = I did not believe them because my judgement & reason which to me constitute the light of Deity, told me I was right in obeying them. Hence I have not apostatized, because I stand there today = It is true I have rendered willing obedience to the requests that have been made of me. I have done so not because I was told to do so only. But because I was told to do so and the telling of the thing was accompanied by the testimony in my soul that it was right. I do not claim that it is fit or necessary in my case that I should see the thing from the beginning—that I should see the tall ladder that reaches into eternity: but it is necessary according to my understanding that I should know sufficient of a measure to feel that it was not wrong. If I do know a thing to be wrong I am willing and have been as I have shown you before to respond to it—

I am perfectly willing to respond to a measure for the sake of unity at the cost of worldly wealth for I think it is worth more than Gold. It is worth everything = The writings that have been read here today contain sentiments that I believe in.

They are mine honestly & frankly expressed. If they are wrong[,] why I am not to blame in that. I do claim in all solemnity and in sincerity that I have not apostatized. The truth is just as dear to me today as it ever was & I am willing and prepared to make more sacrifices. The apostacy from ones religion is to abandon it. The principles I have embraced which I consider are true have led me onward & upward. And here let me say in regards to one point that we do not ignore the priesthood by any means. But we do admit the existence of a power behind the veil from which influences & instructions do come and have always come by which the [sou]l may be guided in its onward path. I say that I have not apostatized, that this is not the spirit of apostacy according to my understanding of it. With regard to the dangerous character of the writings I admit them[;] far be it from me to detract from any thing that is so candidly expressed as by Bro Cannon on this case. He says they are dangerous because they are sophistries mixed with a certain amount of truth. They contain [what] I know [to be true] as far as I am concerned[,] & I feel sure as far a[s] bro Harrison is concerned that we have not condesended to deal in sophistry. We have advocated our sentiments & have not felt that in doing so we were injuring the truth.

I admit they are dangerous if they conflict with that which [others assume] is true: if they combat error in other words[,] as we believe they do[,] they are dangerous to the distruction of that error: but they are not dangerous to the truth = Truth cannot be affected by our puny efforts; it cannot be injured by any number of men. But the point at issue is plain; We have started this Magazine in the first place with the consent and approval of Pres. Young. & it was devoted to a good object in the Com^m^encement [of publication] and has been ever since;

We have freely & fearlessly acted on the ~~rig~~ right that we believed we posessed[,] just as much retained by us as members of this church as by individuals out side of this church[,] to oppose [some] measures, not in a disrespectful spirit, but in a spirit of temperance, moderation & respect to men whom we love, and whose antecedents have been of such a character to inspire us with the purity of their intentions and their honesty as men. If I be sever[e]d from this church I do so [comply] against my solemn protest. We are taught, we have been taught over & over again that it is right [to voice our opinion], that we should have the responding of our own souls to accompany the responding to the requests made at our hands =

It is our privilege and duty = We have been taught over and over again that the great fountain [of knowledge] is within our reach and we can draw from its source light sufficient to lead and guide us from day to day = I have sought there [knowledge and inspiration] with all the sincerity of my soul. I have prayed not only morning & evening. Not only 3 times a day but I have had the spirit of prayer upon me & in my soul and gone forth with God my guard in all matters. I will say that no man has ever claimed that I have done wrong morally; that my character is immoral; that I have been at least any more immoral than my fellow creatures & I trust by Gods grace it will be so; If it were good to pray yesterday it will be tomorrow: if it were good to have sentiments of Kindness & Love yesterday it will be today = I shall endeavor so to live that I shall have the spirit of Kindness, blessing, liberality, and salvation that shall extend to all men as broad as the universe.

E. L. T. Harrison: I shall endeavor to explain the ground upon which I stand which principle and ground I wish to explain. I have manifested a disbelief of the doctrine of the infallibility of the priesthood; I honestly admit that I believe in the priesthood. I believe in the priesthood as a grand institution designed by heaven to teach mankind. I believe in obeying all the light & truth that they bring to my understanding, but I do not believe in according to them the right to dictate me into a course which I consider wrong, morally wrong particularly. There is one principle to day which animates the minds of a great many & is a standard doctrine of the Church & That is that the President with his associates his brethren, his councillors & the twelve [apostles] & others have a right to expel a person from the Church if he does not see eye to eye with them upon matters of doctrine provided he state that difference. I believe that this principle of compulsion is wrong; I believe there is no precedent for it any where = I believe God never furnished a precedent for it; Jesus never did nor any other man = I believe in the first place that it is my right to honestly canvass the teachings of those that are placed over me, seeing that I have to act on those teachings, seeing that eternal salvation rests upon them = Should they council me in matters of money I should consider that of small moment; but when the general principle is laid down, that the President of the Church has the right to exact from me a statement that I believe in the wisdom & divinity of a measure whether I do so [believe in it] or not, I object to that principle; I object to the priesthood being considered to be so authorized = I cannot conceive that they are authorized to that extent. I believe in the right to discuss freely provided I do it respectfully and moderately any measure or principle that may be presented. I do not believe I have a right to be rabbid in regard to my use of vindictive language; but provided I am temperate, provided I accord to others the same previlege I do myself. I believe it matters not how high that man may be in the priesthood, it is my right to respectfully present those views [to consideration] and leave the is^s^ue [to God] =

I believe this in the first place because when I was in the Old Country the Gospel which was offer^e^d to me promised me this right = I go back to the terms of my induction into the Church, the Elders who visited that land told me that this was a land of freedom: you could discuss any thing = Would they cut you off the Church for discussing a principle in this church? It was popery [Catholicism] that did that. We were in the blaze of gospel of light: ["]Come to Utah [and] discuss what you please, but you must obey the ordinances of the Gospel of course and live pure & moral lives[,] and provided you do that[,] you have the utmost freedom of discussion[,] provided you do it in a proper spirit." Whether these were the terms offered to us in England or not my brethren are the best Judges = I will say that they were the terms offered to me and not only to me but the terms that the holy spirit bore witness to as being holy & true, I embraced them because I loved them = We have come here to build up a power of freedom in the world: I did not know I should subject myself to be expelled from the society of God and angles [angels] because I differed from the president of the Church in any of his views, the ordinances & principles of the church excepted = Not only was I confirmed in this view by the contract & vows in which I entered when I embraced the Gospel repenting & being baptized for the remission of sins but I was promised that when I entered the church that I should have such & such liberties: I accepted the contract & today I stand here to claim it.

Not only was I convinced that this was my right and liberty in the Gospel of Jesus Christ but also I was confirmed by observing the spirit manifested in the scriptures; I cannot see that there is any precedent for the head of the church to enforce his views and expel people from the church if they do not agree with him: I cannot see it in any law of right. Why did we embrace the Gospel at first? I[t] was because our Judgement and intellect was convinced; Why say to men discuss & discuss when it is sectarianism[,] and when it is Mormonism think no longer but give way solely to the dictation of the church[?] This is a principle that I want to understand & I shall be guided by the light that is imparted on this subject by my brethren if that light shall seem anything better. I hold that men should be guided entirely by their light

& intelligence. I do not believe that every man should have a revalation every time he does anything. I simply believe that a man should be guided by his highest convictions & if he believes a principle he should follow it provided it be a grand general truth, and he should not accept any principle except the spirit bears witness to it.

How do we know Jesus or God but by the light and knowledge of the principles they present? Their authority is nothing though it may be great and grand in the distant heavens; but we only accept them because they present something higher & nobler than the rest of the world, and I bow to them because their principles are higher; Shall I bow to man beneath "while life and thought and being last or immortality endure?["] [*A Collection of Sacred Hymns*, 1840] I should on the other hand accept truth from a Child if it came along and told me I was wrong. I should bow to it. I should bow to the humblest teachings from the smallest source; but I should not bow to a man because he is the one God has appointed to teach us; I observe mans fallibility: I presume I see as little fallibility in Pres. Young as in any man but I see some; I cannot see but there are points where he appears to miss it: I accord honestly this much. I accord it because it is true[,] not because I wish to flatter: I do not believe in the principle of implicit obedience[,] unconditional obedience without the judgement being convinced[;] hence I see no good effect to result from it. It is said we ought to obey, because we cannot build up Zion, ^without [the observance] of [obedience]. It seems that it would be [a] curious Zion^ that could be built up in that way. If it is apostacy to differ with the President on some points[,] I am an apostate because I honestly differ with him.

I do protest that I differ in a spirit of love and due regard for him; I differ because I cannot help it. I cannot see the wisdom of some of his measures. I differ with him as to workmans wages: I have differed with him on the mineral development of the Territory; and let us say here [that much has been said about me that is untrue]. I do not believe in bringing in lots of people to flood this country in Gold mining. I believe in the development of more solid metals; I believe it would be good for this country to develope Gold in quartz & silver in same way; but I would deplore the flooding of this country with the reffuse of society. I believe it would be one of the greatest curses that could come upon the country. It is only the more solid m^e^tals the Iron, the Copper & the silver in the quartz & the gold in that condition that I believe would be beneficially developed in this Territory:

Well, now brethren my case will be very shortly laid before you; If you cut me off I shall be very sorry for it; but I will not allow you to cut me off from your affections; You shall never see me out of this Territory; Never, never, never, Cut me off if your laws require it, but let me have some of your respect as an honest man = Does not our President profess to be guided by the spirit of Joseph [Smith][?] He is generally accepted as one of that class; He believes he is guided by others in the priesthood who are behind the veil. The spirits of the just[ified] [deceased mortals] made perfect, the spirits of the invisable behind the veil witness to him, & I stand as witness to day that those spirits witness to him & I know that those dead men witness to him whether he denies it or not; It was Jos[eph] Smith[,] the dead man[,] that inspired him to lead this people to the vallies of the mountains = I bear my testimony that mormonism is true as a devine institution = I bear my testimony that Joseph Smith was called of God = I bear my testimony that polygamy is true & eternal; I bear my testimony that this is the gathering place appointed by God, & that Brigham Young is the Legal successor of Joseph Smith = Though I disagree [on one point][,] there is but one point alone & that is in accepting the infallibility of guidence of the Church without any exceptions[,] & therefore you must deal with me according to Justice: But allow me a standing in your affections as ~~an~~ honest man: I wish to present the following little document & that will close the case:—

To all whom it may concern

We the undersigned members of the Church of Jesus Christ of Latter-day Saints[,] temporarily suspended from fellowship on a charge of irregular attendance at the "School of the Prophets[,]" before any further action is taken on our case[,] do present the following declaration of our faith on the subject of Church control.

We hold that it is the right of all members of this Church to refuse to accept any principle or measure presented to them by the Priesthood further than the light of God within them bears witness to the same.

We believe that it is the right of all persons, so long as they obey the ordinances of the Gospel, and live pure and moral lives, to retain a standing in this Church whether they can see the propriety of all the measures of the leaders of the Church or not.

We also believe that it is the right of all members of the church to discuss in the pulpit or through the press—in public and in private—all principles or measures presented to them by the priesthood, provided that they do it in the spirit of moderation and with due regard to the sentiments of others.

We, therefore, hold that it is an illegal and an unrighteous use of the Holy Priesthood to expel any person from the church because they cannot conscientiously admit the divinity of any measure presented by the Priesthood.

We protest against council for the members of this church to watch one another and observe how each vote, or act as calculated to breed suspicion, coldness & distrust between our brethren, and as opposed to that voluntary spirit which is the greatest beauty and glory of the gospel of Christ.

We protest against the inquisitional practise of catechising the members of this church through the [block] Teachers, as to their private views respecting church measures.

And finally we protest against the spirit of compulsion in every form, as well as against the irresponsible investment of power in any person holding the Priesthood.

We claim the right of respectfully, but freely—discussing all measures upon which we are called to act. And if we are cut off from this Church for asserting this right, while our standing is dear to us, we will suffer it to be taken from us sooner than resign the liberties of thought and speech to which the gospel entitles us; and against any such expulsion we present our solemn protest before God & Angels.

As Witness our hands this 23rd Oct. 1869.
E. L. T. Harrison
W S Godbe

W[illiam] S. Godbe[:] In regard to the charge of spiritualism I wish to speak. We do believe in revelation but such only as comes through the channels of the Holy Priesthood and we do not believe in the teachings of spiritualism.

Geo Q. Cannon[:] The charge which has been prefered against these brethren was for harboring the spirit of apostacy. The evidence that has been adduced today to sustain that charge has been in my opinion aboundantly ample. The teachers who visited these brethren and the two apostles who accompanied them all concur, I believe although couched in different language, in stating that the impression left on their minds by the remarks of Bro Godbe & bro Harrison in their interview was that they were indu[l]ging in a wrong spirit in opposing the first Presidency of the church; and that they were on the road to apostacy. The extracts which I have read in your hearing are in opposition to the work of God and the building up of Zion. The articles from which I have read in your hearing sustain the statements of those teachers and of the brethren who accompanied them, and all go to prove that these brethren have been animated whether they know it or not,—and I care not how honestly they may have been actuated in their feelings, whether they know it or not[—]the spirit which has actuated them and indi[c]ted those articles is one that is calculated in its tendency to destroy this work, to destroy the Zion of our God, break down the influence of the Priesthood, and scatter us to the four winds of Heaven. I think[,] my brethren of the High Council[,] that those charges have been amply sustained by the evidence that has been produced.

I do not wonder myself to day in listening to the sophistical speech of Bro. Harrison at the manner in which bro Godbe has been drawn into the meshes of this net. I do not wish to be personal in this matter, but I wish to make a few remarks on this subject. I cannot tell you how long it is since, but I sup[p]ose it is upwards of two or three years ago. Shortly after the "Peep Oday" [magazine] fell through, bro Godbe and myself alluded to bro Harrison. Bro Godbe told me that he took considerable interest in him. I remarked I did also. I thought him capable of great usefulness and could do a great deal of good if used in the right channel, and Bro Godbe told me he (Harrison) was afflicted with skepticism: And from time to time as we met, = and our intercourse was very frequent at that time—he [Godbe] related to me his progress in converting brother Harrison, in using arguments and appealing to him respecting this work. I was pleased & expressed my gratification at the success which he met within his efforts; for I had taken considerable interest in brother Harrison myself, although but slightly acquainted with him personally. I believe this is a similar case to a man drowning in a river. One sees the other drowning and Jumps in to deliver him from the peril in which he is involved, and in making the effort to save his neighbor he is drowned himself. Instead of his convincing brother Harrison, bro Harrison is of too specious a cast of mind for brother Godbe, and he [Godbe] is convinced by him. Brother Harrison is sceptical. There have been remarks made here by him which bring to my mind matters that I have been told of late, since this matter has been agitated, which are to this effect: That he, while East, accompanied by bro. Godbe, had a visitation from somebody behind the veil. A very prominent man's name has been used by brother Harrison, in the testimony that he has borne here, which led me to think there is something in this. I have not attached any importance to this previously, thinking it might be a mere idle rumor like many others. But he testifies in such a solemn man^n^er that he knows that the spirits of dead men witness to President Young[,] whether he [Young] denies it or not[,] that I am led to believe that this rumor is correct and that these men who come here to-day to preach a new Gospel to us, to inaugurate a new era amoungst us, feel they are prompted and sustained by some power we know nothing about, and all this is what men who have had experience in this work have been familiar with in the past. Did you ever know any apostate who did ^not^ make these pretentions? Read the history of this church in the days of Kirtland. Did they object to Joseph as a Prophet, Seer, and Revelator? No: it was by easy steps that they arrived at the rejection of Joseph as a Prophet, Seer & Revelator: To begin with they quarrelled with his temporal knowledge. He was a Prophet Seer and Revelator inspired to teach the principles of righteousness: but in temporal matters he did not have any experience whatever. This is a trick to deceive and herein lies the danger as I remarked before.

It is these brethren professing to have lost faith in the Priesthood that I find fault with, and is the cause of the charge being prefered to-day before this council. Brother Harrison has stated here that he entered into a contract when he joined the Church in England, and that when the Elders made promises to him, he on his part profes^s^ted to perform certain acts, and he questioned now our right to annul that contract. Why not let him do, in other words, as he pleases in the church. As for myself, I consider I hold my membership subject to the will of my brethren who compose this church. If they see anything in a man that they cannot fellowship,—if they see anything in me that is contrary to the welfare of Zion, that is antagonistic to the Gospel of Jesus, they have a perfect right, and it is not despotism, to withdraw that fellowship from me, and sever their connection with me. It is not despotism on the part of the Presidency, it is not despotism on the part of the High Council: but it is the right guaranteed unto them by God our Heavenly Father to withdraw their fellowship from those who do not agree and work with them in building-up the Zion of our God. No matter how many pretentions they may make, no matter how high their pretentions may be to loyalty to the Kingdom of God, nor how honest they may be as individuals whenever the fact is settled in the minds of the brethren and sisters who comprise this church that their influence and actions are opposed to the progress and advancement of the Kingdom of God, they are justified in disfellowshiping them.

Brother Harrison has alluded in his remarks to the fact that when he joined the Church he received certain blessings. Under what authority I would ask did he join it? He joined it under the same authority that now exists. He joined the church under the Presidency of Brigham Young, under the administration of his councillors and the Twelve Apostles; and under the administration of the Elders who went to proclaim the Gospel of Jesus Christ. He obtained his standing in this Church by obeying their counsels and not by any other means. We may say he did not render unconditional obedience. I will not quarrel with him about terms, but he did obtain it only by being obedient to the commands of God, as taught by those Elders, and could not have got into the church by any other means. I care not what Elders told him about freedom and this being a free land; he had to submit to the requirements of those Elders before he could be a member. It is the same obedience that is asked of him today, and no greater requirement than is asked of every man. Does the Priesthood require anything more than it required of us at the waters edge? If it does, I do not understand it. I have been like him, a convert of this Church baptised in it, and I have found that that some confidence I had in the beginning has proven a joy, a peace, a consolation and an endless source of happiness to me from that time unto the present; and I find it is just ^as^ convenient to be obedient now as it was then, and I am not deprived of my agency in the least particle more now than I was then. It does not require me to oppose the work of God, it does not require me to fight against the work of the Lord in order to possess my free agency. <u>We object to these brethren because they fight against the work of God</u>. It is a mistake with them; it is a policy of the devils that will lead them down to hell if they do not repent. I know that this appeals powerfully to the prejudices of the present age. This idea of a free press. Free language. They are catch words that appeal to popular prejudices[;] they are the catch-words of the devil and those who are influenced by him, and who would build up a bullwork against the work of God by saying that the people of God are in bondage when in reality we are as free a people to do right as the sun ever shone upon. But because a man has the liberty to do right, has he the liberty to do wrong? No, not while the watchmen of Zion stand on her walls; not while President Young and his counselors live, have any such rights in this Kingdom and we will withdraw our fellowship from them. We are not assailing a free press; we are not coming in contact with this idea that bro Harrison has so despitefull[y] set forth for he is cunning in his arguments in this matter. Here comes among us a preacher of a new Gospel. Th[e] same President and Quorum and authorities who have guided the church thus far are now going in the dark. It is the old idea. The Church, the doctrine is right, but Joseph is a fallen Prophet. We are comming as the teachers of a new principle[,] [they say]. President Young is not advanced enough; he is beginning to be illiberal and we come now to preach to you a new doctrine. Well, those who want to receive this new Gospel can do so; but as for me and my house, we do not want it; but I am content to be guided by the men that have guided us thus far. I am content to obey the instructions we have thus far received.

Look at the prosperity which abounds around us to-day which is the result of the obedience which has been taught unto us by the Prophet of God. Look at the peace we enjoy, the immunity from our enemies and mobs and difficulties; and shall we stoop to day to question this principle, and say we will have no more of it? Will we receive the Gospel according to St. Harrison? Not in the least. We will follow our old guides; we will follow those whom God has chosen and receive no new men to come in and teach us. I have the voice of the spirit as well as these men. I profess to have revelations; I profess to know the truth and I can bear testimony more than they can or do to-day. I bear testimony that not only was Joseph a prophet of God, but that Brigham is a Prophet of God, and that he is fully inspired to lead this people in these matters; and he has the right to dictate ^[to] us^ as free agents, as

<u>the sons</u> of Almighty God[,] who has chosen this man. It is our right to follow him and be guided by his counsels, especially when he has led us in a path that has been so beneficial unto us from the day we entered into it unto the present time; My brethren of the Council I pray that God may be with us and enable us to understand the truth and maintain it always. Amen.

W[illiam] S. Godbe at the conclusion of bro Cannons remarks, stated that as far as he was able to judge, bro Harrison had not influenced him in his views any more than he had influenced brother Harrison.

Pres. Geo A. Smith: I have been pained to listen to this investigation and the circumstances con^n^ected with it from the fact that it brings back times long gone by. Now the reading of this solemn protest, the defiant manner in which it was read, and the base of falsehoods that it seeks to palm upon the world, is enough to make a mans heart ache. I have been back in my mind to the time of Dr P[hilastus] Hurlb[u]t [Hurlbut] who [in 1833] made solemn protestations of honesty; and I can hear to-day Joseph say, after those protestations were made: "A few days will prove that this man is not honest." And if this man who has read this protest can keep from writing a "Spaulding Story" [theory of Book of Mormon authorship], he will do first rate from the spirit that reigns in his heart. Now brethren for a man to get up among us, to say that there is no liberty of speech, and say that he has [been] turned off, because he believed in liberty of speech, is nonsense. We go back to Kirtland and Nauvoo, we saw the same spirit manifested there. A blacker spirit never reigned in the heart of mortals than reigns in those two men (Godbe & Harrison). It will cover them with the blood of the savior. We know that all the world are against us. We know that every court, sect, and denomination, and all political organizations are for our destruction, but we trust in God. He has lead us through our President Joseph Smith and Brigham Young—through a thousand dangers seen and unseen. We know this, and here rise up some men to unite with the world in getting up a division. The rule on which we ought to work is this: get together and discus[s] what we have to say: and not draw out or sneak out without hearing what is to be said about it. But ^the^ first thing we know[,] we find them publishing and insinuating to the world that the people here are oppressed and that their liberties are taken away and they will unite with all the enemies of Zion to bring down vengeance upon the heads of the Saints. Personally, I have no feelings towards these brethren but those of kindness: but when it comes to the things of God, I have no feelings only to build up Zion, and I protest against any man or any motive or spirit whatever it may be, that will tend to destroy it.

In Kirtland they said Jos[eph] did not know how to manage temporal affairs. He had no right to dictate about temporal matters. And the time was when numbers of Elders embracing the highest order of Priesthood took the ground [and said] that they had a right to question his right to dictate [to] the church in temporal things. They acknowledged that Joseph was a prophet: but they said he had gone into darkness and fallen. They would profess to be full in the faith, they would preach the Gospel and all that, but they would set aside some revelations that were not exactly right in their opinion, and one or two other things. The same tune is heard over again. "Oh! I have such confidence in bro Brigham!" "Such confidence in these brethren" "Such confidence kindness and good feeling!" "I only want to cut their throats!" Did you ever see a man longer faced than William Law? His robe is bloody with the blood of the saints: not a particle more so than those of these men, after a few weeks, if they do not alter. Just as wicked and blind; Yet they do not know it: I see it; and I know and understand it. To think that a man in Israel feels he is justified in throwing this mining question open: ["]Why all the world think we have great mines here." "Come here a hundred thousand hounds! Our mountains are full of gold, iron, copper, and lead, to say nothing of the Balance." Just look at it. Why I should have considered it more manly to have come right out and asked the world to come here to work these Gold mines and cut the throats of the "Mormons," Let a hundred thousand of these hounds come to these mountains and they'd put us in a warm place—I do not want anything of the kind; and I know the man who has the spirit to go to Gold mining and abandon the principle that we are now working upon, to endeavour to produce from the earth all that we use, and learn our people how to live and sustain themselves when Babylon shall fall—the man who undertakes to destroy this principle is as blind as a batt and as ignorant as a man can be. Well, now, that protest that was handed in here is to say to the world and the Church, "We are misled, we have no liberty, we are tied up, we have no freedom of speech. Send an army to protect us; come here and sustain us." It is in plain terms nothing more nor less than a positive lie. This is the freest country there is on the face of the earth: but at the same time, Latter-day Saints do not fellowship a man who draws the sword to destroy them; do not fellowship a man who invites all hell to come and cut out throats; do not fellowship a man who publishes lies concerning us and misrepresents us. We do not fellowship him however honest he may be; because he is blind. I doubt seriously how far his honesty goes; I do actually think there is a studied scheme to divide this Church and break it up; and if there ever was a strong evidence of apostacy, it is in that protest. Butter would not melt in their mouths: their tongues are as sm^o^oth as W[illia]m Laws when he preached about punctuality. How are you going to work to correct a man under such circumstances[;] I see no way: they are perfectly fortified on every side. "We know more than every body else; all the rest of you are fools. The Priesthood that has built up and guided this Church, & gathered us and brought us here is blind, and we have the right to fight against the Priesthood. We have the right to publish as Elders of Israel against Zion. We have all these rights.["] This is what they will say. I say our rights are few. We have the right to do right, and we have no right, as Elders in Israel to do wrong.

Wilford Woodruff: rose to bear testimony that he coincided with the views and sentiments of bro Cannon and President Geo A. Smith.

Orson Pratt bore a similar testimony and remarked that the course brothers Harrison & Godbe were persuing was the same as persued by most other apostates, and if persisted in would lead them to destruction.—

President Brigham Young Said: There is so much to say upon this subject, and few of us are so well acquainted with these matters, such as have been before us this morning that we feel confined to less time than we would like: we would really be pleased if we could ventilate such things before the whole Church so that everyone might hear for himself and all would be able to judge. I will tell you a little story that has been in my mind with regard to the king taking his son to the House of Lords, to let him see how they did there and how they legislated for a nation and how they got along with great national affairs. When the son had sat and heared till he was tired, he said, "Father, what did you bring me here for?" ["]That you might see how little wisdom it takes to govern a nation." I mention this to show you how little wisdom it takes to raise an excitement in the midst of wise men.

You have heard a statement from one of the articles that have been read which says how well every one thinks of those writings: they are so beautiful and lovely to read, and there is a new era dawning, and this that and the other. I think how little wisdom there is in them. It is astonishing, it is marvelous to me that men in this Church can say that they have obtained a witness by the spirit of truth that this is the Gospel of Life & Salvation, and then descend so low as to advance such ideas as are advanced by these brethren. In the case that is before us, we have taken the course to bring it before as many as we could conveniently that Bishops and their Counselors and the teachers, the High Council and the brethren might have an opportunity of seeing for themselves. I will say to these brethren: How will you have your trial? Will you have it before the High Priests, the Seventies, the Apostles, or will you have it before the members of the Church: and leave out the Apostles and the First Presidency? We will try the case that way if you cho[o]se. Or would you like to have the sisters present, and say that the trial shall be by the sisters? And they will judge the matter; or will you have it before the Children? I will try it there, and let them judge the case. It is simple, plain and easy to be ~~de~~ understood.

Liberty! Where is our Liberty? In truth Where is our freedom? In truth: in the truth of God; in truth no matter where it is found[.] Where is our strength? In truth. Where is our power and our wisdom. In truth. It is truth that we want, it is truth that exalts us, it is truth that makes us free, it is truth that will bring us into the Celestial kingdom; and nothing else. We are willing to try this any where. I should be perfectly willing to take this case and try it before the daughters of Israel, and not have one present over fifteen years old; and let them decide the matter. But I will tell you what would be said [by the defendants]. "Why the people are against us, the Old Testament is against us, the New Testament is against us, Jesus is against us." That is what they would say; exactly, those who are brought up for bringing dissention into the Kingdom of God, would say. "The spirit of truth is against us, the Elders of Israel must decide [and they would decide] against us, the people must decide [and they would decide] against us, the sisters in the church must decide against us, and the children would decide against us, and where should we go for a trial?["] I asked bro William [Godbe] and he said they would all decide against him. It is true everyone would decide against them except those who wish to promote wickedness in the land.

You may take the Bible from Adam down to the end of revelations, and whenever the Priesthood of the Son of God has been on the earth there have ^been^ rules and regulations, established for the government, control, guidance and dictation of the Church of God. Everyone acknowledges this. Take the Bible & Book of Mormon, do they sustain the same doctrine? From the beginning to end. Whenever God build[s] up His Church on the Earth, He has a governing and controling power there also; and that power control and supremacy He dictates Himself. Brethren, we are here to day and possess just precisely the same authority as they did in the days of Jesus or any other kingdom that was ever built up[.] ^First^ was the Kingdom of God on the earth. We are possessing the spirit power and privileges now which should govern and control the Church. Who shall lead out in those affairs that pertain to the welfare of Zion? Every man[,] [according to the dissenters]. What confusion, what discord, what discontent, what hatred would soon creep into the bosom of individuals one against the other. Do you know this? Yes. The Children know it, our daughters know it and they would decide against it: We cannot have confusion in the family, if one child has the privilege of dictating I have as much power in this family as my father or mother, and the mother says to one "You go and make the Beds." and to another "Wash up the dishes." Those girls would disobey her orders and think they had as much right to dictate as she had. The Children would understand these things in the family.

Are we the Church & Kingdom of God, the family of Heaven? Yes: we acknowledge it, we say it is so; we have subscribed to it, and we have made no bargain to gather up to Zion to raise confusion. There was no such bargain made in England nor anywhere else. It is false: it is deniable by every Elder in Israel. Bring the Elder that has promised any man if he will be baptised he will have the privilege to come to Zion and raise all the discord he can. I am at the defiance of any man to say that there ever was any such contract made. The building of the storehouse on the Colorado in which a few of the Brethren invested, has been very much dwelt upon. It was a failure, was it? You don't know that. You don't know whether it was a failure or not. We have an object in doing this: we have an influence there; we have a power there, for we are the first ones that ever built in that Ter^r^itory. By & by I expect brother Godbe, if he comes into the Church, will be coming to me and be thankful that ^he^ ever put means into that storehouse. Look at the brethren who went out with the "Mormon Battalion," and those who went up in "Zions Camp." When we went up in ["]Zions Camp" it was all grumbling with some. Where will any good result from this," would say one. "I am Glad I didn't go," said one man: "Well," said I, "one thing I can say, which is this: I have travelled with Joseph a thousand miles, he has led the Camp of Israel: I have watched him and observed every thing he said or did," and said I "for the town of Kirtland I would not give the knowledge got from Joseph from this Journey: and then you may take the State of Ohio and the United States, and I would not give that knowledge for them.["] It has done me good and you good and this was the starting point of my knowing how to lead Israel. I watched every word and summed it up, and I know just as well how to lead this kingdom as I know the way to my own house. It is god within me, and God upon me: God by day and by night, and it is for His Kingdom on the earth. I say this, because it is my right and duty to do it; were it not[,] [I] should not say it: I have never sought but one thing in this kingdom, and that has been to get men and women to obey the Lord Jesus Christ in everything. I do not care what they say of me, if they will live so as to help build up his kingdom. Well, I will say a word or two about the building of that storehouse on the Colorado and this Utah Produce Co[mpany]. That storehouse I am willing to let lie there, it is all right. Just as quick as I can get the means I am willing to pay every man who spent a Dollar in that concern. And as for our produce company. I did what I did for my brethren, to see if we could not lead the Elders to stop their throwing away the means that God had given them.

In relation to this paper business, Bro William [Godbe] says I counseled him to go into it. It is palpably false. I advised him not to do it. I have proof here. I tried to prevail on him not to go into it. Said he, What shall I do with this [16-page weekly] paper[,] [the *Utah Magazine*][?] I told him to sell it. Let brother William have his faith in my management of temporal affairs. He has mentioned time and time again, as have others, wherein I made failures in losing money. I would ask "Who gave you your money? Where did you get it?["] How much did Bro Wm own when he came here? How much did others who invested in those things, own when they came here? Did they have anything? I rather think not; They came to these valleys like most of us, naked and barefooted, as for myself, I owed for the teams that brought my family. Did we run to the gold mines to get capital to raise our grain, to get the timber from the mountains, to make our farms & build our houses? No but this Magazine says go to the gold mines or you cannot do these things. You stay at home[,] brethren that want to, & let those who want to go to the mines do so; and when they have been one or ten years, I will take the ratio of those who have paid attention to their business, and I tell you I can buy every ten of those who go to the mines with one who stays at home. Why did not bro Harrison come and ask the School if they should publish those articles? He seeks to inaugurate a new era, a new kingdom, a glorious kingdom, where every man will be for himself. What is the result when every man is for himself? Why the devil is for the whole of them.

Men who have been in this church as long as a few of us have been have heard the same language, tone, expressions, and declarations made precisely that have been made here by these two brethren. It is everytime. How I love God! They know no more about God than my horse, not one particle, or they would not do as they have done. The spirit of the Lord has gone from them, and the light that was once in them has removed from them, and darkness has taken the place of it. You see brethren how little wisdom it takes to make man apostatise (reads from the Article "Steadying the Ark"). Now, a man who makes such expressions as these is under censure by the spirit of truth. God does not prompt such things at all. Now I wish to correct this in the minds of those present: I will tell you simply so that a child can understand. We are independent creatures; we hold our identity perfectly independent in and of ourselves as far as the organization is concerned being organized or set in motion by the Father or Supreme Being, and this is intended for an independent organization and God operates upon us; and the influences of this Priesthood, which has been defined here as not being anything more than an outward organization, this Priesthood comprehends all things[,] it is in all things, through and around about all things: and it is the government, power, and enlightenment that God dispenses to His creatures here on the Earth and on all others. Now, the Priesthood will not do your thinking, but it will help you to think correctly; and any man who thinks differently knows nothing about it. There is no person that knows anything about the Priesthood that calculates the Priesthood is going to ^do^ the thinking for him or any one. We work in harmony with our Savior. He works in harmony with his Father, and we cooperate with the son for the salvation of ourselves and the human family. The son has according to the wisdom and the design of the Father, become the Savior or the heir of this Earth and all things pertaining to it, and he calls upon his brethren to be co-workers with Him. He works as He is directed by the Father and we are co-workers with him. Jesus has done His work; everyone understands that. He does not do anything in a temporal point of view; and when He was in the flesh He set his disciples to baptise. Certainly when he appeared to Saul of tarus. He did not ordain him nor call him to the ministry; but said he, go to a certain place and inquire of a certain man and he will tell you what to do to be saved. This Priesthood will correct all our ideas and acts in relation to the building up of the Kingdom of God. It is the Plan which God has devised for the salvation of the human family; and the Holy Ghost jointly in and with this Priesthood assists every person to do his work. I will read a little further here (referring to Utah Magazine). Hence if you say to such men [as are assembled here][,] what do you think of such a subject, they will answer. "I do not know, what does the Priesthood say about it." Now this is correct. This has been taught to every person in this Church. That one has the power to decide upon general things, another upon another branch, and another upon another, clear down to the Mother, where she has her children under her, right in her own household, and that is her Kingdom and she presides over it, and that mother has the right to the spirit of revelation to dictate her: and if she has not a sufficient quantity of it to teach them all things, and their father comes in and can tell the children anything, it is his privelege; and if an Elder can do better, it is his privilege. But suppose the President of the Church knows better how to set up a stocking and can teach them how to do it, it is his privilege to do so.

We are not going to seperate the people according to the tenor of these articles, for this would keep the poor poor. I wish to elevate the whole people and I am looking forward to the time when we will put our hand into the one [common] purse. I am teaching that doctrine. I urge it upon the people. If we ever build up Zion, we will be one, I think.

I expect to see the time when everything will be laid at the hands of the Bishops and they will dispence it to the whole wards. I have often stated that the spirit of apostacy is here, and there are men right here in our School [of the Prophets] that will go to Hell. I cannot teach the things of the kingdom. I would have been glad to have opened up the great and glorious things of God: on the earth and in the Heavens. I cannot do it. I am abridged here through the unbelief of my brethren; and the spirit of apostacy. We are not going to permit this[,] you know.

(Reads [from the articles]—"It may be said here [in the magazine articles], that the Gospel is destined to bring us to such a condition, that the motive power of self int[e]rest, which has hitherto been the main spring of the worlds progress[,] is to be superceded by so much of the love of God in everyman's nature, that all will be willing to sink their individuality etc.^"^) Now relative to this I wish to say; there never will such a time come. The only way there is provided in all the economy of Heaven for us to preserve our individuality, is to submit ourselves to the Gospel = The only thing that can sustain and uphold us in the Eternities that are to come, and that will preserve our Identity is perfect submission to the will of God = Those that go down to perdition, those that have had the privelege that our brethren have & turn away and break off by degrees from these pure and Holy principles, will go back to their native element; but I need not have said it. They will taste the second death and lose their identity = Now is this liberty or does it take away our liberty? which is a question that should be understood by all =

All know precisely how to preserve their own form & identity before each other & how to enjoy the Greatest liberty possible. If individuals were to run to E[ast] W[est] N[orth] & S[outh] & every one according to the imagination of his own heart that would be the enlight^en^ment of Nature. My whole nature teaches me to do so. My whole nature speaking after the manner of men & according to the spirit of the world would lead me to destruction. We must have the Lord to rule over us = How do you look at the scriptures? How have you looked at the plan of Salvation? How has it appeared before you, what are your ideas on the plan of salvation that God has devised for the Children of Men to bring them into submission & strict obedience to what he has revealed? Now this prepares a person to become a God & a son of God. For a man to become a god & a son of God & to reign eternally in the heavens requires strict obedience= Will they have dominion? Yes. Crowns? Yes. How little wisdom these Elders of Israel have to think that they must do a wrong to enjoy liberty. Why bless you[,] don't I enjoy my liberty as much as any other man? My liberty is to do right and serve my God & build up his Kingdom; They that h^e^arken to the words of the Lord will go onward and upward and fl[o]urish & increase & inherit; while those who think that they are going to have freedom by being a little wicked & raising a discord will go down to destruction. Live so that the candle of the Lord is always lighted up within you & you will be always right. Live so that this spirit or monitor of right may dictate you all the time. You can see the cunning & craftiness of him that lyeth in wait to deceive = What did Saten say to Mother Eve? Did he not have some truth in his sayings to Mother Eve = Said he "look you here take this fruit and eat thereof. The Gods said you will die[,] but said he[,] your eyes will be opened" if you eat of the fruit = Well now just as quick as she ate this fruit she saw good from evil. She knew good from evil. I know good and Evil, & you know good & Evil. Well now live so that you can discriminate between good & evil. I will tell you one thing if you will live so that the candle of the Lord is lighted up within you from day to day and from Morning till Evening and from Evening till Morning you will never dissent from Brother Brigham.

^I do know that Joseph had a revelation concerning me and a few others in heaven—Said he^ you will never fall from this faith[.] Said he[,] God has seen your labor and rather than you should fall he will take you to himself, so you have the promise through Joseph. I want to say to you that the spirit of the Lord was with me in bringing the people to these Vallies = Now here bro. Harrison tells us that it was spirit of Joseph that came to me; I want to tell you it was the same spirit that Joseph had from the Lord; How quick a man will fall and say [that] which is not true = The spirit of Joseph went with Him, it has gone into the spirit world, but the spirit which dictated Joseph dictates your humble servant, and that spirit guided and directed [me] in bringing the people to these Vallies of the Mountains; Another thing he said which I do not think he me[a]nt, ~~to say~~, he said he did not believe the Priesthood was infallible = I will simply say that the Priesthood is infallible, but Man having the Priesthood may be fallible; I do not pretend to be infallible, but the priesthood that I have on me is infallible; It is from Eternity to

Eternity; and that same priesthood rests upon me that rested upon Joseph, precisely; Joseph has got his own spirit & is in the spirit world; He has not got his body yet [but] he will have it by & by =

We feel pretty well now; when we get further and further advanced we will feel still better = It is a heavy struggle [and] the whole world are upon us. = Only see the political world they are just devising every means they can to crush us = and right in our midst we must have discord = The Enemies of God delight in this paper [*Utah Magazine*]. You have your liberty in this = You have the right to print just what you please, but we have the right to reject it and not have it crammed down our throats. = It is a country of free speech, free press, free trade, and Sailors rights as Joseph used to say. You have the privilege of printing, but we have the right to refuse it; ^you have a right to believe as you please.^ Any man that want[s] to dissent from us has a right to do so. If he is not disposed to go with us, he has a right to go some other way; but we have the same Liberty to go the road the Lord wishes us.= Hear the howl that has been heard since this [economic] cooperation has been introduced. The Gentiles and Jew's and all are crying to the United States that there is no liberty in Salt Lake City. It is our privilege to get our [own] money. It is their privilege to sell [merchandise], and it is my privilege to pass by their stores and buy where I please. They have the liberty to do just as they please; but the liberty that is wanted concerning this paper, is like [what] the Jews & Gentiles stores want. We shall take the liberty of not taking the paper, I think that is what we shall do. I will leave it to the people to do as they have a mind to. I have the right to counsel them and they have the right to take my counsel or let it alone, just as they please. Brethren, I thank you for the time I have occupied in my remarks. We will leave this case to whom? To the Twelve Apostles, the First Presidency, the High Priests, the Seventies? No: we will leave it to the Children, the dau^gh^ters of Israel, and let them judge between you and us. Just as you please. We will leave it right to the Children and let them say whether it is correct or incorrect, and take the revelations God has given to his Children. We are willing to do this and I shall end with it. God bless you Amen.

S[amuel] W. Richards: (for Plaintiffs) The sentiments of bros Godbe & Harrison were such as could not be sustained by the Latter-day Saints. As far as he was concerned they were not sustained.

M[iner] G. Atwood: (for the Defense) He felt sorry these brethren had taken a course so opposed to the spirit of truth. Instead of helping to build up Zion, the policy they had persued would only lend to create dissention in Israel. He was of opinion that the charge had been sustained.

William Eddington: (for Plaintiffs) Endorsed the sentiments of previous speakers, namely, that the charge has been fully sustained. Still he would like brothers Harrison & Godbe to retract their steps, and prayed God might enable them to do so.

John S. Blythe: (for the Defense) As counsel for the defense, he felt as he had always done, a kind and good feeling for the brethren he rose to defend as men; but when it came to principle, he know[s] of nothing but the spirit of God, which is right. He endorsed the sentiments of those who had previously spoken, and left the case, as far as he was concerned, in the hands of the Presidency.

[Counselor in the stake presidency] John T. Caine: The principles that had been advocated by bros Godbe & Harrison, before the Council and in the pages of the ["]Utah Magazine," could only lead us back to Babylon. However much he might respect bros Godbe & Harrison, he could not fellowship the principles they advocated. He supported the other speakers.

[Stake President] George B. Wallace: To his mind the matter was as clear as the sun at noon-day. The c^h^arges had been fully sustained and frankly admitted by Bro Godbe & Bro Harrison. He thought that Lucifer had as much right to retain his standing in the presence of God, after he had rebelled, as these brethren had to be fellowshiped by the people of God after having held and published such sentiments as had appeared in the ["]Utah Magazine;" and those that the Council had listened to from these brethren. Instead of having the spirit of truth to guide them in their actions, they were now subject to evil spirits, and there must have been a cause for it. There must have been something by which the spirit of the Almighty, if they ever had it, ha[s] been caused to depart from them: (bro Harrison & Godbe)

The decission of the [representatives of the High] Council was that bros Harrison & Godbe be cut off from the Church of Jesus Christ of Latter-day Saints, and be handed over to the buffettings of Satan, until they repent.

Jos[eph] L. Barfoot: Moved that the decision be sustained by the [entire] Council, s^e^conded and carried unanimously. The decision was then placed before the whole assembly present, and sustained. When it was requested that those of a contrary mind should raise their hands the following persons lifted their hands: Eli B Kelsey, E[dward] W [Tullidge] & John Tullidge, Jos[eph] Silver, Henry M. Lawrence, & James Cobb. As Eli B Kelsey fully sustained bros. Harrison & Godbe, it was moved by G[eorge] B. Wallace that he be cut off. Seconded by bro Murphy and carried.

After prayer by Pres. Geo A. Smith the Council adjourned till Thursday at 10 Oclock AM.

APPENDIX THREE

MINUTES OF THE SALT LAKE UNITED ORDER, 1874

The following seven entries were recorded on the last pages of the Salt Lake School of the Prophets record book. Additional minutes of the United Order can be found in the Salt Lake Stake records and Historian's Office files at the Church History Library.

June 2, 1874; Tuesday

City Officers of the United Order ~~The School of the Prophets~~ met in the old Tabernacle at 2 oclock pm as per adjournment [the previous day]. Present[:] Prest. B[righam] Young presiding. C[ounselo]rs Geo A Smith & D[aniel] H Wells [and] Ass[istan]t C[ounselo]rs A[lbert] Carrington and Elder John Taylor. After Singing Prayer by Elder Miner Atwood.

Prest B Young said the brethren present are the dictators [directors] ^or officers^ recently appointed in the various wards, ~~in the different~~ to superintend the labours of the people, articles of agreement will shortly be read, as we are anxious to get into a line of operation as soon as possible. Elder D[avid] McKenzie then read the Articles.

Prest. Young ~~asked a few questions of the Prest. Of the 1st Ward, 5 & 6 ward~~ then requested the Officers of the respective wards, to take separate seats with a view of finding out the number of Mechanics ^& farmers^ in each Ward, but they were unprepared to furnish a ~~list~~ complete list, and the 1st Question he wished to ask, was whether we ^had better^ try to organize each branch of business in separate wards, or each ~~of~~ branch throughout the City. ^It was Motioned that we organize in the^ various branches of Industries.

Elder John Taylor, said if we organize according to the above Motion, what becomes of the present organizations in each ward[?]

Elder J[ohn] D. T. McAllister suggested that all workers, ^be organized under one general head^ and all other branches, ~~be organized under one general head for each branches~~ in a similar way.

Elder Orson Pratt if we wished to organize under the laws of the Territory ^we^ must organize separate officers under each branch of Industry.

B[isho]p E[lijah] F. Sheets advocated City Organizations in each branch of labor, on the score of economy—and under such an arrangement, let a general board be organized, even should ^it^ render null and void our present ward organization.

Prest. B Young, wished the brethren to bear in mind the legality of our position, as now organized in wards we are within the scope of Law. In his suggestions, he rather favored the ^ward^ organizations being preserved in tact, even should several wards have to unite together to assist each other. We want our various committees ^selected^ from these brethren, to take hold of the Tannery business, and other branches of Industry forthwith.

Elder O[rson] Pratt said to insure legality in this order every Member must be a shareholder.

Prest. Young said ^what^ was wanted was ^for^ these brethren to get together, and appoint men to take hold of every branch of Mechanism right at once ^by having^ ~~have~~ foremen selected ~~begin at once~~.

He said he wanted to turn over his property as quick as persons are appointed to take hold and operate in this order, when we get thoroughly organized, we shall have no poor in our midst but have our Wives, ^&^ daughters so regulated as to be usefully employed in ^~~making~~^ all kinds of light work.

Elder Jno [John] Taylor Moved & was carried ^Unanimously^ That the Organization of the various Wards remain as they are.

The Meeting was adjourned till next Saturday at one o clock.

Prest. G[eorge] A. Smith suggested that each B[isho]p brings forward at next meeting statistical account of every item pertaining to the business status of the ward.

B[isho]p W Hess enquired if private dwellings would be admitted as Capitol stock in the order.

Prest. Geo A Smith said ~~said~~ yes, but would draw no dividend unless there was a rental received from it.

Benediction by Elder W[illia]m G. Young.

June 6, 1874; Saturday

The Officers of the United Order in ~~the~~ Salt Lake City met in the old~~er~~ Tabernacle at One oclock pm. Present[:] Prest. B[righam] Young presiding [and] D[aniel] H. Wells Ass[istan]t C[ounselo]r A[lbert] Carrington ^Elders^ John Taylor, Orson Pratt & Wilford Woodruff of the twelve [apostles]. C[ounselo]rs D. H. Wells then read the reports of all the City Wards except the 4th, 9th, 14th 16 & 18 wards. After singing Prayer by B[isho]p J[oseph] Warburton.

Prest. B Young said we were on very important business, which was nothing short ~~than business~~ of building up the Kingdom of God; last Tuesday we called for reports from every ward in the City, stating how many Farmers, and Land and Utensils, and how many of each kind of trades, with a view of uniting several Wards together in different branches.

~~It was suggested by Prest. Young that the 1st 2nd 3rd~~ Prest. Young suggested that the Farmers, and Mechanics and every other branch of Industry, [blank].

Motioned and carried That the Farmers meet ^& Gardner &c^ on ~~Thursday~~ ^Wednesday afternoon 4 p.m^ next in the 8th ward School house.

Motioned & Carried That all workers in Wood, & Lumber Merchants meet in the 14th Ward House at 6 pm, Tuesday next. ~~Motioned & Carried That~~

Elder Elias Morris suggested a union of effort amongst the Members of the Order taking shares in the business of Tanning so that it can be commenced immediately, as the Wool and Hides continue to be sent out by the car load. He also stated that many members of this orders he had heard say, they did not ~~now~~ like one article [of agreement] that was read here last ~~School~~ Tuesday—viz that ~~no Capitolist~~ the ~~numbers~~ number of votes should be regulated by the amount of shares held by each member.

Prest. Young explained that it would not certainly be right for one who through economy and industry ~~he~~ had acquired 10,000 ~~th~~ dollars, and he puts that means in an enterprize with others who had only one hundred dollars each, for ~~every~~ him to have no more voice in ~~the~~ its management than those who had so little at stake.

This United Organization is not intended ^to^ last only five or ten years, but for ever and ever. And when a dividend is declared, it was not to be drawn out but added to the Capitol Stock. And as to Ward Stores being a failure, if those who managed them had been strictly honest there is no ward but could easily clear from 10 to 15 per cent. And if our present organization does not succeed it will be our own fault. Unless we are willing to be dictated in our time we shall not be wanted in this order—and when our time is properly contrould we shall at least save right away one fourth of our labor. We shall want store houses built, and what Grain we raise we shall store away, and no one will be permitted to sell it off by any member in this order, but we have got to put away extravagance, and live within our means—and endeavour in all our transactions to have something to sell, Never work on Credit. We must raise our own flax in a suitable place of dampness. This is a life insurance, and insures for ourselves and our children a living as long as we live.

Let one or two wards join together if necessary and build Houses suitable for the poor, ~~and for~~ several in one House, with conveniences for washing Ironing and feeding them comfortable, and find some employment for the aged to knit, making straw Hats, door Mats &c. God had given us every thing that is necessary to make us happy in these Mountains, and all we have to do is to make the most of them.

He intended to put all his property into this Order where the enemy cannot touch it, and was perfectly willing to be dictated by the officers of the order as to how he shall spend his time.

It was suggested that Bros [A. Milton] Musser and [David] McKenzie classify the different branches of labor, and appoint a time and place for each branch to meet, not later than Wednesday next, and to be ~~advertised in tomorrow mornings Herald~~ handed to the Bishops, in time to be advertized at the ward meetings.

Elder Jno. [John] Taylor stated one important item of our organization wherein it is different from similar cooperative institutions in the world, the one joins it with a view of drawing out their dividends, whereas with us there is no drawing out b[ut] left in to increase the Capitol stock for the benefit of the Kingdom of God.

Elder Orson Pratt made a few remarks ~~on some items~~.

The meeting was ~~adjourned sine die~~ Dismissed. Benediction by Elder A Carrington.

June 8, 1874; Monday

The School of the Prophets met in the City Hall at 7 o clock pm. Present[:] Prest. B[righam] Young presiding [and] C[ounselor]rs D[aniel] H Wells[,] Asst C[ounselor] A[lbert] Carrington[,] Also Elder

Wilford Woodruff. After singing Prayer by Elder Geo Nebeker. Singing. The Roll called and 49 members responded.

Elder W Woodruff spoke of the importance ^of^ every one understanding the principle of this united order alike, as he found by conversation with one of the members of the school, we did not.

B[isho]p S[amuel] A. Woolley explained his views, according ~~Prest. B[righam] Young~~ to what he understood from the reading of the constitution on last Tuesday, which were different from the understanding of others.

Prest. B Young said no document or agreement had yet been drawn up, that was at all suited to our wants, we intend to keep trying until we get ^one^ as perfect as the Law will admit of.

B[isho]p S A Woolley then made a few remarks about several revelations in the Doc[trine] & Cov[enants].

Prest. B Young said we want to be one in our operations, to build up Zion, to be an everlasting order—to live as one family, ~~all share and share alike~~. The Lord deals with his ~~bret~~ Children according to their disposition.

Elder David McKenzie made a few remarks on the articles of Agreement, which was read ~~before~~ last Tuesday and the necessity of seeking after ^the^ Spirit that emanates from the priesthood. ~~in~~

Elder Geo B Wallace said inasmuch as God has given us a Man as his Mouthpiece we should be willing to carry out his council, instead of equivocating, and seeking after ancient revelations.

Elder S. A. Woolley made several remarks, which ~~caus~~ called forth some excellent observations from Prest. B[righam] Young pertaining to the safe path for Elders to take, to secure their salvation, and especially in reference to the Union that the Lord is trying to bring about. ~~Prest Young also refered to the reply that he made to Elder Tho[ma]s Taylor, last Tuesday~~.

B[isho]p. A[lonzo] H Raleigh made some sensible remarks on the carrying out of this order, which ^he said^ no doubt will be attended with sacrifice from some, while others may have an easier path, but God has a plan to be carried out, and we are called to carry out a portion of it, we are here to build up Zion, and must submit to his inspirations or we cannot do it. Let us seek to understand the general instructions of the servants of God, and then depend upon the spirit of God to carry out the details of those instructions.

Prest. Young said if there was only 50 men who were willing in this City to unite together in this order, he intended to be one of that number.

Elder W Woodruff said there never was anything revealed to this people, as raised the Devil so universally as this United order. And no one who either acts as Ananias [and Sapphira] did [in withholding money, Acts 5:1–11], or tries to ~~safe~~ draw off and throw cold water upon it, ^but^ what little sap there is, will run out of them.

Prest. B Young said, any one who earnestly desired to know the mind of the Lord on this subject, will have as bright a testimony as anything they ever had in their lives.

Elder Geo B Wallace bore testimony to the above—and stated a happy circumstance that occurred at South Cottonwood yesterday.

Meeting adjourned ~~for one week~~ ^till Saturday next^ at 2 o clock pm. Benediction by Elder Angus M Cannon.

Prest. Young particularly desired the brethren to be open and frank with each other, for that is the way to avoid jealo[u]sy and hard feeling, let us follow every act of kindness, do everything on the principle of honor and honesty, that confidence may be fully established among us.

June 13, 1874; Saturday

The officers of the United Order Met in the Old Tabernacle at 2 o clock pm. Present[:] Prest. B[righam] Young presiding[,] D[aniel] H Wells C[ounselo]r [and] Asst C[ounselo]r A[lbert] Carrington[,] Elder Orson Pratt, Erastus Snow, & Jno [John] Taylor ^of the twelve^ [apostles]. After singing Prayer by Elder Joseph Booth.

Prest. Young gave the privelege for any question to be asked.

B[isho]p S[amuel] A. Woolley enquired, if a Man was in the Order and his family not, could he draw support form the Order for ~~the~~ his family, and if he died, would his family have any claim for their support.

Prest. Young said it was the duty of every man to take care of his family.

Prest. D H Wells enquired if any of the different branches of trade had met, since last meeting, if so, what had been done.

Elder Geo B Wallace, the farmers[,] Gardners &c met this Week, and a sup[erintenden]t was appointed to take the oversight of what farming land should be turned over into the order. John Van Cott was unanimously elected, with the privelege of having two Assistants, E[dwin] D Woolley was elected as one of them.

Horticulture, Geo B Wallace was appointed Superintendent & Bro Gillis & Bro Woodbury his assistants. The [horticulture] meeting was adjourned to next Wednesday in the 8th Ward School house at ½ past 6 pm.

Prest. Young gave some good instructions in regard to having all the farming and Horticultural land put under the best cultivation, and at least should have one Superintendent from each ward &c.

B[isho]p E[dward] Hunter met with the Curriers, Tanners & Harness makers this week. He made some interesting remarks on the Tanning of Hides, and making leather, which business he was satisfied could be gone into with propriety and profit.

Elder A M[ilton] Musser made a few remarks on the same subject, and named that several committees were appointed at that meeting to make various enquiries, and report at next Meeting at City Hall at 6 oclock pm.

Prest. B Young said we wanted to raise what we want to wear, and also what we eat, and as far as possible, live within ourselves and be self sustaining. We will meet next Saturday at 2 oclock, at which time he hoped to have articles of agreement ready to be in every way legal, and have them ready to ^be read^ to the officers of the order. After next Saturday perhaps it would be better to meet in the several trade committees ^in wards^ which would further the ends of business more effectually. He then spoke of the advantages of carrying out the principles of this order, no one being curtailed in their agency by being controuled in our time and means by others. He also vividly held up the wicked & corrupt condition of the Nation, if we could only see things as they are, we should be astonished at the depth of degredation to which the Nation is sunk. He then suggested that himself and Assistants intended to visit the various wards at their ~~various~~ appointed ^places^ and impart what information they could, for the benefit of the brethren.

After singing, Benediction by Elder W[illiam] H. Folsom.

June 20, 1874; Saturday

The Officers of the United Order met in the old Tabernacle at 2 o clock pm. Present[:] Prest. B[righam] Young presiding. C[ounselo]r[s] Geo A Smith & D[aniel] H Wells, Ass[istant]t C[ounselo]r[s] A[lbert] Carrington & Lorenzo Snow, Elders Orson Pratt, ~~hor~~ &

B[righam] Young Jun[io]r, E[rastus] Snow, W[ilford] Woodruff. After singing Prayer by Elder Alex[ande]r Steel.

Elder David McKenzie then read articles of agreement [no longer extant][,] which were somewhat different from those drawn up at St. George.

Elder A Carrington said the above Articles had been carefully drawn up so as to come under the sanction of the law, and although not yet perfect, may be altered or amended at any time by a two thirds vote. This improvement we are called upon to make, is nothing more than we each promised at the water of baptism.

Elder E Snow made some appropriate remarks on the object the Lord has in view by introducing the United order ~~of~~ among the Latter Day Saints, and notwithstanding the greatness and goodness of the plan of operations now sought to be introduced, we find it comes in contact with our traditions, selfishness & love of the World, so that it is very difficult to establish the order of God. He [God] designs however to establish Zion as soon as he can find a people who are willing to be sanctified and prepared for the coming of Christ. He longed to see the day when the same order will exist among the saints, as in the days of Nephi and that of Enoch.

The detail of this order is simply a plan to frustrate the attacks of our enemy, by properly placing out our pickets, and consolidating our forces successfully.

In reply to a Question as to whether a full or partial consecration is intended.

Prest. Young said he intended to put in everything he had on the earth.

Several questions were asked in relation to some articles of the document previously read—~~B[isho]p John Sharp suggested~~

B[isho]p A[lexander] McRae suggested that the articles of agreement be read again, and discussed section by section.

B[isho]p John Sharp ~~suggested~~ Motioned that instead of that, Prest. Young should nominate 12 men ~~to~~ who have time and ability to devote, to carefully examine and revise the Document.

Moved & ~~Seconded~~ Carried That the articles of agreement be read over again. Elder David McKenzie then read them.

~~Question~~. Several questions were asked which caused Prest. Young to make some timely and interesting [blank].

The above Motion was Seconded & Carried and Prest. Young nominated the following committee[:] A Carrington, A[lbert] P Rockwood, O Pratt, Jno. [John] Sharp, Jos[eph] E. Taylor, Lorenzo Snow, B Young Jun[io]r, Erastus Snow[,] W Woodruff, E[dwin] D. Woolley, Isaac Groo, & Jno. [John] Taylor.

B[isho]p E[dward] Hunter advocated prompt action in regard to our Home Manufacturing Industries.

Prest. Young said when the time comes that the Law of God can be fully carried our, the Law will be made known to the people, for them either to accept or reject, and no such criticisms, and objections would be allowed, as we have had here to day, and after being decided to adjourn the Meeting till next Saturday at 2 p m.[,] he particularly injoined upon all present to be punctual to time, and come ~~with~~ filled with the spirit of God to listen to the articles of Agreement, as amended by the Committee.

Benediction by Elder Miner G Atwood.

June 27, 1874; Saturday

The Officers of the United Order met in the old Tabernacle at 2 oclock pm. Asst C[ounselo]r A[lbert] Carrington presiding. Prest. B[righam] Young & Council of the twelve [apostles] being absent at a two days meeting at Brigham City. After singing Prayer by Elder D[aniel] Corbett. Singing.

Elder A Carrington, as Chairman of a Committee appointed last Saturday, stated that in revising the Articles of Association, that being the duty required of them in their appointment, that the Articles had been framed with a view of keeping with the purvue and protection of the laws of our Country, therefore they do not go so far as was previously anticipated, but they are intended as a stepping stone to something more perfect. He regretted the existence of Misgivings and doubts in the minds of some, and as a consequence, some of the most ridiculous rumours have been afloat, these are simple plain self evident principles that we are called upon to subscribe to, and if any who hold responsible offices in trying to carry out those principles practically, should fail to do so satisfactorily, they can easily be removed and others substituted.

The Articles shortly to be read, though not perfect, are as ~~much~~ near so ~~are~~ as they could get them, and the Bye Laws will be prepared as soon as ~~th~~ circumstances will permit.

The Clerk then read the articles.

And after a few more remarks made by Elder A[lbert] Carrington it was Motioned & Seconded That the Articles of Association be adopted as reported by the Committee.

Meeting was adjourned Sine Die. Benediction by Elder H[amilton] G Park.

September 12, 1874; Saturday

The Members of the United Order met in the old Tabernacle at 2 oclock pm as per Notice of Prest. B[righam] Young at Bishops Meeting. Present Geo A Smith presiding. After singing Prayer by Elder Orson Pratt.

Prest. Smith desired of those present who wished to enter into the ~~Order~~ United Order in a good earnest, to hold up their right hand and a Unanimous vote was responded. He then enquired if any Bishop had already commenced ~~under~~ an organization under the recent articles of associations.

Elder Arthur Stayner said in Farmington they had held 3 meetings, and organized their board of directors, and other officers, had partially erected a ~~Tf~~ building for a Tannery[;] at each meeting the articles were carefully read, and a committee of ways and means had been appointed, who were now waiting upon Members of the order, to find out what means could be obtained, after each one had secured their years supply of bread stuff. [The Order] had not yet incorporated.

B[isho]p A[lonzo] H Raleigh said they had held a meeting of Teachers and read the Articles of agreement to them, but had not yet organized under the new constitution.

B[isho]p Anson Call had not taken any definite steps in Bountiful ward, but were waiting rather for a sample in some other ward, so as ~~to~~ not to start until they knew just what to do.

Prest. Geo A Smith explained the cause of the delay, as chiefly arising from the fact of the first Constitution or articles of Association which were not strictly got up according to the Laws of our Country—but where a Capitol of only $5000.00 can be raised in any association, they could easily incorporate under ~~these~~ that. [He realized] it will be necessary for us ^to^ abstain from the purchase of Imported articles, and confine ourselves to those of home manufacture and home production~~—what.~~

Elder A[lbert] Carrington spoke of the necessity of carrying out the will[power] in favor of confining ourselves to the use of home produced articles, the chief drawback to this is pride ^vanity^ extravagance, and a desire to gratify our gentile tastes. But he hoped there was a goodly number who will be willing to deny themselves, for securing the great ^self^ sustaining principle.

He then spoke of the importance of being united though he should prefer going slow rather than run the risk of jumping out of the frying pan into the fire[.] He wished to know that we are going in the right direction, and as fast as circumstances will permit. We must not be discouraged on a/c [account] of being a little slow, for it is much better to go slow and sure, than to run too fast and get into trouble. Nothing but truth, purity and holiness can endure. The object we have ^in view^ is to become one in all things.

Prest. Geo A Smith desired the brethren to commence immediately to organize in the various Associations, and humbly and faithfully try to carry out these self sustaining principles both by precept and example—and if the home missionaries desire to resume their labors to preach through the various wards and settlements, ~~will~~ must communicate with B[isho]p L[orenzo] D[ow] Young.

After singing Benediction by Elder F[ranklin] D Richards.

APPENDIX FOUR

MEETINGS OF THE ST. GEORGE SCHOOL OF THE PROPHETS, 1883

The two dated entries that comprise this appendix appear at the end of the 1883 Salt Lake School of the Prophets minute book. The Salt Lake school met on October 12 and then not again. Why the Salt Lake and St. George schools became inactive so soon after their organization is unclear.

December 23, 1883; Sunday

Minutes of a meeting of the Priesthood held in the sealing room of the Temple of St. George, at 6 P.M. Present: [Temple] president Wilford Woodruff. Apostles Erastus Snow and George Teasdale.

Stake President John D. T. McAllister. Elders Henry Eyring, D[aniel] D. McArthur, John Lytle, Henry Herriman, Henry W. Miller, William Faucett, John Pimm, George Woodword, D[avid] H. Cannon, James G. Bleak, Marius Ensign, Anson P. Win[d]sor, Charles Smith, Robert Gardiner, Walter Granger, Charles A. Terry, Charles W. Smith, Thomas S. Terry, Wilson D. Pace, M[oses] F. Farnsworth, William A. Bringhurst, Marcus Funk, George H. Crosby, W[illia]m H. Thompson, Stephen R. Wells.

Meeting called to order by President W[ilford] Woodruff. Prayer by Apostle Erastus Snow.

Prest. W[ilford] Woodruff said this meeting had been called for a purpose that would be hereafter revealed. It would require the brethren to keep their own counsel. There are ordinances in this house that are sacred and should not be revealed. All the ordinances are sacred, and we must learn to keep our own counsels.

A vote was then taken not to reveal anything that should transpire in our meeting, which was carried unanimously.

Prest. Woodruff said that the time had come for us to enter a higher plane and to understand the further ordinances of the Kingdom of God.

He asked if there was any present who had not obeyed and entered into the law of God (plural marriage). There were none present who had not entered into this covenant. Prest. Woodruff then gave instructions upon the necessity of keeping the Word of Wisdom, and preserving order in our families. He urged the brethren to be kind to their families and just in all their relations with their wives and families. We should all obey the law of tithing and observe all the laws of God, acting consistently in all our doings. Gave some instructions on the Word of Wisdom, the necessity of observing it in its full spirit and meaning, showing the necessity of overcoming all our bad habits and of being obedient to the requirements of the Almighty. Spoke of the necessity of our advancing in the knowledge of God and in the principles of eternal life and of keeping ourselves pure and virtuous.

Apostle Snow said during our visit to the last conference in Salt Lake City the [First] Presidency invited the Apostles, and Presidents of Stakes, to meet with them and we had several meetings. The Apostles had previously met and had freely expressed themselves to them and each other as to their mode of life and actions before the Lord, their conduct toward each other and their families etc., and these brethren were examined concerning their life and obedience to the word of the Lord with regard to Plural Marriage, Word of Wisdom and other things, to see how far they were prepared for the establishment of a School of the Prophets. There had been a man found who had been true and faithful [to the church][,] of the members of the first School of the Prophets, in Kertland. This was Zebedee Coltrin. He related to us, the circumstances of the Word of Wisdom being first given. ["]The Prophet Joseph Smith was in an adjoining room in the school where they were assembled, and came in with that revelation in his hand. Out of the twenty one members that were there assembled all used tobacco more or less except one. Joseph read the revelation and when they heard it they all laid aside their pipes and tobacco and," said Bro. Coltrin, "I have never used it since." It was very interesting to hear him relate the experience of that early school and the circumstances that happened.

President [John] Taylor had diligently sought to understand all the particulars concerning the School of the Prophets, so as to have them properly established. As far as the Presidency and Twelve are concerned they have each taken up a labor with each other to find out how far they were in harmony with the principles of divine truth as revealed from the heavens concerning plural marriage, word of wisdom, our duties to our Families, and the spirit in our houses and homes. Each one scanned himself and his brethren to understand their standing before the Lord. We ought to be exemplary men as we know the principles and the requirements. One principle required of us to consider was had we maintained the principle of plural marriage in our hearts and practice? Did we feel we had lived in this principle in all virtue and purity as well as the word of wisdom? It was not all who were admitted into this holy order who had obeyed this law, in our meeting in the city, but they were in harmony with it and expressed themselves willing to sustain this principle, to honor and obey the law of God. We are required to sanctify ourselves and put ourselves in such a shape that we can present ourselves before the Lord so we can be recommended for an advancement in the Church and Kingdom of God. We must not be the slaves of habit, passion or lust, and must not endulge in that which the Lord has said is not good. In the City all were presented singly as to whether they could be accepted by their brethren as those who would be in harmony with these principles and each other.

Prest. W. Woodruff had not said anything [previously] about the School of the Prophets[,] intending to have asked the brethren of their standing, but as it had been spoken of he would say there had been an attempt to establish a School of the Prophets but men could not keep their own counsel, they betrayed their trust. It is necessary to have men who can keep the law of God and live their religion, being exemplary men and true to their covenants.

Apostle Teasdale felt thankful to God for this privelage of meeting with the brethren in this room. In the past it has seemed impossible to keep our own counsels, some one would betray, but we ought surely to know ^enough^ to keep our covenants, our own counsels. God will not teach us in these schools unless we keep these things to ourselves for they are sacred. We must honor the law of God. We are surely slothful if we have been in the church for some time and have not obeyed the Law of plural marriage. We must have order in our families. Brethren[,] be candid, speak your feelings freely, preach the Gospel by example. Let us love each other as ourselves, not speak evil against the Lord's anointed, exercise righteous dominion over our families and God's heritage, and overcome and keep the whole law of God. Theory will not exalt us, hold each other's interest sacred, live so as to keep ourselves clean and be prepared for the revelations of God who has promised to reveal Himself.

Prest. Woodruff: We have organized one school in Salt Lake City; it is the only one at present. Before I left, in conversing with President Taylor, I was permitted to organize a school at St. George by forwarding the list of names to him for the approval of the Presidency. Plural Marriage and the Word of Wisdom were two important principles to be observed in order to stand in this holy order. He [Woodruff] then called for an expression of the feelings and status of the brethren present.

B[isho]p Marius Ensign had tried to live these principles and was in harmony with and rejoiced in these principles, and the privelage of this meeting. His name was then presented to those who had already become members of the School of the Prophets, and was accepted.

Bro. John Pimm kept the Word of Wisdom and obeyed the law of plural marriage, taught his children the principles of righteousness and was in harmony with the principles advocated. Accepted.

Bro. George Woodward was endeavoring to live these principles and keep the law of God. Accepted.

Bro. W. H. Thompson was very much gratified and mellow in his feelings at being considered worthy to be here. Was living in the law of plural marriage. Had kept most of the Word of Wisdom and [had] given up tobacco some time ago, had indulged in a little tea, but of late had quit everything and desired to conform to everything that was required and to do all he could to become a man of God and proposed with His blessing to be one with his family and assist in building up the Kingdom of God. Had labored as a missionary (under Apostle Orson Pratt in Rhode Island) and at home was willing to do so now. Accepted.

B[isho]p Charles A. Terry had not heard anything but what he could sustain and was in harmony with. He had some trouble in his family but always endeavored to give them good counsel. Endeavored to keep the word of wisdom but occasionally took a little wine in a medicinal manner.

Prest. Woodruff asked the brethren already in the school as he did for every member proposed, if they were willing to receive Bro. Terry into the fellowship of this covenant.

Apostle Snow said the first thing in the word of wisdom is that it is not good to drink wine or strong drink. If we have a habit of using wine we should lay it aside and not use it. Did not require anyone to say they would never taste it again, but not to be in any matter under its influence.

Prest. Eyring expressed himself as to the use of wine that it should never be used only in extreme cases, that our example may not be a license to others.

Bro. Charles A. Terry was accepted.

B[isho]p Granger in times past has used some wine and tea. Had been to conference in Salt Lake City and [in] getting the spirit of the conference had concluded to abstain from all these things and had overcome so as not to need it. He entered into plural marriage and wanted to live the principles advanced. Accepted.

Bro. Stephen R. Wells was pleased to have this privelage. Was in plural marriage. Had kept the word of wisdom strictly, but of late had used a little wine and tea for his infirmities but believed he had power to set it all aside and keep the word of wisdom in its true Spirit and intent thereof. Endeavored to live in harmony with his families, to train his children in the fear of the Lord and the law of plural marriage. Accepted.

B[isho]p Marcus Funk believed in the principles advanced, was in plural marriage and endeavored to do his duty. The word of wisdom he endeavored to live up to. Had not t^o^uched wine on[c]e [in] a month. Was in full fellowship with his brethren and desired to live his religeon. Accepted.

B[isho]p Wilson D. Pace believed he felt just as his brethren. Had not kept the word of wisdom, but he felt that he could keep it according to the spirit and meaning as instructed: Was in plurality, and was in harmony with principles advanced and happy with the privelage of being with the brethren. Accepted.

B[isho]p Charles W. Smith realized that he was in a sacred place. He had received these principles in his heart, he had no appetite for the things prohibited and endeavored to live his religeon. Accepted.

B[isho]p George H. Crosby had been raised in the church and felt honored to have this invitation. Was in full harmony with the principles advanced and the brethren. Made some explanation with regard to his family matters[,] his second wife's leaving. Was in full accord with the principles of plural marriage.

Apostle Snow asked some questions of Brother Crosby which being answered, Bro. Crosby was accepted.

B[isho]p W[illia]m A. Bringhurst esteemed it a privilege and a blessing to be here, was in harmony and full accord with the principles advanced, was in plural marriage and kept the word of wisdom. Accepted.

Bro. A. P. Win[d]sor felt it quite a privelage etc. Coincided with the requirements made, was living in plural marriage. Had quit his Tobacco, 16 years ago. Had quit all the habits spoken of, and was trying to keep the word of wisdom. Accepted.

Bro. William Fawcett was gratified to meet with the brethren etc. Coincided with the principles advanced and was living them to the best of his ability. Could fellowship the brethren already members of the school, etc. (This was in consequence of Prest. Woodruffs requesting all to say that if fellowshipped they could fellowship their brethren.) Accepted.

Prest. D. D. McArthur thanked the brethren for this privelage. Was always in harmony with the principles of "Mormonism." Had never been addicted to drinking. Had quit sometime [ago] to use things not good. Had peace in his family and was trying to keep the law of God. Accepted.

B[isho]p D. H. Cannon was gratified for the confidence the brethren had in him in inviting him to attend this meeting. Has always had a hankering after everything the Lord had said was not good, but was thankful to say he had quit, and was keeping the word of wisdom. Had entered into plural marriage in the fear of the Lord. Had probably been too strict with his family, sometimes a little harsh. Spoke very honestly of his failing, confessing his weaknesses, and said by the help of the Lord he would do His will and keep his commandments. Had always had the fear of the Lord before him, and was in accord with ^all^ the principles and requirements suggested, and with his brethren. Accepted.

Bro. James G. Bleak thanked the Lord and his brethren for the privelage of being here. Had believed in and practiced the law of marriage. Had not always had peace in his family, had some cross^ness^ but was striving to do the best he could to provide, etc. Had had wayward children but had labored with them assiduously, but did [not] know one of them who had turned their back upon the gospel or upon its principles. Had done the best he could before God and his brethren, I think[,] I keep the word of wisdom. Was entirely in fellowship with all present.

Bro. Stephen R. Wells said he could not endorse Bro. Bleak's conduct in his family government. Thought he had not acted as he should and had told him so in his capacity as teacher. Bro. W. H. Thompson was sorry this had come up and explained some family matters.

Prest Woodruff spoke of the difficulties existing in families and difficulties that we could not always controll in our families as we could wish and unless there was something very serious we should have some charity, and gave some very excellent counsel. Bore testimony concerning the integrity of Bro. Bleak.

Bros. Eyring, T. S. Terry, D. H. Cannon, George Teasdale, and Erastus Snow spoke expressive of their feelings and confidence in Bro. Bleak and his judgement in his difficulties. Bro. Snow especially, who was well posted in his affairs, speaking in the kindest manner in justice to Bro. Bleak. Accepted.

B[isho]p Robert Gardiner for some time had watched the spirit and teachings of the leaders and was glad to hear the time had come when we should live nearer to the Lord. Was in plural marriage and had lived up to the spirit of the word of wisdom was proud to be in fellowship with the brethren. Accepted.

Bro. Thomas S. Terry was thankful for the honor of this invitation, was in harmony with the principles taught. Was in plural marriage and it was possible he wanted to have things too much his own way, but was doing to the best of his ability to educate his children and do right. Had not perhaps kept the word of wisdom so closely as he should have done, when since the council held on the 3d of November at the Stake Priesthood meeting where these principles had been refered to by Prest. McAllister, he had kept it straight. Felt willing to try and keep all the commandments of God. Was in fellowship with the brethren and loved them. Accepted.

Bro. Henry W. Miller was thankful to be here with the brethren. Had endeavored to live his religion for many years. Had loved liquor but had overcome it. Had not kept the word of wisdom in all respects, but since the brethren had come back from conference he had kept the word of wisdom. Stated his experience in overcoming habits that were not good. Wanted to do right. Had but a little time to stay with us but wanted the fellowship of the brethren. He had some rude boys [in his family] but was doing the best he could to get along. Was in full fellowship with the brethren. Accepted.

Bro. Charles Smith was thankful that he had been invited. Had lived happy in plural marriage. Had always lived as one family. All my lifetime I have been a temperate man. Tea, coffee or any strong stimulent did not agree with him. Had kept the word of wisdom. His appetite was good and his digestion powers strong, which he attributed to his temperate habits. Was in full fellowship with every man in the room. Accepted.

Bro. M. F. Farnsworth tried to weigh himself carefully since he had been in the room. Was thankful to have the privilege of being here. Had obeyed the law of plural marriage and had lived in peace with his family. Had gained a victory over himself with regard to the word of wisdom, and related his experience in overcoming his natural or unnatural tastes and habits that had beset him, Tried to be kind to his family and live in peace, etc. Was jealous for the rights of the weak and impulsive as his brethren know. Was in full fellowship with every man present. Desired to do the will of God and by His grace overcome every evil propensity and live his religion. Accepted.

Bro. John Lytle had always been a lover of tobacco. Was eighty years old. Had given up his tobacco. But occasionally used snuff for his eyes. Had tried to live up to the principles of the Gospel. Had had two wives but at present had none. Was in fellowship with the brethren. Accepted.

Prest. Henry Herriman would be under the necessity of pleading guilty. Was nearly eighty years old. Thanked God for the spirit and blessing that was resting on the brethren. Knew that plural marriage was correct and desired to keep the law of God, and had called upon Him earnestly day and night but had not kept the word of wisdom, and his children had not been as he could have wished them, but he ^had^ labored faithfully with them. Wanted the fellowship of his brethren and would do the best he could to keep the councils of the Almighty, God being his helper. Was in full fellowship with the brethren. Accepted.

Prest. Woodruff was glad to see this day and time. He expressed great satisfaction at seeing these brethren making the sacrifices they are making. Instructed the brethren to come together tomorrow in fasting and prayer, with clean bodies and garments to have no [sexual] intercourse with their wives. We have heard you express yourselves—you have gained a great victory in overcoming your habits, etc. The Lord requires us to keep the word of wisdom according to the best of our ability. Related his own experience. He had taken up a labor with himself for the time has come for us to keep the word of wisdom as far as we can before the Lord. Come together at 9 A.M. etc.

Benediction by Apostle George Teasdale.

December 24, 1883; Monday

Minutes of a meeting of the Priesthood assembled for the purpose of attending to the ordinance of washing of feet, and for organizing a School of the Prophets, held in the Temple, St. George.

All the brethren who were at the meeting last night assembled in fasting and prayer, and answered to their name at roll call. Prest. Wilford Woodruff presided. "Now let us anew" was sung. Prayer by Prest. Woodruff. "This earth was once a garden place" was sung. The brethren were then listed by age.

Prest. Woodruff then laid aside his coat and vest and girded himself with a towel. All things being prepared, John Lytle, who was the oldest man present, being born on the 18th day of August 1803, then took his seat. Prest. W[ilford] Woodruff washed his feet. He said "By virtue of the Holy Priesthood and in the name of Jesus Christ I wash thy feet according to an Holy Ordinance introduced by our Lord and Savior Jesus Christ with his Deciples when he washed their feet and told them to wash one another, and also by Joseph Smith, the Prophet of the Lord. [It is] an introductory ordinance to the School of the Prophets, and [I] pronounce thee clean from the blood of this generation, and say unto thee, thy sins are forgiven thee, and seal and confirm upon thee all the rights, powers, and privileges associated with this ordinance in the authority of the Holy Priesthood and in the name of the Lord Jesus Christ. Amen.["]

Prest. Woodruff then dried Bro. Lytle's feet while fresh water was prepared by Apostle [George] Teasdale, assisted by Prests. [John D. T.] McAllister and [Henry] Eyring, who had been admitted to the School of the Prophets in Salt Lake City.

The following brethren were then washed in their order:

2	Henry Harriman	born	9 June	1804
3	Henry W. Miller	"	1 May	1807
4	William Fawcett	"	13 Dec.	1814
5	John Pimm	"	13 Sep.	1815
6	George Woodward	"	9 Sep.	1817
7	Anson P. Win[d]sor	"	19 Aug.	1818
8	Charles Smith	"	10 July	1819
9	Robert Gardiner	"	12 Oct.	1819
10	Daniel ^D.^ McArthur	"	18 Apr.	1820
11	Walter Granger	"	4 Aug.	1821
12	Marius Ensign	"	18 Aug.	1821
13	Charles A. Terry	"	10 Nov.	1821
14	Stephen R. Wells	"	26 Dec.	1822
15	Charles N. Smith	"	14 Mar.	1824
16	Thomas S. Terry	"	3 Oct.	1825
17	James G. Bleak	"	15 Nov.	1829
18	Wilson D. Pace	born	27 July	1831
19	Moses F. Farnsworth	"	5 Feb.	1834
20	David H. Cannon	"	23 Apr.	1838
21	William H. Thompson	"	1 May	1839
22	William A. Bringhurst	"	26 Jan.	1839
23	Marcus Funk	"	3 Dec.	1842
24	George H. Crosby	"	25 Oct.	1846

At the completion of the ceremony bread and wine was produced. Remarks were made by Apostle [Erastus] Snow, who gave instructions upon the ordinance of the washing of feet and the sacrament, refering to the "Last Supper" of the Lord Jesus Christ and the instructions given in the Corinthians[,] the organization of the School of the Prophets and the administration of the Sacrament in Jerusalem and Kirtland.

Prest. Woodruff called upon Apostles Erastus Snow and George Teasdale to assist him in the administration of the Sacrament. Apostle Snow asked a blessing on the bread, which was passed around by Bros. Snow and Teasdale. Apostle Teasdale asked a blessing on the wine, and it was passed around.

Prest. Woodruff then gave instructions and stated the effects that had followed this ordinance. Spoke upon the shaking off the dust off the feet and washing the feet in pure water in summer or winter and the judgements of God that had followed. Refered to a revelation that he had had in the wilderness and exhorted the brethren to diligence and faithfulness. Called upon Bro. M[oses] F. Farnsworth to read that revelation [originally recorded in Woodruff's daybook on January 26, 1880].

Bro. M. F. Farnsworth read the revelation, which is in the records of the Temple so not deemed necessary to write here as it was in the record of ^the^ washing of feet under the other circumstances[,] [as part of a testimony against the wicked].

Apostle Erastus Snow refered to the judgments and calamities that had overtaken the people during the last few years. The judgments of God that was amongst the people, earthquakes, tidal waves, cyclones, fires, and calamities and said they would continue; refered to Mr. [Dudley C.] Haskell[,] [US Congressman, R–KS], whose death had been announced, who had been so bitter against the saints and who had opposed Bro. George Q. Cannon when his seat was contested, who had been smitten with an incurable disease that had baffled the skill of the doctors. Gave valuable instructions concerning the work [e]ntrusted to us in these last days. The necessity of unity, faith and prayer. The unseen powers ~~who~~ were assisting in this work behind the vail. The world could go no farther than permitted. In his ministry when mob[b]ed and driven by the wicked he had gone by himself, as commanded, and washed his feet as a testimony against them.

Elder Lytle related some very interesting circumstances that happened in Missouri in the days of the Prophet Joseph [Smith] and his testimony concerning Adam in Adam Ondi Ahman and the altar he built. The place where the ancient of days would sit.

Prest. McAllister said we meet here today, and ^met^ last evening like the brethren did in Salt Lake City. The same ordinance has been attended to. The only man found was Bro. Zebedee Coltrin as said last night whose life had been preserved upon the earth that had been washed by the Prophet Joseph in the first School and had kept himself clean. Spoke upon the necessity of secrecy, and of other names who had been suggested who he would have liked to have been with us, but for reasons were laid over for a while; also upon the obligations resting upon us toward the Lord and each other. Hoped we would from this time hence forth keep the commandments of God.

Apostle Snow spoke upon the necessity of being very particular in the selection of members and gave his reasons why. Hoped the members of this school would be very particular in striving to put away everything that was detrimental to our union and progress. Related his experience in the word of wisdom.

Apostle Teasdale said Bro. Snow had been proposed for the president of the school but his name had not been sustained by the brethren, asked if this should not be so? (Prest. Woodruff answered yes.) He then expressed the joy and the gratitude he had at meeting so many of the brethren who in the providences of God had been brought into this Holy Covenant. God had commanded us to love one another and we should do so, we should cease to find fault put a curb on our tongues and live the principles of righteousness and our example would be a power and we would be a blessing to ourselves, each other and the heritage of God over which we were set. It was a leaven of righteousness that we were entering into. We could but feel how unworthy we were of these blessings when our righteousness was compared to ^that of^ our Redeemer; but hoped we would improve and be faithful to the sacred trust imposed upon us. Exhorted to affection, faithfulness and unity.

Prest. Woodruff presented the name of Apostle Erastus Snow as President of this school. Unanimously sustained. Bro. M. F. Farnsworth as Secretary. Unanimously sustained. Prest. John D. T. McAllister as president in the absence of Prest. Snow. Unanimously carried.

The brethren then retired to behind the vail and were introduced by Prest. Snow to Prest. Woodruff who stood on the steps beside the stand with uplifted hands.

Prest. Woodruff. "Art thou brethren? I salute you in the name of the Lord Jesus Christ, in token or remembrance of the everlasting covenant, in which covenant I receive you to fellowship, in a determination that is fixed, and immoveable, and unchangeable, to be your friend and brother through the grace of God, and in the bonds of love, to walk in all the commandments of God blameless, in thanksgiving, for ever and ever. Amen."

Prest. Snow replied "Art thou a brother? we salute you in the name of the Lord Jesus Christ,["] etc. etc. as above.

"The spirit of God like a fire is burning" was then sang, and Apostle Snow pronounced the benediction. Thus ended a glorious day.

APPENDIX FIVE

BRIGHAM YOUNG DISCOURSE, DECEMBER 20, 1867[1]

The following is an example of the extensive notes taken by George D. Watt in Pitman shorthand at the School of the Prophets, which he kept as part of his job as an official church reporter. After an argument with Brigham Young over wages on May 15, 1868, his shorthand career for the church ended.

Friday. City Hall Dec 20th 1867 1 o'clock
Theological School.
Joseph W Young

Present of the First Presidency[:] Brigham Young, Daniel H Wells. Of the Twelve[:] Orson Pratt. Meeting called to order by President Brigham Young[;] singing "O My Father" etc. Second hymn "Do What is Right."

President Young

It would be [blank]. There are some things for me to say. When this system can be carried out with regard to the spiritual kingdom on the earth we shall have a very strict order [but] we are not [there] now. [Therefore] circumstances [exist] to make the decision to call men in the territory to attend this high school. Consequently we shall admit persons in this school until the time comes when it will be necessary to select out a certain class of men who have proved themselves worthy of the confidence of each other and of the confidence of God.

This people are gathered together under these peculiar circumstances to try them. We have been [and] we are now in a situation for every man to exhibit what is in them. We have a privilege of proving ourselves perfectly honest[,] pure[,] holy[, and] upright before God and we have the privilege of doing little wrong here and little there. We have to prove before the Lord by our acts here on the earth[,] by our conduct[,] by our dealings one with another[,] by our faith[fulness]

1. This discourse is in the papers of George D. Watt, MS 4534, box 5, CHL, and was recently transcribed by LaJean Purcell Carruth. I have silently inserted periods and capitalization. All other edits appear in [brackets]. Appreciation to Carruth and to Matthew J. Grow for making this transcription available.

to our religion[, and] by our integrity to each other and to our God. The outward acts and the [blank] of the [mortal] creature will prove to the heavens whether we are worthy of attaining greater light[,] greater wisdom and more of the knowledge and the wisdom and the glory and the power and the providences of God. We have many great and glorious things revealed to us. We are privileged above all the inhabitants [of the] earth. We have a greater opportunity to show to the world and prove to God[,] angels[,] and each other a stricter <~~strictly~~>love of purity manifesting before the Lord our faith by our works more than other people.

There is nobody else that has this religion[,] nobody else that believes in God in [the] strict sense of word. They do not believe by their works in the Lord as this people do. We prove to the world [and] it is a testimony and argument that is beyond controversy that we have a different path from the rest of the world by our conduct in gathering together. But we are still to prove further by our integrity to our honesty before God [and] to each other that we do love the truth. We know very well a great many embrace this work because it is true. They are convinced it is true. It bears up the pure wherever it goes.

With regard to the things of God[,] it is true we [have many in this valley who] believe this [gospel] because it is the leading religion. It overpowers and overcomes every other faith[,] and we believe it and I guess we will go with the Latter-day Saints[, they say,] and we have a good opportunity to get a living[,] but do they love the truth for sake of it[?] Thousands receive it because they know it is true[,] but have they the love in their souls for the truth[?] We see it proved here all the time before us that people have embraced the gospel of life and salvation because of its mystery and spirit and influence and yet they have not love for the truth. The wheat and tares must grow together until harvest[,] true[,] but who is there that is worthy to receive the things of God? ~~There is many~~

We have a great deal of knowledge with regard to the faith of Christ [and] the gospel of life and salvation[,] and we have a great deal of knowledge with regard to this earth in a great many respects. But who is there that knows and understands the workings of the providences of God to his creatures and the earth[s] that are and were and will be made[?] We do not see the purport and do not understand the most simple things pertaining to the organization of the earth. We know if we sow wheat in good ground and take care of it (in this country that is [with] well water) [we] know we shall have a good crop. But we cannot form the blade or the stock or the husk or kernel. But while we know how to dig down mountains to fill up valleys and do a great many things and how to build houses and cities [and] know how to gain the learning of the day and this philosophy with regard to the arts and sciences. This we naturally understand as other men do. But when we come to the organization of the earth and its existence and understand how it came here [and] what is the power by which it revolves [and] why does it not go to any other planets[,] these laws are not in our possession. We know [if you] take a molded candle [and] you touch fire to it we know that wick burns and makes a light. But we do not know the power of this light and where it comes from. We do not understand these things. So it is with a great many things that are before us that we look upon that we do not understand. The Lord has great and glorious things for the people when they are prepared to receive them.

It is very near time now [that] we go [back] to Jackson County to redeem and build up the center stake of Zion. I felt years ago if the word was to come from the Lord [to] go to Jackson County next year the damndest thieves [would] want to go there. Liars[,] whoremongers[, and] adulterers [would] want to go there and be [the] first men there. If we are permitted to prepare a class of men to go there I shall be glad. I am speaking regarding the moral character of the elders of Israel. I hope we shall have a class of men prepared to go there. I say to the brothers and sisters[,] prepare yourselves to be virtuous and honest and let the [affairs?] of this world alone. I have asked the brethren to observe the Word of Wisdom. I do not think that the spirit of revelation from God [would] ever dictate a man to go there [to Jackson County] that does not observe the Word of Wisdom but [someone says] I want to go and soon you put your name down. I have not the least idea [that] God [would] call a thief to go there [or] that there will come a revelation to build up the kingdoms of this world instead of the kingdom of God. If they go[,] they will go without being called and without the spirit of revelation. I have not the least idea that a liar [will] be called to go there. Will this be of inspiration[?] No but as far as we can spread [the word] we should do [so] and when the people are privileged to go to Jackson

County and build up the center stake of Zion[,] we shall gather the people there and they will come there. But bad and indifferent [people will come] as [they wish] and they will be mixed with us but they will be closely watched. We have said to the brethren will we sustain each other instead of sustaining apostates and men of the world in our mercantile business[?] We will not do it. Those Jews and apostates to day are fed and clothed and make more money than our brethren do. [Will] such men [be] call[ed] to build up the center stake of Zion?

When a temple [will be] built there I am looking for Joseph [Smith]. If we should build a temple of the Lord there I expect to see Jesus and Joseph in the temple and not be manifested to the world [entire?]. Who is prepared to go there to receive visits of angels[?] ~~do~~ Is this people expect[ed] to[?] Just as much as they expect to live [in Missouri,] they are calculating on the time when angels come to visit us. Do you think that they [angels] can have fellowship with liars[,] thieves[,] adulterers[,] whoremongers[,] and those that love to make lies and that will not observe the words of the Lord[?] Will they visit them if we were to organize a class according to the revelations that have been given as far as have been given[?]

A revelation was read the other day [and] 7 sections in that revelation speaks of school of the prophets. If it was organized according to the pattern [given,] no man would be allowed to come into this house until the teacher comes first and prayer [is] offered up. It would be a place built for the purpose and if the scholars came in [they would] be received by the teacher by uplifted hands and if a number came in together in with all humility and [deference?] the test of fellowship would be whether or not they lived according to the revelations God has given to know whether they are brethren. Do you live according to revelations given in all things[?] If you do I hail you as brother and brethren.

The organization now is not perfect but we might gather for [the] purpose of preparing and thinking about it. Here are the elders of Israel[,] here is the First Presidency [and] 12 Apostles and then we take up the other quorums [such as] the President of 70 and high priests and president of stakes and bishops. Here is the leading men of Israel. Now then if we cannot commence to purify and prepare ourselves to be a pure and holy school of the prophets before God we will get what we can and learn what we can and go along until we can get proper men.

Now with regard to our temporal lives here we understand these different organizations in consequence of many surrounding circumstances of parents and [their influence on] children [who] are born into the world natural thieves[,] natural drunkards and liars. You see some mothers that are [close to] bearing a child [but] they want to steal all the time. I know persons in this church of this character that steal in consequence of [circumstances and are pregnant] with child. They are naturally given to these traits. This ~~gospel is~~ gospel is given to cleanse that person from this desire. Another one naturally wants to drink [and] becomes intoxicated. The gospel is expressly [contrary] to that nature[,] this natural appetite that has been produced by the circumstances surrounding the mother and the early education of the child. You see another one addicted to lying[;] they must lie.

When they come to understand[,] the gospel express[ly] ~~taught [illegible]~~ teaches them to overcome this [propensity?]. It is capable of [procuring?] every blessing pertaining to our appetite that we should have in our possession that we can obtain grace in name of Jesus Christ and overcome every such appetite. I heard one of our leading bishops[, after he] first tasted tobacco[, always] had a plug and sold the [product to others]. The gospel is expressly to purify our bodies and ~~our spirits~~ preserve our spirits in purity. If this is the case what shall we do[?] We should apply our lives strictly to the observance ~~in~~ <of> faith in [the] name [of] Jesus to overcome every one of those appetites. A man may be given to desire women[,] some more than others. It is an evil principle and some are ruined with it. The grace of God is expressly to overcome this desire[,] to crucify the deeds of the flesh. There is a cure in the gospel we have embraced for all these appetites. If a man is stingy [and] closely [guards his money] and hates to give anything to the poor and build up the kingdom of God[,] the grace of God is given expressly to engender in the heart of that individual the spirit of liberality [that] the gospel prompts.

We will manifest by our conduct what is in us and God causes those circumstances to show every man before his brethren[,] to show what they are. Should we not seek for grace through faith to overcome every [propensity?] and sanctify ourselves before the Lord. [For/If] I am not talking to the elders of Israel[,] the best class of men can be in this church. I wish they would be removed and we have better men here.

Are the fathers of the ward[,] members of [the] presidency of the high priests[,] of the 70's[, or any] large body of men[, of the] high council [worthy? If not,] where can we get better men[?] And yet we cannot have a school of prophets as it should be. But we are here to see if we cannot prepare ourselves to be worthy to come up near our Father and God [and] to know more of his will concerning us. I want to say these things and there is a great many [more] to say. It is to train ourselves and one another until we come into [all?] holiness[,] until we actually [can] be the servants of God and not the servants of Satan. Amen.

BIBLIOGRAPHY

Abbreviations of frequently cited sources

CHL	LDS Church History Library, Salt Lake City
D&C	Doctrine and Covenants, LDS 2013 edition
FDRJ	Franklin D. Richards journal
GQCJ	George Q. Cannon journal
HOJ	Historian's Office journal
JD	*Journal of Discourses*
JFSJ	Joseph F. Smith journal
JH	Journal History of the LDS Church
SotP	School of the Prophets Records, 1867–1874, 1883, CR 390 5–7, CHL
WWJ	Wilford Woodruff journal.

Adkins Jr., Marlowe C. "A History of John W. Young's Utah Railroads, 1884–1894." Master's thesis, Utah State University, 1978.

Alexander, Thomas G. "A Conflict of Perceptions: Ulysses S. Grant and the Mormons." *Ulysses S. Grant Association Newsletter* 8, no. 4 (July 1971): 29–42.

———. *Things in Heaven and Earth: The Life and Times of Wilford Woodruff, a Mormon Prophet*. Salt Lake City: Signature Books, 1991.

Alexander, Thomas G., and James B. Allen. *Mormons & Gentiles: A History of Salt Lake City*. Boulder: Pruett Publishing, 1984.

Alford, Kenneth L., and Robert C. Freeman. "The Salt Lake Theatre: Brigham's Playhouse." In *Salt Lake City: The Place Which God Prepared*, edited by Scott C. Esplin and Kenneth L. Alford, 97–118. Provo, UT: Religious Studies Center and Salt Lake City: Deseret Book, 2011.

Allen, James B., and Glen M. Leonard. *The Story of the Latter-day Saints*. Salt Lake City: Deseret Book, 1976.

Ambrose, Stephen E. *Nothing Like It in the World: The Men Who Built the Transcontinental Railroad, 1863–1869*. New York: Simon & Schuster, 2001.

Anderson, C. Leroy. *Joseph Morris and the Saga of the Morrisites Revisited.* Logan: Utah State University Press, 2010.

Anderson, Devery S., ed. *The Development of LDS Temple Worship, 1846–2000: A Documentary History*. Salt Lake City: Signature Books, 2011.

Anderson, Devery S., and Gary James Bergera, eds. *Joseph Smith's Quorum of the Anointed, 1842–1845: A Documentary History*. Salt Lake City: Signature Books, 2005.

———. *The Nauvoo Endowment Companies, 1845–1846: A Documentary History.* Salt Lake City: Signature Books, 2005.

Anderson, Lavina Fielding, ed. *Lucy's Book: A Critical Edition of Lucy Mack Smith's Family Memoir*. Salt Lake City: Signature Books, 2001.

Arrington, Leonard J. "Banking and Finance." In Powell, *Utah History Encyclopedia*.

———. *Brigham Young: American Moses*. New York: Alfred A. Knopf, 1985.

———. *From Quaker to Latter-day Saint: Bishop Edwin D. Woolley*. Salt Lake City: Deseret Book, 1976.

———. *Great Basin Kingdom: An Economic History of the Latter-day Saints, 1830–1900*. First published 1958 by Harvard University Press. Salt Lake City: University of Utah Press, 1993.

———. "The Provo Woolen Mills: Utah's First Large Manufacturing Establishment." *Utah Historical Quarterly* 21, no. 2 (April 1953): 97–116.

Arrington, Leonard J., and Davis Bitton. *The Mormon Experience: A History of the Latter-day Saints*. New York: Alfred A. Knopf, 1979.

———. *Saints without Halos: The Human Side of Mormon History*. Salt Lake City: Signature Books, 1981.

Arrington, Leonard J., Feramorz Y. Fox, and Dean L. May. *Building the City of God: Community & Cooperation among the Mormons*. 2nd ed. Urbana: University of Illinois Press, 1992.

Avery, Valeen Tippetts. *From Mission to Madness: Last Son of the Mormon Prophet*. Urbana: University of Illinois Press, 1998.

Bain, David Haward. *Empire Express: Building the First Transcontinental Railroad*. New York: Penguin, 1999.

Barrett, Glen. "Delegate John M. Bernhisel, Salt Lake Physician Following the Civil War." *Utah Historical Quarterly* 50, no. 4 (Fall 1982): 355–60.

Bartholomew, Ronald E. "The Textual Development of D&C 130:22 and the Embodiment of the Holy Ghost." *BYU Studies* 52, no. 3 (2013): 5–24.

Belnap, Daniel L. "'Those Who Receive You Not': The Rite of Wiping Dust Off the Feet." In Belnap, ed., *By Our Rites of Worship: Latter-day Saint Views on Ritual Scripture, History, and Practice*, 209–60. Provo: BYU Religious Studies Center, 2013.

Bergera, Gary James. *Conflict in the Quorum: Orson Pratt, Brigham Young, Joseph Smith*. Salt Lake City: Signature Books, 2002.

———. "Transgression in the LDS Community: The Cases of Albert Carrington, Richard R. Lyman, and Joseph F. Smith—Part 1." *Journal of Mormon History* 37, no. 3 (Summer 2011): 118–61.

Bigler, David L. *Forgotten Kingdom: Mormon Theocracy in the American West, 1847–1896*. Spokane: Arthur H. Clark, 2005.

Biographical Record of Salt Lake City and Vicinity: Containing Biographies of Well Known Citizens of the Past and Present. Chicago: National Historical Record, 1902.

Bitton, Davis. *George Q. Cannon: A Biography*. Salt Lake City: Deseret Book, 1999.

———. *The Ritualization of Mormon History and Other Essays*. Urbana: University of Illinois Press, 1994.

Bradley, Martha Sonntag. *A History of Kane County*. Salt Lake City: Utah State Historical Society, 1999.

———. *ZCMI: America's First Department Store*. Salt Lake City: ZCMI, 1991.

Brown, James S. *Life of a Pioneer, Being the Autobiography of James S. Brown*. Salt Lake City: George Q. Cannon & Sons, 1900.

Brown, Lisle G. "'Temple Pro Tempore': The Salt Lake City Endowment House." *Journal of Mormon History* 34, no. 4 (Fall 2008): 1–68.

Brown, Ralph O. "The Life and Missionary Labors of George Washington Hill." Master's thesis, Brigham Young University, 1956.

Brunson, Samuel D. "Brigham Young vs. the Bureau of Internal Revenue." Working paper, Oct. 2017. Available at the *Social Science Research Network*, www.ssrn.

Buchanan, Frederick S. *Culture Clash and Accommodation: Public Schooling in Salt Lake City, 1890–1994*. Salt Lake City: Signature Books and Smith Research Associates, 1996.

———. "Education among the Mormons: Brigham Young and the Schools of Utah." *History of Education Quarterly* 22, no. 4 (Winter 1982): 435–59

———. "Robert Lang Campbell: 'A Wise Scribe in Israel' and Schoolman to the Saints." *BYU Studies* 29, no. 3 (Summer 1989): 5–27.

Buerger, David John. "The Adam–God Doctrine." *Dialogue: A Journal of Mormon Thought* 15, no. 1 (Spring 1982): 14–58.

———. "'The Fulness of the Priesthood': The Second Anointing in Latter-day Saint Theology and Practice." *Dialogue: A Journal of Mormon Thought* 16, no. 1 (Spring 1983): 10–44.

———. *The Mysteries of Godliness: A History of Mormon Temple Worship*. Salt Lake City: Signature Books, 2002.

Bush Jr., Lester E. "Mormonism's Negro Doctrine: An Historical Overview." *Dialogue: A Journal of Mormon Thought* 8, no. 1 (Spring 1973): 11–68.

———. "The Spaulding Theory Then and Now." *Dialogue: A Journal of Mormon Thought* 10 (Autumn 1977): 40–69.

Bushman, Richard Lyman. *Joseph Smith: Rough Stone Rolling*. New York: Knopf, 2005.

Campbell, Eugene E. *Establishing Zion: The Mormon Church in the American West, 1847–1869*. Salt Lake City: Signature Books, 1988.

Cannon, Abraham H. *Candid Insights of a Mormon Apostle: The Diaries of Abraham H. Cannon, 1889–1895*. Edited by Edward Leo Lyman. Salt Lake City: Signature Books and Smith–Pettit Foundation, 2010.

Cannon, George Q. Journal. Online at Church Historian's Press, www.churchhistorianspress.org.

Chamberlin, Ralph V. *The University of Utah: A History of the First Hundred Years, 1850–1950*. Salt Lake City: University of Utah Press, 1960.

Chernow, Ron. *Grant*. New York: Penguin, 2017.

Church Historian's Office. Historian's Office History of the Church, 1839–circa 1882. Church History Library, Salt Lake City.

———. Journal, 1844–1879. Church History Library.

———. Journal History of the Church, 1830–present. Church History Library.

Cook, Lyndon. *The Revelations of the Prophet Joseph Smith*. Salt Lake City: Deseret Book, 1985.

Cook, Martha Tingey. "Pioneer Bands and Orchestras of Salt Lake City." Master's thesis, Brigham Young University, 1960.

Coontz, Stephanie. *Marriage, a History: From Obedience to Intimacy, or How Love Conquered Marriage*. New York: Viking, 2005.

Cowan, Richard O. "Steel Rails and the Utah Saints." *Journal of Mormon History* 27, no. 2 (Fall 2001): 177–96.

Crawley, Peter. *A Descriptive Bibliography of the Mormon Church*. 3 vols. Provo: BYU Religious Studies Center, 1997–2012.

Crosby, Jeffrey E. *Traveling in the Ministry: An Annotated History and Biographical Essay of the Life of Jesse Wentworth Crosby*. John S. Crosby Family, 1998.

Deseret News. Salt Lake City, 1850–present. Also *Deseret Evening News* and *Deseret Weekly*.

Darowski, Joseph F. "Schools of the Prophets: An Early American Tradition." *Mormon Historical Studies* 9, no. 1 (Spring 2008): 1–13.

Dickson, Robert. "Report of a Mission," Aug. 6, 1872. Missionary Reports, 1831–1900. MS 6104, Church History Library, Salt Lake City.

Dirkmaat, Gerrit J., Brent M. Rogers, Grant Underwood, Robert J. Woodford, and William G. Hartley, eds. *The Joseph Smith Papers: Documents, February 1833–March 1834*. Salt Lake City: Church Historian's Press, 2014.

Dunford, C. Kent. "The Contributions of George A. Smith to the Establishment of the Mormon Society in the Territory of Utah." PhD diss., Brigham Young University, 1970.

Ehat, Andrew F. "Joseph Smith's Introduction of Temple Ordinances and the 1844 Succession Question." Master's thesis, Brigham Young University, 1982.

England, Breck. *The Life and Thought of Orson Pratt*. Salt Lake City: University of Utah Press, 1985.

Evans, Max J. "A History of the Public Library Movement in Utah." Master's thesis, Utah State University, 1971.

Fitch, Thomas. *The Utah Problem: Review of the Course of Judge James B. McKean, and an Appeal for the Surrender of Polygamy*. Salt Lake City: Salt Lake Herald Office, 1872.

Gentry, Leland H., and Todd M. Compton. *Fire and Sword: A History of the Latter-day Saints in Northern Missouri, 1836–39*. Salt Lake City: Greg Kofford Books, 2010.

Godfrey, Matthew C., Mark Ashurst-McGee, Grant Underwood, Robert J. Woodford, and William G. Hartley. *The Joseph Smith Papers: Documents, July 1831–January 1833*. Salt Lake City: Church Historian's Press, 2013.

Gordon, Sarah Barringer. *The Mormon Question: Polygamy and Constitutional Conflict in Nineteenth-century America*. Chapel Hill: University of North Carolina Press, 2002.

Graffam, Merle, ed. *Salt Lake School of the Prophets: Minute Book, 1883*. Salt Lake City: Pioneer Press, 2000.

Grant, Heber J. Diary. Typed excerpts in Quinn Papers, Yale University.

Grow, Matthew J. "Clean from the Blood of This Generation: The Washing of Feet and the Latter-day Saints." In *Archive of Restoration Culture: Summer Fellows' Papers, 2000–2002*, edited by Richard L. Bushman, 131–38. Provo: Joseph Fielding Smith Institute for Latter-day Saint History, 2005.

———. *"Liberty to the Downtrodden": Thomas L. Kane, Romantic Reformer*. New Haven: Yale University Press, 2009.

Grow, Matthew J., Ronald K. Esplin, Mark Ashurst-McGee, Gerrit J. Dirkmaat, and Jeffrey D. Mahas. *The Joseph Smith Papers, Administrative Records: Council of Fifty Minutes, March 1844–January 1846*. Salt Lake City: Church Historian's Press, 2016.

Grow, Matthew J., and R. Eric Smith, eds. *The Council of Fifty: What the Records Reveal about Mormon History*. Provo: BYU Religious Studies Center, 2017.

Grow, Matthew J., and Ronald W. Walker. *The Prophet and the Reformer: The Letters of Brigham Young and Thomas L. Kane*. New York: Oxford University Press, 2015.

Hammond, John J. *Island Adventures: The Hawaiian Mission of Francis A. Hammond, 1851–1865*. Salt Lake City: Signature Books, 2016.

Hansen, Klaus B. *Quest for Empire: The Political Kingdom of God and the Council of Fifty in Mormon History*. East Lansing: Michigan State University Press, 1967.

Hartley, William G. "From Men to Boys: LDS Aaronic Priesthood Offices, 1829–1996." *Journal of Mormon History* 22, no. 1 (1996): 80–136.

———. "Mormons, Crickets, and Gulls: A New Look at an Old Story." *Utah Historical Quarterly* 38, no. 3 (Summer 1970): 224–39.

Head, Franklin H. "What Shall We Do with Our Indians?" In W. W. Catlin, comp. *Echoes of the Sunset Club*, 222–35. Chicago: Howard, Bartels & Company, 1891.

Hedges, Andrew H., Alex D. Smith, and Richard Lloyd Anderson. *The Joseph Smith Papers, Journals: December 1841–April 1843*. Salt Lake City: Church Historian's Press, 2011.

Holzapfel, Richard Neitzel, and Christopher C. Jones. "John the Revelator: The Written Revelations of John Taylor." In *Champion of Liberty: John Taylor*, edited by Mary Jane Woodger, 273–307. Provo: BYU Religious Studies Center, 2009.

Hooten Jr., LeRoy W. "Salt Lake City Old Water Conveyance Systems." Online at *Salt Lake City Docs*.

Howe, Eber D. *Mormonism Unvailed*. With critical comments by Dan Vogel. Salt Lake City: Signature Books, 2015.

Hubbell's Legal Directory ... [including] a Synopsis of the Collection Laws of Each State. New York: J. H. Hubbell, 1877.

Hughes, Evelyn Hawkins. *Thomas Sunderland Hawkins: Biography of a Mormon Pioneer*. Salt Lake City: Hawkins Family Organization, 1994.

Hunter, Edward L., L. W. Hardy, and J. C. Little. "General Tithing Storehouse." Printed letter to bishops, July 8, 1873. Salt Lake City: Presiding Bishop. Church History Library, Salt Lake City.

Hyde, Myrtle Stevens. *Orson Hyde: The Olive Branch of Israel*. Salt Lake City: Agreka Books, 2000.

Irving, Gordon. "The Law of Adoption: One Phase of the Development of the Mormon Concept of Salvation, 1830–1900." *BYU Studies* 14, no. 3 (Spring 1974): 291–314.

Jaques, John. *Catechism for Children, Exhibiting the Prominent Doctrines of the Church of Jesus Christ of Latter-day Saints*. Liverpool/London: F. D. Richards, 1854.

Jenson, Andrew. *Encyclopedic History of the Church of Jesus Christ of Latter-day Saints*. Salt Lake City: Deseret News Publishing, 1941.

———. *Latter-day Saint Biographical Encyclopedia*. 4 vols. Salt Lake City: Andrew Jenson History Company, 1901–1936.

Jessee, Dean C., Mark Ashurst–McGee, and Richard L. Jensen, eds., *The Joseph Smith Papers: Journals, 1832–1839*. Salt Lake City: Church Historian's Press, 2008.

Jones. James P. "John A. Logan: Politician and Soldier." Phd diss., University of Florida, 1960.

Joseph Smith Papers website. "People," at www.josephsmithpapers.org.

Journal of Discourses. 26 vols. London: LDS Booksellers Depot, 1854–1886.

Kimball, Stanley B. *Heber C. Kimball: Mormon Patriarch and Pioneer*. Urbana: University of Illinois Press, 1981.

Kutler, Stanley I., ed. *Dictionary of American History*. New York: Charles Scribner's Sons, 2003. Online at *Encyclopedia.com*.

Larson, Andrew Karl. *Erastus Snow: The Life of a Missionary and Pioneer for the Early Mormon Church*. Salt Lake City: University of Utah Press, 1971.

Leonard, Glen M. "Truman Leonard: Pioneer Mormon Farmer." *Utah Historical Quarterly* 44, no. 3 (Summer 1976): 240–60.

LeSueur, Stephen C. *The 1838 Mormon War in Missouri*. Columbia: University of Missouri Press, 1987.

Ludlow, Daniel H. *Encyclopedia of Mormonism*. 4 vols. First published 1992 by Macmillan. Provo: Brigham Young University, 2007. Online at eom.byu.edu.

Lyman, Amasa M. *Thirteenth Apostle: The Diaries of Amasa M. Lyman, 1832–1877*. Edited by Scott H. Partridge. Salt Lake City: Signature Books, 2016.

Lyman, Edward Leo. *Amasa Mason Lyman, Mormon Apostle and Apostate: A Study in Dedication*. Salt Lake City: University of Utah Press, 2009.

MacKinnon, William P. *At Sword's Point: A Documentary History of the Utah War, 1857–59*. 2 vols. Norman, OK: Arthur H. Clark, 2008, 2016.

Maxwell, John Gary. *The Civil War Years in Utah: The Kingdom of God and the Territory That Did Not Fight*. Norman, OK: University of Oklahoma Press, 2016.

———. *Robert Newton Baskin and the Making of Modern Utah*. Norman, OK: Robert H. Clark, 2013.

Mauss, Armand L. *All Abraham's Children: Changing Mormon Conceptions of Race and Lineage*. Urbana: University of Illinois Press, 2003.

May, Dean L. *Utah: A People's History*. Salt Lake City: University of Utah Press, 1987.

McConkie, Bruce R. *Mormon Doctrine*. 2d edition Salt Lake City: Bookcraft, 1966.

McCormick, John S. "Electrical Development in Utah." In Powell, *Utah History Encyclopedia*.

McCormick, John S., and Gary B. Peterson. *Silver in the Beehive State*. Museum exhibit program. Salt Lake City: Utah State Historical Society, 1988. Online at historytogo.utah.gov.

McPherson, James M. *Battle Cry of Freedom: The Civil War Era*. New York: Oxford University Press, 1988.

Newell, Linda King, and Valeen Tippetts Avery. *Mormon Enigma: Emma Hale Smith*. 2nd ed. Champaign: University of Illinois Press, 1994.

Nichols, Jeff. "'In Defence of God's People If Need Bee': Brigham Young Hampton." *Utah Historical Quarterly* 78, no. 4 (Fall 2010): 344–58.

Nichols, Jeffrey. *Prostitution, Polygamy, and Power: Salt Lake City, 1847–1918*. Urbana: University of Illinois Press, 2002.

Orton, Ferrin Lay. *William Reed Stockbridge Warren: Life Sketch*. Published by the author, 2008.

Packer, Cameron J. "Cumorah's Cave." *Journal of Book of Mormon Studies* 13, nos. 1–2 (2004): 50–57.

Patrick, John R. "The School of the Prophets: Its Development and Influence in Utah Territory." Master's thesis, Brigham Young University, 1970.

Peterson, Charles S. *Take Up Your Mission: Mormon Colonizing along the Little Colorado River, 1870–1900*. Tucson: University of Arizona Press, 1973.

Peterson, F. Ross. *A History of Cache County*. Salt Lake City: Utah State Historical Society and Cache County Council, 1997.

Peterson, John Alton. *Utah's Black Hawk War*. Salt Lake City: University of Utah Press, 1999.

Peterson, Paul H. "Accommodating the Saints at General Conference." *BYU Studies* 41, no. 2 (2002): 5–39.

———. "An Historical Analysis of the Word of Wisdom." Master's thesis, Brigham Young University, 1972.

———. "The Mormon Reformation of 1856–1857: The Rhetoric and the Reality." *Journal of Mormon History* 15 (1989): 59–87.

Pickover, Clifford A. *The Girl Who Gave Birth to Rabbits: A True Medical Mystery*. New York: Prometheus Books, 2000.

Poulsen, Larry N. "The Life and Contributions of Newell Kimball Whitney." Master's thesis, Brigham Young University, 1966.

Powell, Allen Kent, ed. *Utah History Encyclopedia*. Salt Lake City: University of Utah Press, 1994; online at *Utah Education Network*, www.uen.org.

Pratt, Orson. *Divine Authenticity of the Book of Mormon*. 6 vols. Liverpool: By the author, 1850.

———. *The Seer*. Washington, DC, 1853–54.

Pratt, Parley P. *Autobiography of Parley P. Pratt, One of the Twelve Apostles . . . from His Miscellaneous Writings*. Chicago: Law, King, and Law, 1888.

Prince, Gregory A. *Power from on High: The Development of Mormon Priesthood*. Salt Lake City: Signature Books, 1995.

Prince, Stephen L. *Hosea Stout: Lawman, Legislator, Mormon Defender*. Logan: Utah State University Press, 2016.

Pusey, Merlo J. *Builders of the Kingdom: George A. Smith, John Henry Smith, George Albert Smith*. Provo: Brigham Young University Press, 1981.

Quinn, D. Michael. *Early Mormonism and the Magic World View*. Salt Lake City: Signature Books, 1998.

———. *The Mormon Hierarchy: Extensions of Power*. Salt Lake City: Signature Books, 1997.

———. *The Mormon Hierarchy: Wealth and Corporate Power*. Salt Lake City: Signature Books, 2017.

———. Papers. WA MSS-2692, Beinecke Library, Yale University.

———. "The Practice of Rebaptism at Nauvoo." BYU Studies 18, no. 2 (Winter 1978): 226–32.

Reeve, W. Paul. *Religion of a Different Color: Race and the Mormon Struggle for Whiteness*. New York: Oxford University Press, 2015.

Richards, Franklin D. *A Compendium of the Faith and Doctrines of the Church of Jesus Christ of Latter-day Saints*. Liverpool: Orson Pratt, 1857.

———. Journal, 1844–54, 1866–99. MS 1215, Church History Library, Salt Lake City.

Richardson, Arthur. *The Life and Ministry of John Morgan: For a Wise and Glorious Purpose*. Salt Lake City: Nicholas G. Morgan, 1965.

Richardson, James D. *A Compilation of the Messages and Papers of the Presidents*. 11 volumes. Washington, DC: Bureau of National Literature, 1902–1904. Online at *Project Gutenberg*.

Roberts, B. H. *The Life of John Taylor: Third President of the Church of Jesus Christ of Latter-day Saints*. Salt Lake City: George Q. Cannon & Sons, 1892.

Rogers, Jedediah S., ed. *The Council of Fifty: A Documentary History*. Salt Lake City: Signature Books, 2014.

———, ed. *In the President's Office: The Diaries of L. John Nuttall, 1879–1892*. Salt Lake City: Signature Books and Smith–Pettit Foundation, 2007.

Romney, Thomas C. *The Life of Lorenzo Snow: Fifth President of the Church of Jesus Christ of Latter-Day Saints*. Salt Lake City: Deseret Book, 1955.

Salt Lake Herald. 1870–1920.

Salt Lake Tribune. 1871–present.

Scherer, Mark A. *The Journey of a People.* 3 vols. Independence: Community of Christ, 2013.

School of the Prophets. Salt Lake City Records, 1867–74, 1883. CR 390 5–7. Church History Library, Salt Lake City.

———. Salt Lake City Minutes, 1870–74. Typescript by Edyth Romney, in Leonard J. Arrington, Papers, series 9, box 16. Special Collections, Merrill–Cazier Library, Utah State University.

Shipps, Jan. *Mormonism: The Story of a New Religious Tradition*. Urbana: University of Illinois Press, 1985.

Smith, George A. *The Rise, Progress and Travels of the Church of Jesus Christ of Latter-day Saints*. Salt Lake City: Deseret News Office, 1869.

Smith, George D. *Nauvoo Polygamy: "...but we called it celestial marriage."* Salt Lake City: Signature Books, 2011.

Smith Jr., Joseph, et al. *History of the Church of Jesus Christ of Latter-day Saints*. 6 vols. (Period I). Edited by B. H. Roberts. Salt Lake City: LDS Church/Deseret Book, 1902–1912.

Smith, Joseph F. Diary, 1856–81. MS 1325, Church History Library, Salt Lake City.

Speek, Vickie Cleverley. *"God Has Made Us a Kingdom": James Strang and the Midwest Mormons*. Salt Lake City: Signature Books, 2006.

Staker, Mark Lyman. *Hearken, O Ye People: The Historical Setting of Joseph Smith's Ohio Revelations*. Salt Lake City: Greg Kofford Books, 2010.

Stapley, Jonathan A. "Adoptive Sealing Ritual in Mormonism." *Journal of Mormon History* 37, no. 3 (Summer 2011): 53–117.

———. "'Pouring in Oil': The Development of the Modern Mormon Healing Ritual." In *By Our Rites of Worship*, edited by Daniel L. Belnap, 283–316. Provo: BYU Religious Studies Center, 2013.

Stout, Wayne. *Hosea Stout: Utah's Pioneer Statesman*. Salt Lake City: By the author, 1953.

Strack, Don. *Ogden Rails: A History of Railroading at the Crossroads of the West*. Cheyenne: Union Pacific Historical Society, 2005. Online at *UtahRails.net*.

Swanson, Vern G. "The Development of the Concept of a Holy Ghost in Mormon Theology." In *Line Upon Line: Essays on Mormon Theology*, edited by Gary James Bergera, 89–101. Salt Lake City: Signature Books, 1989.

Third Annual Catalogue of the Officers and Students in the University of Deseret. Salt Lake City: University of Deseret, 1871.

Thornton, W. W. *The Law of Pure Food and Drug, National and State*. Cincinnati: W. H. Anderson, 1912.

Tullidge, Edward W. *History of Salt Lake City*. Salt Lake City: Star Printing Company, 1886.

———. *Life of Brigham Young; or Utah and Her Founders*. New York: By the author, 1876.

———. *Tullidge's Quarterly Magazine*. Salt Lake City, 1880–85.

Turner, John G. *Brigham Young: Pioneer Prophet*. Cambridge: Harvard University Press, 2012.

Union Vedette. Salt Lake City, 1863–67.

Van Wagoner, Richard S., editor. *The Complete Discourses of Brigham Young*. 5 vols. Salt Lake City: Smith–Pettit Foundation, 2009.

———. "The Making of a Mormon Myth: The 1844 Transfiguration of Brigham Young." *Dialogue: A Journal of Mormon Thought* 28, no. 4 (Winter 1995): 1–24.

———. *Sidney Rigdon: A Portrait of Religious Excess*. Salt Lake City: Signature Books, 1994.

Van Wagoner, Richard S., Steven C. Walker, and Allen D. Roberts. "The 'Lectures on Faith': A Case Study in Decanonization." *Dialogue: A Journal of Mormon Thought* 20, no. 3 (Fall 1987): 71–77.

Walker, Kyle R. *William B. Smith: In the Shadow of a Prophet*. Salt Lake City: Greg Kofford Books, 2015.

Walker, Ronald W. "The Liberal Institute: A Case Study in National Assimilation." *Dialogue: A Journal of Mormon Thought* 10, no. 4 (Autumn 1977): 74–85.

———. *Wayward Saints: The Godbeites and Brigham Young*. Urbana: University of Illinois Press, 1998.

Watt, Ronald G. *The Mormon Passage of George D. Watt: First British Convert, Scribe for Zion*. Logan: Utah State University Press, 2009.

Watt, Ronald G., and Kenneth W. Godfrey. "'Old 42': The British and European Mission Headquarters in Liverpool, England, 1855–1904." *Mormon Historical Studies* 10, no. 1 (Spring 2009): 87–99.

Webster, Noah. *American Dictionary of the English Language*. New Haven: S. Converse, 1828.

Weightman, Gavin. *The Frozen-water Trade: A True Story*. New York: Hyperion, 2003.

Welch, Thomas Weston. "Early Mormon Woodworking at Its Best: A Study of the Craftsmanship in the First Temples of Utah." Master's thesis, Brigham Young University, 1983.

White, Richard. *The Republic for Which It Stands: The United States During Reconstruction and the Gilded Age, 1865–1896*. New York: Oxford University Press, 2017.

Whitney, Orson F. *History of Utah*. 4 vols. Salt Lake City: George Q. Cannon and Sons, 1892–1904.

Woodruff, Wilford. *Wilford Woodruff's Journals, 1833–1898*. Edited by Dan Vogel. 11 vols. Salt Lake City: Benchmark Books and Smith–Pettit Foundation, forthcoming.

Woolley, Samuel A. Papers, 1846–1899. MS 1556. Church History Library, Salt Lake City.

Young, Brigham. Office Files, 1832–1878. CR 1234. Church History Library, Salt Lake City.

Young, John R. *Memoirs of John R. Young: Utah Pioneer, 1847, Written by Himself*. Salt Lake City: Deseret News, 1920.

INDEX

Devery S. Anderson is also co-editor of a three-volume documentary series:

Joseph Smith's Quorum of the Anointed, 1842–1845
The Nauvoo Endowment Companies, 1845–1846
The Development of LDS Temple Worship, 1846–2000

and a recent book on Mississippi's most notorious lynching, *Emmett Till: The Murder That Shocked the World and Propelled the Civil Rights Movement.*

He has been at work for several years on a soon-to-be completed biography of early Mormon herbal physician Willard Richards, who became official clerk to Joseph Smith, Church Historian, and was in jail with him at the church founder's assassination. In Utah, Richards, an apostle since 1840, was a member of the church presidency under Brigham Young, the first postmaster of Salt Lake City, and founding editor of the *Deseret News*. Anderson's biography is expected in 2020–21.

A B C D E F G H I J K L M
N O P Q R S T U V W X Y Z

a b c d e f g h i j k l m
n o p q r s t u v w x y z

The titles in *Salt Lake School of the Prophets* are set in Democratica, a typeface designed in 1991 by Miles Newlyn for the Emigre foundry. It was chosen for its oddities and stroke variations that are reminiscent of characters from the Deseret alphabet. The sample below is from the 1869 Deseret alphabet edition of the Book of Mormon (Alma 18:26 in the modern edition).